Canada: The State of the Federation 2001

Canadian Political Culture(s) in Transition

Edited by

Hamish Telford
and Harvey Lazar

Published for the Institute of Intergovernmental Relations
School of Policy Studies, Queen's University
by McGill-Queen's University Press
Montreal & Kingston • London • Ithaca

Canadian Cataloguing in Publication Data

The National Library of Canada has catalogued this publication as follows:

Canada : the state of the federation

Annual.
1985-
Continues: Year in review, ISSN 0825-1207.
ISSN 0827-0708
ISBN 0-88911-851-5 (2001 issue ; bound).—ISBN 0-88911-863-9 (2001 issue : pbk.)

1. Federal-provincial relations—Canada—Periodicals. 2. Federal government—
Canada—Periodicals. I. Queen's University (Kingston, Ont.). Institute of
Intergovernmental Relations

JL27.F42   321.02'3'0971   C86-030713-1 rev

The Institute of Intergovernmental Relations

The Institute is the only organization in Canada whose mandate is solely to promote research and communication on the challenges facing the federal system.

Current research interests include fiscal federalism, the social union, the reform of federal political institutions and the machinery of federal-provincial relations, Canadian federalism and the global economy, and comparative federalism.

The Institute pursues these objectives through research conducted by its own staff and other scholars, through its publication program, and through seminars and conferences.

The Institute links academics and practitioners of federalism in federal and provincial governments and the private sector.

The Institute of Intergovernmental Relations receives ongoing financial support from the J.A. Corry Memorial Endowment Fund, the Royal Bank of Canada Endowment Fund, Power Corporation, the Government of Canada, and the Government of Ontario. We are grateful for this support which enables the Institute to sustain its extensive program of research, publication, and related activities.

L'Institut des relations intergouvernementales

L'Institut est le seul organisme canadien à se consacrer exclusivement à la recherche et aux échanges sur les questions du fédéralisme.

Les priorités de recherche de l'Institut portent présentement sur le fédéralisme fiscal, l'union sociale, la modification éventuelle des institutions politiques fédérales, les nouveaux mécanismes de relations fédérales-provinciales, le fédéralisme canadien au regard de l'économie mondiale et le fédéralisme comparatif.

L'Institut réalise ses objectifs par le biais de recherches effectuées par son personnel et par des universitaires de l'Université Queen's et d'ailleurs, de même que par des conférences et des colloques.

L'Institut sert de lien entre les universitaires, les fonctionnaires fédéraux et provinciaux et le secteur privé.

L'institut des relations intergouvernementales reçoit l'appui financier du J.A. Corry Memorial Endowment Fund, de la Fondation de la Banque Royale du Canada, de Power Corporation, du gouvernement du Canada et du gouvernement de l'Ontario. Nous les remercions de cet appui qui permet à l'Institut de poursuivre son vaste programme de recherche et de publication ainsi que ses activités connexes.

CONTENTS

v   *Foreword*

vii   *Contributors*

I   Overview

3   1.   Canadian Political Culture(s) in Transition and the State of
the Federation
Hamish Telford and Harvey Lazar

II   Federal Politics

35   2.   The Liberal Chameleon: From Red Tories to Blue Grits
Reg Whitaker

51   3.   Four Dimensions of Political Culture in Canada Outside
Quebec: The Changing Nature of Brokerage and the Definition
of the Canadian Nation
Matthew Mendelsohn

83   4.   Say Goodbye to the Dream of One Canada: The Costly Failure
to Purchase National Unity
Patrick James and Michael Lusztig

111   5.   The Reform Party/Canadian Alliance and Canada's Flirtation
with Republicanism
Hamish Telford

III   Regional Perspectives

141   6.   Atlantic Canada at the Start of the New Millennium
Jennifer Smith

163   7.   Quebec's Changing Political Culture and the Future of
Federal-Provincial Relations in Canada
Daniel Salée

199   8. The Evolution of Ontario's Confederal Stance in the Nineties:
          Ideology or Continuity?
          Hugh Segal

217   9. Social Democracy in a Neo-Conservative Age: The Politics of
          Manitoba and Saskatchewan
          Nelson Wiseman

241 10. British Columbia: Affordable Resentment, Growing Options,
          Diverging Interests
          Gordon Gibson

IV New Identities

265 11. The Evolution of Charter Values
          Paul Howe and Joseph F. Fletcher

293 12. Mosaic and Melting-Pot: The Dialectic of Pluralism and
          Constitutional Faith in Canada and the United States
          Samuel V. LaSelva

313 13. Framing Citizenship Status in an Age of Polyethnicity:
          Quebec's Model of Interculturalism
          Alain-G. Gagnon and Raffaele Iacovino

343 14. Communities in Conflict: Nova Scotia after the
          Marshall Decision
          Ian Stewart

367 15. Where One Lives and What One Thinks: Implications of
          Rural-Urban Opinion Cleavages for Canadian Federalism
          Fred Cutler and Richard W. Jenkins

V   Chronology

393 16. Chronology of Events January 2000 – December 2000
          Victoria Crites

FOREWORD

This year's *Canada: The State of the Federation* examines the shifts in Canadian political culture over the last couple of decades and their impact on Canadian politics and intergovernmental relations. As with *Canada: The State of the Federation 1998/99: How Canadians Connect*, this volume does not focus narrowly on the conduct of intergovernmental relations; it examines the state of the federation in a more overarching way. Political culture defines the environment within which governments operate, and the constraints and opportunities placed on them by public demands. We believe that the analyses contained herein will shed some light on how the wider world of Canadian politics impacts on the relatively secretive processes of Canadian intergovernmental relations. General observers of Canadian politics as well as intergovernmental relations specialists should thus benefit from the analyses.

Canadian political culture is changing in various ways. The political, economic, and social values of Canadians seemed to have shifted over the past twenty years. Canadians have become more conservative in their economic thinking, but social attitudes have, if anything, become more progressive. These changes have important implications for the federal party system. Moreover, while Canadians overwhelmingly want their governments to cooperate, we also believe that the new political culture in Canada, especially in regard to taxation and public spending, is constraining the space for intergovernmental negotiations and manoeuvring. The chapters here illuminate the difficulties of managing the federation during a time of fiscal retrenchment.

As in other years, a chronology of major events in the federation is provided. It covers the period from January 2000 to December 2000.

The editors would like to thank all the people who contributed to the production of this volume. In particular, I wish to note that Hamish Telford played a leading role in conceiving the volume and seeing it through to publication. This explains why he is the first-named of the two co-editors. Patti Candido and Mary Kennedy applied their expertise to the organization of the conference for the initial dissemination of the chapters and subsequently to the tedious process of preparing the revised chapters for publication. Their unfailing dedication to the project made the production of this volume possible. The conference participants, the discussants and the anonymous reviewers supplied the authors with valuable feedback at critical junctures in the production process. Valerie Jarus, Mark Howes and Marilyn Banting managed the desk-top publishing, cover design and copy-editing and Catherine Côté translated the abstracts for each chapter into French. Collectively, they transformed the rough pages into the book.

Harvey Lazar
September 2002

CONTRIBUTORS

Victoria Crites graduated from the University of British Columbia with a Political Science Honours Degree. She is now in the Political Science Master's program at the University of British Columbia.

Fred Cutler is Assistant Professor of Political Science at the University of British Columbia.

Joseph F. Fletcher is Associate Professor of Political Science at the University of Toronto.

Alain-G. Gagnon is Professor in the Department of Political Science at McGill University and is a member of the Research Group on Multinational Societies. In 2002, he is Visiting Fellow with the Institute for Research on Public Policy, Montreal.

Gordon Gibson is Senior Fellow in Canadian Studies at the Fraser Institute in Vancouver.

Paul Howe is Assistant Professor of Political Science at the University of New Brunswick.

Raffaele Iacovino is a PhD candidate in the Department of Political Science at McGill University.

Patrick James is Professor of Political Science at the University of Missouri, Columbia.

Richard W. Jenkins is a Senior Consultant at Ekos Research Associates in Ottawa.

Samuel V. LaSelva is Professor of Political Science at the University of British Columbia.

Harvey Lazar is Director of the Institute of Intergovernmental Relations at Queen's University.

Michael Lusztig is Associate Professor of Political Science at Southern Methodist University.

Matthew Mendelsohn is Associate Professor in the Department of Political Studies and Director of the Canadian Public Opinion Archives at Queen's University.

Daniel Salée is Professor of Political Science and Principal of the School of Community and Public Affairs at Concordia University.

Hugh Segal is President of the Institute for Research on Public Policy and Ivey Fellow at the School of Policy Studies, Queen's University.

Jennifer Smith is Professor and Chair of the Department of Political Science at Dalhousie University.

Ian Stewart is Professor of Political Science at Acadia University.

Hamish Telford teaches political science at the University College of the Fraser Valley, and is Research Associate of the Institute of Intergovernmental Relations at Queen's University.

Reg Whitaker is Distinguished Research Professor Emeritus, York University, and currently Adjunct Professor of Political Science, University of Victoria.

Nelson Wiseman is Associate Professor of Political Science at the University of Toronto.

I

Overview

1

Canadian Political Culture(s) in Transition and the State of the Federation

Hamish Telford and Harvey Lazar

Ce chapitre soutient que la culture politique canadienne a effectué un virage particulier au cours des deux dernières décennies. Les Canadiens se sont déplacés vers la droite par rapport aux enjeux économiques, notamment en ce qui a trait aux questions de taxation et de dépenses publiques, alors qu'au même moment, ils se tournaient vers la gauche pour ce qui touchait les questions sociales. Ce déplacement vers la gauche par rapport aux questions sociales explique la fragmentation du système de partis fédéral tandis que les pressions pour un réalignement fiscal et une baisse d'impôt ont réduit la marge de manœuvre intergouvernementale quant au fédéralisme fiscal. Ainsi, même si les Canadiens souhaitent par-dessus tout que leurs gouvernements coopèrent et qu'il y a effectivement collaboration intergouvernementale, ironiquement, cette nouvelle culture politique canadienne contribue aussi à exacerber les tensions entre les paliers de gouvernements quant aux affaires fiscales. Ce tournant particulier de la culture politique a donc un impact important sur les relations intergouvernementales canadiennes.

INTRODUCTION

This volume examines the changes in Canadian political culture over the last two decades and their impact on Canadian politics and intergovernmental relations. Political culture can be a useful instrument to explain a variety of phenomena, such as changing party systems and general trends in public policy. In essence, political culture defines the public environment in which governments operate. "In a substantive sense," Elkins and Simeon suggest, "culture may help to explain the scope and content of government activity."[1] With the dramatic party system change in 1993, increasing continental integration, and the rise of globalization, one might very well expect Canadian political culture to have changed over the past 20 years.

After assuming office in 1993, Jean Chrétien's Liberal government endorsed the free trade agreement with the United States and Mexico, and it quickly moved to slay the federal government's budgetary deficit, partly by reducing transfer payments to the provinces. Some provinces moved to tackle their deficits earlier than Ottawa and some moved a little later. But during the 1990s, almost all provinces acted forcefully on the fiscal front, including the Conservative governments in Ontario and Alberta, the New Democratic Party (NDP) government in Saskatchewan and the Liberal government in New Brunswick. Many commentators thus concluded that Canadian politics was swinging decidedly to the right toward neo-conservatism.[2]

A number of the chapters in this volume support the contention that Canadian political culture has swung to the right over the past 20 years. Various chapters indicate that a broad consensus has emerged among Canadians that government deficits needed to be eliminated and that overall government debt should be reduced; that freer trade has generally been positive for Canada; that lower taxes are required to stimulate investment, to maintain productivity growth, and to remain competitive with the United States; that governments should relinquish their business enterprises and deregulate important segments of the economy; and generally that governments should be managed in a more responsible and business-like fashion, in accordance with the ideas associated with the new public management. In this process, large cuts were made to major social programs. This all suggests that Canadian political culture has indeed swung to the right.

Political culture, however, is not unidimensional. The evidence presented here suggests that Canadians from coast to coast to coast have embraced the political values entrenched in the *Charter of Rights and Freedoms*; that they have endorsed the principle of official bilingualism, even if they have not figured out how to provide constitutional recognition of Quebec's distinctiveness; that they are comfortable with the advances made by women over the past four decades; that they have accepted the unclosetly of homosexuality; that they are broadly sympathetic to Aboriginal peoples, even if there is no agreement on how to provide redress to Aboriginal communities; and that they cherish the multicultural dynamic of Canada. Notwithstanding the contention that Canadians have swung toward neo-conservatism on economic matters in the past two decades, the analyses here also indicate that Canadians have adopted increasingly progressive social attitudes in relation to bilingualism, multiculturalism, and homosexuality. That is, Canadians have stepped a little to the "left" and have become more progressive in their approach to human rights, at least when these rights are expressed in individual terms. Canadians are admittedly still suspicious of the group claims made by Aboriginal peoples and Quebecers.[3] The new social progressivism in Canada, while very real, thus still has its limits.

While the new political consensus in Canada captures a wide swath of the Canadian polity, it by no means captures everyone. Social democrats who do not embrace the principles of freer trade, deficit elimination, lower taxes and the new public management remain isolated and radicalized. On the other hand, social conservatives continue to feel frustrated by the mainstream consensus around secular, liberal values. Canadians outside the mainstream, especially large numbers of Aboriginal peoples and the more staunch sovereignists in Quebec, are also feeling increasingly isolated, and many are articulating their distinct identities more vehemently than in the past. How the Canadian mainstream will respond to these disaffected groups remains an open question at this time.

Nevertheless, we believe that the analyses in this volume support the contention that the traditional centrism of Canadian political culture has rotated on its axis over the past two decades. It would appear that Canadians have shifted to the right on economic issues and questions of taxation and public spending, while social attitudes seem to have moved to the left at the same time. The inspiration for this argument emerges from Reg Whitaker's discerning chapter on the federal Liberal Party in this volume, which is wonderfully entitled "The Liberal Chameleon: From Red Tories to Blue Grits." Professor Whitaker concludes, "if the Liberals have moved to the right on economic policy as the centre of gravity in the country has shifted rightward, it is also the case that the Liberals have shifted 'leftward' (if that is the correct term) on social and cultural issues as the country has shifted in that direction."

These shifts to the right on economic issues and to the left on social issues are almost certainly not of equal magnitude. In highly unscientific fashion, we would suggest that Canadian political culture has shifted two steps to the right on economic issues and perhaps one step to the left on social issues and human rights. (We use the word "left" here to denote general social progressiveness, as opposed to moral traditionalism.) We believe these shifts have important implications for Canadian politics and intergovernmental relations. We shall argue that the leftward shift on social attitudes helps explain the fragmented federal party system, while the logic of fiscal retrenchment and the pressures for lower taxes have reduced the room for intergovernmental manoeuvring on questions of fiscal federalism. While Canadians overwhelmingly want their governments to cooperate,[4] and there is much evidence of intergovernmental collaboration, the new political culture in Canada, especially in relation to beliefs about taxation and thus public spending, ironically serves to exacerbate intergovernmental tension. Political culture and the wider world of Canadian politics thus have a very real impact on the relatively secretive world of intergovernmental relations.

WHAT IS POLITICAL CULTURE?

Political culture is one of the more nebulous concepts in political science. Nelson Wiseman has reported that more than 250 definitions of political culture exist in the literature.[5] For our purposes, the definition of political culture provided by David Bell is succinct, inclusive, and intuitive. "Political culture," Bell says, "consists of the ideas, assumptions, values, and beliefs that condition political action."[6] Put another way, political culture is a "mindset,"[7] which establishes the parameters of politics in society. In short, political culture defines "the general purposes of government and the kinds of processes and substantive decisions that are acceptable and legitimate."[8]

There are two broad approaches to the study of political culture. The first approach is premised on survey research and statistical analyses. In this approach, a relatively large number of individuals are asked specific questions about their political values and beliefs. The standard replies may be interpreted as political culture. The second approach is more general, and perhaps more holistic. This approach may entail an examination of history, popular culture, literature, geography, education, and other social aspects of society, including political socialization. The holistic approach could also include an examination of political institutions and public policy trends. In terms of their respective strengths and weaknesses, these two approaches to political culture are essentially mirror opposites. The survey approach provides hard data, but it may lack contextual richness; the holistic approach usually provides a richer description of the social context, but it may be impressionistic and not empirically grounded. The combination of both approaches is highly desirable, but usually beyond the means of an individual researcher.

Beyond definition of and approaches to political culture, there is also confusion about the purposes of studying political culture. Part of this confusion stems from the dual character of political culture. On the one hand, political culture may be merely descriptive. In this sense, political culture tells us that a "group exhibits a given range and distribution of (largely unconscious) assumptions about its political life."[9] While these descriptions may be interesting, the real allure of political culture as a concept is its potential to explain political phenomena. The deployment of political culture as an explanatory variable, however, can be problematic. Elkins and Simeon argue persuasively that political culture should only be turned to for explanation after institutional and structural variables have been considered, or in conjunction with such explanations.[10] Furthermore, they warn that political culture should not be asked to explain too much. They suggest that political culture cannot explain macro-political phenomena such as "stability, democracy, authoritarianism, and level[s] of economic or political development"[11] On the other hand, political culture cannot account for micro-political behaviour such as individual attitudes either. Elkins and Simeon argue that political culture may be useful in explaining mid-range political phenomena, such as the creation of political institutions and policy-making.

In addition to careful selection of the dependent variable, Elkins and Simeon stress that political culture as an explanation can only be employed in a comparative context.[12] Political culture may explain interesting differences in the political processes among countries. Within countries, political culture may be employed to explain regional variations in the political system. Alternatively, the comparison may be temporal. Variations in the political system over time may be explained by changes in political culture. In this latter sense, "the logic of comparison is maintained," as Elkins and Simeon note.[13]

In our study, all of the contributors work with the idea of political culture at a general and intuitive level, in keeping with the definition provided by Bell above. The majority of chapters adopt a holistic approach of one sort or another. Some are primarily historical, others are more philosophical, while others are more attuned to policy and political economy trends. However, three of the chapters are also statistical in nature. The combination of approaches helps illuminate the many facets of political culture. Some of the chapters are focused on federal politics, while others examine politics and political culture in the different regions of the country. The remaining chapters examine various non-spatial dimensions of Canadian political culture, particularly the role of multiculturalism and the impact of the Charter.

The focus in all of these cases is on the evolution of political culture in Canada from the early 1980s to the present. The year 1982 provides a convenient point of departure. The introduction of the Charter in that year provides the context – though not necessarily the explanation — for many of the social changes witnessed in the country over the past 20 years, but it also roughly demarcates the point of transition from Keynesian economic strategies to a neo-liberal/neo-conservative framework in the Canadian policy process. In other words, the primary line of comparison is temporal. Both in method and objective, we believe that the study falls neatly within the guidelines established by Elkins and Simeon.

DEFICIT REDUCTION POLITICS: THE NEW RIGHT HAND OF CANADIAN POLITICAL CULTURE

It has long been believed that "Canadian politics is regional politics."[14] While more recent studies tend to refute the findings made by Simeon and Elkins,[15] regionalism is still frequently positioned as an explanatory variable in Canadian political science. The Canadian election studies continue to reveal regional voting patterns,[16] and Herman Bakvis has detailed the regional considerations in the formation of the federal Cabinet.[17] Furthermore, Michael Lusztig has argued that the presence of distinct "mega-constitutional orientations" in

the different regions of Canada confounded the attempts at constitutional reform in the 1990s.[18] More recently, in a *Globe and Mail* opinion piece, Michael
Bliss essentially resurrected Simeon and Elkins's analysis and provocatively
characterized Quebec and the Atlantic provinces as comprising the backward
and stagnant "Old Canada," while portraying Ontario and the west as the forward and innovative "New Canada."[19] The studies in this volume, however,
suggest that on the level of broad economic values and social attitudes, if not
identity, Canadians are now more similar than the traditional regional characterizations of the country imply.

Jennifer Smith explicitly uses Bliss's argument as her point of departure.
In her chapter, she argues persuasively that political culture in Atlantic Canada
has modernized and is now broadly similar to political culture in the rest of
Canada. She notes correctly that the shift toward new public management and
fiscal responsibility began with Frank McKenna's Liberal government in New
Brunswick, and not in Ontario or Alberta as commonly believed. Smith reports that the other governments in Atlantic Canada have or are in the process
of managing their deficits and debts, and that the region is enjoying unprecedented economic growth. Notwithstanding these efforts the Canadian
Alliance continues to perpetuate old myths about the region. While some might
characterize Nova Scotians' dalliance with the NDP in federal and provincial
elections in the 1990s as a longing for traditional government largesse, Smith
suggests that the NDP's modest electoral successes in Nova Scotia are indicative of the population's willingness to experiment with political alternatives.
In short, it is suggestive of a political culture in transition.

In Ontario, Mike Harris's Conservative Party swept to power in 1995 on
the strength of its "common sense revolution." The new government moved
quickly to cut taxes and government spending; it reduced the size of the provincial civil service; it restructured municipalities in the name of cost-saving;
and it pursued a vigorous agenda of privatization. These policies have become the hallmarks of neo-conservative economic thinking in Canada, and
they have been adopted to a greater or lesser extent by most other governments in Canada. In the process of actualizing the common sense revolution,
the Harris government soon found itself embroiled in a very public conflict
with the federal government, primarily over transfer payments for health care.
While Ontario objected strenuously to the transfer cuts, the federal government replied that if Ontario required more funds for health care it should not
have made such deep tax cuts.

The rivalry between the Conservative government in Ontario and the Liberal government of Canada was interpreted by many as an intense ideological
conflict, and a significant departure from Ontario's traditionally centrist orientation. In his chapter, however, Hugh Segal suggests that this conflict was
structurally motivated and not ideological or personal. Segal argues that the
conflict was caused primarily by the economic recession in Ontario and the

concomitant decline of revenue, and he maintains that any party that had the misfortune of governing Ontario at this juncture would have pursued the same line with Ottawa. Indeed, he notes that the conflict was set in motion when Bob Rae's NDP government articulated its notion of "fair shares federalism." The conflict deepened when Mike Harris became premier. This was a conflict about sharing money at a time when both governments were working assiduously to eliminate their deficits and reduce taxes. Arguably, however, the primary difference between Ontario's Conservative government and the Liberal government of Canada was strategic: should tax cuts come before or after the elimination of the deficit? The intensity of their dispute demonstrates the difficulty of managing the federation during a period of fiscal retrenchment.

While the Harris government aggressively challenged the federal government on the issue of transfer payments, Segal insists that Premier Harris has maintained Ontario's traditional position of constructive engagement on the question of "national" unity. He points in particular to Harris's insistence that he would not accept a new transfer agreement with Ottawa in September 2000 unless it was acceptable to Quebec.

Nelson Wiseman contends in his chapter that "political culture is stable, enduring, and cross-generational." Notwithstanding the processes of globalization and continental integration, Wiseman argues that the social democratic tradition in Manitoba and Saskatchewan and the conservative tradition in Alberta have endured. This is reflected in the fact that Manitoba and Saskatchewan continue to elect NDP governments, while Alberta votes solidly for the Conservative Party and has been the bedrock for the Reform Party/Canadian Alliance. However, Wiseman also suggests that the social democratic tradition in the eastern prairies is different than in other parts of the country. He argues that social democrats in the prairies have demonstrated an aversion to public debt starting with the Regina Manifesto. Wiseman states "Saskatchewan's CCF-NDP, along with its Manitoba NDP counterpart, have a record of vigilance and probity in public finance," and he notes that Roy Romanow's NDP government in Saskatchewan was "the first in the west to balance its budget." Wiseman also reports that the NDP governments in Saskatchewan and Manitoba have demonstrated a willingness to experiment in public policy, including health care, and they have become somewhat more decentralist in relation to the federation. While Wiseman believes that it is incorrect to describe the NDP in Saskatchewan and Manitoba as "neo-conservative" parties in disguise, it would also seem that the governing ideology of the NDP in these provinces is consistent with the prevailing economic thinking in the rest of Canada.

Gordon Gibson argues in his chapter that British Columbia has historically punched below its weight in the federation, but he anticipates this will change with the election of the Liberal Party in the spring of 2001. Gibson reports that British Columbians are increasingly frustrated with the "absent-minded gorilla" that governs the nation with scant regard for British Columbia, and he suggests that British Columbians are especially suspicious of the federal government's orientation to Aboriginal policy. Furthermore, he presents evidence that new immigrants to the province are increasingly adopting a "BC-first" attitude, and that the East Asian community in particular is strongly supportive of the pro-market economic policies espoused by the BC Liberal Party and the Canadian Alliance. He thus expects the tension between British Columbia and the rest of Canada, especially the federal government, to grow. While the Aboriginal issue is certainly sensitive, the Campbell government to date has tried to work cooperatively with Ottawa, especially on the softwood lumber issue. On the whole, in fact, the new Liberal government has been preoccupied with its domestic agenda during its first year in office.

While Gibson's analysis may well be borne out in due course, one could also make an alternative argument with the same evidence. In this scenario, British Columbia under the NDP was the outlier in the federation. While the governments in other parts of Canada worked assiduously to eliminate their deficits (primarily through spending reductions), the NDP in British Columbia tried to spur economic growth (and thereby raise government revenue) through public spending. While other governments privatized, deregulated, and introduced user-fees for public services, the NDP government in British Columbia not only maintained public hydro and government auto insurance, it froze hydro and insurance rates as well as university tuition. In short, the NDP strategy in British Columbia was diametrically opposed to the strategies pursued by the other governments of Canada, including the federal government. With the landslide election of the Liberal Party in 2001, British Columbia is now pursuing the public management strategy adopted to greater or lesser extents by the other governments of Canada in the 1990s. In this regard at least, British Columbia has belatedly fallen in line with the rest of the country.

The ebb and flow of Quebec nationalism in the past decade has been dramatic. When Lucien Bouchard assumed the leadership of the sovereignist forces in the last referendum campaign, he very nearly carried the "Yes" side to victory but, when he resigned as premier in January 2001, many commentators pronounced the end of the sovereignty movement. While the claims made by these commentators are certainly exaggerated, Daniel Salée reports that significant changes are occurring in the discourse of Quebec nationalism and in the purportedly distinct Quebec model of governance. The sovereignty movement in Quebec has since the 1980s tried to project a civic nationalism, but it has frequently been perceived and portrayed by others as a crass ethnic nationalism. The movement's cause has not been aided by the unfortunate comments made by prominent sovereignists from time to time, most notably Jacques Parizeau's provocative remarks on the night of the last referendum. In an effort to overcome the negative connotations of ethnic nationalism, sovereignist leaders have striven to present a humane civic nationalism, which "celebrates diversity, promotes the integrity of minority cultures, and posits at the same time the Quebec state as the rallying point with which all can and should identify." But, Salée writes, "to the extent that [civic nationalism] waters down Quebec's pre-political collective identity ... it also dulls the sense of outrage and injury necessary to galvanize political energies in support of Quebec sovereignty."

If the promotion of civic nationalism weakens the quest for sovereignty, the logic of the North American and global economic market also leads Quebec to adopt economic policies similar to those of other Canadian governments. While the Government of Quebec still seeks to forge a consensus between business and labour on economic policy, Salée writes that many policies of the government "reflect an unequivocal penchant for neo-liberalism. Unmitigated support for free trade, zero deficit in public finance, important budgetary restrictions in public health, social assistance and education, and major structural and administrative changes in the welfare functions of the state, which increasingly require individuals to face the negative consequences of economic restructuring on their own, have been the mainstay of the current government's approach to socio-economic management." While Salée refers to these policies as "neo-liberal," they are virtually indistinguishable from the so-called "neo-conservative" policies pursued by governments in the rest of Canada. The terms would appear to be interchangeable. Salée's analysis accounts nicely for the stunning rise of the Action Démocratique in the spring of 2002.

In sum, Salée indicates that Quebec's distinct style of socio-economic management, which has been a core feature of Quebec's nationalist project since the Quiet Revolution, may be fading in the face of global and regional integration. While the social and economic policies of the Government of Quebec may now be broadly similar to policies pursued in the rest of Canada, nobody should expect the distinct Quebec identity to dissipate. Indeed, as Salée notes, nationalism has been "a permanent fixture of modern Quebec's political imagination and, in all likelihood, will continue to do so," even if it is not clear at this time how that will manifest itself.

Patrick James and Michael Lusztig detail how the burden of fiscal deficits felt by the provinces was also felt by the federal government. They suggest that social spending in Canada was not merely a Keynesian instrument to offset downturns in the economy, but that it was also intended to forge "national" unity. While deficit financing was adopted by most advanced democracies in the 1970s, the unique political situation in Canada may have prevented the federal government from tackling the deficit aggressively until it was an absolute economic necessity. While they acknowledge that the federal Liberal government has now curbed its profligate spending habits, they fear that the retrenchment is not sufficiently deep or institutionalized. Telford's chapter reveals that the neo-conservative discourse of deficit elimination, debt reduction, and tax cuts was introduced to the federal party system by Preston

Manning and the Reform Party, while the chapter by Whitaker details how this agenda was largely and successfully appropriated by the federal Liberal Party.

Governments across the country have all moved to curb their deficits. Most of those that were unable or unwilling to eliminate budget deficits were unceremoniously evicted from office. Opposition parties that articulated alternative economic approaches withered in the polls, most notably the federal NDP. Influential factions of the federal NDP dismiss any proposals to reconcile market principles with social democracy as opportunistic and vulgar "Blairism." While thousands of people in the public sector demonstrated noisily as their jobs and salaries were cut, a broad social consensus emerged that government debt could not accumulate indefinitely, although most Canadians still support publicly financed social programs, especially medical care and education. In crude terms, Canadians abandoned their postwar flirtation with "tax and spend liberalism" and replaced it with an economically more prudent "tough-love liberalism." While most Canadians did not embrace the full set of neo-conservative policy prescriptions, they undoubtedly stepped to the right on the basic questions of taxation and public spending.[20]

The rightward shift in economic thinking in Canada, of course, is consistent with the rise of globalization. Political regionalism in Canada was historically buttressed by distinct regional modes of production, each with their own set of interests and policy preferences. The creation of a continental and global market has seemingly imposed a single economic logic on all the regions and governments of Canada. It is not clear whether Canadians actually embrace this logic or simply believe that it is futile to resist it, but the vast majority of Canadians have accepted trade liberalization and see it as a key component of prosperity.[21] In this sense, globalization appears to be eroding the distinct regional political cultures in Canada.

THE REBALANCING OF MARKET AND STATE

Why did Canadian political culture shift to the right in the 1980s and 1990s, at least in relation to the broad questions of public finances? Beginning in the 1980s, governments across Canada began to re-think the role of the state and the way in which they manage the public sector. The impetus for this change arose from several sources. At the macroeconomic level, there was a growing recognition that significant elements of the post-World War II policy paradigm were no longer providing the expected results. Rates of inflation had risen during the 1970s. By the early 1980s, annual budget deficits had become the norm and public debt was beginning to mount rapidly. Financial markets began to lose confidence in the outlook for the Canadian economy and in the value of the Canadian dollar. By the mid-1980s, reducing deficits and taming public debt had become a growing part of the rhetoric of governments.

A second source was the concern that government programs were also having unintended consequences. A relatively generous federal system of unemployment insurance, in conjunction with provincial welfare systems, was increasingly criticized as discouraging work effort. There was similarly a growing worry that the combined effect of federal and provincial regulations was acting as a drag on the economy, unnecessarily inflating business costs and discouraging entrepreneurship and innovation. Government ownership of large enterprises — airlines, railways, oil companies, and hydro — also began to seem outmoded. And indeed action was taken on all three fronts, with reforms and large cutbacks to unemployment insurance and welfare, with significant deregulation (e.g., the demise of the National Energy Program) and re-regulation (e.g., financial services, transportation, and energy), and with major Crown corporations like CN, Air Canada, and Petro-Canada being privatized and large airports and some harbours turned over to municipalities and other local authorities.

A third impetus was the recognition that the conditions that had given rise to many government programs no longer prevailed. The postwar welfare state had been premised on the widespread prevalence of two-parent, one-earner families. By the 1980s, family structure was much more heterogeneous and the role of women in society had changed dramatically. There was also a growing view that governments alone lacked the capacity to meet some of the new public policy challenges. Either because of their technical knowledge, or their intimate relationship with clients and customers, the cooperation of nongovernmental actors from the business and voluntary sector was seen as increasingly necessary in implementing public policies.

Not all of the change pressures originated from within Canada. Internationally, successive General Agreement on Tariffs and Trade (GATT)/World Trade Organization (WTO) rounds of trade liberalization further opened Canada to the winds of global competition. The Canada-US Free Trade Agreement and the North American Free Trade Agreement added to these pressures. Moreover, by the 1990s, trade agreements were as much about harmonizing internal regulatory regimes as they were about traditional border measures. Changing technology was, at the same time, enabling capital markets to move huge sums of money from country to country in a matter of seconds. Whether one liked or disliked this new efficiency, it became part of the context within which all governments conducted their business.

A common perception within government during these years was that it had become too hierarchical and unduly rigid. The change pressures thus resulted in important adjustments, both in government rhetoric and in programs. With regard to rhetoric, there was much talk of deregulation, privatization, market mechanisms, lower taxes, partnerships, and the like. Within government structures, flatter organizations became a focal point of discussion, as did a greater interest in arm's length agencies and contracting-out. Behind this, there was a sense that the state was just trying to do too much. Among federal and provincial officials, for example, the "steer, don't row" thesis of Osborne and Gaebler's *Reinventing Government* circulated widely through the corridors of power.[22] As a set of ideas, the New Public Management looked to private initiative and markets to play a larger role in achieving public purposes.

In the 1990s, the Canadian state, at both federal and provincial/municipal levels, stopped growing. And by the late 1990s, it had shrunk substantially as a share of the economy. At the federal level, program spending as a share of gross domestic product (GDP) had fallen from around 18 percent of GDP in the early 1990s to around 12 percent, a drop of one-third. At the provincial/ local level, the drop was from around 29 to 23 percent of GDP over the same period.

Support for these changes came from two overlapping but distinct quarters. On the one hand, there were voices that are variously referred to as neo-liberal and neo-conservative. From this perspective, the goal was to reduce taxes and government spending and make government a much smaller part of the economy and society as a desirable end in itself. Relying much more heavily on the instruments of the new public management fit well with this policy orientation. For those in this camp, perhaps initially well represented by the Reform Party of Canada, government was often the problem and not the solution. And to the extent that government was the solution, it was best to carry out at the provincial and local levels where the public will was more easily ascertained. Provincial governments led by Ralph Klein in Alberta and Mike Harris similarly can be identified with this view. A sharp veer to the political right on matters of political economy was a matter of ideological conviction.

A second group pursued at least a part of this agenda in order to restore public finances and to make the state more efficient and effective in meeting traditional objectives. For this group, the shift to the right was a secular (as opposed to ideological) response to fiscal necessity and the apparent defects of Taylorism and complex and at times bloated public bureaucracies. The objectives of public policy were not being changed, but the means for doing so were being adjusted to reflect current fiscal conditions and new knowledge about what works and what does not work. Thus, for example, de-layering large hierarchical organizations and contracting-out certain services were thought to be promising mechanisms for achieving improved results for every dollar of expenditure. This group includes the federal government under Jean Chrétien and arguably also Brian Mulroney. A number of provincial governments might be included in this camp, including parties with quite different labels, from the New Democratic Party in Saskatchewan and later Manitoba, to the Parti Québécois, to some Liberal and Conservative parties (such as the Newfoundland Liberals led by Brian Tobin).

Whether the move to smaller and less interventionist government was prompted by perceptions of unfortunate necessity or preferences to make government much smaller, the record speaks for itself. During the 1980s and 1990s, program spending was reduced substantially, state corporations were sold off, regulation reviewed and in places cut, programs were out-sourced, and tax burdens began to ease. On matters of political economy, the performance of federal and provincial governments took a significant turn to the right. Given the ability of governments who made this shift to be re-elected, including the federal Liberals, the PQ in Quebec, the Conservatives in Alberta and Ontario, among others, these governments appear not to have been out of step with their electorates.

The rightward shift in Canadian political culture was motivated by the changes in the Canadian economy and the state of public finances, and it was initiated primarily by business groups, governments, and professional economists. Voters across the country, however, apparently were willing to accept that governments needed to be restructured and that deficit elimination was necessary. In other words, voters opted-in to the new government thinking. This new public view toward taxing and spending inevitably has an impact on the federal government's fiscal relationship with the provinces. While there are always tensions about the amount of interprovincial sharing mediated through the federal government, these tensions are easier to manage during periods of fiscal expansion than during periods of fiscal retrenchment.

SOCIAL ATTITUDES: THE PROGRESSIVE LEFT HAND OF CANADIAN POLITICAL CULTURE

From a political economy perspective, Canadian culture has shifted unmistakably to the right. But a political economy analysis alone would overlook significant changes in social attitudes in Canada over the last few decades. After the Charlottetown Accord referendum, Canadians were exhausted by the mega-constitutional debates of the Trudeau-Mulroney era. Suffering from constitutional fatigue, Canadians demanded that governments address the fundamental economic issues confronting the federation, and they made it abundantly clear that they wanted governments to cooperate in intergovernmental matters. At the same time, however, there is considerable evidence that Canadians embraced much of the substance of mega-constitutional politics, especially bilingualism, multiculturalism, and political equality.

New social attitudes started emerging in the 1960s; they were re-enforced by the Charter; and they have deepened, and perhaps become entrenched, over the past 20 years. Fifty years ago, the nuclear family, with a working father and stay-at-home mother, was the foundation of social life in Canada; ethnically Canada was more homogeneous (more European and more Christian);

and Aboriginal people on reserves had not yet obtained the right to vote in federal elections. But the second wave of feminism propelled many women into university and subsequently into professional occupations; successive waves of immigration from the non-western world transformed Canada into a visibly multicultural society; and Aboriginal people have become engaged in Canada's constitutional odyssey, although their goals have still not been fulfilled. The recognition these groups received in the *Charter of Rights and Freedoms* indicates that these dramatic social changes were embraced by most Canadians.

Paul Howe and Joseph Fletcher report that public support for the Charter has remained very high, notwithstanding considerable criticism of the Supreme Court by some commentators.[23] Their survey data indicate that 83 percent of Canadians thought the Charter was "a good thing for Canada" in 1987, while in 1999 support was pegged at 82 percent. While their data also reveal support for traditional values and respect for authority, Howe and Fletcher argue that this support is rather more ephemeral in nature and that a strong belief in equality rights drives the overall support for the Charter.

The evolution of Charter values in the past 20 years is perhaps most evident with the acceptance of homosexual rights. Twenty years ago most homosexuals were "in the closet." Now there are support groups for gay and lesbian students in many high schools and even junior high schools. Even primary school children are being taught to accept and tolerate sexual diversity. Homosexuality has also become part of popular culture in Canada. Many entertainers are now open about their homosexuality, and many new television shows portray homosexual characters. Gay pride parades have become one of the largest public events of the year in many Canadian cities.

Homosexual activists have successfully exploited the Charter and the courts to advance their equality claims. Indeed, David Rayside claims that "Canadian lesbians and gays have won more progress through political and legal systems than their counterparts in either Britain or the United States, and for that matter in all but a few countries in the world."[24] In the near future, it is entirely possible that the courts will sanction homosexual marriage under the equality provisions of the Charter. In a recent British Columbia case, Mr. Justice Pitfield ruled that preventing homosexual marriage was an infringement of Charter equality rights, although in this instance he determined that the discrimination was "reasonable" under section 1.[25] In *Halpern et al.* v. *the Attorney General of Canada*, the Ontario Superior Court of Justice (Divisional Court) ruled in July 2002 that prohibiting same-sex marriages could not be saved by section 1. The Government of Canada is appealing the decision. A recent poll revealed that 65.4 percent of respondents supported same sex marriages. A majority of respondents (53.1 percent) indicated that they supported the adoption of children by same-sex couples. The transformation of Canadian attitudes was underscored by Christian Bourque, the vice-president of

Leger Marketing (which conducted the poll), when he told *The Globe and Mail*, "I don't think a pollster would even have asked the question about same-sex adoption 20 years ago. Nobody would even have considered it."[26]

While the second wave of feminism was initiated in the 1960s, women made considerable advances in the 1980s and 1990s, and they continue to make gains. The proportion of women in Parliament increased from 0.4 percent in 1968 to 18.3 percent in 1993; Audrey McLaughlin became the first woman to lead a federal political party in 1990; Rita Johnston became the first female premier in Canada in 1991, followed by Catherine Callbeck in 1993; Kim Campbell became prime minister in 1993; Bertha Wilson became the first female Supreme Court Justice in 1982; today three of the nine justices of the Supreme Court are women, including the Chief Justice; Jeanne Sauvé became the country's first female governor general in 1984, followed by Adrienne Clarkson in 1999; Jocelyne Bourgon became the first female clerk of the privy council in 1994; Pat Carney became the first female president of the Treasury Board in 1988, followed by Lucienne Robillard in 1999; Marlene Catterall became the first female government whip in 2000; and Sheila Fraser became the first female auditor general in 2001. Women now constitute a majority of students enrolled in Canadian universities. Women have slowly moved into "non-traditional" occupations such as corporate executives, astronauts, airline pilots, and combat soldiers. We do not suggest that women have now obtained substantive equality. To the contrary, there are considerable gains still to be made. The point that we wish to make is that women continued to make advances in Canadian society throughout the 1980s and 1990s and, most importantly, these advances were supported and celebrated by an overwhelming majority of Canadians.

The face of Canada has changed too. While the federal government has promoted official multiculturalism for 30 years, multiculturalism is much more of a reality in Canadian society today than it was in 1970. A large proportion of people living in cities like Vancouver and Toronto identify languages other than English as their mother tongue, and about 40 percent of the people in the city of Montreal identify languages other than French as their mother tongue. Three-quarters of the non-French-speaking population in Montreal are allophones. New Canadians are now participating in Canada's governing institutions. The first turban-wearing Sikh entered Parliament in the 1990s, and in 2000 Ujjal Dossanjh became the first Indo-Canadian premier in Canadian history. Indeed, if one overlooks Joe Ghiz (who was partly of Lebanese origin), Dossanjh was the first visible minority to lead a provincial government, a fact celebrated by many in British Columbia and across Canada. By contrast, when Larry Grossman ran for the leadership of the Ontario Conservative Party in 1985, people wondered openly if Ontario was "ready" for a Jewish premier.[27] The different receptions granted to Grossman and Dossanjh indicate just how significantly Canadian attitudes have evolved within just two decades. While visible minorities did not always find it easy to settle in Canada, as Bharati Mukherjee makes clear in the preface of *Darkness* (her 1985 collection of short stories),[28] multiculturalism is now celebrated in many aspects of Canadian popular culture, including beer commercials.[29]

Samuel LaSelva argues that the acceptance of multiculturalism in Canada is foundational. LaSelva notes at the start of his essay that "multiculturalism can be part either of a mosaic or a melting-pot." He builds his analysis of these metaphorical models with an examination of multiculturalism in Canada and the United States, and he concludes that each country has produced "radically different brands of pluralism" because they have different "constitutional faiths." These distinct constitutional faiths stem primarily from the fact that "Canada is both a multinational and a territorial federation, whereas the United States has never been a federation of peoples." LaSelva concludes that "fraternity" has played a special role in Canada. The notion of fraternity has not only held English and French Canada together, he argues, it has facilitated the acceptance of multiculturalism.

There is a perception that the new social attitudes concerning feminism, homosexuality, multiculturalism, and Aboriginal people are a phenomena of the large urban centres in Canada. However, Fred Cutler and Richard Jenkins find in their study that the real picture is considerably more complex than commonly imagined. They discovered first that there are conservative and liberal voices in both rural and urban communities. Second, they did find a rural-urban gap on questions concerning "moral traditionalism," especially in relation to homosexuality. In short, urban respondents are more tolerant of homosexuality than rural dwellers. A similar gap exists in relation to urban and rural perspectives on Aboriginal peoples. However, the gap narrows considerably in relation to multiculturalism, and it appears not to exist at all on the accommodation of Quebec in the federation. Much of the gap can be explained by differing levels of education, and the gap that does exist is much smaller than one would imagine; it is in the order of 10 percent on most questions. Cutler and Jenkins thus conclude that "the intolerant rural hick is a straw man."

The conclusions reached by Cutler and Jenkins are in keeping with a modernizing society and globalizing world. The "national" media, both print and television, is now so ubiquitous that rural and urban people in Canada generally obtain their news from the same sources. They watch the same television shows; they see the same movies; and listen to the same music. Rural and urban Canadians can surf the WorldWideWeb from the comfort of their own homes. In short, rural and urban Canadians are bombarded daily with the same cultural messages. This is reinforced by rural-urban migration. For the most part, it is young people who migrate to the cities in search of better education and employment opportunities, and with better communication networks it is easy to stay in touch with family and friends back home on the farm or in the village. With children and grandchildren in the cities, older Canadians in rural communities now have compelling reasons to visit the city more often, and with better transportation networks it has never been easier to travel back and forth between rural and urban communities. This rural-urban interaction serves to expose rural Canadians to the new social attitudes in the city. The new social attitudes may also be transmitted through provincial education standards, which are established in relatively cosmopolitan provincial capitals. In short, the boundaries separating rural and urban Canada are no longer sharply demarcated. The boundaries are now extremely porous and traversed many times every day. One can only imagine that over time the gap in rural-urban social attitudes will continue to shrink, if it ever existed in the first place.

In sum, Canadians have adopted more progressive attitudes on a variety of social issues over the past 20 years. In contrast to the new neo-conservative attitudes toward the economy and public finances, social attitudes concerning gender equality, homosexuality and multiculturalism have moved perceptibly to the left. This is consistent with Nevitte's finding that "moral permissiveness" has increased in Canada.[30] As the chapter by Reg Whitaker ably demonstrates, the Liberal Party under Jean Chrétien has not only embraced neo-conservative economic policies, it has endorsed the new and more progressive social attitudes and defended the Supreme Court's Charter decisions on these issues, while the Reform Party/Canadian Alliance has struggled with these new social attitudes, as explained in the chapter by Telford.

While some of the more conservative provincial governments have been displeased with Supreme Court rulings, especially in homosexual rights and same-sex benefits cases, none resorted to use of the "notwithstanding" clause of the Charter to override court decisions on matters of human rights. The Charter as a political instrument still evokes some controversy in Quebec, although there is broad public support for equality and individual rights. A conflict may arise between the federal government and British Columbia over Aboriginal rights, as Gordon Gibson discusses in his chapter but, for the most part, there is little intergovernmental conflict on human rights issues. It would thus seem that the leftward shift in social attitudes has helped support relatively harmonious federal-provincial relations on human rights issues.

UNIVERSAL VALUES BUT MULTIPLE IDENTITIES?

The studies in this volume lend support to the claim that Canadian political culture has stepped to the right on questions of economic policy and fiscal management but stepped to the left on social issues (as distinct from social policy). Again, we wish to stress that the movement to the right has probably been greater than the move to the left, but both shifts are perceptible and significant. In every province, voters have expressed a desire for government to better manage public debt, and support for Charter values, particularly the equality provisions, is comparably high in all regions of the country. Arguably, these are emerging as universal values in the Canadian context. Put another way, Canadian political culture appears to be more homogeneous. It would seem that the processes of globalization and the post-Cold War concern for human rights are eroding the historical regional political cultures of Canada, at least in relation to economic values and social attitudes.

Are we finally witnessing the decline of regionalism in Canada? It would be premature to make that call, and we certainly do not have the evidence to support such a strong claim. Moreover, notwithstanding the convergence of economic values and social attitudes across Canada, regional identities are likely to persist, and some non-territorial identities may well become more pronounced. A number of structural and institutional variables may perpetuate regional and non-territorial identities. Regional political parties, such as the Alliance and the Bloc Québécois, will almost certainly reinforce regional identities; the continuation of distinct provincial party systems may also preserve distinct provincial identities.[31] The forces of globalization, furthermore, do not necessarily lead to economic policy convergence. To the extent that there are distinct regional political economies, or uneven distributions of wealth across the regions, globalization may impact the regions differentially and drive them further apart.[32] And, of course, the historical processes of socialization can work to maintain distinct identities long after the objective differences between groups have vanished. After all, the Scots are still Scots three centuries after the Act of Union, not to mention after many generations since the virtual disappearance of the Gaelic language in Scotland. In short, the issue of identity is distinct from questions of values and attitudes. Regional identities are thus likely to persist in Canada at some level, especially in Quebec.

The status of Canada's Aboriginal people is perhaps the most compelling identity issue in Canadian politics today, as the chapter by Ian Stewart on the fallout from the Marshall decision in Nova Scotia makes abundantly clear. While Howe and Fletcher report that Canadians are very supportive of Charter equality rights, Stewart suggests that there is an "absolutist quality" associated with the discourse of rights. The adjudication of rights is widely interpreted in the general public as a zero-sum contest, notwithstanding the Supreme Court's general disposition to balance contending interests. Disputes over rights thus tend to be polarizing, especially when there are economic rewards to be won and the contesting parties are relatively poor. All too often, First Nation reserves are located in impoverished rural areas and, while the surrounding non-Aboriginal community may be economically better off, these non-Aboriginal communities are frequently dependent on a declining natural resource industry. As resource industries are often the only game in town, Aboriginal peoples are increasingly wanting to participate in these sectors, which means that the ever-shrinking pie now has to be shared more ways.

The conflict over rights, however, goes much deeper, as Stewart elaborates in his chapter. While Canadians support the equality values embedded in the Charter, they understand these rights to apply universally to individuals. In this regard, Canadians are quintessentially liberal, and they have been very reluctant to accept particularistic and collective rights. In short, many Canadians are struggling with the idea of justice based on difference, notwithstanding their support for multiculturalism. For many Canadians, a differential distribution of rights smacks of inequality and injustice. Stewart has documented how these conflicting theories of justice were articulated by Aboriginal and non-Aboriginal communities in Nova Scotia following the Marshall decision, and he doubts that the impasse will be resolved any time soon. The differing identities and experiences have given rise to sharply different perceptions of justice, and this cleavage does not seem confined to Nova Scotia. It is sadly replicated across the country, and it has the power to weaken the strong support for the Charter, as Howe and Fletcher document in relation to Charter support in Quebec and British Columbia, two provinces that have been rocked by conflict with Aboriginal peoples.

The chasm between Aboriginal and non-Aboriginal peoples in Canada may in fact be deepening. Aboriginal peoples, as Stewart notes, are increasingly couching their claims as "inherent" rights. This perspective has been critiqued,[33] and some have tried to find some middle ground,[34] but it does not alter the fact that a crisis of legitimacy now exists between Aboriginal peoples and the Canadian state. If Aboriginal grievances are not redressed satisfactorily, the social and economic costs will be enormous, as the Royal Commission on Aboriginal Peoples argued. On the other hand, many Canadians are reluctant to endorse expensive proposals for Aboriginal self-government, such as the ones made by the Royal Commission on Aboriginal Peoples, especially in this era of fiscal conservatism. In other words, the issue of Aboriginal governance is also partially a fiscal issue as well as a human rights issue.

The chapter by Alain Gagnon and Raffaele Iacovino reminds us again that Quebec is still a distinct society. In particular, they argue that the promotion of multiculturalism in Quebec serves a very different social purpose. Gagnon and Iacovino maintain that Quebec has developed a model of *interculturalism* that is radically different than the model of multiculturalism practised in the rest of Canada. While multiculturalism accepts cultural diversity as an individual responsibility and a private matter, Gagnon and Iacovino suggest that interculturalism promotes a diversity of cultural collectivities in the public sphere, while at the same time sustaining the viability of a French-speaking society on an English-speaking continent. For Gagnon and Iacovino, interculturalism works to reinforce the distinct identity of the Québécois.

In short, while there is evidence of a rightward shift in matters related to the economy and public finances, and a leftward shift in approaches to human rights and social attitudes, it is also the case that this coming together on values does not equate to an erosion of language-based, regional or other identities. If anything, Aboriginal identities have become much more prominent over the past 20 years; Quebec retains a distinct personality and is more than likely to remain unique; and regional identities persist in Atlantic Canada and the west. The question of accommodation is thus still central to Canadian politics, but Matthew Mendelsohn fears that Canadian political parties have abandoned the traditional models of accommodation. Most distressingly, Mendelsohn argues that the Liberal Party has "since 1968 defined itself in opposition to the accommodation of groups that do not support a strong central government as their patron. It has staked out one well-defined pole on the political spectrum in opposition to all perceived threats to a strong Canadian state, namely Quebec nationalism, western devolutionist sentiment, and, from 1968 until the mid-90s, North American integration." In short, he contends that the Liberal "Party is committed to a particular view of the Canadian nation with little tolerance for alternative conceptions." And he notes, alarmingly, that "the 1993, 1997, and 2000 federal elections are the only elections in Canadian history where a party has formed a majority government but has failed to win a majority of seats in either Quebec or western Canada." Mendelsohn accepts Whitaker's proposition that the Liberal Party has successfully capitalized on the new economic and social consensus, but he fears that the Liberal Party's capacity to broker interregional accommodation has declined. This does not bode well for those groups left outside the new political consensus.

CANADIAN POLITICAL CULTURE AND THE FEDERAL PARTY SYSTEM: BLUE GRITS VERSUS RED TORIES?

As Canadians have shifted to the right on economic values and somewhat to the left on social attitudes, the federal Liberal Party under Jean Chrétien has moved in lock-step with public opinion. Paul Martin was a more successful "conservative" finance minister than Michael Wilson but, at the same time, the Liberal Party has steadfastly eschewed the moral traditionalism advocated by the Reform Party/Canadian Alliance. As Whitaker says, the Liberals under Chrétien have become very successful "blue grits." While the Liberals have undoubtedly benefited from a fractured opposition in the last three elections, the analyses in this volume suggest that they were not elected simply by default.

Preston Manning and the Reform Party can take some credit for influencing the new economic discourse in Canada, but it only provided modest electoral results for the party. As Canadians have moved to the right on economic and fiscal issues, they may be somewhat more in line with the economic philosophy of the Reform Party/Canadian Alliance, but in as much as Canadians have moved to the left in social attitudes, the social conservatism of the Alliance is further away from the Canadian median. The new leader of the

Alliance, Stephen Harper, apparently prefers to campaign on conservative economic issues and avoid questions of moral traditionalism. This strategy may have helped him win the Alliance leadership, but it is not clear that Harper's strategy will propel the party to victory. The left flank of Canadian political culture is probably too robust to ignore.

The federal NDP is positioned as the mirror opposite of the Reform Party/ Canadian Alliance. As Canadians have shifted to the right on economic questions, the NDP is now further away from the Canadian median on economic and public finance issues, although it is now perhaps closer to the median on social issues than it used to be. In the last four federal elections, the NDP has championed itself as the greatest defender of medicare and other social programs. As the polls indicate that Canadians are supportive of medicare, the NDP cannot fathom why they have not been more successful in the polls. Some NDP stalwarts seem to believe that the party has faltered because it has moderated its policies. These activists argue that the party's electoral fortunes can only be improved if it adopts more strident left-wing policies. If the analyses in this volume are correct, these prescriptions are seriously misguided.

The conclusions reached here, however, may provide some succour to the federal Conservative Party. While many social conservatives are loath to support Joe Clark, he appears to have a better read on contemporary public opinion in Canada than any of the contenders in the last two Alliance leadership races. Clark is trying to resurrect a truly progressive conservatism. The party's fiscal conservatism was evident in its election manifesto, while Clark's progressivism was openly displayed when he led Calgary's gay pride parade in the spring of 2001. In short, Clark is trying to create a broad-based party parallel to the Liberals, running from fiscal conservatism to social liberalism. Clark is undoubtedly aware that the Tories are the party of second choice for most Liberal voters.[35]

How the Bloc Québécois fits into this picture is not clear. The chapter by Salée indicates that the same pattern of economic conservatism and social liberalism in Canada exists also in Quebec. The Parti Québécois has certainly sloped in these directions, and the Quebec Liberal Party is apparently on the same angle. The Action Démocratique may in fact be positioned best to capitalize on the new political culture. The Bloc Québécois perhaps styled itself as a somewhat more progressive party on economic issues, but quebecers were not voting for the Bloc for these reasons, but to defend Quebec's interests, irrespective of left- or right-wing considerations. Quebecers' affection for the Bloc appeared to weaken in the 2000 election. The Bloc only obtained half the vote and half the seats in Quebec in 2000, and some *Blocistes* believe that the party should probably be folded if its support drops any further.[36]

The analyses here suggest that the Liberal Party has a lock on the federal party system for the foreseeable future. The Canadian Election Study has arrived at the same conclusion.[37] What are the implications for the federation of continued Liberal hegemony? Under Jean Chrétien, and most of his probable successors, we would expect "steady-as-she-goes" policy. The Liberals appear committed to a "balanced" approach to tax cuts, spending increases, and debt reduction. The Liberals under Chrétien also appear to prefer a pragmatic "problem-solving" approach to governing the federation rather than governing from first principles. On a large variety of important issues and programs, the Liberal government has worked cooperatively with the provinces, trying to solve problems one at a time through specific intergovernmental agreements.

But on "higher order" questions, the Liberals have been reluctant to engage with the provinces and other groups. And when pushed on symbolic issues or cross-cutting issues, they have tended to push back. The Liberals do not seem to be in any rush to develop self-governance for Aboriginal peoples. The Liberals display no desire to recognize Quebec's distinctiveness constitutionally and they have laid down the law on unilateral secession. The Liberals have also summarily rejected the assertion made by the provinces that there is a vertical fiscal imbalance in the federation.

The weakness of the other parties in the system suggests that the Liberals may again be reading the mood of the country more accurately. There does not seem to be much demand for greater centralization or more decentralization, nor does there seem to be much appetite to recognize Quebec's distinctiveness constitutionally or establish Aboriginal self-government, notwithstanding the public's support for official bilingualism and general sympathy for Aboriginal peoples. If anything, there is pressure to take a tougher line against Quebec and Aboriginal self-government. The Canadian Election Study reports that only 9 percent of Canadians outside Quebec think "more"should be done for Quebec, while 39 percent opted for "less"; 43 percent supported the status quo.[38] Canadians overwhelming rejected the Tories more favourable approaches to Quebec and the provinces generally in 1993, and they have yet to embrace the more province-friendly orientation of the Alliance (apart from Alberta and British Columbia). On the other hand, Canadians have not responded to the NDP's desire to strengthen the social role of the central government or the NDP's more favourable disposition to the First Nations. The general social progressiveness we have described in Canada is thus limited by the staunch individualism displayed by most Canadians and the associated scepticism of group claims. Nevertheless, the opposition parties seem either too fragmented or out of step with Canadian public opinion to launch a serious challenge to the governing Liberals.

CANADIAN POLITICAL CULTURE AND INTERGOVERNMENTAL RELATIONS

Other things being equal, one might expect the general convergence on political values to have a positive impact on the state of the federation and the conduct of intergovernmental relations. Of course, in the real world, other things are not always equal. For one thing, as already noted, a convergent direction on values does not have anything to say about identities. Perhaps more importantly, the practice of intergovernmental relations in the past decade has been strained by the politics of fiscal retrenchment and the desire for lower rates of taxation. While Canadians overwhelmingly want their governments to cooperate, the new political culture in Canada appears to have given the federal and provincial governments less room to manoeuvre where money issues are concerned.[39]

While many individuals inside government, especially in line ministries, understand the virtue of intergovernmental cooperation, the strong public pressure for intergovernmental cooperation has also undoubtedly helped governments to cooperate in broad areas of public policy. The consensus of federal, provincial, and territorial finance ministers meant that through much of the 1990s, there was little disagreement among governments about the desirability of fiscal restraint, with the possible exception of British Columbia under the NDP. In the aftermath of continental free trade, the broad consensus among governments regarding the need for competitive markets helped facilitate the intergovernmental Agreement on Internal Trade (AIT). There was also little dispute among federal and provincial governments regarding the idea that the state, whether federal or provincial, needed to be made more efficient. This led to a new focus on outcomes (however hard in practice it might be to achieve), accountability, and transparency in federal-provincial agreements. In addition to the AIT, intergovernmental agreements have been reached in other areas, including social policy (e.g., the Social Union Framework Agreement; National Child Benefit; homelessness and social housing arrangements; the labour market development agreements; a new Health Accord), the environment (the Environmental Harmonization Agreement), and the management of natural resources. The media and opposition parties look for disputes, not agreements. This may help to explain why so little attention is focused on these broad areas of intergovernmental cooperation.

Quebecers also want the two orders of government to cooperate, and a great deal of business has been effectively carried out between the Government of Canada and the Government of Quebec in recent years. The Government of Quebec has signed many arrangements with Ottawa, ranging from the AIT, a bilateral labour market training and development agreement, to the February 1999 Health Accord, the September 2000 First Ministers' Agreement on Health, and the autumn 2000 business plan associated with the federal-provincial climate change efforts as a result of commitments at Kyoto (a plan that Ontario did not sign on to). While in general the Government of Quebec declares it is much more open to one-on-one bilateral deals than to multilateral agreements in which Quebec is one government in ten or thirteen (if the territories are included), it is also inevitably influenced by the content of what is on the table. In the five agreements noted just above, four were multilateral. They were signed because they fit with Quebec's economic agenda (AIT and perhaps the climate change plan) or fiscal needs (the health deals). At the same time, the Quebec government has chosen not to sign several other agreements, including the Canada-Wide Accord on Environmental Harmonization, the National Child Benefit, and the F/P/T Agreement on Early Childhood Development. The continuing salience of Quebec nationalism, and the conventional Quebec interpretation of the 1867 bargain, helps to explain the latter deals that have not been struck. Nonetheless, the number of items on which the governments of Canada and Quebec have been able to reach agreement is significant.

In short, public pressure has helped to support relatively peaceful and cooperative intergovernmental relations over a wide swath of public policy in the post-Charter era. At the same time, however, the public's desire for intergovernmental cooperation has obviously not been sufficient to create an era of complete harmony in the federation or of easy intergovernmental relations. In this regard, a major source of contention is money. Anthony Birch once stated that "The problem of finance is the fundamental problem of federalism."[40] This statement appears to be as true today as it was 50 years ago. Indeed, the problem has undoubtedly intensified over the past two decades as a result of fiscal retrenchment and the public's aversion to further tax increases.

Coming out of the recession of the early 1980s there was a conviction at the federal level that there was a vertical fiscal imbalance in the federation and that it favoured the provinces. Thus, on several occasions in the 1980s the federal government more or less unilaterally reduced the planned rate of increase in its transfer payments to the provinces. Provincial governments received these actions poorly. The 1990 cap on the Canada Assistance Plan transfers to non-Equalization-receiving provinces also furthered the provincial perception that Ottawa was an untrustworthy fiscal partner. By the time of the large transfer reductions associated with the introduction of the Canada Health and Social Transfer (CHST), provincial governments had become deeply convinced that they could no longer trust the federal government on fiscal matters.

Our purpose here is not to discuss in detail the merits or demerits of Ottawa's actions. Rather, it is simply to note that since the CHST, the provinces have worked with one another in a cooperative manner, notwithstanding differences among them, to "get back" the monies they believe to be owed to them.[41] The provinces also attempted to impose some limits on the federal spending power through their initiative that led to the Social Union Framework Agreement. And to varying degrees they have campaigned publicly against the federal government concerning the current division of revenues.[42] Although the federal government responded with large increases in transfer payments to the provinces as its finances improved, the federal actions are viewed by provinces as an inadequate reply to their needs. There thus remains an atmosphere of profound mistrust among the provinces in respect of fiscal relations with the federal government.

The intergovernmental battle over health care is closely linked to the larger intergovernmental fiscal relationship. The controversy has mainly to do with whether the federal government is paying its fair share of provincial medicare costs. It is, of course, also about other things, including the federal role in interpreting and enforcing the *Canada Health Act* and the possibility of a greater role for the private sector in delivering health services. Both of these items, however, are linked to the fiscal issue.

The division of revenues between federal and provincial governments, at any point in time, is not a zero-sum game in the sense that if one order of government alters its tax revenues, this does not necessarily result in changes in the revenues of the other order of government by an equivalent amount.[43] However, it appears that governments are reluctant to raise taxes these days in the face of tax-exhausted voters, and tax competition from the United States. The result is that governments, especially provincial governments, behave as if the division of revenues is a zero-sum game, and they are demanding that Ottawa explicitly transfer revenues or tax room to them instead of raising more of their own revenues. The word "explicitly" is crucial here. In his 2000 budget, the federal finance minister announced a large five-year program of tax reductions. When Paul Martin made his announcement, an option open to the provinces was to occupy at least some of the room that the federal government was vacating. But none did so. Nor, from the public record, does it appear that any seriously contemplated so doing. In other words, they were not willing to take the political flak or the economic risk for treating Ottawa's tax cuts as a tax transfer in their favour even though they believed the federal government had been treating them very unfairly in relation to intergovernmental transfers.

It is undoubtedly more difficult to sustain harmonious fiscal relations between federal and provincial governments during periods of fiscal retrenchment than during periods of fiscal plenty. The more general hypothesis that emerges from this argument, however, is that the federal government and the provinces have been constrained by the more conservative economic culture, especially on fiscal matters, that has prevailed in the federation over the last decade and longer.

What can we conclude from this analysis? The trends in contemporary political culture help to explain the harmonious intergovernmental relations across a wide swath of public policy in recent years. The extent of what is working well should not be underestimated. But the convergent trend in some important dimensions of political culture has also contributed to a fractious set of intergovernmental relations on the sharing of the fiscal pie. And convergent trends around social attitudes have not taken nationalist and regionalist politics off the political agenda. With Quebec nationalism relatively quiescent at present, Aboriginal self-governance appears destined to be the major mega-constitutional challenge over the coming few years. This issue affects some provinces more than others, and it may well introduce a new set of inter-governmental tensions over the next decade as the governments of Canada and Aboriginal nations seek a just solution for Aboriginal peoples. As for non-constitutional politics, intergovernmental relations seem destined to swirl around fiscal issues for the foreseeable future.

NOTES

The authors would like to thank Bob Young, Reg Whitaker, Matthew Mendelsohn and Ian Stewart for the helpful comments they provided on various drafts of this chapter.

1. David Elkins and Richard Simeon, "A Cause in Search of an Effect, or What Does Political Culture Explain?" *Comparative Politics* 11, 2(1979):143.

2. Alexandra Dobrowolsky, "Political Parties: Teletubby Politic, the Third Way, and Democratic Challenge(r)s," in *Canadian Politics in the 21st Century*, ed. Michael Whittington and Glen Williams (Toronto: Nelson Thompson Learning, 2000).

3. We want to stress that we distinguish between social attitudes on human rights questions and attitudes on social policy. While attitudes on social issues such as feminism and homosexuality may have shifted somewhat to the left in the past few decades, attitudes toward social policy appear to have swung to the right in accordance with the view that governments need to be more fiscally responsible.

4. See, Centre for Research and Information on Canada, *Portraits of Canada, 2001*, p. 22.

5. Nelson Wiseman, "Provincial Political Cultures," in *Provinces: Canadian Provincial Politics*, ed. Christopher Dunn (Peterborough: Broadview Press, 1996), p. 23.

6. David Bell, "Political Culture in Canada," in *Canadian Politics in the 1990s*, ed. Michael Whittington and Glen Williams (Toronto: Nelson Canada, 1995), p. 105.

7. Elkins and Simeon, "A Cause in Search of an Effect, or What does Political Culture Explain," p. 128.

8. Bell, "Political Culture in Canada," p. 106.

9. Elkins and Simeon, "A Cause in Search of an Effect, or What does Political Culture Explain," p. 131.

10. Ibid., p. 139.

11. Ibid., p. 140.

12. Ibid.

13. Ibid.

14. Richard Simeon and David Elkins, "Regional Political Cultures in Canada," *Canadian Journal of Political Science* 7, 3(1974):397; see also John Wilson, "The Canadian Political Cultures: Towards a Redefinition of the Nature of the Canadian Political System," *Canadian Journal of Political Science* 7, 3(1974).

15. Ian Stewart, *Roasting Chestnuts: The Mythology of Maritime Political Culture* (Vancouver: University of British Columbia Press, 1994).

16. Neil Nevitte *et al., Unsteady State: The 1997 Canadian Federal Election* (Toronto: Oxford University Press, 2000).

17. Herman Bakvis, *Regional Ministers: Power and Influence in the Canadian Cabinet* (Toronto: University of Toronto Press, 1991).

18. Michael Lusztig, "Constitutional Paralysis: Why Canadian Constitutional Initiatives are Doomed to Fail," *Canadian Journal of Political Science* 27, 4(1994).

19. Michael Bliss, "The Fault Lines Deepen," *The Globe and Mail,* 2 May 2000, p. A15.

20. Nevitte found that support for free market principles and meritocracy has increased in Canada. While this suggests a movement to the right on economic issues, he reports that Canadians do not perceive their rightward shift when asked to place themselves on the left-right spectrum. See Neil Nevitte, *The Decline of Deference* (Peterborough: Broadview Press, 1996), p. 118.

21. Matthew Mendelsohn and Robert Wolfe, "The Aftermyth of Seattle: Public Opinion on Globalization and Trade Liberalization," *International Journal* (June 2001).

22. David Osborne and Ted Gaebler, *Reinventing Government: How the Entrepreneurial Spirit is Transforming the Public Sector* (Reading, MA: Addison-Wesley Publishing Company, 1992).

23. F. L. Morton and Rainer Knopff, *The Charter Revolution and the Court Party* (Peterborough: Broadview Press, 2000).

24. David Rayside, *On the Fringe: Gays and Lesbians in Politics* (Ithaca: Cornell University Press, 1998), pp. 105-06.

25. See, *Egale et al.* v. *Attorney General Canada et al.*, BCSC 1365 (2001).

26. Alexander Panetta, "Poll Reveals Doubt on Gay Adoption," *The Globe and Mail,* 16 July 2001, p. A4. The poll actually revealed that support for homosexual equality rights rose to 75.7 percent when the contentious issues of marriage and adoption were excluded from the equation. It is often believed that Alberta is more conservative than other provinces, but even here the government refrained from employing the notwithstanding clause in response to the Vriend case. While the government was under pressure from certain quarters to reverse the court's decision, evidently the government concluded that the majority of Albertans would not tolerate the suppression of equal rights for homosexuals.

27. Rosemary Speirs, *Out of the Blue: The Fall of the Tory Dynasty in Ontario* (Toronto: Macmillan, 1986), p. 43.

28. Bharati Mukherjee, *Darkness* (Toronto: Penguin Books, 1985).

29. The concept of multiculturalism is still the subject of serious critiques from time to time. See Neil Bissoondath, *Selling Illusions: The Cult of Multiculturalism in Canada* (Toronto: Penguin Books, 1994); Richard Gwyn, *Nationalism without Walls: The Unbearable Lightness of Being Canadian* (Toronto: McClelland & Stewart, 1995). For a refutation of these critiques, Will Kymlicka, *Finding Our Way: Rethinking Ethnocultural Relations in Canada* (Toronto: Oxford University Press, 1998).

30. Nevitte, *Decline of Deference*, p. 217.

31. R.K. Carty and David Stewart, "Parties and Party Sytems," in *Provinces. Canadian Provincial Politics*, ed. Christopher Dunn (Peterborough: Broadview Press, 1996).

32. See Harvey Lazar and Hamish Telford (eds.), *The Impact of Global and Regional Integration on Federal Political Systems* (Kingston: Institute of Intergovernmental Relations, forthcoming).

33. Tom Flanagan, *First Nations? Second Thoughts* (Montreal: McGill-Queen's University Press, 2000).

34. Alan Cairns, *Citizens Plus: Aboriginal Peoples and the Canadian State* (Vancouver: University of British Columbia Press, 2000).

35. Nevitte *et al., Unsteady State*.

36. From a personal conversation with a prominent Bloc official.

37. André Blais *et al., Anatomy of a Liberal Victory: Making Sense of the Vote in the 2000 Canadian Election* (Peterborough: Broadview Press, 2002), p. 204.

38. Ibid., p. 104.

39. A recent survey asked Canadians the following question: "Thinking about how governments make decisions, which of the following do you think would be best for Canada: One, the *federal* government should have the final say on some things, the *provincial* governments on others, and they should both stay out of each other's way; or two, both levels of government should *work most things out together*."

	Final Say (%)	Work Together (%)	Don't Know (%)	Number
BC	13	86	1	325
Alberta	17	82	1	327
Man/Sask	11	88	1	450
Ontario	17	81	2	403
Quebec	30	65	4	1,001
Atlantic	6	93	1	434

These polling numbers are from Fred Cutler and Matthew Mendelsohn, "Unnatural Loyalties? The Governments and Citizens of Canadian Federalism," forthcoming in the edited volume on the work of Alan Cairns.

40.   Anthony Birch, *Federalism, Finance and Social Legislation in Canada, Australia, and the United States* (Oxford: Oxford University Press, 1955), p. xi.

41.   See, for example, "Redesigning Fiscal Federalism – Issues and Options," paper submitted to premiers by the provincial and territorial ministers of finance, 1999/2000.

42.   For example, the Government of Ontario ran newspapers ads and the Government of Quebec appointed a Commission on Fiscal Imbalance.

43.   It is worth recalling that both orders of government have a constitutional right to tax what are today the most lucrative tax bases. While it is true that the revenues of provinces that have entered into tax collection agreements with Ottawa will be automatically affected when the federal government adjusts its definition of tax income, it is also the case that the provinces can adjust their tax rates or other parts of their tax system to offset the revenue effects of any tax changes coming from Ottawa.

II

Federal Politics

2

The Liberal Chameleon:
From Red Tories to Blue Grits

Reg Whitaker

Le gouvernement libéral de Jean Chrétien projette une image vraiment floue de sa politique publique. Les libéraux ont toujours prétendu être des centristes pragmatiques, mais depuis 1993, ce gouvernement libéral a été particulièrement difficile à catégoriser. Il a adopté plusieurs des politiques économiques de son prédécesseur conservateur, incluant celles auxquelles il s'était énergiquement opposé lorsqu'il était dans l'opposition: le libre-échange et la TPS en étant deux exemples frappants. Remarquablement, l'adoption de ces politiques, qui avait causé de sérieux dommages politiques au gouvernement Mulroney, lui a procuré un bénéfice politique. Bien que la question du bon moment ait été importante pour expliquer cet état de fait, plus importante encore a été sa capacité de comprendre que le centre politique est une cible mouvante. Les libéraux de Chrétien ont correctement prévu un déplacement vers la droite de l'opinion publique quant à la politique fiscale et ont ainsi substantiellement amoindri l'Alliance canadienne en volant leur plate-forme fiscale, comme l'avaient fait certains gouvernements libéraux passés en devançant le NPD sur la gauche. Cependant, ce serait une erreur de croire que les libéraux sont tout simplement devenus un gouvernement de l'aile droite. Sur les enjeux sociaux et culturels, ils ont été alertes en se plaçant eux-mêmes à la gauche de l'Alliance, au diapason de l'opinion publique. Le succès des libéraux n'est pas seulement attribuable à la faiblesse et à la fragmentation de l'opposition, mais plutôt le résultat d'une habileté extraordinaire à se positionner au centre d'une société canadienne changeante.

The Liberal government of Prime Minister Jean Chrétien has a blurred ideological image. This may be fitting for a centrist party, but it has led to confusion among analysts and difficulties in situating the current government in relation to the Canadian political culture. To some, the Liberals are conservative wolves in liberal clothing, while to others they are liberal wolves in conservative disguise. To others, they seem to lack all direction and definition. Chrétien is no political visionary and the government he leads usually places itself prudently but closely behind, rather than dangerously in front of, developing public opinion. By examining the Liberal record in the context both of history and of the changing global environment, the Liberal government assumes some shape, although in ways that defy traditional left-right categories. In the early twenty-first century, the Liberals remain what they were for much of the twentieth century, the government party.[1] As such, they are ideological chameleons, taking their colours from their context. But they are hardly monochromatic: given contemporary diversity and turmoil, the Liberal chameleon turns out to be variegated and nuanced in its shading.

A LIBERAL SUCCESS STORY?

As the Chrétien government advances through its third term of office, it is, by many objective standards, a success. Politically, Prime Minister Chrétien has won three consecutive back-to-back majority governments, a feat not matched by any federal leader in peacetime since Sir Wilfrid Laurier almost a century ago. At no time in previous history has the opposition been so fragmented, impotent, and self-destructive.

In terms of economic policy, the Liberals turned a serious budgetary deficit situation, which had plagued previous Liberal and Conservative governments, into a budgetary surplus position just past the end of its first term. Having achieved this surplus, the Liberals have been able to restore the provincial transfers on health care they had cut to tackle the deficit, made large tax reductions, sustained moderate increases in spending on social programs, and begun paying down the cumulative debt and thus reducing the debt to gross domestic product (GDP) ratio. Unemployment, the bane of earlier governments for decades, has declined in later Liberal years. Inflation seemed, by the late 1990s, to have become largely a threat of the past. It is a mark of Liberal success in economic policy, that Finance Minister Paul Martin, responsible for executing major cutbacks in the first term, is now the most popular single federal political leader, outstripping the prime minister himself.[2]

In international trade, Canada moved from consolidation of NAFTA to taking a leading role in the advancement of a broader Free Trade of the Americas Agreement (FTAA). Throughout most of this time, Canada has enjoyed large trade surpluses with the rest of the world. In foreign policy, the former minister of foreign affairs, Lloyd Axworthy, established a distinctive role for Canada abroad with a human security agenda and new notions of "soft power."

The one policy area that had suggested Liberal weakness was the grave threat of Quebec secession, especially after the near victory of the sovereignists in the 1995 Quebec referendum, and the relative feebleness of the federal Liberals in Quebec confronting the Bloc Québécois in francophone Quebec. Yet by the time of the Liberals' third electoral victory in 2000, the threat of secession had diminished dramatically. The Liberals had passed the *Clarity Act*, setting relatively tough rules for future referenda, without rousing any pro-sovereignist backlash in Quebec; in the 2000 election, they were able to improve their electoral fortunes somewhat in francophone Quebec at the expense of the Bloc; and Chrétien's formidable adversary, Lucien Bouchard, retired as premier.

In federal-provincial relations, the high-octane — and high risk — era of mega-constitutional revision is over. Smaller scale, piecemeal constitutional changes, such as Quebec and Newfoundland's revisions to the status of denominational schools, or the federal government's transfer of manpower training to the provinces, have been shown by the Liberals to be possible under the constitutional status quo. Moreover, the Social Union Framework Agreement was signed by all provinces save Quebec. There were no conflicts on the order of the Ottawa-Alberta energy battles of the 1970s and 1980s. Although Ontario under Tory provincial rule was emerging as something of an antagonist to Ottawa, this was balanced by the overwhelming propensity of Ontario voters to opt for the Liberals at the federal level.

At a more intangible level, after eight years of Liberal governance, the country seems more tranquil, less agitated and less surly than it was when Chrétien took over — although this may represent a turning away from politics more than a contentment with the political system (declining voter turnout would indicate the latter). The 2000 election campaign, mired in attacks on personal integrity, struck a low and negative tone. Yet this only served to emphasize the lack of substantive issues on which the opposition parties could make any dent on the Liberal record. If the election was unusually petty, it was because the Liberals comfortably held all the big issues. The country, by and large, was unmoved, or repelled, by the personal attacks, and those who did vote produced another mandate for Chrétien.

HOLDING THE CENTRE AGAINST CENTRIFUGAL FORCES

Of course, not everyone would agree with these characterizations. A majority of voters have throughout the Chrétien era supported other parties. Even if regional support was won back in Atlantic Canada in 2000 (after a stinging rejection in 1997, and after restoring employment insurance benefits), Quebec remains a Liberal soft spot, and the west has produced diminishing returns. Sections of the media remain highly critical, ranging from the active, relentless hostility of the *National Post* to a less ideologically driven propensity on the part of other print and electronic media to focus on negative reporting of potential corruption or the "arrogance of power." Nor is there any shortage of complaints about policy failures or shortcomings emanating from the opposition parties, the media, business, unions, social movements, academics, and the various think-tanks and research institutes. Yet when all the free advice is tabulated, it quickly becomes apparent that much of it is self-cancelling, that is, some call for deeper tax cuts while others call for more social spending; some insist that increased productivity should be at the top of the agenda, while others demand that a decade of lost real wages and benefits be recouped. There are only a few issues that seem to mobilize a clear majority, and when they do emerge, as with deficit elimination and salvaging the health-care system, the Liberals are very adept at getting to the front of the parade. Otherwise, they have been careful to maintain a "balanced" approach in the new era of fiscal surpluses between new spending, tax cuts, and debt reduction, a formula that permits flexibility without commitment to any single overriding priority. In short, the Liberals appear to be a classic centrist government, steering resolutely down the middle.

This centrist formula was cast into sharp relief against the more programmatic opposition parties when Paul Martin announced to the House of Commons in 1998 the "official" demise of the deficit. The opposition party leaders rose in turn to attempt to put their own partisan spin on what was manifestly a triumph for the government. Not surprisingly, each claimed that credit lay elsewhere than with the Liberals, but in each case the choice was ideological. The Reform and Conservative leaders said that it was the long-suffering Canadian taxpayer who had borne the brunt of deficit fighting through a crippling tax burden: now was the time to reward these efforts through immediate tax relief. The Bloc Québécois insisted that it was the provinces, that is, Quebec, that had borne the brunt of the deficit fight through lost transfers and subsidies: now was the time to restore all these monies to the provinces. The New Democratic Party (NDP) leader attested that the deficit had been defeated on the backs of the poor and the working class through deep cuts to social programs: now was the time to restore these programs and extend them. The Liberal response was textbook centrism: each of the opposition parties was, in its own way, right. It was not the Liberals who had killed the deficit, it was "Canadians," and this included taxpayers, the provinces, and those who benefited from social programs. All had done their part, and now all should receive some recompense, but in a balanced way, tempered with sound fiscal prudence, lest there be any slippage back to the bad old days.

THE MOVING CENTRE, FROM MULRONEY TO CHRÉTIEN

Does the Liberal government, as a successful catch-all brokerage party, simply exhibit the virtues of pragmatism, the political utility of sticking to the centre? However alluring this may be as a simple, no-fuss explanation, there are problems. The Progressive Conservative governments of Brian Mulroney, from 1984 to 1993, were constructed along similar lines. Indeed, Mulroney started from a much more secure base in 1984, with majorities in every region and every province of the country. Mulroney too was notoriously pragmatic, much to the despair of ideologues to his right, as he failed to live up to the exacting standards of Reaganism and Thatcherism in slashing social program entitlements. Yet within nine years, his coalition had splintered spectacularly asunder, with its two main wings — western conservatives and Quebec nationalists — both breaking off to form new, more ideological parties. The equally pragmatic Chrétien Liberals have not only avoided the fate of a brokerage that failed, but today it is the opposition that is splintering and floundering.

One explanation for the greater success of the Liberals is structural. Mulroney's alliance with the so-called "soft" nationalists of Quebec proved to be inherently unstable and ultimately self-destructive. The Liberals have never made deals with nationalists, which has left their Quebec base smaller but more stable, while allowing them to maintain their English-Canadian coalition unencumbered by the need to appease Quebec nationalist demands. Meech Lake was the populist anvil upon which the Mulroney Tories were hammered. When Alliance leader Stockwell Day began overtures to Quebec nationalists in 2000, Prime Minister Chrétien could barely contain his enthusiasm: "go right ahead," he advised, "go again down the path of Meech and Charlottetown — but you won't find the government following you."

The Liberals have also been sensitive to the point that the centre is itself a constantly moving target, that anyone who wants to stay in the "middle" must be prepared for persistent readjustments and policy shifts to keep up with and even to keep just slightly in front of public opinion. This also means that a Liberal government has no scruples about shifting rightward when the centre of political gravity has itself been shifting rightward. Thus the paradox, infuriating as it must be to Mulroney and his former ministers in retirement, that policy initiatives taken in his government were later capitalized upon by the Liberals, despite having generally opposed the same initiatives while in opposition.

In the matter of deficit elimination, the Tories had talked the talk of neoliberal retrenchment, but shrank from the necessary means to actually achieve results in the face of widespread public backlash — including the Liberals, who painted the Tories as heartless reactionaries, and pledged to defend social programs. In office, the same Liberals took the bold step of eliminating block transfers to the provinces on health, postsecondary education, and welfare, and replacing them by the Canada Health and Social Transfer (CHST), which lopped more than $6 billion off Ottawa's bill from 1996 to 1998. At the same time, Employment Insurance (EI) was overhauled, with reductions in benefits and increases in contributions from workers. There were deep cuts to the public service, with more than 50,000 jobs eventually eliminated. Of course, drastic effects on social programs were widely felt, especially in the health-care sector, although there is evidence that the provinces had actually made most of the cuts in health care prior to the bite of the CHST.[3] The EI cuts led to retribution against the Liberals by angry Atlantic voters in the 1997 election, although their majority was preserved nationally. But the success of the government in achieving deficit elimination, coupled with clear signs of a general economic recovery by the late 1990s, seemed to have taken the sharp edge off opposition. Except for the transitory regional protest in the Maritimes in 1997, the NDP, which might otherwise have been the natural beneficiary of class-based protest against the contraction of social programs, was barely able to keep its head slightly above water, and indeed has posed such a small political threat to the Chrétien government as to have been almost entirely ignored since 1993.

Two Mulroney initiatives that generated massive popular opposition were the Canada-US Free Trade Agreement (FTA) and the imposition of the Goods and Services Tax (GST). So ferocious was the opposition to these measures that Parliament had to be either bypassed, in the case of the FTA, or restructured, in the case of the GST. When the Liberal-dominated Senate forced the Tories to put the prospective FTA on the agenda for the 1988 election, the three-party, first-past-the-post electoral system resulted in another Tory majority government. But as a quasi-referendum on free trade, 1988 showed that a majority of voters supported the two anti-free-trade parties, everywhere except Quebec and Alberta. Instrumental in galvanizing this anti-free-trade sentiment had been the passionate opposition articulated by Liberal leader John Turner. In 1993, the Liberals promised in their *Red Book* of election pledges to "renegotiate" both the FTA and its proposed extension into the North American Free Trade Agreement (NAFTA), to obtain four major concessions. The *Red Book* went on to state that "abrogating trade agreements should only be a last resort if satisfactory changes cannot be negotiated."[4] Notwithstanding a failure to achieve most of the concessions demanded, one of the first acts of the new Liberal government was to endorse NAFTA. Indeed, wholehearted assent to economic globalization has been a hallmark of the Chrétien-Martin governments, symbolized for publicity purposes in the various "Team Canada" trade missions abroad, and culminating in the enthusiastic leadership shown by the Liberals in encouraging the expansion of NAFTA into the proposed FTAA at the controversial Quebec City meeting in the spring of 2001. The industry minister, Brian Tobin, in a moment of unusual candor, told a conference held to commemorate the original FTA negotiation, that Brian Mulroney had been right in 1988 and the Liberals wrong. Although Mulroney gracefully accepted the apology, it must have been cold comfort.

In order to force the GST through a Liberal Senate which had suddenly awakened to widespread public anger about the new tax, the Mulroney Tories had to resort to the desperate measure of "packing" the upper house with additional new senators pledged to vote for the GST. Given the bad image of the unelected Senate in the populist public eye, and concerns over wasteful expenditures and political patronage, this procedure was, depending upon one's point of view, either courageous or foolhardy. It was a contribution to the rapidly deteriorating position of the Progressive Conservative party, which ended in its huge debacle of the 1993 election.

The Liberals, sensing partisan blood, pledged themselves in their 1993 platform to "replace" the GST with a system that "generates equivalent revenues, is fairer to consumers and to small businesses, minimizes disruption to small business, and promotes federal-provincial fiscal cooperation and harmonization."[5] In office, desultory efforts to fiddle with the optics of the unpopular tax were soon abandoned after three Atlantic provinces consented to its "harmonization" with provincial sales taxes. The GST is now as established a part of the federal revenue system as free trade is the centrepiece of commercial policy. Yet apart from the bizarre incident of one minister, Sheila Copps, who had incautiously pledged to resign her seat if the GST were not killed, having to be re-elected in an unnecessary by-election, the political fallout from this Liberal turnabout appears to have been limited.

On the constitutional front, the Mulroney government twice pushed forward boldly, with the Meech Lake and Charlottetown initiatives, only to be rebuffed by provincial and popular antagonism. These turned out to be high-stakes gambles — Meech was later described by Mulroney as "rolling the dice" — and failure cost the Conservatives dearly. The Liberals were somewhat ambivalent at the time: former Prime Minister Pierre Trudeau was the chief antagonist of both initiatives; Chrétien personally failed to endorse Meech, although the Liberals officially backed Charlottetown. Yet in the face of their near-defeat by the sovereignists in the Quebec referendum of 1995, the Chrétien government did embrace constitutional change to recognize Quebec's status within federalism as a "distinct society" (the most controversial aspect of Meech in English Canada), and a Quebec constitutional veto, first via a non-binding parliamentary resolution in November 1995, and then with Intergovernmental Affairs Minister Stéphane Dion's commitment to securing constitutional recognition of Quebec's distinctiveness. While this was never given any priority by a government unwilling to rouse the hornets' nest of constitutional revision, it is also the case that at the philosophical level at least, the Chrétien Liberals have executed a *volte-face* from Trudeau-era doctrine in the direction of at least tepid endorsement of Mulroney's constitutional initiatives for which the Tories paid such a stiff price. The Liberals, as usual, managed to emerge relatively unscathed.

Why did the Conservatives pay such a heavy price for implementing policies that their Liberal successors have conserved and even extended while collecting political credit? There are a number of possible answers to this. One is simply a question of timing, always an important political variable.

Experience of free trade has made Canadians less fearful of its effects than they were at its uncertain outset in 1988, and more aware of its tangible benefits. Despite the sometimes violent demonstrations by anti-globalization activists at Quebec City in 2001, the Chrétien government is quite confident that it has majority support from Canadians for extending free trade to the proposed FTAA, and public opinion data would seem to bear this out.[6] Canadians have hardly learned to love the GST, but they have learned to live with it, and have forgiven, or perhaps forgotten, the Liberals' two-faced response to it, in and out of office. The Liberals' deficit-cutting measures were launched at a time when both elite and public opinion were finally ready for them, which had not been the case when the Tories came into office in the mid-1980s.

It is also a question of style of leadership. The Mulroney Conservatives were vocal and aggressive in pushing their policies at the rhetorical level, even if they were sometimes hesitant and vacillating in execution. Canadians responded resentfully and anxiously to the constant barrage of change being thrust upon them, and especially to the "in-your-face" style of Mulroney. The Chrétien Liberals have been more low-key and managerial in style, eschewing ideologically tinged rhetoric while concentrating on quiet implementation. The Conservatives pushed a deficit-elimination agenda with belligerent neo-liberal rhetoric that belied an ineffective record of performance. Paul Martin, on the other hand, has kept the rhetorical heat rather low, while systematically achieving results. His success thus appears as a triumph of sound managerial pragmatism, rather than as a vindication of an abstract economic ideology that tends to create as many enemies as friends when spelled out.

LIBERALISM'S AMBIGUOUS "CENTRE-LEFT" CREDENTIALS

One characterization of the Liberal government's propensity to steal its Conservative predecessors' policies and make them its own, is to stress an alleged discontinuity in Liberal philosophy after its return to office in 1993. By this account, the Liberals in opposition to Mulroney were in continuity with a moderately left-centrist position that has allegedly epitomized the Liberals in the modern era. The Chrétien Liberals are described as wolves in sheeps' clothing, as a species of "Blue Grits" to match the so-called "Red Tories" of the right. Despite tinges of old left-liberal rhetoric still clinging around the margins of the government, the prime minister, and especially the finance minister, have completed the restructuring of Canadian public policy along outright neo-liberal lines. This is the claim of the NDP leadership, as well as of the various factions within and around the party that seek a renewal of social democracy along more radical lines. It is rejected by the faction in the NDP (represented most clearly by former Saskatchewan Premier Roy Romanow) that is not opposed in principle to some accommodation with the Liberals. It is an argument that is rarely heard openly on the right, either from the Canadian Alliance or the Progressive Conservatives, but its validity is sometimes tacitly, if unhappily, admitted each time another piece of conservative clothing is brazenly stolen away and tried on for size on the government benches. Right-wing ideologues in and around the Alliance, and in the editorial offices of the *National Post,* used to insist that the Grits were still the same old tax-and-spend socialists, but even they seem reconciled to admitting that their nemesis is "centrist."[7] The Liberals themselves try to obfuscate and elude ideological characterization altogether by describing themselves in banal terms, such as the "radical middle," the "middle way," "balance," etc.

Partisan colouring aside, how good is the evidence for sharp ideological discontinuity post-1993? Upon closer examination, the argument is based upon a number of dubious assumptions about history, about context, and finally, about the actual record of the Chrétien Liberals.

The idea that the Liberals have traditionally followed a centre-left course rests on a certain selective reading of history. Liberal behaviour at certain specific conjunctures is cited. Mackenzie King carefully picked off Progressives in the 1920s, and more dramatically, kicked off the era of the postwar Keynesian welfare state when the old CCF posed a serious electoral threat on the left in the latter years of World War Two. In the mid-1960s, the embattled minority governments of Lester Pearson countered the newly formed NDP with the second wave of welfare state programs, including medicare and the Canada Pension Plan.[8] Pierre Trudeau solved a minority government problem from 1972 to 1974 by governing in tacit coalition with the NDP, and moved in the direction of a more interventionary stance on the economy in his last government, from 1980 to 1984, with the National Energy Program and foreign investment review. As late as 1988, a former Bay Street lawyer, John Turner, led the Liberals into a passionate anti-free-trade campaign fiercely opposed by big business; Turner did not win office, but he did pre-empt the NDP from gaining second place, which had seemed possible at the outset of the campaign. These examples can be set against that of Paul Martin bringing down his tough deficit-fighting budgets while herding the Reform caucus in front of him as human shields, or Martin making huge pre-election tax cuts in his 2000 mini-budget to cut the Alliance's electoral appeal off at the knees.

Selective snapshots can, however, be misleading. It is true that at particular conjunctures in the past, circumstances encouraged the Liberals to move leftward and they were able and willing to take advantages of these opportunities. But it is hardly the case over the longer haul that Liberal governments consistently governed from the left-centre. Mackenzie King's government after 1935 was deeply conservative in the face of the Great Depression, in sharp contrast to the more creative and improvisational New Deal administration in the US. The Liberal governments of Louis St. Laurent, from 1949 to 1957, were managerial, businesslike, and fiscally conservative — by present-day standards, almost stingy in protecting the public purse against claimants, however deserving. In 1957, for instance, the Tories inveighed successfully against "six-buck Harris," a reference to the small increase cautiously permitted old age pensioners by the finance minister, Walter Harris. For most of the past seven decades, it is the Liberals who have been the pre-eminent party of business, measured by which party receives the lion's share of corporate donations to campaign funds. The period from the late 1970s through the 1980s when the Conservatives assumed that role, appears in retrospect as anomalous. The Chrétien-Martin Liberals of the early twenty-first century are in direct continuity with the St-Laurent-C.D. Howe Liberals of a half century ago.

THE SHIFTING INTERNATIONAL CONTEXT

If present-day Liberalism seems weighted toward the more conservative side of Liberal history, it is important to look at the context. A successful centrist party is like a chameleon, taking its colour from its surroundings. If the Reform/Alliance have been the CCF/NDP of the post-1993 parliaments, this is a reflection of a shift in the political culture. The dynamic on the margins has shifted rightward, and it is here that many of the new movements and ideas in the 1990s were to be found. The Liberals, always in the past alert to co-opt signs of movement on the left, alertly applied the same strategy after 1993 to the emerging forces to their right. This shift was facilitated by a history of policy failure in experiments in interventionism: the National Energy Program of the early 1980s, for instance, was a disaster, not just for the vituperative reaction it raised and still raises in the west, but in terms of achieving its own announced objectives. Greater public scepticism about the capacity of governments to achieve results through big, bureaucratic, expenditure programs, an attitude assiduously fed by the business media, was also generated by the perception of a long series of statist projects gone awry, or missing their targets. It is particularly among elites that disillusion with governments has proceeded furthest,[9] and it is also the elites that are most sensitive to the effects of government policies on business confidence and international finance. It is not surprising that the Liberals in office have been chary of involvement with big-ticket, *dirigiste* programs, although this hardly distinguishes them from other parties at the federal or provincial levels (including provincial NDP governments).

On the other hand, selective, targeted government support for the private sector to enhance global competitiveness has not been abandoned as a viable policy option. From the 1993 *Red Book* through to the Speech from the Throne in 2001, the Liberals have emphasized a strong federal role in enhancing the "innovative economy" through education and skills training, tax inducements to encourage research and development, and provision of infrastructural support for the "innovative" sector.[10] This is the new Liberal model of how government should operate in relation to the "new" economy, which has gone hand in hand with further privatization and deregulation (extending and deepening a trend begun under the Mulroney Tories).

There has also been an important international context for this shift. The Trudeau Liberals in their final, interventionary phase in the early 1980s, were actually moving diametrically away from the policy directions of Canada's closest neighbours and allies, the US and the UK, which by 1981 were both under the neo-liberal regimes of Reagan and Thatcher. The Chrétien governments coincided from 1993 to 2000 with the Democratic administrations of Bill Clinton, and by 1997 with the "New" Labour government of Tony Blair in Britain. This time there was considerable Liberal policy congruence with ruling parties with whom the Liberals feel very comfortable. In the American and British cases, centre-left parties had succeeded to office after forceful, innovative right-wing "revolutions" had transformed the policy landscapes. They accepted the changes, by and large, making no particular effort to reverse or even amend most of their predecessors' innovations. Various formulations, such as the Third Way[11] have been put about to explain (or rationalize) why there was to be no going back on the core elements of neo-liberal governance in the era of globalization. Left-wing critics excoriate this "betrayal," while others justify it as sensible realism, but the 1990s do seem to have marked a turning point, the consolidation of neo-liberalism under social-democratic or liberal, rather than conservative, auspices. There are historical precedents. Liberal or social-democratic Keynesianism triumphed in the immediate postwar era, after the traumas of worldwide depression and world war, but was presided over by Republican and Conservative governments in the US and UK by the early 1950s. Neither Eisenhower nor Churchill/Eden/Macmillan saw fit to reverse many of the changes brought about by their somewhat more leftish predecessors, forming a consensus that would eventually give way only to concerted and radical neo-liberal onslaughts in the late 1970s and 1980s. In the shift toward the "new economy" and globalization at the end of the millennium, political parties are similarly adapting, and in the process shifting the centre of political gravity. The Chrétien Liberals are fully in step with these wider trends. But this is not the end of the story.

WINNING THE CULTURAL WAR

The "wolf in sheep's clothing" characterization of the shift of the centre-left misleads if taken too literally. To take the US example: if the Clinton Democrats accepted much of the legacy of the Reagan revolution in relation to fiscal and monetary policy, they rejected the other, socially conservative, side of the Reagan revolution. The religious right, with its intolerant attitudes toward multiculturalism and feminism, its anti-abortion and anti-homosexual zealotry, and its persistent dabbling on the fringes of racism, had pitted itself in a "cultural war" against an America of multi-ethnic diversity and cultural pluralism. The Republican party had brazenly and successfully played the "race card" in national politics from the Nixon era in the 1960s through to the use of the infamous Willie Horton ad in the 1988 campaign of George Bush, Sr. In general, it could be said that throughout the Reagan-Bush era, the Republican Party was divided between free-market and "moral majority" wings, which managed to coexist for the most part, but which were mutually contradictory on a number of issues. The Clinton Democrats accepted much of the neo-liberal economic agenda, but strongly rejected the moral majority agenda on the cultural and social front. In opposition, it was the moral majoritarians who first gained ascendancy in the Republican Party under the congressional leadership of Newt Gingrich. But ultimately, they overplayed their hand disastrously in the attempted impeachment of Clinton in the Lewinsky affair. That was the biggest battle of the cultural wars, and the right was routed. The "real" America had decisively moved on and away from the conservative model of the religious right. It is fascinating to note that in the 2000 Republican campaign for the White House, social conservatism was largely downplayed, if not in some cases, abandoned altogether. Diversity and multiculturalism had become keywords in the new symbolic discourse of Republicanism, and the newly elected president was quick to make racial and cultural diversity one of the leading standards for his political appointments. American experience thus indicates that ideological shape shifting is by no means a one-way process.

In the Canadian case, the Chrétien Liberals may have assiduously stolen the policies of the right on deficits and tax cuts, but on cultural and social issues, they have differentiated themselves from their right-wing rivals at every opportunity. The Mulroney Conservatives could not be described as strongly motivated by social conservative causes, even if their caucus possessed a "family values" group. This relative indifference to the moral crusades of the religious right was itself one of the causes of the breakdown of the Tory party in the west and the rise of the Reform Party. Opponents of multiculturalism, large-scale immigration, abortion, and homosexuality, wanted a vehicle to express their views and concluded that they needed to go outside the traditional Conservative Party structure to do so. Since 1993, the Canadian right has been split between two parties that espouse neo-liberal economics but are divided over social conservatism. The Tories under Joe Clark eschew all identification with the religious right, and on social issues may well deserve the old appellation of "Red Tories." The Reform Party under Preston Manning was wary of giving too much ground to its social conservatives, but when the Canadian Alliance opened up its leadership in a primary-style election, religious conservatives and "right-to-lifers" flocked to put one of their own, Stockwell Day, in charge of the new party.

In the 2000 election, the Alliance Party and Day were ambushed by the Liberals on the social conservative issues, the acceptability of which within the Alliance was not matched among voters outside the party. When the Liberals stressed a campaign of "values" — especially diversity, tolerance, and multiculturalism — they knew they had a winner. They also had a distinctive record to submit to public scrutiny. From the beginning, the Chrétien Liberals have embraced identification with social liberalism, especially when it does not carry a huge price tag. For instance, one of the important acts of their first term was to pass the national gun registration legislation, which was defended explicitly in the feminist context arising out of the massacre of 14 women at the Montreal École Polytéchnique. Extension of gay rights was another achievement (even if falling short of explicitly altering the definition of marriage).[12] And the very idea of a referendum to re-criminalize abortion was used as a club with which to bludgeon Stockwell Day during the election. Moreover, the Liberals have selected for government support certain target groups, as with the $2 billion promised the cultural industries by Sheila Copps in 2001, some of whom constitute veritable red flags to the social conservatives. The Axworthy foreign policy was another component of the "liberal" Liberal record, projecting onto the international stage ideas of human security that resonate very strongly with many Canadians, and mobilizing public support for such causes as peacekeeping missions and the landmines treaty that speak to liberal social values.[13]

This kind of political differentiation, if not pushed too far in front of public opinion, as the prudent Liberals are careful to avoid, is a win-win situation for the Chrétien government. It serves to indicate to women, to minorities, and to liberal urban voters generally, that the government is defending tolerance and diversity against enemies on the opposition benches. At the same time, with their fiscal record, they can defend their right flank with fiscal conservatives who are themselves dubious about evangelical social conservatism. Finally, another welcome by-product is that by being seen to block the religious right, the Liberals also pre-empt some of the space on the left otherwise available to the NDP. So effective have the Liberals been with their "values" agenda that in the aftermath of the 2000 election, Stockwell Day's leadership of the Canadian Alliance is being severely challenged by dissident forces within the caucus and the party who, among other things, see Day's social conservatism as an albatross around the Alliance's neck. It is also clear that any prospective merger between the Alliance and the Conservative Party will only happen if the social conservative agenda is cast aside, or at least buried very deeply.

CONCLUSION

If the Liberals have moved to the right on economic policy as the centre of gravity in the country shifted rightward, it is also the case that the Liberals have shifted "leftward" (if that is a correct term) on social and cultural issues as the country has shifted in the same direction. Unlike their Conservative predecessors, the Liberals have proven to be extremely adept in their traditional role as chameleons of the political centre. It is a mark of Liberal absorptive capacity and adaptability that, in the first year of their third majority mandate, political criticism of the government has tended to shift toward a critique of a nascent "one-party state," and lamentations over the lack of any credible or effective opposition. There are indeed very real questions to be addressed to the Liberal hegemony and its implications for Canadian democracy, but until any one group in opposition can find the means to construct as faithful a replica of mainstream public opinion as can be glimpsed in the Liberal Party, the questions will remain unanswered.

POSTSCRIPT: AFTER SEPTEMBER 11

The terrorist attacks on the World Trade Center and the Pentagon on September 11, 2001 radically altered the policy agendas of all western countries, including Canada. National security has once more become the highest priority, as in two world wars and the early stages of the Cold War. Canada immediately joined in the coalition formed to prosecute a new war on terrorism, and dispatched 2,000 servicemen and women to the Afghan theatre of operations. A sweeping package of anti-terrorism legislation was rushed before Parliament, including provisions for preventive arrest and investigative hearings that greatly extend the powers of the state at the expense of individual rights. Calls for a "security perimeter" around North America that would establish harmonized immigration security rules and enforcement between Canada and the United States became irresistible, despite the clear challenge this poses to Canadian sovereignty.

In this crisis atmosphere, in which one dominant policy paradigm was being suddenly superceded by another, the federal Liberals have once again demonstrated the requisite degree of agility and flexibility to maintain their hegemonic position in national politics. The prime minister's cautious but firm approach, eschewing rhetoric but laying the groundwork for substantive action, was initially denounced by the opposition and condemned by media pundits — until polls came in showing strong public approval. The Liberals have once again struck a balance between the conservative opposition, inside and outside Parliament, who attributed softness and lack of resolve to the government, and on the other side, a minority — among them the NDP — that opposed military responses to terrorism in favour of the United Nations and international courts.

An inner, or war Cabinet, under the direction of Foreign Affairs Minister John Manley has taken charge of instituting the new national security priority.

Here, the Liberals can draw on long traditions of governance in times of national security crisis: World War Two, much of the Cold War, and the October 1970 Crisis, were all managed by Liberal governments that balanced national security with civil liberties. While that balance has sometimes been a matter of controversy in the past, the Liberals have been adept at negotiating this always difficult passage, and it would seem that once again the Canadian public is willing to entrust their confidence in a party that avoids extremes in either direction. For instance, the pressures from the Americans for perimeter security have been cautiously met in Ottawa, despite demands from the right for instant and unconditional acceptance, and cries from the nationalist left that any cooperation would constitute a sellout of sovereignty. The Liberals know that elements of perimeter security are unavoidable, but will seek to negotiate *quid pro quos* with the US that will retain some safeguards for Canada.

Even in times of great crisis, perhaps especially in such times, the Liberal chameleon demonstrates an adaptability and staying power that is the despair of its opposition, left and right.

NOTES

1. This was a phrase I coined a quarter of a century ago to describe the Liberal Party in the Mackenzie King-Louis St. Laurent era (R. Whitaker, *The Government Party: Organizing and Financing the Liberal Party of Canada, 1930-1958* (Toronto: University of Toronto Press, 1977). I used the term then mainly to describe the organizational relationship between party and state, but I also pointed to an apparent ideological tendency of Liberal governments to depoliticize politics, to strive for an ideal of an apolitical public life. This observation certainly resonates with the current Liberal government.

2. In a COMPAS poll, 19 June 2001, Martin, with 31 percent, led all other contenders for the Liberal leadership, including Prime Minister Chrétien, who came in second with only 17 percent.

3. See Katherine Fierlbeck, "Cost Containment in Health Care: The Federalism Context," in *The Canadian Social Union: Canadian National Health Goals and Objectives*, ed. Duane Adams (Kingston: Institute of Intergovernmental Relations, 2001), pp. 131-78. Fierlbeck does indicate that the CHST cuts had a "chilling effect" on federal-provincial relations and seriously disrupted planning for the medium- and long-term future of health care.

4. The Liberal Party of Canada, *Creating Opportunity: The Liberal Plan for Canada* (Ottawa, 1993), p. 24.

5. Ibid., p. 22.

6. COMPAS, 10 April 2001, found that supporters of the proposed FTAA at the Quebec City meeting led opponents by 2 to 1 (54 percent to 22 percent, with one-quarter of the sample undecided). Matthew Mendelsohn and Robert Wolfe, "Probing the Aftermyth of Seattle: Canadian Public Opinion on International

Trade, 1980-2000," Working Paper No. 12 (Kingston: Queen's University, School of Policy Studies, 2000) make a much more subtle case that Canadians accept that trade liberalization provides economic benefits, but are more doubtful and hesitant about the potential social, cultural and democratic impacts of expanded free trade arrangements. They conclude that governments can capture public support if they can provide a credible narrative to explain trade liberalization in non-threatening terms. This is what the Chrétien government has been trying to accomplish.

7. For example, in a recent editorial lamenting Liberal dominance, the *National Post* editor-in-chief argues that "A one-party state, even when that one party is as electorally successful and *as resolutely centrist* as the Liberals, cannot adequately represent all Canadians." Kenneth Whyte, "One-party rule isn't an option," *National Post*, 25 June 2001 [emphasis added].

8. Penny Bryden, *Planners and Politicians: Liberal Politics and Social Policy, 1957-1958* (Montreal: McGill-Queen's University Press, 1997) downplays the electoral threat of the CCF as instigating Liberal action in implementing medicare and the Canada Pension Plan.

9. Frank Graves, "Rethinking Government as if People Mattered: From 'Reaganomics' to 'Humanomics,' " in *How Ottawa Spends, 1999-2000: Shape Shifting: Canadian Governance Toward the 21st Century*, ed. Leslie A. Pal (Toronto: Oxford University Press, 1999), pp. 48-50.

10. *Creating Opportunity*, pp. 42-61; Liberal Party of Canada, *A record of Achievement: A Report on the Liberal Government's 36 Months in Office* (Ottawa, 1996), pp. 36-55; Liberal Party of Canada, *Opportunity for All: The Liberal Plan for the Future of Canada* (Ottawa, 2000), pp. 7-13; Speech from the Throne to open the 1st Session of the 37th Parliament (Ottawa, 30 January 2001). Leslie Pal suggests that "innovation and research were among the key themes" of the Speech. Leslie A. Pal, "How Ottawa Spends 2001-2: Power in Transition," in *How Ottawa Spends, 2001-2002: Power in Transition*, ed. Leslie A. Pal (Toronto: Oxford University Press, 2001), p. 14.

11. Anthony Giddens, *The Third Way: The Renewal of Social Democracy* (Cambridge: Polity Press, 1998).

12. Miriam Smith, "The Liberal Government and Rights Claims: The Lesbian and Gay Case," in *How Ottawa Spends, 1998-99: Balancing Act: the Post-Deficit Mandate*, ed. Leslie A. Pal (Toronto: Oxford University Press, 1998), pp. 293-314. In 2001, a Leger Marketing poll indicated that 75.7 percent of Canadians agreed that homosexuals deserve the same rights as heterosexuals, and 53 percent agreed that they should have the right to adopt children. An executive of the polling firm declared that "if we had done the poll 15 years ago — my God, how different the results would have been!" Alexander Panetta, "Poll reveals doubt [*sic*] on gay adoption," *The Globe and Mail*, 16 July 2001.

13. Fen Osler Hampson, Norman Hillmer, Maureen Appel Molot (eds.), *Canada Among Nations 2001: The Axworthy Legacy* (Toronto: Oxford University Press, 2001).

3

Four Dimensions of Political Culture in Canada Outside Quebec: The Changing Nature of Brokerage and the Definition of the Canadian Nation

Matthew Mendelsohn

Dans ce chapitre, l'auteur analyse le conflit de valeurs au Canada en dehors du Québec et distingue quatre dimensions à ce conflit, soit les politiques économiques, les valeurs sociales, la définition de la démocratie et la définition de la nation. Cette dernière dimension est particulièrement complexe et peut se manifester de différentes manières, que ce soit au niveau du soutien envers «l'esprit d'accommodement», surtout en ce qui a trait au Québec, en attitudes envers les minorités ou les Autochtones ou encore en termes de vision du rôle du gouvernement fédéral. Selon l'analyse des données, les débats quant aux définitions de la nation canadienne et de la démocratie auraient été nettement décisifs lors des derniers choix électoraux. Qui plus est, toutes les disputes quant à la définition de la nation canadienne se rejoignent en un désaccord commun en ce qui a trait à la force du gouvernement fédéral et des élites fédérales, que ce soit pour les tenants du nationalisme québécois, du sentiment régional, du populisme ou encore de l'intégration nord-américaine. Depuis 1968, les libéraux ont manœuvré afin de monopoliser un côté de ce débat, mais actuellement, aucun parti n'occupe l'autre côté et ne semble parler pour tous les opposants. Le point de rupture du conflit politique au Canada se situe entre les centralisateurs pan-canadiens et les décentralisateurs, formés des nationalistes québécois, des populistes de l'Ouest et des supporteurs d'une plus grande intégration nord-américaine. La grande difficulté pour l'Alliance canadienne est qu'en dehors du Québec, ceux qui soutiennent le plus l'intégration nord-américaine et la décentralisation en faveur des gouvernements provinciaux sont également ceux qui supportent le moins le nationalisme québécois. Ceux qui instinctivement supportent les mesures pour aider le Québec sont aussi ceux qui supportent instinctivement un gouvernement fédéral plus fort. L'auteur avance que la nature du compromis s'est transformée de multiples façons et explique comment cela prend place à l'intérieur des partis libéral et de l'Alliance canadienne, et soutient qu'aucun d'eux ne représente le parti du compromis et de l'intégration.

It is generally believed that an important element of Canadian political culture historically has been support for compromise. Canada's most pressing
existential challenge has been the management of centrifugal forces, and a
variety of processes and institutions, such as "brokerage" parties, elite accommodation, and executive federalism, are all infused with the belief that
one must integrate diverse communities in the governing process and ensure
that no group is permanently excluded from political power. While these integrative elite processes have been important for managing conflict and
governing, whether mass opinion supports integrative processes remains
unclear and unmeasured. In fact, the frequent rationale for elite-driven integrative processes is that mass opinion would not appreciate the need for the
subtle compromises necessary for keeping the country together. It has therefore been assumed that Canadian political culture is characterized by elite
processes designed to manage centrifugal forces, and by mass opinion that
refuses to demonstrate a spirit of accommodation. This paper challenges both
of these assumptions, arguing that elite processes have not promoted accommodation in a traditional sense, and speculating that mass opinion may be
more accommodating than often presumed.

In section one, I map out the patterns of value conflict that characterize
political culture in Canada outside Quebec. I will be interested in four dimensions of conflict: economic policy, social values, elitism, and conflicts over the
definition of the nation. This latter may manifest itself in a variety of ways, such
as support or opposition for "the spirit of accommodation," particularly in regards
to French Canada (and, more recently, Quebec) or in terms of the role of the
federal government in thwarting regionalism or North American integration.

In the second section, I discuss how the nature of "brokerage," "accommodation," and "the definition of the nation" are being transformed. At first blush,
the rise of the Reform Party in 1993 seemed to imply that an ideological type
party had emerged from the right to contest the brokerage of the Liberals and
Conservatives and the integrative forces at work in the political culture. Upon
closer examination, we will see that it is also the putative brokerage party —
the Liberals — that had rejected the notion of the accommodation of groups
in favour of an alternative conception of brokerage. This has gone relatively
unnoticed because many confuse the notion of a "centrist" and "catch-all"
party (which the Liberals certainly are on many issues) with the notion of a
"brokerage party." Since 1968, the Liberals have not sought to accommodate
those with differing views of the Canadian nation, the element within the political culture most in need of careful management by a brokerage party. The
Liberals and Alliance both make appeals based on a pan-Canadian civic nationalism that integrates citizens as individual rights-bearers, rather than as
members of subnational communities, but they differ on some issues related
to the definition of the Canadian nation. The Liberals accept a more diverse
cultural tradition, while the Alliance appeals to a more unified, common

Canadian tradition.[1] But the Liberals' understanding of brokerage has changed since 1968. As the party of the centre, it rejects provincial claims and is prepared to offer accommodation to only those groups that share its definition of the nation and look to the federal government as champion, namely, linguistic minorities and ethno-cultural communities. The Alliance, on the other hand, has been seeking to transform itself into a brokerage party, but one that offers accommodation only so long as citizens reject group and collectivist claims and accept a common, undifferentiated Canadian tradition, though for its part it is prepared to represent diverse regional and provincial communities and the periphery. Both parties' appeals leave out significant sections of the Canadian population.

In the third section, I test whether I am right that these four dimensions exist in Canada outside Quebec and how they relate to vote choice in 1997 and 2000. The evidence presented will suggest that conflicts over definitions of the Canadian nation and democracy, particularly the former, are the enduring features of the political culture that distinguish Reform/Alliance supporters from Liberal voters, and, to a lesser extent, Tories and New Democrats. Debates about Quebec, the role of the federal government, and the power of the Canadian political establishment have been crucial factors affecting party performance. The Alliance has failed to make significant breakthroughs east of Manitoba or in multicultural urban Canada in part because of socially conservative positions, but also because of their treatment of questions related to the definition of the Canadian nation. It is not that their positions on Quebec are far from those of the average voter in English-speaking Canada — they are not — but that these positions prevent the coalition-building with forces in Quebec necessary to win national elections in Canada. These positions in regards to Quebec also prevent national success because they inhibit the ability to build alliances with key groups in Ontario and Atlantic Canada. This is because a sufficiently large number of Canadians support brokerage and accommodation under most circumstances to prevent an ideological type party from having national success, even if this party's positions with regard to Quebec or immigration are not far from those of the average voter.

I advance a number of cascading arguments. First, it has often been demonstrated that one of the hallmarks of Canadian political culture has been its centrism, moderation, and lack of ideology.[2] This is true, as far it goes, on issues of economic policy. But Canada has been characterized by deeply ideological, divisive disagreements over the role of the federal government, the recognition of the periphery, and the place of French Canada.

Second, the emergence of the Reform Party along with the decline of the Conservatives in 1993 has highlighted important realities of Canadian political culture. The diverse nature of Canada's political culture created the need for brokerage parties that transcend regional or ethnic interests. The emergence of Reform has been a damaging decade-long distraction because the party could not integrate diverse groups, and the lack of a real brokerage alternative to the Liberals allowed the latter to indulge in some of its worst instincts and abandon accommodation with relative impunity. There are only two possible winning coalitions in Canada, and Reform/Alliance represents neither. The Liberals continue to articulate a vision of brokerage governed by diversity, individualism and the recognition of groups that look to the federal government — linguistic minorities and ethnocultural communities — for protection. The other winning coalition is less coherent but is also broadly acceptable to Canadians: it makes similar appeals as the Liberals but contends that the federal government and federal elites have become too powerful. Since 1968, the Liberals and Tories were both brokerage parties, differing on the definition of the Canadian nation, with the Liberals' coalition a fairly coherent collection of those who looked to the federal government as their champion and the Conservatives a somewhat less coherent coalition of those who looked to their provincial governments. These are the two potential winning coalitions in Canada, and Reform rose to prominence by attacking the compromises, coalition-building, and deal-making of both variants of brokerage. The party's position is not sustainable because it owes its initial success to the rejection of the very brokerage that one must embrace in order to win national elections and govern. There are intense moments of political conflict when parties that make majoritarian appeals can have some success in the periphery, as witnessed in the 1990s, but such parties are not sustainable because they do not appeal to the spirit of moderation that is usually present throughout the country. Moreover, appeals to one unified Canadian cultural tradition are doomed to fail because they push away too large a constituency of Canadians, and make inroads into Quebec impossible.

Third, although the battle within the Alliance during the summer of 2001 was in part over the leadership of Stockwell Day, it was more substantively a debate about accommodation. It is not clear that those MPs who left the Alliance caucus and later branded themselves the Democratic Representative Caucus, were any more centrist on questions of economic or social policy than those who remained. However, they were prepared to accept watered down versions of these policies in a partnership with the Conservatives if it meant that they were more likely to form a government. It was a disagreement over what *type* of party it should be — ideological or brokerage? Those prepared to moderate their platform for the purposes of building a partnership with the Conservatives had come to believe that in order to have a chance of electoral success, they had to embrace the *sine qua non* of Canadian political culture: compromise and brokerage. The great challenge for the Canadian right is that the Liberals have a monopoly on the brokerage of pluralism. The Conservatives of Stanfield, Clark, and Mulroney made appeals to those who rejected the dominance of the federal government and federal elites, but the coalition was revealed as incoherent when it came to power because it had offered specific accommodations for Quebec nationalism. The alternative for any second brokerage party must be to articulate a vision that appeals to both devolutionists and nationalists, one that offers collective protections to Quebec without using the language of differential treatment. One of the two forms of brokerage must be embraced in order for a party to win national government.

DIMENSIONS OF POLITICAL CULTURE IN CANADA

POTENTIAL DIMENSIONS

Students of elections have identified a large number of underlying ideological dimensions to electoral politics. The two most consistently cited are economic policy and cultural values. Within the realm of economic policy, one can think of state intervention in the economy, the distribution of the tax burden, and support for social programs. Within the realm of cultural values, one can think of issues such as abortion, treatment of crime, moral traditionalism, and the place of ethnic minorities.[3] The economic dimension is easily interpreted through a traditional left-right conceptualization, while cultural politics can be characterized as a communitarian conflict between "left-libertarian" secular and "right-authoritarian" traditional values.[4] The comparative literature has been quite explicit that these two dimensions structure European political conflict, with Kitschelt contending that he, "[does] not see *any other dimensions*" (italics in original).[5] Canadian observers would certainly see echoes of these two dimensions in the 2000 Canadian election during debates on issues of "economic" and "social" conservatism. In most European countries, these two dimensions in fact become unidimensional because parties to the right on economic policy tend also to be to the right on social values,[6] while in the US, there also appears to be a single "liberal/conservative" dimension on social and economic questions in congressional voting patterns.[7]

The Canadian literature has not been as explicit as the comparative literature. For the 1988 election, Johnston and his colleagues identify three elements within the political culture that provoke conflict: commercial policy, "class issues," and conceptions of nationality and the place of French Canada. Attitudes toward Quebec have been particularly important in structuring the Canadian party system.[8] Yet this is clearly fuzzy because commercial policy and class issues overlap, while commercial policy includes (in 1988) feelings about the United States, potentially a measure of conceptions of nationality. Moreover, at least according to the 1988 data presented by Johnston and his colleagues, the issue of abortion was not related to any of these questions, suggesting that moral traditionalism may be a different dimension.

Nevitte and his colleagues have clarified which dimensions are key to political conflict in Canada, including free enterprise, moral traditionalism, the place of women, the place of Quebec, attitudes toward outgroups, Canada's relationship with the United States, cynicism, and regional alienation.[9] These are plausible, and Nevitte and his colleagues provide some evidence for their importance,[10] but again, some may be related to each other (moral traditionalism and the place of women for example, or cynicism and regional alienation). A categorization of two dimensions oversimplifies the complexity of Canadian political culture, while a categorization of innumerable dimensions makes the concept of "dimension" difficult to apply.

In addition to the dimensions dealing with economic and cultural politics, I suggest two others must be considered if one is to understand the nature of Canadian political culture and party competition today. First, disagreements about the definition of the Canadian nation have manifested themselves in a number of interrelated ways. They are in part a debate over the role of the federal government: Does Canada need a strong central government? They have also manifested themselves in a debate over differentiated equality and the character of the Canadian identity: Is Canada binational (or multinational)? Are Canadians really just individual members of one nation? Should this nation be thought of as pluralistic? What these elements have in common — the role of the federal government, as well as the place of Quebec, Aboriginal peoples and multicultural communities — is actually an overriding disagreement in regard to how one should accommodate groups that do not identify strongly with the federal government or a "common Canadian tradition."

Attitudes toward elites and "the public" must be considered as a fourth dimension of conflict. This dimension relates to issues of populism, anti-elitism, party democracy, and public participation, what Nevitte *et al.* refer to as "cynicism." Throughout Canadian history, the Progressives, the Cooperative Commonwealth Federation (CCF), and the Reform/Alliance have all at various times appealed to innate populism — particularly in the Canadian periphery — and rejected elite decision-making and some of the principles of party government. The issue has been central to the success of many new parties.[11] Frontier societies traditionally have little respect for traditional institutional procedures, and this cultural tradition is still present in the western periphery.

I thus suggest we think of political culture and conflict in Canada outside Quebec as structured by four dimensions. The economic dimension of political conflict is well understood, but a large number of issues — direct democracy, immigration levels, abortion, same-sex benefits, the policies of the parole board, gun control, Aboriginal fishing rights, recognition of Quebec as a distinct society — have been lumped together as part of a dimension of "cultural politics." I suggest they represent three additional underlying dimensions: first, support for moral traditionalism and order as opposed to secular values and social permissiveness; second, attitudes toward elites; and third, attitudes toward the definition of the Canadian nation, which itself can be complex because it encompasses issues such as the place of ethnocultural communities, the place of Quebec, the place of Aboriginal peoples, relations with the United States, and accommodation more generally. All of these issues come together in a disagreement over the strength of the federal government and federal elites in opposition to their challengers, namely Quebec nationalism, regional sentiment, populism, and North American integration. Since 1968, the Liberals have managed to monopolize one side of this divide, but currently no one party occupies the other.

The issue of social permissiveness figured prominently in the 2000 election, but, unlike its frequent prominence during American elections, it has not historically been an issue during Canadian elections. The presence of the Reform Party, and even more so Stockwell Day, proved to be a glorious opportunity for the Liberals and a distraction from the real choices facing Canadians within the mainstream of Canadian political culture. It is a reality of Canadian political culture, understood in its broadest terms as the interaction between political parties, the mass media, and mass opinion, that issues of social conservatism cannot be successfully mobilized by Canadian parties. Issues related to elites and the definition of the nation can, as long as one accepts the principle of accommodation in some capacity, either the Liberals' or Tories' variant. Once in office, neither party has been particularly successful at accommodating diverse communities, but, nonetheless, a successful Canadian party must evoke one of these two traditions of accommodation in voters' minds. Issues related to the definition of the nation are likely to be placed back on the agenda, as the issues related to morality and the renunciation of human impulse, placed on the agenda by the Reform Party, fade.

THE IMPORTANCE OF ACCOMMODATION AND ELITISM IN CANADA

Brokerage has been crucial to the successful governing of Canada, and attitudes toward brokerage have been an implicit fault line of Canadian politics. Although voters would not express their feelings in the terms I use here, the clash between those who believe in brokerage parties and those who do not has been a theme of Canadian politics and an important disagreement over the definition of the nation. This clash over brokerage has historically manifested itself in attitudes toward French Canada. It has also manifested itself in terms of affective reactions to "compromise," with some voters adamantly rejecting the spirit of compromise that often characterizes political decision-making and others happily accepting the deal-making process. Those parties that do not believe in brokerage, however, have never been able to come to power federally because they are not able to build successful coalitions. A large part of the motivation for individuals' voting decisions during the 1992 Charlottetown referendum was predicated on attitudes toward the deal-making and compromise process.[12] But while it has been documented that Americans do not like the messy deal-making that characterizes the real world of decision-making,[13] it is not at all clear that Canadians share this same antipathy. Although some characterize the defeat of the Charlottetown Accord as evidence that a majority of Canadians are not prepared to go along with delicate compromises, there are a variety of other credible explanations for its defeat,[14] and it is well-established that parties can rarely win office during an election without embracing moderation and some form of brokerage (the election of Unionists in 1917 being the one exception).

Attitudes toward the political elite were also crucial in influencing the 1992 referendum vote.[15] Populist discourse in third-party platforms regularly emerges in Canada, directed toward issues of public participation and anti-elite sentiment.[16] The 1997 election study team found that the dimension that they labelled "cynicism," conceptually very similar to what I have called "attitudes toward elitism," was the strongest ideological predictor of Liberal voting (with those professing less cynicism far more likely to vote Liberal) and, along with attitudes toward Quebec, the strongest ideological predictor of Reform voting. On the face of it, much of the popular and media interpretation of the 1997 election as a disagreement between economic policy and social values was misguided. Although these issues may have been the source for some vote switching among less committed partisans, what distinguished Reform from Liberal voters were questions about the definition of the Canadian nation and the role of elites, increasingly, elites associated with the federal government. The inherent regionalism within the political culture of Canada[17] has facilitated the creation of strong provincial governments often in opposition to federal actions. Between 1968 and 1993, it was the Conservative Party that allied itself with these regionalizing forces and provincial governments. Reform/Alliance has not been able to construct a wide coalition to appeal to the very real provincialist sentiments in Quebec and Atlantic Canada, because the party has shunned brokerage.

It is widely acknowledged that in the 1990s Canadians became "increasingly disenchanted with elite-dominated, consensus-driven politics."[18] The implication is that Canadian political culture is currently characterized by a populist rejection of elite decision-making and a majoritarian rejection of accommodation, a shift therefore in mass opinion on both dimensions. There is some survey evidence that the public has organized its views in this way, with attitudes toward accommodation of Quebec correlated with cynicism and attitudes toward elites.[19] And at the level of basic personality types, cynicism and a rejection of outgroups likely go together. However, it is possible that the correspondence in public opinion between the two dimensions — attitudes toward accommodation and toward elitism — may be a product of how elites have structured political conflict in Canada by linking the two values in the concept of "elite accommodation."[20] It is possible to formulate a coherent discourse that appeals to the participatory and the integrative dimensions.[21]

In Canada, "elite" and "accommodation" have gone together for a variety of historical reasons. The Loyalists who came to Canada had no faith in "the people" and the democratic movement. In Quebec after 1840, populist democratic elements were an unimportant force for over a century. The English, loyal to Britain, along with French Canadians had little faith in popular democracy and *simultaneously* had to figure out how to live together politically. Elite and accommodation became the way things got done in the United Canadas.[22] Later patterns of settlement in western Canada were different and more conducive to a populist, plebiscitarian, anti-elite sentiment. These contrasting cultural origins of Ontario and the Maritimes as opposed to the western provinces continue to find echo in electoral politics today. This cleavage — support or opposition to elitism — is conceptually distinct from the cleavage regarding accommodation, in particular, accommodation of Quebec, although the two have gone hand in hand for legitimate, historical reasons. When western populists have rejected elites, they have also by historic necessity had to reject the brokerage undertaken by these elites. Although Canada is now characterized by a less deferential political culture than it was 30 years ago,[23] there is no evidence of which I am aware that documents a similar decline in support for accommodation. In fact, if one believes that citizens are now more likely to manage complex information and engage in negotiation in increasingly non-hierarchical organizational structures (both in the family and at work), support for the value of accommodation may in fact be increasing. Unfortunately, such values have not been systematically measured and tracked over time, so this must remain speculative at this point.

THE CHANGING NATURE OF BROKERAGE IN CANADA

As Carty and his colleagues have pointed out: "The pattern that has emerged in Canada requires that much of the accommodation between ... clashing identities take place within parties rather than between them."[24] Two forces in the postwar period that facilitated this task of intra-party brokerage were Red Tories and Business Liberals, both of whom prevented their respective parties from becoming ideological on economic questions. Both factions believed in elitism and brokerage, both sought to suppress the regional and linguistic cleavages through pan-Canadian appeals, and both were infused with the ideology of elite accommodation. Although both groups may have had class interests, these were muted by their participation in wider, catch-all parties. It will be my contention that since 1968, with the exception of a brief time during the Mulroney interregnum in the Conservative Party, no party has successfully made appeals using the language of accommodation as traditionally understood in Canada. In particular, both the Liberals and the Alliance reject recognition of Quebec's national status.

THE LIBERAL PARTY AND BROKERAGE

Because the Liberal Party is a catch-all, centrist party, prepared to move strategically to the right or left on the economic dimension depending on the appeal of their main rivals, some have confused its recent incarnation for a traditional brokerage party. This confusion is also a product of the fact that on the social dimension, the Liberals have clearly followed rather than led public opinion on issues such as abortion rights, same-sex marriage, and euthanasia, albeit while embracing secularism. On the economic and social dimension, then, the Liberals have been centrist. On the other two dimensions, however, the claim that the Liberals are a brokerage party is exaggerated. The two dominant ideological commitments of the Liberals for over three decades have been the defence of a strong central government — a vertical rather than a horizontal vision of federalism — and a rejection of Quebec's national status. If historically the two major groups in Canada most in need of accommodation by an effective brokerage party, that is, those two major groups most likely to become disaffected from the federation, have been Quebec francophones and western Canadian Protestants of northern European origin, the Liberals have failed to offer any type of accommodation.

The party thought of as the *sine qua non* of brokerage has in fact since 1968 defined itself in opposition to the accommodation of groups that do not support a strong federal government as their patron. It has staked out one well-defined pole on the political spectrum in opposition to all perceived threats to a strong Canadian state, namely Quebec nationalism, western devolutionist sentiment, and, from 1968 until the mid-1990s, North American integration. As in most countries, the great nationalizing and centralizing projects have been met with resistance in the periphery, and the Liberals have been the party of the centre. The party is committed to a particular view of the Canadian nation with little tolerance for alternative conceptions. During the Pearson era there was a great deal of discussion about how best to accommodate the collective aspirations of Quebec, and the formal recognition of duality was considered, along with elaborate opting-out procedures for Quebec. These efforts were abandoned by Trudeau and then Chrétien, because they believed that the best way to keep Canada together was through a vigorous defence of federal institutions against what they saw as the forces of disintegration. Although it is true that a more accommodating wing exists within the party, reflected in the Pepin-Robarts Commission and by those who supported the Meech Lake Accord, the Liberals have not been successful at winning government with this wing in power.[25] The Trudeau/Chrétien wing, which believed that their vision would promote accommodation, misread the political culture. The ideology is too narrow to offer real accommodation to the periphery, although it is sufficiently expansive to keep them in power and thus discourage innovation.

Since 1968, the Liberals have evolved from a party of accommodation to a party of diversity. By embracing diversity and rejecting one overriding Canadian tradition, the party has managed to make itself barely acceptable to some francophone Quebecers who are rightly concerned about the discourse of an undifferentiated Canadian nation. In English-speaking Canada, this evolution enabled the party to retain its base among those who manifest a spirit of ac-commodation and reject a unified cultural Canadian tradition, but it has proved unable to respond to the majority's aspirations in either Quebec or western Canada. The party was prepared to accommodate diversity, as long as this diversity was expressed within the framework of loyalty to a strong central government. The party's discourse thus appealed to the spirit of accommoda-tion inherent in many Canadians, while being rejected by the very groups supposedly in need of accommodation. The great misfortune of Pierre Trudeau's discourse was that he appealed to those in English-speaking Canada who were open to accommodating Quebec, and directed this goodwill toward an ideology that rejected accommodation.

The irony, then, is that the putative national brokerage party has had a nar-row definition of the Canadian nation and has opted for a vision of accommodation that is at odds with the reality of the political culture. While it is no doubt true that "Reform, along with the Bloc Québécois ... shattered the old brokerage-style system, which had been predicated on bridging the national divide and neutralizing the national question,"[26] it was the Liberal Party that abetted this destruction. While the Liberal Party officially supported the Meech Lake and Charlottetown Accords, powerful forces within the party did not offer support to the Tories' accommodation, but instead adopted a discourse similar to that of the Reform Party's rejection of compromise-building. Carty *et al.*[27] are certainly right that Canada's three most recent elections demonstrate a rejection of intra-party brokerage, but they exaggerate when they lay the blame solely on the Bloc and Reform/Alliance who "exist to articulate, and even exacerbate, ethno-linguistic and regional tensions,"[28] while letting the Liberals off the hook: "The Liberal party has remained firmly in the accommodative tradition, trying to encompass as diverse a coalition as possible."[29] Since 1968, the Liberals have been full participants in the Cana-dian game of exacerbating ethno-linguistic and regional tensions. The Liberals may continue to see themselves as a party of elite accommodation but they do not use a discourse of accommodation and have demonstrated little tolerance for those with different views of the country.

The party has, however, using the discourse of the Charter, attempted to accommodate individual Canadians of diverse backgrounds to the Canadian federation through shared rights and a pan-Canadian identity. This has been the discourse of civic Canadian nationalism, with some allowance for multiculturalism and Aboriginal nationalism, which has appealed to Canadi-ans' moderation. Within this discourse there is little place for recognition of Quebec's national status or demands from the periphery for a more horizontal style of federalism. The 1993, 1997, and 2000 federal elections are the only elections in Canadian history where a party has formed a majority govern-ment but has failed to win a majority of seats in either Quebec or western Canada. On occasion, the most successful Canadian governments have won majorities in both the west and Quebec; at a minimum, they have had majority representation from one of these two regions. To have relatively thin representation from both areas reveals a governing party incapable of responding to the aspirations of citizens most in need of accommodation. As we will see, the Alliance also claims to reject the accommodation of groups, appealing instead to an undifferentiated liberal individual. One is therefore left with no dominant party that makes appeals to the brokerage and accommodation of national groups.

THE CANADIAN RIGHT

The presence of Red Tories in the Conservative Party acted as an important check against their emergence into an ideological type party in the postwar period. Their presence in the Conservative Party acted as an important reassurance to many voters, who could then feel comfortable voting Tory when they grew tired of the Liberals. The rise of the Reform Party changed this dynamic, with the party lacking a faction that tempered the neo- (and theo-) conservatives. Since 1993, the major "conservative" party has been an ideological party with no tradition of, or support for, brokerage and explicitly built on attacking brokerage. Although previous parties in Canada have also on occasion presumed that Canada features a majoritarian and homogenous political culture, they have not been able to have success at the federal level.

It has been well-documented elsewhere[30] that the "unite the right" efforts seem to have missed the underlying ideological foundations of party politics in Canada. When asked directly, most Conservative voters in 1997, particularly in Ontario, preferred the Liberals to Reform as their second choice. Conservative voters were closer to Liberal than Reform voters on cultural, economic, and social issues, particularly the latter. What the analysis of the CES team hints at, but does not make explicit, is the question of brokerage. The Alliance is not only "too conservative" on social issues for a strong majority of Canadian voters; it is my suggestion that they are also too ideological in their approach and too unwilling to engage in brokerage.

The fact that we have not properly measured "attitudes toward accommodation" as one key element of the debate over the definition of the Canadian nation has potentially led to incomplete conclusions about the motivations of voting decisions. The 1997 election study team concluded that Ontario voters and western voters had basically the same attitudes toward Quebec, and therefore, ideological differences on this question could not explain Reform's inability to break through in Ontario. They concluded that the difference between voters in Ontario and the west was that Ontario voters simply did not accord much importance to the question. Voters in the west used their attitudes toward Quebec as an important determinant of their vote, while those in Ontario did not.[31] However, it is possible that there was another dimension, namely, attitudes toward compromise, that went unmeasured. The story told by Nevitte and his colleagues may need to be qualified: Ontario voters did not use these attitudes toward Quebec to influence their vote because their ideological commitment to compromise and brokerage trumped the former. The CES team found that 28 percent of Ontario voters said that the Reform Party was "too extreme" to even consider voting for. This contrasts with 1 percent for the Liberals, 2 percent for the Tories, and 7 percent for the NDP. The 28 percent who found Reform "too extreme" is virtually identical to the percentage of Ontario voters who found the secessionist Bloc too extreme to consider voting for, a damning fact for the party. All citizens have a variety of competing considerations battling for prominence. Even those voters who do not much like Quebec may also want to vote for a party that does not, in their view, "threaten national unity," and by a margin of 49–30 percent, Ontario voters felt that Manning was a threat to national unity.

Attempts by the Reform Party in the early 1990s to supplant the Conservatives and transform the party of the right from a traditional brokerage party to a party of ideology dominated by two competing forces — moral traditionalists and neo-conservatives — could not succeed within the context of Canadian political culture because the party had not come to terms with the complexity of the Canadian nation and accommodation. The notion of a united right denies the extreme moderation of many voters whose natural home is the political centre and who have no interest in continually choosing between stark options. But this comfort with the political centre is more than simply economic or social "moderation"; it is in fact a comfort with brokerage and a deep instinct toward accommodation. It is a real commitment to a particular definition of the Canadian nation and its identity. This commitment is occasionally punctuated by issues which call to mind Canadians' tribal loyalties, such as occurred in the debate over conscription or the Meech Lake Accord. But these moments are interruptions and cannot exist for long in duration; if they do, the country does not survive. So, by definition, any party that succeeds due to the mobilization of these powerful tribal emotions cannot come to power (though the Unionist government of 1917 managed to pull off this trick). It is, of course, possible for a centre-right coalition to come to power in Canada, but only once it first articulates a credible vision that is accommodating of the many facets of Canadian nationhood.

The challenge for the Alliance since the 1997 federal election was often framed as one of ridding itself of the image of social conservatism. This oversimplifies the problem, and assumes a two-dimensional space. In fact, opinion leaders in central Canada are secular, adopt a conciliatory and accommodative language, and resist more popular democracy. The appeal that the Alliance's economic policies may have for some central Canadian opinion leaders is dwarfed by not one but three countervailing dimensions.

In the period following the 2000 federal election, many in the Alliance came to recognize the importance of brokerage. Although the Alliance is likely to continue to reject all form of group rights, and argue that new immigrants, Aboriginal peoples, and Quebecers should be integrated into an undifferentiated Canadian nation, a successful brokerage party will likely need to avoid these issues because they detract from efforts at re-branding. There is room on the Canadian landscape for a second brokerage party to rival the Liberals that argues that the interests of provincial communities need to be better accommodated through better respect for the federal principle. By so doing, it may be able to appeal to Quebec nationalists, without ever speaking directly to the question of Quebec specifically. For any centre-right, centre, or centre-left coalition to come to power in Canada, it must come to terms with this fault line and navigate it successfully. Since 1968, those Canadians who have not accepted primary loyalty to a strong central government have found a home in the Conservative Party, and, on occasion, regional third parties. A successful alternative to the Liberals must appeal to all groups that do not identify with the national project of the Liberals, and the Alliance has proved unable to do so.

THE NEW CONTOURS OF BROKERAGE

On most questions related to the definition of the Canadian nation and brokerage, the Liberals and the Alliance are remarkably similar: they both articulate a discourse of individual rights, pan-Canadian civic nationalism, and no national recognition of Quebec. Where they differ is, first, on issues related to the protection of collective rights for ethno-cultural communities, Aboriginal peoples, and linguistic minorities, with the Alliance more supportive of one unified common Canadian tradition;[32] and second, on the role of the federal government. The Liberals and Alliance currently define themselves in opposition to each other on the question of the federal principle, interest group politics, and a common Canadian tradition. By embracing a definition of the nation characterized by one common Canadian tradition, the Alliance cannot succeed in Quebec and cannot make headway in other communities that support the spirit of accommodation, but because of its defence of a strong centre, the Liberals can have little success in francophone Quebec and Protestant western Canada.

Johnston and his colleagues[33] have remarked that "Incoherence has always been the price of successful brokerage." Although the Conservatives' coalition of the 1980s was infused with incoherence, the Liberals' coalition is quite coherent in its defence of the federal government and federal elites. What is particularly incoherent is that somehow many have looked to the Liberal Party to be a party of accommodation, when, since 1968, it has been the party that most explicitly rejects the accommodation of differing definitions of the Canadian nation. The Liberal Party's definition of brokerage and the Canadian nation remains coherent, yet the primary challenge — the accommodation of Quebec rather than French Canada — has gone through a dramatic evolution.

Our confusion — seeing the Liberal Party as the party of accommodation despite its adamant rejection of the principle — may stem from the fact that the Liberals have been the party of French Canada and diversity for most of the twentieth century. Those voters outside Quebec instinctively supportive of French Canada and multiculturalism have seen the Liberal Party as their home. When the accommodation of Quebec, rather than French Canada, became the country's central issue, many Liberal voters sympathetic to French Canada became prepared to accommodate Quebec, despite the fact that the party leadership became increasingly sure in its rejection of this approach. The Liberals have continued to remain barely viable in Quebec because they reject a unified cultural tradition and continue to have an accommodative wing, despite the fact that this wing has not been able to win power.

Questions related to social conservatism, like abortion, which were quite prominent in the 2000 federal election, are not likely to play as large a role in the future. All parties have now made it clear that they are secular, competing for a similar pool of voters. Even the Alliance, which can count on the support of social conservatives, has no room to make gains among social conservatives and must expand its appeal to an increasingly secular population. The political culture cannot support a party that directs its appeal to moral traditionalism. Instead, a successful alternative brokerage party must be seen to be secular and articulate a vision of the Canadian nation that appeals to those disenchanted with the Liberals' national project. A second credible brokerage alternative to the Liberals will adopt a discourse of respect for the federal principle, in an attempt to rebuild the Conservative alliance of the 1980s, a discourse that remains attractive to Tories.

The debate over the character of the nation will pit the Trudeau vision against the provincialist vision, without this debate being clouded by a debate over Quebec's national status or by a debate over social conservatism. This debate will also coincide perfectly with the Alliance's appeal to democratic and populist values in opposition to an elitist federal government. The natural fault line for political conflict in Canada is between the pan-Canadian centralizers and the devolutionists, made up of Quebec nationalists and western populists (as well as those supportive of greater North American integration). The great difficulty for those who supported the Meech Lake Accord has been that the constituency in Canada outside Quebec that is naturally sympathetic to Quebec, and which has been prepared to recognize Quebec as a distinct society, is also more supportive of a strong federal government and weaker provinces. Therefore, those who instinctively support measures to help Quebec are also more likely to instinctively support a stronger federal government. The Trudeau/Chrétien Liberal coalition is coherent because one can simultaneously support a strong federal government and accommodation with French Canada in the form of national bilingualism and protection of linguistic minorities.

EXPLORATORY ANALYSIS

The best way to resolve the question of how many dimensions of conflict exist is through empirical investigation. This must begin with correlation and factor analysis between a large number of well-constructed measures. Unfortunately, well-crafted items on all of the issues I have discussed have not been asked in one survey. This necessitates an exploratory empirical analysis, some of which will remain speculative. I will make use of the best available data: the 1997 Canadian Election Study (CES), which asked a large number of relevant questions — though no ideal measure of what I describe as support for accommodation — and the 2000 Centre for Research and Information on Canada (CRIC) survey, which asked a large number of questions on Canadian values and the Canadian nation. I will highlight how parties' voters differ, and, by so doing, I am not suggesting that the parties or their platforms are entirely consistent: many in the Alliance leadership have sought to attenuate their rejection of multiculturalism and many in the Liberal leadership have shown more flexibility toward Quebec. These observations are correct, but by identifying the enduring ideological differences between partisans, I will highlight key features of Canadian political culture.

Table 1 presents the results of an exploratory factor analysis conducted on a large number of variables from the 1997 CES. Factor analysis is highly influenced by which variables are included, and one should consider these results suggestive only. Five underlying dimensions emerged, and I have labelled them populism, accommodation, social conservatism, deficit, and taxes. The most important point to take out of this table is that social conservatism, populism (or cynicism about elites), and accommodation (or attitudes toward minorities) do not load on the same factor, but remain separate. This provides some evidence that one should avoid lumping all of these issues together in a dimension of "cultural politics." Note that two different factors emerge on the economic dimension. This may have been particular to the 1997 election and the unique role played by the issue of the deficit, or, alternatively, economic reasoning may be more complex than is generally presumed. For my purposes, however, I will continue to think of the economic dimension as one dimension and retain my fourfold conceptualization.

In Table 2, I regressed the underlying factors onto the vote from 1997. From this table, one should retain the extreme polarization between Liberals and Reform, particularly on the question of populism. On the question of accommodation, the polarization also clearly exists, but it is the NDP that is the party of minority accommodation. What is also striking is the far more muted polarization on the economic and social dimensions between the Liberals and Reform. The Conservatives present a particularly interesting pattern in 1997: their voters are the least distinct ideologically, and the combination of ideology, region, and social structure explain far less of the Tory vote. The

Table 1: Exploratory Factor Analysis: What are the Dimensions of Political Conflict in Canada Outside Quebec?

	Populism	Accommodation	Moral Traditionalism	Deficit Reduction	Tax Reduction
Do parties keep their promises?	**0.56**	-0.09	-0.02	0.00	0.06
Satisfied with democracy in Canada?	**0.53**	-0.19	0.06	-0.16	0.10
MPs soon lose touch	**0.63**	-0.06	-0.14	0.11	-0.01
People like me have no say	**0.69**	-0.08	0.12	0.00	0.09
Government doesn't care	**0.77**	-0.11	0.10	-0.04	0.11
Politicians are ready to lie to get elected	**0.68**	-0.07	0.07	0.00	0.04
How much should be done for Quebec?	-0.18	**0.68**	0.03	-0.02	-0.04
How much should be done for racial minorities?	-0.04	**0.70**	-0.16	0.00	0.02
How much should be done for Aboriginals?	0.01	**0.67**	-0.04	-0.14	-0.01
Should we accept more immigrants?	-0.20	**0.44**	-0.12	0.03	-0.12
Support distinct society	-0.16	**0.61**	0.03	0.05	-0.13
Only married people should have children	0.02	-0.08	**0.83**	0.07	0.06
Women should stay home with kids	0.09	-0.10	**0.81**	0.04	0.01
Social programs/deficit trade-off	0.02	0.00	0.12	**0.81**	0.11
Reducing deficit is important	-0.06	-0.08	0.00	**0.82**	0.07
Cutting taxes is important	0.16	-0.07	0.03	0.07	**0.80**
Social programs/tax cut trade-off	-0.01	0.14	-0.04	0.10	**0.78**
Eigenvalue	3.40	1.80	1.40	1.20	1.00
Cumulative percent of explained variance	20.30	31.20	39.50	47.10	53.10

Note: Extraction Method: Principal Component Analysis. Rotation Method: Varimax with Kaiser Normalization.
Source: Data from Canadian Election Study, 1997.

Table 2: Ideological Dispositions and the Vote in Canada Outside Quebec: 1997

	Liberal	Reform	NDP	Conservative
Populism	-0.61 (0.06)ᵃ	0.62 (0.08)ᵃ	0.17 (0.08)ᶜ	-0.10 (0.07)
Accommodation	0.21 (0.06)ᵃ	-0.64 (0.08)ᵃ	0.53 (0.08)ᵃ	0.08 (0.07)
Social Conservatism	-0.04 (0.06)	0.30 (0.08)ᵃ	-0.21 (0.05)ᶜ	0.15 (0.07)ᶜ
Deficit Reduction	-0.12 (0.06)ᶜ	0.25 (0.08)ᵃ	-0.46 (0.08)ᵃ	0.06 (0.07)
Tax Reduction	-0.15 (0.06)ᵇ	0.28 (0.08)ᵃ	-0.39 (0.08)ᵃ	0.17 (0.07)ᶜ
Atlantic	-0.18 (0.27)	-0.87 (0.42)ᶜ	-0.27 (0.35)	0.94 (0.33)ᵇ
Ontario	0.41 (0.23)	-0.28 (0.33)	-0.61 (0.32)	0.19 (0.31)
Manitoba/Saskatchewan	-0.18 (0.27)	-0.08 (0.36)	0.46 (0.34)	0.06 (0.35)
Alberta	-1.00 (0.28)ᵃ	1.20 (0.33)ᵃ	-0.91 (0.39)ᶜ	0.72 (0.32)ᶜ
British Columbia	0.16 (0.26)	0.72 (0.34)ᶜ	-0.43 (0.36)	-0.74 (0.39)
Catholic	0.71 (0.13)ᵃ	-0.53 (0.18)ᵇ	0.19 (0.19)	-0.44 (0.16)ᵇ
No religion	0.27 (0.17)	-0.14 (0.20)	0.19 (0.23)	-0.33 (0.21)
Income	-0.01 (0.02)	0.02 (0.02)	-0.03 (0.02)	0.02 (0.02)
Female	0.03 (0.03)	-0.13 (0.04)ᵃ	0.12 (0.04)ᵇ	-0.03 (0.03)
Constant	-1.00 (0.27)ᵃ	-1.60 (0.35)ᵃ	-2.10 (0.37)ᵃ	-1.70 (0.34)ᵃ
-2 log likelihood	1748.346	1157.151	1010.952	1346.283
Cox and Snell R sq.	0.13	0.18	0.09	0.05

Note: Logit coefficients reported, standard errors in parentheses.
ᶜ $p < 0.05$; ᵇ $p < 0.01$; ᵃ $p < 0.001$.

Source: Data from Canadian Election Study, 1997.

Conservatives continued to make pan-Canadian brokerage-style appeals (or at least the composition of their electorate so suggested). On the economic dimensions, the NDP electorate was very different than other parties' supporters. Across the board, populism and accommodation were the most pronounced fault lines, highlighting that both the Reform and the Liberals were appealing to fairly coherent constituencies in regards to their views on the definition of the Canadian nation and public participation.

The evolution of the party system is apparent in these results. Tory voters and Reform voters point the same way on the economic and social dimensions, while Liberal and NDP voters point the same way on these two dimensions. However, on populism, it is Liberals and Tories who point the same way, while Reform and NDP supporters also point the same way. Here we have a clear demonstration that the Tories and Liberals share similar dispositions on elitism, while Reform has challenged that consensus. We also see that NDP supporters are more sceptical of elitism, much like Reformers. However, on the dimension of accommodation, NDP and Reform partisans diverge dramatically. We therefore clearly see that NDP partisans are simultaneously more participatory and accommodating of diversity.

One final thing deserves mention in Table 2: on each of the five factors, the Reform Party controls one pole. The Tories never control even one pole, while the Liberals and the NDP control some (Liberal voters are the most elitist, while NDP voters are the most accommodationist, socially liberal, and economically liberal). This is in part why Reform — and to a lesser extent the NDP — are often portrayed as extreme. On each of the four dimensions of political conflict — economic, social, populism, and accommodation — Reform controls one pole. While the Liberals may be at one extreme on one question, they are centrist on others. The Tories were in the difficult position in 1997 of controlling no pole, and hence having no loyal electorate. The Liberals have been in an excellent position: control a pole on one or two dimensions so that they can count on a loyal electorate with a commitment to a well-defined conception of the Canadian nation, but avoid the "extremist" label by centrism on the economic and social dimensions which have figured prominently during recent election campaigns.

Table 3 reports correlations from the 2000 CRIC survey on a large number of questions central to our understanding of accommodation and the definition of the Canadian nation. The first thing to point out is that the populism variable and the accommodation variables are *not* correlated, highlighting again the distinctiveness of these dimensions. However, the variables which measure support for devolution and the federal government are highly related to the populism variable. This is an important finding about the evolving nature of Canadian political culture. Some have suggested that the 1990s featured a rejection of elite accommodation, a simultaneous rejection of elitism and accommodation. I have argued elsewhere that the public rejected elitism but

Table 3: Correlations Between Variables (2000)

	(2)	(3)	(4)	(5)	(6)	(7)	(8)	(9)
No private health care (1)	0.19[a]	-0.03	0.03	0.04	0.17[a]	0.07[c]	0.14[a]	0.11[a]
Canada should be less like US (2)		-0.03	0.02	-0.09[b]	0.16[a]	0.06[c]	0.11[a]	0.08[b]
Treat Natives exactly the same (3)			0.11[a]	0.04	-0.05	-0.10[b]	-0.06[c]	-0.11[a]
Accept fewer immigrants (4)				0.04	-0.09[b]	-0.16[a]	-0.11[a]	-0.11[a]
Public should be involved in decisions (5)					-0.15[a]	0.00	0.04	-0.13[a]
Feds should have more power (6)						0.02	0.10[b]	0.28[a]
Quebec can be satisfied with goodwill (7)							0.08[b]	0.08[b]
Social programs, not tax cuts or debt (8)								0.10[b]
Trust feds to protect programs (9)								

Note: [c] $p < 0.05$; [b] $p < 0.01$; [a] $p < 0.001$.

Source: Data from Centre for Research and Information on Canada, 2000.

was still quite open to accommodation.[34] The findings presented in Table 3 clarify what has been going on. It is not a rejection of elites and a rejection of accommodation that have gone hand in hand, but elites and the federal government. This distinction is crucial. Those who believe in public participation are more likely to distrust the federal government — personified by the Liberals since 1993 — and support devolution, but are *not* more likely to support lower levels of immigration, Aboriginal rights, or accommodation toward Quebec. The debate concerning the definition of the Canadian nation in the early 1990s was characterized by discussions of Quebec's national status. Today, the debate is far more likely to focus on the role of the federal and provincial governments more generally, and on these issues there *is* a relationship between populism and the definition of the Canadian nation, with populists calling for devolution. The federal government is today understood by many Canadians as representing the Canadian elite, and those who reject this elite are more likely to simultaneously reject the elite's definition of the Canadian nation — a strong federal government — and its definition of democracy — party discipline and little public participation. Other correlations of note include the strong relationship between variables measuring accommodation toward Quebec and Aboriginal peoples, as well as support for immigration. This provides evidence that many Canadians continue to use affective responses to outgroups to structure their thinking about politics.

Table 4 presents regression results from the 2000 election. Although CRIC did not ask a vote intention question, I was able to combine the CRIC survey on issues related to federalism with the Environics' vote intention question asked as part of their omnibus survey.[35] Several results central to my argument should be noted. First, the Alliance vote is by far the most heavily structured by these ideological dimensions, highlighting that its voters are far more ideologically pure than one would find in a traditional brokerage party. Second, attitudes toward the federal government and the distribution of powers provide the sharpest distinction between the Liberal and Alliance vote, suggesting that disagreements over the definition of the Canadian nation and the role of the federal government continued to be important elements of the political culture structuring political conflict. Third, the Alliance continues to be very much the party of those who support increasing the role of the public, while the Liberals and the Tories represent the older party model, appealing to those with less trust in the public. Fourth, attitudes toward Quebec remain very important for Alliance supporters. Fifth, while Alliance supporters have a distinct set of attitudes with regard to Quebec, their attitudes toward Aboriginal issues and immigration are far less distinct.

Figures 1 and 2 map these dimensions of political conflict and party positions. The positioning of the parties is based on where their own partisans fall on these dimensions.[36] Figure 1 presents the economic and social dimensions, based on two questions from the 1997 CES (a question measuring opinion on

Table 4: Ideological Explanations of the Vote in 2000 in Canada Outside Quebec

	Liberal	Alliance	NDP	Conservative
No private health	0.37 (0.16)[c]	−0.76 (0.18)[a]	0.64 (0.32)[c]	0.05 (0.27)
Less like US	0.03 (0.11)	−0.45 (0.12)[a]	0.24 (0.21)	−0.06 (0.19)
Natives no different	−0.31 (0.16)[c]	−0.24 (0.19)	−0.41 (0.27)	0.98 (0.34)[b]
Fewer immigrants	−0.01 (0.12)	0.13 (0.15)	−0.09 (0.20)	0.36 (0.21)
No public involvement	0.26 (0.10)[b]	−0.32 (0.13)[b]	0.16 (0.16)	0.34 (0.16)[c]
Centralize powers	0.60 (0.12)[a]	−0.70 (0.15)[a]	−0.34 (0.20)	0.01 (0.21)
Goodwill to Quebec	0.09 (0.15)	−0.62 (0.19)[a]	0.29 (0.26)	0.26 (0.26)
Social programs	0.10 (0.16)	−0.96 (0.24)[a]	0.14 (0.26)	−0.09 (0.29)
Trust feds	0.89 (0.19)[a]	−0.83 (0.31)[a]	0.20 (0.31)	1.10 (0.46)[c]
Constant	−2.50 (0.61)[a]	4.00 (0.74)[a]	−4.00 (1.10)[a]	−5.70 (1.10)[a]
−2 log likelihood	1036.176	743.311	437.144	458.494
Cox and Snell R sq.	0.12	0.16	0.06	0.03

Note: Logit coefficients reported, standard errors in parentheses.
[c] $p < 0.05$; [b] $p < 0.01$; [a] $p < 0.001$.

Source: Data from Environics' Omnibus, supplemented by Centre for Research and Information on Canada, 2000.

Figure 1: A Rough Mapping of Economic and Social Politics in Canada Outside Quebec (correlations based on 1997 CES)

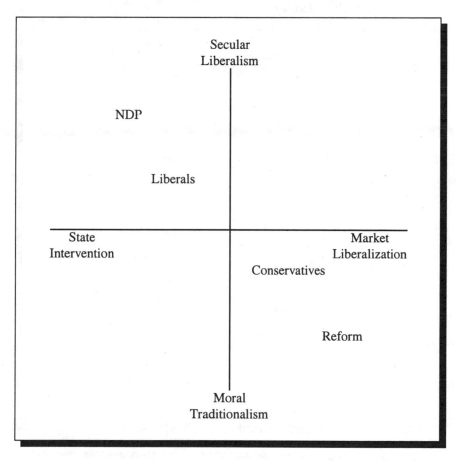

taxes versus social programs, and a question measuring whether only married people should have children). The positioning is exactly as many might expect. By looking at this figure alone, one might conclude that the competitive space in 1997 was in fact unidimensional, moving from the NDP, which was on the left on both dimensions, to the Liberals, then the Tories, and finally to Reform, which was the most to the right. This unidimensional mapping, however, fails to depict the complexity of the Canadian ideological landscape; recall that it was the other two dimensions that allowed us to most clearly distinguish different partisans.

**Figure 2: A Rough Mapping of Populist and Integrative Politics in
    Canada Outside Quebec (correlations based on 2000
    Environics survey)**

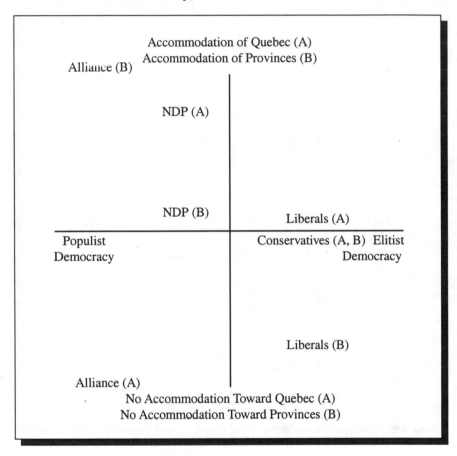

Figure 2 presents results from questions in the 2000 CRIC study, using the
question regarding public participation in decision-making to tap into the
populism dimension, and using two different questions regarding the definition of the nation, one based on support for accommodation of Quebec, the
other based on support for devolution of powers toward the provinces. The
placement of Alliance and Liberal partisans changes dramatically depending
on which question regarding the definition of the Canadian nation is at play.
The Liberals are clearly the party of a strong central government, while the
Alliance supports devolution. But the Alliance also is quite resistant to Quebec
accommodation. The dysfunction of the Conservative coalition of the 1980s

is apparent: those most supportive of stronger provincial governments were also those who were least supportive of accommodating Quebec. This coalition, however difficult to sustain, is the natural brokerage alternative to the Liberals. Within an electoral context, it remains viable so long as its focus remains the role of the federal government rather than the special place of Quebec. Simply because neither Preston Manning nor Stockwell Day were able to build a successful coalition with parties in Quebec in no way negates the fact that this is the only natural governing alternative to the Liberals.

The 2000 election appears to have given us a prelude to coming debates, with the Liberals defending a strong federal government against all those who might attack it. Whether the NDP has a place in this debate is far from clear. At first glance, they have the potential to occupy a quadrant on their own: those who are generally supportive of accommodation toward Quebec and other minorities, and those who support public participation — an ideological grouping that has had no real spokesperson in Canada. However, this grouping is comparatively small. Moreover, the evidence suggests that in Canada, public participation is closely associated with devolution, and devolution has been historically resisted by the NDP that saw a strong federal government as being key to the protection of national social programs. On questions of economic and social policy, and the accommodation of Canadian diversity, the NDP has natural allies in the Quebec nationalist movement, yet the party remains closely associated with a strong federal state. Yet the evidence presented in Table 4 suggests that the remaining NDP partisans are not as committed to a strong central state as they once were, and the path ahead for the NDP may lie in advocating devolution, public participation/democracy, secular values, and the accommodation of groups.

It is also striking that the upper-right quadrant — the quadrant that represents the ideology of elite accommodation — remains virtually vacant, although the Tories come closest to situating themselves in this space. Where Tory and Alliance supporters are most likely to differ is on questions of public participation in decision-making. Looking only to Figure 1, one might come to the conclusion that party leaders could easily split their differences on social and economic issues and arrive at something of a consensus. However, on questions of populism, as well as questions of the definition of the Canadian nation, their respective partisans are wide apart. It is on these questions where the greatest challenges lie, and it is these questions that have meant doom for previous Blue coalitions.

The Appendix presents results from a number of survey questions that could be understood as tapping attitudes toward accommodation. In 1996, Canadians outside Quebec by very strong majorities accepted the idea that different provinces might be allowed to exercise different powers (questions 10 and 11). However, in 1999 and 2000, when questions were asked which attempted to mirror the debates over differentiated equality and Aboriginal peoples,

Canadians outside Quebec by sizable majorities rejected Aboriginals' differential status (questions 3 and 12). These results are suggestive: the discourse of undifferentiated equality is deeply anchored and parties challenge this philosophy at their peril. At the same time, Canadians are sensitive to the different situations of different provinces, and provided that asymmetry does not imply formal "special status," a highly flexible federalism is consistent with Canadians' values. The Meech Lake Accord was understood as a "special deal," and Canadians outside Quebec are very resistant to this idea. They are not, however, resistant to the idea that different provinces, cities, and communities may develop their own unique institutional and procedural arrangements to respond to their own challenges — what could be understood as functional, instrumental, or generalized asymmetry.

CONCLUSION

Writing about party competition and public opinion is perilous during this period of fluidity, as discussions continue between the Alliance and the Conservatives regarding cooperation, the NDP considers its future, and the Liberal Party considers a change of leadership that may turn power over to a leadership team more open to Quebec nationalism. Yet all actors have to confront a number of fairly stable elements of the political culture as they consider their options, and my goal has been to highlight these realities.

A primary conflict within the Canadian political culture is over the definition of the nation and what role the federal government should play in national life.[37] The Liberal Party has established hegemony by occupying one pole of this debate and attracting the loyalty of the many Canadians supportive of a continuing strong role for the federal government, its close relationship to the Canadian elite, and an affirmative representation of diversity and pluralism. This coalition, despite some internal tensions, has remained largely coherent because of a shared conception of the Canadian nation and an overriding commitment to compromise and brokerage on economic and social questions, despite their rejection of compromise on issues related to the definition of the nation itself, particularly the place of Quebec and the provinces in confederation, and the role of the public in decision-making.

The alternative coalition is less coherent because its manifestation can take place in one of a number of different ways, each of which places different strains on this coalition. So long as the coalition merely reflects the periphery and those who have less allegiance to a strong federal government, it remains coherent and a credible alternative government. However, when this coalition focuses on other elements within the political culture, namely Quebec, but also potentially multicultural communities, its coherence breaks down. It breaks down in part because it loses key allies, but also because it appears to reject brokerage and compromise and becomes an ideological party, one that can hold its base but frightens moderate elements within the Canadian political culture who prefer to vote for a brokerage party.

Both the Alliance and Liberals attempt to communicate to Canadian voters that they are pan-Canadian parties who believe in finding accommodation and compromise between all regional and national groups, though both have histories that belie these pretensions. To many in the west and in Quebec, the Liberals' claim that it is a party capable of representing all Canadians is not credible. Likewise, the Alliance's appeal to one undifferentiated Canadian cultural tradition communicates to voters in Quebec and ethnocultural communities that they are not welcome, and in 2000 the Alliance continued to have difficulty in western Canada attracting francophones, those of non-European background, and Catholics. The Liberals claim that the Alliance does not respect the diversity of Canada, while the Alliance claims that the Liberals do not respect the regions. Neither, however, speaks for the recognition of subnational communities. In order for any alternative to the Liberals to have national success it must clear a high hurdle: it must re-brand itself as a brokerage party that combines a belief in devolution with populism, and present a program that offers accommodation to Quebec all the while avoiding issues that make specific mention of Quebec's status. It must avoid these issues not because it is far away from the median Ontario voter, but because the articulation of these issues prevents bridge-building with potential allies in Quebec and threatens its chances in Ontario because many of these voters support accommodation as a fundamental value.

The elections of 1887, 1891 and 1896 offer parallels. At the time, the Conservatives were the party of the centre and the Liberals represented the periphery, provincial rights, and North American integration. But the Liberals could not win national government because they lacked a key element of that coalition, namely Quebec. It was only by gradually bringing francophone Quebec voters into this coalition, a coalition that sought to accommodate Quebec as well as the western periphery by avoiding sectional politics, that the Liberals were able to secure national government in 1896. This required a delicate balancing act. In particular, the Liberals needed to downplay the nationalism of Honoré Mercier when campaigning outside Quebec, much like Mulroney had to mute the nationalism of his Quebec representation when campaigning in the west. But Laurier's 1896 coalition was viable, it appealed to accommodation, and this coalition — which now finds its home in the right-of-centre parties — represents the natural governing alternative to the brokerage of the present-day Liberals.

NOTES

I thank John Meisel for his very helpful comments on an earlier draft of this paper, and Jon Clancy for his research assistance. I am indebted to the editors, Fred Cutler, and the anonymous reviewer who provided generous and insightful comments. Their probing suggestions forced me to turn a paper that was largely a collection of observations into a far more coherent and empirically supported work.

1. See Telford, this volume.

2. Harold D. Clarke, Jane Jenson, Lawrence Leduc and Jon Pammett, *Absent Mandate* (Toronto: Gage Publishing, 1984).

3. A leading American scholar includes the following hotly debated issues in the realm of cultural politics: "the legality of abortion, government funding of controversial forms of artistic expression, the place of gays and lesbians in society, policies aimed at promoting equality for women and minorities, the defense of traditional values in education and the family, concerns over violence and sex in films and television." Dennis Chong, *Rational Lives: Norms and Values in Politics and Society* (Chicago: University of Chicago Press, 2000).

4. Herbert Kitschelt, *The Transformation of European Social Democracy* (Cambridge: Cambridge University Press, 1994).

5. Ibid., p. 296.

6. Ibid., p. 140.

7. Keith T. Poole and Howard Rosenthal, "D-NOMINATE after 10 Years: A Comparative Update to Congress: A Political-Economic History of Roll-Call Voting," *Legislative Studies Quarterly* 26, 1(2001):5-29.

8. Richard Johnston, André Blais, Elisabeth Gidengil and Neil Nevitte, *The Challenge of Direct Democracy: The 1992 Canadian Referendum* (Montreal: McGill-Queen's University Press, 1996), p. 172; See also Richard Johnston, "Canadian Elections at the Millennium," *Choices* (Montreal: Institute for Research on Public Policy, 2000).

9. Neil Nevitte, André Blais, Elisabeth Gidengil and Richard Nadeau, *Unsteady State: The 1997 Canadian Federal Election* (Toronto: Oxford University Press, 2000), pp. 48-65.

10. Ibid., pp. 138-42.

11. David Laycock, *Populism and Democratic Thought in the Canadian Prairies, 1910 to 1945* (Toronto: University of Toronto Press, 1990).

12. Johnston, Blais, Gidengil and Nevitte, *The Challenge of Direct Democracy.*

13. John R. Hibbing and Elizabeth Theiss-Morse, *Congress as Public Enemy: Public Attitudes Toward American Political Institutions* (Cambridge: Cambridge University Press, 1995).

14. Matthew Mendelsohn, "Public Brokerage: Constitutional Reform, Public Participation, and the Accommodation of Mass Publics," *Canadian Journal of Political Science.* 33, 2(2000):245-73.

15. Johnston, Blais, Gidengil and Nevitte, *The Challenge of Direct Democracy.*

16. Laycock, *Populism and Democratic Thought in the Canadian Prairies, 1910 to 1945.*

17. David Elkins and Richard Simeon, *Small Worlds: Provinces and Parties in Canadian Political Life* (Toronto and New York: Methuen, 1980).

18. R. Kenneth Carty, William Cross and Lisa Young, *Rebuilding Canadian Party Politics* (Vancouver: UBC Press, 2000), p. 8.

19. Nevitte, Blais, Gidengil and Nadeau, *Unsteady State: The 1997 Canadian Federal Election*, p. 92.

20. Matthew Mendelsohn and John McLean, "Reconcilable Differences: Federalism and Public Consultation," in *Federalism and Democracy*, ed. David Stewart and Paul Thomas (Winnipeg: University of Manitoba Press, 2001).

21. John Forester, *Critical Theory, Public Policy, and Planning Practice: Toward a Critical Pragmatism* (Albany: State University of New York Press, 1993).

22. Gordon Stewart, "The Origins of Canadian Politics and John A. Macdonald," in *National Politics and Community in Canada*, ed. R. Kenneth Carty and P. Ward (Vancouver: UBC Press, 1986).

23. Neil Nevitte, *The Decline of Deference* (Toronto: Broadview, 1996).

24. Carty, Cross and Young, *Rebuilding Canadian Party Politics*, p. 84.

25. The division between the Paul Martin and Jean Chrétien wings of the party is bitter and personal. But it is easy to exaggerate the personal aspect to these conflicts. The animosity between their respective partisans stems from a conflict not over economic or social values, but over the Meech Lake Accord. It is this disagreement in regard to accommodation that animates conflict within as well as between parties.

26. Neil Nevitte, André Blais, Elisabeth Gidengil, and Nadeau, *Unsteady State: The 1997 Canadian Federal Election*, p. 90.

27. Carty, Cross and Young, *Rebuilding Canadian Party Politics,* p. 6.

28. Ibid., p. 35.

29. Ibid., p. 85.

30. Nevitte, Blais, Gidengil and Nadeau, *Unsteady State: The 1997 Canadian Federal Election*, chap. 8

31. Ibid., pp. 94-95.

32. See Telford, this volume.

33. Richard Johnston, André Blais, Henry E. Brady and Jean Crête, *Letting the People Decide: Dynamics of a Canadian Election* (Montreal and Kingston: McGill-Queen's University Press, 1992), p. 73.

34. Matthew Mendelsohn, "Public Brokerage: Constitutional Reform, Public Participation, and the Accommodation of Mass Publics."

35. One should also note that CRIC did not ask a question that measured social conservatism.

36. The placement of the parties is based on the percentage point difference between those who intend to vote for the party and the mean. The end points of the axes are fixed at 20-point divergences from the mean.

37. How parties deal with economic questions, such as taxation and social programs, will, of course, remain crucial to their potential success, although the Liberals, Tories, and Alliance have tended to converge on these issues in important ways. Parties' positioning on moral questions related to the family will become increasingly less relevant to parties' discourse as the Alliance is forced to recognize that dealing with these issues within the context of an election campaign is unsustainable given the value structure of Canadian voters.

APPENDIX
CRIC Questions, October 2000

1) In your opinion, should Canada allow privately-owned companies to deliver some health-care services in Canada, or should the health-care system be operated entirely as a public program?
   Allow private 33%; Keep public 63%; DK 4%.

2) In the future, would you like to see Canada become more like the United States, less like the United States, or would you like things to remain as they are?
   More like 11%; Less like 49%; Remain unchanged 37%; DK 2%.

3) Do you think that Aboriginal peoples should have some type of preferential access to hunting and fishing grounds in areas where they have traditionally lived, or do you think that when governments regulate access to hunting and fishing grounds they should treat everyone the same?
   All equal 66%; Preferential access 31%; DK 2%.

4) Do you think Canada should accept more immigrants, fewer immigrants, or about the same number as we accept now?
   More 12%; Fewer 31%; Same 55%.

5) If the general public was more involved in decision-making on our big national problems, do you think we would be more likely to solve our problems, less likely to solve our problems, or that it would make no difference?
   More likely 47%; Less likely 19%; No difference 32%; DK 2%.

6) In your opinion, does the federal government have too much power, do the provincial governments have too much power, or is the balance between them about right?
   Feds have too much 29%; Provinces have too much 12%; About right 52%; DK 5%.

7) Which of the following statements more closely reflects your own opinion?
   Almost nothing will satisfy Quebec; it wants everything and will always keep asking for more 52%; With some effort on the part of the rest of Canada, Quebec can be made to feel happy within Canada 44%; DK 4%.

8) If governments have budgetary surpluses, which of the following three things should be the highest priority?
   Cutting taxes 25%; Paying down the debt 43%; or Putting more money into social programs 31%; DK 1%.

9) Which government do you trust more to protect the programs you care about? Is it:
The federal government 20%; The government of your province 28%; Both equally 31%; or Neither 20%; DK 1%.

10) Sometimes people talk about "equality of the provinces." Some people say this means that each province has to be treated identically, otherwise we don't have true equality. Others say we can still have true equality even if different provinces have different powers to meet their specific circumstances. This could mean special powers for Quebec over the French language. Insight, 1996.
Identical treatment 32%; Different treatment is possible 64%; DK 4%.

11) Sometimes people talk about "equality of the provinces." Some people say this means that each province has to be treated identically, otherwise we don't have true equality. Others say we can still have true equality even if different provinces have different powers to meet their specific circumstances. This could mean special powers for Quebec over the French language, BC over the fisheries, or Alberta over oil. Insight, 1996.
Identical treatment 24%; Different treatment is possible 72%; DK 4%.

12) Which of the following two statements comes closest to your own view: As Canada's first people, Aboriginal peoples should be entitled to special consideration in some areas, such as access to hunting and fishing grounds; or: All Canadians should have exactly the same rights, otherwise we do not have true equality. CRIC, 1999.
Same rights 68%; Special consideration 31%; DK 2%.

4

Say Goodbye to the Dream of One Canada: The Costly Failure to Purchase National Unity

Patrick James and Michael Lusztig

Une composante importante de la vision du Canada de Trudeau était la notion qu'une société juste devait fournir des compensations financières pour ses membres les moins privilégiés. Même si l'État-providence fut mis en place avant l'ère Trudeau, sa vision d'une communauté nationale florissante, notamment grâce à de généreuses dépenses publiques, fait maintenant partie intégrante de la politique culturelle canadienne. Trudeau croyait également que les dépenses reliées aux programmes sociaux parviendraient à diminuer les clivages et rapprocher les diverses communautés ethniques du Canada. Cependant, dans ce chapitre, James et Lusztig soutiennent qu'il existe aussi des effets pervers importants quant à l'utilisation de l'État-providence pour créer et maintenir un sentiment fort de communauté nationale.

With the exception of Sir John A. Macdonald, and possibly William Lyon Mackenzie King, no Canadian prime minister made a greater mark on Canadian politics than Pierre Trudeau. Trudeau governed at a time when the country faced its greatest constitutional crisis since Confederation. The means by which he sought to address this crisis — wide-scale cultural, constitutional, and economic reform — left a seemingly indelible mark. In brief, Trudeau sought to institutionalize his vision of the "Just Society," an exercise that bound constitutional issues with those of political culture and public spending. The latter is of immediate interest here. This chapter seeks to evaluate the success of Trudeau and his successors to achieve social cohesion through the national coffers.

At its core, Trudeau's vision of the "just society" was the idea that circumstance should not distort any individual's ability to participate in, and benefit from, the fruits of the national community. It built upon a prevailing sense of pan-Canadian nationalism that had been developing through the postwar era and had found a home in the Liberal Party of Canada (although the basic concept also was embraced by some within the Progressive Conservative Party, most notably John Diefenbaker).[1] According to this pan-Canadianism, all Canadians, regardless of mother tongue, ethnicity, region of residence or social class, were to have a common sense of what it meant to be Canadian. Not only was this just, but it would build bonds of nationhood strong enough to withstand the centrifugal forces associated with ethno-linguistic dualism, Canada's traditionally dominant line of social cleavage. Similar to John Diefenbaker's conception of Canada,[2] Trudeau envisioned a nation of "unhyphenated Canadians" whose primary loyalty would be to a commonly held sense of what it meant to be Canadian. Canada would not be a community of communities. Instead, there would be "One Canada" to which all other loyalties would be subordinated.[3]

Among the most important components of this pan-Canadian vision was the notion that a just society would provide *financial* compensation for its least privileged members. Obviously Trudeau was not the architect of the welfare state in Canada. Save for regional development and multicultural initiatives, he did not provide impetus for a great deal of new social spending, at least in comparison to historically prominent and expensive programs such as universal pensions and publicly insured health care.[4] Nor was he the first to conceive that social cohesion in Canada might be purchased through public spending. Universalism in social programs was a cornerstone of what Jenson[5] calls the citizenship regime of the early postwar era.[6] However, Trudeau came to power just as the real threat of separation emerged in Quebec. This confluence of events — the existence of a generous welfare state, the emerging threat of Quebec separatism, and Trudeau's articulation of the Just Society — conspired to create a virtual path dependence for successive governments' strategies with respect to economic and social policy.

This vision of a national community bound together, in part, through the generosity of the public purse, has become an integral part of Canadian political culture.[7] Equally important was the sense that, consistent with the modified evolutionary welfare hypothesis (to be discussed below), public spending could help to bind the dominant ethnic cleavage in Canada. As this chapter argues, however, the use of social program spending as a means of creating and maintaining a sense of national community has generated grave side effects or, as they are known to students of political economy, negative externalities.

While social program spending has a palliative effect in the short term, it eventually becomes more than optimal and thus harmful. The law of diminishing returns, in other words, mandates that more and more spending is necessary to create less and less social cohesion. Indeed, public spending in an age of post-materialist, "Charter politics" attracts ever greater demands on the state.[8] These demands actually create a centrifugal dynamic of their own. Increasingly, groups such as feminists, Aboriginals, "third-force" Canadians[9] and those of alternative sexual preferences have mobilized to parlay constitutional recognition into a moral imperative to be compensated, at least in part, out of the commonweal.

In addition, public spending becomes increasingly difficult in an age of globalization. The North American Free Trade Agreement (NAFTA) in particular has coincided with, if not necessarily exacerbated, the productivity gap between Canada and the United States. This disparity, we argue below, is at least in part a function of supraoptimal public spending. Other countries have recognized the relationship between globalization and the limitations on public spending. The political economy of inefficient allocation is straightforward: because capital (necessary for the construction of a viable tax base[10]) is mobile, whereas clientele groups of the state are not, governments have responded to globalization by creating more capital-friendly environments. Indeed, over the past 20 years, a number of societies with generous levels of public spending (including Australia, Britain, Denmark, New Zealand and Sweden) have recognized the economic imperative of welfare state retrenchment. In Canada, however, the link between national cohesion and public spending aimed toward redistribution of income, especially in the aftermath of a series of controversial constitutional initiatives, has limited the government's manoeuvrability in this regard. While the recent reforms of the Chrétien government suggest that the federal government may also recognize these imperatives, it is too early to suggest that welfare state retrenchment in Canada has been institutionalized.

What are Canada's options in response to the externalities generated by the use of social program spending to purchase national unity and constitutional peace? One option, which has been apparently favoured in a sustained way within some quarters of the Liberal Party, is to expand public spending. However, economic reality suggests severe long-term limitations for this option. Another idea is to examine the successful free-market reforms that have taken place in other "small states in big trouble."[11] In Australia, Denmark, New Zealand and Sweden, left-wing governments engaged in welfare state retrenchment in response to economic imperatives. Meaningfully for present purposes, these reforms, which partially entailed devolving greater responsibility for welfare to local governments, were realized without serious political backlash against the national governments. While the Chrétien government has largely followed the second option, we argue that it could, and should, go further. Specifically, the Chrétien reforms appear insufficiently institutionalized. A return to difficult times, or even a shift within the Liberal Party power structure, could see a return to traditional high-spending ways.

This chapter unfolds in six sections. The first outlines Trudeau's (pan-Canadian) philosophy of nation-building in the context of the so-called modified evolutionary welfare hypothesis. The second focuses more directly on evolutionary theory in relation to the political economy of the welfare state.

Section three discusses the history of social welfare provision in Canada through the Mulroney era. The fourth section examines the role of the Chrétien government, acknowledging the difficult spending decisions that it has made, but demonstrates also the fact that further retrenchment is necessary. The fifth and penultimate section is prescriptive, demonstrating the political and economic benefits that accrue to national governments that stop using public money to purchase social cohesion. Finally, the sixth section summarizes the findings.

NATIONAL UNITY AND PUBLIC SPENDING

Trudeau's vision of a Just Society mandated construction of an overarching sense of national community designed to meet a number of threats that militated against a universal commitment to Canadian nationalism. The most prevalent were the cultural influence of the United States; regionalism, as manifested in the movement toward province-building in the postwar era; and most importantly, the growing nationalism and isolationism that emerged from the Quiet Revolution in Quebec. Trudeau's response to these threats consisted, in the main, of four initiatives.[12]

First, as a cultural "protectionist," Trudeau attempted to forge a national culture by distancing Canada from the United States, both in terms of domestic and international politics.[13] This nationalism was most evident in policies such as the Third Option, in which Canada sought to pursue a foreign policy independent of the United States, the creation of the Foreign Investment Review Agency (FIRA) and the Canadian Radio-Television and Telecommunications Commission (CRTC), and the increased presence of the federal government in the oil patch following the National Energy Program (NEP).[14]

Second, Trudeau sought to undercut the role of provincial governments by attempting to create a direct relationship between individual citizens and the federal state through the constitutionalization of a charter of rights. From the genesis of this policy as a position paper when Trudeau was minister of justice,[15] through the failed 1971 Victoria Charter, until entrenchment in 1982, Trudeau's political career was characterized by his desire to entrench constitutional rights.[16]

Third, even as he sought to ensure that the Just Society provided a universal and homogenous set of rights, he was equally concerned that it not enforce ethnic or linguistic homogeneity. This commitment to pluralism was realized through bilingualism and multiculturalism,[17] and was manifested most obviously through the 1969 *Official Languages Act*, as well as numerous provisions in the *Charter of Rights and Freedoms*.[18]

Finally, and most pertinently for present purposes, Trudeau sought to make use of high levels of social program spending in Canada, as well as to expand and entrench critical features of the welfare state in Canada. For Trudeau, social program spending was the mortar that bound the Just Society. Indeed, Banting is quite authoritative upon the point of social program spending constituting the basis of a unique Canadian national identity:

> In Canada, social programs have been seen primarily as a means of integration across territorial lines. Social programs represent one of the few spheres of shared experience for Canadians, an important aspect of our lives which is common, irrespective of our language and religion. Moreover, the inter-regional transfers underpinning these programs have represented an affirmation that — despite geography, economics, and demography — we are a single people, with a common set of benefits and obligations.[19]

A more sinister interpretation, however, is that the government merely sought to set itself up as the "national paymaster." In this capacity, it sought to replace the market as the ultimate arbiter of decisions regarding resource allocation. Indeed, this centralization-of-power theme, the ability to act as social engineer, epitomizes Trudeau's entire meta-constitutional agenda.[20] On the other hand, independent of Trudeau's political philosophy, there was also a strong institutional incentive for Trudeau and his successors to follow what we call the modified evolutionary welfare hypothesis.[21]

EVOLUTIONARY THEORY AND THE POLITICAL ECONOMY OF THE WELFARE STATE

Two general paradigms predominate in the literature on the distribution of public resources. The first, evolutionary theory, is based upon the assumption that governments have an incentive to distribute resources narrowly, that is, in a way that is ethnically exclusionary. Put differently, evolutionary theory anticipates that people will be more disposed toward providing support for those they perceive as kin, fictive or otherwise.[22] Thus, within the theory, social spending for those who appear similar to oneself is justified as a positive act in terms of inclusive fitness. By contrast, the more diverse the society, the less obvious it is that, on average, members of one's own group — real or fictive — will be the beneficiaries of social program spending. Therefore, from an evolutionary perspective, the basic hypothesis is that *more* ethnically heterogeneous societies should feature *lower* levels of welfare provision because of the role expected for ethnic nepotism in diminishing altruism.[23]

The second, more familiar, general paradigm is known as consociation. The logic here is precisely the opposite of evolutionary theory. While governments may have a narrow incentive to engage in parochial distribution of public resources, this is nested within a larger imperative to maintain systemic stability. Thus, governments are expected to engage in broad, proportional distribution of public resources to all politically relevant (however this is determined) social groups.[24] At its core, consociational theory mandates four main rules: (i) elites must construct universally inclusive (however defined) grand coalitions; (ii) each member of the grand coalition must have a veto; (iii) public resources must be divided proportionally; (iv) each relevant societal subsection must be allowed a high degree of autonomy.[25]

An examination of the Trudeau and post-Trudeau years suggests that neither general paradigm fully captures reality, although the consociational model comes closer. However, it is difficult to argue that Canada fulfills all the conditions associated with consociation. Indeed, conditions (i) and (ii) are realized only through a very relaxed definition of the term "grand coalition." Moreover, although the logic of federalism allows for condition (iv) to be met, federalism alters the consociational compromise in a way that causes public spending to be not only proportionally distributed (condition (iii)), but also *accelerated*. This is an important point for the issue at hand and suggests a further conceptual distinction between consociation and what we observe in Canada during the Trudeau and post-Trudeau years.

Thus, it may be argued without a great deal of controversy that federalism creates the potential for conflicting loyalties among citizens.[26] Where national and subnational governments have radically different meta-constitutional philosophies, moreover, potential for fragmentation is magnified. As Meadwell[27] notes, subnational governments provide excellent vehicles for the mobilization of alternative visions of the country. This occurred during the US Civil War; it also captures nicely the separation crisis in Quebec. Belgium is another excellent case in point.[28]

Under these conditions, there emerges a strong incentive for the national government to use its spending power to bind the wounds of the nation. Subnational governments, in turn, might have no incentive to oppose increments in federal spending if they benefit from such allocations as well. Thus a very *diverse* federation might be the most obvious candidate of all for social program spending in excess of the optimal. As Richards notes: "When major interests in particular regions threaten secession, it is an understatement to say that politicians have difficulty in exercising the discipline necessary to achieve fiscal balance. Reliance on deficits as a tactic to patch over social divisions is a strong temptation."[29]

As such, we posit that the Trudeau and post-Trudeau years are consistent with what we call the modified evolutionary welfare hypothesis (MEWH), which suggests that diversity (ethnic or otherwise) actually will lead to *increased* distribution of public resources. Moreover, where socially relevant subgroups enjoy institutionalized autonomy, as in federal systems, the potential for public spending to compensate for the perceived centrifugal effects of diversity will be higher still. More important than the conceptual tweaking associated with the MEWH, however, is the prescriptive lesson it provides.

The MEWH provides the best perspective from which to understand social program spending during the Trudeau years. Social program spending increased dramatically in Canada until, and perhaps even beyond the time, it encountered upper limits based on economic viability. This is to be expected, since the federal government would have an incentive to believe that the strategy would work but only at somewhat higher levels of welfare provision. In other words, continuing failure to achieve national unity and constitutional cohesion could be rationalized as a function of inadequate supply of key public goods such as health, income-maintenance, and education. The inability to recognize that further increases in spending ultimately would result in futility does not distinguish federal leaders from the many other people who deal with persistent problems by doing more of what has not worked so far. Given the amount of time and money already invested in national integration through social program spending, the federal government's refusal to abandon the strategy until forced into that decision by economic necessity actually becomes quite understandable.

THE DEVELOPMENT OF SOCIAL WELFARE PROVISION IN CANADA

Regional disparity traditionally has been the defining characteristic of Canadian political economy. The Atlantic provinces long have lagged behind the rest of the country in living standards. While generally better off in economic terms, the western provinces have a history of resenting what they view as excessive control over the Canadian economy by the central provinces of Ontario and Quebec.[30] In response to this tension, Canadian governments have engaged in equalization payments to the "have-not" provinces since the 1950s. These transfers by the federal government are intended to help the poorer provinces provide public services at levels equivalent to those of their wealthier counterparts.[31] The magnitude of the payments is considerable; in 1994–95, for example, 23 percent of total federal transfers to the provinces took the form of equalization.[32]

With respect to social spending, the Great Depression represents the first major turning point in Canadian history. Prior to the difficult economic times of the 1930s, the federal government had a limited role in social programs. It started with regulatory policies intended to create a national market and later provided limited workers' compensation, mothers' pensions and federal/provincial pensions to veterans and the needy among the elderly. The hardships endured by millions during the Depression reduced inhibitions about "social engineering" by the federal government. By 1940, as recommended by the Rowell-Sirois Commission, the federal government had assumed responsibility for unemployment insurance and federal leadership continued in the development of social welfare policies through the mid-1960s.[33] The *Unemployment Insurance Act* (1940) was followed by the *Family Allowance Act* (1944) which, according to a study that generally favours welfare spending, "opened the door to demands for more programs of this type.[34]

Pensions came under concurrent jurisdiction (albeit with provincial predominance) in 1951. In 1965 the Canada/Quebec Pension Plan came into being and went into force across all provinces in 1967. In the health-care sector the federal government produced a National Health Grants program in 1948. The *Hospital Insurance and Diagnostic Services Act*, passed in 1957, enunciated four basic principles about coverage. In order to qualify for federal cost-sharing of eligible provincial expenses, coverage had to be comprehensive, universal, portable, and publicly administered. Finally, in the late 1960s, Ottawa passed the *Medical Care Act*, which established public medical care insurance with a 50 percent cost-share by the federal government.[35]

Financing of postsecondary education evolved in much the same way as health care. Beginning in 1952, federal support for postsecondary education took the form of block grants. Each province received a sum of money for operating costs of postsecondary education "without any detailed conditions or strings attached." From 1967 through 1977 the federal grants were based on a formula that provided 50 percent of expenditures.[36]

Two other important federal welfare programs came into being during the 1960s. Introduced in 1966, the Canada Assistance Plan (CAP) established that Ottawa would pay 50 percent of expenditures on social assistance to people identified by the provinces as being in need. In that same year, in addition to Old Age Security and the Canada/Quebec Pension Plan, the Guaranteed Income Supplement (GIS) transferred extra funds to old age pensioners whose income was below a certain threshold level. The GIS represented an especially major change because the federal government in effect had instituted a negative income tax for at least some of its citizens.[37]

The Liberal governments of the 1960s and early 1970s "revised and expanded" unemployment insurance, family allowances, assistance programs and pensions.[38] The Pearson and Trudeau regimes also created programs for housing.

Trudeau, in particular, introduced a *qualitative* change in social welfare through development of highly targeted programs that moved dramatically into new areas. The Local Initiatives Program (for public works), Opportunities for Youth (in which young people "invented" jobs), Youth Perspectives (a summer employment program) and New Horizons (a program providing "leisure activity for the aged"), all came into being in close proximity near the start of the 1970s.[39] The overall impact of these and other social programs is summed up by Noël and Graefe:

This multiplication of programs and interventions entailed a sufficiently large increase in public spending to speak of a qualitative change. Indeed, while government spending on health, welfare and education stood at 6.5% of GNP in 1951 and 11.6% in 1961, by 1971 it had reached 19.4%.[40]

All of this occurred against the backdrop of Trudeau's commitment to "left-wing" projects that, in his words, "I had been dreaming about for a long time."[41] The series of programs upgraded and created by the Trudeau minority government from 1972 to 1974 represented the high-water mark of the Canadian welfare state.[42]

This is a natural point at which to revisit the metaphor of the federal government in general and Trudeau in particular as the would-be national paymaster. Is there reason to see what has just been reported as an attempt to purchase national unity? Obviously, at a certain level, this assertion is beyond proof. It would not have been in the interest of either Trudeau or his inner circle ever to acknowledge such a connection. The next best thing is circumstantial evidence, and some of it is very compelling.

Consider, for example, the establishment of the Department of Regional Economic Expansion (DREE) in 1969. The DREE provided grants and loans "to develop infrastructure and attract industry to low-income regions."[43] Trudeau appointed Jean Marchand, a close friend who also happened to be from Quebec, as the first minister for the new portfolio. The creation of this ministry, which distorted natural economic processes in the interest of regional equalization, almost certainly worked to the relative advantage of Quebec and other provinces with failing industries in remote areas. Unemployment Insurance (UI) reform in 1971 had much the same character. Benefits rose from about 40 percent of insured earnings to about two-thirds, with the qualifying period being reduced to as little as eight weeks and the benefits period being increased to as long as 51 weeks. Even Jim Coutts, a great admirer of Trudeau and liberal welfare policies, acknowledged that the plan had "faults," one of which was to "discriminate against unemployed people in high-employment areas."[44] As in the case of DREE, the UI reform tended to redistribute benefits toward Quebec, which had a traditionally higher rate of unemployment than some other provinces.

While neither of the preceding examples can prove a tendency toward "buying support," the huge deficits that began in the Trudeau era and program creation point in the direction of motivated bias.[45] The regime did not try to legislate in the direction of efficiency. Instead, the policies of the Trudeau era emerge as redistributive in both time and space. First, funding social programs through deficits amounts to an "inter-generational transfer,"[46] in which living (and voting) beneficiaries are privileged at the expense of those who are either members of future generations or at the very least are not as yet voting. Second, the content of certain high-profile programs, such as DREE and UI reform, points to an attempt to redistribute revenue toward marginal supporters in areas most likely to benefit from the new initiatives, including Quebec, where Trudeau's regime competed for public favour against an increasingly hostile separatist movement.

By the mid-to-late 1970s, federal spending — regardless of what motives it had — appeared to be out of control. From 1964 to 1975, the federal civil service increased from 200,000 to 330,000, or by 65 percent.[47] Social spending, in particular, assumed a high profile: hospital insurance, medicare and postsecondary education had become so costly that a sense of crisis prevailed in Ottawa. No longer did the federal government see it as feasible to support essentially open-ended spending programs through a commitment to cost-sharing. As a product of federal-provincial negotiations, Ottawa passed the Federal-Provincial Fiscal Arrangements and *Established Programs Financing Act* (EPF) in 1977, which set up tax transfers and a cash transfer connected to the gross national product.[48] In order to limit its commitments and discourage drastically increasing provincial outlays that had been driving the upward spiral, the federal government under the EPF no longer committed to a specific share of the cost of hospital, medical, and postsecondary education programs.[49]

By the mid-to-late 1980s, deficit reduction had become a federal priority. In 1973, the federal government ran a deficit and the deficits continued into the 1980s. By 1984, the deficit had reached $38 billion, with a national debt of over $200 billion.[50] This leads naturally into a discussion of the Mulroney years, that is, 1984 to 1993.[51] Did this regime, from the Conservative rather than Liberal Party and strongly supported by business interests, interrupt the long-term upward spiral in the public sector? Overall, the answer turns out to be "no."

Brian Mulroney came to power at a time when the mind-set of the western world already had shifted considerably away from the Keynesianism of the post-World War II era. Stagflation in the 1970s had opened the door to new ways of thinking.[52] By the end of 1980, neo-conservative governments had come to power in the two countries with the greatest influence in setting trends for Canadian public policy, namely, the United States and United Kingdom. Thus Mulroney took office in 1984 against the backdrop of an international environment that demanded greater government efficiency *and* a domestic setting with traditions that supported the continuation of an activist federal government. Sentiments in favour of social programs and against deregulation did not hold sway only among those identified with the Liberals and NDP; rather, even prominent Cabinet ministers, such as Joe Clark and Flora McDonald, put forward such views and constituted a *de facto* "Red Tory" faction within the new government.[53]

Conservative policy over the two mandates can be described, for such reasons, as cross-pressured. The Tories created the Atlantic Canada Opportunities Agency (ACOA) in their first term, a regional development agency intended to deal with at least some of the lingering regional complaints about economic disparity.[54] This looks, at least on the surface, to be in the same tradition as DREE. Yet the same federal government moved early in its first mandate toward trade liberalization with the US — a response to international imperatives in favour of more limited government and less regulated commerce — and achieved that goal with the Free Trade Agreement (FTA) of 1988. Even with such a momentous change, however, the Mulroney government could not achieve a level of economic performance sufficient to make lasting progress on deficit control. The factors contributing to the large Canadian deficit included "increasing interest payments on the debt, increases in cyclical expenditures such as unemployment insurance, and various tax breaks and deferrals that have resulted in a significant loss of federal revenues relative to GDP."[55] Although it did make incremental progress during the first term in office, the Mulroney regime ultimately either could or would not make spending cuts at the levels required to bring the deficit under control.

Figures from the second Mulroney government (1988–93) reveal that major restrictions in government spending, at least in relation to revenue, would not be forthcoming. Graham's authoritative tracking of budgetary expenditures in 1990–91, for example, shows a 3.4 percent increase from the preceding year.[56] Furthermore, the provinces continued to disapprove of efforts to make significant reductions in income-tested programs and unemployment insurance. This view — and the perceived need to respond to it — comes out clearly in more specific figures from the 1990–91 budget expenditures. While the budget froze the per capita EPF transfers to all provinces at the 1989–90 level for the next two fiscal years, equalization payments remained untouched and the so-called "have-not" provinces (i.e., all but Alberta, Ontario, and British Columbia) escaped the 5 percent ceiling placed on CAP transfers.[57] In response to regional concerns, members of the Mulroney Cabinet voiced strenuous objections and managed to discourage any decisive actions in each budgetary season.[58] Budgetary pressures, however, continued to build in the 1990s.

While the deficit had been reduced on a yearly basis in the first Mulroney mandate, that success ended with the onset of recession in 1990. Revenues dropped and interest charges on the deficit increased.[59] As the recession intensified, spending pressures began to build; ministers had proposed about $15 billion in policy initiatives by the fall of 1992 and wanted action. The failed Charlottetown Referendum in October 1992 generated increased political uncertainty and contributed to the downward economic spiral, and the deficit increased to almost $15 billion above the projected level. The Conservative government had to increase its EPF cash transfers to several provinces by approximately $2 billion to meet its obligations.[60] Thus, by the end of the Mulroney regime in 1993, it became obvious that no genuine reversal in deficit spending had been achieved.

Mulroney, as a bridge between Trudeau and Chrétien, shares some traits with each but also seems different in at least one important way. All three of these prime ministers came from Quebec and each made great efforts to purchase the support of that province. Mulroney's record, for instance, included the extremely expensive bilateral immigration deal, the above-noted "cap on CAP" (which did *not* affect Quebec), the CF-18 contract and so on. Mulroney, however, also differed from Trudeau in terms of at least a stated adherence to more conservative economic principles, embodied most directly in the FTA with the US and the later North American Free Trade Agreement. This difference, however, makes Mulroney's own spending practices all the more noteworthy. He did not engage in a frontal assault on the Canadian welfare state, as would have been expected from a genuine neo-conservative. In short, the power of the MEWH appears to be sustained even when someone qualitatively different, at least in ideological terms, sits in the Prime Minister's Office. Neither Mulroney nor his pro-business supporters in the Tory caucus ultimately dared to take hold of the "third rail" of Canadian politics — the welfare state.

A SEA-CHANGE?

During the early years of his administration, Chrétien's government took measures to control spending, most notably with respect to social services. The Canada Health and Social Transfer (CHST) in the 1995 federal budget suggested that Ottawa was moving toward a reduction in its commitment to medicare, which produced tensions with anxious provincial leaders. The CHST merged the EPF and CAP into one block transfer program and ended the practice of requiring availability of welfare services to all in need.[61] Medicare constituted a centrepiece in the government's successful attempt to reduce the federal deficit. Between 1994 and 1997, it is estimated that the Chrétien government trimmed $7 billion from its health-care budget.[62]

The obvious effect was to create a new source of federal-provincial tension. Diminished federal funding of health care generated a centrifugal demand for greater provincial autonomy. For example, Alberta, Manitoba, Newfoundland, and Nova Scotia all began to allow clinics to engage in extra-billing of patients (known as "facility fees") in defiance of Ottawa's prohibition of such practices. More systematically, the provinces began to clamor for more input into the administration of new and existing spending initiatives in areas of provincial jurisdiction under the auspices of the so-called Social Union Framework Agreement (SUFA).[63]

The SUFA, announced in early 1999 and signed by every province except Quebec (which supported the plan to the extent that it served to devolve greater control to the provinces, but did not accept it in its final form), established a new framework for social program spending in Canada. SUFA, which contains a three-year review clause, contains a number of provisions. First, the federal government agrees not to introduce new joint spending initiatives without the agreement of a majority of the provinces. Second, each province will have the authority to design its own blueprint for the administration of the new initiative. Thus, Ottawa might propose the broad parameters of a new program, but the details will be left to the individual provinces. Third, although not part of the SUFA *per se*, but as part of a related agreement, the provinces will receive more funding for health care in return for a commitment to spend the extra money on medical care. The federal government will retain the ability to influence the administration of health care, but will allow for mediation over conflicts such as those concerning extra-billing and the establishment of private clinics.

It is too soon to determine whether or not social spending reductions of the 1990s represent a social policy "realignment." However, it is safe to conclude that the SUFA will not serve as a great deterrent to the federal spending power. There is no population floor for the provincial majority needed for new federal spending initiatives. Moreover, the federal government retains the right to penalize provinces that fail to conform to national standards for social programs (although such standards themselves are the product of federal-provincial agreement). As Dunn notes: "To a remarkable extent — at least when one considers all the discussion on the social union — the *status quo ante* prevailed."[64] Thus, it is possible to conceptualize the "collaborative federalism" of the Chrétien years as "pan-Canadianism with a bit of regional diversity." If we have witnessed a sea-change in Canadian social policy, in other words, it has not been accompanied by a great deal of institutional change.[65]

With respect to program-spending reductions, the Chrétien government has had a generally responsible record, although, again, the results feature some interpretive ambiguity. Program spending across all levels of government as a percentage of gross domestic product (GDP) fell markedly from its peak in 1992 (46 percent) to 36.4 percent in 1999.[66] While this is impressive by Organisation for Economic Co-operation and Development (OECD) standards, and indeed places Canada below the OECD average for the second half of the 1990s, it is worth noting that Canada continues to commit a significantly higher portion of its GDP to program spending than does the US. Indeed, the US committed only 27.3 percent of GDP to program spending.[67] Given that the US is far and away Canada's leading trading partner, not to mention the reservoir of Canada's "brain-drain," it represents the most meaningful baseline of comparison.[68]

Whether the Chrétien government will continue to reduce program spending is an open question. In September 2000, the federal government committed to increase spending on health care. Moreover, while the government backed off of its commitment to a national daycare program, in the run-up to the 2000 election it launched the Early Childhood Development Initiative that pledges $2.2 billion over five years to a variety of programs including child care.[69] Indeed, according to some in the Liberal Party, increased social program spending is the optimal means for the party (and hence federalists) to regain political support in Quebec.[70] In other words, at least for some, the time is ripe for a renewed commitment to purchasing national unity out of the public purse. Prime Minister Chrétien's trial balloon in the aftermath of the 2000 election, which floated the old idea of a national guaranteed annual income, is a good illustration of this point. On the other hand, at least for now, fiscal conservatives appear to be ascendant within the government. Tax cuts, and not an increased fiscal burden, appear to be the order of the day.

While the Chrétien government may have tamed the budget deficit, and thus the most obvious negative consequences of overspending, it is important to bear in mind that Canada still suffers from a large public debt and attendant service charges which, as noted earlier, eat up a significant percent of total federal public spending. In turn, debt-servicing has obligated Canada to maintain a large annual revenue stream in the form of a prohibitive tax structure. This generates two negative externalities: an incentive structure that leads highly educated Canadians to seek work south of the border, and tensions between the federal government and the provinces, most perniciously Quebec.

Globalization, and particularly NAFTA, have exposed serious flaws in Canada's profligate spending patterns. For example, large numbers of highly skilled, mostly young, Canadians educated at the expense of the Canadian taxpayer are finding that the US economy provides opportunities they could not realize at home.[71] As Serge Nadeau, chief economist for Industry Canada, recently noted, real income per capita in Canada is roughly 25 percent less than in the United States.[72] Moreover, if one considers that far more Americans than Canadians are living below the poverty line, it is logical to posit that Nadeau's figures understate the national differential in living standards for the middle class. In other words, those who qualify for readily available Temporary NAFTA (TN) visas, on average will see their living standards increase by more than one-fourth as a function merely of crossing the border for employment. For some professions, the figures are considerably higher.[73] Moreover, while average after-tax incomes in Canada fell by roughly 5 percent in the 1990s, US incomes rose by an average of 10 percent.[74] While precise measurements are difficult to obtain, there is sufficient evidence to generate suspicion about the Chrétien government's oft-repeated position that there is no "brain drain" from Canada to the United States.[75] At the very least the problem is visible enough to have been recognized in the first page of Canada's entry in *Nations of the World* (2000), a handbook published in the UK.

The brain-drain question remains controversial and is an important corollary to the MEWH. Helliwell, for example, finds that the number of Canadian-born US residents has declined markedly since 1980, which would seem to cast doubt on the idea of a brain drain. Aside from that study, which focuses on aggregate numbers, the evidence is very much in the opposite direction.[76] Schwanen shows that in the critical area of science and engineering university graduates, a quality gap is emerging, with many of the most qualified (often most senior) of Canada's graduates heading to the United States and being replaced by immigrants who require a number of years of language and skills training before being able to match the performance of native North Americans.[77] As Schwanen notes, "although immigration is beneficial to the Canadian economy, it does not, by itself, negate the cost of science and engineering emigration."[78]

The most recent and authoritative study sums up emigration from Canada to the US in the following way:

> The country does, however, appear to be losing a significant fraction of its labour market elite, at least as judged by individuals' incomes, with fully 0.89 percent of all tax payers earning $150,000 or more in the last full tax year preceding their departure leaving the country, which contrasts with the .12 departure rate for all tax filers taken together.... The evidence presented above shows that the brain drain is not particularly large in terms of the total numbers involved [i.e., consistent with Helliwell] or the general "quality" of the majority of leavers, but that there are a number of important types of "knowledge workers" who are leaving in substantial numbers, whose departures represent the loss of substantial public investments in terms of those individuals' education and job experience, and whose skills will be missed. These include health sector workers, especially physicians and nurses, university professors, cutting edge R&D and high-tech workers, and high income individuals in general.[79]

As more professionals head south of the border in search of higher returns on their (educational) investments, so too have numerous other investors (and, less obviously, potential investors). As a consequence, there is an emerging productivity gap between Canada and its largest trading partner, the United States.[80] In the 1970s and 1980s, productivity differentials between Canada and the United States narrowed; the past decade has seen a reversal of that trend. Higher levels of taxation in Canada have contributed to the fact that investment by businesses in machinery and equipment is lagging behind that in the United States and other developed countries. In turn, this has undermined the relative efficiency of worker output in Canada. Put differently, according to Nadeau, lower productivity explains 96 percent of the variance in cross-border living standards.[81]

Perhaps even more pernicious is that declining living standards exacerbate problems of social cohesion in a country that is already badly divided after more than three decades of experimentation with the MEWH. As times get harder, more and more groups make demands on the state, further taxing the ability of the government to satisfy special interests. In the 1970s, alarmists called this phenomenon "post-pluralist malaise" or the "crisis of ungovernability."[82] Two decades

of hindsight suggest that the condition is controllable through austerity measures such as those practised in Britain under Margaret Thatcher, or in the
"small states in big trouble" discussed below. Even so, the problem is potentially politically destabilizing.

The danger in Canada is that the most relevant special interests are provinces, some of which are increasingly unhappy with the economic status quo.
Regional resentment in Canada does not appear to have diminished in the
wake of Trudeau's attempt to create "One Canada." A 1997 POLLARA poll,
for example, found that roughly 50 percent of British Columbians believe that
their province is the victim of a raw deal from Confederation; one-quarter
believe that BC would be better off economically if it separated from Canada.[83]
Similarly, the governments of Alberta and Ontario have been at the forefront
of a running battle with Ottawa about their dissatisfaction with the inequity of
their share of transfer payments.

OPTIONS

While the Chrétien government appears to have taken advantage of good economic times to distance itself from the MEWH strategy, two dangers remain.
The first is that upon the manifest restoration of economic health, the government will seek to use surplus revenues to its own political ends. While the
proposed cuts to the federal income tax make this unlikely, it is also clear that
tax remissions are a source of division within the government. The second,
more likely, danger is that as economic times get tougher, the government
will revert to the familiar strategy of using federal dollars to purchase political peace. We suggest that the Chrétien reforms would be less vulnerable to
reversal if Canada were to devolve more fully to the provinces the capacity to
provide social programs. This would entail, broadly speaking, shifting tax
points and other revenue-generating capacities to the provinces as a means of
allowing them to meet their constitutional obligations.

The experience of other "small states in big trouble"[84] provides important
prescriptions for Canada. One reason why welfare retrenchment is so difficult
politically is that the state's policy manoeuvrability is, in the words of Cairns,[85]
embedded in a network of vested interests.[86] Policies, in other words, remain
static even as the environment in which they operate is dynamic.

An obvious example is the set of policies associated with the welfare state
in an age of globalization. Indeed, this disequilibrium was recognized by the
small states and led to their attempts to "create more autonomy for the central
state by breaking up the broad social base of support for the welfare state."[87]
More specifically, this autonomy was realized by devolving responsibility for
social welfare provision to subnational governments as a means of shifting
the locus of political backlash. Again, in the words of Schwartz:

Decentralizing operational authority forces local agencies and localities to use their new operational autonomy to prioritize activities within global budgetary constraints. This disperses political conflict away from central government and to the localities, where small groups will fight over their particular interests.... Put crudely, if the former system of quasi-monopoly provision of state services encouraged the use of voice by making exit difficult, the new system is intended to encourage consumers to exit from specific providers in order to prevent them from using voice on the central state.[88]

What are the advantages to devolution of welfare responsibility to the provinces? Most patently it would eliminate an important source of conflict between the federal government and Quebec. Quebec has long argued that the Constitution provides the provinces with exclusive jurisdiction over the provision of most social welfare, and that the provinces' autonomy is undermined by too much federal control in that area. Satisfying a long-standing constitutional demand of Canada's least satisfied province cannot be a bad thing for national unity, especially since doing so has attendant benefits.

The first such attendant benefit is that devolution of authority for welfare provision would necessarily obligate the federal government to transfer revenue-generating capacity (probably in the form of taxation points) to the provinces. Limiting the federal revenue stream, then, would help to "tie the hands" of the historically profligate federal government. Concomitantly, it would provide fewer areas of jurisdiction for the creative spending of federal tax dollars.

A second, and more important, benefit is that it would shift the locus of conflict from the federal to the provincial arena. Given the tough reforms necessary to maintain economic viability (all the more worrisome against the backdrop of Quebec separatism) it is preferable that the provinces be in the front lines of the battle over fiscal reform. This would undermine the rather effective argument advanced by separatists that, economically speaking, Confederation is not working.

This leads to the third attendant benefit: it would force the provinces, including Quebec, to better get their economic houses in order. This is more productive than having provinces sit on the sidelines taking "potshots" at the federal government. Moreover, in the case of Quebec, it would underscore to residents of that province that hard decisions regarding public spending are not merely a function of intergovernmental politics. Moreover, making such hard economic choices is not conducive to a successful referendum on separation. Indeed, it would further exacerbate tensions within the Parti Québécois among those who wish to postpone the referendum until Quebec resolves its economic difficulties and those who demand an immediate referendum.

All of this leads back to the assertion from Banting,[89] noted at the outset of this chapter, about the deep and abiding commitment to social welfare as a form of "negative nationalism" directed toward the United States (or perhaps,

"Toryism"[90]). This mind-set will continue among elites regardless of what specific quantitative indicators might say about spending at any given time. Consider just two examples from academe, where, for better or worse, the ideas translated into policy ultimately will tend to originate. In an otherwise analytical essay on the Canadian case, Noël and Graefe assess studies that characterize provision of social welfare as substantial as focusing on "what went right in Canada, rather than on what went wrong."[91] Finnie's evaluation of various possible responses to the Canadian brain drain is another instance: reduced public spending as a result of tax cuts, for example, presumably would jeopardize "the ability to walk the streets almost anywhere at any time, the advantages of better public health, the full insurance aspect of a more generous safety net, and other such benefits."[92] Furthermore, "significant cuts in social spending would also diminish the deep satisfaction which many Canadians feel by being part of a society where equality of opportunity, compassion for the disadvantaged, cultural identity and other goals related to common purpose and social justice are given more central place." All of the preceding assertions by Finnie are put forward with neither evidence nor acknowledgment of counter-arguments; for advocates of the Just Society — regardless of what it might be called now — some truths are just self-evident.

CONCLUSION

This chapter has explored Canada's commitment to use public spending to maintain constitutional cohesion. It has argued that the MEWH, while theoretically appealing, ultimately cannot be sustained. National unity and constitutional peace based on the provision of social program spending ultimately obligates the government to engage in levels of welfare provision that become supraoptimal and ultimately have a destabilizing effect. This problem is exacerbated, or at least hastened, by globalization. Given these facts, then, the lesson derived is that any re-commitment to the MEWH in the aftermath of a successful battle against the budget deficit appears to be destined to failure.

Despite 30 years of high social program spending, the conflict between Quebec and the rest of the country persists. The pronouncements of the new premier of Quebec, Bernard Landry, at least as of this time of writing, would appear to reinforce that point dramatically.[93] Indeed, provincial governments cooperated with exaggerated welfare provision for many decades because cost-sharing with Ottawa made it possible to pile up debt and postpone the consequences of fiscal irresponsibility. Only in the last decade, when both internal and external pressures combined to indicate that an upper boundary on debt accumulation grew imminent, did the federal government begin to put limits on new spending. It is not yet clear that these limits have been institutionalized.

What, then, are the implications of this study? Decades of overspending have not produced a higher degree of national integration.[94] Instead, as might be expected, provincial and federal governments are at odds over how to deal with the fallout from long-term supraoptimal provision of various public goods. It almost goes without saying that such conflict is only exacerbating regional tensions that already exist. The national parliament is now almost fully "balkanized" and another referendum on Quebec sovereignty remains a distinct possibility. It is ironic that decades of profligate spending serve to limit the federal government's current room for manoeuvre in trying to address regional concerns. Moreover, we are no closer now than we were 30 years ago to meta-constitutional consensus.

The unfortunate experiences of successive Canadian federal governments, especially as contrasted to those of the "small states in big trouble," suggest that a fundamental reorientation of Canadian welfare provision may be essential to protect against economic forces that easily could exacerbate regional tensions. Speaking more generally, based on the Canadian experience, throwing money at ethno-linguistic tensions is a tempting course of action but one that ultimately will not succeed. Ethno-linguistic conflicts, it would seem, cannot be resolved through pork barrel politics. The harsh reality is that the Dream of One Canada is over; that of a united and prosperous one, however, need not perish as well.

NOTES

We would like to thank Christine Carberry, Harvey Lazar, Alain Noël, Ian Sirota, Hamish Telford and an anonymous reviewer for their helpful comments.

1.   David E. Smith, "Party Government, Representation and National Integration in Canada," in *Party Government and Regional Representation in Canada*, ed. Peter Aucoin (Toronto: University of Toronto Press, 1985).

2.   John G. Diefenbaker, *One Canada: Memoirs of the Right Honourable John G. Diefenbaker, The Years of Achievement 1956 to 1962* (Toronto: Macmillan, 1976).

3.   Pierre E. Trudeau, "Say Goodbye to the Dream of One Canada," in *With a Bang, Not a Whimper*, ed. Donald Johnston (Toronto: Stoddard, 1988); Guy Laforest, *Trudeau and the End of a Canadian Dream*, translated by Paul Leduc Browne and Michelle Weinroth (Montreal: McGill-Queen's University Press, 1995).

4.   As Moon and Sayers point out in a study of Australia, aggregate indicators such as expenditures and public employment may not be the most accurate measurements of the *scope* of government activity. A focus on state government in Australia reveals that ministerial portfolios can provide a more meaningful assessment of scope. See Jeremy Moon and Anthony Sayers, "State Government Convergence and Partisanship: A Long Run Analysis of Australian Ministerial Portfolios," *Canadian Journal of Political Science*, forthcoming 2002.

5.   Jane Jenson, "Reading the SUFA Through Policies for Children: Towards a New Citizenship Regime," *Policy Options* (May 2000):48-50.

6.   See also Smith, "Party Government, Representation and National Integration in Canada," pp. 29-33. Indeed, the case can be made that nation-building was one of the objectives of postwar welfare state construction. Absence of a separatist threat subordinated national unity to the more immediate objectives of safeguarding against the economic pathologies of the 1930s. Still, the federal government articulated the relevance of welfare spending to national unity in its proposals to the 1945 Dominion-Provincial Conference on Reconstruction. Upon noting the importance of "social security proposals" to both humanitarian and macro-economic concerns, the proposal suggests: "Less tangible, perhaps, but in some ways most important of all, they would make a vital contribution to the development of the concept of Canadian citizenship and to the forging of lasting bonds of Canadian unity." Canada, *Dominion-Provincial Conference on Reconstruction. Proposals for the Government of Canada* (Ottawa: King's Printer, 1945), p. 28.

7.   Keith Banting, "The Social Policy Divide: The Welfare State in Canada and the United States," in *Degrees of Freedom: Canada and the United States in a Changing World*, ed. Keith Banting, George Hoberg and Richard Simeon (Montreal: McGill-Queen's University Press, 1997), p. 267.

8.   For a discussion of the effects of post-materialism and/or the Charter on Canadian politics see Ian Brodie and Neil Nevitte, "Evaluating the Citizens' Constitution Theory," *Canadian Journal of Political Science* 26(1993):235-59 and Alan C. Cairns, "A Defence of the Citizens' Constitution Theory: A Response to Ian Brodie and Neil Nevitte," *Canadian Journal of Political Science* 26(1993):261-67.

9.   See Alan C. Cairns, "Constitutional Minoritarianism in Canada," in *Canada: The State of the Federation 1990*, ed. Ronald L. Watts and Douglas M. Brown (Kingston: Queen's University Institute of Intergovernmental Relations, 1990); Patrick James, "Rational Choice? Crisis Bargaining Over the Meech Lake Accord," *Conflict Management and Peace Science* 16(1998):51-86; Patrick James, "Evolutionary Theory and the Provision of Public Goods: The New Science of the Canadian Constitution" (Werner Reimers Institute, February, 1999); Patrick James, "The Chain Store Paradox and Constitutional Politics in Canada," *Journal of Theoretical Politics* 11 (1999):5-36.

10. Charles E. Lindblom, *Politics and Markets: The World's Political-Economic Systems* (New York: Basic Books, 1977).

11. Herman Schwartz, "Small States in Big Trouble: State Reorganization in Australia, Denmark, New Zealand, and Sweden in the 1980s," *World Politics* 46(1994):527-55.

12. Many of these ideas are articulated in Trudeau's early writings; see, for example, Pierre Elliot Trudeau, *Federalism and the French Canadians* (Toronto: Macmillan, 1968).

13. Pierre Elliot Trudeau, *Memoirs* (Toronto: McClelland & Stewart, 1993), pp. 358, 360.

14. Eric M. Uslaner, *Shale Barrel Politics: Energy and Legislative Leadership* (Stanford, CA: Stanford University Press, 1989); Patrick James, "The Canadian National Energy Program and Its Aftermath: A Game-Theoretic Analysis," *Canadian Public Policy/Analyse de Politiques* 16(1990):174-90; Patrick James, "Energy Politics in Canada, 1980-1981: Threat Power in a Sequential Game," *Canadian Journal of Political Science* 26(1993):31-59; Patrick James, "A Reply to "Comment on 'Energy Politics in Canada, 1980-1981: Threat Power in a Sequential Game,'" *Canadian Journal of Political Science* 26(1993):65-68; Jeffrey Church, "Comment on 'Energy Politics in Canada 1980-1981: Threat Power in a Sequential Game,'" *Canadian Journal of Political Science* 26(1993):60-64.

15. Canada. Department of Justice. *A Canadian Charter of Human Rights* (Ottawa: Queen's Printer, 1968).

16. Trudeau's commitment to the idea that individual liberties must be respected in a just society predates his political career. As early as 1959 Trudeau was quoted as saying: "The Just Society is the kind of society freedom would establish.... A Just Society is one toward which every citizen must work, and the first condition of such a society is that of respecting the liberty of individuals." Pierre Elliot Trudeau, *Conversations With Canadians*, ed. Ivan Head (Toronto: University of Toronto Press, 1972), p. 12. Even more explicit is a quote from one of Trudeau's closest advisors: "The attachment of Canadians to a sense of national community, and to a belief in the strength of shared values, claims, obligations and opportunities, is a fundamental objective of a nation-building quest. The Charter was the Ark and the Covenant in the federal vision." Thomas Axworthy, "Colliding Visions: The Debate over the Charter of Rights and Freedoms, 1980-81," in *Litigating the Values of a Nation: The Canadian Charter of Rights and Freedoms*, ed. Robin Elliot and Joseph Weiler (Toronto: Carswell, 1986), p. 14.

17. The antecedents of this initiative are to be found in the Royal Commission on Bilingualism and Biculturalism. Canada. Royal Commission on Bilingualism and Biculturalism, *Report* (Ottawa: Queen's Printers, 1967). Trudeau himself declared in a 1971 House of Commons speech that: "National unity, if it is to mean anything in the deeply personal sense, must be founded on confidence in one's own individual identity; out of this can grow respect for that of others and a willingness to share ideas, attitudes and assumptions. A vigorous policy of multiculturalism will help create this initial confidence. It will form the base of a society which is based on fair play for all." Trudeau, *Conversations With Canadians*, p. 32.

18. Specifically sections 16–23, 28.

19. Banting, quoted in Melville McMillan, "Economic Threats to National Unity: from Within and Without," in *Beyond Quebec: Taking Stock of Canada*, ed. Kenneth McRoberts (Montreal: McGill-Queen's University Press, 1995), p. 286.

20. See Michael Lusztig, "Canada's Long Road to Nowhere: Why the Circle of Command Liberalism Cannot be Squared," *Canadian Journal of Political Science* 32 (1999):451-70.

21. James, "Rational Choice? Crisis Bargaining Over the Meech Lake Accord."

22. Evolutionary theory is generally consistent with the primordial interpretation of
     ethnicity. Ethnic identity, from this perspective, supersedes instrumental con-
     cerns and continues to be relevant even in the face of supranational economic
     integration. The most sustained and effective application of primordialism as a
     concept to the analysis of inter-ethnic cooperation and conflict appears in John
     Stack, ed., *Ethnic Identities in the Contemporary World* (Westport, CN: Green-
     wood Press, 1981). See also John Stack, ed., *The Primordial Challenge: Ethnicity
     in the Contemporary World* (New York: Greenwood Press, 1986) and John Stack,
     "The Ethnic Challenge to International Relations Theory," in *Wars in the Midst
     of Peace: The International Politics of Ethnic Conflict*, ed. David Carment and
     Patrick James (Pittsburgh: University of Pittsburgh Press, 1997).

23. Salter sums up the results of research on social spending (and altruism more
     generally) as related to ethnic heterogeneity and places it in the larger context
     of evolutionary theory: "The negative relation between racial diversity and con-
     tribution to public goods might be a more tenacious version of the problem faced
     by emerging polities, that of *including* families and clans to extend their loyalty
     to the civic sphere." Frank Salter, "Symposium Idea," unpublished manuscript,
     1999. Masters also notes the consensus among empirical studies that higher lev-
     els of diversity ultimately have negative consequences for a society's commitment
     to welfare spending. Roger D. Masters, "Why Welfare States Rise — and Fall:
     Ethnicity, Belief Systems, and Environmental Influences on the Support for
     Public Goods," unpublished manuscript, 1999. The most widely accepted study
     appears to be R.E. Hero and C.J. Tolbert, "A Racial/Ethnic Diversity Interpreta-
     tion of Politics and Policy in the States of the U.S.," *American Journal of Political
     Science* 40 (1996):851-71, which suggests that hostility to ethnic minorities plays
     a major negative role in provision of social welfare benefits. The finding is given
     further credibility by the results obtained by Sanderson. Stephen K. Sanderson,
     "Ethnic Heterogeneity and Public Spending: A Cross-National Study," unpub-
     lished manuscript, 1999.

     On the basis of a sample of 121 states, welfare spending appears to be linked
     negatively to ethnic heterogeneity when controls are included for the standard
     positive factors: GNP, labour unionization and level of democracy. The findings
     of Schubert and Tweed produce an interesting curvilinear effect with respect to
     support for the United Way in a sample of localities in the US. A threshold
     effect appears to exist with respect to the negative effects of diversity on chari-
     table donations. Only when a minority reaches 10 percent of the overall
     population is a further increase in its size associated with a decline in altruism
     as measured by support for the United Way. James N. Schubert and Michael
     Tweed, "Ethic Diversity, Population Size and Charitable Giving at the Local
     Level in the United States," unpublished manuscript, 1999.

24. Consociational theory was first articulated by Lijphart. Arend Lijphart, *The Poli-
     tics of Accommodation: Pluralism and Democracy in the Netherlands* (Berkeley:
     University of California Press, 1968). Some perceived theoretical relevance in a
     number of countries, including Canada. For a discussion of consociation in
     Canada, see Kenneth McRae, ed., *Consociational Democracy: Political Ac-
     commodation in Segmented Societies* (Toronto: McClelland & Stewart, 1974);

for an application to Canadian constitutional politics see Michael Lusztig, "Constitutional Paralysis: Why Canadian Constitutional Initiatives are Doomed to Fail," *Canadian Journal of Political Science* 27(1994):747-71 and Michael Lusztig and Colin Knox, "Good Things and Small Packages: Lessons from Canada for the Northern Irish Constitutional Settlement," *Nations and Nationalism* 5 (1999):543-63.

25. Arend Lijphart, *Democracy in Plural Societies: A Comparative Exploration* (New Haven: Yale University Press, 1977), p. 25.

26. Of course, it could be argued just as reasonably that a highly divided polity will opt for federalism, to prevent sweeping changes in favour of whatever faction takes power. These arguments are not contradictory; rather, the two together might be regarded as components of a reinforcing cycle of causation.

27. Hudson Meadwell, "When Voice Encourages Exit: Nations and Legislatures in the Developed West," in *Regionalism and Party Politics in Canada*, ed. Keith Archer and Lisa Young (Toronto: Oxford University Press, 2001).

28. John Richards, "Now That the Coat Fits the Cloth ... Spending Wisely in a Trimmed-Down Age," *C.D. Howe Institute Commentary* (June 2000), p. 143.

29. Ibid., p. 13.

30. Quebec and Ontario are seen by many residents of the other provinces and the territories as being economic beneficiaries of long-standing political hegemony. This was especially true in the aftermath of the NEP, and is the basis of what has commonly been called western alienation; see Roger Gibbins, *Prairie Politics and Society: Regionalism in Decline* (Toronto: Butterworths, 1980), ch. 5; J.F. Conway, *The West: The History of a Region in Confederation*, 2d ed. (Toronto: Lorimer, 1994), ch. 8.

31. In fact, the federal government has provided grants in support of provincial governments dating back to Confederation. The importance of these grants, however, has been eclipsed by equalization payments.

32. William W. Joyce and Richard Beach, eds., *Introducing Canada* (Washington, DC: National Council for the Social Studies, 1997), p. 86.

33. Canada. Royal Commission on Dominion-Provincial Relations, *Report* (Ottawa: Queen's Printers, 1940); Donald V. Smiley, "Introduction," in *The Rowell-Sirois Report*, ed. Donald V. Smiley (Toronto: McClelland & Stewart, 1963); Carolyn Tuohy, "Social Policy: Two Worlds," in *Governing Canada: Institutions and Public Policy*, ed. Michael Atkinson (Toronto: Harcourt Brace Jovanovich, 1993), p. 287.

34. Alain Noël and Peter Graefe, "Aus dem Schatten des Nachbarn: Der Wohlfahrtsstaat in Kanada," in *Der Gezügelte Wohlfahrtsstaat. Sozialpolitik in Reichen OECD-Demokratien*, ed. Herbert Obinger and Uwe Wagschal (Frankfurt and New York: Campus Verlag, 2000), p. 6. This study appears in German and quotations from it follow the English translation provided by Alain Noël.

35. Joan Price Boase, "Social Security to Social Insecurity," in *Profiles of Canada*, ed. Kenneth G. Pryke and Walter C. Soderlund (Toronto: Irwin Publishing, 1998),

pp. 200-01; Paul Barker, "The Development of the Major Shared-Cost Programs in Canada," in *Perspectives on Canadian Federalism*, ed. R.D. Olling and M.W. Westmacott (Scarborough: Prentice-Hall, 1988).

36. Rand Dyck, *Canadian Politics: Critical Approaches*, 2d ed. (Toronto: Nelson, 1996), p. 78.

37. Boase, "Social Security to Social Insecurity," p. 202; Barker, "The Development of the Major Shared-Cost Programs in Canada."

38. Noël and Graefe, "Aus dem Schatten des Nachbarn: Der Wohlfahrtsstaat in Kanada," p. 6.

39. Jim Coutts, "Expansion, Retrenchment and Protecting the Future: Social Policy in the Trudeau Years," in *Toward a Just Society: The Trudeau Years*, ed. Thomas S. Axworthy and Pierre Elliott Trudeau (New York: Penguin, 1990), pp. 192-93. Trudeau, *Memoirs*, p. 156.

40. Noël and Graefe, "Aus dem Schatten des Nachbarn: Der Wohlfahrtsstaat in Kanada," pp. 6-7.

41. Trudeau, *Memoirs*, pp. 164-65.

42. Jim Coutts, who served as Principal Secretary to Trudeau, described the 1973 Orange Paper on social policy as a "sweeping review, tantamount to a blueprint for the future." The document included "major strategies" for employment, social insurance, income supplementation, income support, and employment and social services. (Coutts, "Expansion, Retrenchment and Protecting the Future," p. 186.)

43. Lloyd Axworthy, "Regional Development: Innovations in the West," in *Towards a Just Society: The Trudeau Years*, ed. Axworthy and Trudeau, p. 242.

44. Jim Coutts, "Expansion, Retrenchment and Protecting the Future: Social Policy in the Trudeau Years," p. 189.

45. The accumulated budget deficits, which continued under Brian Mulroney, contributed to Canada's large public debt. By 1996, Canada's debt-to-GDP ratio was third highest in the OECD (Richards, p. 1). Indeed, Canada's debt-servicing cost rose to 15.4 percent of total spending by 1996-97. By 1999–2000, it was still 14.8 percent (Canada. Statistics Canada, *The Daily*, 26 July 2000).

46. Todd Sandler, *Global Challenges* (Cambridge: Cambridge University Press, 1997).

47. Kenneth McDonald, *His Pride, Our Fall: Recovering from the Trudeau Revolution* (Toronto: Key Porter Books, 1995), p. 47.

48. Trudeau, *Memoirs*, passim.

49. George E. Carter, "Financing Health and Post-Secondary Education: A New and Complex Fiscal Arrangement," in *Federalism in Canada: Selected Readings*, ed. Garth Stevenson (Toronto: McClelland & Stewart, 1989), p. 436; Boase, "Social Security to Social Insecurity," p. 202.

50. McDonald, *His Pride, Our Fall: Recovering from the Trudeau Revolution*, p. 48.

51. The brief governments of Prime Ministers John Turner and Kim Campbell are excluded from the analysis because neither lasted long enough to establish an identity in terms of social policy.

52. Isabella Bakker, "The Size and Scope of Government: Robin Hood Sent Packing?" in *Canadian Politics in the 1990s*, 3rd ed., ed. G. Whittington and Glen Williams (Scarborough: Nelson Canada, 1990), pp. 425-26.

53. Ibid., pp. 427-28.

54. Katherine A. Graham, "Discretion and the Governance of Canada: The Buck Stops Where?" in *How Ottawa Spends, 1989-1990: The Buck Stops Where?* ed. Katherine A. Graham (Ottawa: Carleton University Press, 1989), p. 5.

55. Bakker, "The Size and Scope of Government: Robin Hood Sent Packing?" p. 425.

56. Katherine A. Graham, "Tracking the Second Agenda: Once More with Feeling?" in *How Ottawa Spends, 1990-91: Tracking the Second Agenda*, ed. Katherine A. Graham (Ottawa: Carleton University Press, 1990), p. 9.

57. Ibid. p. 11.

58. Tuohy, "Social Policy: Two Worlds," in *Governing Canada: Institutions and Public Policy*, p. 301.

59. David McLaughlin, *Poisoned Chalice: The Last Campaign of the Progressive Conservative Party?* (Toronto and Oxford: Dundurn Press, 1994), p. 41.

60. Ibid., p. 43.

61. Daniel Cohn, "The Canada Health and Social Transfer: Transferring Resources or Moral Authority Between Levels of Government?" in *Canada: The State of the Federation 1996*, ed. Patrick C. Fafard and Douglas M. Brown (Kingston: Institute of Intergovernmental Relations), pp. 169, 175.

62. *Toronto Star*, 9 December 1997.

63. See Jenson, "Reading the SUFA through Policies for Children: Towards a New Citizenship Regime," pp. 48-50; Harvey Lazar, "The Social Union Framework Agreement and the Future of Fiscal Federalism," in *Canada: The State of the Federation 1999/2000, Toward a New Mission Statement for Canadian Fiscal Federalism,* ed. Harvey Lazar (Montreal: McGill-Queen's University Press, 2000).

64. Christopher Dunn, "FYI: SUFA? DOA," *Policy Options* (May 2000):50.

65. Ibid.; Antonia Maioni, "The Social Union and Health Care," *Policy Options* 2000(April):39-41.

66. John Richards, "Now That the Coat Fits the Cloth ... Spending Wisely in a Trimmed-Down Age," p. 3.

67. Ibid., p. 3

68. This chapter will not attempt to answer the question of whether Canada, at any given phase of its development, should be regarded as a relatively high or low spender on social welfare in a cross-national sense. The reason is the incredibly

high level of complexity that results from efforts to quantify *net* social expenditure at the national level. A recent and compelling study by Adema identifies three kinds of social expenditure (public, mandatory private and voluntary private), discusses a wide range of issues that arise in calculation (such as the tax system and indirect benefits) and includes an overview of how to derive net social expenditure that includes no less than eleven steps, several of which include relatively arcane and even arbitrary components that are much more familiar to economists than political scientists. Even after all of these complicated steps, Canada ranks ahead of the US (the most salient point for comparison) in terms of gross public social expenditure — 18.6 percent versus 15.8 percent of GDP factor costs for 1993–95. More general statements about where Canada would stand relative to other OECD states should be made (if at all) with extreme caution, given the sensitivity of the data to different measurement regimes. Willem Adema, "Net Social Expenditure," Labour Market and Social Policy Occasional Papers No. 39 (Paris, France: Organisation for Economic Co-operation and Development, 1999), pp. 13, 18, 24, 28, 31.

69. Liberal Party of Canada, Official Website, at <www.liberal.ca> (2000).

70. *National Post*, 5 October 1999.

71. Daniel Schwanen, "Putting the Brain Drain in Context," *C.D. Howe Institute Commentary* (April 2000):140.

72. *National Post*, 24 September 1999.

73. See Don Wagner, "Do Tax Differences Cause the Brain Drain?" *Policy Options* 2000(December):33-41.

74. *National Post*, 30 September 1999.

75. See Mahmood Iqbal, "Are We Losing Our Minds?" *Policy Options* (September 1999):34-38; Don DeVoretz, "The Brain Drain is Real and it Costs Us," *Policy Options* (September 1999):18-24; Wagner, "Do Tax Differences Cause the Brain Drain?"

76. John F. Helliwell, "Globalization: Myths, Facts and Consequences," *C.D. Howe Institute Benefactors Lecture* (23 October 2000).

77. Schwanen, "Putting the Brain Drain in Context."

78. Ibid., p.10; see also Iqbal, "Are We Losing Our Minds?"

79. Ross Finnie, "The Brain Drain: Myth and Reality — What It Is and What Should Be Done," School of Policy Studies, Working Paper No. 13 (Kingston, Ontario: Queen's University, 2001), pp. 4, 5.

80. Productivity rates capture aggregate economic output net of costs.

81. *National Post*, 24 September 1999.

82. Samuel Brittan, "The Economic Contradictions of Democracy," *British Journal of Political Science* 5 (1975):129-59.

83. *National Post*, 20 December 1997.

84. Herman Schwartz, "Small States in Big Trouble: State Reorganization in Australia, Denmark, New Zealand, and Sweden in the 1980s," pp. 527-55.

85. Alan C. Cairns, "The Embedded State: State-Society Relations in Canada," in *State and Society: Canada in Comparative Perspective*, ed. Keith Banting (Toronto: University of Toronto Press, 1986).

86. Ikenberry makes a similar argument in the context of the United States during the oil crisis of the 1970s. G. John Ikenberry, *Reasons of State: Oil Politics and the Capacities of American Government* (Ithaca: Cornell University Press, 1988); see also Paul Pierson, "The New Politics of the Welfare State," *World Politics* 48 (1996):143-79.

87. Schwartz, "Small States in Big Trouble: State Reorganization in Australia, Denmark, New Zealand, and Sweden in the 1980s," p. 529.

88. Ibid., p. 530.

89. Banting, "The Social Policy Divide: The Welfare State in Canada and the United States."

90. See Hamish Telford, this volume.

91. Noël and Graefe, "Aus dem Schatten des Nachbarn: Der Wohlfahrtsstaat in Kanada," p. 26.

92. Finnie, "The Brain Drain: Myth and Reality – What It Is and What Should Be Done," p. 7.

93. These statements include surreal, even bizarre, assertions about economic relations with the rest of Canada. For example, Landry regards the $1.5 billion received by his province in the latest transfer of funds from Ottawa — with the overall total for so-called "have-not" provinces being $1.8 billion — as proof that Confederation has impoverished Quebec. At no point is the possibility that Quebec's own history of deficit spending and huge public sector might have weakened its long-term economic competitiveness. In sum, it would be difficult to imagine more compelling evidence in favour of the MEWH than these recent assertions by the premier of Quebec.

94. For a comparative assessment of Canada's profligate spending in the fourth quarter of the twentieth century, see Richards, "Now That the Coat Fits the Cloth ... Spending Wisely in a Trimmed-Down Age."

5

The Reform Party/Canadian Alliance and Canada's Flirtation with Republicanism

Hamish Telford

Gad Horowitz avait très bien démontré que le socialisme canadien représentait une synthèse des formes distinctives canadiennes du conservatisme et du libéralisme. Ces idéologies ont traditionnellement été représentées dans le système de partis canadien par les progressistes-conservateurs, les libéraux et les néo-démocrates et ont collectivement été perçues comme la constellation complète des idéologies de la culture politique canadienne. L'arrivée du Parti réformiste (devenu par la suite l'Alliance canadienne) au début des années 1990 a représenté un important défi pour les analystes de la politique canadienne puisque ce parti ne semblait pas correspondre à la typologie élaborée par Horowitz. Ce chapitre examine la question selon laquelle le Parti réformiste/Alliance canadienne pourrait être considéré comme une toute nouvelle synthèse du libéralisme et du conservatisme. On pourrait qualifier cette nouvelle idéologie de néoconservatrice ou encore de néolibérale, mais il semble plus approprié de la qualifier de néoconservatrice. De plus, le Parti réformiste/Alliance canadienne semble représenter une forme canadienne distincte de républicanisme. Ce parti a mis l'accent sur une définition particulière de l'égalité politique, et il a offert aux Canadiens une nouvelle compréhension des traditions politiques canadiennes. La présence d'un quatrième pôle idéologique en politique canadienne a toutefois contribué à rendre encore plus difficiles les tentatives d'accord constitutionnel durable au Canada. Finalement, l'auteur de ce chapitre soutient que l'institutionnalisation du républicanisme néoconservateur du Parti réformiste/Alliance canadienne contribuera probablement à diviser la droite politique au Canada.

INTRODUCTION

In his famous essay "Conservatism, Liberalism, and Socialism in Canada: An Interpretation," Gad Horowitz presented a provocative analysis of (English) Canadian political culture and its relationship to the Canadian party system. In brief, Horowitz employed Louis Hartz's founding fragment thesis to suggest that the first British settlers in Canada, especially the United Empire Loyalists, brought with them a peculiar "tory touched liberalism." Over time, socialism emerged dialectically in Canada as a synthesis of Canadian liberalism and the "tory touch." Horowitz suggested finally that conservatism, liberalism, and socialism were institutionalized in Canada's main political parties, the Progressive Conservatives, the Liberal Party, and the New Democratic Party (NDP).

Horowitz was roundly criticized through the 1970s, and he addressed his critics in a subsequent article.[1] However, he has come under attack again more recently. Janet Ajzenstat and Peter J. Smith have declared that "the tory touch thesis is bad history and poor political science."[2] They contend by contrast that Canada's political culture has been influenced by an indigenous form of *republicanism*. While Ajzenstat and Smith make a valuable contribution to our understanding of Canadian political culture, they may have thrown the baby out with the bath water with their critique of Horowitz. The main problem with Horowitz's analysis is that it is now outdated. As it stands, the Horowitz thesis does not seem to account for the presence of *neo-conservatism* in Canada, as manifested in the Reform Party, now the Canadian Alliance.

It will be argued in this chapter, however, that neo-conservatism in Canada can be explained in Horowitz-like fashion as a new synthesis of liberalism and Tory conservatism. Once a fourth ideological pole has been added to the Horowitz model, the theoretical gap between Horowitz and his recent critics, such as Ajzenstat and Smith, may not be so great. In short, the neo-conservatism of the Reform Party/Canadian Alliance can be interpreted as a modern manifestation of Canadian republicanism. It appeared in the early 1990s that the Reform Party and its particular brand of conservatism republicanism was set to transform Canadian political culture but, as a new decade unfolds, it seems that the Reform Party/Canadian Alliance is destined to be just another episodic flash of republicanism. Nevertheless, the analysis will also demonstrate that strong differences of opinion remain between Alliance republicans and Conservative Tories, especially on the constitutional question, which will make uniting the right a serious political challenge.

CANADIAN POLITICAL CULTURE: THE HOROWITZ THESIS

Gad Horowitz's interpretation of Canadian political culture rests on the "fragment" thesis developed by Louis Hartz in his studies *The Liberal Tradition in America* and *the Founding of New Societies*. For Hartz and Horowitz, the key to understanding new societies is to locate "the point of departure" of the first settlers from Europe. Horowitz contends that "the ideologies borne by the founders of the new society are not representative of the historic ideological spectrum of the mother country. The settlers represent only a fragment of that spectrum."[3] Horowitz claimed this is significant because "a new society which leaves part of the past behind it cannot develop the future ideologies which need the continued presence of the past in order to come into being. In escaping the past, the fragment escapes the future."[4] In short, "the ideology of the founders is thus frozen, congealed at the point of origin." Horowitz contends that the founding ideology largely determines the political culture of the new society.

Horowitz acknowledged that "liberalism is the dominant element in the English-Canadian political culture" but he insisted that "non-liberal British elements have entered into English-Canadian society *together* with American liberal elements at the foundations."[5] He admitted that he cannot identify the precise "point of congealment" in English-Canadian political culture but, he maintained, "the important point is this: no matter where the point of congealment is located in time, the tory streak is present before the solidification of the political culture, and it is strong *enough* to produce *significant* 'imperfections,' or non-liberal, un-American attributes of English-Canadian society."[6]

Horowitz suggested that American liberalism is premised on rugged individualism, fierce egalitarianism, hostility toward central authority, market capitalism, republican democracy, and, perhaps somewhat incongruently, an enlightened rationalism. On the other hand, he continued, "if English-Canadian liberalism is less individualistic, less ardently populistic-democratic, more inclined to state intervention in the economy, and more tolerant of 'feudal survivals' such as the monarchy, this is due to the uninterrupted influence of toryism upon liberalism."[7] The key characteristics of toryism, according to Horowitz, include an acceptance of elitism, inherited social status, acceptance of authority, a belief in tradition, an organic view of society, and a willingness to use the state for economic development and regulation. Horowitz argued that the principles of Toryism modified Canadian liberalism from the pure American form, while at the same time it became dialectically entangled with this liberalism to produce a distinctly Canadian form of socialism. According to Horowitz, Canadian "socialism is an ideology which combines the corporate-organic-collectivist ideas of toryism with the rationalist-egalitarian ideas of liberalism."[8]

Nelson Wiseman has distilled and simplified Horowitz's argument.[9] Wiseman's synopsis of Horowitz's thesis provides a snapshot of the ideological landscape in Canada. Each of the main ideologies in Canada, in their pure forms, includes a bundle of values and principles. Conservatism, or Toryism, is premised on an organic-collectivist view of society, which stresses cooperation and the priority of community, while liberalism is premised on rational-individualism and economic competition. Toryism is further predicated upon authority, hierarchy, and tradition, while liberalism stresses equality and freedom. Wiseman, following Horowitz, states that "Canadian socialism synthesized antithetical aspects of liberalism and toryism. It combined the rationalist-egalitarian outlook of classical liberalism with the organic-collectivist outlook of classical conservatism or toryism."[10] (See Figure 1.)

Figure 1: The Horowitz-Wiseman Interpretation of Canadian Ideological Traditions

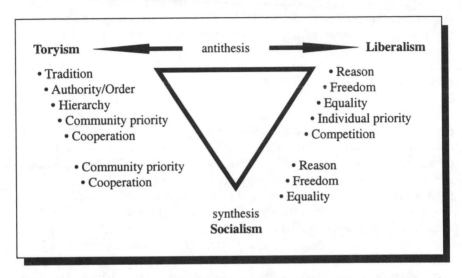

Source: Nelson Wiseman, "Political Parties," in *Canadian Politics in the 1990s,* ed. Michael S. Whittington and Glen Williams (Toronto: Nelson Canada, 1995).

In Horowitz's analysis, these ideologies were represented to a greater or lesser degree in Canada's main political parties. He argues that "it would not be correct to say that toryism is *the* ideology of the [Conservative] party," but "if there is a touch of toryism in English Canada, its primary carrier has been the Conservative Party."[11] "The key to understanding the Liberal party in Canada," contends Horowitz, "is to see it as a *centre* party, with *influential* enemies on both the right and left."[12] Horowitz suggested that the Liberal Party is ideologically pragmatic, and that historically it has relied on the opposition for policy innovations. He concludes, "when the left is weak, as before and after the Second World War, the centre party moves right to deal with the Conservative challenge; when the left is strengthened, as during the war and after the formation of the NDP, the centre moves left to deal with that challenge."[13] This ideological flexibility has positioned the Liberals as the "party of government" in Canada, at least in the twentieth century.

While Horowitz provided a sweeping heuristic analysis of Canadian political culture and political parties, it is difficult to see where the Reform Party/ Canadian Alliance fits into his picture. Does this mean his analysis of Canadian political culture was wrong, or is Canadian political culture in a process of transformation? I will attempt to answer these questions after a brief review of a new critique of the Horowitz thesis.

THE NEW REPUBLICAN CRITIQUE OF THE HOROWITZ THESIS

Janet Ajzenstat and Peter Smith have argued forcefully that "the 'tory touch' thesis gets Canadian history wrong. It cripples Canadians' understanding of Canada's identity, and precludes informed debate about current issues."[14] They suggest, following developments in American historiography, "the challenge to 19th century liberalism arose from a republican ideology on the political left, rather than toryism on the right."[15] Thus, they say, "it is our contention that understanding the republican idea of democracy, and the constitutional response to it, is the key to Canadian political history, the Canadian identity, and Canadian politics today."[16] In fact, they claim, "there is no toryism in Canadian political history, and none in Canadian politics at present, not even a 'touch.' "[17]

Modern republicanism is most closely associated with the American revolution, especially Thomas Jefferson. For Jefferson, the enduring moral of the American revolution was that ordinary people must always be vigilant against central authority. Unlike James Madison, Jefferson "found it impossible to regard popular majorities as dangerous or to think about the powers of government in positive ways."[18] Jefferson tended to regard the constitutional settlement of 1787 as a nearly unacceptable constraint against the people. Furthermore, unlike Madison, "Jefferson denied the principle of judicial review and argued that the provisions made for amending the Constitution were the only proper procedures for deciding all questions of constitutionality."[19] "In his more radical moments," in fact, "[Jefferson] seemed to believe that all fundamental constitutional questions should be settled by a popular referendum, since the doctrine of popular sovereignty empowered only the people at large to render such judgments."[20] While Pettit argues that republicanism "is not inherently populist,"[21] Jeffersonian republicanism clearly rests on a faith in the *demos*.

Where does republicanism fit in the constellation of western political ideologies? David Ericson suggests that "republicanism is related to liberalism as species to genus."[22] He thus presents republicanism, liberalism, and what he calls pluralism as distinct ideologies. Ajzenstat and Smith suggest that "liberals emphasize the importance of institutional restraints to moderate greed and ambition."[23] In short, "liberals believe that the best way to curb greedy politicians is to have a good constitution."[24] "Civic republicans," they assert, "view politics through a vastly different prism. In contrast to the liberal emphasis on moderation of behaviour through institutional constraints, civic republicans put their trust in social constraints."[25] More specifically, republicans believe that the ambition of politicians can only be restrained by virtuous and publicly active citizens.

Republicanism also has distinct communitarian features.[26] In republican thought, "the public happiness can be defined organically, as a single good which subsumes the private interests of all citizens of a political society and uniquely determines the optimal public policy in any given situation."[27] The republican project is thus necessarily premised on "a highly homogeneous citizen body," as opposed to liberalism, which tolerates diversity, and pluralism, which embraces diversity.[28] Ajzenstat and Smith elaborate that republicanism envisages "a one-class society of small property owners, farmers, and independent craftsmen."[29] In order to ensure homogeneity and public participation, the ideal republic is thus small. Federalism is frequently advocated by republicans to maximize the advantages of size, while ensuring discrete homogeneous units.[30]

For republicans, "civic virtue is the essential quality of citizenship," whereas virtue is a private matter for liberals and pluralists.[31] The republican objective is thus to create "a regime of civic virtue," which provides a single moral code for all members of the community and ensures that "people are disposed to serve, and serve honestly in public office."[32] In this manner, "civic republicanism promises to rescue government from the hands of the powerful and privileged."[33] In short, the republican project aims to institutionalize in government the common sense and decency of the common people. As an ideology of and for common folk, republicanism is fiercely egalitarian.[34] "That all men are created equal," as Jefferson wrote in the Declaration of Independence, is a "self-evident" republican "truth."

Pettit insists that republican liberty is about non-domination. He suggests that Isaiah Berlin's notion of negative liberty,[35] the principle of non-interference, is a political fantasy. Pettit suggests that "all law is a form of interference."[36] The key is not whether a law interferes with people's liberty, but whether it unfairly subordinates them. Thus, the primary objective of the republican project is to prevent "arbitrary power." This of course was the objective of the American revolution. In conclusion, Pettit claims that the republican democracy is not premised so much on the consent of the governed, "but rather on the contestability by the people of everything that government does: the important thing to ensure is that governmental doings are fit to survive popular contestation, not that they are the product of popular will."[37]

The republican tradition is most closely associated with the United States. While republicanism appears to be emerging as a significant force in Australia, it is generally not associated with monarchical societies. It has certainly not hitherto been recognized as a major current in Canadian political thought, although it will be suggested below that it has been at least an episodic phenomenon in Canadian political history.

REFORMING HOROWITZ: NEO-CONSERVATISM AND CANADIAN POLITICAL CULTURE

Where does the Reform Party/Canadian Alliance fit in the Horowitz-Wiseman spectrum of ideologies in Canada? Wiseman suggests that "in popular parlance what is usually labelled today as conservatism — the policies of Mike Harris's Conservatives or Preston Manning's Reformers — is yesterday's liberalism."[38] But this is not a very satisfactory answer. What liberalism were they attempting to conserve? Trudeau? Pearson? King? Laurier? Hardly. Rawls? Dworkin? Berlin? Mill? Locke? I don't think so. Preston Manning may well have been trying to revive the social credit tradition in Canada, but that was not a liberal tradition. In fact, Preston Manning seemed to defy ideological categorization. He was variously described as a populist,[39] a Christian fundamentalist,[40] a right-wing conservative,[41] while Tom Flanagan suggested that Preston Manning was "eclectic in his thinking."[42]

It is my contention that the Reform Party/Canadian Alliance represents a distinct ideological orientation that combines elements of traditional conservatism and classical liberalism in a new synthesis. If we look at the Horowitz-Wiseman description of political ideologies in Canada (see Figure 1), it is quite clear that the Reform Party/Canadian Alliance articulates some of the basic tenets of conservatism. In particular, Reformers support a certain conception of Canadian tradition, and they have a strong predilection for authority and order.[43]

The Reform Party's support for Canadian tradition was displayed with its unabashed reverence for the Maple Leaf flag, even though it is a new flag. Indeed, Reform MPs lobbied to adorn their desks in the House of Commons with flags. The Reform vision of Canada was perhaps most evident in the party's support for the RCMP: "The Reform Party supports the traditional role of the Royal Canadian Mounted Police as a police force representative of and responsive to the populations it serves in Canada's regions."[44] As the leader of the Canadian Alliance, Stockwell Day articulated strong support for the traditional role of the Canadian Armed Forces. The Reform Party also placed great emphasis on its immigration policies, saying "immigrants should possess the human capital necessary to adjust quickly and independently to the needs of Canadian society and the job market"[45] Preston Manning declared that Reform Party principles and policies were designed to restore Canadians' "pride and love for Canada."[46] In sum, Preston Manning and the Reform Party, and now the Canadian Alliance, have presented a quintessentially conservative picture of Canada, a picture for which many Canadians feel some nostalgia.

The Reform Party/Canadian Alliance notion of tradition is perhaps more evident in its support for the family. While most Canadians would support the concept of "family," Reformers advocate a traditional understanding of family. The Reform Party stated unambiguously, "a family should be defined as individuals related by blood, marriage, or adoption. Marriage is the union of a man and a woman as recognized by the state."[47] The Reform Party also declared that "government programs, policies, and legislation should serve to strengthen and protect the Canadian family, and furthermore, that pertinent government bills and regulations be accompanied by a family impact assessment."[48] The Canadian Alliance policy declaration repeats these statements almost verbatim, and it adds that "the family unit is essential to the well being of individuals and society, because that is where children learn values and develop a sense of responsibility." Reformers, especially Stockwell Day, have been very uneasy, to say the least, about non-traditional notions of family. They are not comfortable with gay rights, as indicated by their opposition to the Supreme Court's decision in the Vriend case; they adamantly oppose gay marriage; and they wish to prevent the adoption of children by gay couples. In short, reformers support the traditional nuclear family, which was presumed to have been the norm in Canada some time in the past.

Social order is also a primary value for most Reformers. The Reform Party certainly stressed the "law and order" issue in its campaigns, as did the Canadian Alliance in the 2000 federal election. The Reform policies included longer prison sentences, including consecutive sentences rather than concurrent sentences, less opportunity for parole and greater supervision of released prisoners, greater police powers of investigation, fewer rights for prisoners, and the repealing of the *Young Offenders Act*. The Canadian Alliance has stated, "we will make providing safety and security for Canadians, their families and their property the overriding objective of the criminal justice system," and it promises that "law enforcement agencies will be given the resources they need to fight crime." The Alliance has also declared that "the rights of victims of crime must take precedence over those of criminals." The aforementioned support that Reformers provide to the RCMP and the Canadian Armed Forces is indicative of their belief in social order and authority. The establishment of a traditionally ordered society is perhaps the underlying *raison d'être* of the Reform Party/Canadian Alliance.

The Reform Party/Canadian Alliance support for tradition and order/authority demonstrates that the party is at least partially conservative, as defined by the Horowitz-Wiseman scheme. The other values in the Tory bundle of principles, however, do not seem to apply to the Reform Party/Canadian Alliance. The conservative acceptance of social hierarchy, in particular, is mitigated by the Reform/Canadian Alliance's emphatic belief in the equality of individuals. For Preston Manning this was a God-given belief: "my perspective and contributions will reflect Christian convictions such as the following: that human beings are of infinite value, [and] that all human beings are of equal value in the sight of God and entitled to equal treatment under the law."[49] Respect for the equality of individuals was repeated at least twice in Reform's list of 22 core principles, and Manning insisted that "the guarantee of equality for all Canadians" was the key to "national unity."[50] "Reformers," he clarifies, "support 'equality of opportunity' not 'equality of results.' "[51] The Canadian Alliance has similarly declared its commitment to the "true equality of citizens." Although equality has been a core component of liberal thought since the American and French revolutions, the rhetoric of equality in Canada in the 1990s was appropriated by the Reform Party, while liberals began to defend the concept of *difference*.

While Tories have a belief in community and cooperation, Reformers seem more inclined toward individual priority and competition, although they do have a specific understanding of community, as will be discussed below (see also Mendelsohn in this volume). The Reform Party/Canadian Alliance is a strong supporter of market principles. Preston Manning has written, "we believe that an open, free-market economy, combined with a genuinely democratic political system, offers the best possible chance for individuals to pursue their goals in life."[52] The Reform Party declared, "we believe that the creation of wealth and productive jobs for Canadians is best achieved through the operations of a responsible, broadly-based, free-enterprise economy in which private property, freedom of contract, and the operations of free markets are encouraged and respected."[53]

Stockwell Day has stated that when he was young, "I leaned toward socialistic [*sic*] thinking. Over time I realized that if you really want to see people move ahead and create opportunities and take care of their families, you have to have freedom of enterprise, freedom of opportunity, and that's what the Canadian Alliance is talking about."[54] Indeed, in the 2000 federal election, the Canadian Alliance promised to "create an economic climate in which businesses can thrive and grow" by providing a low, single income tax rate, "eliminating unnecessary regulations and minimizing government interference in the labour market," abolishing affirmative action programs, "pursuing free and open trade at home and abroad, including the elimination of inter-provincial trade barriers," and "securing access to international markets through the negotiation of trade agreements," withdrawing "government from areas of the economy where the private sector could deliver the same services more efficiently," and creating "a smaller and more efficient federal government." These *laissez-faire* market policies are more congruent with classical liberalism than the paternalistic *noblesse oblige* of traditional Toryism.

While Horowitz and Wiseman maintain that Canadian socialism represents a distinct synthesis of the communitarian and cooperative aspects of traditional Toryism with the classical liberal principles of reason, freedom, and equality, the Reform Party/Canadian Alliance appears to have made a distinctively new synthesis of Toryism and liberalism by combining the Tory beliefs in tradition and order/authority, with the liberal principles of equality, individual priority, and market-based competition (see Figure 2). In sum, Reformers have a traditionally conservative view of society and a liberal belief in market economics. What should we call this liberal-conservatism or conservative-

Figure 2: A Revised Interpretation of Canadian Ideological Traditions

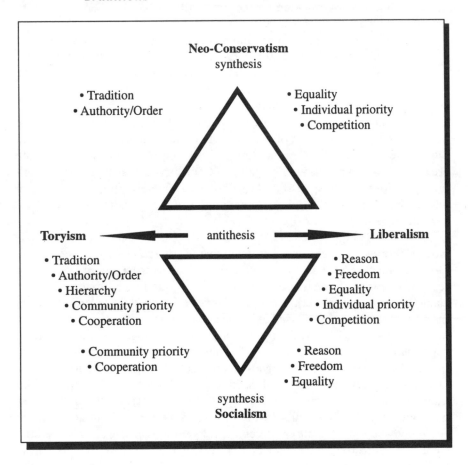

liberalism? Tom Flanagan reports that Preston Manning "never refers to himself simply as conservative," although he "will accept the label of *social conservative*,"[55] and it is probably safe to conclude that most Reformers define themselves as conservative. On the basis of self-identification, it thus seems appropriate to refer to Reformers ideologically as *neo-conservatives* as opposed to *neo-liberal*s. Furthermore, neo-conservatism appears to be a distinct ideological orientation in the Canadian political spectrum, notwithstanding Wiseman's assertion that Reformers are just "yesterday's liberals."

POPULISM IN THE REFORM PARTY/CANADIAN ALLIANCE: A CANADIAN REPUBLICANISM?

The Reform Party/Canadian Alliance has not been motivated simply by neo-conservatism. Preston Manning has stated that his "personal political convictions are rooted in the populist political tradition of western Canada."[56] "Curiously," however, "Manning has never laid down a concise definition of populism, even though it is the central concept in his political thought."[57] Indeed, Manning is so committed to the concept of populism that he has indicated that he decided to wait for a new populist movement to sweep across the Prairies rather than engage in traditional party politics.[58] While populism is a particularly nebulous concept, it will be suggested here that Manning's distinctive amalgamation of populism and neo-conservatism gives rise to a sort of Canadian republicanism, which is in keeping with the historical republican tradition in Canada described by Ajzenstat and Smith. For his part, Preston Manning was fond of situating his politics in what he called the "reform" tradition in Canada, which included the likes of William Lyon Mackenzie, Louis-Joseph Papineau, Louis Riel, William Aberhart, Ernest Manning, W.A.C. Bennett, and John Diefenbaker.[59] These are some of the people Ajzenstat and Smith identify as constituting Canada's "republican" tradition.

Populism is a political program that attempts to translate the wishes of the *populus* into public policy.[60] In keeping with the tenets of republicanism, then, populism relies on the common sense of the people. Indeed, the Reform Party adopted this as a core principle:

> We believe in the common sense of the common people, their right to be consulted on public policy before major decisions are made, their right to choose and recall their own representatives and to govern themselves through truly representative and responsible institutions, and their right to directly initiate legislation for which substantial public support is demonstrated.[61]

The party maintained that "public policy in democratic societies should reflect the will of the majority of the citizens as determined by free and fair elections [and] referenda." Furthermore, the party declared that "the duty of elected members to their own constituents should supersede their obligations to their political parties." Notwithstanding Preston Manning's repeated assertions that the Reform Party was a party of principles, unlike the "traditional" parties, the above statements offer no vision of the good life, other than the suggestion that the *populus* is always *right* and *virtuous*. There is no space here for leadership, for a dispassionate determination of the public good, or for a Canadian good greater than the sum total of 301 constituency goods.

Preston Manning apparently regarded populism as a *methodology* rather than an *ideology*.[62] As a political method, populism can be harnessed to virtually any ideology, although the objective in each instance is "to redefine and reconstitute the processes of democracy."[63] The Reform Party consequently adopted a number of policy resolutions that, if adopted, would have reshaped the dynamics of the democratic process in Canada. The party was committed to fixed four-year electoral terms, except in the event of the government losing a motion of non-confidence; it promised to hold a referendum to determine if Canadians were satisfied with the first-past-the-post electoral system and, if not, a subsequent referendum to choose a new electoral system; the party also supported the introduction of legislation that would allow constituents to recall their member of Parliament; and they wanted binding referenda on government legislation, when demanded by the *populus*, and a citizen's initiative whereby citizens could introduce legislative proposals by referendum. Following Thomas Jefferson, the Reform Party has also expressed scepticism at the role of the Supreme Court in interpreting the constitution. Thus, it proposed "that Parliament be given back its rightful place as the supreme body for creating and *interpreting* the laws of Canada and that the courts should be returned to their proper role of *applying* and *administering* the law."[64] These policies have subsequently been embraced by the Canadian Alliance.

These proposals would have changed Canada's system of representative democracy to a simple system of delegated democracy. A system of delegated democracy can only work if the citizens care sufficiently to participate actively and virtuously in the political process. Without their active engagement, the system will stagnate and, if they are not virtuous, the system will slide into a tyranny of the majority. The Reform Party's agenda was premised on the cardinal assumptions of republicanism. Reformers, especially Preston Manning and subsequently Stockwell Day, were convinced that if given the opportunity, citizens would participate actively and conscientiously in the political system. The decline in voter participation in recent elections casts some doubt on this assumption.

A corollary of the populist belief that the *populus* is always right is the contention that the *populus*, or the *demos*, is, or at least should be, *one*. This is also a core belief of republican thought. This, in fact, was the first principle of the Reform Party: "We affirm our commitment to Canada as one nation, indivisible."[65] Flanagan reports that Preston Manning unconsciously followed a logic of *monism*, "a philosophy of oneness." "This monistic populism," he suggests, "seems to stem from Manning's evangelical Christianity," although it may also follow from his experience in Alberta politics where "one party has always functioned as the representative microcosm of the provincial society."[66] On the other hand, Reform's commitment to Canada as "one nation" is remarkably similar to John Diefenbaker's notion of "One Canada." Diefenbaker may also be considered a populist-republican, although perhaps a little less populist and quite a bit more Tory than Preston Manning. Nonetheless, Diefenbaker insisted, "I have always considered the official policy of separating our country into various racial groups to be a curse on the realization of a united Canada. One Canada, one nation, my Canada, your Canada, cannot be a hyphenated Canada."[67] On this point, at least, Diefenbaker and Manning are indistinguishable.

Republicanism places great emphasis on the integrity of political figures and here again the Reform Party fits the mould. The party stated as a core principle, "we believe in public service — that governments, civil servants, politicians, and political parties exist to serve the people, and that they should demonstrate this service commitment at all times."[68] In keeping with the republican tradition of public service frugality, the Reform Party opposed the generous pension programs for members of Parliament, and it was highly critical of the expense allowances accorded to MPs and Senators. Indeed, it stated that "until a balanced budget is achieved, the salaries and expenses of government MPs and their offices should be frozen."[69] In short, the Reform Party followed Pettit's prescriptive republicanism "under which people are disposed to serve, and serve honestly in public office."[70]

Canadian republicans have frequently been derided as American imposters,[71] and Horowitz suggested that "the secret dream of the Canadian liberal is the removal of English Canada's 'imperfections' — in other words, the total assimilation of English Canada into the larger North American culture."[72] Preston Manning has been similarly excoriated. Trevor Harrison decries Reform's "incipient pro-Americanism" and suggests, "the most openly 'Americanized' Reformer is Preston Manning, a man whose political ethos is fundamentally republican and who, indeed, frequently quotes from American political heros," including Abraham Lincoln.[73] Manning is indeed an admirer of Lincoln, who inherited the republican mantle from Jefferson, but this does not mean Manning wished to transform Canada into a new United States. The criticism is fatuous. Canadians have embraced other American political concepts, namely democracy and federalism, without becoming Americans. Thus, while the Reform Party/Canadian Alliance may have exhibited republican tendencies, it is a distinctly Canadian republicanism.

Nelson Wiseman has dismissed Ajzenstat and Smith's analysis of the republican tradition: "from the vantage point of the tory-liberal-socialist paradigm, the distinction between liberalism and republicanism is secondary ... both liberalism and republicanism or civic humanism share cardinal liberal assumptions about man and society. Neither tories nor socialists share them."[74] However, the vast majority of Canadians endorse a number of overarching principles. Almost all Canadians believe in the rule of law, democracy, parliamentary government, and most accept the principles of federalism and constitutionally entrenched rights, as well as the capitalist mode of production. These important principles are embraced by the conservative-liberal-socialist ideologies in the Horowitz-Wiseman dialectic, and by neo-conservatives in the Reform Party/Canadian Alliance. To this extent, then, almost all Canadians are *liberals* of one description or another.[75]

Thus, the question is, do we wish to highlight the *differences* or the *similarities* among Canadians? In comparison to other societies, it may be worth noting that Canada is essentially liberal but, if we do not acknowledge our ideological differences, we cannot account for our politics. Without at least somewhat different perspectives on human nature, there is no basis for political disagreement, conflict, and competition. The Reform Party/Canadian Alliance has presented to Canadians a political platform that entails a conception of the good life that is fundamentally different from the other political parties, and consequently it has provoked considerable disagreement and conflict in the political arena, as we shall see in the following sections. It thus seems appropriate to describe the Reform/Alliance blend of populism and neo-conservatism as a variant of republicanism that is distinct from the other political traditions in Canada, including liberalism and conservatism.

THE POLITICS OF EQUALITY IN THE CANADIAN PARTY SYSTEM

In the 1993 election, "the Reform Party and the Bloc Québécois smashed through the brokerage system."[76] The Reform Party and the Bloc Québécois emerged as a result of Mulroney's failed attempts at mega-constitutional reform. The Bloc emerged directly from the collapse of the Meech Lake Accord, while the Reform Party received large boosts in its initial popularity from its opposition to Meech and subsequently the Charlottetown Accord. The politics of Quebec are thus integral to the Reform Party's success and central to its conflict with the Conservative Party.

Preston Manning and the Reform Party, and now the Canadian Alliance, habitually depict Canada as a federation of equal provinces and citizens, and the party has opposed any constitutional reforms that deviate from this formulation. Manning, sensitive to accusations that his party was anti-Quebec, has stated that he opposed the Meech Lake Accord for its "top-down, closed-door approach to constitution making," its rigid amending formula, and the lack of Senate reform, and he adds "that none of these three objections to the Meech Lake Accord ... refers to the province of Quebec."[77] He suggests that "at the root of the rejection of Meech Lake in the West was *mistrust* — of the process, of the politicians involved, and of the words and phrases cobbled together by that process and those politicians."[78]

Manning's opposition to the Meech Lake Accord, however, ran much deeper than concerns about the process. He states that "in western Canada, there is virtually no acceptance of the concept of Canada as some sort of marriage between the French and the English."[79] He thus claims there is no appetite in the west to accept Quebec as a "distinct society," especially if that recognition "was to confer upon the government of Quebec constitutional powers not conferred on other provinces."[80] In fact, Manning goes much further in his critique of federal government efforts to accommodate Quebec. He declares that "Reformers believe that going down the special status road has led to the creation of two full-blown separatist movements in Quebec.... It has led to desires and claims for 'nation status' on the part of hundreds of aboriginal groups.... It has led to a hyphenated Canadianism that emphasizes our differences and downplays our common ground, by labelling us English-Canadians, French-Canadians, aboriginal Canadians, or ethnic Canadians — but never Canadians, period."[81] As such, he suggests that "since the mid-1960s, virtually every constitutional initiative taken by the federal government to make Quebec feel more secure at home in Confederation has increased western alienation and made an ever-increasing number of other Canadians feel less at home."[82] Survey evidence, furthermore, indicates that Reformers are less inclined to accept special status for Quebec than supporters of other parties.[83]

The Meech Lake Accord and the distinct society clause in particular provoked a debate between liberal and communitarian conceptions of community and political equality.[84] Liberals contend that the state should not endorse particular conceptions of the good life. In other words, liberals believe that the state ought to remain neutral in its relations with the citizenry. Communitarians, on the other hand, argue that the state ought to recognize the distinct cultural communities within society. Radical communitarians believe that cultural groups are intrinsically meaningful and thus ought to be accorded constitutional recognition,[85] while moderate communitarians contend that the state should recognize only culturally vulnerable groups as a means of cultural preservation.[86] From these basic premises, liberals advocate the equality of individuals and individual rights, while communitarians support the notion of group rights and the equality of communities.

If we place the Canadian political parties within the liberal-communitarian debate, the Reform Party/Canadian Alliance falls on the liberal side, while the Conservative Party, in keeping with its Tory heritage, falls on the communitarian side. Tories, as depicted in Figure 1, have an abiding belief in community priority and cooperation. The Tory sentiment was captured perfectly by Joe Clark's famous description of Canada as a "community of communities." While Brian Mulroney claimed before he entered public office that "I do not believe in a theory of two nations, five nations, or ten nations.... Nor do I believe in any concept that would give any one province an advantage over any other," he maintained that "Québec is different. It is not strange or weird, it is just different. And the difference is rooted in language and culture. That is why the preservation and enhancement of these two instruments are so vital."[87] The distinct society clause in the Meech Lake Accord reflected Mulroney's acceptance of Quebec as an integral but unique community in Canadian society, while the more complex Canada clause in the Charlottetown Accord gave institutional expression to Joe Clark's belief in Canada as a community of communities. Preston Manning's opposition to the

Meech Lake and Charlottetown Accords was rooted in his conception of Canada as *one* community. As mentioned above, Manning's neo-conservative republicanism is a communitarian philosophy but, as Flanagan notes, it is a *monistic* communitarianism, as opposed to the *pluralist* communitarianism of Brian Mulroney or Joe Clark.

The suggestion that differences of opinion exist between Reform/Alliance and Conservative supporters has been made by a number of people (including Mendelsohn in this volume). Nevitte *et al.* have determined from opinion survey research that the "three sets of issues that stand out as separating Conservative voters from Reform supporters are law and order, moral traditionalism, and accommodating diversity."[88] In particular, they suggest that "the sharpest differences [*sic*] between supporters of the two right wing parties appear on the Quebec question."[89] They thus conclude that "the prospects are dim for a Reform-Conservative merger."[90] The contribution of the analysis made here is that Reform/Alliance and Conservative perspectives on the Canadian political community, and particularly the role of Quebec, are not merely superficial differences of opinion that may be overcome for political expediency. The different conceptions of political community presented by Reformers and Tories are fundamental and probably irreconcilable.

NEO-CONSERVATIVE EQUALITY VERSUS LIBERAL EQUALITY

Preston Manning's opposition to the Meech Lake and Charlottetown Accords bears at least a superficial resemblance to Pierre Trudeau's blistering attacks on the two accords.[91] But their respective critiques are motivated by different ideological assumptions. A careful analysis of their critiques will reveal crucial differences between Trudeau's quintessentially liberal perspective and Manning's neo-conservative republicanism. Contrary to popular opinion, Trudeau was perfectly willing to recognize Quebec's sociological distinctiveness:

> that Quebec is a distinct society is totally obvious. The inhabitants of the province live in a territory defined by its borders. The majority speak French. They are governed under a particular system of laws. And these realities have been pivotal in the development of a culture which is uniquely theirs. These are inarguable facts, arising from two centuries of history marked by intense struggles and juridico-political stubbornness.[92]

For Trudeau, Quebec's distinctiveness is a sociological reality. He objected only to recognizing Quebec's distinctiveness in *law*. In Trudeau's estimation, once Quebec was legally recognized as a "distinct society" the courts would be asked to define the meaning of these words and their effect on the individual rights guaranteed in the Charter. Trudeau argued that

> the Charter, whose essential purpose was to recognize the fundamental and inalienable rights of all Canadians *equally*, would recognize henceforth that in the

Province of Quebec these rights could be overridden or modified by provincial laws whose purpose is to promote a distinct society and more specifically to favour the "French-speaking majority" that has "a unique culture" and "a civil law tradition."[93]

With the constitutional recognition of Quebec as a distinct society, Trudeau feared that "Canada henceforth will be governed by two Constitutions, one to be interpreted for the benefit of Canada and one interpreted for the preservation and promotion of Quebec's distinct society — two Constitutions, two Charters, promoting two distinct sets of values."[94] In short, he stated, "the possibility of building *one Canada* will be lost forever."[95]

Both Trudeau and Manning, and liberals more generally, have been accused of ignoring "difference." Iris Marion Young has argued that "the principle of equal treatment originally arose as a formal guarantee of fair inclusive treatment. This mechanical interpretation of fairness, however, also suppresses difference."[96] Since Young's ground-breaking work, critics of liberalism have insinuated that a concern for political equality promotes *sameness* at the expense of *difference*. The *liberal* conception of society and politics, however, is premised on the assumption of diversity. Ronald Dworkin has argued that "since the citizens of a society *differ* in their conceptions [of the good life], the government does not treat them as equals if it prefers one conception to another."[97] And Amy Gutmann has suggested that the liberal conception of justice "represents the fairest possible *modus vivendi* for a pluralistic society."[98] Liberalism not only assumes diversity, but some liberals value diversity as a guarantee of freedom. Lord Acton, who was Trudeau's source of intellectual inspiration, argued, "the co-existence of several nations under the same State is a test, as well as the best security of its freedom."[99]

How can we distinguish Trudeau's concern for political equality from Manning's articulation of equality, and by extension the meaning of political equality endorsed by the Reform Party/Canadian Alliance? Their espousal of political equality can only be differentiated if we situate their understanding of equality within the larger bundle of values that define their ideological orientations (see Figure 2). As a liberal, Trudeau not only valued equality, he valued *individual liberty*. In the liberal ideological framework, individuals are equally free to pursue their own identity, subject only to the rule of law. Manning's conception of equality was tempered by his neo-conservative belief in *tradition*, especially his singular understanding of Canadian tradition and his social conformism. In the neo-conservative framework, individual freedom of action is confined to the marketplace; outside the marketplace, individuals are expected to conform to a common identity and set of social values. In this conception, individuals are indeed only equal to be the same. Manning's neo-conservative conception of equality thus does not permit difference, while Trudeau's liberal conception of equality allows for difference, at least in social practice if not in law.

Manning's singular understanding of tradition, and his concomitant intolerance of difference, is consistent with the theoretical weakness of republicanism. Ajzenstat and Smith suggest that "the notion that one communal way of life is to be preferred above all condones the suppression of political dissent and opposition."[100] And if one reads Iris Marion Young more closely, it becomes apparent that she too is concerned about monistic conceptions of community. She suggests that "community represents an ideal of shared public life, of mutual recognition and identification.... The impulse to community often coincides with a desire to preserve identity and in practice excludes others who threaten that sense of identity."[101] Thus, "the ideal of community," she continues, "also suppresses difference among subjects and groups."[102] For Young, it is the concern for equality *and* the ideal of community that suppress difference but, as has been demonstrated above, the concern for equality does not necessarily subsume difference. It depends on the wider bundle of values held in society or espoused by a party or regime. In particular, it depends upon whether the party endorses individual liberty and a pluralist community, or whether the party espouses a singular social tradition and a monistic notion of community.

THE EQUALITY OF INDIVIDUALS VERSUS THE EQUALITY OF PROVINCES

One last point needs to be elaborated. Unlike Pierre Trudeau, the Reform Party/Canadian Alliance has not been entirely consistent in its campaign for political equality. Trudeau only advocated the equality of individuals, while the Reform Party declared its support for both the equality of citizens *and* provinces, and so too has the Canadian Alliance.[103] These two concepts can converge and mutually support each other, but they can also diverge and contradict each other. If one province is accorded special recognition or powers, the state will not be treating all of its citizens equally; the citizens of that province will have entitlements, perhaps only symbolic, unavailable to citizens in other provinces. As such, the equality of citizens is strengthened when the provinces are accorded the same constitutional powers.

On the other hand, the equality of provinces, especially equal provincial representation in the Senate, would weaken the equality of citizenship. Citizens in the smaller provinces would be accorded relatively more representation in the Senate than citizens in the larger provinces. Furthermore, an equal Senate could produce profoundly undemocratic results. For example, the combined total representation of the five smallest provinces, representing no more than 15 percent of the population of Canada, could defeat legislation passed by the House of Commons, which is supposed to be representative of the population. While some might argue that this is a justifiable arrangement to prevent the "tyranny of the majority," this is not the ideology of the Reform Party/Canadian Alliance. Indeed, Preston Manning has argued that "safeguards" are required "to protect Canadians against 'the tyranny of minorities.' "[104] Moreover, the Reform/Alliance agenda for greater public participation through referendums is designed to ensure majority rule. The notion of an equal Senate thus contradicts the Reform/Alliance's populist platform.

The fundamental tension in the Reform/Alliance position is that the provinces, while constitutionally entrenched entities, are simply groups or communities. It is not clear why the Reform/Alliance would recognize and support these communities but not other communities. Why are Reformers willing to recognize the provinces of Canada, but not the nations of Canada? It cannot be that provinces already have constitutional recognition; Aboriginal groups also have constitutional recognition, as does the French language, which is the primary basis for Quebec's claim as a nation. If Reformers are concerned simply about the equality of citizens, there is no need to speak about the equality of provinces. However, if they are serious about extending the notion of provincial equality, they must be prepared to accept demands for equality from other sorts of groups and communities.

THE NEW IDEOLOGICAL LANDSCAPE AND CONSTITUTIONAL RECONCILIATION IN CANADA

After the failures of the Meech Lake Accord and the Charlottetown Accord, Jean Chrétien decided to avoid mega-constitutional settlements. While this has proved to be a successful short-term political strategy, a mega-constitutional settlement will likely be required some time in the future to resolve Quebec's place in the federation, and to meet the demands of other groups and regions in the country. What does the rise of neo-conservatism in the Reform Party/ Canadian Alliance, as well as in the Ontario and Alberta Conservative Parties, portend for a possible constitutional reconciliation? Assuming that neo-conservatism remains vibrant into the future, and Toryism and socialism do not disappear entirely, the ideological landscape in Canada is now much more complex.

Although Preston Manning and the Reform Party benefited tremendously from the high degree of constitutional cynicism present in Canada in the early 1990s,[105] Manning was largely motivated by the desire to obtain a lasting constitutional settlement in Canada. Indeed, Manning fancied himself as a constitutional "mediator."[106] In the mid-1970s, Manning drafted a report for the Canada West Foundation in which he articulated a "deal model of confederation."[107] In this report, Manning advocated the construction of a "National Unity Matrix" in which each region of the country — Atlantic Canada, Quebec, Ontario, the west, the Northern Territories, and Canada — would stipulate its primary political/economic "aspirations and concerns" and the concomitant policy/constitutional proposals required to fulfil these aspirations. Manning hoped that the governments of Canada could utilize the matrix to negotiate a

constitutional settlement. His belief was that each region could obtain its desired constitutional amendments, in exchange for supporting the demands from
the other regions.

If one imagined a matrix of the constitutional demands of each region in
contemporary Canada and distilled it into a package of constitutional reforms,
it would probably look a lot like the Charlottetown Accord. Indeed, Manning
wrote in 1991, "the Deal Model of Confederation would suggest that if any
'historic compromise' is possible ... it would consist of four elements: a limited
recognition of Quebec's distinctiveness, a Triple-E Senate, a limited (defined)
recognition of the rights of aboriginals to self-government, and provision for
a national referendum on new constitutional arrangements."[108] The irony is
that Manning and the Reform Party opposed the Charlottetown Accord.

Tom Flanagan hints that Manning may have been at least somewhat favourably disposed to the Charlottetown Accord, and that "he would have preferred
to stay out of the [Charlottetown] fight."[109] This is not surprising given how
close the Accord resembled Manning's deal model of confederation. Flanagan
reports that Manning thought Reform could exploit the provisions in the accord for a new Senate, and he was worried about the constitutional fatigue in
the country.[110] Reform supporters, however, were dismayed by the accommodations made for Aboriginal peoples and the recognition of Quebec as a distinct
society in the accord and, as their opposition became known, Manning was
forced into leading the "No" campaign. Manning's opposition to the accord
represented a rejection of his deal model of confederation, which had motivated him for almost two decades prior to the Charlottetown Accord.[111]
Manning's experience with the Accord illustrates the difficulties of leading a
populist party, and makes a mockery of Manning's insistence that he was a
politician of principle.

While Manning's approach in the deal model of confederation was obviously not that different from Joe Clark's approach to constitution-making,
Manning's proposals were frequently dismissed as "simplistic." Sharpe and
Braid state, "ultimately, Manning and his party provide simplistic reactions
to the complexity of modern Canada. This is both their appeal and their failure, for their goals could only be achieved if Canada itself were suddenly
simpler — stripped of ethnic loyalties, feminist hopes, Québécois dreams,
and all the other collective aspirations that define the country today."[112] There
seem to be two common assumptions that guide the processes of mega-
constitutional reform in this country, the first of which is dubious at best and
the second incorrect. The first assumption is that Canada constitutes a complex society. Assuming that this is "true" for the sake of argument, the second
assumption holds that Canada consequently requires a complex constitutional
solution. This was obviously Joe Clark's assumption during the Charlottetown
negotiations. These assumptions give rise to what might be called "Canada's
constitutional fallacy."

The challenge in constitution-making is to obtain an "overlapping consensus."[113] The fundamental premise of identity politics is that different social groups hold different political assumptions and values. In short, they each have distinct world views. In a homogeneous society, there will be one world view, with near universal agreement on primary values. The space for an "overlapping consensus" is thus large. As more world views are added to the picture, the space for an "overlapping consensus" is reduced. If Canada is truly a diverse country, with multiple belief constellations, the space for an "overlapping consensus" will be small, and this space will *shrink* as the country becomes more complex (see Figure 3). The emergence of the Reform Party/Canadian Alliance and its distinct conception of the Canadian political community has served to reduce the space for an overlapping constitutional

Figure 3: The Inverse Relationship between Diversity and the Space for an Overlapping Constitutional Consensus

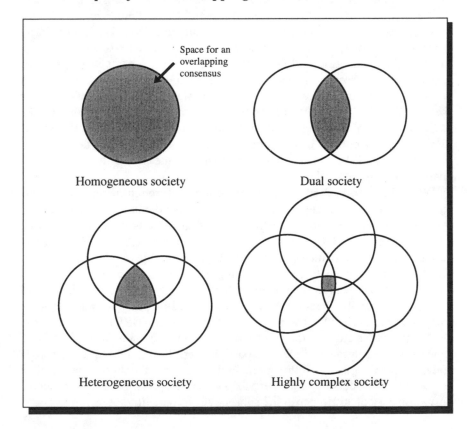

Space for an overlapping consensus

Homogeneous society

Dual society

Heterogeneous society

Highly complex society

consensus. It has meant that a collective statement about the *good life* is all but impossible in Canada. A constitutional reconciliation is thus only possible if the actors involved seek to obtain a relatively simple *modus vivendi* that focuses on the basic means by which diverse communities can co-exist and fulfil their aspirations.

CONCLUSION

Gad Horowitz provided a sweeping portrait of Canadian political culture and party politics, at least for the period in which he was writing. However, as Ajzenstat and Smith have ably demonstrated, Horowitz did not consider the episodic moments of *republicanism* in Canada. Perhaps he would have been able to incorporate a fourth dimension into his analysis if he had chosen to give any consideration to the erstwhile Social Credit movement. Nonetheless, when Preston Manning established the Reform Party in the late 1980s, he provided a modern institutional expression to the fourth dimension of Canadian political culture in the form of a neo-conservative republicanism. In the early 1990s, it appeared that the Reform Party and its particular brand of neo-conservatism was set to transform Canadian political culture. The Reform Party certainly influenced the discourse surrounding government budgeting, especially deficit reduction and tax cuts, and it complicated the processes of constitutional reform in the early 1990s. In relation to fiscal policy at least, notwithstanding the unpopularity of Preston Manning in some quarters, the Reform Party was the party of innovation in the early 1990s, although the Liberal Party stole Reform's thunder by eliminating the deficit. In this sense, Canadian party politics has continued to function as Horowitz described it, except that the Liberal Party has been poaching ideas from the right rather than the left (see Whitaker, this volume).

When the Reform Party failed to make a breakthrough in central Canada, Preston Manning took the bold step of re-branding the party as the Canadian Alliance but, unexpectedly, Stockwell Day dramatically won the leadership of the new party. While Day's obvious charisma and apparent bilingualism fanned the hopes of Alliance supporters, he was not able to take the party any further in the 2000 election than Manning had done in the previous two elections. After the election, Day's lustre faded quickly. Through the spring of 2001, a number of Alliance MPs defected, including party stalwart Deborah Grey, and established the Democratic Reform Caucus (DRC), which sat with the Conservative Party in the House of Commons. The members of the DRC evidently lost confidence in Day as party leader. He was subsequently forced to tender his resignation, although he indicated immediately that he intended to re-seek the leadership of the party. However, the party membership elected former MP Stephen Harper in the subsequent leadership race.

After his stunning first ballot victory, Stephen Harper met with Conservative leader Joe Clark to discuss possible strategies of inter-party cooperation. In a deft move, Harper proposed a much tighter integration of the two party caucuses than Clark could countenance. When Clark rejected Harper's proposal, thus dashing hopes of "uniting the right," the members of the Democratic Reform Caucus returned to the Canadian Alliance. While Harper does not openly espouse the social conservative moral concerns articulated by Manning and Day, he does not ascribe to the values embedded in Clark's Toryism either. The ideological chasm between the two parties thus remains wide.

While Harper's leadership appears to have steadied the Alliance Party in the short term, the party's electoral misfortunes to date (and possibly in the future) may run deeper than the leader. While the other three dimensions of Canadian political culture have proven to be significant and enduring, notwithstanding the fact that the socialist tradition in Canada is only half as old as the liberal and conservative traditions and only ever about half as strong, the republican tradition in Canada has been fleeting and episodic. Conservative republicanism either does not appeal to a sufficient number of Canadians, or it is only attractive at particular historical moments. History would thus suggest that the neo-conservative republicanism of the Canadian Alliance will not appeal to enough Canadians to produce an electoral majority. Thus, as in the past, the Alliance may be destined to be a third party, and it may just fade away in the years to come like the Social Credit previously.

If the political right in Canada has any hope of challenging the current hegemony of the Liberal Party, Tories and Alliance supporters will have to put their differences aside and combine forces. Party strategists working toward this end are fond of suggesting that the platforms of the two parties are broadly similar. Even if that is largely true, the analysis in this paper suggests that the remaining gap between the party philosophies is profound. Tories and Alliance republicans have fundamentally different conceptions of the country. These differences can only be set aside as long as major constitutional questions are left in abeyance, but as soon as the constitutional file is re-opened the differences between Tories and Alliance republicans will almost certainly re-surface. Canadian political culture will thus likely remain fragmented into the foreseeable future.

NOTES

The author would like to thank Nelson Wiseman and the two anonymous reviewers for the helpful comments they provided on earlier drafts of this chapter.

1.   Gad Horowitz, "Notes on 'Conservatism, Liberalism, and Socialism in Canada,' " *Canadian Journal of Political Science* 11, 2(1978).

2.   Janet Ajzenstat and Peter J. Smith, "The 'Tory Touch' Thesis: Bad History, Poor Political Science," in *Crosscurrents: Contemporary Political Issues*, ed. Mark

Charlton and Paul Barker (Toronto: ITP Nelson, 1998), p. 90. For another recent critique of Horowitz from a different angle, see Elizabeth Mancke, "Early Modern Imperial Governance and the Origins of Canadian Political Culture," *Canadian Journal of Political Science* 32, 2(1999).

3.   Gad Horowitz, "Conservatism, Liberalism, and Socialism: An Interpretation," *Canadian Journal of Economics and Political Science* 22, 2(1966), p. 141.

4.   Horowitz, "Conservatism, Liberalism, and Socialism: An Interpretation," p. 144.

5.   Ibid., p. 156; emphasis original.

6.   Ibid., p. 154; emphasis original.

7.   Ibid., p. 162.

8.   Ibid., p.144.

9.   Nelson Wiseman, "Political Parties," in *Canadian Politics in the 1990s*, ed. Michael S. Whittington and Glen Williams (Toronto: ITP Nelson, 1990); Nelson Wiseman, "Tory-Touched Liberalism: Political Culture in Canada," in *Crosscurrents: Contemporary Political Issues*, ed. Charlton and Barker.

10. Wiseman, "Political Parties," p. 233.

11. Horowitz, "Conservatism, Liberalism, and Socialism: An Interpretation," p. 156; emphasis original.

12. Ibid., p. 162; emphasis original; see also Whitaker in this volume.

13. Horowitz, "Conservatism, Liberalism, and Socialism: An Interpretation," p. 168.

14. Ajzenstat and Smith, "The 'Tory Touch' Thesis: Bad History, Poor Political Science," p. 84.

15. Janet Ajzenstat and Peter J. Smith, "Liberal-Republicanism: The Revisionist Picture of Canada's Founding," in *Canada's Origins: Liberal, Tory, or Republican?* ed. Janet Ajzenstat and Peter J. Smith (Ottawa: Carleton University Press, 1995), p. 1.

16. Ajzenstat and Smith, "Conservatism, Liberalism, and Socialism: An Interpretation," p. 84.

17. Ibid.

18. Joseph P. Ellis, *American Sphinx: The Character of Thomas Jefferson* (New York: Vintage Books, 1996), p. 122.

19. Ibid., p. 331.

20. Ibid., p. 265.

21. Philip Pettit, *Republicanism: A Theory of Freedom and Government* (Oxford: Clarendon Press, 1997), p. 8.

22. David F. Ericson, *The Shaping of American Liberalism* (Chicago: University of Chicago Press,1993), p. 2.

23. Ajzenstat and Smith, "The 'Tory Touch' Thesis: Bad History, Poor Political Science," p. 87.

24. Ibid.

25. Ibid.

26. Pettit, *Republicanism: A Theory of Freedom and Government*, pp. 120-26.

27. Ericson, *The Shaping of American Liberalism*, p. 11.

28. Ibid., p. 13.

29. Ajzenstat and Smith, "Liberal-Republicanism: The Revisionist Picture of Canada's Founding," p. 8.

30. Ericson, *The Shaping of American Liberalism*, p. 14.

31. Ibid., p.12.

32. Pettit, *Republicanism: A Theory of Freedom and Government*, p. 20.

33. Ajzenstat and Smith, "Liberal-Republicanism: The Revisionist Picture of Canada's Founding," p. 8.

34. Pettit, *Republicanism: A Theory of Freedom and Government*, pp. 110-11.

35. Isaiah Berlin, *Four Essays on Liberty* (Oxford: Oxford University Press, 1969).

36. Pettit, *Republicanism: A Theory of Freedom and Government*, p. 271.

37. Ibid., p. 277.

38. Wiseman, "Tory-Touched Liberalism: Political Culture in Canada," p. 73.

39. Trevor Harrison, *Of Passionate Intensity: Right-Wing Populism and the Reform Party of Canada* (Toronto: University of Toronto Press, 1991).

40. Sydney Sharpe and Don Braid, *Storming Babylon: Preston Manning and the Rise of the Reform Party* (Toronto: Key Porter Books, 1992).

41. Murray Dobbin, *Preston Manning and the Reform Party* (Toronto: James Lorimer and Company, 1991).

42. Tom Flanagan, *Waiting for the Wave: The Reform Party and Preston Manning* (Toronto: Stoddart Publishing, 1995), p. 15.

43. In this chapter, the word "Reformers" will be used as short hand to describe the supporters of both the Reform Party *and* the Canadian Alliance.

44. Reform Party, *The Blue Book: Principles and Policies of the Reform Party* (Calgary: Reform Party, 1999), p. 16. Richard Sigurson has reported that the 1991 Reform Blue Book read, "The Reform Party supports the preservation of the distinctive heritage and tradition of the Royal Canadian Mounted Police by retaining the uniformity of the dress code. Changes should not be made for religious or ethnic reasons" (Richard Sigurdson, "Preston Manning and the Politics of Postmodernism in Canada," *Canadian Journal of Political Science* 17, 2(1984), p. 268, note 42). This policy was intended to prevent Sikhs from wearing their traditional turbans in the RCMP and Aboriginals from wearing braids.

45. Reform Party, *The Blue Book: Principles and Policies of the Reform Party*, p. 42. The Reform Party, especially in its early days, was frequently tripped up by the question of immigration. The party was perceived as supporting a somewhat Eurocentric immigration policy on the assumption that this would support Reform's traditional picture of Canada. It is thus interesting to note that the Canadian Alliance did not articulate a position on immigration in its Policy Declaration, 2000.

46. Reform Party, *The Blue Book: Principles and Policies of the Reform Party*, p. 4.

47. Ibid., p. 41.

48. Ibid.

49. Preston Manning, *The New Canada* (Toronto: Macmillan, 1992), p. 105.

50. Reform Party, *The Blue Book: Principles and Policies of the Reform Party*, p. 4.

51. Manning, *The New Canada*, p. 314.

52. Ibid.

53. Reform Party, *The Blue Book: Principles and Policies of the Reform Party*, p. 7.

54. Quoted in the *The Globe and Mail*, "Day Embraces Tory Converts to Alliance," 21 August 2000, p. A4.

55. Flanagan, *Waiting for the Wave: The Reform Party and Preston Manning*, pp. 10-11.

56. Manning, *The New Canada*, p. 2.

57. Flanagan, *Waiting for the Wave: The Reform Party and Preston Manning*, p. 22.

58. Manning, *The New Canada*, p. 7.

59. Ibid., p. 26.

60. For further discussions of Reform populism see Flanagan, *Waiting for the Wave: The Reform Party and Preston Manning;* Harrison, *Of Passionate Intensity: Right-Wing Populism and the Reform Party of Canada*; Peter McCormick, "The Reform Party of Canada: New Beginning or Dead End?" in *Party Politics in Canada*, ed. Hugh Thorburn (Toronto: Prentice-Hall Canada, 1991); Thérèse Arseneau, "The Reform Party of Canada: Past, Present and Future," in *Canada: The State of the Federation 1994*, ed. Douglas M. Brown and Janet Hiebert (Kingston: Institute of Intergovernmental Relations, 1994); David Laycock, "Reforming Canadian Democracy? Institutions and Ideology in the Reform Party Project," *Canadian Journal of Political Science* 17, 2(1984); and Steve Patten, "Preston Manning's Populism: Constructing the Common Sense of the Common People," *Studies in Political Economy* 50 (1996) and "The Reform Party's Re-imagining of the Canadian Nation," *Journal of Canadian Studies* 34 (1999):1.

61. Reform Party, *The Blue Book: Principles and Policies of the Reform Party*, p. 8.

62. Flanagan, *Waiting for the Wave: The Reform Party and Preston Manning,* p. 24.

63. Laycock, "Reforming Canadian Democracy? Institutions and Ideology in the Reform Party Project," p. 19.

64. Reform Party, *The Blue Book: Principles and Policies of the Reform Party*, p. 37.

65. Ibid., p. 6.

66. Flanagan, *Waiting for the Wave: The Reform Party and Preston Manning,* pp. 34-36.

67. John G. Diefenbaker, *One Canada: The Memoirs of the Right Honourable John G. Diefenbaker, The Crusading Years 1895-1956* (Toronto: Macmillan, 1975), p. 218.

68. Reform Party, *The Blue Book: Principles and Policies of the Reform Party*, p. 9.

69. Ibid., p. 36.

70. Pettit, *Republicanism: A Theory of Freedom and Government*, p. 20.

71. Kenneth McNaught, *The Penguin History of Canada* (London: Penguin Books, 1998), pp. 86-87.

72. Horowitz, "Conservatism, Liberalism, and Socialism: An Interpretation," p. 154.

73. Harrison, *Of Passionate Intensity: Right-Wing Populism and the Reform Party of Canada*, pp. 172-73. Harrison continues, "Manning's intentions would seem to be to make Canada into a country very similar, if not indistinguishable, from the United States," and his "New Canada would be modelled on the American 'melting-pot' " (ibid., p. 173). In fact, Harrison suggested that Reform's extreme populism was a form of *nativism*, which he defines as "a conjunction of nationalism with prejudicial attitudes based on ethnicity, religion, or race" (ibid., p. 164). He concludes that many "Reformers view the party's policies, and even Manning's public utterances, as possessing an inner code, the meaning of which signals an intent to return to a predominantly Anglicized, white nation" (ibid., p. 175).

74. Wiseman, "Tory-Touched Liberalism: Political Culture in Canada," pp. 76-77.

75. Richard Van Loon and Michael Whittington, *The Canadian Political System: Environment, Structure, and Process*, 4th ed. (Toronto: McGraw-Hill Ryerson, 1987), pp. 112-13.

76. Neil Nevitte *et al.*, *Unsteady State: The 1997 Canadian Federal Election* (Toronto: Oxford University Press, 1999), p. 85.

77. Manning, *The New Canada*, p. 239.

78. Ibid., p. 240; emphasis original.

79. Ibid., p. 313.

80. Ibid., p. 309.

81. Ibid., p. 304.

82. Ibid., p. 120.

83. Nevitte *et al.*, *Unsteady State: The 1997 Canadian Federal Election*, p. 100.

84. Hamish Telford, "Liberalism versus Communitarianism and Canada's Constitutional Conundrum," *Journal of Canadian Studies* 33, 3(1998).

85. Michael MacDonald, "Should Communities Have Rights? Reflections on Liberal Individualism," *Canadian Journal of Law and Jurisprudence* 4(1991):2; Vernon Van Dyke, "The Individual, the State, and Ethnic Communities in Political Theory," *World Politics* 29 (1977):3; Vernon Van Dyke, "Collective Entities and Moral Rights: Problems in Liberal-Democratic Thought," *Journal of Politics* 44 (1982):23.

86. Charles Taylor, "Shared and Divergent Values," in *Options for a New Canada*, ed. Ronald L. Watts and Douglas M. Brown (Toronto: University of Toronto Press, 1991); Will Kymlicka, *Liberalism, Community and Culture* (Oxford: Clarendon Press, 1989).

87. Brian Mulroney, *Where I Stand* (Toronto: McClelland & Stewart, 1983), p. 59.

88. Nevitte *et al.*, *Unsteady State: The 1997 Canadian Federal Election*, p. 8. Mulroney, *Where I Stand*, p. 59.

89. Nevitte *et al.*, *Unsteady State: The 1997 Canadian Federal Election*, p. 100.

90. Ibid., p. 98.

91. Pierre Elliott Trudeau, *With a Bang not a Whimper* (Montreal: Stoddart Publishing, 1988); Pierre Elliott Trudeau, *Towards a Just Society* (Toronto: Penguin Books, 1990); Pierre Elliott Trudeau, *A Mess that Deserves a Big No* (Toronto: Robert Davies Publishing, 1992).

92. Trudeau, *Towards a Just Society*, p. 434.

93. Ibid., p. 436; emphasis added.

94. Trudeau, *With a Bang not a Whimper*, p. 99.

95. Ibid., p. 99; emphasis added.

96. Iris Marion Young, *Justice and the Politics of Difference* (Princeton: Princeton University Press, 1990), p. 11.

97. Robert Dworkin, "Liberalism," in *Liberalism and Its Critics*, ed. Michael Sandel (New York: New York University Press, 1984), p. 64; emphasis added.

98. Amy Gutmann, "Communitarian Critics of Liberalism," *Philosophy and Public Affairs* 14 (1985):313.

99. Lord Acton, *Essays on Freedom and Power* (Cleveland: Meridian Books, 1940), p. 160.

100. Ajzenstat and Smith, "Liberal-Republicanism: The Revisionist Picture of Canada's Founding," p. 9.

101. Young, *Justice and the Politics of Difference*, p. 12.

102. Ibid., p. 12.

103. For an excellent discussion about provincial equality, see Jennifer Smith, "The Meaning of Provincial Equality in Canadian Federalism," *Institute of Intergovernmental Relations Working Papers*, 1 (1998).

104. Manning, *The New Canada*, p. 320.

105. Nevitte *et al.*, *Unsteady State: The 1997 Canadian Federal Election*, p. 97.

106. Flanagan, *Waiting for the Wave: The Reform Party and Preston Manning*, p. 2.

107. Preston Manning, "A Realistic Perspective of Canadian Confederation" (Calgary: Canada West Foundation, 1977).

108. Manning, *The New Canada*, p. 309.

109. Flanagan, *Waiting for the Wave: The Reform Party and Preston Manning*, p. 46.

110. Ibid., p. 101.

111. Manning wrote in 1991, "when, as leader of the Reform Party of Canada, I am called upon to discuss the constitutional development of Canada and proposals for constitutional change, I still draw to a large extent on knowledge gained and conclusions reached as a result of fifteen years of viewing federal and provincial concerns and aspirations using the national unity matrix and the Deal Model of Confederation" (Manning, *The New Canada*, p. 88).

112. Sharpe and Braid, *Storming Babylon: Preston Manning and the Rise of the Reform Party*, p. 195.

113. John Rawls, "The Idea of an Overlapping Consensus," *Oxford Journal of Legal Studies* 1 (1987).

III

Regional Perspectives

6

Atlantic Canada at the Start of the New Millennium

Jennifer Smith

Est-ce que le Canada atlantique est enlisé dans le paradigme «Vieux-Canada» avancé par l'historien Michael Bliss? Dans ce chapitre, la réponse est un NON retentissant. Le «Vieux-Canada» est décrit comme étant économiquement frêle, politiquement rétrograde et corrompu, démographiquement stagnant et plus ou moins un boulet pour le reste du pays. Mais les données quant au Canada atlantique des années 1990 démentent cette image. Au niveau économique, la région est prospère grâce à une combinaison de développements, incluant l'industrie côtière du pétrole et du gaz et la concentration d'entreprises de nouvelles technologies et de communications dans des centres urbains comme Halifax et Moncton. Les gouvernements de la région poursuivent tous les mêmes principes de l'agenda néoconservateur: la privatisation de certains services publics, la réorganisation des services publics sur un modèle axé sur le client et des budgets équilibrés. Seule exception: les baisses d'impôts, qui sont encore hors d'atteinte. Au niveau politique, il y a du changement en cours en Nouvelle-Écosse, alors qu'elle passe d'un système traditionnel à deux partis à un système compétitif à trois partis à la suite d'un NPD incroyablement fort. Bien sûr il y a encore une continuité. Toutefois, on peut tirer comme conclusion que les seules pratiques du «Vieux-Canada» qui subsistent, sont encore celles du — bon — Canada.

> More than ever, Canada has become politically two countries. The dividing line is ... between Old Canada, which consists of Quebec and the Atlantic Provinces, and New Canada, which stretches from Ontario to British Columbia.[1]

Historian Michael Bliss elaborated this observation in an article ominously entitled "The Fault Lines Deepen." In his estimation, only one federal political party, the governing Liberal Party, has any chance of straddling the political fault lines. The remaining parties are confined either to Old Canada (Progressive Conservative Party, New Democratic Party, Bloc Québécois) or to New Canada (Canadian Alliance).

In the Bliss paradigm, the Old-New distinction is rooted in history and in economic and cultural factors. Old Canada is a product of the seventeenth and eighteenth centuries; New Canada is a product of the nineteenth and twentieth centuries. Old Canada still possesses a slow-growing economy while New Canada is a positive engine of economic dynamism and growth. Old Canada prefers big government and continues to practise the corrupt politics of government grants — to get votes, to encourage businesses, or to reward friends. New Canada prefers small government and citizen self-reliance. New Canada is growing fast in population and is friendly to immigrants and multiculturalism. Bliss omits to comment on this aspect of Old Canada, although the demographics there are known to be slow-moving by comparison.

It appears, then, that the New is the future, and that the west and Ontario are driving the country's destiny, and the Old is the past, and stuck in the mud. This is an unhappy conclusion, at least for those living in Old Canada. They might not mind being regarded as traditional. But no one wants to be considered passé, although being passé is the least of the Bliss indictment. And it *is* an indictment. Here is Bliss: "The political culture of Old Canada is the culture of the government grant, the subsidy to business, the handout to the unemployed, the handout to your political friends. In Atlantic Canada and Quebec, politicians are proud of the activities of HRDC, content to play the old patronage games."[2]

Lest it be thought that the Old Canada idea is a silly stereotype that is not worth a second glance, it is worth recalling the power of stereotypes in politics. Stereotypes are symbols, or shorthand ways of characterizing individuals and even, or especially, whole communities. In his study of the use of symbols in politics, Murray Edelman wrote: "It is characteristic of large numbers of people in our society that they see and think in terms of stereotypes, personalization, and oversimplifications, that they cannot recognize or tolerate ambiguous and complex situations, and that they accordingly respond chiefly to symbols that oversimplify and distort."[3] In other words, much of the power of a stereotype is rooted in its unidimensionality, and so is its prejudicial effect.

Stereotypes are worth combatting. That being so, it is fair to ask whether the Bliss stereotype reflects a sound appreciation of the political culture of Atlantic Canada at the start of the new millennium. Do political attitudes remain unchanged? Do political practices remain unchanged? Has the region remained essentially untouched by the major economic and political developments of the last decade? Or has it responded to them by fashioning major public policy changes and changes in governmental organization? The purpose of this chapter is to pursue these queries by focusing on the decade of the 1990s and scanning the record of public attitudes, electoral politics, and the efforts of governments to "re-invent" themselves. The record offers some empirical evidence to use in evaluating the Bliss paradigm. At its core, however, the paradigm is normative. Bliss strongly implies that the new Canadian ways are good and the old Canadian ways are bad, and this implication is taken up in the conclusion of the chapter.

REGIONALISM

Some would find difficulty with the idea of describing the four Atlantic provinces as one region, to say nothing of breezily lumping it with Quebec in an entity called Old Canada. It is undoubtedly the case that Bliss is prepared to make his points at the expense of caricature and over-simplification. However, even if he is given some leeway in this respect, which I propose to do, there remains the problem of the concept of regionalism in relation to Atlantic Canada that needs to be addressed before the analysis gets underway.

In Atlantic Canada there are four provinces, each with a pedigree that predates Confederation. This means four governments, four capital cities and four sets of economic and social institutions. Unquestionably these provincial institutional apparatuses substantially outweigh the regional one. They are like centres of gravity, and their effects on the organization of economic, political and social life can hardly be overestimated. Certainly little interest has been expressed in abandoning them for a political union, a bright idea that surfaces from time to time.[4]

In addition to the institutional factor, which is heavily weighted on the provincial side, there are the inhabitants themselves, and whether they are disposed to identify with the province or with the region. The question is a complicated one, not least because there are communities within the provinces, like the Acadian communities in Nova Scotia and New Brunswick; the Aboriginal communities in the Maritime provinces and Labrador, Cape Breton Island, also part of Nova Scotia; and the Black communities in Nova Scotia. These communities are important sources of individual identities. Further, the results of survey research over the years are mixed.[5] Nevertheless, there is some evidence to support the view that provincial identities outweigh any sense of regional identity, notwithstanding the fact that across the four provinces the majority of the population is of British or Irish descent.[6] That being so, it might be wondered whether it is acceptable to treat the four Atlantic provinces as a region at all.

Janine Brodie has defined the concept of region "as an interpretation of politics that prioritizes the condition of the territorial entity rather than relations among groups of people defined in non-territorial terms, such as gender, class, or race."[7] The existence of regional institutions would help to support such an interpretation. On this dimension, support for the idea of an Atlantic region is slim, but not negligible. To begin, the composition of the Senate of

Canada is region-based. In 1867 there were three regions — Ontario, Quebec and the Maritime provinces — each assigned 24 seats. The Maritime region, initially comprised of Nova Scotia and New Brunswick, was meant to include Prince Edward Island (PEI) as well, and eventually it did. Newfoundland only joined the federation in 1949, and it was assigned six seats on its own. So there is a Maritime region in Senate representation, although not an Atlantic region. However, recent developments in relation to the amendment of the constitution indicate that, in some minds at least, Maritime is growing into Atlantic.

None of the formulas entrenched in the constitution that are applicable to its amendment is region-based; region-related, maybe, but not region-based. However, recently the entrenched formulas were encrusted with a statutory hurdle, and it *is* region-based. The federal *Act Respecting Constitutional Amendment*, passed in 1996, was part of the fall-out from the result of the Quebec referendum held the previous November, in which the sovereignist option failed to pass by the merest whisper. The purpose of the Act is to assign (some would say restore) to Quebec a veto over constitutional amendments. This is accomplished by the requirement that the federal government gain specified provincial and regional approvals before submitting to the House of Commons a resolution to amend the constitution in accordance with the amending procedures entrenched in the constitution. In its original form, the bill treated Ontario and Quebec as regions in their own right, following the old Senate model, and the four western provinces as one region, which caused an uproar in British Columbia and Alberta, two provinces that see themselves in more elevated terms than that implies. The federal response was to make British Columbia a region on its own, like Ontario and Quebec, and to put Alberta together with Manitoba and Saskatchewan in a Prairie region where the majority rules, which is tantamount to giving Alberta a regional veto. The other region is Atlantic Canada, in which consent is defined as the agreement of two of the four provinces which together possess 50 percent of the population of the region.

A final bit of institutional evidence that is very recent indeed is the establishment of a successor to the Conference of Atlantic Premiers, namely, the Council of Atlantic Premiers. In May 2000, the four Atlantic premiers launched the new council in an effort to coordinate their public policy positions and thereby strengthen their voice in national political circles. The Council of Maritime Premiers, which was established in 1971, is to remain in place for now.[8] A certain hedging of bets might be detected here. The old conference was a handy organization for the inclusion of the Newfoundland premier in meetings with the Maritime premiers. Its transformation into the Council of Atlantic Premiers suggests some strengthening of support for the idea of the four-province region, although the smaller Maritime council remains in the event of unforeseen conflict with the newest regional colleague.

In addition to the institutional evidence of regionalism, there is also the historical record of regional responses to region-wide crises or opportunities. An early example was the Maritime Rights movement in the 1920s, which developed in response to the crisis of the deindustrialization and marginalization of the Maritime economies that followed in the wake of changes made in key national transportation policies during and after World War I. Maritime Rights was a political movement that was destined to fail in the attempt to alter policy at the national level, although it did manage to prod the federal government into taking some compensatory measures on the region's behalf.[9] In another example in the 1960s, it was more a matter of responding to opportunities. Acting on the statist economic thinking of the day, all four eastern governments engaged in extensive efforts to foster industrial development by offering inducements of various kinds to existing and prospective businesses to locate in their respective provinces. In the 1990s, it has been a matter of crisis again, specifically the marked deterioration in the state of public finances with which all four governments have had to cope. On the basis of these examples, James Bickerton concludes that "regionalism becomes salient when established relations with extra-regional economic and political actors become unstuck or de-stabilized, making them subject to a heightened politicization in which common regional interests and concerns are granted greater prominence."[10]

On the bases of the institutional setting and the historical record — rather than any notion of a regional identity in the minds of the inhabitants — it is possible, following Brodie, to assume an interpretation of the politics of the Atlantic region and to test the Bliss interpretation of the politics of the region, beginning with political attitudes. Do Atlantic Canadians possess "Old Canada" attitudes?

REGIONALISM AND POLITICAL ATTITUDES

In 1974 Richard Simeon and David Elkins published data that support the Old Canada thesis. They found that in Newfoundland, New Brunswick, and to a lesser extent Nova Scotia — the data from PEI were too small to count — the orientation of respondents toward government reflected lower efficacy and trust levels than those of respondents elsewhere in the country.[11] Even when controls for factors like class, age, education, gender, community size, and party identification were introduced, the regional pattern persisted.

As Ian Stewart points out, the study has been cited many times, including in texts on provincial politics.[12] As a result, it has influenced perceptions about the political culture of Atlantic Canada. And how might it have influenced perceptions? Unquestionably the normative inference of the findings is negative. Simeon and Elkins define political efficacy as "a sense that one can be personally influential in politics, can make one's voice heard, and can be effective,"[13] in other words, upstanding citizenship in a healthy liberal-democratic polity. By contrast, feelings of inefficacy block active citizenship. On trust, Simeon and Elkins query the extent to which "citizens feel government and politicians to be competent, concerned for, and interested in their welfare and worthy of respect."[14] Low levels of trust in government indicate a low opinion of government.

It might be thought that grim findings like these simply point to bad government. In their conjectures on the causes of the findings, Simeon and Elkins consider that they might be rooted in the cumulative, negative experiences of citizens with government or, alternatively, in electoral and political-party systems that discourage widespread political participation. They also raise the possibility of European settlement patterns, specifically the impact of Loyalist emigration to the Maritimes during and after the American Revolution. However, the lengthiest consideration by far is given to the economic factor, in particular "the dividing line formed by the Ottawa River [that] separates rich from poor, developed from undeveloped."[15] Now we are in Bliss country. The suggestion is that the relative poverty of the Atlantic region, its high proportion of poor and ill-educated citizens, the stagnating population levels, the lack of a dynamic urban and industrial core coupled with extensive rural subsistence living, and the vulnerability in the face of economic decisions made elsewhere — all economic negatives — have combined to generate the widespread disaffection from the political system tapped by the study.

None of this is to say that the study was somehow inaccurate at the time. On the contrary, it was a significant and revealing examination of regional political cultures. The question is whether it still conveys an accurate picture of the political culture. By 1994, Stewart thought that it did not. Using data going forward to 1984, he found instead that the variations among the regions in relation to political trust, political efficacy, and political interest had been declining since 1968 and had become quite minor. He saw convergence rather than divergence. As a result, he concluded that "the notion that Atlantic Canadians are a uniquely disaffected lot, distinguishable from other Canadians by their low levels of political trust and political efficacy, should clearly be put to rest."[16]

However, more recently this notion has been resurrected by Elisabeth Gidengil and her colleagues in a study based on data gathered during the 1997 general election. Gidengil and company are struck by the marked regionalization of the vote in the election. Region of residence, they find, was a stronger predictor of the vote than any of the typical social background characteristics like religion, ethnic origin, level of education, and so on. They are particularly intrigued by the gap in the vote for Liberal candidates between Ontario (50 percent) and Atlantic Canada (33 percent), a 17-point gap. They find that about two-thirds of the gap can be attributed to election-specific factors, the two most important being perceptions of economic conditions and evaluations of the performance of the governing Liberal Party since its election four years earlier. Briefly, in Atlantic Canada there was significant concern about the loss of jobs and the viability of existing social programs, and the effort of the federal government to reduce the deficit was not warmly welcomed. In Ontario, by contrast, voters evinced optimism about the economic future, were more appreciative of deficit reduction and were focused on issues like fighting crime and preserving national unity.[17]

Significantly, Gidengil and company also find that much of the rest of the gap can be attributed to differences in political culture between the two regions on two dimensions. First, Atlantic Canadians exhibited more cynicism about the political process than did Ontarians. Second, and unlike Ontarians, they perceived that the federal government treated their provinces worse than the other provinces. The analysts conjecture that differences like these are products of long experience and therefore unlikely to change easily. In the meantime they form the horizon of opinion in which electoral judgements are made.

It must be stressed that the higher measure of political cynicism in Atlantic Canada picked up in the1997 election study is just that — higher by comparison with Ontario. Political cynicism is everywhere. In his analysis of the data gleaned from the *World Values Surveys* taken in 1981 and 1990, Neil Nevitte demonstrates that in advanced western societies, there has been a decline in public confidence and public trust in government, which is part and parcel of a decline in deference to the authority traditionally exercised by elites.[18] Others have confirmed the decline, including Frank Graves, president of Ekos Research Associates, although Graves cautions against placing too much emphasis on it with respect to government, since he finds that government has fared better in the public's estimation than religious and educational institutions and the media.[19] However, his data tap into feelings of economic insecurity that are worth pausing to consider.

As noted above, Gidengil and company show that Atlantic Canadian residents were much more worried about job losses than Ontarians, for whom the concern was not even statistically significant. This is consistent with Graves' findings on insecurity. He defines insecurity to include not only economic insecurity but also more general fears about the future and the changes that it might entail for community, identity, and values. Significantly, he finds that insecurity increasingly is a function of social class and region. "The East-West security divide," he writes, "is roughly demarcated by the Ottawa River."[20] This is the Old Canada-New Canada divide.

There is nothing so conclusive about any one set of findings that it overrules other findings. There may well be attitudinal differences that are rooted in long-standing regional economic differences. However, these attitudinal differences may be patchy. They may persist within the larger context of the erosion of interregional differences in political culture, in other words, within the larger context of value convergence. Further, the traditional attitudes that do persist might lag or even mask change that is underway, for example, in the electoral arena.

ELECTORAL POLITICS

THE FEDERAL ARENA

At the federal level, the vote in Atlantic Canada in the 1997 general election has captured the attention of analysts like Bliss, who see it as a kind of luddite or dated response to new developments in a brave world. In order to assess the validity of such a judgement, it is useful to review a little electoral background.

Until 1997 in the Maritimes, and then the Atlantic region, the twentieth century belonged to the Liberal and Conservative Parties. Sometimes they were competitive, and sometimes not. And in any given election there were likely to be variations among the provinces. For example, from its entry into Confederation in 1949 until 1968, Newfoundland was nearly a Liberal preserve. It is astonishing to consider that in the first general election held there in 1949, the Liberals got only five of seven seats with a popular vote of 71.9 percent. They missed out in St. John's, where the anti-Confederate and business vote managed to elect two Conservatives.[21] Meanwhile, in the other three provinces the Conservatives had come back from a rather prolonged slump to move past their rivals in the 1957 and 1958 general elections. Then New Brunswick, always a Liberal stronghold, slipped back into the Liberal fold in 1961. Nova Scotia and PEI, for their part, remained winning provinces for the Conservatives through to the 1984 general election.[22] And so on. There is no need to run through the results of election after election. The point is that only two parties were really in the race. In 1997, this changed to three parties.

The NDP's success in 1997 could not be foreshadowed by the 1993 election. In that election, the Liberals, who defeated the incumbent Conservatives and went on to form the government under Prime Minister Jean Chretien, polled well in Atlantic Canada, capturing 31 of 32 seats — only popular Conservative MP Elsie Wayne held out in Saint John — with huge popular vote percentages in the provinces that ranged from a high of 67.3 percent in Newfoundland to a low of 52 percent in Nova Scotia. The Conservatives, on the other hand, took the most famous drubbing of any political party in Canadian political history, winning only two seats of a total of 305 — Wayne's and leader Jean Charest's in Brome, Quebec. Obviously in Atlantic Canada some of the Conservative vote went to the Liberals. Where else in the region did it go? Certainly not to the NDP. The party's percentage of the popular vote ranged from a high of 6.8 percent in Nova Scotia to a low of 3 percent in

Newfoundland, less than half of its vote in 1988. Some of the Conservative vote went to the new western-based Reform Party, established in 1987 under the leadership of Preston Manning. While the Reform Party gained only 1 per cent in Newfoundland and in PEI, it gained 13.3 percent in Nova Scotia and 8.5 percent in New Brunswick. Together the Reform and Conservative vote amounted to about one-third of the total in each of the region's provinces.

Ironically, the two parties — the NDP and the Conservative Party — which did so poorly in the 1993 election throughout the country as well as in Atlantic Canada were the same two that bounced back in 1997 in the region. The NDP story was the more dramatic of the two. In 1993, in keeping with tradition, the party had elected no one in the region. In 1997 the party gained eight seats, six in Nova Scotia and two in New Brunswick. The remarkable vote percentages ranged from a high of 30.4 percent in Nova Scotia to a low of 15.1 percent in PEI. The Conservatives, for their part, picked up 13 seats (12 more than in 1993) and increased their popular vote shares in each of the provinces. In Nova Scotia, the combined Conservative and Reform Party share was 40 percent while in New Brunswick it was 48 percent.

Since the Conservative Party gained a total of 20 seats in the election, or 18 more than the previous outing, the 13-seat Atlantic component was hardly a negligible contribution. The same could be said of the NDP, which rebounded from nine seats in 1993 to 21 seats in 1997, eight being from the Atlantic region. In post-election analyses, the parties were stamped as Atlantic Canadian parties. In the case of the Conservatives, the immediate reason was the sheer weight of the regional complement. In the case of the NDP, it was because the eastern seats were new seats, including the new leader's seat in Halifax, and because the new leader, Alexa McDonough, had led the Nova Scotia NDP for 13 years. The question is why these two parties, nominally so disparate, *both* did so well in the same region in the same election.

The significance of the question lies in the fact that in the past the anti-government vote has always gone to the alternative traditional party. In other words, the traditional party out of office was the default option. In 1997, apparently, there were two default options. One explanation, at least for Nova Scotia and New Brunswick, was the effect of the Reform Party, and the extent to which it drained support from the Conservative vote. Given the dynamics of the single-member-plurality (SMP) system which is Canada's electoral system, it is quite possible that a combined Conservative-Reform vote would have deprived the NDP of some of their seat gains. However, the fact of the matter is that the Reform Party and the Conservative Party delivered different messages in the campaign. The Reform Party stuck to its neo-conservative message in the east, stressing the need to lower taxes, pay down the public debt, fight crime, pursue the decentralization of the federation rather than focus on the accommodation of Quebec, and reform the parliamentary system of government. The Conservatives also promised to cut taxes, and made that promise the central plank of their campaign. But the issue did not work for them. Reform owned the issue, and in any event it was not a salient one for most voters.[23]

However, the Conservatives also attacked the Liberal government for cutting social programs and for failing to tackle the high unemployment plaguing some areas of the region, and for breaking its promise to eliminate the goods and services tax (GST). Their best issues revolved around the concerns about social programs and unemployment, although the electoral benefits were largely confined to Atlantic Canada. There, according to Nevitte and company, it was the Conservatives rather than the NDP who benefited from feelings of insecurity about unemployment.[24] In any event, in positioning themselves to the left of the Liberals on social issues, the Conservatives were closer to the NDP than to Reform. Indeed, in the east the key distinction between the Conservatives and the NDP was the national unity issue, with the Conservatives emphasizing the need to take a more accommodative approach to Quebec than the Liberal government, and the NDP preferring to avoid the issue altogether. The Conservative leader, Jean Charest, never shrank from discussing the unity issue even though it was not found to be highly ranked in importance among voters outside Quebec.[25]

The 1997 election left observers wondering whether the Reform Party would ever make inroads in the region; whether the Conservatives were really making an eastern-based comeback; and whether the NDP could sustain and build on its gains in the region. The next general election, which was held in November 2000, produced some answers. In the runup to the election, the Reform Party made a deliberate effort to transform itself into a national party with a new name, the Canadian Alliance, and a new leader, Stockwell Day, who had left his post as the treasurer in the Conservative government of Alberta to seek the leadership of the new party. In the east, the gambit failed. In Nova Scotia, the party's share of the popular vote barely moved, registering 9.6 percent in 2000 as opposed to 9.7 percent in 1997. In New Brunswick, it was 15.7 versus 13.1; in PEI, 5 versus 1.5; in Newfoundland, 3.8 versus 2.5.

Understandably, these figures yielded the Alliance no seats in Atlantic Canada, although the party did come out of the election with six seats more than the 60 it had going in — seats gained elsewhere. That more or less answers the inroads question for now. By contrast with the Alliance, the Conservatives slumped nationally, losing seats (down to 12 from 20) and votes (down to 4 percent from 6.6). In Atlantic Canada, the region so critical to them, they went into the election with 13 seats and wound up with nine. Their share of the popular vote was steady in Nova Scotia and PEI, off slightly in Newfoundland and a little more in New Brunswick. It was not a comeback. The NDP fared as badly as the Conservatives nationally, losing seats (down to 13 from 21) and votes (down to 4.3 percent from 7). In the Atlantic region, the party halved its seats from eight to four, thereby failing to consolidate its gains in 1997.

The big winner, of course, was the Liberal Party, with their third election victory in a row. In each of the Atlantic provinces, it strengthened its share of the popular vote and gained an additional eight seats, giving it a total of 19 in the region. The Liberals ran an "Old Canada" campaign in the region, bringing in Cabinet ministers to tout the benefits of being on the government side, like the former premier of Newfoundland and then Industry minister, Brian Tobin (he has since resigned the Cabinet), and proposing to soften some of the rules that govern access to employment insurance, an obvious pitch in rural areas that experience high seasonal rates of unemployment. Moreover, they could point to a strong economy on their watch, and the significant income-tax cuts announced prior to the election call, a popular move everywhere. Indeed, the puzzle is why the Liberals did not do even better. In Dartmouth, for example, the former Senate majority leader, Bernie Boudreau, argued the advantages of government over opposition to no avail, failing to oust the sitting NDP member.

The record of the last three federal elections in Atlantic Canada, then, is not exactly an Old Canada tune. Moreover, the NDP gains in 1997, gains that were pared but not eliminated in 2000, deserve reflection. The federal NDP, which is after all a social democratic party, has been marginalized in this neo-conservative period of Canadian political life, particularly in the context of an economy that, until quite recently, has been booming. The party is thought to have little to contribute to contemporary public policy-making, in particular to issues like the privatization of public services, the regulation of the financial sector of the economy, or tax reduction. As a result, it is easy to interpret its gains in Atlantic Canada as an Old Canada refusal to accept change. However, it must be stressed that a few short years ago these very gains would have been heralded as a fresh, modern breakthrough in a politically traditional part of the country. As noted earlier, in 1994 Ian Stewart argued that there has been an *erosion* of the traditional political culture in the region. Thus there was an erosion of the traditionalism so inimical to the prospects of an ideological party. Having made that point, he was then faced with explaining why the NDP was still an electoral failure. Stewart offered the intriguing suggestion that the NDP was a "prisoner of the past." He meant that the NDP might still suffer from the lingering effects of a hostile, if dying, traditionalism.[26] If Stewart was right, then the NDP's recent success — its escape from the years of "free-floating failure" — is related to a changing political culture, not a stagnant one. Developments at the provincial level bear this out.

THE PROVINCIAL ARENA

To some analysts, the most important characteristic of the region provincially is the existence of three Conservative governments in PEI, Nova Scotia, and

New Brunswick. They regard these governments as an important harbinger of events to come at the federal level, following the cycle thesis according to which provincial electorates choose governments of a different political stripe than the federal government, which eventually falls too, at which point the cycle begins again.[27] Presumably Newfoundland, which has a Liberal government, is counter-cyclical. Alternatively, like Bliss, they regard the Conservative governments as little more than Old Canada evidence because the provincial Conservative parties are closer to the federal Conservative Party than they are to the new Canadian Alliance, the aspiring national successor to the old western-based Reform Party and the political home of neo-conservatism.[28]

For my purposes, the cycle thesis is neither here nor there. More important is the Old Canada notion, because it masks two factors of fundamental importance in understanding developments in the region since 1987. One is the election of administrations that have essentially pursued a neo-conservative agenda. The other is the rise of the provincial NDP in Nova Scotia.

It is important to focus on the fact of neo-conservative administrations, beginning with the election in 1987 of the Liberals in New Brunswick who were led by Frank McKenna. In the 1987 election the Liberals took every seat, defeating the discredited Conservatives who had held power since 1970. Whether or not New Brunswickers were fully aware of it, the new premier held strong and consistent anti-statist, pro-market views. If ever there was an administration openly favourable to the business agenda, it was McKenna's. Unlike his federal colleagues, McKenna supported the proposed free trade agreement with the United States in the 1988 general election. He pursued deficit reduction, cutting public service jobs, eliminating or amalgamating agencies, privatizing services, and holding down public sector wages. He also pursued job creation, essentially by getting businesses to locate in the province. His energetic efforts in this respect drew national attention, largely because they were so focused on communications firms engaged in activities like telemarketing, customer ordering and billing, and data processing — and because he had some success. Finally, he pursued changes to social programs in a manner consistent with his views on how to reposition the province's workforce for the "new economy" era. There was an emphasis on education and retraining to help people overcome reliance on the old combination of casual labour and unemployment insurance, and even workfare programs designed to compel participants to jettison welfare dependency.[29]

Policies such as these are instantly recognizable as part of the neo-conservative agenda and common currency among governments today. They were not common currency among Canadian governments in 1987, which makes the McKenna example a significant one. His governments set the neo-conservative standard for Atlantic Canada, and one by one the other governments followed suit — later, unhappily, in fits and starts — but they followed suit. In the end there was no other choice because in the early 1990s the federal government began instituting significant cuts in transfers to the provinces for social programs. Faced with these cuts, on one side, and their own mounting deficits and debts,[30] on the other, the provincial governments needed to focus on painful and old-fashioned goals like balancing budgets. PEI balanced its budget in the spring of 2000. The government of Nova Scotia has yet to meet that benchmark. However, it aims to do so by fiscal 2002–03. Meanwhile, in its budget for 2000–01, it expects the deficit to run to $199 million. In Newfoundland, the budget for 2001–02 shows a projected deficit of $30.5 million, the smallest for many years.

The partisan stripe of the governing party in office seems not to matter a great deal in terms of the adoption or not of a neo-conservative agenda. Frank McKenna won three elections before stepping down in 1997. Two years later his successor, Camille Theriault, sustained an unexpected defeat at the hands of the youthful Bernard Lord, who led the Conservative Party to victory. The new government is following the same conservative financial policies as its predecessors: its spring budgets in 2000 and 2001 each showing a surplus. In Newfoundland the Liberal Party has been in power since 1989. In PEI there was a switch from the Liberals to the Conservatives in the middle of the decade. Nova Scotia has been more tumultuous, moving back and forth between the Conservatives and the Liberals. Nevertheless, no matter what their partisan stripe, all of the provincial governments either have produced budget surpluses or are moving in that direction, principally by cutting personnel and program expenditures, raising taxes, implementing new user fees for various services[31] and, at the millennium, generally benefiting from booming economies. As a result, it appears unwise on the basis of the low levels of support in the region for the old Reform Party and now the Canadian Alliance to conclude that Atlantic Canada has rejected the neo-conservative agenda. Many in the region might not like the agenda. But the fact of the matter is that provincial governments — which are elected, after all — have pursued it. The discipline of the neo-conservative agenda, then, has been as much a part of the region's experience as elsewhere. That leaves the second point — the rise of the NDP in the provincial politics of Nova Scotia.

The NDP's success is significant because it represents an observable change in the political-party system from a competitive two-party system to a competitive three-party system. The facts are these. The CCF, the predecessor of the NDP, contested its first election in Nova Scotia in 1941, gaining three seats and 7 percent of the popular vote. That set a pattern that continued for many elections, the party capturing somewhat more or less than 10 percent of the popular vote and none to three seats. The 1974 election inaugurated a new phase in which the party, now the NDP, consistently gained more than 10 percent although still very few seats, ranging from one to four.

The big change came in the provincial general election in March 1998. The governing Liberal Party, under the leadership of a new premier, Russell MacLellan, suffered extensive losses, dropping from 40 seats in the 52-seat house of assembly to 19 seats on the basis of a popular vote of 35.3 percent. The NDP soared from four seats to 19 with 34.6 percent, while the Conservative party increased its number from nine to 14, with 29.8 percent.[32] Premier MacLellan formed a minority government, met the assembly, and with the help of the Conservatives, got a budget passed. The following year, however, the Conservative Party pulled the plug. Its leader, John Hamm, stated that he could not support a budget that was not balanced. As a result, an election was set for July 1999, an election that the Conservatives won, gaining 30 seats and 39.2 percent of the popular vote. The Liberals and the NDP both fell back, the Liberals with 11 seats and 29.8 percent, and the NDP with 11 seats and 29.9 percent.[33]

In the case of the NDP, the obvious question is whether its new-found support is set to endure. Much of the new support is located in metropolitan Halifax, although the party has made inroads in rural areas of the province, too. Since the long-term demographic trend is the steady increase in the population of the metropolis, this is just as well, success there being essential for any party. A final point to be made about the NDP is its moderate social-democratic character under the leadership of Robert Chisholm, who replaced long-time leader Alexa McDonough in 1996. For example, in the 1999 election, an aspiring NDP ran a restrained campaign, promising little except the prudent management of public monies, and reforms to health care and education that would have to be financed without new taxes or raises in the sales tax or the income tax. Indeed, some alleged that the party was running the classic, low-key "front runner's" campaign, emphasizing strategy over traditional policy positions. Even if the allegation was justified, it serves only to demonstrate the party's perception at the time of where on the political spectrum it ought to locate itself, the answer being moderately left of the two main parties. All three parties were converging toward the ideological centre, each trying to present itself as the better manager of public finances.

In the wake of the NDP's disappointment at the results of the 1999 electoral outing — many thought the party had a crack at winning government — Robert Chisholm decided to step down and in July 2000 the party chose Helen MacDonald, a teacher from Cape Breton, as his successor in a closely fought contest among four aspirants. However, she had to relinquish the leadership after her loss in a by-election forced her to try to lead the party from outside the legislature. Now the party is looking for another leader. Some observers might persist in regarding the rising prospects of the NDP as an indicator of the popularity of old-style, debt-and-deficit politics. The better view, however, is to interpret them as a signal from a public which seems prepared to consider a departure from the old two-party mould.

GOVERNMENT STRUCTURES

An important part of the public agenda in the last two decades is the objective of smaller government. The efforts made to gain the objective range from straightforward cuts in the number of civil service positions as well as cuts in the number of programs on offer to the use of the private sector to deliver programs formerly administered by government to the adoption of business procedures in the evaluation of how well government works.

Despite the growing problems of public finance in the 1980s, the federal government only began pursuing the sorts of measures just identified in the early1990s in an effort to get its own finances under control and to meet the new challenges of the day, the most obvious being the technological revolution underway. The provincial governments have been engaged in similar efforts, including the governments in the Atlantic region, whose efforts to downsize their bureaucracies were particularly painful in the context of the economic recession in the opening years of the decade. In addition, the same governments are still wrestling with the old problem of the role of patronage in staffing the civil service.

The most spectacular assault on patronage came from Liberal Premier John Savage in Nova Scotia, spectacular because it ended in his own demise as leader. When Savage assumed office in 1993, the Liberal Party had been out of power for 15 years. The new premier, a medical doctor and an experienced municipal politician, had made a commitment to end patronage practices in the campaign. Taking office, he was hit immediately with demands from Liberal partisans for road patronage, perhaps the oldest and most resilient political tradition in the province. In this area, senior positions and contracts fell outside of public service hiring and bidding procedures. As a result, a change in government ordinarily signaled a complete change in workers, supervisors and contract-holders. The Savage government managed to bring road work within the ambit of public service procedures, albeit in the wake of unhappy partisans who found this denial of the spoils of office galling.[34] However, it should be noted that there was enough slippage under Savage's Liberal successor, Premier MacLellan, to inspire the Conservatives to include a plank in their 1999 campaign platform to "establish a proper, non-partisan process for ensuring that rural roads and highways meet the needs of Nova Scotians and support economic development."[35] The new Conservative government's record on this front is not yet clear, although to date Premier Hamm has not been the target of disaffected Conservative partisans over roads.

Road work is the public face of patronage; as important as the contest between patronage appointments and merit-based appointments in the rest of the public service. Here, too, the Savage government advanced substantial reforms, replacing the old Civil Service Commission with a new staffing regime in a newly established Department of Human Resources. In addition to the expressed need to protect appointments from political interference, the new regime was designed to permit the delegation to departments of authority over various aspects of staffing and personnel administration. According to one close observer of these matters, the new regime is in line with public management reforms in other Westminster systems, and it has contributed to a "greater professionalism" in the staffing function.[36] Nevertheless, it must be kept in mind that in Nova Scotia the premier appoints the deputy ministers, and in doing so he signals to the public service as a whole the government's attitude on the issue of public service professionalism versus partisan loyalty in the staffing of the most senior government positions.

The Atlantic governments have also engaged in restructuring themselves. This has been part and parcel of the effort at downsizing and the adoption of new public management ideas drawn from business models. A notable example of restructuring is PEI, where successive governments have gone about implementing some of the recommendations of the Program and Expenditure Review Commission, which reported to the Liberal government in 1987. The commission was nothing if not up-to-date. In addition to the advocacy of smaller government doing fewer things, it applied the market paradigm to the governing process, transforming citizens into cost-conscious consumers, civil servants into employees competing with private sector employees in terms of wages and benefits, and government into competitive service provision. It has been pointed out that the commission's ideas were more radical than the restructuring efforts that flowed in its wake.[37] Nevertheless, these efforts have been substantial, and pursued by Liberal and Conservative governments. In addition to the inevitable downsizing of government, they include the use of non-departmental agencies, the employees of which are not necessarily covered by the traditional civil service standards of employment; pay reduction schemes; and a reorganized personnel management system designed to inject business-style flexibility into the deployment of government employees. Newfoundland, too, has undergone its version of the new public-management-style reforms, initially under the auspices of the governments of Clyde Wells, 1989–96. Wells' successor, Brian Tobin, continued in the same vein. His government established a series of task forces on governance in the spring of 1997 and subsequently undertook to implement the recommendations, a number of which concern human-resources development in the career public service.[38]

New Brunswick has been a leader in the organization of modern government, including the development (during Premier Louis Robichaud's tenure, 1960–70) and maintenance of a "top-flight public service."[39] When Liberal leader Frank McKenna took office in 1987, he was concerned to reposition the province economically to meet the challenges posed by reduced federal transfers to the province, on the one hand, and the global, free trade economy, on the other. In connection with government and the public service, this included downsizing; reorganization measures; the privatization of selected services, including the building and maintenance of schools and prisons; the introduction of performance-based incentives for management; and decentralization in the use of financial resources by managers. An energetic reformer, McKenna was prepared to experiment with the repertoire of techniques in the new public management approach.

As the foregoing material indicates, the governments of the Atlantic provinces have not turned their backs on the governance paradigm of our day. On the contrary, they have adopted it and found ways to execute it. They have downsized, privatized, contracted-out the delivery of various goods and services, and introduced market-style incentives within the organization of the public service. As a result, the only leg on which the Old Canada charge can rest is patronage. Have Atlantic governments eliminated patronage? No. Have they made any efforts to minimize it? Yes. Have the other Canadian governments eliminated it? No. Will the governments ever eliminate it? No. So long as Canadians retain free government and political parties, the elected officials will be inclined to work with their political friends.

CONCLUSION

While much of the evidence belies the Old Canada charge, there is other evidence that appears to favour it, some of it quite recent. An example is the activity of the governing federal Liberal Party, which continues to spend money on the region through the Atlantic Canada Opportunities Agency (ACOA). ACOA, of course, is the *bête noire* of the neo-conservatives because it is a government agency established to assist regional economic development with the use of public funds. To neo-conservatives it is a visible manifestation of statist and anti-market thinking. It is also the latest in a long series of federal regional development initiatives dating back at least to the establishment of the Department of Regional Economic Expansion (DREE) in 1969.

Over the years there have been some successful development programs.[40] Nevertheless, in general the conclusion is a record of failure, a result for which various technical and administrative reasons have been advanced.[41] Looming large as a factor in the failure is the political factor, that is, the politicization of regional economic development. In an early analysis of ACOA, Herman Bakvis emphasized the agency's function in serving the Cabinet ministers from the Atlantic region by enabling them to be stronger advocates of the region's needs. He also warned that "unless carefully managed, bureaucratic resources placed in the hands of ministers for regional purposes can end up being used in highly parochial fashion. Rather than promoting the welfare of the region as a whole, or even particular provinces, the benefits of having access to bureacratic expertise may well end serving the needs only of the minister's riding."[42] Highly publicized ACOA grants in federal ministers' ridings during the 1990s appear to have borne out Bakvis' warning. The agency is dismissed with contempt by editorial writers.[43] And in the 1997 federal election, the Reform Party vowed to eliminate it.[44] Nevertheless, in old-economy style, in the months preceding the general election in November 2000, the federal Liberals announced a $700 million economic development strategy for Atlantic Canada to be administered by ACOA,[45] a move immediately denounced by Premier Harris of Ontario as "another example of taxpayers' dollars just being wasted."[46] Cynics could only nod and murmur — *plus ça change.*

Meanwhile, the Atlantic premiers managed to contribute to Old Canada cynicism about the region when they established the Council of Atlantic Premiers, an organization discussed earlier in the chapter. The council is intended to advance cooperative behaviour among the provincial governments in terms of policies in the region. But the intention is also to generate strength through unity in dealings with the federal government, particularly the effort to extract more dollars from it. Indeed, as a local newspaper reported none too suavely, "Squeezing cash from Ottawa tops agenda for Atlantic council."[47] This provoked a swift response from the president of the Atlantic Institute for Market Studies (AIMS), who wrote: "These guys still don't get it. The old regime is dying all around them, and still they bang out the old tunes on the fiddle."[48]

Undoubtedly there are a few old tunes about, but there are also new ones. A more balanced view is to appreciate the new as well as the continuities. The new developments include a perceptible shift in public attitudes away from low levels of trust, efficacy and interest in politics to levels commensurate with the norm in the rest of the country; some interesting departures in voting patterns in recent federal and provincial elections, largely in relation to the NDP; the development of a competitive three-party system in Nova Scotia; and the reorganization and reduction in size of the public service as well as an emphasis on alternative ways of delivering public services. Provincial governments have not turned away from the perceived need to diminish the role of the state in society in the effort to cope with the burden of debts and deficits. Instead they have attempted to respond to it, and in so doing adopted some of the market-oriented justification that lies behind it. Moreover, they have acted in the context of economies that, for decades, have been far less robust than is the case in other provinces.

Speaking of provincial economies, it must be pointed out that the region has been experiencing strong growth recently, in part owing to the effects of the booming offshore oil and gas industry and related pipeline developments. In their budgets for 2001–02, Nova Scotia and New Brunswick are forecasting economic growth at 2.3 percent and 2.1 percent, respectively. PEI has seen three consecutive years of growth on the order of 3 percent per year, and is projecting 2 percent for 2001. Newfoundland and Labrador came off a very strong year in 2000 that saw a 5.3 percent growth rate, and the forecast is 2 for

2001. As indicated, the offshore oil and gas industry is highly significant in all of this, and there is more to come. In addition to the Hibernia and Sable projects, there is the Laurentian sub-basin still to be tapped. The sub-basin, said to be 60,000 square kilometres in the deep water south of the Grand Banks, is believed to encompass some nine trillion cubic feet of natural gas and 700 million barrels of oil, much larger than any of the finds to date. Currently, Newfoundland and Nova Scotia are wrangling over the marine boundaries of the sub-basin before a three-member, federally-appointed tribunal.[49]

Given the record of change as well as continuity in the region, the empirical claim of the Bliss paradigm is unsustainable. And the moralizing dimension loses its bite, too. Taken on its own, the moralizing means little anyway. For example, Bliss says that the New Canada effort to shrink government is part of the drive to liberate individuals and the private sector and to learn how to be truly competitive in a global economy. He compares this to the Old Canada preference for strong government, which he thinks encourages deference over competitiveness. This is not the place to undertake a foray onto the terrain of moral philosophy. Still, where would Bliss be if deference were simply an outward indicator of a large concern for the well-being of the community, while muscular competitiveness turned out to be the mark of moral indifference to anything beyond self-interest.

NOTES

1. Michael Bliss, "The Fault Lines Deepen," *The Globe and Mail*, 2 May 2000, p. A15.

2. Ibid.

3. Murray Edelman, *The Symbolic Uses of Politics* (Urbana, IL: University of Illinois Press, 1967), p. 31.

4. See Jennifer Smith, "The Economic Case for Political Union in Atlantic Canada," in *Has the Time Come? Perspectives on Cooperation*, ed. Maurice Mandale and William J. Milne (Fredericton, NB: Atlantic Provinces Economic Council and the Vaughan Chair in Regional Economics, 1996), pp. 9-19.

5. See Ian Stewart, "Simeon and Elkins Revisited: Regional Political Cultures in Canada," in his *Roasting Chestnuts: The Mythology of Maritime Political Culture* (Vancouver: UBC Press, 1994).

6. James Bickerton, "Atlantic Canada: Regime Change in a Dependent Region," in *Canadian Politics*, 2d ed., ed. James P. Bickerton and Alain-G. Gagnon (Peterborough: Broadview Press, 1994), pp. 427-28; Murray Beck, "An Atlantic Region Political Culture: A Chimera," in *Eastern and Western Perspectives*, ed. David Jay Bercuson and Phillip A. Buckner (Toronto: University of Toronto Press, 1981), pp. 147-68.

7. Janine Brodie, "Regions and Regionalism," in *Canadian Politics*, ed. Bickerton and Gagnon, p. 410.

8.   Chris Morris, "Atlantic Premiers Launch New Alliance," *Chronicle-Herald*, Halifax, 15 May 2000, p. A1.

9.   For a full account of the subject, see Ernest R. Forbes, *The Maritime Rights Movement, 1919-1927: A Study in Canadian Regionalism* (Montreal and Kingston: McGill-Queen's University Press, 1979).

10. Bickerton, "Atlantic Canada: Regime Change in a Dependent Region," p. 429.

11. Richard Simeon and David Elkins, "Regional Political Cultures in Canada," *Canadian Journal of Political Science* 7,3(1974):415.

12. Stewart, "Simeon and Elkins Revisited," p. 8.

13. Simeon and Elkins, "Regional Political Cultures in Canada," p. 404.

14. Ibid., p. 405.

15. Ibid., p. 433.

16. Stewart, "Simeon and Elkins Revisited," p. 22.

17. Elisabeth Gidengil, André Blais, Richard Nadeau and Neil Nevitte, "Making Sense of Regional Voting in the 1997 Canadian Federal Election: Liberal and Reform Support Outside Quebec," *Canadian Journal of Political Science* 32,2 (1999):262.

18. Neil Nevitte, *The Decline of Deference: Canadian Value Change in Cross-National Perspective* (Peterborough: Broadview Press, 1996), p. 67.

19. Frank L. Graves, "Rethinking Government As if People Mattered: From 'Reaganomics' to 'Humanomics,'" in *How Ottawa Spends, 1999-2000 — Shape Shifting: Canadian Governance Toward the 21st Century*, ed. Leslie A. Pal (Toronto: Oxford University Press Canada, 1999), p. 42.

20. Ibid., p. 44.

21. J.M. Beck, *Pendulum of Power: Canada's Federal Elections* (Toronto: Prentice-Hall, 1968), p. 271.

22. I am relying on the data presented in James Bickerton, Alain-G. Gagnon and Patrick J. Smith, *Ties That Bind: Parties and Voters in Canada* (Toronto: Oxford University Press, 1999).

23. See Neil Nevitte, André Blais, Elisabeth Gidengil and Richard Nadeau, *Unsteady State: The 1997 Canadian Federal Election* (Toronto: Oxford University Press, 2000), p. 83.

24. Ibid.

25. Ibid., p. 84.

26. Ian Stewart, "Free-Floating Failure: The NDP in the Maritimes," in *Roasting Chestnuts*, p. 62.

27. Stephen Muller, "Federalism and the Party System in Canada," in *Canadian Federalism: Myth or Reality*, ed. J. Peter Meekison (Toronto: Methuen, 1968), pp. 123-24.

28. Michael Bliss, "The Long, Empty Future of the Tories," *National Post*, 13 May 2000, p. B4.

29. Rand Dyck, *Provincial Politics in Canada: Towards the Turn of the Century*, 3rd ed. (Toronto: Prentice Hall Canada, 1996), pp. 200-01.

30. J. Stefan Dupré, "Taming the Monster: Debt, Budgets, and Federal-Provincial Fiscal Relations at the *Fin de Siècle*," in *Provinces: Canadian Provincial Politics*, ed. Christopher Dunn (Peterborough: Broadview Press, 1996), pp. 379-97.

31. Allan M. Maslove and Kevin D. Moore, "Provincial Budgeting," in *Provinces: Canadian Provincial Politics*, ed. Dunn, pp. 321-50.

32. Nova Scotia, Chief Electoral Officer, *Report: Return of General Election for the House of Assembly: Thirty-Fourth General Election, 1998* (Halifax, NS: Government Printers, 1998), p. 262.

33. Nova Scotia, Chief Electoral Officer, *Report: Return of General Election for the House of Assembly, Thirty-Fifth General Election, 1999*, Volume 1 (Halifax, NS: Government Printers, 1999), p. 248.

34. Peter Aucoin, "Nova Scotia: Government Restructuring and the Career Public Service," in *Government Restructuring and Career Public Services*, Monograph No. 23, ed. Evert Lindquist (Toronto: The Institute of Public Administration of Canada, 2000), pp. 232-33.

35. Nova Scotia, Progressive Conservative Party, *Strong Leadership: A Clear Course*, 1999, p. 4.

36. Ibid., p. 244.

37. John Crossley, "The Career Public Service in Prince Edward Island: Evolution and Challenges," in *Government Restructuring and Career Public Services*, ed, Lindquist, p. 220.

38. Christopher Dunn, "The Newfoundland Public Service: The Past as Prologue?" in *Government Restructuring and Career Public Services*, ed. Lindquist, pp. 201-03.

39. Donald Savoie, "New Brunswick: A "Have" Public Service in a "Have-less" Province," in *Government Restructuring and Career Public Services*, ed. Lindquist, p. 260.

40. See Donald J. Savoie, "Regional Development: The Case of Prince Edward Island," in *The Maritime Provinces: Looking to the Future*, ed. Donald J. Savoie and Ralph Winters (Moncton: The Canadian Institute for Research on Regional Development, 1993), pp. 189-212.

41. James Bickerton, "Regionalism in Canada" in *Canadian Politics*, ed. Bickerton and Gagnon, p. 226.

42. Herman Bakvis, "The Maritimes: Looking to Ottawa with Clout," in *The Maritime Provinces*, ed. Savoie and Winter, p. 274.

43. "Atlantic Canada's Bind," *The Globe and Mail*, 22 May 2000, p. A12.

44. Reform Party of Canada, *A Fresh Start for Canadians*, 3rd ed. (Calgary: Reform Fund Canada, Official Agent for the Reform Party of Canada, 1997), p. 7.

45. Shawn McCarthy, "Atlantic Canada Gets $700-million Boost: PM Calls it an Investment but Critics Say Real Aim is to Lift Sagging Liberal Fortunes in Region," *The Globe and Mail*, 30 June 2000, p. A6.

46. Mark MacKinnon, "Alliance Pulls its Punches Criticizing Atlantic Spending," *The Globe and Mail*, 30 June 2000.

47. Chris Morris, "Premiers Team Up to Have 'Bigger Impact,'" *The Chronicle-Herald*, Halifax, 16 May 2000, p. A8.

48. Brian Crowley, "Not Quite Ready to Kick the Habit," *The Globe and Mail*, 19 May 2000, p. A15.

49. Stephen Bornais, "Nova Scotia Draws the Line: Province on Offensive as Seafloor Boundary Dispute Hearings Open," *The Daily News*, 13 March 2001, p. 4.

7

Quebec's Changing Political Culture and the Future of Federal-Provincial Relations in Canada

Daniel Salée

La question nationale et le désir de souveraineté ne semblent plus avoir la même profondeur politique qu'ils ont déjà eu dans la conscience collective des Québécois. On peut se demander si le nationalisme québécois et la culture politique collectiviste qu'il informait jadis constituent encore des facteurs déterminants dans la manière dont la province aborde ses rapports avec le reste du Canada. Cet article soutient que bien que les revendications nationalitaires et la pugnacité historique du Québec à l'égard du Canada ne soient pas sans effet, des changements significatifs dans la perception qu'ont d'eux-mêmes les Québécois ont affecté le discours et les pratiques nationalistes et ont conduit à l'émergence de visions contradictoires de la communauté politique québécoise. L'unité de pensée et les consensus qui ont déjà animé les actions du Québec à l'endroit d'Ottawa semblent s'étioler et n'ont plus nécessairement l'impact recherché quand vient le temps d'affronter le gouvernement fédéral. Cet article identifie et analyse trois transformations importantes de la culture politique québécoise qui expliquent cet état de choses et qui pourraient bien influencer la nature et l'orientation des rapports du Québec avec Ottawa au cours des années à venir : la reformulation du discours nationaliste québécois, l'érosion de la cohésion sociale et la fragmentation concomitante de l'appartenance politique et, enfin, la reconfiguration des principes de gestion sociale et économique qui ont guidé le développement du Québec au cours des dernières décennies. Divers scénarios quant à l'avenir des rapports Québec-Canada sont évoqués en conclusion à la lumière de l'évolution possible de ces transformations.

INTRODUCTION

Political developments in Quebec since the 1995 referendum may prompt some to anticipate that the days of protracted confrontation between Quebec and Ottawa are soon coming to an end. Indeed, the relatively poor showing of the Bloc Québécois in the November 2000 federal election, the steady decline in levels of popular support for the sovereignty option,[1] polls indicating that

Quebecers would prefer to look for solutions to the constitutional impasse within the institutional confines of Canadian federalism,[2] their indifference over the enactment of Bill 99, the National Assembly's response to the *Clarity Act*,[3] and Premier Lucien Bouchard's own admission of failure at bringing about sovereignty in his resignation speech on 11 January 2001 may appear to some observers and commentators as telling signs that the Quebec sovereignist movement is teetering on the verge of irrelevance or, at least, that nationalist sentiments are currently of little import in Quebec's political life. In addition, during the past year, some prominent public intellectuals close to, or supportive of, the sovereignty movement have essentially disavowed the dream of an independent Quebec, and proposed instead that Quebecers explore other avenues of self-affirmation within the institutional confines of Canadian federalism.[4]

As students of Canadian and Quebec politics know well, Quebec's relationship with the rest of Canada in the second half of the twentieth century has been largely shaped by a culture of antagonism and resistance that owed much to Quebec's multifaceted but sustained bid for national self-affirmation. In its various incarnations, usually as a perceived threat to the unity of the Canadian state and the country's social cohesion, Quebec nationalism has had considerable bearing on the internal and constitutional dynamics of the Canadian federation over the past four decades.[5] But should the political occurrences of the past year be interpreted as indications of a shift in Quebec's political culture that may be about to lead to a major transformation of the relationship between Quebec and the rest of Canada? As this volume takes stock of changes in Canada's political culture(s) and their impact on the state of the federation, two questions obviously stand out with regard to Quebec: Are Quebec nationalism and its attendant political culture of collective rights claims still significant factors in the province's relations with Ottawa and the rest of the country? Are they likely to determine the nature of Quebec-Canada relations and influence Canada's constitutional agenda in the foreseeable future?

In answer to these questions I argue in this essay that while nationalist claims and the historic pugnaciousness of Quebec's political attitude in matters of national unity should not yet be discounted, they are engulfed in a cloud of indeterminacy which, at this juncture at least, makes it difficult to assert with confidence what the basis and outlook of future Canada-Quebec relations will be. As the political history of Quebec since the 1980 referendum attests, one would be ill-advised to forecast the disappearance of the sovereignist movement and nationalistic claims from the province's political landscape. Despite the fading fortune of sovereignists and their option during the better part of the 1980s, Quebec nationalism re-emerged forcefully at the time of the debacle of the Meech Lake Accord and picked up enough steam in the ensuing years to nearly win the day in the 1995 referendum. Although the nationalist sentiments of Quebecers may seem fickle at times, nationalism has remained a permanent fixture of modern Quebec's political imagination and, in all likelihood, will continue to be so. However, the last decade has been witness to some degree of change in collective self-perception, which has affected the nationalist discourse and practices, and led competing visions of the political community and differing conceptions of social and economic management to oppose each other in the political arena. Quebec is not the consensus-driven society that eager nationalist politicians often portray it to be. Common grounds that formerly brought socio-political actors to speak with one voice in response to Ottawa are eroding, defusing in the process any semblance of unity Quebec might need to challenge the federal government credibly.

Hence, although it is not possible to anticipate with definite certainty the shape of things to come with respect to Quebec-Ottawa relations, there is movement within Quebec. Trends and undercurrents that are likely to have an influence are emerging and, in some cases, are even firmly taking hold. In this chapter I propose to map out what are perhaps the three most significant ones, namely the reformulation of the nationalist discourse, the erosion of social cohesion and the fragmentation of political belonging, and the reconfiguration of social and economic management. I look at each of these in turn and conclude by examining scenarios that can be derived from their possible evolution and applied to Quebec-Canada relations.

As should become clear, the notion of political culture that guides my analysis eschews traditional concepts and analytical approaches that are well-entrenched in the specialized literature. Rather than emphasize individual and institutional behaviour, individual or collective psychology, public opinion and levels of political participation, I take political culture as evolving out of the particular ways in which individuals and groups in any society formulate, negotiate, realize and impose the competing claims they make upon one another and upon the general direction of society. The political culture of a given society is cast in the particular dialectical dynamics of power that oppose social agents in their bid to shape the public agenda to their advantage and benefit. In this sense, political culture refers to the "historically contingent practices and beliefs that give legitimacy to political structures and political authority to individuals and 'interests,' and which, in turn, political actors use creatively to affect public policy or, more generally, public life."[6] By definition, then, a political culture is not static; it is likely to change according to transformations in socio-economic hierarchies and patterns of social and political domination.

THE "NEW" QUEBEC NATIONALIST DISCOURSE

As a result of the bad press and negative image associated with nationalistic and ethnicity-driven upheavals in many parts of the world in recent years, a number of political philosophers and social theorists, in the West particularly, have felt compelled to uphold the virtues of nationalism, stress its liberal nature, insist on its emancipatory potential, or point out its openness to diversity.[7] Others concerned with the particularistic and chauvinistic outlook of strictly defined, essentialist, national identities have proposed to anchor the national community in overarching, broad-based, legal, civic and above all democratic principles to which any reasonable person can readily adhere,[8] and which can reach beyond the limited identities comprising a society (multicultural ones in particular). Though their respective views are not necessarily unified conceptually, they are united in their desire to lay the moral and normative foundations most likely to favour social cohesion and solidarity in increasingly plural and diverse societies. Their work is influential, and politicians whose socio-political goals and advancement hinge on the recognition and affirmation of an independent nation find in their theorizing much support for the renewed, broader, and more inclusive sense of the national community they like to advocate.

Quebec's leading nationalists and current sovereignist government are a case in point. Over the past two decades, the nationalist discourse elaborated both by the state and intellectuals in Quebec has progressively rejected, at least in public documents, the traditional, ethnic and cultural connotations, which, until about the early 1980s, essentially informed Quebec nationalism. Accordingly, today Quebec nationalists claim to understand *la nation québécoise* no longer as the sum total of an historically determined, common cultural experience shared mainly by French-speaking Quebecers, but as the gathering, through citizenship, of reasonable and equal social and political beings around rational, democratic institutions upon which they all have agreed, regardless of their differences and diverging interests. In this sense, the nation is presented as a plural and heterogeneous political community, and as a civic project to be accomplished within given, geographic or territorial boundaries. This means, concretely, that everyone and anyone who lives within the Quebec territory is considered a citizen,[9] hence a *Québécois*, an appellation which is no longer reserved to identify only the French Canadians of old. Quebec's "new" nationalism encourages pluralism beyond the historical, culturally determined confines that used to define *la nation québécoise*, celebrates diversity, promotes the integrity of minority cultures, and posits at the same time the Quebec state as the rallying point with which all can and should identify.[10] Political self-determination, and eventually, the full independence of the Quebec state from Canada are matters for all Quebecers to decide and not simply the francophone majority. Implicit in this view of things is the idea that Quebecers, regardless of their origin or background, have to work together to develop a *culture publique commune*, a common civic culture, based on universal values to which everyone can readily subscribe (democracy, open civic participation, equality between men and women, freedom of speech, socioeconomic solidarity), with the French language as the central vector of its reproduction and transmission.[11]

This relatively new expression of Quebec nationalism vindicates the will of most liberal proponents of nationalism to make it a morally, intellectually and politically sustainable project. The emphasis of current Quebec nationalism on pluralism meets the liberal requisite of unimpeded individualism, its insistence on democratic citizenship satisfies the liberal faith in universal values, and its aspiration for a common civic culture fulfills the fundamentally integrative bent of the liberal state. While it can be said that for an extended period of the province's history, nationalism in Quebec bore the unequivocal imprint of ethnicity and justified what some would see as quasi-tribal attitudes, it is also true that nationalist exhortations led to a large movement of self-affirmation, democratic emancipation and social change in the 1960s and 1970s. Quebec nationalism went from a conservative defence of French-Canadian social, cultural, and moral values against the British ruler, to confident, self-possessing, at times aggressive, claims of self-determination and political independence for the socio-economic promotion of French-speaking *Québécois*. Today, Quebec nationalism is still imbued with this forward-looking attitude, and has enlarged its original conception of national identity to include all who live and reside in the Quebec territory as equal and full partners in nation-building. This sense of the Quebec nation has pervaded public documents and policies for over a decade now, and no nationalist leader or intellectual would entertain, at least officially, any other view of the nation. The type of nationalist discourse that currently holds sway in Quebec is premised on inclusiveness and openness to diversity.[12]

Critics and political opponents of Quebec nationalists routinely dispute this view of things and insist that no matter how urbane and politically advanced Quebec nationalism appears in theory, it is in fact parochial, inward-looking and xenophobic.[13] They argue that despite its high-minded, inclusive references to all-encompassing citizenship, it remains ultimately geared toward and conceived for "old stock" francophone Quebecers. The new brand of Quebec nationalism is but the brain-child of a state-engineered, public relations strategy designed to hide its true nature and cajole public opinion.

Critics and foes notwithstanding, while it is not improbable that public image considerations play a role, the emergence of civic nationalism in Quebec's political discourse is a more complex phenomenon and is best understood as the result of the combined action of several factors related to the general process of socio-economic transformation experienced by Quebec society in the past three or four decades.

In the 1960s and 1970s French-speaking Quebecers gained remarkable confidence in their abilities to exercise control over their personal and collective destinies.[14] As they succeeded in imposing their culture and language as the primary conduits of social and economic life, the English progressively ceased to figure as the oppressive other against whom their own identity was defined and made sense. Targeting the English and Anglo dominance as the source of

French Canadian woes (as pre-modern and early modern Quebec nationalists often tended to do) appeared increasingly ineffective and futile by the 1980s as socio-economic power started shifting clearly in favour of French-speaking Quebecers, and elements of Anglophone culture began to be considered more as potential tools to penetrate international markets and further Quebec's economic development than as instruments of oppression of an hostile neighbour. This gradual disappearance of the English as symbolic foe contributed to a relative de-ethnicization of *Québécois* claims and national identity. Nowadays, sovereignist and nationalist appeals are more likely to challenge the Canadian federal government over administrative and jurisdictional issues than to focus on the Anglophone minority over matters of collective solidarity or inter-groups equity. While references to ethnic consciousness may still have currency in public discourse, they do not constitute as significant a stimulus of nationalist mobilization as they once did.

The influx and increased visibility of immigrants in many sectors of Quebec's social and economic life have also influenced the transformation of the nationalist discourse, if only for sheer political reasons. In the wake of their defeat in the first referendum on independence in 1980, nationalist leaders became aware that if immigrants were not made somehow to feel that they are an integral part of Quebec society, they would never support the sovereignist project. This in itself was a powerful incentive to modify the traditional, nationalist discourse and make it more inclusive. Nationalist leaders clearly understood after 1980 that immigrants and minorities could not be counted out of any democratic attempt at turning Quebec into an independent country. Indeed, the state's immigration policies and general approach toward ethnocultural minorities since then have by and large reflected a new and greater sensitivity to the social reality of immigration as well as a more ready willingness to address and satisfy the political demands of diversity.[15] The language policy of the late 1970s opened the way in this regard, for it allowed for a much more considerable degree of interaction between immigrants and the rest of the population than had been the case until that point. By requiring immigrant children to attend French schools, language legislation progressively socialized immigrants and several minority groups into the francophone mainstream, bringing larger segments of these constituencies to take a more active and more direct part in the social, cultural, and economic life of Quebec society.[16] French-speaking Quebecers have become, with time, less likely to look upon immigrants and minorities as a threat to the integrity and permanence of Quebec's majority culture. Many among them have developed as a result an increasingly positive attitude toward immigration and ethnocultural diversity and are less prone to differentiate between "us and them," at least in public settings and situations.[17] There has been in fact a significant evolution in public mentality toward immigration, which has translated into greater social acceptance of immigrants and a narrowing of the symbolic gap between majority and minorities. While this does not imply that ethnicity has become irrelevant in public discourse,[18] or that civic integration is a total success,[19] or even less that socio-economic exclusion on the basis of ethnocultural differences has been eradicated,[20] this evolution has led to a conception of the Quebec nation as encompassing — in principle at least — far more than the French-speaking majority. The political program of the sovereignist Parti Québécois, for example, now clearly acknowledges that the Quebec people is made up of every individual who resides within Quebec territory;[21] up until that time its notion of the Quebec people included primarily Quebecers of French origin to whom were added, almost like an afterthought, all those who had joined them and shared in their culture.[22]

The expressed will of Quebec's economic elite to face up to the challenges and imperatives of economic globalization can also be cited as another factor accounting for Quebec nationalism's emphasis on citizenship. The nationalist state policies of the 1960s and 1970s largely contributed to the social and political ascent of a new class of francophone capitalists who, since the early 1980s, have come to prevail in the economic and political affairs of the province.[23] This new economic elite has been particularly anxious to tackle new markets and expand its international economic horizon.[24] Its eagerness in this regard heightened its sensitivity to global pressures, made it more open to the world, and led it to realize as a result the limitations a narrowly defined conception of the Quebec nation could impose not only on the province's ability to grow, but also on its own prospects: too strong a focus on ethnicity or particularism could turn Quebec nationalism into a liability. Hence, the current insistence of Quebec's nationalist discourse on citizenship largely reflects the concern of Quebec's economic elite to defuse the "dangers" of the postmodernist and postcolonialist claims that have come to pervade Quebec's political landscape. These claims presumably contribute to the fragmentation of the unity of the political community, bring about political instability, and compromise the quality of the socio-political environment needed for the market to thrive.[25] Like the economic elite of most contemporary western societies, Quebec's capitalists are more comfortable with the integrative bent and universalist pretenses of liberal-democratic citizenship.

One can dispute whether Quebec's new nationalism is really civic, whether it can ever be, or whether ethnicity is bound to remain a significant dimension of any nationalistic expression. Be that as it may though, the civic nationalist discourse is real. It implies a qualitative shift in the way the nationalist intellectual and political elites are conceiving Quebec, and in what they are asking the population to understand Quebec to be. Gone are the visceral, emotional appeals to bond as a linguistically and culturally distinct people. This may appear to many as a good thing and a sign of democratic progress. But gone also is the spark that has motivated successive generations of Quebecers to mobilize in support of what they saw as a "struggle" of national liberation against the Anglo-Canadian "oppressor"; the same spark, in fact, that ignited several federal-provincial confrontations and constitutional conflicts between Quebec and Ottawa.

The civic nationalist discourse is offering Quebecers a legalistic project couched in a formal, purportedly neutral sense of liberal-democratic citizenship. Paradoxically, though it seeks to broaden the nation, to make it as politically compelling and inclusive a category as possible, civic nationalism as formulated by its Quebec proponents insists rather on the jurisdictional and territorial essence of the Quebec nation. It calls on Quebecers to support not so much a renewed sense of political belonging, but turf wars waged by political apparatchiks and bureaucrats in Quebec City and Ottawa. It implicitly asks them to choose not so much between two very distinct visions of nation (Quebec versus Canada) or two very distinct social projects — one, Quebec's, which would be significantly better than the other — but between two civic logics, two conceptions of socio-economic management, and two underlying concerns for social cohesion that are basically identical, and differ only in terms of who is formulating them.

Quebec civic nationalists endorse in fact the same fundamental values and guiding principles of political community and social cohesion that inform the current, prevailing vision of the Canadian state on issues of national unity; that is, unadulterated reason and "common sense," the fusion of social and ethnocultural singularities into one unified conception of the community, and the dominance of liberal-democratic norms of socio-political transactions.[26] This is not to suggest that Quebec and Ottawa are so similar that the days of administrative and constitutional wrangling are over. But if the whole Quebec nationalist project boils down simply to asserting jurisdictional boundaries and administrative prerogatives, and if the respective, internal logics driving the Quebec state and the Canadian state become increasingly blurred and indistinguishable, the Quebec public may well wonder, what, then, is the point of nationalism, and, by extension, of pursuing sovereignty?

On the face of it, civic nationalism may seem like a more "advanced," more civilized form of communal expression, but to the extent that it waters down Quebec's pre-political collective identity — that very same identity in defence and promotion of which much of Quebec's political mobilizations of the past four decades against Ottawa were championed — it also dulls the sense of outrage and injury necessary to galvanize political energies in support of Quebec sovereignty. As *indépendantiste* political philosopher Serge Cantin noted recently, "the new credo of an open, plural, multi or transcultural Quebec nation undermines the very project it purports to advocate by gradually stripping it of its *raison d'être*. Indeed it implies that we should disappear on account of altruism, that we should renounce, in the name of democracy, the very principle of democracy, that is the right of peoples to self-determination and self-government."[27]

Cantin's lament is obviously rooted in a fundamentally ethnic, almost nostalgic understanding of the Quebec nation, but nevertheless it cogently underscores the paradox of civic nationalism in Quebec. Without a robust and unequivocal ethnocultural identity thoroughly pervading the collective sense of self, can the will to sovereignty be fully carried out; can it translate into appropriate and meaningful political action capable of truly dismantling the Canadian federation? Clearly, Quebec sovereignists are faced with an interesting challenge. By making Quebec into a civic nation, they have modernized Quebec nationalism, but they also seem to have diluted its ability to persuade Quebecers to engage in a vigourous tug-of-war with Canadian federalism. It may not be impossible that, in the long run, the new, civic sense of nation will bring about a revitalized sense of collective self capable of enjoining Quebecers to resist Canada. At this particular juncture though it is not clear that this is a likely outcome: neither ethnocultural minorities nor "old stock" Quebecers seem ready to endorse the new conception of the Quebec nation fully, the former because they simply do not trust the state's encompassing recasting of the Quebec political community,[28] and the latter, because it propounds an image of the Quebec nation which requires that their existence be somehow downplayed. Although the outlook of what is in store is still largely unfathomable, it seems safe to surmise that the further Quebec's overall political identity will develop from its original, pre-political incarnation, the more unlikely the province will be to articulate its relationship with the rest of Canada in terms of the historical, ethnoscultural duality of the country. Civic nationalism — provided that it is indeed as genuine a feature of Quebec political culture as the official discourse would have us believe — might essentially be making this duality and the dynamics of confrontation that usually ensued, irrelevant.

THE FRAGMENTATION OF POLITICAL BELONGING AND THE DIFFICULT UNITY OF THE POLITICAL SUBJECT

For the better part of the often stormy postwar history of federal-provincial relations, Quebec political leaders could generally assume that they were speaking to Ottawa and the rest of Canada with the full backing of a constituency that was fairly clear about its identity, where it stood within the Canadian federal system, what to expect from it and what to try and gain from it. Of course the strategies they utilized to further Quebec's interests did not necessarily meet with every Quebecer's approval, and, most of the time, the population remained — and still is — fundamentally divided as to the proper course of action needed to deal with Canada. The result of the 1995 referendum highlights this point remarkably. But by and large Quebec political leaders could count on a fairly high degree of consensus over issues such as group identity or the essence of *Québécois*. They could address the rest of Canada with the confidence that the apparent legitimacy such a consensus afforded them: through it, they could claim, Quebec was speaking with one voice on whatever issue was at contention with Ottawa. Unsurprisingly, in most conventional analyses of Quebec-Canada relations, Quebec appears as a rather monolithic political community, imbued with particular traditions and an unequivocal sense of collective self. The Quebec identity is rarely presented as contested, or in the process of transforming itself; the social and ideological contours of "Quebecness" are usually well delineated, taken for granted, practically immutable.

From the point of view of Quebec sovereignists and those who tend to approach Quebec's dealings with Canada from a position of antagonism and competition, this image of collective unity is, understandably, quite indispensable. Within Quebec, the credibility of the whole sovereignist argument rests on its ability to convince the largest number of Quebecers that the Canadian federation is detrimental to their individual and collective well-being. Outside Quebec, the political clout of sovereignists hinges on maintaining the impression that Quebec is one and undivided, and unquestioningly constitutes a distinct national group and political community. Failing success on both fronts, their case against the Canadian state obviously stands little chance of being taken seriously. Today, more perhaps than at any other point in time, the biggest political challenge of Quebec sovereignists is to create a believable, sustainable and most of all effective sense of collective identity. As the foregoing discussion points out, significant alterations in the ethnocultural fabric of Quebec society and a greater openness to social pluralism and diversity led in recent years to a widening of the terms of reference of Quebec identity. It is no longer proper to present Quebec in its primordial guise as the home of "old stock," French-speaking Quebecers. To the extent that the Quebec collective identity now appears inevitably more polymorphous and variegated, it is also more difficult and hardly reasonable in fact to preserve the traditional, ethnicity-based mantle of unity and social cohesion, which was so crucial in justifying and legitimizing the uncompromising stance of successive Quebec governments vis-à-vis Ottawa and the rest of Canada. Indeed, the customary invocation of historical claims might now seem pointless and the recourse to strategies of unyielding confrontation with Ottawa, hardly defensible.

From the strict perspective of Quebec-Canada relations, civic nationalism and its attendant plea for a common public culture offer in a way a convenient response to the political challenge faced by sovereignists. Politically, the civic nationalist discourse works on two fronts: it allows sovereignists to escape the charge of seeking to build a political community founded on the ethnicity of one group, by positing Quebec as an intrinsically and positively plural and diverse society; but it also deflects the political consequences of the democratic obligation of recognizing the existence of multiple political and cultural allegiances, by proclaiming that they can all be subsumed into a common public culture that encompasses all of Quebec's "limited identities." In other words, as the old discourse of ethnocultural cohesion, which long informed Quebec's traditional claims against Ottawa, becomes morally untenable in the heightened liberal-democratic politics of recognition, civic nationalism provides an alternative, universalistic narrative of unity focused on the integrative capacity of the Quebec state as the source of citizenship and social cohesion for all who live in Quebec. Operating as a dual discourse of diversity and unity, it sends a clear message to Ottawa: Quebec society may be internally plural, but the Quebec state speaks for all with one voice. If anything, sovereignists can insist their claims are even stronger and more legitimate than ever before, for the Quebec state duly represents all Quebecers regardless of origin, culture, and time of residence.

But does it? Does the Quebec state constitute a national, encompassing, civic space with which every resident of Quebec readily identifies? Suppose we ignore for a moment the perennial difficulties encountered by sovereignist leaders within the context of the Canadian political process to get Quebec recognized as a self-determined political community. Still, the very idea of Quebec as an independent, self-contained, civic space with universal appeal would be confronted with the same kind of obstacles facing liberal democracies nowadays. In fact, the politics of identity which largely determines the contemporary political dynamics compounds Quebec's historical problem of political recognition, for as social theorist Anna Yeatman noted, "the identity and boundaries of the political community are now subject to politics in ways which both destabilize any appearance of a consensualist national tradition and bring to light the historically changeful artifice by which such traditions are constructed."[29]

Therein lies the crux of the problem for sovereignists. The unity of the political subject and the paradigm of citizenship and belonging that it entails are fast becoming targets of reprobation in modern-day politics. Quebec sovereignists are operating on the basis of a universalist, consensus-driven, Enlightenment discourse at a time when this kind of political narrative, the institutional arrangements it favours and the social hierarchies it justifies are facing enormous resistance throughout the western world.[30] Quebec sovereignty is being challenged not simply because it implies the dismantling of the Canadian state, an unacceptable option for many obviously, but also because insofar as it rests on the fundamental will to create an all-inclusive, universalistic and rationalist civic space, its conceptual underpinnings are under siege.

That is particularly evident on the issue of a common public culture. The Quebec state may well proclaim with the best of inclusivist intentions that Quebecers are united beyond their different identities and allegiances through

French language as the principal vector of public transactions and shared values (democracy, equality of men and women, etc.), but that view is extremely problematic for significant segments of the population. Enjoined by the state to embrace a "moral and civic contract" that essentially urges them to adopt Quebec's historically determined and pre-established set of social and political norms, immigrants, members of ethnocultural minorities and non-francophone Quebecers feel unfairly targeted and forced into endorsing a normative framework that seems extraneous to them. They often react by denouncing the whole notion of a common public culture and by deploring the Quebec state's insistence on French as a common language. They reprove the whole thing as a perverse bid to de-legitimize difference and identity claims, assert the social hegemony of the French ethnic majority, and, in the end, homogenize Quebec society to the advantage of the latter. Some in fact contest that there should even be a common public culture. Representatives of some First Nations, for example, completely deny that the Quebec state has any jurisdictional power over them. They want nothing to do with Quebec's civic and national aspirations, for they essentially see Aboriginal people as separate national entities. The same can be said of the partitionist idea which, idiosyncratic and shaky as it may be, still reflects a profound unwillingness on the part of many to embark into a French-based, majoritarian political nation.

Some analysts have argued that the general opposition of immigrant groups, ethnocultural minorities, Anglophones and First Nations to the sovereignist civic project results from a deliberate and successful political strategy conceived by the federal government. It consists in downplaying Quebec's claims by encouraging ethnic minorities, through the multiculturalism policy, to formulate particularistic claims of their own.[31] Canadian multiculturalism, so the argument goes, puts Quebec's national aspirations on the same footing as the claims of any ethnocultural group. Not only does it ethnicize Quebec's political will to self-determination which tends to make it less morally sustainable in a purportedly liberal democratic political system — but it also negates Quebec's alleged status as one of Canada's "founding nations." In such a context, as no hierarchy of identity claim is possible, members of ethnocultural communities feel confident that they can rightfully oppose Quebec's will to nation.[32] The Canadian state's multiculturalist discourse has succeeded in convincing them that Canada, and not a subaltern jurisdiction, is their primary and most fundamental site of civic and political existence. The argument concludes that Quebec's status within Canada is problematic: so long as Quebec will remain part of Canada, the federal strategy will constantly work to thwart any attempt made by the Quebec state to integrate minority ethnic groups into a fully Quebec-based civic space. As such, it will continuously inhibit the emergence of a genuine Quebec citizenship and prevent, among members of ethnocultural minorities, the development of a feeling of belonging to the Quebec political community.[33]

One can hardly deny that the political particularities of the Quebec-Canada relationship play a role in shaping the civic allegiance of minorities in Quebec. Because of the imperatives of their respective national project, both Quebec and Canada are vying for the support of ethnocultural communities; both claim them as integral to their national core. The stakes are high indeed: in the 1995 referendum even minimal endorsement for sovereignty by ethnocultural communities could have tipped the scale in favour of the "yes" forces. Ethnocultural communities clearly represent important pawns that oppose Quebec and Ottawa in the power struggle. Still, it is misleading to explain the resistance of ethnocultural communities to the national and civic project of Quebec essentially in terms of the adversarial nature of Quebec-Canada relations, or on account of Ottawa's success at checking the political objectives of Quebec nationalism. First of all, such a view incorrectly assumes that all immigrants and members of ethnocultural communities uncritically and unequivocally embrace Canada's multiculturalism and sense of nation; it is simply not the case.[34] But more importantly, it neglects and misjudges Quebec's own internal societal dynamics. Thanks to its own Charter of Rights and Freedoms, its policies of institutional accommodation and employment equity, its recognition of Quebec's Aboriginal peoples as nations, and a few other such initiatives, the Quebec state, like the Canadian state, also encourages minorities to express their claims, to seek entitlements, rights and means of empowerment, and to participate directly in the shaping of the Quebec civic space. That, of course, is a good thing. However, on this score, Quebec is caught in the conundrum which faces most contemporary liberal democracies: it sets for itself fairly high standards of openness to pluralism and diversity, but it remains unwilling or unable to satisfy fully the requirements that such openness implies. The unsettled disputes over several Aboriginal social and economic claims,[35] the continued economic marginalization of racialized minorities and the slow progress in matters of employment equity[36] are but just a few cases in point.

Quebec, like most of its liberal democratic counterparts (including Canada), is incapable of solving the tension extant in modern societies between the dictates of universalism and particularistic claims. This inability only reinforces the frustration of minority claimants, and furthers their resolve to oppose any broad and encompassing policy or political design that excludes them, or that does not take their interests into account to their satisfaction. Although the civic and political project of Quebec sovereignists appears itself as a particularistic challenge in the wider context of the Canadian state, it is construed by minority groups within the political boundaries of the Quebec state and society as an attempt at imposing ideological parameters of social and political behaviour over the definition and development of which they had little or no influence. From their perspective, the attitude of the Quebec state smacks of *dirigiste* socio-political engineering. It is at odds with the "rights

discourse" that has come to prevail in North American politics, and it is contrary in spirit to the Quebec state's own discourse about freedom of choice,
tolerance, and respect for otherness. For many minority groups, opposing Quebec's civic and political project then is not so much tantamount to an
unqualified acceptance of Canada or the Canadian state — although some are
prompt to read it as such — as it is the mark of their dissatisfaction with the
social and political assumptions which lie behind the liberal democratic, unitary conception of the Quebec state.

This said, one should be careful not to exaggerate the implications of the
foregoing for the immediate future. Quebec remains a fairly homogeneous
society where the majority of the population continues to be quite clear about
its identity and sense of political belonging. The unwillingness of minorities
to consent unquestioningly to the sovereignist civic project must not obscure
the fact that on the ground, in everyday life, the French-speaking majority
coexists in relative harmony with members of ethnocultural minorities and
that, as noted above, some degree of social integration of immigrants is taking place. Clearly, Quebec is not a society about to founder in the throes of
inter-ethnic or intercultural rivalries.

Nevertheless, Quebecers'sense of collective identity is undergoing a transformation. It no longer rests on symbolic foundations as secure or as stable as
it may once have appeared. The political prominence of the question of ethnocultural minorities in public debates over the meaning and contents of Quebecness obviously indicates that the recasting of Quebec's collective identity in a
way that would satisfy and rally everyone is far from being a done deal. But
beyond the vagaries of Quebec's internal situation, broader, more contextual
considerations must be added to get the full picture of the difficulty facing the
Quebec state in maintaining the image of socio-political unanimity it needs to
project in its dealing with Ottawa and the rest of Canada. Much of it has to do
with globalization.

Experts are divided over the real effects of globalization on the enduring
character and continued suitability of the nation-state as a sovereign structure
of societal interaction. To some the forces of globalization are inexorably and
fundamentally altering the parameters of citizenship and the nation-state;[37] to
others, though weakened internally and externally, the nation-state remains
an essential and relevant political unit.[38] Still, most people tend to agree that
globalization questions at least the relative autonomy of the nation-state upon
which rests national citizenship; that it undermines the distinctiveness and
originality of national cultures; and that it fosters the rapidly increasing mobility of people across national borders.[39] In this sense, one can assume that
globalization works in two ways with regard to Quebec. As in most countries,
it exposes society to the imperatives of the international economy, and per-
force, to the pressures they exercise on the autonomy of the nation-state —
which obviously cannot bode too well for anyone aspiring to create a sovereign

nation-state. But more significantly, it enhances the political challenges of ethnocultural diversity to the unity of the political subject. The very logic of globalization encourages the engagement of immigrants in transnational socio-political practices. Many maintain strong social, economic, cultural or political ties with their country of origin, and their sense of belonging is consequently shared between here and elsewhere. A recent longitudinal survey of 1,000 immigrants who arrived in Quebec in 1989 revealed, for example, that 93 percent of respondents report sustained involvement with their country of origin for family, business or professional reasons.[40] There is nothing intrinsically wrong with that of course; it is in fact rather normal. But as other studies also indicate, the maintenance of transnational ties, practices, and networks within the host country contributes to creating tensions between the demands of citizenship in the new country (i.e., the state injunction to pledge allegiance, to adopt a new identity and to develop a new sense of belonging), and the enduring appeal of the country of origin.[41] This can suggest that transnational action brings a kind of hybridity nature to the Quebec nation; that alone breaks away from the usual images and representation of Quebec's collective identity. It suggests as well, though, that for many individuals the real emotional anchor of national attachment remains with their country of origin. They either feel disconnected from the civic project of Quebec nationalists, or at a complete loss to grasp the "intricacies" of Quebec-Canada relations; they are simply disinterested in the "stakes" involved in Quebec's historical claims.[42] As the preceding discussion underlines, the fact that Quebec nationalism is a hard sell with immigrants is a complex issue, and this disinterest cannot entirely account for it. However, to the extent that globalization can and will multiply or segment the allegiances of individuals, it does compound the political unity problem of the Quebec state.

Be that as it may, one should be careful not to overstate the role of immigrants and ethnocultural minorities on this score. There is at least one other emerging factor which casts additional doubts over the long-term ability of the Quebec state to maintain the political unity necessary to engage productively with Ottawa. The shifting attitude of native Quebecers vis-à-vis the political status of the language issue deserves attention in this respect. French has long been, and continues to be, a pivotal marker of collective identity in Quebec and an important stake in Quebec-Canada relations. The cultural pervasiveness and political strength of French has significantly contributed to Quebec's claim of distinctiveness within Canada; it has time and again provided a powerful justification for demanding a special status, or calling for independence. But throughout most of modern Quebec's history, the political significance of French as a marker of collective identity hinged largely on the presence of English, and the fairly deep-seated perception that it was the language of the oppressor. Quebecers' sense of themselves has been shaped to no small extent in opposition to the considerable socio-historical weight of

English-speakers in Quebec and the economic hegemony of their elite. The process of French language affirmation of the 1960s and 1970s was fuelled largely by resentment and the will to free francophones Quebecers from the socio-economic yoke of the English. Unsurprisingly, French-English conflicts often made the stuff of unity debates and constitutional controversies. Today, however, the opponents of French language, and thus of francophone Quebecers, are no longer easily identifiable institutions, corporations, or individuals whom one can conveniently point to as the source of French-speakers' personal and collective woes, and against whom one can readily rise up. The "threat" to French does not come from the arrogant, old English-speaking economic elite, which in fact has virtually disappeared as a socially and politically relevant group. Anglophone Quebecers have by and large adapted to and accepted the progressive and democratic transfer of social power that has gradually favoured francophone Quebecers over the past four decades.[43] Public laments against the "imposition" of French tend to emanate from isolated individuals or Anglo-rights associations whose legitimacy within the English-speaking population of Quebec is limited,[44] and who, as a result, are hardly taken seriously by the large majority of French-speaking Quebecers.

Except perhaps for a fairly small core of politically marginal radical nationalists, the English as an emblematic figure of anti-French or anti-Quebec sentiments and action no longer has the mobilizing appeal among francophone Quebecers it may have had in the early days of modern Quebec nationalism. If English is a threat in Quebec today, it is a depersonalized one, brought about by the tidal wave of global culture, the new knowledge-based economy, communication technology and trade. In this sense it is a threat that francophone Quebecers experience along with almost all non-Anglophone cultures around the world. It may be disturbing to some, but it can hardly be presented as an Anglo-Canadian conspiracy to eradicate French Quebecers or contain their national aspirations.[45] The impact of this reality within the purview of Quebec-Canada relations is clear: as the domestic political salience of the language issue abates, or seems no longer specific to the Quebec situation, the Quebec state loses an important determinant of the social and political cohesion that has been so essential historically in levelling credible and politically efficient claims against Ottawa.

The years ahead might well prove to be quite dispiriting for Quebec political leaders intent on questioning Canadian federalism and driving the national unity question back onto the country's political agenda. If the preceding analysis of the transformation of key aspects of Quebec's political culture is correct, they will most likely have a hard time garnering the necessary level of public support to justify the uncompromising and at times vehement attitude they favour in dealing with Ottawa. What they see as egregious federal encroachments on the Quebec people's right to self-determination may well have a rather faint echo in Quebec's public opinion. The rather anemic public reaction to the federal *Clarity Act* and to Quebec's legislative response to it is in itself a telling indication that on matters of federal-provincial relations, the public and political leadership do not necessarily share the same concerns.

REPACKAGING SOCIO-ECONOMIC MANAGEMENT: THE "QUEBEC MODEL," FEDERALISM AND CIVIL SOCIETY

The final aspect of Quebec political culture that is of relevance to the future dynamics of Quebec-Canada relations has to do with the ways in which the Quebec state has managed the pressures of accelerating socio-economic change during the past decade or so.[46] In Quebec, as in most western polities, globalization, economic restructuring, the fiscal limits of the welfare state and difficulties in maintaining the levels of social and economic achievements reached during the previous decades have opened the way to a serious reconsideration of prevailing social hierarchies, modes of socio-economic redistribution and patterns of institutional relations between social groups and economic stakeholders. Since the late 1990s, the current Quebec government has regularly boasted that it has successfully addressed the challenges at hand by maintaining and improving on what it calls the "Quebec model." In general terms, the expression evokes the state-driven approach which originated during the years of the Quiet Revolution and contributed to the modernization of Quebec society and economy. In its latest incarnation, it implies more specifically that Quebecers believe that solidarity is a central value of their collective lives and must remain so, that *concertation* (that is, discussing and solving problems together) is a Quebec trademark way to achieve the greater goals of society, and must continue to be so, that the state should be actively involved in promoting economic development, along with the cooperative movement, the labour movement and all who are committed to the social economy, that this model is unique, and a defining characteristic of the only francophone jurisdiction in North America, and that it has been beneficial to all Quebecers and has allowed them to grow as a united political community.[47]

The notion of the Quebec model works as a metaphor for social cohesion and the distinctiveness of the Quebec people. The government uses it to underscore both how socially and politically different and united Quebecers are in dealing with contemporary socio-economic problems, and how deleterious Canadian federalism is for a jurisdiction that tries to adopt solutions suitable to its own circumstances. The Quebec-model argument insists that, contrary to what occurs almost everywhere else, consensus on issues of general concerns is achieved in Quebec by bringing together all the stakeholders of society (state, business, unions, community organizations, women, elderly citizens, youth, immigrants and ethnocultural minorities) to participate in defining original global public policy orientations; but the increasingly centralistic tendencies of the Canadian state prevent Quebecers from developing fully and jeopardize their opportunities to further enhance their social and economic potential.

Critics might argue that there is much political posturing in the government's references to the so-called Quebec model. The notion is meant largely as an ideological tool to mobilize Quebecers against Ottawa and the Canadian federal system (and, as such, it conveniently ignores that some of Quebec's socio-economic accomplishments of the past decades benefited in varying measures from the input of the federal state, and from the administrative and jurisdictional autonomy afforded to provinces by the Canadian constitution in key sectors of activity). Whether there is indeed a model of socio-economic development that is distinctly Quebec's own is open to debate,[48] but in fairness there is more to the Quebec model than mere ideological fiction. Recent and ongoing research in economic sociology shows that, starting in the 1980s, the Quebec state has encouraged and even actively promoted several initiatives of socio-institutional innovations aimed at fostering local business and economic development, curtailing unemployment, and enhancing social solidarity. These initiatives rest on extensive social partnerships usually involving the state, private corporations, unions and the community sector. They are real, viable, and have resulted in institutional practices that, in many ways, distinguish Quebec in North America.[49]

Different examples are cited as illustrations of Quebec's unique economic policy-making process among which are the *Forum pour l'emploi*,[50] the *Fonds de solidarité*,[51] a dynamic cooperative movement,[52] and more recently the shift to the social economy. In 1996, the government convened business, labour and the community sector at a socio-economic summit designed to elaborate strategies of economic management.[53] Participants agreed that the government should implement measures necessary to reach a zero-deficit situation within the following four years. Premier Bouchard maintained that this was essential to achieve the "winning conditions" toward an eventual referendum on sovereignty. In return, following political pressures from the community sector,[54] the government resolved to facilitate the advancement of the social economy by directly supporting the *Chantier de l'économie sociale*, an independent body bringing unions and community organizations together to promote the emergence and consolidation of social enterprises.[55]

Most specialists and scholars in the field tend to portray the government's involvement with the social economy as an example of the Quebec state's commitment to include civil society in economic policy decisions, and maintain social solidarity without giving in to the imperatives of market competitiveness. To them, the state's latest interventions in the social economy represent a renewal of the Quebec model and a positive, enabling and potentially more democratic reconfiguration of socio-economic hierarchies between the state, business, labour, and the community sector. Although their work rests on prudent analyses and qualified evaluations of the situation, it often conveys the impression that a fairly broad political consensus permeates Quebec society on issues of socio-economic management and on fundamental societal priorities, thus reinforcing the image of Quebec as a tightly knit, unitary political community. The existing literature on the Quebec social economy shies away from openly sharing the government's political conclusions about the allegedly negative impact of Canadian federalism on the further development of the Quebec model, but in the end it provides, willingly or not, the evidence the government readily uses to proclaim that Quebec society is socially cohesive and distinct, and that nothing but sovereignty can safeguard the model and allow Quebec to thrive.

While it is difficult to sort out the actual role that Quebec's broad-based approach to decision-making on matters of socio-economic policy played in the province's economic performance, some noticeable changes have occurred over the past decade. As the government likes to point out, the Quebec economy has become far more export-oriented, with export and manufacturing shipments having moved from labour and resource-intensive industries to capital and technological intensive ones; research and development as a share of gross domestic product (GDP) has grown faster in Quebec than in the rest of Canada as the number of firms active in research doubled between 1990 and 1995, and the adoption of general applied technologies more than doubled since 1989; the economic and industrial culture has evolved toward more cooperative labour-management relations[56]; and the unemployment rate has gone down nearly three percentage points in the past few years.

The policy consensus that seems to have materialized around issues of socio-economic management by the end of the 1990s obtains from three factors. First, the greater willingness exhibited during most of the 1980s and 1990s by the state, business, and labour elite to transcend their objective differences and collaborate on major policy questions created a general political environment more conducive to social accommodation. Second, following two highly confrontational and politically difficult decades in the 1960s and 1970s, Quebec's labour movement became increasingly pervaded after the early 1980s with a sense that the state of public finance and the general economic situation left the working class with little choice but to agree to social and economic compromises which they would have rejected in the past — an attitude which, presumably, paved the way to the new culture of accommodation mentioned above. On account of credibility and consistence, the labour movement also restricted its own ability to exercise its traditional prerogatives as social and political critic after siding with the government on the national question and associating with nationalist forces at the time of the 1995 referendum. Finally, one cannot underestimate Premier Bouchard's brokering skills and talent at political persuasion: during his tenure he made use of his charisma and on many occasions wagered his own reputation to create as wide a coalition of socio-economic interests as possible in the hope of bringing about the "winning conditions" in preparation for another referendum on sovereignty.

To some extent then, the political culture of consensus that has progressively come to characterize the policy process in Quebec owes much to the relative political weakness of the labour movement and associated community groups. It is in a way a fragile consensus which depends essentially on whether labour, the community sector, and progressive social forces in general are still prepared to believe the government's supposed commitment to social solidarity. This is not a given, for the government's ability to nurture and sustain this consensus further is facing important challenges. Indeed, despite fairly remarkable global economic results and the government's repeated engagement toward social solidarity, Quebec's development model has hardly been a social success. A look at some socio-economic indicators brings the limitations of the social economy and the Quebec model in general into clearer focus. A recent analysis of Quebec's economic performance shows that in spite of an annual real economic growth rate of 2.1 percent since the early 1980s, Quebec's relative situation in contrast to the rest of Canada and the US is deteriorating. Between 1981 and 1999, Quebec's real GDP has increased by 45.2 percent while the GDP in the rest of Canada increased by 64.2 per cent during the same period. Quebec's GDP accounted for 24 percent of Canada's GDP in the early 1980s; by 1999 it had slipped to 21.9 percent. However, it is on the employment front, the basic plank of the whole social economy approach, that one gets a more tragic sense of the shortcomings of the Quebec model. Again, for the 1981–99 period, the total number of jobs in Quebec grew by 20.4 percent, but in comparison, job creation grew by 31.3 percent in the rest of Canada, and by 33 percent in the US. Between 1990 and 1999, the number of new (part-time and full-time) jobs increased by 6.9 percent in Quebec, but by 12.4 percent in the rest of the country and in the US. In other words, Quebec's economy has systematically created less jobs than Canada's economy for the past two decades. Though Quebec comprises one-quarter of the Canadian population, it created less than one-fifth of all the new jobs in Canada between 1981 and 1990 and barely one-sixth for the period 1990–1999. Similarly, inasmuch as full-time jobs alone are considered in this broad picture, it appears that they increased by 9.2 percent in Quebec in comparison to 14.2 percent in the rest of Canada between 1981 and 1990; for the period 1990–99, they increased by only 5.2 percent as opposed to 10.5 percent in the rest of Canada. Quebec was responsible for the creation of 18 percent of all the new full-time jobs in Canada for the period 1981–90; that proportion dropped to 13.9 percent for the 1990s. In order for Quebec to post an employment rate equivalent to that of the rest of Canada or the US — it is currently at 55.5 percent, compared to 60.8 percent for Canada and 64 percent for the US — at least 14 percent more jobs (that is roughly 469,000) are needed immediately.[57]

Such socio-economic indicators force a sobering evaluation of the purported benefits of the Quebec model. To some critics, it is nothing but a model of economic exploitation and political domination.[58] They see state-sponsored social partnerships as demagogic smoke screens which compel labour and the community sector to buy into social, economic, and even political compromises that work in the end against their objective and class interests. The celebrated social economy, they further argue, only keeps workers and the economically marginalized in precarious economic circumstances. Even the most successful experiments in social economy remain largely local and limited in scope. They may help those involved in them to break out of the vicious cycle of economic dependence, they may even strengthen community bonds and make individuals feel good about themselves, but they rarely reach beyond the people who partake in them; they hardly amount to a global, universally endorsable model of social and civic overhaul. The interest of the government in the social economy is basically motivated by its perceived potential ability to lighten the social welfare burden of the Quebec state (by making people find their own way out of economic dependence), without questioning the logic and the process that have created the situations of glaring socio-economic inequality in the first place. The social economy liberates the state from its previous commitments to the segments of the population that it can purportedly no longer support, and saves it from having to transform or reconsider the exclusionary mechanisms at the root of the opposition between solidarity and scarcity in capitalist economies. In this sense, the social economy is an ideology of social cohesion working to the advantage of the neo-liberal agenda of the state.

Scholars with a natural sympathy toward Quebec's institutional innovations in socio-economic management also warn that the apparent shift to consensual decision-making should not obscure the fact that concerted action does not imply the absence of conflict or clashes between competing interests. Despite the emergence of a broadly agreed upon and uniform public discourse on employment, the importance of re-enabling civil society and the necessity to reform governance structures in Quebec, it is not clear that all stakeholders have the same understanding of that discourse. On one side, there are those, mostly from the private sector, whose economic interests are firmly entrenched in globalization and the internationalization of market exchanges. Their view of Quebec's development is fundamentally neo-liberal in nature. They strongly believe that all institutional transformations of the Quebec economy must be primarily geared toward enhancing the province's international competitiveness. To them, the social economy is good insofar as it can check the tendencies to social fragmentation and encourage private initiative. On the other side are those whose typical milieu are social enterprises, nonprofit organizations and local, small- and medium-sized enterprises; they naturally associate with the labour movement and the community sector. Their view of globalization hinges much less on achieving international competitiveness at all costs, but focuses on finding means to promote local social solidarity and empower individuals and communities.[59]

Although the government claims to be equally sensitive to the vision of both groups, many of its actual policies reflect an unequivocal penchant for neo-liberal measures. Unmitigated support for free trade, zero deficit in public finance, important budgetary restrictions in public health, social assistance and education, and major structural and administrative changes in the welfare functions of the state, which increasingly require individuals to face the negative consequences of economic restructuring on their own, have been the mainstay of the current government's approach to socio-economic management. These are not sitting well with a growing number of civil society organizations which are questioning the government's policy decisions in no uncertain terms. The government's emphasis on consensus conceals with increasing difficulty the existence of smoldering tensions between the nationalist governing elite who applies the neo-liberal policy agenda and progressive forces who reject it.

Will these tensions erupt soon? It is hard to say at this stage, although some radical and left-leaning groups have become more and more vocal and dissatisfied with the government's policy stance on a number of social and economic issues. In the fall of 1997, for example, 600 disaffected left nationalists met to create a new political movement, the *Rassemblement pour une alternative politique* (RAP), with well-known, retired unionist Michel Chartrand at its head. A few RAP representatives ran in the November 1998 provincial election — with Chartrand opposing Premier Bouchard in his own riding — to no avail, but they got their message across. In November 1997, 1500 representatives of more than 20 community and anti-poverty groups held a *Parlement de la rue* (street parliament) for a whole month across from the National Assembly to denounce the government's social policies. In February 2000, a coalition of groups on the political left, the *Coalition autonome populaire jeunesse* (Autonomous Popular Youth Coalition) organized a parallel summit to protest the government's "Youth Summit" which convened, following a familiar pattern, Quebec's major stakeholders to discuss policy solutions to youth unemployment, education, and job training. Organizers and participants at the "counter summit" decried the government's neo-liberal policies and commitment to integrate Quebec into the global economy in conformity with the rules of such executive agreements as the North American Free Trade Agreement (NAFTA), the World Trade Organization (WTO) and the still tentative Free Trade Area of the Americas (FTAA). They eventually clashed with the Quebec City police force.

The latest movements of protest have also gone global. In the spring of 1998 and again in the fall of 2000, Quebec-based youth and anti-globalization organizations disrupted the Montreal meetings of the Multilateral

Agreement on Investments (MAI) and the G20. Similarly, the *Fédération des femmes du Québec* (Quebec Women's Federation) initiated and organized in 2000 the Women's World March, a peaceful protest aimed at sensitizing governments to the difficult socio-economic situations of women around the world, and at exposing the negative human consequences of economic globalization and the neo-liberal economic policies adopted by national governments. Several other Quebec civil society groups were very heavily involved in the preparation of the "People's Summit," to counter the April 2001 official Summit of the Americas held in Quebec City to discuss the FTAA, and they took an active part in the many anti-globalization, political demonstrations surrounding the event.

Despite the variety of their actions and objectives these and other left-inspired protest initiatives all reprove the policy choices of the Quebec government, distrust its alleged commitment to social solidarity, and condemn its emphasis on international competitiveness and blind faith in free market mechanisms. The depth of their popular support, or the extent to which they will evolve into a well-organized political alternative (or even into an entirely new civic culture) are still quite unclear. But their very existence is undoubtedly shattering the image of societal consensus which the Quebec government is so eager to project; they partake of a conceptual paradigm that is basically at odds with the fundamental values and norms of civic engagement that mould the liberal democratic outlook of Quebec nationalists. To many of the individuals involved in this process of resistance, particularly those whose actions focus on transnational issues, the whole Quebec-Canada question is disconnected from their experience on the ground (despite the obvious link between national and transnational policy questions). In terms of federal-provincial relations, it is more likely that they will not follow the nationalist elite in their "struggle" against Ottawa, partly in protest against the government's management of the province, but also because the chronic Quebec-Ottawa imbroglio appears of limited relevance in the "grand scheme of things." This is not to say that the new protest groups are inherently federalist. Many of them are not, or they simply could not care less whether the unity of the Canadian federal union is preserved or not. They are just as vehement in their critique of the Canadian state to the extent that they consider that it too favours neo-liberal policy choices. Their critique of the Quebec state therefore cannot be appreciated in terms of "anti-Quebec," or "anti-sovereignty," and "pro-Canada" sentiments; it operates at a broader and more general political level.

For the sovereignist political elite, this can translate into quite a setback in the long run. The sovereignty movement could always count on the support of a large coalition of left forces as long as the Parti Québécois donned the mantle of social democracy with some credibility. The political sovereignty of Quebec was also considered by most people on the left as a necessary step for the emancipation and empowerment of Quebec's labouring and economically disadvantaged classes. Some still believe that; it is the case of the RAP, for example. But as the Parti Québécois no longer appears as a plausible vehicle of social change to increasing segments of the Quebec left, sovereignists are losing natural allies. Premier Landry chided members of the new-left coalition turned political party in June 2001 for creating the risk that the sovereignist vote be divided in an eventual general election.[60] He was still reeling from the defeat inflicted the Parti Québécois a few weeks earlier in a by-election in a Montreal riding that had regularly supported the sovereignist party since the 1970s. Although the Liberal Party representative won, the setback was largely attributed to the unexpectedly good standing of the relatively unknown "new-left," sovereignist but independent candidate who, with nearly 24 percent of the vote, moved ahead of the Parti Québécois contender and was blamed for having "split" the sovereignist vote. Should this kind of outcome occur again on a wider basis, Landry's fear is that not only will the societal consensus needed to launch credible charges against Ottawa likely dwindle, but any interest or support for the kind of jurisdictional battles the Quebec state has waged might wane irremediably.

CONCLUSION

Some might be tempted to infer from the preceding that the days of the Quebec sovereignist movement are numbered, and that Quebec-Ottawa relations are about to become less tense, less vindictive or less subjected to the relentless assaults of a disgruntled, regional political elite. It is not an improbable scenario. This chapter has attempted to show that there are indicators which might lead one to believe that the purchase of Quebec nationalism on the collective imagination is no longer what it used to be, that Quebec nationalists themselves are sending ambiguous signals as to what the Quebec nation really is, and that the consensual bent of the Quebec political culture is not as definite as it might look. The basic point that I tried to make is a simple one: in light of what appear to be real, qualitative changes in Quebec political culture, it will be increasingly difficult for sovereignists to muster the unequivocal support they need to stand up to Ottawa and achieve their ultimate political goal. This point was made painfully clear by Lucien Bouchard in his resignation speech. If that analysis is correct, it seems indeed conceivable that Quebec's historical contention with Ottawa will soon subside on account of insufficient levels of nationalist fervour, and because of an arising sense of alienation toward the Parti Québécois.

This is a scenario that weary defenders of the Canadian union no doubt would like to see materialize. But it is not the only plausible one. The shift in Quebec's political culture described in this chapter could also produce a significantly different outcome. Challenged by failing popular support, sovereignists could very well beat the nationalist drum with added vigour in a more or less desperate attempt to re-ignite the flame. This would unavoidably translate into more political stalemates and more jurisdictional clashes between Quebec and Ottawa. Under Bernard Landry's stewardship especially, that is a distinct possibility; his confrontational style and fiery rhetoric vis-à-vis Ottawa are well known. Of course, that kind of approach might just further alienate the Quebec people from the sovereignists, but that is immaterial in a sense: as long as the Parti Québécois remains in power nothing can really prevent its leadership from provoking a showdown with Ottawa. Still, this scenario could also evolve in a different way. Precisely because of popular disaffection, sovereignists (or Jean Charest's Liberals for that matter, assuming they would get elected the next time around) could decide to try the avenue suggested by public intellectuals like Jean-François Lisée and Christian Dufour: make the best of the Canadian federal system without ever relenting on the distinct nature of Quebec's national identity, and constantly seek the best possible advantages for the province. Canadians may at least gain from that the assurance that Quebecers would not try to secede. It does not mean, though, that Quebec-Canada relations would be more amicable as Quebec would most likely favour more or less extreme forms of asymmetrical federalism for which Canadians in general have had until now rather lukewarm sympathy at best.

Looking at a longer time line there is a third scenario that may be harder to fathom, but which, nonetheless, is not inconceivable. As the traditional consensus breaks down, it is not impossible that in the long run a new approach or paradigm (or new ones) will form. This chapter has mostly emphasized that the nationalist rhetoric seems to be losing its appeal, but what of the citizenship discourse? At present Quebec nationalists are trying hard to merge conceptually the Quebec nation with citizenship — with mitigated success as we saw. Nevertheless Quebec is perhaps the only provincial jurisdiction in Canada right now where lively debates over the nature and content of political belonging are occurring. These debates are not in vain. They suggest that there is an ongoing public reflection on the underlying, defining terms of the political community. It is not impossible in fact that at the end of the process Quebecers will have reshaped their political space not so much as a *national* space, which has tended historically to meet with internal resistance, but as a primarily *civic* space, which in many ways would be a convenient way out of the perplexing conundrum of ethnocultural identities. Only time will tell whether things will indeed thus unfold. But as socio-cultural integration patterns of newcomers to Quebec increasingly tend to favour the French-speaking majority, they also indicate that in the ensuing blend, issues of national or group identity might become irrelevant.

If such were to be the case Quebecers might be more likely to see themselves as citizens first, and one can assume that the Quebec nation would be a
far less compelling notion to apply in dealing with Ottawa. Would things be
easier with Ottawa if Quebec were a civic space as opposed to a national
space? Not necessarily. Even as a civic space Quebec might well continue to
develop its own priorities and agendas that would clash with Canada's. The
difference would be that they would no longer be formulated as national affirmation claims, but more with a view to protecting bureaucratic or jurisdictional
prerogatives or boundaries. This trend was already in evidence during Lucien
Bouchard's tenure as premier. Quebec's dissatisfaction in the social union
dossier, for example, was almost exclusively focused on primarily administrative and bureaucratic issues.[61]

When discussing Quebec-Canada relations, most analysts readily assume
that Quebec poses a threat to Canada's union. In the background of their studies of Canadian federalism often looms an implicit concern, which is shared
by most Canadians outside Quebec: what is Quebec likely to pull out of its
sleeves that will have us concerned again over the fate of the country? As
Quebec "mutates" into a civic space as opposed to a properly national political space, one could well reverse the question and ask in what way does Canada
pose a threat to the civic integrity of Quebec? The guiding logic of the Quebec civic space may well not correspond to that enforced over time by the
Canadian state. The point is, modern Canadian federalism rests mainly on a
dynamics of jurisdictional opposition and conflict between the central government and the provinces: even if Quebec eventually does away with its
nationalistic claims, there is no reason to believe that it would make for
smoother relations between Quebec and Ottawa.

Clearly, the foundations of Quebec political culture, broadly defined, are
going through some alterations which may indicate that Quebec's customary
way of relating to Canada will also change. Those who anticipate a quieting
of Quebec-Canada relations as a result might be in for a disappointment.

NOTES

The author wishes to thank Harvey Lazar, Hamish Telford and an anonymous reviewer
for their comments and suggestions.

1. G. Gagné and S. Langlois, "L'état de l'appui à la souveraineté du Québec," in
    Québec 2001, ed. R. Côté (Montreal: Fides, 2000).

2. According to a Léger and Léger poll commissioned by Radio-Canada and re-
    leased in April 2000, 71.2 percent of Quebecers believe that Canadian federalism
    can be renewed, and 68.2 percent think that efforts should be made to find a
    third way between sovereignty and current federal practices in Canada. (Quoted

in J. Maclure, "Le Projet nationaliste en transition : la fin des vaches sacrées?" in *Québec 2001*, ed. Côté, p. 93).

3. It was adopted by the National Assembly as an *Act respecting the exercise of fundamental rights and prerogatives of the Quebec people and the Quebec state*. It clearly "specifies that only the Quebec people, acting through its own political institutions, has the right to decide the nature, scope, and mode of exercise of its right to self-determination, and that no other parliament or government may reduce the powers, authority, sovereignty or legitimacy of the National Assembly."

4. C. Dufour, *Lettre aux souverainistes québécois et aux fédéralistes canadiens qui sont restés fidèles au Québec* (Montreal: Stanké, 2000); J.-F. Lisée, *Sortie de secours. Comment échapper au déclin du Québec* (Montréal: Boréal, 2000). Jean-François Lisée, a prominent Quebec journalist, was a key strategist of the "yes" side during the 1995 referendum and one of the main advisors to Premier Bouchard until he resigned in September 1999. No longer convinced that the sovereignist movement was steering the right course he later published a rather provocative book, *Sortie de secours*, in mid-winter 2000, which argues that the referendum strategy pursued by the Parti Québécois is a mistake. While he does not abandon his sovereignist conviction and still believes in the necessity of national affirmation for Quebec, he now thinks that Quebecers stand to gain more and shed this feeling of failure that ails them by working within the Canadian federal system. Christian Dufour, ENAP professor, political commentator and high-profile pro-sovereignty contributor to public debates about the future of Quebec and Canada for over a decade is also on record for adopting a similar position in his latest *Lettre aux souverainistes québécois et aux fédéralistes canadiens qui sont restés fidèles au Québec*. Despite his scathing attack against the Canadian political system for its allegedly inherent tendency to marginalize and keep Quebec in a minority situation, he suggests that the sovereignty project is dead and that it might now be more productive for Quebecers to explore the possibilities of asymetrical federalism seriously.

5. L. Balthazar, "The Faces of Quebec Nationalism," in *Quebec State and Society*, 2d ed., ed. A.-G. Gagnon (Scarborough: Nelson Canada, 1993); F. Rocher, "Le Québec et la Constitution: une valse à mille temps," in *Bilan québécois du fédéralisme canadien*, ed. F. Rocher (Montreal: VLB éditeur, 1992); J. Webber, *Re-Imagining Canada* (Montreal: McGill-Queen's University Press, 1994).

6. D. Farber, "Political Culture and the Therapeutic Ideal," *Reviews in American History* 23, 4(1995):681.

7. W. Kymlicka, *Multicultural Citizenship* (Oxford: Oxford University Press, 1995); D. Miller, *On Nationality* (Oxford: Oxford University Press, 1995); Y. Tamir, *Liberal Nationalism* (Princeton: Princeton University Press, 1993); C. Taylor, "Nationalism and Modernity," in *Theorizing Nationalism,* ed. R. Beiner (Albany, NY: State University of New York Press, 1999).

8. J. Habermas, "Citizenship and National Identity: Some Reflections on the Future of Europe," in *Theorizing Citizenship*, ed. R. Beiner (Albany, NY: State University of New York Press, 1995).

9.   Citizenship in this context is taken in its generic sense. As a provincial jurisdiction of the Canadian state, Quebec cannot formally deliver citizenship status. Legally, only the Canadian state can. However, the current government's insistence on dealing with its various constituencies as *citizens* says much about the will to sovereignty that pervades its actions and self-perception. In June 2000, the minister responsible for civic relations and immigration launched a public document for discussion in a general public consultation scheduled to take place in September 2000. This document simply entitled *La citoyenneté québécoise* suggests the legal, institutional and symbolic parameters that should ideally comprise a new Quebec citizenship. It is presented and understood by the government as the first step toward the establishment of a formal, Quebec-based citizenship.

10. In spite of its 1977 language legislation and subsequent amendments, which make French the only official language of public transactions in Quebec, force immigrants to attend French schools, and make corporations have commercial signs and publicity in French only, the nationalist (and currently governing) Parti Québécois has been committed to protecting the rights of Anglophones to an English-language education, to providing service in English in the health-care system and various state agencies, and to allowing the use of English, as well as French, in the National Assembly. In addition, the Quebec state, following the Parti Québécois initiative in the mid-1980s, officially recognizes Quebec's Aboriginal communities as nations, with a full panoply of rights including autonomy within Quebec society, the protection of their languages, cultures and traditions, the right to hold and control land, and the right to participate fully in economic development on their own terms. Finally, the Quebec state has since 1975 a Charter of Rights and Freedoms which guarantees the protection of all fundamental rights for everyone living in the Quebec territory.

11. This is clearly stated in the political platform of the Parti Québécois (see Parti Québécois, *Le Québec dans un monde nouveau* (Montreal: VLB Éditeur and Parti Québécois, 1993), p. 54-60; Parti Québécois, *La volonté de réussir* (Montreal: Parti Québécois, 1997), section B. For a fuller, more academic and varied exposition, see C. Bariteau, *Québec 18 septembre 2001* (Montreal: Québec-Amérique, 1998); G. Bouchard, *La nation québécoise au futur et au passé* (Montreal: VLB éditeur, 1999); A. Légaré, "La souveraineté: nation ou raison," in *Québec: État et société*, ed. A.-G. Gagnon (Montreal: Québec-Amérique, 1994); M. Sarra-Bournet, ed., *Le pays de tous les Québécois* (Montreal: VLB éditeur, 1998); and M. Seymour, ed., *Nationalité, citoyenneté et solidarité* (Montreal: Liber, 1999); and M. Seymour, ed., *La nation en question* (Montreal: L'Hexagone, 1999).

12. Balthazar, "The Faces of Quebec Nationalism."

13. D. Francis, *Fighting for Canada* (Ottawa: Key Porter Books, 1996); W. Johnson, *A Canadian Myth: Quebec, Between Canada and the Illusion of Utopia* (Montreal: Robert Davies Publishing, 1994); M. Richler, *Oh Canada! Oh Quebec! Requiem for a Divided Country* (Toronto: Penguin Books, 1992).

14. J. Létourneau, "La nouvelle figure identitaire du Québécois. Essai sur la dimension symbolique d'un consensus social en voie d'émergence," *British Journal of Canadian Studies* 6, 1(1991):17-38 and "Le Québec moderne: un chapitre du

grand récit collectif des Québécois," *Revue française de science politique* 42, 5(1992):765-85.

15. M. Labelle, "Politiques québécoises et diversité," *Cahiers du programme d'études sur le Québec* 13 (Montreal: McGill University, 1998).

16. A. Norris, "Rallying Anglos. Signs and Battles of the Anglo-Rights Movement Resonate Less with Younger English Quebecers," *The Gazette*, 5 June 1997.

17. Several surveys of public opinion have regularly shown over the past decade that Quebecers in general are positively inclined toward immigration and ethnocultural minorities. Intercultural and interracial contacts are on the increase and even encouraged, particularly within the Montreal area (where the bulk of immigrant population lives) and among the younger and more educated segments of the population. Close to two-thirds of the population (three out of four respondents in the Montreal area) have a supportive and open attitude toward immigration. Respondents favouring exclusion and discriminatory policies usually account for small proportions of the samples — less than 6 percent. J. Joly, *Sondage d'opinion publique québécoise sur l'immigration et les relations interculturelles,* Collection Études et recherches, no. 15 (Quebec: Direction des communications, ministère des Relations avec les citoyens et de l'Immigration, 1996); J. Joly and M. Dorval, *Sondage sur l'opinion publique québécoise à l'égard des relations raciales et interculturelles,* Collection Études et recherche, no. 6 (Quebec: Direction des communications, ministère des Communautés culturelles et de l'Immigration, 1993). This is a stark contrast with the more reserved and negative attitudes that generally prevailed prior to the 1990s. D. Bolduc and P. Fortin, "Les Francophones sont-ils plus "xénophobes" que les Anglophones au Québec? Une analyse quantitative exploratoire," *Canadian Ethnic Studies* 22, 2(1990):54-77. In fact, Quebecers tend to be on the whole more accepting of immigration and will more readily recognize it as having a positive effect on society than any other Canadians. See D. Palmer, *Canadian Attitudes and Perceptions Regarding Immigration: Relations with Regional Per Capita and Other Contextual Factors,* Citizenship and Immigration Canada (Ottawa: Minister of Public Works and Government Services, 2000).

18. G. Elmer and B. Abramson, "Excavating Ethnicity in *Québécois,*" *Quebec Studies* 23(1997):13-28.

19. I. Molinaro, "Contexte et intégration. Les communautés allophones au Québec," *Globe. Revue internationale d'études québécoises* 2, 2(1999):101-24.

20. M. Labelle and D. Salée, "Immigrant and Minority Representations of Citizenship in Quebec," in *Citizenship Today: Global Perspectives and Practices,* ed. T. Aleinikoff and D. Klusmeyer (Washington, DC: Carnegie Endowment for International Peace, 2001); J. Renaud, *Ils sont maintenant d'ici. Les dix premières années au Québec des immigrants admis en 1989* (Québec: Ministère des Relations avec les Citoyens et de l'Immigration, 2001).

21. Parti Québécois, *La volonté de réussir.*

22. C. Bariteau, "Le Québec comme nation politique, démocratique et souveraine," in *Penser la nation québécoise,* ed. M. Venne (Montreal: Québec-Amérique, 2000), p. 232.

23. Y. Bélanger, "Economic Development: From Family Enterprise to Big Business" in *Quebec State and Society*, ed. Gagnon; A.-G. Gagnon and K.Z. Paltiel, "Towards Maîtres chez nous: The Ascendancy of a Balzacian Bourgeoisie in Quebec," *Queen's Quarterly* 93, 4(1986):731-49.

24. This is perhaps best illustrated by its unmitigated support of free trade with the US. Indeed, while the issue of free trade was vehemently debated and opposed in English Canada, most social and political forces in Quebec unequivocally endorsed it. Free trade is largely perceived in Quebec, particularly by nationalists, as a useful and effective instrument of economic development and affirmation. See K. Holland, "Quebec's Successful Role and Champion of North American Free Trade," *Quebec Studies* 19(1995):71-84; D. Latouche, "Quebec in the Emerging North American Configuration," in *Identities in North America: The Search for Community*, ed. R.L. Earle and J.D. Wirth (Stanford: Stanford University Press, 1995); P. Martin, "When Nationalism Meets Continentalism: The Politics of Free Trade in Quebec," *Journal of Regional and Federal Studies* 5, 1(1995):1-27; and F. Rocher, "Continental Strategy: Québec in North America," in *Quebec State and Society*, ed. Gagnon. Other studies show that Quebecers, by and large, are quite open and willing to be exposed to external influences, particularly from the United States, and are convinced of the necessity to be connected to the world. See Groupe de recherche sur l'américanité (GRAM), "Recherche sur l'américanité des Québécois," *Le Devoir,* 14, 15 and 16 July 1998 and L. Balthazar and A.O. Hero, *Le Québec dans l'espace américain* (Montreal: Québec-Amérique, 1999).

25. D. Salée, "NAFTA, Quebec, and the Boundaries of Cultural Sovereignty: The Challenges of Identity in the Era of Globalization," in *Joining Together, Standing Apart. National Identities After NAFTA*, ed. Dorinda G. Dallmeyer (The Hague: Kluwer Law International, 1997).

26. There is, of course, a political difference between Quebec and Canada that cannot be downplayed. Quebec's will to full citizenship and insistence on social cohesion must be appreciated in the context of its perennial attempt at establishing itself as a self-contained and self-determined political community. Canada's approach on the other hand is mainly motivated by a fundamental concern to preserve and strengthen historical, political and symbolic boundaries that serve as defining markers of the country's statehood and sense of nation. Still, there is little difference in terms of the inner logic of civic and political homogeneization at play in both cases. For a fuller exposition of Canada's emphasis on citizenship and social cohesion, see M. Labelle and D. Salée, "La citoyenneté en question: l'Etat canadien face à l'immigration et à la diversité nationale et culturelle," *Sociologie et sociétés* 31, 2(1999):125-44.

27. S. Cantin, "Pour sortir de la survivance," in *Penser la nation québécoise,* ed. M. Venne (Montreal: Québec-Amérique, 2000), p. 92. Author's translation of the following: "Mine de rien, le nouveau credo de la nation québécoise ouverte et plurielle, multi- ou transculturelle, mine le projet qu'il prétend servir, en le privant peu à peu de sa raison d'être.... Car il implique que nous disparaissions par altruisme; que nous renoncions, au nom de la démocratie, au principe même de la démocratie, au droit des peuples à disposer d'eux-mêmes, à se gouverner."

28. D. Salée, "Quebec Sovereignty and the Challenge of Linguistic and Ethnocultural Minorities: Identity, Difference and the Politics of *Ressentiment,*" *Quebec Studies* 24(1997):6-23.

29. A. Yeatman, *Postmodern Revisionings of the Political* (New York: Routledge, 1994), p. 90.

30. See, for example, B. Barber, *Jihad vs. MacWorld. How Globalism and Tribalism are Reshaping the World* (New York: Ballantine Books, 1995); M. Horsman and A. Marshall, *After the Nation-State: Citizens, Tribalism and the New World Disorder* (London: HarperCollins, 1994); S. Huntington, *The Clash of Civilizations* (New York: Simon and Schuster, 1996), and R. Kaplan, *The Coming Anarchy* (New York: Random House, 2000).

31. M. Labelle and J. Levy, *Ethnicité et enjeux sociaux* (Montreal: Liber, 1995), p. 331 et sq.; K. McRoberts, *Misconceiving Canada. The Struggle for National Unity* (Toronto: Oxford University Press, 1997).

32. Y. Abu-Laban and D. Stasiulis, "Ethnic Pluralism Under Siege: Popular and Partisan Opposition to Multiculturalism," *Canadian Public Policy/Analyse de Politiques* 18, 4(1992):367-68; M. Labelle, "Pluralisme, intégration et citoyenneté. Enjeux sociaux et politiques à propos du Québec," in *La diversitéé linguistique et culturelle et les enjeux du développement*, ed. S. Abou et K. Haddad (Beyrouth: AUPELF/UREF, Université Saint-Joseph, 1997); F. Rocher, "Continental Strategy: Québec in North America," in *Quebec State and Society*, ed. Gagnon.

33. M. Labelle, G. Rocher and F. Rocher, "Pluriethnicité, citoyenneté et intégration: de la souveraineté pour lever les obstacles et les ambiguities," *Cahiers de recherche sociologique* 25(1995):213-45.

34. Recent field work interviews with politically and socially active Montreal area members of ethnocultural communities reveal a significant degree of suspicion vis-à-vis the injunctions of the Canadian state in favour of national unity and Canadian citizenship. See M. Labelle and D. Salée, "Immigrant and Minority Representations of Citizenship in Quebec," in *Citizenship Today: Global Perspectives and Practices*, ed. T. Aleinikoff and D. Klusmeyer (Washington: Carnegie Endowment for International Peace, 2001). For an exposition of the various critiques leveled at multiculturalism policy see Abu-Laban and Stasiulis, "Ethnic Pluralism Under Siege: Popular and Partisan Opposition to Multiculturalism." See also the critical analyses of H. Bannerji, *The Dark Side of the Nation: Essays on Nationalism, Multiculturalism and Agency* (Toronto: Canadian Scholars Press, 2000); and R.J.F. Day, *Multiculturalism and the History of Diversity* (Toronto: University of Toronto Press, 2000) to appreciate the theoretical and empirical limits of Canadian multiculturalism.

35. D. Salée, "Identities in Conflict: The Aboriginal Question and the Politics of Recognition in Quebec," *Ethnic and Racial Studies* 18, 2(1995):277-314.

36. During the 1990s, unemployment figures for immigrants remained higher than what the general population experienced (between 5 and 7 percent higher); this kind of situation was almost unheard of in the preceding decades. Recent immigrants (after 1986) even had to contend with rates of unemployment that were

nearly twice the general average. The same can be said for members of racialized minorities, some of whom, Blacks and people of Latin American origin for example, face levels of unemployment that are almost three times as high (26 and 29 percent compared to a general rate of 10 to 11 percent). In addition, the rates of participation in the labour market for both immigrants and members of racialized minorities are between 3 and 4 percent lower than the general average (62.3 percent compared to 58 and 59 percent). Similarly the percentage of people from racialized minorities working full-time, year round is also lower (48 percent) than that of the general population (53 percent). These figures indicate a clear under-utilization and even mis-utilization of immigrants and members of racialized minorities in the Quebec economy. When they are employed, members of racialized minorities in particular are overrepresented in low-paid, precarious, menial jobs requiring little or no special skill. Very few are found in middle and upper management positions, or in coveted, well-paid public sector jobs, this, in spite of the fact that, overall, they tend to be better educated than the general population. In Montreal, while 13 percent of the population can boast a university degree, more than 18 percent of people from racialized minorities are university-trained; yet, of the three largest Canadian cities where racialized minorities are found in significant numbers (Toronto, Montreal, Vancouver), Montreal is the one city where the unemployment rate for this group is the highest. Unsurprisingly, the income gap between the immigrant population and non-immigrants has increased steadily since the early 1980s. At that time, the average income of immigrants was 10 percent lower than that of the general Quebec population. In the 1990s it was almost 25 percent lower. The contrast is even starker when income differentials are broken down by groups: the average income of the population of African origin is 12 percent lower (it was 3 percent higher in the early 1980s). It is 47 percent lower for immigrants from the Caribbean, 40 percent lower for people from Latin America and 33 percent lower for Asian immigrants. Other statistics show that the income of members of racialized minorities is 17 percent lower than the general population. Comparatively, the average income of immigrants from Europe and the US has always been and continues to be superior to that of non-immigrants. High unemployment, unsteady job situations and lower incomes have unavoidably led to the growing marginalization of ethnocultural minorities from the economic mainstream and increased their dependency on social welfare. Most of the 1980s and 1990s were difficult times in Quebec. Corporate and state downsizing or restructuring and economic slowdown led to relentlessly high levels of unemployment across the board (among the highest in Canada), and heavier reliance on state programs of income security. Members of ethnocultural minorities were hit hard. Between 1981 and the mid-1990s, the number of immigrant households relying on social assistance increased by 420 percent, while it only grew by 42 percent for households whose head was born in Canada. About one immigrant household in seven now depends on welfare in Quebec, as opposed to one in twenty-five, twenty years ago. These figures are drawn from Conseil des Communautés culturelles et de l'Immigration, *Le logement et les communautés culturelles. Analyse de la situation* (Québec: Editeur official, 1992); *L'immigration et le marché du travail. Un état de la question* (Québec: Editeur official, 1993); *La capacité du*

Québec d'accueillir de nouveaux immigrants en 1995, 1996, 1997 (Québec: Editeur official, 1994); Conseil des relations interculturelles, *L'équité en emploi: de l'égalité de droit à l'égalité de fait* (Montreal: Conseil des relations interculturelles, 1999), both are government bodies.

37. K. Ohmae, *The Borderless World* (New York: HarpersCollins, 1991) and *The End of the Nation State: The Rise of Regional Economies* (New York: Harper Collins, 1995); V. Schmidt, "The New World Order, Incorporated: The Rise of Business and the Decline of the Nation-State," *Daedalus* 124, 2(1995):75-106; Y.N. Soysal, *Limits of Citizenship: Migrants and Postnational Membership in Europe* (Chicago: University of Chicago Press, 1994).

38. L.E. Guarnizo and M.P. Smith, "The Locations of Transnationalism," in *Transnationalism from Below*, ed. M.P. Smith and L.E. Guarnizo (New Brunswick, NJ: Transaction Publishers, 1999); M. Mann, "Has Globalization Ended the Rise of the Nation-State?" *Review of International Political Economy* 4, 3(1997):472-96; S. Sassen, *Globalization and Its Discontents* (New York: The New Press, 1998).

39. S. Castles and A. Davidson, *Citizenship and Migration: Globalization and the Politics of Belonging* (New York: Routledge, 2000), pp. 6-9

40. J. Renaud, *Ils sont maintenant d'ici. Les dix premières années au Québec des immigrants admis en 1989* (Québec: Ministère des Relations avec les Citoyens et de l'Immigration, 2001).

41. M. Labelle and F. Midy, "Re-reading Citizenship and the Transnational Practices of Immigrants," *Journal of Ethnic and Migration Studies* 25, 2(1999):213-32.

42. M. Labelle and D. Salée, "La citoyenneté en question: l'Etat canadien face à l'immigration et à la diversité nationale et culturelle," *Sociologie et sociétés* 31, 2(1999):125-44.

43. G. Stevenson, *Community Besieged: The Anglophone Minority and the Politics of Quebec* (Montreal: McGill-Queen's University Press, 1999), p. 309.

44. A. Norris, "Rallying Anglos. Signs and Battles of the Anglo-Rights Movement Resonate Less with Younger English Quebecers," *The Gazette*, 5 June 1999.

45. A. Dubuc, "La loi 101 est au bout de son rouleau," *La Presse*, 14 February 2, p. A-18.

46. This section borrows in part from Salée, "Transformative Politics, the State, and the Politics of Social Change in Quebec," in *Changing Canada: Political Economy as Transformation*, ed. Wallace Clement and Leah Vosko (Montreal: McGill-Queen's University Press, forthcoming).

47. Parti Québécois, *Vers la souveraineté: assurer l'avenir du modèle québécois* (Montreal: Parti Québécois).

48. The controversy over the Quebec model was sparked in mid-1999 after Quebec Liberal Party leader, Jean Charest, suggested that the government's approach to socio-economic management was inherited from the Quiet Revolution and was in dire need of a serious overhaul. His views were echoed by high profile

politicians and public intellectuals such as Senator and former Cabinet minister
Claude Castonguay, *La Presse*'s Editor Alain Dubuc and columnist Claude Picher,
and a few others who essentially argued that the current way of doing things was
counterproductive and hampered Quebec's further modernization. Some even
claimed that there is no such thing as a Quebec model, that Quebec is no different than most western democracies when it comes to social and economic
development, and that if there is indeed a Quebec model, that is nothing to brag
about given the province's relatively poor performance on most key economic
indicators. Premier Lucien Bouchard lashed out at these critics implying in no
uncertain terms that any criticism of the Quebec model should be interpreted as
an attack on Quebec identity and as an attempt at dissolving it into the wider
Canadian vision of the nation. Since then other politicians and academics have
joined the fray from time to time as the debate tends to re-emerge whenever
Quebec identity seems at stake.

49.   G.L. Bourque, *Le modèle québécois de développement* (Sainte Foy: Presses de
l'Université du Québec, 2000); Y. Comeau, L. Favreau, B. Lévesque and M.
Mendell, *Emploi, économie sociale, développement local. Les nouvelles filières*
(Sainte-Foy: Presses de l'Université du Québec, 2001); L. Favreau and B.
Lévesque, *Développement économique et communautaire. Economie sociale et
intervention* (Sainte-Foy: Presses de l'Université du Québec, 1996); B. Lévesque
and M. Mendell, *La création d'entreprises par les chômeurs et les sans-emploi:
le rôle de la microfinance*. Research report submitted to the International Labor
Organization (Montreal: Centre de recherche sur les innovations sociales dans
l'économie sociale, les entreprises et les syndicats (CRISES), 2000).

50.   The *Forum pour l'emploi* (Forum for Jobs) was a non-governmental group created in the late 1980s and comprised mainly of representatives from the labour
movement and private corporations. It promoted joint action to fight unemployment and significantly influenced governmental economic strategy.

51.   The *Fonds de solidarité* is an investment fund created by the *Fédération des
travailleurs du Québec* (Quebec Federation of Labour) with money supplied by
workers and the Quebec public. With over $3 billion in assets it focuses all its
investments on Quebec-based enterprises. Individuals investing in the *Fonds* can
avail themselves of attractive tax breaks offered by both the Quebec and federal
governments.

52.   The *Mouvement Desjardins* (credit unions) initiated in the early twentieth century is the best-known success story of the Quebec cooperative movement. Built
with the small savings of ordinary people, it now ranks among the most important Canadian financial institutions.

53.   Since the late 1970s the Quebec government has held several such socio-economic summits. They represent one of the distinctive features of the Quebec
model. They are usually broad-based although more sectoral meetings have also
been convened. Their policy effectiveness varies and depends on the state of the
social tensions between the participants. Early experiments have achieved mitigated results. See A.B. Tanguay, "Concerted Action in Quebec, 1976-1983:
Dialogue of the Deaf," in *Quebec State and Society*, ed. Gagnon. More recent

meetings throughout the 1990s seem to have provided the policy and political consensus the government was seeking.

54. Particularly from the women's movement through *La marche des femmes contre la pauvreté,* and from the Comité d'orientation et de concertation sur l'économie sociale (Lévesque and Mendell, *La création d'entreprises par les chômeurs et les sans-emploi: le rôle de la microfinance,* p. 21).

55. In Quebec, social enterprises are understood as non-profit organizations and co-operatives whose primary objectives include social as well as economic benefits for the communities and regions in which they are located.

56. P. Graefe, "The Contradictory Political Economy of Minority Nationalism: Quebec's Economic Nationalism Reconsidered." Paper presented at the annual meeting of the Association for Canadian Studies, 29 May 2000, p. 13.

57. Marcel Boyer, *La performance économique du Québec: constats et défis* (Montreal: CIRANO, 2001), pp. 3-5.

58. L. Boivin and M. Fortier, eds., *L'économie sociale: l'avenir d'une illusion* (Montreal: Fides, 1998); R. Paquet, "Les emplois de l'économie sociale: forme de démocratisation du travail ou exploitation d'une main-d'oeuvre qualifiée?" *Économie et solidarités* 30, 1(1999):78-94; J.M. Piotte, *Du combat au partenariat: interventions critiques sur le syndicalisme québécois* (Québec: Nota Bene, 1998).

59. Comeau *et al., Emploi, économie sociale, développement local. Les nouvelles filières,* pp. 243-44.

60. On 9 and 10 June 2001, the Ralliement pour l'alternative progressiste (RAP) officially became a political party, establishing itself as a broad coalition including the Green Party, the Parti de la démocratie socialiste and the Quebec Communist Party. Though it is putting forward a radical platform on social and economic issues, it is committed to Quebec sovereignty.

61. A.-G. Gagnon and H. Segal, eds., *The Canadian Social Union Without Quebec: 8 Critical Analyses* (Montreal: IRPP, 2000).

8

The Evolution of Ontario's Confederal Stance in the Nineties: Ideology or Continuity?

Hugh Segal

La position ontarienne en matière de relations fédérales-provinciales sous le gouvernement Harris n'était pas aussi profondément motivée par des considérations idéologiques que certains l'ont cru. Lorsqu'on la replace dans un contexte historique plus large, en prenant en considération les traditions établies sous la gouverne de Davis, Peterson, puis de Rae, on constate que plusieurs des traits caractéristiques de ces administrations ont continué à influencer les grandes tendances philosophiques, fiscales et redistributives de la période Harris. En fait, les initiatives prises par les néo-démocrates semblent être celles qui ont le plus d'importance pour comprendre la position du gouvernement Harris — une indication supplémentaire que cette position n'était pas, en substance, étroitement idéologique.

INTRODUCTION

There are a host of factors that shape a province's stance toward federal-provincial relations in Canada. Some are historical and cultural; others are situational and reflective of electoral fortunes and other political challenges. Most are portrayed by both the federal government and provinces as matters of deep and compelling principle. But it has been my general experience in politics that while historical, cultural and principled questions are frequent, questions that relate to money and who gets to spend it are more fundamental and pervasive. Simply put, whenever one hears a statement from officials or politicians that the matter at hand is about principle and not money, it is usually about the money. That bias should be clearly set out for readers of this analysis. The differences over the 1990s between Premiers Michael Harris, Bob Rae, and David Peterson — representing the three major political traditions in the province of Ontario — were not totally unrelated to their respective ideologies. But it seems both logical and fair to conclude that had Bob Rae governed during times that were as economically expansive as those in the Peterson years and the later Harris years, he would have had a broader range of options and very different issues relative to federal-provincial priorities. Similarly, it can be argued that had Mike Harris governed during a period of prolonged recession his approach to Ottawa may well have been very different both in tone and substance.

In accepting this viewpoint, you need to put in perspective the arguments of the spin doctors of the various governments and their counter-spinners in the editorial boards, who use ideology and/or party policy as pretexts for what in the end may well be structurally determined federal-provincial policies. I am not a determinist on the issue, but I do believe that the vast body of evidence argues for a mix of factors. But, with respect to Ontario and Confederation during the 1990s and the changing positions of the three governments that served during that period, this analysis will advance the case that the mix of factors was profoundly more structural than ideological. In other words, the policies pursued by Ottawa would have led to essentially the same response in Ontario regardless of what political party was in power.

THE DAVIS VERSUS RAE CONTEXT

In the late 1970s and early 1980s, the Davis government was involved in intense negotiations with Ottawa on the constitutional file and energy policy. The election of the Clark minority government in 1979 was in no small measure tied to William Davis's campaign support in Ontario's federal seats. The energy dispute of that period between Ottawa and Queen's Park of that period was in some ways a result of Alberta's constitutional concern about provincial hegemony over natural resources, but was also not inconsistent with Davis's attack on Pierre Trudeau's excise tax of ten cents a gallon during the 1975 Ontario election. The release of a paper on energy pricing by the Ontario government at the annual premiers' conference in August 1979, just a few weeks after Joe Clark's election, both infuriated Alberta and fatally (but unwittingly) wounded Joe Clark's Ontario electoral prospects in 1980. Given the political situation, the Davis government would have felt that any failure to champion the Ontario industrial and consumer interest on energy pricing would be seen as a partisan rollover for the federal Tories.

At the same time, the Alberta government, with the only solid majority among the three main governments involved, Alberta, Ontario, and Canada, was propelled by a traditional and totally justifiable defence of provincial jurisdiction over natural resources. Any embrace of a two-price system where Canadians paid less than the world price for Alberta resources would be a subsidy paid by future generations of Albertans to the eastern provinces — a birthright violation no Alberta premier could have been seen to willingly endorse. From Ontario's perspective, the creation years earlier of the Ottawa Valley Line by the Diefenbaker administration, which forced all consumers and industries to the west of that line to buy energy from the substantially more expensive Alberta energy basin rather than from cheaper Middle East and Venezuelan sources, constituted a subsidy to the process of exploration and resource development in Alberta. That contribution, Davis argued later, earned Ontario consumers a "Canadian price" for oil and gas.

If one accepts that the role of political culture is to provide "a range of acceptable values and standards upon which leaders can draw in attempting to justify their policies,"[1] it is clear that this stance by Davis was not about the right-left spectrum at all. It was about championing the consumer and the requirement of some Canadian interest on energy pricing. The classic pragmatism of Ontario's political culture was dominant at this particular juncture. It was a pragmatism that federal Liberals and Ontario Conservatives understood, but Clark did not. This dispute paralysed the Clark administration, creating a 20-point lead for the Trudeau Liberals in Ontario, which was simply insurmountable in the 1980 election. The fact that the election was precipitated by a defeat in the House of Commons for the Clark government over a budget that contained an 18 cents per gallon excise tax reduced the probability of meaningful Ontario Conservative support for the Clark re-election effort, in view specifically of Davis's opposition to the excise tax increase imposed by the Trudeau administration earlier.

Before the advent of the Reform Party of Canada later in the 1980s, close to 55 percent of those Ontarians who voted federally for the Liberal Party voted provincially for the Progressive Conservative Party. That was particularly true under the essentially moderate policies of the Davis administration. While flare-ups between the two administrations were not infrequent — proposed PLO (Palestine Liberation Organization) attendance at a UN Law Enforcement Conference in 1974; the revenue guarantee dispute in 1976 between Darcy McKeough for Ontario and Donald Macdonald for the federal government; general disagreement over fiscal and budgetary policy throughout the 1970s and 1980s — the tendency of voters to split their federal and provincial vote in Ontario has a long and distinguished tradition, especially in more urbanized areas. It is noteworthy that despite the suggestion Ontario has moved radically to the right since the election of Mike Harris in 1995 the same voting patterns continue, only more so as a result of fragmentation of the opposition parties in Ottawa. In the federal elections of 1997 and 2000, regions of Ontario that sent heavily Progressive Conservative delegations to Queen's Park elected federal Liberals to Ottawa. The traditional pragmatic balance of the Ontario voter between federal Liberals and provincial Conservatives continues to survive.

When the defeat of the Clark administration came — for reasons not unrelated to the dispute with Ontario on energy matters — and the Liberals were restored in Ottawa, Ontario assumed a more conciliatory and cooperative approach to confederal issues. This was not unrelated to William Davis's own approach — being, as he often put it, "a Canadian first." Ontario's confederal orientation at this time was also significantly influenced by the 1980 referendum in Quebec on sovereignty association. Unlike 1995, when the federal government actively discouraged participation of other provincial governments in the referendum process, the 1980 effort involved various premiers, including Bill Davis, Peter Lougheed, and Richard Hatfield, making a series of visits and speeches in Quebec about the kind of constitutional change they desired, and how they would collaborate with Quebec on constitutional matters after a "Non" vote. Those interventions, as well as relatively close coordination with the Quebec federalist leader Claude Ryan, a negative characterization of female opponents to sovereignty by the "Yes" side, along with Pierre Trudeau's forceful presence, produced an unambiguous "Non" vote and a clear sense of obligation in Ontario to contribute to and energize constitutional change.

In sum, the confluence of constitutional and energy issues in the 1979–81 period produced a positive confederal orientation in Ontario. The government of Ontario became an enthusiastic partner in constitutional change; it favoured renewing a responsible role for the federal government; it opposed excessive decentralization; and it accepted Quebec's desire for significant cultural, linguistic, and constitutional protections. In short, the Government of Ontario helped establish some momentum for constitutional reform, which culminated with the patriation of the constitution in 1982. David Peterson's Liberal government maintained the proconstitutional change bias of the previous Conservative governments.

The circumstances surrounding the election of the Rae government in 1990 were profoundly different. That government followed a spendthrift Liberal administration that had won its own 1987 majority after having been levered into power in 1985 with the help of the New Democratic Party (NDP). Bob Rae inherited a burgeoning Ontario deficit at the beginning of what was an overall recession in Ontario. The election of Ontario's first social democratic NDP government was the result of several factors. The traditional first-past-the-post electoral system allowed a majority government to be formed with less than 40 percent of the popular vote. The premature election call by the Liberals lacked a meaningful script. Splinter parties like the Family Coalition and Christian Heritage, which focused on issues like abortion, siphoned away as much as 4 or 5 percent of the vote for traditional parties (especially the Conservative Party), which produced unexpected rural wins for NDP candidates. Mike Harris had just been chosen to lead the third-place and financially overburdened Ontario Progressive Conservative Party, and he focused during the election on hammering Liberal tax policies in a way that rebuilt parts of the Tory base but produced an anti-Peterson voter fervour that further helped the

New Democrats. With the Mulroney government in its post-Meech and pre-Charlottetown funk, and because Mr. Peterson had been intimately involved with the Meech Lake agreement and its collapse, the anti-incumbent mood worked substantially to Bob Rae's advantage. Another vital part of the NDP victory was the high regard in which Rae was held. His persona was associated with fairness, affability, and relative moderation, especially when compared to previous NDP leaders in Ontario and elsewhere.

The decision of the Peterson administration to increase spending well beyond the level of inflation had heated up the provincial economy in a way that forced the Bank of Canada to apply higher interest rates to dampen down a serious inflationary spiral. This activity not only slowed the economy but also produced the twin scourges for the Rae government of collapsing revenues precisely as costs for matters like welfare and health care began to rise substantially. The recession that hit the Rae government — and, in the process, also contributed to the demolition of the Kim Campbell government in Ottawa — produced a more difficult frame of reference for Queen's Park, with revenues collapsing, costs increasing, and a social democratic administration determined to address social injustice. The Rae administration's early decision to embrace a $10 billion dollar deficit as the appropriate instrument to at least bridge the time gap until the economy came back, combined with a longer recession than most had predicted, resulted in a very tattered fiscal capacity which could not but undermine the *noblesse oblige* patina Ontario had worn with such comfort in the past.

There was early relief in the Rae administration at the election of a federal Liberal government in 1993 which took all but one of Ontario's 103 seats and would be utterly dependent on holding those in any future election. However, as federal Finance Minister Paul Martin set about the process of restraining federal transfers, especially the Canadian Health and Social Transfer (CHST), it became apparent to the Ontario government that this was little more than a continuation of the Wilson/Mazankowski regime, perhaps even worse so far as Ontario was concerned.

In February 1994, Premier Rae wrote to all federal MPs from Ontario,[2] laying out a litany of unfairness and calling upon them to "make a choice and to send a message to the people of Ontario. Let them know, through your upcoming budget, that you will end the discriminatory policies of the former Conservative government, and treat the people of Ontario fairly."[3] Among the discriminatory issues he raised were:

- Ottawa capping the Canada Assistance Plan in Ontario, allegedly producing extra cost for Ontario of $1.7 billion per annum;

- Ottawa only spending 27 percent of its training budget in Ontario, despite the province having 38 percent of the national workforce and 36 percent of the unemployed;

- Ontario receives 55 percent of Canada's immigrants while receiving only 38 percent of federal funding.

The doctrine of "fair shares federalism" was launched with this initiative and with a budget paper that accompanied the last budget of the Rae administration in April 1995. That effort consisted of a line-by-line comparison of the amount of Ontario's tax contributions to Ottawa and the amount invested by Ottawa in Ontario, accompanied by a comparative statistic about Ontario's population or its percentage of the workforce or some other statistic that conveyed a sense of unfairness for the Ontario taxpayer.

In fact, the April budget paper, while noting that a percentage of Ontario's $15 billion contribution in excess of return to the province was "a legitimate reflection of sharing the wealth,"[4] goes on to point out in significant detail that while Ontario contributed 43 percent of Ottawa's total receipts from all domestic sources, only 31 percent of Ottawa expenditures return to Ontario. "Fair shares federalism" had been born. In terms of Ontario's political culture, New Democrats, who are usually strong proponents of a strong central government, were also forced by both fiscal and economic reality to engage Ottawa on the issue of fairness. In so doing, they conformed fully to the political pragmatism that drove Bill Davis on energy in 1979–80.

STRUCTURAL AND IDEOLOGICAL INTERPLAY

It is likely that an endless dialectic on what is structural and what is ideological could emerge in almost any area of public policy analysis. For the purposes of this analysis I treat structural determinants as those that would have forced any Ontario government to react in a particular way notwithstanding its political affiliation. Ideological determinants are those that are less impacted by externalities and more directed from the core of party belief. While some argue that there is little the current Harris government has done that is not ideological, accepting the role of ideology does not necessarily diminish the importance of structural issues — namely those that would invoke a similar response from any Ontario administration whether of the left or the right, or any shade in between.

During the negotiations leading up to the Charlottetown Accord, Ontario proposed a social charter as an appropriate inclusion in the Canadian constitution. There are few observers who would not agree that the Social Charter accurately reflected Bob Rae's view as a social democrat of what Canada's basic law should proclaim. As Bob Rae said in the Premier's Message accompanying the release of the charter:

> The basic reason for a social charter is simply this: we want to make sure some of our most important achievements, like medicare and universal education, are protected and guaranteed. Putting them in a constitution is a way of saying that

being a Canadian citizen means more than having just a formal set of rights. It means giving constitutional teeth to our common sense of what you are entitled to simply because you're a Canadian.[5]

Whether that is deemed ideological or not, it expresses fundamental views about the nature of society that cannot but be central to the way that premiers would respond to any cuts in transfer payments or cost-sharing formulas that diminished Ontario's capacity to keep up its own end relative to its own population. When confronted with increasing fiscal pressure, Premier Rae embraced the novel approach of achieving savings and cost-control through the option of unpaid days off as opposed to job cuts or layoffs. This was Rae's "social contract." The notion of a strong and vital social obligation within the context of federal-provincial relations or within the realm of Ontario's domestic fiscal and social policies was not only central to the overall government view advanced by the Rae administration but also a more fundamental part of its core ideology than more traditional social democrat nostrums such as nationalization or increasing the role of the state.

Does this ideological preference for social contracts become an underpinning for the "fair shares federalism" that motivated Rae's letter to the MPs or the April 1995 budget paper with its accounting critique of the federal government? Here I conclude that the transfer from social charter to fair shares federalism was both structural and ideological. It was structural in the very strong sense of a deep and relentless recession, the worst in Ontario since World War II, and an even stronger concern that Ontario was having its capacity to sustain its part of the social contract buffeted by revenue collapse and an increase in need. When it became clear that the federal Liberals would go substantially further in cutting transfers than the previous federal Conservative government to the detriment of Ontario, Premier Rae had few other options but to pursue a strong accounting process that detailed what would constitute fair treatment for the province.

It is hard to see how a provincial government of Progressive Conservative or Liberal allegiance could have taken any other meaningfully different path. It may very well be that the point of departure for Ontario's confederal stance was driven by an ideological commitment to basic social entitlements, but in the end it was the hard and compelling structural realities that determined the position on which the Rae government ended its federal-provincial dialogue.

On the Meech Lake Accord, as an opposition party leader and later during the Charlottetown negotiations as premier, Bob Rae played an engaged, creative and positive role, creating critical bridges between Ottawa and other provinces and specific bridges between the entire process and Canada's First Nations. The failure of the Charlottetown referendum ended the period of countrywide constitutional creativity for some time to come, as did the election of a sovereignist Quebec government in the ensuing years. But Ontario had serious fiscal issues to address in the years that followed the end of

Charlottetown, and structural realities made the course taken essentially unavoidable.

Arrayed against the backdrop of Ontario's political culture, Premier Rae's actions did not exceed the normal parameters of the pragmatic bias that drove that culture. Ontario's position with respect to fairness did not differ because Conservatives had yielded to Liberals in the election of 1993. The driving force behind Rae's fair shares federalism was the domestic requirement to keep the basic social bargain in Ontario and the fiscal realities of that bargain — two drivers essentially consistent with Ontario's dominant political culture.

ROOM TO MANOEUVRE IN THE NEW ECONOMY

The election of the Harris government in 1995 was not, as has been suggested on occasion, a massive move to the right by the provincial electorate. If anything, it can be viewed as both a move to the centre and a result of a poorly executed campaign on the part of the Ontario Liberal Party. The Liberals under Lynn McLeod began the pre-election and writ period with a compelling first-place position, leading both the second-place New Democrats and third-place Progressive Conservatives by healthy two-digit gaps. The Conservatives had published, consulted upon, and disseminated a policy platform innocuously called *The Common Sense Revolution*, which was focus group tested enough to be more about extolling the centrist values of common sense than setting the heather afire with talk of revolution. In its main underpinnings, namely a tax cut and stability in education and health funding, it appealed primarily to the traditional Tory core and to the soft centre-right faction of Ontario's Liberal voting coalition. Here the Harris campaign team sought merely to recreate the voting pattern in Ontario of voting Liberal federally and Progressive Conservative provincially that had largely dominated the Davis elections of 1971, 1975, 1977, and 1981 — except that the Tories in Ontario in 1995 started with massive Liberal dominance of Ontario's federal seats. While the common sense revolution presented a coherent script, it was not taken terribly seriously coming from a third-place party.

But it was a script, something the Liberal Party chose to enter the election season essentially without. And while revisionist history has on occasion claimed this to have been a tectonic shift in Ontario's politics, it was a script that advocated levels of spending that approximated the relative levels of the Davis administration, hardly known as a narrow right-wing regime. The Liberal leader herself, and the party's campaign strategy, portrayed McLeod almost as the incumbent. As Rae, the premier, was actually the incumbent (and ran a spirited and focused campaign), the only party available for those looking for any change at all was the Progressive Conservatives. Playing into the Tories' electoral opportunity was the traditional split-vote tendency that has been a large part of Ontario electoral history. The presence in Ottawa of a recently elected federal Liberal majority government only increased the likelihood that Ontario voters would seek the traditional balance at provincial election time, by not choosing Liberals provincially.

The Conservatives ran a disciplined and well-organized campaign underlying the themes most likely to pry votes from the soft Liberal camp to Tory candidates across the province. The New Democrats averted a complete collapse through the effective campaign, integrity and popularity of Premier Rae. The Liberals failed to execute a coherent campaign. The result, a Tory majority, was therefore about many things. But it is clear that there is no evidence to suggest that it was the result of a meaningful ideological shift or any change in political culture.

The Tories moved with relative haste to begin cutting various areas of government expenditure, notably welfare for the able-bodied, so as to reduce deficits and finance tax cuts. In moving on expenditures, the government continued what the Rae government had latterly advanced and joined, an emerging consensus on the need to achieve some measure of fiscal discipline — a consensus that crossed both provincial and partisan lines.

By that point in the decade, Frank McKenna in New Brunswick and Roy Romanow in Saskatchewan, a Liberal and New Democrat respectively, had already shown substantially more fiscal discipline than the Conservatives they had replaced. The Harris administration was in a sense a new arrival in a sea of consensus about the need to reduce government spending and borrow in order to lever public fiscal balance in support of economic expansion writ large. Where the Harris administration was outside the consensus was in having a tax cut along with fiscal constraint as opposed to waiting until after fiscal balance had been achieved. This more Reaganesque policy was highly responsive to a middle-income voter cohort that felt income taxes were steadily on the rise while provincial services were at best stalled or being reduced in scope.

The continued federal focus on expenditure reduction saw the reduction of transfers to the provinces at a rate greater than the reduction in federal own-account spending. And while Ottawa would pay politically in the 1997 election in Atlantic Canada for some of the cuts it made in the shift from Unemployment to Employment Insurance and the modification of eligibility thresholds, there was a clear perception in the provinces that Ottawa was using provincial transfers and diminished forward liabilities to put its own fiscal house in order.

In an August 1996 speech in Calgary to the Chamber of Commerce, barely a year after being elected, Premier Harris stated the Ontario view in a very precise way:

We've learned from other countries. We've learned from Canadian premiers. Gary Filmon of course, and from Frank McKenna and, dare I say it, even Roy Romanow. Each of these leaders has acted to change the way government operates in his jurisdiction.[6]

The premier chose not to be as complimentary to the federal government:

I believe that the types of policies we are implementing in our own provinces have huge potential if they were to be implemented imaginatively and courageously by all levels of government, particularly by the federal government. To date, the federal government has cut spending primarily by reducing transfers to the provinces. I will never criticize them for cutting spending if it is part of a fair and genuine plan to balance the federal budget. But as our minister of finance pointed out at the last Finance Ministers' Meeting, the federal government is cutting payments to the provinces for health, education and social programs by 42.2 percent while the rest of its own program spending is being reduced by only 1.3 percent![7]

A full year since the defeat of the Rae government, yet despite the talk of a new ideology and a "common sense revolution," Premier Harris's perspective on federal-provincial transfers was essentially the same as Rae's view. And while the principle of parity in cuts would have been differently applied by the Conservative premier (it is not at all clear that Premier Rae would have called for federal program cuts to be of the same magnitude as cuts in transfers to the provinces), the issue of "the money" and the fairness was still very much at the core of Ontario's position.

In anticipation of the Annual Premiers' Conference in Jasper, Premier Harris laid the groundwork for an evolution in the Ontario confederal stance away from the traditional Davis position in favour of a stronger federal government:

If this country is to enter the next century ready for the real challenges of the new global economy ... we must all co-operate. We need all provincial, territorial, and federal governments working together to create jobs, hope, growth and opportunity for all Canadians ... Ontario recently released a paper by Professor Tom Courchene of Queen's University — a university that now has Peter Lougheed as its chancellor, by the way. Professor Courchene looks at the feasibility and practicality of developing accords between governments, which would lay out a clear set of rules and guidelines for managing the country without a unilateral approach by Ottawa or without intrusive federal legislation in areas of provincial jurisdiction.[8]

While various premiers felt moved to attack the Courchene paper, the similarities in the underlying principles of that paper, the Calgary Declaration signed by the premiers a year later, and the Social Union Framework Agreement agreed to by Ottawa and nine of the provinces in 1999 are quite compelling and important. Harris's support for and championing of the interprovincial principle followed a year of work by a ministerial council on social reform co-chaired by the Hon. Diane Cunningham of the Ontario Cabinet and the

Hon. Ken Rostad of Alberta. The championing of interprovincial social policy engagement is really a response to what provinces viewed as a capricious cutting of transfers in a way that made managing the internal social contract in each province more difficult.

Ontario became an enthusiastic supporter of a more interprovincial approach to social policy and an advocate for more provincial independence in economic and fiscal policy. In some respects, however, this latter evolution is also an unavoidable structural response to Ottawa's focus on maintaining its unilateral federal redistributional programs while cutting transfers to the provinces as equalization was maintained. With social expenditures constituting the lion's share of provincial budgets and with federal transfers either cut or frozen at levels unreflective of the increase in demand or provincial client realities, provinces clearly had to reform the cost side of their programs while working to more fully maximize the investment and ensuing economic growth necessary to sustain the spending capacity they needed even for reformed social service delivery structures and programs. For an unequalized province like Ontario, badly hit by the recession and feeling demonstrably short-changed in terms of federal transfers, a greater focus on its own income-generation capacity — that is, economic growth and development — was both a logical and unavoidable shift. Indeed, it would push Ontario to seek the appropriate manoeuvrability around key economic instruments, such as taxation and specified tax treatment of key and strategic tax areas.

Ontario's traditional focus on competitiveness with the neighbouring American states in both social programs and economic productivity was heightened by the increased north-south pull after the Free Trade Agreement and the North American Free Trade Agreement. This reality forced Ontario to seek to reduce uncompetitive aggregate taxation levels and, more importantly, fed the heightened domestic perception of excessive taxation among investors and entrepreneurs. While tax cuts obviously have considerable electoral appeal, it is hard to believe that Ontario could have endured the cumulative federal and provincial tax burden on the provinces and have remained competitive in the North American economy. The need for more provincial flexibility in economic instruments was in a sense a direct result of the increased pressure brought upon provincial programs by Ottawa's transfer policies. The need to gain greater flexibility and develop the instruments that would allow provincial policies in support of economic growth defined the way the decade ended, and the kind of federal-provincial posture that Ontario would take into the new millennium.

It could reasonably be concluded that elements of Ontario's traditional political culture — stability on the political spectrum, support for core pragmatism, and being "Canadian First" — were being tilted at this time by the joint focus on greater integration with the United States in terms of tax competitiveness and a reduced federal presence. But on deeper reflection it is not clear that conclusion holds up. The focus on tax cuts so as to maintain competitiveness in the Great Lakes Region is really just a 1995 version of the Davis administration's opposition to a world price for energy in 1979. In other words, this was more about conforming to the operative and traditional political culture in Ontario than moving away from it.

ONTARIO SEEKS NEW INSTRUMENTS

While Ontario strongly supported greater intergovernmental cooperation, as expressed in the Calgary Declaration and the Social Union Framework Agreement, the Government of Ontario also believed it required new instruments to improve Ontario's competitive position in the North American economy. In its 1997 budget, the Ontario government announced that it would seek new fiscal arrangements with the federal government so as to improve Ontario's economic competitiveness. And because it was in a budget, it takes on more importance than the rhetoric of finance ministers' meetings or partisan speeches. A budget instantly becomes a pillar of provincial policy and a dye through which all subsequent provincial policy must be examined.

In the 1997 Budget Speech, Treasurer Ernie Eves made three requests of Ottawa:

> In its most recent budget, the federal government actually reduced the amounts of a gift to a Crown foundation that can be claimed for an income tax credit from 100 percent of income in a year to 75 percent. While that budget followed Ontario's lead by providing incentives for conventional charitable giving, its treatment of Crown foundations is not appropriate.... We have asked the Federal government to administer a tax credit for Ontario to address this problem.... The federal government has said no. Our request means no cost to the federal government since we would pay for administration and only the Ontario tax would be affected. It also means that the federal government is attempting to prevent Ontario from encouraging giving to charitable foundations by making changes to our own provincial tax system.[9]

This specific request and refusal had an impact on provincial charities like hospitals and universities seeking the same charitable status as federally chartered charitable organizations that had set up federal Crown foundations to maximize the deductibility to the donor. The desire to establish provincial Crown foundations for some 19 high-profile organizations had been the direct result of a consultation led by the minister's parliamentary assistant. Ottawa bureaucratic recalcitrance at the time was not only intrinsically frustrating and apparently arrogant, but it was also visible to the leaders of Ontario's business and philanthropic elite. While a matter generally of secondary importance in the larger provincial scheme of things and just another irritant by Ottawa, it was the kind of "on the side of the angels" issue few provincial governments could fail to embrace and exploit.

This dispute also formed the basis for a structural proposition relative to Ontario's own provincial income tax. In that same budget, Ontario cited other areas where Ottawa had refused Ontario's requests for flexibility. Ontario had asked for an easily accessed check-off box for those taxpayers who wished to donate tax refunds to lower the debt, and Ottawa had said there was no room on the form. Ontario had also asked for a simple, easily understood design for administering the Fair Share Health Care Levy and Ottawa's response had been "not now."[10] At this time, the Government of Ontario also informally notified the federal government that unless it was prepared to loosen up a bit, Ontario would have to seriously consider withdrawing from the current common tax collection arrangements. A paper in that same budget talked about the issues related to an Ontario withdrawal.

Ontario also used the 1997 budget to send a strong message to Ottawa on the negative impacts of policy divergence. The federal government's payroll taxes, especially high Employment Insurance premiums, and the need for federal tax cuts were all precisely enumerated in the Treasurer's speech. And, in a fashion that would have made Bob Rae proud, issues of fairness in federal expenditures in Ontario were also raised. It cited the differentials between what an unemployed person receives in New Brunswick, British Columbia, and Ontario, showing Ontario at the lowest level.[11] Similar concerns were expressed relative to employment training dollars available per capita to Ontario compared to Quebec.[12] The interest cost to Ontario of Ottawa collecting Ontario's taxes and holding until remittance — no remittance made until $1.5 billion are collected — was also raised in the 1997 budget speech.[13]

The 1997 budget barrage can be seen as an accumulation of a series of irritants that, when taken together, began to suggest a serious and mounting federal restraint upon Ontario's capacity to use the tax system to advance a more competitive fiscal and economic plan. In order to understand the ledger from the provincial perspective, it is important to understand the degree to which structural policy shifts from Ottawa (and here I use structural in the sense of fiscal and revenue effects that will persist well into the future) accumulated to produce an abiding sense of frustration. France St-Hilaire has commented on the structural burden in this way:

> At the end of the day, we are left with:
> - a federal government that has withdrawn significantly from the financing of health, post-secondary education and social assistance;
> - a federal government that has reneged on its stabilization role in the economy and implemented policies which undermine the risk-sharing aspects of our federal system;
> - provincial governments that must bear greater expenditure responsibilities — for instance, they now have to deal on their own with the problems associated with the long-term unemployed — and that are more exposed than ever to the fiscal effects of future recessions;

- a context where 'have' provinces in response to previous cases of unfair treatment and added fiscal pressures are increasingly unwilling to tolerate federal
  redistributive schemes of any kind.[14]

Ontario's search for new instruments is not particularly new, as Tom
Courchene carefully documented in a recent analysis of the personal income
tax (PIT) issue.[15] Nor is Ontario alone in having sought its own tax system —
or at least talking about seeking its own system. But in a sense the search for
new instruments reflects the growing roles that local governments have in
attracting and maintaining high value-added investment and retaining and sustaining the human capital vital to sustaining economic growth and quality of
life. Quebec has long spoken about the need for "*les instruments du société*"
by which it means the economic and social levers vital to sustaining the socio-
economic and cultural "exigencies" of a modern pluralist French-speaking
society in North America.

As the new decade began, and Ottawa responded to both the Calgary Declaration, the Social Union Framework Agreement, and the concerns about
re-investment in health, it is clear that the toughening up of Ontario's confederal
stance was at least in part a natural evolution, more structural than ideological
and largely in response to a new kind of federal unilateralism that seemed
basic to Ottawa's deficit reduction strategy.

THE CONCILIATORY INTERLUDES

It would be factually incorrect to look at the last decade of federal-provincial
relations relative to Ontario without highlighting the significant points of in-
tersection between Ontario and Ottawa. It is also important to point out how
those differed from earlier points in recent history, and to try and understand
how those points of difference provide a more comprehensive appreciation of
the evolutionary thrust over the decade as a whole. The balance in those peaks
and valleys are shaped by the core — the essentially pragmatic and non-
ideological nature of Ontario's political culture.

Premier Peterson's steadfast support of the Meech Lake Accord, which
contrasted sharply with his stout opposition to free trade, reflected Ontario's
traditional way of separating its economic concerns and disputes from the
needs of the nation overall, most especially national unity. Peterson and his
Liberal government paid dearly for that support, as did a number of incumbent administrations that supported the Meech Lake Accord. Premier Rae
advanced the Charlottetown Accord with equal vigour when he was in
government and generally associated himself with the federalist position in
Quebec, even when Prime Minister Chrétien's unclear strategy made that particularly difficult. Premier Harris was as supportive as could be possible to

the federalist cause in Quebec during the 1995 referendum despite being told wrongly by Ottawa (along with the other premiers) until the very last few hours that everything was going well. That Harris was less encouraging when the prime minister sought support for a rushed motion in the House of Commons right after the near-disastrous referendum that would enshrine distinct society and regional vetoes should not be surprising.

Ontario's policy toward Quebec, dating from John Robarts and embracing Messrs Davis, Peterson, Rae, and Harris is one of both constructive engagement and collaboration with the next largest province in confederation and a measured approach to the issue of federal-provincial balance. Rushed federal measures — ill-conceived or born in panic and confusion — are as popular with the present-day Ontario premier as the ill-conceived and repressive *War Measures Act* was with John Robarts. While Ontario is a reliable ally in defence of the legitimacy of the confederal union, it is not, nor has it ever been, a willy-nilly hallelujah chorus for slapdash trigger-happy excess from any federal administration.

In the negotiations that culminated in the Calgary Declaration, Ontario was a constructive and engaged participant working toward creative and practical compromises in the Ontario tradition. It is fair to conclude the very same about the Social Union Framework Agreement. Premier Harris (and his son) attended the large pro-Canada demonstration in Montreal the week before the 1995 referendum in Quebec, and on the night of the referendum Harris clearly stated Ontario's traditional confederal stance:

> tonight's close win for the "NO" option is no reason for complacency. Canadians over the last number of weeks, and Quebeckers in their decision today, have clearly told us the status quo is not acceptable. We have a collective duty to address how our federation might better serve all Canadians.... [A]long with Quebeckers, Ontarians earnestly believe that the way the federation is managed must be substantially changed for the better.[16]

The similarity of Premier Harris's position after the 1995 referendum to that of Premier Davis after 1980 and the similarity of Premiers Rae and Peterson on issues like Meech and Charlottetown (with Harris as a Conservative MPP and party leader voting for both) speaks eloquently to the pervasive and non-ideological nature of Ontario's political culture on the core question of national unity.

It is very hard to weigh the main events in both the Rae and Harris periods and conclude that ideology stood in the way of collaboration when appropriate or that ideology exacerbated the nature of those disagreements that were structural in both origin and impact. Similarly, Ottawa's decision to relent in discussions over taxation on "tax on tax" and permit "tax on base," which had the effect of freeing provinces to have their own provincial tax rates for personal income, as well as the decision to distribute conciliatory health funding at the time of the Social Union Framework Agreement on a per capita basis, were noteworthy gestures reflective of legitimate Ontario concerns. Indeed, the decade was not devoid of gestures of conciliation from both sides. But it also ended with irritants in health care, immigration funding, training funding, and tax policy — all of which might flare up at any time.

THE WAY AHEAD

While it is difficult to predict the exact future of federal-provincial relations, including relations between Toronto and Ottawa, a reflection on the past decade may well reveal a particular prism though which to scan the way ahead. Where would federal-provincial relations have been if Ottawa, either in the form of Don Mazankowski or Paul Martin, had sat with the provinces and jointly explored a mutually cooperative path through the high waters of looming deficits and cascading federal and provincial debt? What if unilateralism had not been Ottawa's chosen point of entry and consistent path through the decade? What if the Social Union Framework Agreement had been preceded by a confederal plan for fiscal balance that was a collective effort? What would the state of federal-provincial relations be today? Surely no worse.

What is clear is that the structural policy changes created by Ottawa's unilateralism will now combine with rapid changes in the world economy and the need for provinces to move deftly to secure local economic and social advantage to put even more strain on federal-provincial relations. How Ottawa deals with its mounting surplus and how Ottawa seeks to build consensus with the provinces relative to issues like debt reduction and tax policy will determine the structural realities that will shape Ontario's emerging stance in the present decade. Ontario's economic vision must extend more north-south than east-west, and more global and hemispheric than just confederal or bilateral. The evidence from the nineties indicates most clearly that ideology will have little more than a peripheral impact on how Ontario responds to or engages with the rest of our federation during that period. And the pervasive themes of Ontario's political culture — relative moderation, pragmatism, and balance — will only be ignored at their own peril by those who seek public favour or legitimacy.

NOTES

I would like to thank Bradley Axmith, a graduate in History from Concordia University who assisted with some of the research for this chapter.

1.   David V.J. Bell, *Roots of Disunity: A Look at Canadian Political Culture* (Toronto: McClelland & Stewart, 1979), p. 277.

2. Ontario. Ministry of Intergovernmental Affairs, Media Release. 2 February 1994.

3. Ibid.

4. Ontario. Ministry of Finance. *Ontario Budget* (Toronto: Queen's Printer for Ontario, April 1994).

5. Ontario. Ministry of Intergovernmental Affairs. Media Release, 13 February 1992.

6. The Hon. Michael Harris, Address to the Calgary Chamber of Commerce, 20 August 1996.

7. Ibid.

8. Ibid.

9. Ontario. Ministry of Finance, *Budget Speech of the Minister, 1997 Budget* (Toronto: Queen's Printer for Ontario, 1997).

10. Ibid.

11. The average benefit in New Brunswick was $13,100; in BC, $6,500; in Ontario, $4,800. All figures are for 1996.

12. The figures are $1,060 per Quebec unemployed worker and $850 per Ontario counterpart.

13. Interest costs were cited by the minister as over $100 million for Ontario on an annual basis.

14. France St-Hilaire, "Comment," in *Stretching the Federation*, ed. Robert Young (Kingston: Institute of Intergovernmental Relations, Queen's University, 1999), p. 192.

15. Thomas Courchene, "The PIT and the Pendulum: Reflections on Ontario's Proposal to Mount Its Own Personal Income Tax System," in *Stretching the Federation*, ed. Young, pp. 129-186.

16. Office of the Premier of Ontario, Media Release, 22 August 1995.

9

Social Democracy in a Neo-Conservative Age: The Politics of Manitoba and Saskatchewan

Nelson Wiseman

Ce chapitre s'intéresse à la culture politique du Manitoba et de la Saskatchewan à travers les prismes idéologiques du néoconservatisme et de la social-démocratie. Un fossé culturel existe entre les traditions relativement collectivistes de ces provinces et les préférences plutôt individualistes de l'Alberta. Cette situation a conduit à des choix électoraux différents et des propositions divergentes en ce qui a trait au système fédéral canadien. Est-ce que la vague néoconservatrice des dernières décennies a érodé les différences historiques et contribué à une convergence idéologique? Pour y répondre, ce chapitre reprend les points de vue des gouvernements, des partis et des citoyens envers les enjeux fédéraux et rend compte des différentes conditions socio-économiques des provinces des Prairies.

In recent decades, Canada and the western world have been buffeted by the ideology of neo-conservatism. This influences the tone and content of political discourse and the workings of the Canadian federation. Ideologies such as neo-conservatism refer to abstract ideas or principles; political culture refers to the works and ideas of specific groups of peoples.[1] Political culture may be considered as an independent variable that has helped to shape the Canadian federation.

The three Prairie provinces, their peoples and their culture, have historically been lumped together as a single identifiable and distinctive entity. The thesis of this chapter is that, broadly speaking, two distinct political cultural traditions have arisen on the prairies that have pointed to dramatically different directions for the Canadian federal system. The eastern Prairies, Manitoba and Saskatchewan, have developed and sustained a strong collectivist tradition that may be counterposed to the strong individualist tradition that has taken hold in Alberta. Manitoba and Saskatchewan have been voices for strong central government and an active role for the state, both provincial and federal.

Alberta has been a voice for smaller government and a more decentralized and classical federal system. These distinct cultural dispositions have been reinforced by the relative wealth of Alberta and the relative poverty of the other two provinces. A question that emerges against the backdrop of recent international and external forces — globalization, continental economic integration, and the growth of large transnational corporations in the agricultural and other sectors — is: Has the neo-conservatism of the last two decades eroded the social democratic culture of Manitoba and Saskatchewan and reinforced the conservative culture of Alberta?

At the beginning of the twenty-first century, the two leading neo-conservative and Conservative governments in Canada were in Alberta and Ontario. Between them, in Manitoba and Saskatchewan, two self-styled social democratic regimes held sway. Twenty years earlier, in 1981, Conservatives also governed Alberta and Ontario. Manitoba and Saskatchewan were also governed then by the social-democratic New Democratic Party (NDP). From this perspective, what stands out is the ideological contrast of Manitoba and Saskatchewan and its apparent durability. If the federal Liberals have been the natural government party for the past century, then the NDP has been the natural government party of Saskatchewan since 1944, holding office in each of the past seven decades. In Manitoba, the NDP has been in office more than out of it since 1969, also governing in every decade since then. With the exception of British Columbia, this is striking in comparison with other provinces.

There is no single overriding political tradition on the prairies. The three Prairie provinces have always been diverse politically. Right-wing parties have dominated Alberta since the 1930s in what C.B. Macpherson characterized as a quasi-party system.[2] Alberta rallies around one provincial party, practising the "Politics of Consensus"; Saskatchewan's practice is "Parties in a Politically Competitive Province".[3] Manitoba has gone from having a provincial party system like Ontario's (the NDP as the weak third sister) to one like Saskatchewan's and British Columbia's (an ideologically polarized two-party system). That the right-wing party in Saskatchewan has changed — from the Liberals in the 1960s to the Conservatives in the 1980s to the Saskatchewan Party in 1999 — merely confirms the prevalence and persistence of ideology over partisan labels. The Prairies gave birth to the Reform Party, but the appetite for it and its neo-conservatism proved relatively depressed in Manitoba and Saskatchewan. Consider the 1993 federal election: Reform swept the overwhelming majority of seats in Alberta, but Saskatchewan elected more NDP MPs than Reformers and more than the rest of Canada. In the 2000 election, the eastern Prairies' relative receptivity to social democracy continued. Although the Alliance Party performed better than the NDP, the latter captured 26 percent of the Saskatchewan vote, triple its national average. In Manitoba social democrats won four seats, more than in any other province and as many as the Alliance.

One way to downplay the significance of the NDP's hold on office in Saskatchewan and Manitoba is to see it as having been swept up itself in the neo-conservative temper of recent times. The charge that the CCF-NDP has lost its once radical edge, that it is not very different from its partisan competitors, is an old one. Mackenzie King and Louis St. Laurent thought of the CCF as "Liberals in a hurry." One book dismissed it as *A Protest Movement Becalmed* [4] in the 1960s. The Waffle movement's expulsion from the NDP in the 1970s was depicted as another rejection of socialism.[5] Whatever the merits of assessments of the NDP's conservatization, they do not account for its institutionalization on the eastern Prairies. The Progressives, Social Credit, the United Farmers parties, and smaller more recent splinters like the Western Canada Concept and the Confederation of Regions Parties have all presented blueprints for revising the Canadian federation. All of them have come and gone or faded, but the NDP has endured. It is firmly entrenched in the political cultures of Manitoba and Saskatchewan. Why?

PRAIRIE POLITICAL CULTURE

The continuing electoral viability of Prairie social democracy implies that there is no single, unified, English Canadian political culture. It is regionally fragmented. Each province might be seen as its own unique small political world.[6] Survey research, however, suggests the opposite: that the mass political beliefs of Canadians, if not their voting behaviour, are remarkably similar. While Canadians appear to have some basic values in common, distinctive patterns of cultural orientations toward politics and governments are discernible. This raises the question: Is Prairie political culture what its residents say as reported by surveys or is it reflected in how they vote and what their political leaders say and do? A related issue is whether Prairie political culture should be seen as rooted in the past or ahistorically, as whatever Prairie residents think in the here and now.

Michael Ornstein has argued that, with the exception of Quebec, distinct provincial/regional political cultures based on ideological differences do not exist despite the appearance thrown up by history and studies of parties' exhortations and popularity. On the basis of opinion surveys in the 1980s, he concluded that "The presence of social democratic parties does not reflect greater present-day support for social democratic policies."[7] His findings are counter-intuitive. Ornstein's survey questions probed, among other things, government cutbacks, redistributive tax policies, welfare and unemployment, perceptions of corporate and union power, foreign investment, and the distribution of federal and provincial powers. He found that, in placing responses on a left-right scale, Atlantic Canadians were more leftist than western Canadians. The wording of his questions and what they measure, however, are problematic. As one example, he defined the preference for more provincial power as left-wing. His survey suggests a glaring dissonance between party systems and public opinion: relatively leftist Atlantic Canadians perpetuated the Liberals and Conservatives, "ins versus outs" parties that are ideologically indistinguishable. Meanwhile relatively rightist western Canadians opted for a left-right, polarized party system. In Ornstein's cosmology, the election of NDP governments on the prairies is not a case of bucking trends because the west lacks a distinctive left-wing popular ideology. He explains NDP success by explaining it away, by dismissing the party as "cautious" and not a force for socialism. In brief, this is yet another version of the "protest movement becalmed" analysis.[8] For Ornstein, the relative leftism of Atlantic Canadians and the relative conservatism of westerners is attributable to economic status: Atlantic Canadians are relatively poor and westerners relatively wealthy. This is logical but inconsistent with his finding that, within the west, relatively poor "Manitoba and Saskatchewan are to the right of [relatively wealthy] British Columbia and Alberta."[9] His data have the residents of Saskatchewan, followed by Manitobans, as the most right-wing in Canada. Survey research would have us believe that residents of Manitoba and Saskatchewan have elected governments whose social-democratic principles they disavow.

Gad Horowitz mined Louis Hartz's rich ideological fragment theory to account for Canada's socialist streak, its socialist touch. He did so by locating its ideological genesis in Canada's minoritarian Tory streak, born of classical British conservatism with its communitarian, cooperative, and collectivist bias.[10] On the relatively open and more egalitarian Prairie frontier, however, more than in Canada as a whole, it was classical liberalism or what is now commonly labelled neo-conservatism that prevailed. That is the wellspring of the Prairies' plebiscitarian populism. Prairie society was formed in a more modern era, less tradition-bound and always more radical than the Tory-anchored Maritimes and Ontario. The Prairies, where Canadian socialism has been strongest, are precisely where Canadian Toryism has been weakest. The Hartz-Horowitz thesis appears to founder on the eastern Prairies. Similarly, it cannot account for the relative weakness of contemporary neo-conservatism in the region in comparison with Alberta and Ontario. The fragment theory might be rescued in the prairie setting by pointing to the directly imported British labour-socialist strain in its political culture and attributing it to its earlier origins in Britain's collectivist age.[11]

The fragment thesis does illuminate differences *within* the Prairie region. The existence of distinctive provincial political subcultures does not contradict the notion that some ideas have spanned the three Prairie provinces. Manitoba, as the Ontario of the Prairies,[12] featured an Ontario-centred Tory-touched liberalism. This contrasted with Alberta's Americanness where liberal populism, an ideology wholly unalloyed with Toryism, prevailed. In that province, the United Farmers (UFA) were led by an American (Henry Wise Wood) and inflationary monetary theories were popularized by another American Albertan who had been the populist governor of Kansas (J.W. Leedy). The UFA had more American-born directors than either native Canadians or Britons.[13] In later decades Calgary's prestigious and influential Petroleum Club, from 1955 to 1970, featured nine Americans among its 15 presidents.[14] Such differences among the Prairie provinces take us back to their settlement patterns and help to account for voting and ideological preferences, or political culture, throughout the twentieth century. They provide insight into why the Reform and Alliance Parties have been so strong in Alberta and relatively weak in Manitoba. In 2000 for example, in Manitoba and Ontario and unlike provinces further west, the federal Liberals captured more seats than the Alliance.

Political culture is stable, enduring, and cross-generational.[15] It is transmitted. In this respect, Prairie political culture is no different from culture elsewhere. To understand the Prairies' social democratic exceptionalism, one must revisit the Prairies' formative years, a century ago. It was a time when the west grew exponentially and Wheat was King. In the first decade of the twentieth century, Winnipeg's population tripled, Vancouver's quadrupled, and Regina's increased tenfold. Calgary, which had fewer than 5,000 souls, is now on the cusp of one million. The four main sources for Prairie settlement were Ontario, Britain, continental Europe, and the United States. The Ontario impact was greatest in Manitoba. Ontarians brought the Mounted Police, put down Riel's Métis rebellions of 1870 and 1885, and settled the best lands along the tracks of the CPR. They brought their "grit" Liberal and Conservative partisan biases. They led the fledgling provincial governments. Ontarians made up the majority of legislators, government administrators, and were the early ruling class in both Manitoba and Saskatchewan. An example of Ontarian cultural transplantation was Hugh John Macdonald, John A.'s son and Manitoba's premier as the twentieth century dawned. Every Manitoba premier after that, until Ed Schreyer of the NDP in 1969, was either Ontario-born or of Ontario parentage. The Prairies were not so much a party to the federation as they were an extension of it. The early wheat economy demanded more than the Ontarians could offer, so other immigrants, preferably British, were aggressively solicited.

The turn-of-the-twentieth-century British who came to the prairies were quite unlike the British influx to Upper Canada in the first half of the nineteenth century. These new Britons were largely urban and working-class, steeped in the labour-socialist politics of Britain's new and ascending Labour Party. They quickly established Prairie versions of the party. The British labour-socialist impact was greatest in the west's cities: Winnipeg, Vancouver, Calgary. The British ethnic character of early labour-socialism cannot be exaggerated: Between 1919 and 1945, not a single Labour alderman in multi-ethnic polyglot Winnipeg was of German, Ukrainian, or Polish descent. In the 1920s, 85 percent of Labour's aldermen were British-born; in the 1930s, 70 percent.[16]

Although the older pioneering generation died off, its partisan social-democratic fidelity did not. It was inherited and expressed in elections by subsequent generations in the very same neighbourhoods.[17] Many ideological strains circulated on the Prairies, but it was the seed planted by British socialists that took root.

Oddly, on account of Saskatchewan's rural character, the British impact there played itself out even more forcefully. Each of the three Prairie provinces had approximately equal numbers of British-born residents, but Saskatchewan had as many Britons operating farms as Manitoba and Alberta combined.[18] The political implications of settlement, rural or urban, were substantial: the systematic underrepresentation of urban areas in legislatures meant that no matter how popular the labour-socialist impulse might be in the cities, it would not prevail. The Britons' *rural* impact in Saskatchewan meant they could offer a competitive political alternative to the Liberal-Conservative politics of the transplanted Ontarians in a way that Manitoba's Winnipeg-based Britons could not. Thus, Saskatchewan produced the radical Farmers Union of Canada whose motto was "Farmers and workers of the world unite"[19] and whose founding leader was a British unionist railway worker. Two socialist Britons in Saskatchewan's rural and small-town setting were Tommy Douglas and M.J. Coldwell, future federal CCF-NDP leaders. The pressing political issue of those days for socialists was neither the distribution of federal and provincial powers nor regional grievances. It was the redesign of the national socio-economic system with the view of reducing disparities. There were not enough British socialists in Saskatchewan, however, to catapult the party to power. The pivotal swing vote for social democracy in the 1940s and later years came from the large and previously politically deferential continental Europeans: Ukrainians, Germans, Dutch, Scandinavians, Russians. Saskatchewan had relatively more of them than either Manitoba or Alberta. Their politics of deference gave way with acculturation, intermarriage, and assimilation. The same occurred in Manitoba but, as there were fewer such European farmers, they and their children's "ethnic revolt"[20] did not occur until 1957 federally and 1969 provincially when John Diefenbaker and Ed Schreyer changed the faces of western Canadian and Manitoban politics.

The early ethnic and religious biases of Prairie politics were shattered. Those of British ethnic origins no longer enjoy the privileged status and unchallenged leadership they once had in the Prairies' vertical mosaic. For the first time in the late 1990s, all Prairie premiers — Filmon, Romanow, Klein, Doer — were of non-British or mixed ethnic origins. One implication of this for the politics of Canada's federation is the at-best marginal official sympathy and, more common popular hostility to bilingualism, "founding peoples" theory, "distinct society," and other perceived Quebec-centred concerns. One survey in the 1980s revealed that more than four in five of those in Manitoba and Saskatchewan — a significantly higher ratio than in any other province — felt the federal government had given "too much attention" to Quebec.[21] The increasing social and political equality of individuals on the Prairies, whatever their ethnic origins, nourished another notion of equality — that of provinces. Ironically, this proposition belies the Prairies' origins as territorial colonies of Ottawa.

The glue once linking populist farmers and the urban working classes was the Protestant Social Gospel. Preached in Labour and People's Churches, it stretched across the Prairies, but drew few non-Anglo-Saxons and could not dispel suspicion between city and country. Overtaken by secularism, the social gospel gave way to the gospel of social planning against a backdrop of Depression and war. Manitoba's CCF leader offered social ownership as did the party's national brain trust, the League for Social Reconstruction. [22] Saskatchewan served as a postwar provincial laboratory for social democratic social and economic policy. It pioneered social security in the form of hospitalization and Medicare and its labour legislation was the most pro-union of any North American jurisdiction. It adopted the first provincial Bill of Rights and expanded government's economic sphere by creating a large stable of Crown corporations.[23]

Manitoba and Saskatchewan have not been major immigration receptacles for over three-quarters of a century, but Canada's changing face has affected them too. Recent Asian immigration and the rise of "identity politics" since the 1970s — gays, women, Aboriginals, the disabled, visible minorities — have led social democrats to see class lived as race, gender, and ethnicity. The NDP came to identify with social movements and "equity-seeking" groups. Allan Blakeney touted financing advocacy groups "which then turn around and hammer the hand that fed them [as]...good social policy."[24] This contrasts starkly with Reform's neo-conservative suspicions of "special interest groups." If there is a new ideological polarization in civil society, one driven by non-regional identities and the social rights-based activism of "Charter Canadians," Prairie social democrats embrace it. Some might argue that the adoption of "identity politics" has changed the internal culture of the NDP, making it a coalition of "special interests." In contrast, neo-conservatives resist such claimants and are suspicious of activist "law-making" courts entertaining them.

Aboriginals stand out as a systemically disadvantaged group. Their personal income levels are but 60 percent of the western provinces' averages.[25] They make up less than 4 percent of Canadians but are more than 10 percent of the populations of Manitoba and Saskatchewan, by far the highest provincial percentages.[26] The NDP in those provinces has been more successful in capturing their support than the other, more conservative, parties. The Manitoba Conservatives in 1995 attempted to undercut this by illegally funding counterfeit "independent" Aboriginal candidates. The ensuing scandal helped defeat the Conservatives in 1999. Neither Aboriginals nor most other residents of the Prairies' inner cities have much sympathy for neo-conservatism's individualism and its recipe for constricted government. Reform/Alliance success since 1993 has been precisely in those areas where the CCF-NDP has always been relatively weaker or marginal.

Agrarian Socialism[27] is a misnomer for Prairie social democracy. Many Saskatchewan farmers flocked to the CCF in the 1940s, but the party always fared better in the cities than the rural areas. This is quite unlike the Alliance Party, Reform, and Social Credit. Farmers proved to be bit players, not stars, in the social-democratic constellation. The number of Saskatchewan farms declined precipitously, from 170,000 to 70,000 between the 1950s and 1970s, but the CCF-NDP tradition persisted. It was the farm vote that deprived the NDP of power in 1986 when its vote total exceeded that of the Conservatives. The Saskatchewan NDP eked out a minority government in 1999, but it did so, remarkably, without winning a single farm constituency in the most agrarian of provinces. Similarly, in Manitoba, the NDP was elected in 1999 on the strength of urban popularity. The party has never won a farm seat in the rich southwestern wheat belt homesteaded by Ontarians over a century ago. What boosted the NDP in both provinces in the 1990s were provincial electoral boundaries that displayed less bias in favour of small rural constituencies than other provinces.[28] Nevertheless, agriculture — however shrunken its base (only 3 percent of Manitobans labour in primary food production) — has a critical multiplier effect on Prairie economic fortunes. It is embedded in the Prairie psyche. NDP governments thus lobby Ottawa continuously and aggressively for federal farm aid. Another part of the Prairie agrarian heritage is the cooperative movement. In Saskatchewan it has a leftish veneer. The province has by far more members of non-financial cooperatives than any other province.

SOCIAL DEMOCRACY AND NEO-CONSERVATISM

Neo-conservatism is associated with the shrinkage of the state, the ascendancy of markets over politics, and the primacy of the individual over the collectivity. The populist incarnation of neo-conservatism champions egalitarianism and depreciates elitism. Within the neo-conservative panorama, there are differences between social or moral conservatives and libertarians. The former treasure social conformity and traditional values; the latter would leave issues of personal morality — abortion, homosexuality, euthanasia — to individual choice. Neo-conservative policy outcomes, according to social democrats, produce greater inequality in conditions, widening the gap between the wealthy and the poor. This is antithetical to social-democratic values. Social democracy is associated with broadening rather than narrowing the public sphere. Among socialists too there are differences. There are those who are ever suspicious of capitalism as hopelessly irredeemable and those who want to harness and humanize it. On the prairies, as in Canada generally, the dominant democratic-socialist outlook since the Winnipeg General Strike has been social democracy rather than revolutionary socialism or syndicalism. Since the Second World War, social democrats have been influenced by the so-called managerial revolution. The predominant social-democratic tendency has been to postulate that the social and developmental objectives motivating public enterprise may be attained most effectively through government's regulatory powers and indirect management. Some have defined this as "functional socialism."[29] Moreover, there has arisen among social democrats, as well as neo-conservatives, a depreciation and critique of public managers as not necessarily more responsive to the public interest than private managers.

Neo-conservatism has recently exhibited global momentum. Nonetheless, popular sentiments may often be at odds with it. Witness the resurgence of social-democratic governments in Western Europe and the relatively liberal Democrats recapturing the White House in the 1990s. People and places adversely affected by neo-conservatism have been understandably unenthusiastic about it, from Scotland and Harlem to Atlantic Canada and the eastern prairies. Neo-conservatism is not a consequence of what people have wanted or how they have voted. It is what governments are doing. Ironically, some conservative economists are questioning whether neo-conservatism has triumphed or failed.[30] Governments of all stripes have been pushed to deregulate, privatize, de-unionize, outsource public functions, and cut back on social entitlements. Social democrats defend the instrumentality of the state, but have behaved more or less as other governments have out of a sense of compulsion or "realism." It is dictated by the new enveloping global economic order. Some social-democratic parties, as in the Antipodes, have embraced globalization. English Canada's has resisted. The pressures of globalization, however, affect all governments. This has fed TINA ("There is no alternative"). In this context, social democracy is in difficult straits, swept up in a neo-conservative vortex, defying national or localized control. Globalization represents the institutionalization of technological neo-conservatism in the form of unrestricted capital flows. Social democrats might note that history shows that such a trend is not necessarily permanent.[31] Prairie history reminds us that TINA is not novel. Social Credit confronted it in its quixotic quest for monetary reform and gave up. Ernest Manning went from being Alberta's Social Credit premier to being a director of one of Social Credit's formerly reviled big central Canadian banks.

The blossoming and unchecked mobility of global capitalism has forced stocktaking among social democrats. Capitalism's contradictions have not led to its implosion. What are the implications for social democratic objectives and the prospect for their attainment? TINA has created a hybrid, or perhaps a monster, in social-democratic thinking. Original ideals are tempered with a pessimistic cynicism about achieving them. Social democrats downplay their visionary objectives and feed neo-conservatism's momentum. But social democrats do not necessarily eradicate their values. The repressed may return. Social-democratic thinking, even when difficult to locate in the *policies* of social-democratic governments, may be in abeyance, akin to a recessive gene or remission in a cancerous situation. On the other hand, as new generations emerge, there may be little knowledge of or caring for social democrats like Tommy Douglas. Winnipeg schools and government buildings sport the names of socialist legends like J.S. Woodsworth, One Big Union leader R.B. Russell, and farmer-socialist E.A. Partridge (who popularized the term "cooperative commonwealth"),[32] but their names evoke few memories among youth.

Just as the CCF was influenced by early British Fabianism, the NDP is now tilting to latter-day Fabian thinking. The federal NDP associates with Tony Blair's "Third Way"[33] which merges the essential values of the centre and centre-left. There is no jettisoning, however, of the centre-left's traditional values of social justice, solidarity, and progress. Long-standing concerns — poverty, the conditions of the work world, social disorder, the need for deeper democratic reform, environmental degradation, and the evolving roles of women and technology — remain. What are changing are some of the established social-democratic approaches such as public ownership, comparatively high taxation regimes, and the privileging of producers' interests at the expense of consumers. Social democracy's orientation maintains its Keynesian concern with macroeconomic stability. What is falling away is the insistence on state interference as preferable to *laissez-faire*. The new tack is to lessen rather than increase people's dependence on the state. Support for funding educational infrastructure is justified in the pursuit of "higher" educational standards. Social democrats are increasingly open to forming partnerships with the private and voluntary sectors, to reconciling social compassion with individual ambition and enterprise.[34]

For the NDP there is also the question of the appropriate role for organized labour, one of its founding partners, in the party's organs. Should it continue to have a place of privilege, placing restraints on the party's behaviour as a government? In Manitoba and Saskatchewan, organized labour is not the force it is in Ontario, but it has favoured and been favoured by NDP governments. The link is reflected in Gary Doer, whose career led him directly from heading the Manitoba Government Employees Association to NDP Cabinet minister and eventually the premiership. The Pawley government, of which he was a leading member, legislated, according to *The Globe and Mail*, "the most pro-union [labour laws] in the country (with the possible exception of Quebec)."[35] The tie with labour is fraying however: the health funding policies of Roy Romanow's NDP were challenged by unionized nurses and others in the public sector. Allan Blakeney argued for a neo-corporatism that borrows from the Swedish model.[36] In it, government and peak labour and business organizations cooperatively develop a national industrial strategy that also entails federal-provincial cooperation. This would require organized labour and business to move beyond the adversarial North American collective bargaining model. Resisted by market-oriented neo-conservatives, this approach is also viewed suspiciously by many union leaders and leftists as impractical in the context of Canadian capitalism.

Neo-conservatism and social democracy share a common populist thread on the prairies. Prairie populism once had right-wing and left-wing faces. Only the right-wing version took root. As in the United States, but in a less pronounced manner, Prairie populism has Christian evangelical predilections: Aberhart, the Mannings, and Stockwell Day. The once potent anti-big-business populism of the left and right is now muted. Some say social democracy has lost its soul and its gospel. Agrarian socialism and the People's and Labour Churches are long gone. Right-wing populism is not. It informed the Reform Party's neo-conservatism. It defines government, unions, and organized "special interest" groups other than those of business as enemies of the little man. The Prairie agrarian cooperative movement, like populism, attracted radical rightists and leftists. For the rightists, big bourgeois interests like financial institutions threatened their *petit bourgeois* status as small independent commodity producers. For leftists, the cooperative movement was perceived as a building block on the road to a socialist commonwealth. Alberta's populists throughout the twentieth century have preferred voluntary cooperatives and marketing schemes for agricultural products. Their more social democratically inclined Saskatchewan neighbours have preferred compulsory ones. They divided on the issue in the 1920s over the wheat pools, in the 1980s over free trade, and in the 1990s over barley marketing.[37] Once again, the political cultural ridge on the prairies was exposed.

Neo-conservatism has, with some success, identified itself with fiscal prudence and tarred social democracy with the brush of fiscal profligacy. Image and fact do not correspond insofar as the Prairies are concerned. The CCF's Regina Manifesto condemned public deficits for their "perpetuation of the parasitic interest-receiving class." Saskatchewan's CCF-NDP, along with its Manitoba NDP counterpart, have a record of vigilance and probity in public finance. This contrasts with their provincial Conservative counterparts and NDP governmental experience in Ontario and BC. The Lyon Conservative government of the late 1970s and early 1980s ran up the largest public debt until then in Manitoba history. So too did Saskatchewan's Devine Conservative regime in the 1980s. Under Conservative governments in both provinces in the 1980s and 1990s, bonds were downgraded by rating agencies. In Saskatchewan, the neo-conservative sin of fiscal mismanagement was compounded with criminal wrongdoing. In the most glaring scandal in provincial history, a number of Cabinet ministers including a former deputy premier were convicted of misappropriating public funds for partisan purposes. Disgraced, the party disbanded, its energy and foot soldiers moving to the Saskatchewan Party.

In office, the neo-conservative Conservatives privatized many long-established Crown corporations and outsourced various government services.[38] But it was under the Romanow NDP that the province became the first in the west to balance its budget. While Mike Harris's neo-Conservatives in Ontario increased provincial debt by over $20 billion in the latter half of the 1990s, Saskatchewan's NDP government reduced its provincial debt by $4 billion, or more than a quarter.[39] In addition to Saskatchewan's fiscal straits, any activist social-democratic socio-economic agenda in the province has been constrained by recession, the dismantling of the Crown corporation sector, and the restrictions imposed by Canada's free trade agreements. Saskatchewan's "gain" in the *Constitution Act 1982*, section 92A, paradoxically undermined a rationale for public ownership by facilitating provincial taxation of resource enterprises without having to own them. NDP governments also turned to casinos for revenue, an idea that would have revolted social gospellers.

A certain convergence of neo-conservative and social-democratic thinking is exemplified in the work of John Richards. Elected as NDP in 1971, he soon exited the party on the left to sit as an independent socialist. By the 1990s, he was a business professor associated with the right-wing C.D. Howe Institute. He remained in the social-democratic fold, but lamented what he considered the irresponsibility and growing incredibility of the federal NDP's economic analysis and policy prescriptions. He argues for *Retooling the Welfare State*,[40] for reconciling the continuing importance of welfare with fiscal conservatism. He defends the collective, public role of the state but insists that social democrats have to face up to government failures as well as the market failures they dwell on. Unwavering in his social-democratic commitment to greater equality of condition, Richards depicts the welfare state as a flawed work-in-progress but one with continuing relevance. Its social programs are vital because a circumscribed neo-conservative state and capitalism cannot deliver a decent life for most people. Roy Romanow pointed to Richards's thinking as contributing to sharpening and clarifying social-democratic analyses and values and doing so without illusions.[41]

On the partisan front, there is also evidence of social-democratic movement toward the centre. The old strategy, based on developments in early twentieth-century Britain, was to realign the party system so that the Liberal Party would fracture, with its progressives gravitating to the NDP and its reactionaries absorbed by the Conservatives. What has possibly happened is a reverse takeover. Left-liberal thinking is overtaking social-democratic politics rather than socialism seducing liberals. Where once the CCF-NDP disparaged both the Liberals and Conservatives as tweedledum and tweedledee rightists, the NDP has come increasingly to seek some common cause with the Liberals. This is not unprecedented on the Prairies: the Manitoba CCF was briefly a party to a coalition government in the 1940s. Elsewhere, in Ontario, the NDP signed an accord with the Liberals to oust the Conservatives in the 1980s.

Evidence of partisan convergence came in the aftermath of Saskatchewan's 1999 election. It returned the NDP, but in a minority position. They coalesced with the small but sufficient contingent of Liberals. This may be a precursor to federal developments if the Liberal majority falters. Liberal minority governments were propped up by the NDP in the 1960s and 1970s, but the arrangements were informal and fluid. They may become formal, as in Saskatchewan, where the leaders of both parties have sat at the Cabinet table. That would be a first in federal politics. But would that undermine or further the apparent hegemony of neo-conservatism? The Prairies, as in so many other areas of policy and public administration, may point the political and ideological way to Canada's future in federal politics.

SOCIAL DEMOCRACY AS A FEDERATION

The NDP's organizational structure reveals something of its view of a federation's operation and purpose. The party, like the Cooperative Commonwealth *Federation* before it, is an integrated federal one quite unlike the Liberals and Conservatives. The latter are largely confederal parties. Their provincial and federal namesakes tend to be functionally and legally separate organizations. They have separate offices and membership lists in all of the larger provinces. Regionally and historically, the older parties are more integrated in the Maritimes than in the West.[42] The NDP is the most tightly knit of the parties. One becomes a federal NDP member by virtue of one's provincial membership. There are no distinct and separate federal party members as there are in the other parties. Moreover, the NDP's membership criteria preclude membership in any other party at any level of government. The NDP shuns cross-partisans — those belonging to one party federally and another provincially. The other parties pursue them. The other parties are more likely to have differing policy positions at the federal and provincial levels and across provinces. In the NDP, in contrast, the federal and provincial wings of the party are more likely, but not always, united across the federal-provincial divide on issues. They were on both free trade and Meech Lake in ways the other parties were not.

The integrated federal dimension of the NDP dovetails with its self-image as part of a broader international political movement. It sees itself as more than just a national political party. Along with fraternal parties in more than 140 states, the NDP is part of a global coalition of social-democratic parties of which more than two dozen have held or shared national power. The Socialist International (SI) is nearly a century and a half old. All its members are structured as mass parties. They are theoretically built from the bottom up by members sharing common principles rather than as cadre parties revolving around leaders and their prerogatives. The SI's membership of approximately

100 million makes it the world's largest coalition of political forces.[43] Every card-carrying member of the NDP is a member. Neo-conservatism has no similar organizational vehicle. It is less of a conscious, coherent, and consistent political movement. But is the NDP actually or only theoretically a mass party? As the opposition party in the late 1980s, the Saskatchewan NDP had 38,000 members or nearly 6 percent of the electorate. This was roughly equivalent to the Saskatchewan CCF's membership in the 1940s.[44] In power in the mid-1990s, however, membership dropped to fewer than 27,000 or less than 1 percent of the electorate. In no other province does the NDP, despite its mass party model, have a membership equalling even 1 percent of the electorate.[45] Party membership in the older Liberal and Conservative Parties, once an inchoate notion, now often exceeds NDP provincial memberships. Their inflated membership lists, however — as with the Alberta's Conservatives which boasted more than 100,000 members in 1992 — are driven by leadership contests rather than ideological commitment. They rise and fall dramatically.

An example of the NDP behaving as a philosophically distinctive national force was the emergence of a cadre of social-democratic public administrators and planners. NDP governments in Saskatchewan, Manitoba, BC, and Ontario employed some of them at the highest levels of their provincial bureaucracies after they served in comparable positions in other NDP-governed provinces.[46] No other party points to such a cross-provincial phenomenon. This speaks to a national and ideological consciousness that transcends the parochialism of provincialism.

ATTITUDES TO THE FEDERATION

Have alleged changes in Canadian political culture in the direction of neo-conservatism meant changes in Prairie attitudes to the federation? Attitudes and opinions are more fickle than fundamental values and deeply rooted belief systems, but they too fall under the broad rubric of political culture. Social scientists strive to measure as well as understand them. Certainly the individual rights discourse spawned by the *Charter of Rights and Freedoms* and the increasing marketization of the state have currency on the eastern prairies as they do elsewhere. Despite the rise of the Reform and Alliance Parties, however, it is difficult to locate hard evidence that residents of the eastern Prairies are any more suspicious of the federal centre than they once were.[47] Indeed, a 2001 survey by the Canada West Foundation revealed more Manitobans satisfied with the current balance of power between the federal and provincial governments than Manitobans opining that Ottawa was too powerful.[48] An example of differences between Alberta on the one hand and its easterly prairie neighbours on the other regards attitudes to the federal equalization program. A 2001 survey by the Centre for Research and Information in Canada revealed that fewer than one in three Albertans "strongly supported" it as opposed to half of those on the eastern prairies.[49]

One way of examining the eastern prairies' place in the federation is by looking at public attitudes. Another is to look at the postures of their governments. If one did not know that Saskatchewan and Manitoba had a penchant for social-democratic regimes, one might think that their residents think politically much like Canadians elsewhere. On the basis of both national and cross-national survey research Canadians appear more similar than dissimilar in their political attitudes. Canadians, wherever they live, have thought their province puts more into Confederation than it gets out of it. Politically however, they behave quite differently in terms of the kinds of political parties they elect. Survey research cannot account for such differences so it discounts the political culture significance of partisan choice. More illuminating surveys point to provincial and partisan differences rather than similarities. In 2000, Environics surveyed Canadians' orientations toward their country and province of residence. "Do you feel that you are more a citizen of Canada," read the question, "or more a citizen of [province]?" This is a false proposition in its assertion that citizenship may be provincial, something it is not. Nevertheless, respondents were forthcoming. With the exception of Quebec and Ontario, responses in the other regions/provinces were more similar than they were different.[50] Ontarians logically exhibit relatively weak provincial identification: in Ontario, national consciousness fed by the media and corporate behemoths overwhelms regional or provincial consciousness. *Maclean's*, *The Globe and Mail*, the *National Post*, CBC, CTV, the banks, the National Ballet School, etc., are Ontario-based but project national pretence and consciousness. Ontario and Quebec are "inner" Canada. The others are the "outer provinces."[51] Substantially higher levels of provincial identification in Quebec may be attributed to language, cultural distinctiveness, and centuries of continuous settlement.

One might expect residents of Saskatchewan, Manitoba, and Atlantic Canada to have a stronger identification with Canada than Ontarians because of their relative dependence. Manitoba and Saskatchewan's relative have-not status is a trait shared with the Atlantic region. In the early 1990s, per capita incomes in Saskatchewan fell below Nova Scotia's. There is a greater sense of regional vulnerability and exposure in Manitoba and Saskatchewan than there is further west. And realistically so. Whereas federal transfers as a percentage of provincial government revenues in 1990s were lower in the "far west" than in any other province — 13 and 15 percent — they accounted for more than double that — between 28 and 30 percent — in the "near west."[52] These material differences are mirrored attitudinally when it comes to projecting provincial economic futures: only one in five Saskatchewanians and fewer than one in three Manitobans expressed optimism in 2001. In contrast, six in ten Albertans did.[53]

On issues related to federalism and neo-conservatism, however, partisan cleavages among respondents are more significant than their province of residence. More than seven in ten Alliance voters in the West felt, in 2001, that the federal government had too much power. In contrast, only 42 percent of western NDP members and 34 percent of western Liberals agreed. On globalization's effects, western social democrats stand out: whereas significant majorities of Alliance, Liberal and Conservative voters saw increased global trade as beneficial to Canada, only a minority of NDP members thought so.[54] Alliance voters are also the most likely to see "the west" as a distinct region; NDP voters are the least likely.[55] Since NDP governments have held sway on the eastern Prairies, such sentiments among their partisans have had to be accommodated.

Cries of western separatism have always been weaker, barely discernible, in Manitoba and Saskatchewan than in Alberta and BC. The latter's relative wealth and distance more easily feed fanciful, if still marginal, notions of autonomy. Surveys in the 1990s gauging public support for decentralization of the federation showed that westerners — along with Quebecers and as opposed to Ontarians and Atlantic Canadians — were more likely to prefer additional provincial government powers. However, the inner (or near) and outer (or far) wests differed: in Alberta and BC more decentralization was favoured by 55 and 50 percent respectively while in Saskatchewan and Manitoba it was 44 and 43 percent.[56] Are these significant differences or merely matters of degree? The results were much the same in the Canada West Foundation's 2001 survey.

Differences within the west on the federal question are more pronounced at the level of governmental policy than of public opinion. Saskatchewan in particular has historically endorsed a strongly centralized federation. Manitoba too embraced that vision when the Rowell-Sirois Commission canvassed federal-provincial relations.[57] Alberta and BC have been more in the "province-building" camp, asserting provincial rights and a more circumscribed federal role. The Douglas CCF government favoured the federal centre in the 1940s, consistent with national CCF thinking at the time.[58] Douglas's successor, the conservative Liberal Ross Thatcher, adopted no less a centralist, if not a socialist, bias.[59] Saskatchewan's centralism seemed somewhat tempered in the 1970s and 1980s in its determination to wrest greater control and taxation of its resource industries[60] and in the run-up to the constitution's patriation. By this time, the provincial state was well ensconced, fortified in its delivery of social programs by substantial tax resources and federal transfers. Saskatchewan, however, also maintained a stake in some long-established federal policies. When Ottawa eliminated the Crow rate in the 1980s — the effective subsidy for grain shipments for nearly a century — the NDP government organized an intense campaign to keep it. Allan Blakeney's NDP articulated a view of the national interest that contrasted with Trudeau's centralist view that only Parliament speaks for all Canadians on the national interest. It was also different from the view of the Quebec and far west province-builders: the national interest is but the cumulative interests of the provinces. Blakeney defined it as an amalgam of federal and provincial interests. He propounded a role for the provinces that had not been part of the earlier socialist vision of Canada.

Like Saskatchewan, Manitoba has also looked to and been dependent on Ottawa's largesse. It adopted a centralist bias but has not pressed it forcefully and persistently. An intriguing articulation was Ed Schreyer's idea of "functional capacity" overriding "fiscal capacity"; by this, he meant that jurisdiction in any area was to be determined on the basis of what was most practical from the program recipients' perspective rather than that of competing governments. He was also receptive to asymmetrical federalism.[61] Decentralization and the Senate reform proposals of the Alberta government and the Reform/Alliance Parties have not stirred the eastern Prairies. In 40 years of constitutional conferencing between 1950 and 1990, one strains to find either in the agendas of Manitoba governments.[62] In all four western provinces, there is more public enthusiasm for increased federal-provincial cooperation than for either Senate or parliamentary reform.[63] The centralist thrust in social-democratic thinking revealed itself in the imbroglio of Meech Lake. Left-wingers in the Manitoba NDP opposed the Accord fearing an evisceration of the federal spending power.[64] Manitobans — like most Canadians — have been more driven by the practical consequences of public policy than by the lure of constitutional reform. In the run-up to the Charlottetown Accord, for example, a parliamentary committee toured the province, but hardly anyone showed up. Those who did, the co-chair complained, were keen to express views on everything *but* the constitution.[65]

Over time Prairie social democrats have come to a more decentralist position on the federal question. Centralization was originally part of social-democratic theory, but so too was democratic participation at the local level. Social democracy cannot restore the sovereignty of the nation-state in a neo-conservative era, but it is well-positioned on the eastern prairies to defend the integrity of the provincial welfare state. The federal principle with its dispersal of policy jurisdictions militates against effective national planning. During the Depression, corporate interests used constitutional legal arguments in favour of provincial jurisdiction to frustrate federal efforts at national economic planning. Such planning, however, proved indispensable during the war. Social democracy's focus then shifted from economic planning to social security as the welfare state grew and provincial governments offered opportunities once unimagined. As Canada decentralized in recent decades, social democrats were sometimes leaders and sometimes were swept along.

A related explanation for social democracy's shift to preferring a more decentralized federation has to do with the NDP's political triumphs in Saskatchewan seen against the backdrop of its federal prospects. Thinking globally and acting locally means using the levers of provincial government rather than waiting and praying for an NDP government in Ottawa. Saskatchewan was innovative in health-care policy, labour law, and in public administration. It introduced Canada to medicare and the institutionalized Cabinet.[66] Such innovations influenced the federal Liberal and other provincial governments. An upshot of the Saskatchewan CCF-NDP's defeat in 1964 was Ottawa's snapping up some of the province's professionally competent and social democratically inclined public administrators such as A.W. Johnson and Tom Shoyama, who went on to help construct the national social safety net system. In the neo-conservative 1990s, when the NDP held power in four provinces, social democrats perceived and presented provincial governments as ramparts for an alternative agenda. They mused that social democracy's brightest prospects were to be found in securing provincial victories and then using them as stepping stones to national success.

Slow economic growth, dependence on federal transfer payments, a relatively stagnant population, as well as a social-democratic legacy have militated against the eastern prairies becoming a bastion for neo-conservatism. Its residents continue to believe in a strong national community and to contribute to its definition. In this regard, however, the region is not strikingly distinctive. In differentiating themselves from Americans, English Canadians often point to medicare as a symbol of an alternative perception of the public good. The program was born on the prairies and then spread east and west in spite of the recalcitrance of Conservatives Ernest Manning and John Robarts.[67] As the twenty-first century began it was culturally consistent with the past that Alberta, rather than Manitoba or Saskatchewan, was proposing medicare's partial privatization. The latter governments were also committed to cost-containment, but their rhetoric stressed that universal, accessible, and comprehensive health care is a public good and not a private marketable commodity. Manitoba and Saskatchewan have always been less keen on the idea that the federal government has little to contribute to fashioning health policy beyond the transfer of unconditional funds. Saskatchewan and Manitoba are relatively small, making up but 6 percent of Canadians and Canada's gross domestic product (GDP). In contrast, Alberta and BC account for a quarter of the national GDP. Saskatchewan and Manitoba's roles in federal politics and policies however — from medicare to Meech Lake — have been profound and pivotal in the federation's evolution.

The neo-conservative ideological wave of the past two decades has both moderated and contributed to sustaining the social-democratic culture of Manitoba and Saskatchewan. It has simultaneously reinforced Alberta's historical conservatism, its predilection for "rugged individualism," and the celebration of "free enterprise." On the policy front, Albertans have looked more posi-tively at American-inspired formulations such as the flat tax, an equal and elected Senate, plebisciterian democracy, and were the first to deregulate elec-tricity rates. Paralleling western America's drive for expanding state rights (known as the "sagebrush revolution" during the Reagan era), Alberta has consistently engaged in the discourse of provincial rights.

These differences in broad provincial cultural inclinations have been but-tressed by changing social and economic conditions. Saskatchewan, once a magnet for immigrants and an engine of national economic growth, long ago became a laggard on both scores. It now has the west's oldest population, attracts relatively few interprovincial and international migrants, and is heav-ily dependent on the federal centre. Yet, it continues to sustain a substantial and relatively collectivist and egalitarian social ethic. Such a value system is consistent with difficult times, as in the current farm crisis. In Alberta, where the income disparities between rich and poor are greater than they are in ei-ther Manitoba or Saskatchewan, and where the west's youngest provincial population lives, there is a robust preference for the private sphere over the public domain. Alberta advances local self-reliance and individual choice over collective effort and social solidarity. Such a disposition is compatible with Alberta's wariness of federal power and initiative. Manitoba has stood eco-nomically between the other two Prairie provinces but, over time, has become more like Saskatchewan. Culturally too, its original Ontario-inspired, Tory-touched liberalism has been partially eclipsed. Urbanization and rural demographic decline have aided that province's long-established but once mi-nority social-democratic base in Winnipeg, a city that now comprises more than half the seats in the provincial legislature. The notion of a common Prai-rie experience, culture, and political response once had some currency. Today it is clearly not tenable. This is most obvious when we look at the contrasting ideological stripes of the governing provincial parties and the peculiar politi-cal dynamics within each of the Prairie provinces. The Prairie provinces both impel and react to federal developments in culturally diverse ways. The neo-conservative tone of recent vintage has not changed that. Indeed, the neo-conservative impulse has been tempered in Saskatchewan and Manitoba, Canada's bastion of social democracy.

NOTES

I am grateful to the editors, Leslie Seidle, and an anonymous reviewer for comments on earlier drafts of this chapter.

1.   David V.J. Bell, "Political Culture in Canada," in *Canadian Politics in the Twenty-First Century*, 5th ed., ed. Michael Whittington and Glen Williams (Toronto: Nelson, 2000), p. 279.

2. C.B. Macpherson, *Democracy in Alberta: Social Credit and the Party System* (Toronto: University of Toronto Press, 1953).

3. J. Anthony Long and F.Q. Quo "Alberta: Politics of Consensus" and John C. Courtney and David E. Smith, "Saskatchewan: Parties in a Politically Competitive Province," in *Canadian Provincial Politics: The Party Systems of the Ten Provinces*, 2d ed., ed. Martin Robin (Scarborough: Prentice-Hall, 1978).

4. Leo Zakuta, *A Protest Movement Becalmed: A Study of Change in the CCF* (Toronto: University of Toronto Press, 1964).

5. Robert Hackett, "The Waffle Conflict in the NDP," in *Party Politics in Canada*, 4th ed., ed. Hugh G. Thorburn (Toronto: Prentice-Hall, 1979).

6. David J. Elkins and Richard Simeon, *Small Worlds: Provinces and Parties in Canadian Political Life* (Toronto: Methuen, 1980).

7. Michael D. Ornstein, "Regionalism and Canadian Political Ideology," in *Regionalism in Canada*, ed. Robert J. Brym (Toronto: Irwin, 1986), p. 79.

8. Alan Whitehorn, "An Analysis of the Historiography of the CCF-NDP: The Protest Movement Becalmed Tradition," in *Building the Co-operative Commonwealth": Essays on the Democratic Socialist Tradition in Canada*, ed. J. William Brennan (Regina: Canadian Plains Research Centre, 1984), pp. 1-24.

9. Ornstein, "Regionalism and Canadian Political Ideology," p. 79.

10. Gad Horowitz, *Canadian Labour in Politics* (Toronto: University of Toronto Press, 1968), ch. 1. There are many commentaries on and criticisms of the Hartz-Horowitz thesis, including its alleged assumption of cultural homogeneity, the notion of cultural congealment, and its dialectical conceptualization of historical change. See, for example, H.D. Forbes, "Hartz-Horowitz at Twenty: Nationalism, Toryism and Socialism in Canada and the United States," *Canadian Journal of Political Science* 20 (1987):287-315. Gerald Friesen and Roger Gibbins have identified forces such as modernization, urbanization, and mass media as undermining the existence of a shared political culture. See Gerald Friesen, *The Canadian Prairies: A History* (Toronto: University of Toronto Press, 1984); and Roger Gibbins, *Prairie Politics and Society: Regionalism in Decline* (Toronto: Butterworths, 1980).

11. Samuel H. Beer, *British Politics in the Collectivist Age* (New York: Alfred A. Knopf, 1965). On the closing cultural gap between Canada and the United States, see Seymour Martin Lipset, *Continental Divide: The Values and Institutions of the United States and Canada* (New York: Routledge, 1990).

12. W.L. Morton, *Manitoba: A History,* 2d ed. (Toronto: University of Toronto Press, 1967), ch. 9.

13. W.L. Morton, *The Progressive Party in Canada* (Toronto: University of Toronto Press, 1967), p. 39.

14. Howard Palmer, *Alberta: A New History* (Edmonton: Hurting, 1990), p. 306.

15. Heinz Eulau, *The Behavioral Persuasion in Politics* (New York: Random House, 1963), ch. 3.

16. J.E. Rae, "The Politics of Class: Winnipeg City Council, 1919-45," in *The West and the Nation: Essays in Honour of W. L. Morton*, ed. Carl Berger and Ramsay Cook (Toronto: McClelland & Stewart, 1976), pp. 235-36.

17. Nelson Wiseman and K.W. Taylor, "Class and Ethnic Voting in Winnipeg during the Cold War," *Canadian Review of Sociology and Anthropology* 16, 1 (February 1979):60-76.

18. Robert England, *The Colonization of Western Canada* (London: P. S. King, 1936), pp. 280-81. See also *Census of Canada, 1921*, vol. 5, Table 58, p. 80.

19. Morton, *The Progressive Party in Canada*, p. 276.

20. Donald Swainson, "Ethnic Revolt: Manitoba's Election," *Canadian Forum* 49 (August 1969):98-99.

21. Ornstein, "Regionalism and Canadian Political Ideology," pp. 62 and 68.

22. S.J. Farmer, *Social Credit or Social Ownership* (Winnipeg: 1936); League for Social Reconstruction, *Social Planning for Canada* (Toronto: Thomas Nelson and Sons, 1935).

23. Gordon W. MacLean, *Public Enterprise in Saskatchewan* (Regina: Crown Investments Corp. of Saskatchewan, 1981).

24. Allan Blakeney, "The Social Democratic Challenge: To Manage Both Distribution and Production," in *Social Democracy Without Illusions*, ed. John Richards *et al.* (Toronto: McClelland & Stewart, 1991), p. 55.

25. Robert Roach and Loleen Berdahl, *State of the West: Western Canadian Demographic and Economic Trends* (Calgary, AB: Canada West Foundation, April 2001), at <www.cwf.ca>.

26. Statistics Canada, *1991 Census, Canada's Aboriginal Population*, Cat. No. 94-326 (Ottawa: Supply and Services Canada, 1991).

27. Seymour Martin Lipset, *Agrarian Socialism: The Cooperative Commonwealth Federation in Saskatchewan*, rev. ed. (Garden City, NY: Anchor, 1968).

28. Rand Dyck, *Provincial Politics in Canada: Towards the Turn of the Century*, 3rd ed. (Scarborough: Prentice-Hall, 1996), Table 12.7, p. 651.

29. Gunnar Adler-Karlson, *Reclaiming the Canadian Economy: A Swedish Approach through Functional Socialism* (Toronto: Anansi, 1970).

30. William Watson, "Has Neo-conservatism Failed?" *Policy Options* (March 2001).

31. Linda Weiss, *The Myth of the Powerless State* (Ithaca, NY: Cornell University Press, 1998).

32. E.A. Partridge, *A War on Poverty* (Winnipeg: Wallingford Press, 1925).

33. Tony Blair, "What the Third Way Stands For," *The Globe and Mail*, 21 September 1998. See also Tony Blair, *The Third Way: Politics for a New Century* (London: Fabian Society, 1998).

34. Bob Rae, *The Three Questions: Prosperity and the Public Good* (Toronto: Viking, 1998).

35. "Labour and Politics 'Fused' in Manitoba," *The Globe and Mail*, 22 February 1988.

36. Blakeney, "The Social Democratic Challenge: To Manage Both Distribution and Production," pp. 52-53.

37. "Producer Vote Supports Single-Desk Sale of Barley," *Agrivision* (Ottawa: Agriculture and Agri-Food Canada, April 1997), and "One Vote Could Decide Barley Marketing," *Agriweek* (Winnipeg), 11 November 1997.

38. James M. Pitsula and Ken Rasmussen, *Privatizing a Province: The New Right in Saskatchewan* (Vancouver: New Star, 1990).

39. Janet McFarland, "Unyielding Fiscal Policies are Romanow's Greatest Legacy," *The Globe and Mail*, 28 September 2000.

40. John Richards, *Retooling the Welfare State* (Toronto: C.D. Howe Institute, 1998)

41. Roy Romanow, back cover text, in *Social Democracy Without Illusions*, ed. Richards *et al.*

42. Rand Dyck, "Links Between Federal and Provincial Parties and Party Systems," in *Representation, Integration and Political Parties in Canada*, ed. Herman Bakvis (Toronto: Dundurn, 1991).

43. Michel Rocard, "Does Social Democracy Have a Future?" in *The Future of Social Democracy: Views of Leaders from around the World*, ed. Peter H. Russell (Toronto: University of Toronto Press, 1999), pp. 14-15.

44. Lipset, *Agrarian Socialism*, p. 244.

45. R.K. Carty and David Stewart, "Parties and Party Systems," in *Provinces: Canadian Provincial Politics*, ed. Christopher Dunn (Peterborough: Broadview, 1996), Table 1, p. 69.

46. Among others who have served as deputy ministers in at least two of the four provinces: Marc Eliesen, Michael Decter, Michael Mendelson, Jay Kaufman, George Ford, Charles Kang.

47. On the ideology of the Reform Party, see Richard Sigurdson, "Preston Manning and the Politics of Postmodernism in Canada," *Canadian Journal of Political Science* 27, 2 (June 1994).

48. Canada West Foundation, "The West and Federalism — Survey Data," 15 May 2001, at <www.cwf.ca>.

49. Centre for Research and Information in Canada (CRIC), *CIRC Survey of Western Canada* (April 2001), at <www.ccu-cuc.ca>.

50. Environics, *Focus Canada*, April 2000.

51. Stephen G. Tomblin, *Ottawa and the Outer Provinces: The Challenge of Regional Integration in Canada* (Toronto: James Lorimer, 1995).

52. Statistics Canada, *Provincial Economic Accounts, Annual Estimates 1988-1992*, Cat. No. 13-213 (Ottawa: Supply and Services Canada, 1994).

53. Canada West Foundation, "Is the West a Region?" 25 April 2001, at <www.cwf.ca>.

54. Canada West Foundation, "The West and Globalization: How Should the West Compete?" 2 May 2001, at <www.cwf.ca>.

55. Canada West Foundation, "Is the West a Region?"

56. Roger Gibbins and Sonia Arrison, *Western Visions: Perspectives on the West in Canada* (Peterborough: Broadview, 1995), pp. 102-03.

57. Manitoba Provincial Treasurer, *Budget Speech, 1937.*

58. *Dominion-Provincial Conference (1945 and 1946)*, Dominion and Provincial Submissions and Plenary Conference Discussions, in *Building a Province: A History of Saskatchewan in Documents*, ed. David E. Smith (Saskatoon: Fifth House, 1992), p. 419.

59. Constitutional Conference, Proceedings, 8-10 December 1969, in *Building a Province*, ed. Smith, pp. 423-24.

60. *"Canadian Industrial Gas & Oil Ltd.* v. *Government of Saskatchewan*, 1978," in *Federalism and the Charter: Leading Constitutional Decisions*, ed. Peter H. Russell *et al.* (Ottawa: Carleton University Press, 1989), pp. 188-89.

61. *Constitutional Conference, Proceedings, Third Meeting*, Ottawa, 9-10 December 1969 (Ottawa: Queen's Printer, 1970), pp. 34-40, 86-88, 123-24, 127-28, 130, 140, 190-01, 219, 236.

62. Nelson Wiseman, "In Search of Manitoba's Constitutional Position, 1950-1990," *Journal of Canadian Studies* 29 (Autumn 1994):85-107.

63. CRIC, *CIRC Survey of Western Canada*, pp. 11-12.

64. Gerald Friesen, "Manitoba and the Meech Lake Accord," in *Meech Lake and Canada: Perspectives from the West*, ed. Roger Gibbins (Edmonton: Academic Printing and Publishing, 1988) pp. 53-57; and Paul Thomas, "Manitoba: Stuck in the Middle," in *Canada: The State of the Federation, 1989*, ed. Ronald L. Watts and Douglas M. Brown (Kingston: Queen's University, 1989), ch. 4.

65. "Committee Travels Far, Hears Few," *Winnipeg Free Press*, 6 November 1991.

66. Christopher Dunn, *The Institutionalized Cabinet: Governing the Western Provinces* (Montreal: McGill-Queen's University Press, 1995).

67. Malcolm G. Taylor, *Health Insurance and Canadian Public Policy: The Seven Decisions that Created the Canadian Health Insurance System* (Montreal: McGill-Queen's University Press, 1978), pp. 338-40, 375.

10

British Columbia: Affordable Resentment, Growing Options, Diverging Interests

Gordon Gibson

Les politiques de la Colombie-britannique ont eu historiquement peu d'importance dans le courant dominant de la fédération canadienne. Ce fait est partiellement attribuable à une succession de gouvernements provinciaux qui furent soient indifférents, hostiles ou tout simplement ignorants de la façon dont les intérêts nationaux pouvaient affecter gravement la Colombie-britannique. Cela découlait également d'une certaine négligence du gouvernement fédéral à son endroit. Toutefois, des changements économiques, une démographie aiguillonnée par l'immigration et une politisation des nations autochtones changeront diamétralement le rôle de la Colombie-britannique au sein de la fédération. La Colombie-britannique se fera alors pingre par nécessité économique, et plus conservatrice par tempérament. Ce nouveau programme sera ensuite vigoureusement poursuivi par le nouveau gouvernement libéral de Colombie-britannique.

INTRODUCTION

Since the securing of the Canadian flank on the Pacific Ocean with the entry of British Columbia into Confederation in 1871, the politics of this province have been of little importance to the mainstream issues of the federation. Some of our more colourful figures have provided intermittent amusement for other Canadians, but we have had little influence of substance. This chapter will argue that conditions are set for a major change in the province's national role.

We have, of course, seen precursors of how western Canada as a whole could have real influence. The first small wave came with the Progressives, who never enjoyed much BC support and were rapidly absorbed by the traditional parties. The two more durable influences were also spawned on the Prairies, but unlike the Progressives, enjoyed strong BC support as well. As a result they have come to influence the national agenda.

The story of the CCF/NDP on the national scene is well known. There can be absolutely no doubt that this party shaped Canadian public policy toward the left, far beyond its minor electoral success. The strong base of trade unionists and expatriate British socialists in BC contributed mightily to the success of the movement, though this force is now arguably spent.

The story of the Reform/Alliance Movement is still being written. Also invented on the Prairies (though much more Alberta in this case) and also with massive BC support, Reform/Alliance has moved much further and faster than the New Democratic Party (NDP), and has already had a like effect on policy, in this case pushing toward the right rather than the left. (The politics of public finance and immigration have been totally changed by the entry of the new party, to name but two issues.)

But neither of these great forces captures the true regionalism of British Columbia. Their foundations are principled rather than territorial. The impact of British Columbia *as a province* on the national scene has been minimal. As set out most recently by Philip Resnick, in concurrence with a long line of scholars,[1] the official face presented by British Columbia to Canada was an ineffective one — sometimes sulky, sometimes ineffectively demanding, sometimes off the wall.

The reasons for this posture in the first 80 or so years of Confederation are of little current consequence but still contribute a residual background sentiment. They turned largely on the difference between the importance British Columbians naturally enough placed upon their own concerns, and the very minor importance, also naturally enough, accorded those same issues by national governments of any stripe. We were simply not important to anyone but ourselves in national terms, and this relative lack of attention fostered resentment.

The political realities underlying the federal attitude were two. First, there were not many votes in the BC of those days. In the second place the few BC votes there were tended to be *unreliable*, in the sense of not being easily amenable to standard central government pressures and blandishments. BC voters by and large simply did not need Ottawa, and acted accordingly.

With the years of extraordinary growth that began in the 1950s, carrying BC from 8.3 percent of Canada's population in 1951 to the 13.2 percent of today, and as the wealth of the province grew more than proportionally, the political calculus notionally ought to have changed, but it did not. Neither economics nor politics required a change in the traditional view.

As far as the economy was concerned, BC was not as closely integrated into the general Canadian scheme as most provinces (always having had relatively more US and Asian commerce), and in the one thing that did matter to the federation — the extraction of taxes — the central government had all the powers it required with no local cooperation required.

And while the numbers grew, the BC voters remained unreliable. In that sense they also became increasingly dangerous, but by traditional political thinking it was hard to know what to do about that.

However, the key factor in the relative lack of influence of BC on the federation ("back when" and to this day) lay in a succession of provincial governments that were by turns indifferent to, antagonistic toward or just plain ignorant of issues of the federation that critically affect BC interests. For example, W.A.C. Bennett famously forbade his deputy ministers to make phone calls outside the province without authorization and routinely avoided what were then known as Dominion-Provincial Conferences.

The two socialist administrations during the period had an additional burden beyond the usual indifference, antagonism and ignorance cited above.[2] For ideological reasons they believed in big government and central solutions, and the central government has generally stood ready to offer as much of either as needed. On the other hand they had to live in a local political climate that contained a good deal of anti-Ottawa sentiment (though nevertheless strongly *Canadian* in loyalty). The upshot was that the socialist administrations were not so much indifferent as erratic. The antagonism (especially in the Glen Clark years) and ignorance remained.

The one great exception to the above became for many the proof that there was no point in BC playing the federation game. During the constitutional conferences of the late 1970s the government of Bill Bennett, building especially upon the views of Bennett himself along with Minister Rafe Mair and Deputy Mel Smith, long-time constitutional advisor to the province, proposed what are arguably the most imaginative and thoughtful ideas for constitutional reform originating with any government since Confederation.[3]

For its pains in this regard the BC government was met with indifference from most in the intergovernmental industry, and "who do you think you are?" from some.[4] This rejection was not a political success for Mr. Bennett, and the lesson was not lost on his successors.

The net effect is that for all of its history in Canada, BC has been the "outsider" of the federation. Matters of the greatest moment to the province — tax policy, immigration policy, equalization, distribution of federal spending, international trade issues, the balance of power between the two orders of government — all of these received the benign or willful neglect of governments in Victoria. This 130 years has been the period of "affordable resentment." That is about to change.

CHANGING UNDERLYING REALITIES

There is a traditional British Columbia, which is probably still the dominant concept held by other Canadians, and the new BC, which is the reality.

Traditional BC was based on large natural resource industries and a habitual and often bitter atmosphere of contestation both between managers and workers, and in the political sphere. Notwithstanding this grossly inefficient way of conducting an economy and the business of government, the resource rents of the province per capita were so high that the affordable resentment expressed nationally within the federation could carry on as a characteristic of the *internal* operating approach in the province as well.

The polarization, which has been the curse and dominant characteristic of BC politics for almost 70 years (since the formation of the CCF), has served to support the continuity of bitter contestation in politics long after the "affordability" ended. For as is obvious, when population doubles, resource endowment per capita halves. Adding to this, the natural propensity of governments and industry to "high-grade" resources in earlier times to maximize short-term payout guarantees an even faster decline in resource rents per person. And adding the significant recent additions to the resource extraction cost structure by an increasingly effective environmental regime, affordability drops yet further. Indeed, BC's personal income per capita has declined from over 30 percent above the Canadian average 60 years ago to about par today. Amazingly, our gross domestic product (GDP) per capita is today only 95 percent of the Canadian average.[5] This is a revolution, and it hurts.

The new BC is not only more populous but is also poorer. It also has a rapidly changing industrial structure. The resource industries remain important, but tourism and technology and small manufacturing are growing dramatically and represent the province's future. Alas, while the new industries promise to be more sustainable, the wage structures are much lower.[6]

For whatever reasons — the government blames the "Asian flu"; the opposition blames government policies — BC has done terribly badly over the past decade in economic terms. Not only have personal incomes dropped below the Canadian average, but over the period 1992–99 (all under the NDP administration) the average Canadian disposable income per capita grew by 12.1 percent while that of the average British Columbian grew by only 4.8 percent.[7]

The comparison with the United States is even more cruel. BC relates most directly to Washington State, where we travel and trade extensively. Washington State has none of the problems of inner city poverty or other negative social conditions allegedly prevalent in the United States. These factors usually cited to prove Canadian superiority are absent in this particular cross-border comparison. Seattle is an altogether delightful, prosperous, and civilized city.

But alas, even measured in terms of purchasing power parity (a far gentler comparison than the official exchange rate) the average Washingtonian's disposable income is *80 percent higher than the average British Columbian's.* No talk of medicare or less equal income distribution — both appropriate caveats — can paper over such an enormous gap. Anecdotal evidence suggests a southern drain of talent from BC in some professions.

The first "new reality" for BC is a dramatic economic underperformance that is felt throughout BC society. People know things are not going well. There is as yet no sweeping consensus on whom to blame, but there is a clear sense that things have to change. Politicians and trade unionists are having the most difficulty drawing the inevitable conclusions. In the run-up to the 2001 provincial election, businesses were simply accommodating reality, sometimes by waiting out the provincial government, sometimes by growing elsewhere.

But there is a second "new reality" which greatly mitigates the gloom of the first. BC has been "discovered." Vancouver is now regularly cited as one of the world's great cities, a success story of man as well as nature. The beauty of the hinterland is gaining a growing international fame, as visitation attests. The political climate in the province is therefore by no means one of depression, nor is there a sense of living in a culture of losers. The sense is more one of unfulfilled potential, which does continuing battle, even within the soul of many individuals, with another and often conflicting wish to preserve the wilderness, restrain growth, and so on. The difficulty is, the population growth continues and no one has offered any plausible way to stop it; which brings us to the third "new reality."

The population base of a society is the greatest single determinant of its political, social, and economic characteristics. Normally trends in economics — globalization, technology, and so on — move more quickly than trends in demographics, however, and are therefore the more notable engines of change; not so in the BC of recent decades.

Table 1: Populations of BC and Canada, 1951–2000 ('000s)

	Canada	BC	%
1951	14,163	1,179	8.3
1961	18,363	1,640	8.9
1971	22,040	2,259	10.2
1981	24,921	2,842	11.4
1991	28,127	3,404	12.1
2000	30,667	4,052	13.2

The astounding rate of growth — almost a quadrupling — of British Columbia's population would surely affect its political, social and economic characteristics even if there were no change in the composition of the population in terms of ethnic mix, source (i.e., local or immigrant), and aging. Sheer critical mass can change a society in important ways.[8]

But that is not the whole story. While BC's population has been showing aging trends similar to the rest of Canada, the ethnic and source indicators are dramatically different. We are used to thinking of Canada as an "immigrant society," but for most of the country (outside Toronto, where the immigrant effect is considerable, but less than in BC) giving any reality to this description really requires going back 100 years. Most Canadians, and their parents, have been here for quite awhile.

Not so in BC. Immigrants (i.e., persons foreign-born and granted landed status) now make up over one-quarter of the population of the province.[9] This is matched only by Ontario. No other province comes close. Our immigrant population *growth rate* between the census data of 1991 and 1996 was 25 percent. (Ontario had a 15 percent growth rate over the same period.) Net international migration is now the most important contributor to BC's growth.

In addition, most of these immigrants are very new. Almost two-thirds of the immigrant population in 1996 had arrived in the previous 25 years. This is an astounding number. Moreover, the composition of recent immigration is very different from traditional sources. As recently as 1968, 83 percent of annual immigration to BC came from Europe (mostly), the United States, and Australia. Only 13 percent came from Asia. By 1999, the figures had reversed, with the Europe/US/Australia figure being at 18 percent, and the Asian number growing to 76 percent. These "third reality" numbers also clearly constitute a revolution.

The net result by the time of the 1996 census saw a huge change in the ethnic mix of the province. The situation is clouded by the questions asked. People are able to give single or multiple ethnic origins, and can now include "Canadian" as one of these.[10] The data indicate that it is largely the descendants of British stock who choose the new "Canadian" label, at least so far. If one takes the "single-origin" data as a proxy for overall distribution of ethnicity, the British/Canadian/European cohort stood at about 68 percent of the total in 1996. The Asian group stood at about 26 percent. (Of these, the East Asian group, overwhelmingly Chinese, comprised 19 percentage points, and the South Asian group, overwhelmingly East Indian, made up the remaining 7 points.) Just ten years before, the distribution was dramatically different, standing at 82 percent "European" as compared to 13 percent "Asian."[11]

All of this is obviously important, but what to make of it in political terms? No one really knows, but some comments and conjectures follow:

1.   History suggests that newcomers move only slowly into the political process. There is therefore a "lag" effect, but the activities of political parties

in chasing the "ethnic vote," generally, a proxy word for newcomers, gives empirical evidence of its growing importance.

2. The balance of Chinese to East Indian populations from the above figures is just a bit less than 3:1. Most of the Chinese immigration has come from Hong Kong or, latterly, Taiwan. Both of these areas are famously market-oriented economies, and in that sense at least, conservative economies. India on the other hand has traditionally been well-known as a centrally planned and regulated economy (to the extent it can be said to be planned at all, in practice), with a very different political culture including a more activist state.[12]

3. Voluntary immigrants (as distinct from refugees), by the very fact of their mobility, are likely to be somewhat more adventurous/entrepreneurial than the average for their society of origin.

4. Immigrants, almost universally, consider that they are coming to *Canada*, not to this or that province. The distinctions between the two orders of government, and the divided loyalties that they engender among many Canadians, take some time to learn.

5. Immigrants, again almost universally, are not steeped in traditional Canadian attitudes toward such unique local questions as the role of the British Crown, Aboriginals, and other Canadian value sets stemming from our particular history. That would make a fascinating study on its own, but for the purposes of this essay and British Columbia politics, the important point is that immigrants do not share the collective Canadian guilt on the Aboriginal issue. Indeed, many immigrants have come from places where their own estate was worse.

6. Immigrants are not evenly distributed throughout British Columbia. They tend overwhelmingly to concentrate in the Lower Mainland. This naturally also ensures the concentration of the political effect.

At a guess, the "on-balance" effect of the above over time is likely to be toward a gradually more conservative society in British Columbia. Moreover, notwithstanding the initial exclusive identification of immigrants with Canada rather than any single province such as BC, the primacy of provincial administrations in commercial and market matters, plus the growing demographic differences of BC from the rest of Canada may well foster an eventual on-balance adoption of "BC First" attitudes to at least the same extent as traditional British Columbians.

Finally under the "new realities" heading, British Columbia is subject to all of the great world trends affecting Canada generally. Chief among these, at a very high level of abstraction, are globalization and technology. The impact of globalization, buttressed by the *Pax Americana*, is such that economic influence is draining away from the national state, as national levers such as tariffs, taxation, and monetary policy are increasingly standardized with the rest of the world and therefore become less effective in defining the economic ground rules. Provincial and local governments are also losing influence by comparison with market allocation mechanisms and the private sector, but they at least can still hang on to resource and real property policy — fixed factors — and expenditure patterns for some continued influence.

The impact of technology shows up in two ways. First, distributed production (as opposed to the old centralized model) has become possible and even essential in many businesses. At the same time, specialization and cross-border networking and alliances proliferate.

Second, the astonishingly increased reach and lowered pricing of communications has not only facilitated the dispersion of economic activity, but has also, equally importantly for political purposes, led to one of history's greatest challenges to individual identity. The easy and cheap availability of the cultural resources of the entire planet to virtually anyone in the developed world has expanded our horizons immensely.

On the other hand however, this same cultural availability — dominated as it is by "superstars" of economic power or of the intellect or of celebrity — makes it increasingly difficult for the individual to answer the question "Who am I?" in a manner that suitably places him or her in an understandable context. Compared to the whole world, any one of us seems unimportant. The practical response to this is a new strengthening of the concept of understandably sized "community" — whether political, geographical, cultural or spiritual.

We see these forces all over the world. They are by no means unique to Canada. But the importance for the Canadian federation and British Columbia's role therein is that these forces — and all are very powerful ones — are on balance decentralist. This does not mean that subsidiarity has become a one-way street, or that national or supranational orders of government are becoming irrelevant. It *does* mean that decision-making power is shifting downward. It is shifting most of all to free markets (the care and feeding of which is rapidly becoming the most important responsibility of governments), but in the public sector, power is shifting from larger governments to smaller ones, simply and irresistibly because of the way the world is changing.

THE ABSENT-MINDED GORILLA AND THE GOBLET TO BE DRAINED

The "absent-minded gorilla" is Ottawa. The central government is immensely powerful, and yet seems largely forgetful of its Pacific Coast province. Programs and expenditures are designed for areas that are either more needy (as seen from the centre) or of greater political consequence. Even allegedly "national" programs such as Employment Insurance (EI) are clearly fine-tuned with Quebec and the Atlantic in mind. Agricultural programming is designed for the Prairies and Central Canada. Industrial development, cultural development (film industry support, for example) and technology policies are widely believed in BC to be disproportionately centred on Ontario and Quebec. Federal procurement of goods and services from the province, according to provincial government figures, is only about half of what should be expected based on our population.

One must not make too much of this — certainly these things are less important than the affirmative action taken by the central government with respect to BC, to be dealt with below, but this sort of benign neglect as perceived from BC does give rise to a constant low-level irritation.

The "goblet to be drained" is a famous phrase of Premier W.A.C. Bennett. This, he said, was how Ottawa viewed BC. What are the facts of the relationship, and how do these facts colour BC's present and future attitude to the federation? In considering this we should look first at the impact that the federation, by way of its central government, has on the province of BC and its citizens. Consider first, and then leave aside the programs of general application such as trade and monetary policy, foreign policy, the military, the Criminal Code, the Post Office, payments to seniors, Statistics Canada, drug certification, EI (even with all its regional distortions), and the like. These things are all important, but largely undifferentiated. The only political impact they have on the federation — and this is of great consequence — is that because of programs like these, British Columbians share the views of most Canadians that the federal government is a sort of underwriter of security and order. To the extent it is true that we all have multiple political allegiances, these programs explain the national loyalty. (I do not discount the influence of inertia and sentiment. Indeed, these are the principal glues binding Canada. However, they are brittle connectors, not resistant to shock and subject to fatigue over time.)

Now consider the ways that the federation, through its central government, interacts with BC in ways that are unique to this province. There are many programs in this category too, but only three are important. Those are the fishery, immigration, and Aboriginal affairs.

The main importance of the fishery is symbolic. The industry accounts for less than 1 percent of the provincial GDP. But in symbolic terms the fishery, and in particular the salmon fishery, is seen as part of the soul of British Columbia. There may be someone outside the federal bureaucracy who is prepared to argue that the central government has done a good job of running the BC fishery over the years, but I have not met or heard of that person.

Immigration has been briefly dealt with as to numbers, but we should also look at the broader context. A society is defined by its population base. Everything else — power structures, wealth creation, cultural achievement — flows from that base. There is nothing more fundamental. Since the early part of the twentieth century when widespread mobility throughout the world became technically and economically possible, states have jealously guarded their control over their population base. There is a libertarian argument that this is an improper thing to do, and a property rights argument that validates the practice, but the fact of the importance of controls on immigration to virtually every state in the world is incontrovertible.[13]

Under the constitution of Canada immigration is a shared jurisdiction with federal paramountcy, but as a practical matter no province but Quebec has even attempted to have a significant influence on admissions. By way of its immigration policies over the past generation, the central government has literally changed the face of BC society. Curiously, there is no reason to believe that this was anything more than a side effect and unintended consequence of a simple pursuit of ethnic votes in selected ridings, particularly in Toronto. The gradual shift over time (by both Liberal and Conservative governments, but particularly the former) to framing immigration policy to address the interests of recently arrived Canadians (i.e., "family reunification," which translated into ethnically specific immigration) instead of the interests of all Canadians (i.e., usefulness to Canada as a whole) led to the demographic changes described in a previous section.

The upshot from British Columbia's point of view has so far generally been a happy one, and surely one of the most peaceable ethnic readjustments on record. There have been plenty of kitchen table mutterings about this, of course, related to race and jobs, but a high level of tolerance coupled with rising real estate prices fuelled by the newcomers (allowing "old-stock" British Columbians to retire to the sunny Okanagan or Vancouver Island with a condo, small boat, and term deposit) kept things on an even keel. Latterly there is a growing pride in the new multiracial mix in this province.

But three things remain. The first is that the BC population base was changed without consulting British Columbians. (BC has, of course, had representatives in Parliament throughout this exercise, but they have never had much influence, even when in government, which mostly they have not been.) Whether the outcome is good or bad, something very important has happened without our input, and that is alarming for those who think about such things.

"Those who think about such things" — basic matters such as who your neighbour is —constitute a very large part of the population. This concern about lack of influence at the centre is fed not only by immigration but by other policy files, but that general concern is a large part of the underpinning for the rise of the Reform Party in BC.

The second thing that remains is that of settlement cost. However the dialogue on the *long-run* economic impact of immigration is sorted out (and it appears to depend importantly on the age and skill-set composition of the newcomers), the *short-run* impact is clearly costly to the host province. Provinces pay these bills, and English (or French) language education, social services, and infrastructure requirements for newcomers are considerable whatever their origin. The federal appetite for immigrants has laid a net cost on British Columbians of double that of the average Canadian.

The third consideration is the most important of all to our topic of political culture, and perhaps as well the most unintended of all of the consequences. If the speculation of an earlier section is in the correct direction, it appears that the Asian migration of the late twentieth century may bolster the BC right as surely as the British working-class migration of the early twentieth century turned the province's politics to the left. This will have provincial electoral consequences early on, and federal consequences as immigrants and their descendants lose their gratitude to the (largely Liberal) politicians who admitted them to Canada.[14]

In the matter of the "goblet to be drained" the facts are simple and imposing. When the BC Ministry of Finance adjusts Statistics Canada's interprovincial accounts for the impact of the federal deficit or surplus, BC sends about $22 billion in tax revenue to Ottawa every year, and receives something less than $19 billion back in benefits, measured by the most generous direct and indirect attributions. For example, BC's share of the military, embassies, foreign aid, Ottawa overhead, and so on are all counted as benefits to BC.

The net drain of about $3 billion is almost 3 percent of our GDP. If this seems not too bad for a "rich" province, recall that it is higher than any annual deficit ever incurred by a BC government. In addition, we are no longer rich. Recall as well that our GDP per capita now stands *below* the Canadian average, at only 95 percent.

One might argue that we have brought this unhappy state on ourselves by our curious choice of provincial governments, but as the equalization formula generally works in this country, the more incompetent any given province's economic system, the more support is given. BC receives no equalization, however, and suffers a net drain instead. (So too do Alberta and Ontario, but these provinces are far richer than the average.)

The heaviest burden of all on British Columbia flowing from the federation acting via its central government is in the area of Aboriginal affairs, to which I now turn.

CITIZENSHIP AND ABORIGINAL AFFAIRS

In an error of historic and tragic dimensions, the *British North America Act* singled out one race of Canadians and assigned responsibility for (section 91(24)) "Indians and lands reserved for the Indians" to the central government. 1867 was a racist, sexist, and bigoted time. Chinese, Jews, women, Catholics and Indians — all were thought inferior to the Anglo-Saxon male and discriminated against. But only Indians were mentioned in the constitution. All of the rest — Chinese, Jews, women, Catholics — are just fine in the year 2001. The constitutional ability to treat one subgroup of Canadians differently under the law has permitted governmental actions — often well intentioned — that have fostered the separate and unequal path of the Indian people. That the federal administration of Indian affairs has been a human tragedy is common knowledge. The results have been much less felt in Central and Eastern Canada, though the Atlantic is getting a taste of things to come in the wake of the *Marshall* decision.[15]

What is less well-known is the impact of the reserve system on western Canada, and the even greater impact of the land and treaty question in BC.[16] Unlike much of the rest of Canada,[17] most of BC's territory was never covered by treaties with the Indian inhabitants. Instead, small parcels of land were arbitrarily set aside as reserves. There is a grievous history of sharp dealing and broken promises even with respect to the few lands that were assigned.

BC has about 200 distinct Indian bands averaging perhaps 700 members per band, typically with about 50 percent on-reserve and the rest off, mostly in urban settings. The "land question" has never gone away, and has served to focus the attention and energy of BC Indians in a manner unknown in the rest of Canada.

The gradual evolution of Supreme Court of Canada (SCC) decisions added impetus to this movement. Then the constitutional amendments of 1982 and 1984 not only entrenched yet-to-be-defined entitlements, but made the Supreme Court of Canada — very definitely a non-BC institution — the effective lawmaker with respect to Indian matters.

Within a period of ten years, Indian land claims progressed from an arcane branch of the law to a matter of intense economic concern in the province. Claims to land title were launched which covered more than 100 percent of the province. (Some barren areas and some existing treaty areas were not covered, but there are considerable overlaps in the claims.) Most of the productive area of the province outside the northeast Peace River country is covered.

With an appetite for land (based as much on modern aspirations as on traditional usage) came a complementary appetite for Indian government. These two demands came together in the landmark *Delgamuukw* case. The SCC declined to rule on the plea for a declaration that Indian governments had an inherent right of sovereignty over traditional territories. However, the court did speak as to land claims.

The 1997 decision said the following: Aboriginal title exists in BC. The extent is undefined. The court proposed several tests for determining where title exists in law, but expressed a preference for negotiation. The court also said that for good and justified public purpose Aboriginal title could be infringed, but only to that extent, and only upon payment of compensation. No one has any very good idea as to what lands and what compensation might be involved, nor how all of this applies to lands alienated in the past.

This judgement landed in the midst of a long and complex treaty negotiation process between Canada, BC, and a majority (but by no means all) of Indians in the province, as represented by about 50 of the bands. The federal government has taken a negotiating position since the 1970s, also adopted by BC, that it will discuss only the future. Additional land, cash, self-government — all can be on the table, but not title from the past, nor compensation for the past. The Indian participants had reluctantly accepted this.

Suddenly the SCC said that the past exists in law, with claims for title and compensation having legal force. The result has been that negotiations have, as of September 2001, been mostly paralyzed ever since. Some local dealings continue, and some emergency accommodations are made in response to blockades, so-called "illegal" (but is it?) logging, and so on.

The current Liberal government in Ottawa and the former NDP government in British Columbia made a pre-*Delgamuukw* agreement with the Nisga'a tribe that provided for considerable lands and cash, and a form of Indian government with elements of sovereignty. The first judicial challenge in the Supreme Court of British Columbia has led to a decision in favour of the treaty-makers, including a judicial view that some elements of Indian sovereignty survived Confederation. No one knows where this may lead, and the case is under appeal.

The pre-Nisga'a settlement formula was $70,000 per Indian in cash and resources. Nisga'a clocked in at about $100,000 but, as mentioned, this was set pre-*Delgamuukw*. The Nisga'a benchmark would see total BC settlement costs of about $15 billion. My guess is that the *Delgamuukw* standard could run to $50 billion.

The issue of who pays is significant. BC has historically taken the position that Term 13 of the Terms of Union loads all such costs onto Ottawa. The NDP government in 1993 reversed this position and entered into an agreement that would see the province paying about half, mostly in lands. No one at that time contemplated the escalation in values involved.

The issue of Indian government is even more significant. In a survey taken for the federal government by the Angus Reid organization in the fall of 1999, only 25 percent of Canadians thought that Indians should be entitled to ethnically based governments denied to any other ethnic group. In an earlier survey Reid found a general Canadian generosity for the settlement process, but then an ongoing and strong expectation by 73 percent of respondents that Indians would thereafter be ordinary Canadians in a political sense. This perception goes directly to the question of Canadian citizenship. Are we one nation, are we two ("founding nations"), are we many nations, or are we any of the above depending on the issue?

The polling numbers above and much other data suggest that "equality" is the current watchword for the public. The difficulty is that this concept does not square with the solutions currently contemplated by the parties at the treaty tables. This is a very difficult issue. The solutions will be hard to reach and painful, because expectations on the two sides of the bargaining table are so very far apart. This is not the forum for that debate. But the politics of it all in BC and in the federation are hugely important. It is an area where the policies and the interests and intergovernmental relationships of BC and Canada are fraught with conflict and complexity.

THE RISE OF THE POPULIST MARKETEERS

British Columbia politics have until recently been characterized by a socialist/non-socialist polarization at the provincial level and a vague anti-Ottawa, anti-Toronto sense at the federal level. The typical BC MLA has been non-socialist, whatever the label du jour to that end, and the typical MP has been anti-Ottawa.

There have been exceptions of course. In the Trudeau sweep in 1968 the whole country ignored traditional patterns and voted for an imaginary figure who didn't really exist except in the hopes of the voters. There have also been two periods of socialist government, but each was supported by only 40 percent of the voters and elected as a result of divisions among the non-left voters. But BC voting patterns have generally been negative — anti-socialist on balance and anti-Ottawa outsiders. There is some evidence that this is changing.

The Reform/Alliance Party provides the clearest case. The movement is indeed still based on anti-Ottawa sentiment and a wish for more clout at the centre, but coherent positive elements are woven in as well. The first relates to the way decisions are made on issues of public policy. There is a strong wish for more pervasive and direct attention to public sentiment — hence the "populist" label. There is also a distrust of big government and a belief in decentralization and the free market and individual responsibility — hence the "marketeer" part of the moniker.

All of this remains leavened, in the typical Canadian way, by many constraints. For example, the market is well and good, but morality must not be lost sight of. The market is well and good, but the famous Canadian aversion to risk inhabits the soul of the Alliance member at least to some extent. We do all love our medicare and want the state to look after us, pick up the pieces where we fail and keep us safe from environmental and other risks. Aside from some hard-line purists, the populist marketeers often exhibit the same preference for the "soft option" in any tough area of public policy choice, rather than knowingly distressing anyone. And of course, Ignorance and Apathy remain the parties of choice of a great many British Columbians, as in any other part of the country.

But with all of these caveats there is a genuine difference of worldview here from the old Liberal/Tory/NDP concepts. The Reform/Alliance view is much more decentralist, and much more centred on the individual. The old-line approach was much more centralist, and much more centred on the *institution* — to do good things for the individual, of course, but it did not always work out that way.

The implications for relationships inside the federation are obvious. Decentralization implies a shift of power away from the centre. Emphasis on the individual implies a concentration on transparency and accountability that is quite foreign to the old style of the "hidden level of government," that is, federal-provincial relations. Emphasis on the individual implies a turning of Indian policy on its head. Current policy values the collectivity, Indian governments, and the "institutions" of the Indian industry. An individual-based policy looks to the welfare of the individual, leaving the collective reliant on the voluntary support and unlegislated goodwill of those individuals. All of these things suggest a revolution in some of the most basic patterns of relationships within our federation.

Turning to the provincial level, the "populist marketeer" phrase fits rather well with the provincial Liberal Party,[18] although provincial Reform would claim a stronger right to the "populist" label. But for our purposes the populist component is less important than the marketeer aspect. The provincial Liberal Party is philosophically oriented toward smaller government and decentralist and market-oriented solutions. They have developed such concepts as a Charter of Rights for municipal governments.

In Indian policy there is much similarity in the provincial Liberal approach to that of the Reform/Alliance Movement. Again, the basis is the welfare of the individual, not necessarily the collective. Provincial Liberal policy is very strong in its denial of the propriety of race-based government. It supports the treaty process, but pays a good deal more attention to the practicalities of how new arrangements would actually work, and eliminating the overlapping jurisdictions and entanglements being created both by the courts and by negotiators in the current treaty process. This policy would be in harmony with an Alliance government at the federal level, and in contrast to that of an ongoing Liberal administration in Ottawa.

Importantly, the party leader and the senior members who will likely be involved with questions affecting Canadian federalism believe that BC has been far too quiet and uninvolved as a player in the intergovernmental games. The election of a Liberal government in BC in the spring of 2001 implies a more vigorous BC participation in the affairs of the federation. This will be buttressed by a stronger economy. A new provincial government with the stated policies of the provincial Liberals should on balance provide a positive factor for business investment in contrast to the clearly negative influence of the NDP administration.

PULLING THE THREADS TOGETHER

To recap some of the main propositions in this survey:

- BC has punched considerably below its weight in the affairs of the federation.

- There has been little reason for the central government to be concerned with this; quite the contrary.

- There have been significant changes in demographics and economics to strengthen BC's role.

- Institutional factors,that is, failings in successive BC governments, have guaranteed an ineffective role.

- The edge in resource wealth, which has allowed BC its "affordable resentment," has vanished. BC is no longer insulated by riches from a need to play the federation game, and indeed is inspired by a new relative poverty vis-à-vis the Canadian average and, even more so, our immediate American neighbours.

- BC nonetheless has a confident mood, hoping to fix the above.

- Demographic trends have both added to the weight of the province in Canada, and laid the groundwork for an ongoing shift in the political climate in a conservative direction.

- While we have not seen an end to the usefulness of two-way subsidiarity, world trends are driving all jurisdictions in the direction of decentralization.

- The current relationship with the federation and especially the federal government gives rise to very significant adverse consequences, particularly in the fields of fiscal flows and Aboriginal issues.

- Important changes in the institutions of party politics, and in particular the rise of the Alliance federally and the BC Liberal Party provincially point to a potential new openness to BC ambitions and decentralization at the centre, and an insistence on these things from the BC government.

Given the above, it is timely to consider how this newly defined British Columbia will work within the federation. After all, to change things one needs allies.

One potential ally could be a new federal government. This could be either a post-Chrétien Liberal administration, or a conservative version in due course. One or the other is clearly on the radar screen of the next few years. Either would loosen the rigidity of the old federal model. And federal governments are likely to pay more attention in the future to BC. No longer based solely on negative motivations, BC voters have become more "reliable." For the moment that means support for the Alliance, but through appropriate policy or personnel changes and internecine warfare on the right, the federal Liberals could become contenders.

The BC-Canada relationship with respect to the Aboriginal issue is a case by itself. It cannot be overstressed how important this file is to the province, and how deeply it is embedded into the voting motivations of the ordinary citizen and the investment intentions of the resource industries today. The rest of Canada mostly does not understand the immense importance of the issue to British Columbia. The land base and to an extent the social order are in play.

In this context, it matters greatly whether the new government of British Columbia and the Liberal government in Ottawa turn out to be in harmony or in opposition on this file. In the former case there will be major and wrenching changes in the approach to Aboriginal questions. In the latter there will be major federal and provincial differences. There will be no effective short-term appeals to the voters through an election in either case, since BC representatives, federal and provincial, will surely support the position of the provincial government, while the national electorate is not engaged with the issue.

On other intergovernmental issues for BC the surer allies are Ontario, Quebec, and Alberta. The six client-state provinces will continue to make common cause with Ottawa as long as the paymaster relationship continues, however much that may harm their fundamental interests.[19] The four large provinces have many common causes of their own, however,[20] and of course they contain 85 percent of the population of Canada. United they will not be gainsaid in any reasonable approach to federalism supported by their various electorates.

Historically, Ontario and Quebec were the joint movers of the "large-province" interests. With the ascendancy of sovereignist governments in Quebec this has become more difficult, though transient alliances have surfaced. Alberta and Ontario have not forged a durable partnership as yet, and BC as a large-province "wild card" has been a positively disruptive influence.

In the ongoing federal/provincial game, Ottawa has always held the upper hand. In part this has reflected the ability of the federal government to "wave the flag" of Canada. In part it has been the judicious application of the spending power to reward friends, punish others, and gain favour with the voters. And in part the Ottawa ascendancy has come from the ability of the central government to speak with one voice, while the provinces were usually divided.

"The flag" is still there for Ottawa, though interestingly a recent survey of over 3,000 westerners (Canada West Foundation, June 2001) found primary political identification to be biased much more strongly to "local," "provincial," or "the west" (selected by a total of 65 percent) than to "Canada" (selected by 28 percent).[21]

The spending power seemed even to be expanded in its usefulness for federal domination of the political agenda with the signature of the Social Union

Framework Agreement of 1999. For the first time ever the provinces (except Quebec) officially blessed the spending power, and astonishingly validated its use *in areas of provincial jurisdiction* with as few as six provinces with 15 percent of the population giving approval. That agreement was poisoned by the isolation of Quebec as a non-signatory. No derivative agreements have been reached under its terms, and it seems unlikely that any will prior to its review date in February 2002.

In fact restraints on the future use of the spending power will probably be determined by the third factor — the relative political organization and capacity of the two levels of government. At the federal level, a new administration with a bias either more strictly respectful of sections 91 and 92, and/or of a decentralist philosophy could exercise voluntary restraint. At the provincial level, a common approach between the four large provinces would exercise a similar, but non-voluntary restraint of a political nature on the central government.

The position of Quebec in this regard is well known. The positions of Ontario and Alberta are quite similar to those of Quebec, but they tend to back away in the crunch. The Social Union Agreement was a prime example. And the position of British Columbia in recent years has been absolutely subversive of any large-province concordat.

The BC factor is poised for dramatic change. The NDP administrations of the past decade have been uninterested and erratic in the business of the federation. They have generally favoured central authority, consistent with a socialist philosophy. From this point of view, decentralist large provinces have been either "right-wing" or "separatist," and not suitable for the receipt of BC support, lest they undermine medicare or even Canada itself.

The accession of a Liberal government in BC will likely bring a far tougher-minded approach in pursuit both of decentralization and of BC's particular interests in the federation. Early evidence was provided by Premier Campbell's almost immediate visit to Ottawa with a team of ministers to canvass the important aspects of the federal-provincial relationship.

This new element could well have a catalytic effect. The Harris-Bouchard alliance at the time of the First Ministers' Conference on health- care cost-sharing in September 2000 was clearly an important initiative that proved that the two largest provinces, if determined, could exercise a veto. We cannot as yet know whether this spectacular alliance was a "one-off" or the renewal of the historic Ontario-Quebec axis running from Mowat and Mercier until effectively terminated by Ontario's Leslie Frost 50 years ago. It is quite certain that if the alliance is revived, it will dramatically change federal-provincial relations, but the Quebec "national question" makes this problematic until (if and when) resolved. In this regard, the chapter by Daniel Salée in this volume is suggestive of possible new dynamics emanating from Quebec as Quebec's political culture continues to evolve.

BC is likely to become an aggressive participant in this large-province front, which may induce the cautious Ralph Klein of Alberta to begin asserting the interests of his own province more forcefully, in which case the provinces could even begin to "drive the bus" of the federation.

Who will BC seek out as its principal allies? Will it be the west (above all, Alberta, another rich province) or Ontario and/or Quebec? Peter Meekison has pointed out that BC has always in modern times considered itself a "region" as much as a province.[22] This was vividly illustrated by W.A.C. Bennett's dramatic unveiling of a "Five Region" map of Canada[23] at a Dominion-Provincial Conference in 1959. It was received with amusement. In the negotiations of 1971, BC insisted on being a "region" for the purpose of Supreme Court judge quotas, in 1978 its Senate proposals were based on regions, and BC outrage induced the federal government to add a fifth (BC) region to the law governing federal approval of constitutional amendments.

This regional business does not sit well with Alberta. Just as cooperation with Quebec is constrained by the national question, so is cooperation with Alberta constrained by the regional question. Interestingly, the evolving view of the provinces as being formally equal but different in weight — "special" in some way, each of them — may point a way forward.

What is important to note in all of the above is that the new BC attitude and its insistence on being closely involved in the affairs of the federation should not be seen as depending on personalities. While it is true that a changed BC attitude as described is most congenial to Liberal leader Gordon Campbell and his senior lieutenants, in this they but reflect a changing BC. In fact, it is the distant and chaotic approach of the NDP administration of the past decade that has been the anomaly.

World trends in globalization and technology and BC trends in demographics and economics all underwrite the above changes. BC will be leaner and meaner by economic necessity, and more conservative by temperament. These different tendencies will result in a major change in the role that BC plays in the future operation of the Canadian federal system.

NOTES

1. Philip Resnick, *The Politics of Resentment* (Vancouver: IRPP/UBC Press, 2000).

2. David Barrett, 1972–75, and Mike Harcourt, Glen Clark, Ujjal Dosanjh, 1991–2000.

3. The Allaire Report to the Quebec government went considerably further, but was never adopted as government policy. Quebec Liberal Party, Constitutional Committee (J. Allaire, Chair), *A Québec Free to Choose: Report of the Constitutional Committee* (Quebec: Quebec Liberal Party, 1991). The same is true of Claude Ryan's Beige Paper, produced a couple of years after the Bennett

documents. Quebec Liberal Party, Constitutional Committee, *A New Canadian Federation* (Montreal: Quebec Liberal Party, 1980).

4.   Rafe Mair tells a fine anecdote to illustrate how seriously the BC proposals were really taken. In the first year, they were presented in eight slim volumes. Mel Smith, sensing the minimal impact, suggested they be resubmitted the following year to the next in a series of constitutional conferences, unchanged, but in a single volume. Mair well recalls the compliments he received for the "new" work.

5.   Personal income is slightly higher compared to the rest of Canada than GDP/capita because of external remittances not based on local productivity.

6.   Technology holds out the promise of huge returns, but capturing those depends upon maintaining firms in BC to technological maturity. Too often they leave or are bought out at an earlier stage. The reasons for this are a matter of major political debate.

7.   The figures in this and the following two paragraphs are taken from *A look at incomes in British Columbia* (BC: Business Council, July 2000).

8.   It is interesting to note that the population of BC today is 1,000,000 souls larger than that of the Thirteen Colonies at the time of the Declaration of Independence.

9.   The following data is from publications of *B.C. Stats*, the statistics branch of the Ministry of Finance, based on census data.

10.   In 1996 in BC, about 56 percent of respondents gave single-origin answers.

11.   Aboriginal Canadians plus a few persons of miscellaneous origin make up the small difference to 100 percent in each case.

12.   This tradition has begun to change in recent years.

13.   One of the most convincing indices of the growing "federalism" of the European Union is the way in which the Schengen Convention member states have been willing to subordinate this power to the overall Union.

14.   It should not be imagined that this development will be too long delayed. Even today, immigrants who have been in Canada for a couple of decades and therefore more likely to participate in the political process complain in the editorial pages of British Columbia newspapers about the "lax" new standards of admission depreciating the value of their own, hard-earned entry.

15.   See chapter by Ian Stewart in this volume for some discussion of that issue.

16.   For a detailed treatment of many of these issues, see www.fraserinstitute.ca for availability and downloading of several articles by this author.

17.   Except for eastern Quebec and most of the Atlantic provinces, where BC-type problems may in due course surface.

18.   It should be noted that the provincial Liberal Party has no organic links with the federal party of the same name, though there are significant overlaps in personnel. Most of its current support comes from British Columbians who used to vote Social Credit. The provincial Reform Party also is and was unaffiliated with either the Alliance or the previous national Reform Party.

19. See McMahon, *Looking the Gift Horse in the Mouth; The Impact of Federal Transfer Payments on Atlantic Canada* (Halifax: Atlantic Institute for Market Studies, 1996).

20. An end to conditional cost-shared programs and a restriction of equalization to the formal program of that name being foremost, with a demand for a greater handle on federal jurisdictions that affect the provinces a close second.

21. I recognize that these data differ considerably from what some other surveys have reported. However, the different results probably are linked to the way the question was asked. In particular, the Canada West Foundation allowed respondents to identify with local as well as provincial identities.

22. Personal correspondence with author.

23. BC, the Prairies, Ontario, Quebec, the Atlantic.

IV

New
Identities

11

The Evolution of Charter Values

Paul Howe and Joseph F. Fletcher

Les sondages révèlent que le soutien accordé à la Charte canadienne des Droits et Libertés reste aussi élevé en 1999 qu'il l'était en 1987, et ce, malgré des jugements judiciaires controversés et un déplacement apparent vers la droite de la culture politique canadienne au cours des années 1990. Les auteurs cherchent à expliquer ce phénomène en s'attardant à l'évolution des opinions et des valeurs au cours de cette période de douze ans.

Différents courants s'avèrent être à l'œuvre. L'appui envers les libertés civiles reste essentiellement constant durant cette période, alors que l'importance accordée aux principes de tradition et d'autorité a augmentée, tout comme l'opposition au concept général de droits à l'égalité. Ces changements n'étaient toutefois pas accompagnés d'une hostilité croissante envers les droits de groupes spécifiques. En fait, dans l'ensemble, les groupes minoritaires ont bénéficié d'un plus grand support de l'opinion publique en 1999 qu'en 1987. Ce dernier changement de l'opinion publique est d'ailleurs enraciné dans l'effet de cohorte — il y a un soutien plus élevé pour les droits à l'égalité chez les jeunes que chez les groupes plus âgés, associé à un soutien stable chez les cohortes à travers le temps — ce qui suggère que ce changement est sérieux et que de futurs revirements sont improbables.

Les liens entre les différents types de valeurs et le soutien à la Charte indiquent également une variation significative. En 1987, le soutien accordé aux droits à l'égalité était un facteur plus déterminant envers le soutien à la Charte que les autres types de valeurs; cette différence était encore plus prononcée en 1999. De sorte que l'évolution de l'opinion publique en faveur des droits à l'égalité est donc partie intégrante du soutien continu envers la Charte.

INTRODUCTION

Despite recent criticisms directed at the *Canadian Charter of Rights and Freedoms*, public support remained high over the 1987 to 1999 period. In 1987, 83 percent of Canadians thought the Charter was "a good thing for Canada," 12 percent thought it was a bad thing, and the rest were unsure.

Twelve years later, 82 percent thought it a good thing, 11 percent a bad thing, and the remainder were unsure.[1]

What underlies the deep support for this central pillar of the Canadian political landscape? Political culture — the underlying values, predispositions and beliefs that shape attitudes toward actors and institutions in the political sphere — is likely part of the story. Common sense would suggest that people's opinions on fundamental value- and rights-based questions must figure among the determinants of Charter support. But if this is so, the story is not without wrinkles. For while the Charter is meant to be an embodiment of rights and values on which there is general consensus, its application in specific instances, via judicial rulings, has caused considerable controversy. Canadians differ over the priority that should be given to gay rights, Aboriginal rights, the rights of the criminally accused, and so on, and these differences likely structure attitudes toward the Charter. Indeed, it is somewhat puzzling, given the volume and vehemence of recent value-based criticisms, that Charter support remains as strong as ever.

In seeking to understand this resilience, two datasets are used in the analysis below, from surveys conducted in 1987 and 1999.[2] This allows for not only a cross-sectional view of the underpinnings of Charter support at two different points, but also the identification of trends in those underpinnings over time.[3] From this longitudinal analysis, tentative assessments are drawn as to what might happen to Charter support in the future.

While our principal concern is to understand continuing Charter support, we do so by examining change and continuity in basic value orientations, an integral components of Canadian political culture. Thus, our contribution is twofold: to shed light on the evolution of Canadian political culture over the past 12 years — a worthwhile enterprise in its own right — and to outline why Charter support remains high today, with an eye to assessing whether this is likely to continue into the future.

VALUE CHANGE IN CANADA

One dominant and influential perspective on value change in western democracies is that developed by Ronald Inglehart, which holds that postmaterialist values are slowly replacing the dominant materialist orientations of the past. Since the end of World War II, basic needs for physical security and material well-being have been largely met in these societies, leading to greater emphasis on postmaterialist concerns. Postmaterialists assign higher priority to self-expression and individuality and exhibit diminished respect for authority and tradition. This value change has abetted the mobilization of previously marginalized groups, including ethnic minorities, homosexuals, and women — a process dubbed the "new politics" — and engendered greater sympathy in the general population for such groups. The postmaterialist phenomenon is held to be rooted in generational dynamics, as those cohorts that have experienced material privation and physical insecurity (older ones) are less likely to embrace postmaterialist values than those that have not (younger ones). The stability of these value orientations over time means that population turnover — the replacement of older cohorts by younger ones — will lead to the continued ascendance of postmaterialist values.

In Canada, the postmaterialist account of value change has not been widely applied. The most extensive treatment is Neil Nevitte's *Decline of Deference*, which traces changes in Canadian values over the 1981 to 1990 period and finds confirmation of the postmaterialist thesis.[4] Instead, there has been as much emphasis on the Charter itself, and its transformative impact on Canadian political culture. By providing opportunities for political mobilization to a variety of social groups, the Charter, so the argument runs, has privileged certain identities and political claims over others, and in so doing, effected a seismic shift in Canadian political culture.[5] Generational differences in the Charter's impact are not typically considered in this more institutionally oriented literature, but it would be reasonable to posit that the Charter's impact would be greatest on younger Canadians, who have grown up with the Charter and imbibed its basic premises from the earliest age. If there are some differences between the two accounts,[6] they share a common implication: there has been increasing sympathy for Charter-based values that is deeply rooted and unlikely to change. In either view, the ongoing high levels of support for the Charter are no mystery and future trends are easy to predict.

But against these theoretical accounts, there has been an apparent swing to the right in the 1990s, most obviously evidenced by the rise of the Reform Party (now the Canadian Alliance).[7] Some scholars have suggested that the Charter, as interpreted by the courts, has brought about changes that run directly counter to the value preferences of most Canadians.[8] At the very least, it is reasonable to wonder if support for Charter values remains as strong today as it has been at points past.

That the Alliance is the most outspoken critic of certain Charter values and the new politics raises one possible hypothesis. It has been suggested that Reform/Alliance supporters are, on average, older than other parties' supporters;[9] and as noted above, younger cohorts are said to be more sympathetic to postmaterialist values. It may be, then, that the debate over Charter-based values which has been unfolding lately is generationally-structured, with younger Canadians largely sympathetic to those values and the backlash of the 1990s coming primarily from older Canadians who are less supportive. In terms of future predictions, this would suggest that support for Charter values and the new politics is likely to remain strong (assuming, of course, that age differences represent cohort effects not age effects, as the postmaterialist literature would suggest).

How do we go about investigating these questions? Our data are not structured in accordance with the postmaterialist literature; the design principle was to re-create questions asked at an earlier point (1987) for a rather different purpose. Indeed, the standard questions used to categorize respondents as materialists, postmaterialists, and of mixed preferences do not appear on the surveys.[10] Yet the survey items do speak to many of the values held to be linked with postmaterialist orientations — in particular, attitudes toward authority and tradition and views on various outgroups that have made considerable gains in the past couple of decades. Our focus is on the evolution of these attitudes and how they relate to Charter support. The analysis is presented in three sections:

1.   First, an overview is provided of the evolution, from 1987 to 1999, of Canadian opinion on various value- and rights-oriented questions. To what extent is there evidence of a right-wing backlash over this period? We find *prima facie* evidence of such a backlash in the markedly higher value placed by Canadians upon authority and tradition. But there is also evidence that points the other way: support for civil liberties has remained constant over the period, while support for equality rights, on most measures, has increased.

2.   The evolution of these values is then examined in greater detail by tracking attitudes within birth cohorts over time. Are the predictions of postmaterialist and Charter-transformation accounts borne out? The answer to this question forms the basis for tentative predictions about future values trends in Canada and consequently Charter support.

3.   Finally, the relationships between different values and Charter support at two points in time (1987 and 1999) are considered. The causal linkages thus identified help explain why Charter support remains high today.

RIGHTS AND VALUES: THE EVOLUTION OF CANADIAN OPINION

The data in the analysis below are drawn from two surveys. The Charter Project consists of a series of surveys conducted in 1987 that measured attitudes on a host of rights- and value-based issues.[11] The *IRPP Survey on Courts and the Charter* involves a single survey conducted in 1999 that replicated numerous questions from the Charter Project for the express purpose of longitudinal analysis.[12]

Table 1 shows the change from 1987 to 1999 on some relevant items, previously linked with postmaterialist orientations, that appeared on both surveys.[13] On the civil liberties front, the data would suggest that while opinion is divided on all three questions, attitudes have been relatively stable over the 12-year period. Indeed, the first item, concerning free speech (C1), shows no

Table 1: Canadian Attitudes Toward Rights and Values, 1987 and 1999

		1987	1999
Civil Liberties			
C1. Free speech ought to be allowed for all political groups even if some of the things that these groups believe in are highly insulting and threatening to society.	Basically agree	52	51
	Basically disagree	46	46
	Don't know	2	3
C2. I would like you to consider now an instance where the police see a young man they do not recognize walking very near a house where they know drugs are being sold. They search him and find he is carrying drugs. Do you think this search is a reasonable search, or does it violate the young man's rights?*	Reasonable search	59	53
	Violated his rights	40	46
	Don't know	1	1
C3. Consider this case: The police asked an obviously drunk driver to take a breathalyzer test without telling him that he had a right to consult a lawyer. Should a judge allow the breathalyzer evidence to be used in court or should he exclude it, even if the driver may go free as a result?*	Allow evidence	68	71
	Exclude evidence	29	28
	Don't know	4	2
Equality Rights			
E1. We have gone too far in pushing equal rights in this country.*	Basically agree	30	40
	Basically disagree	68	57
	Don't know	2	4
E2. How important is it to guarantee equality between men and women in all aspects of life?	Very important	72	70
	Somewhat important	23	25
	Not important	5	5
	Don't know	–	1
E3. How important is preserving French and English as the two official languages of Canada?	Very important	48	44
	Somewhat important	31	34
	Not important	21	21
	Don't know	1	1
E4. How important is it to make a special effort to protect ethnic and racial minorities?*	Very important	42	52
	Somewhat important	44	39
	Not important	12	9
	Don't know	2	1
E5. Should native peoples be treated just like any other Canadian, with no special rights, or should the unique rights of Canada's native peoples be preserved?*	Like any other Canadian	50	59
	Unique rights preserved	47	39
	Don't know	3	2
E6. Do you approve or disapprove of allowing homosexuals to teach in school in (respondent's province)?*	Approve	50	73
	Disapprove	47	23
	Don't know	3	4
Tradition and Authority			
T1. How important is preserving traditional ideas of right and wrong?*	Very important	58	72
	Somewhat important	35	24
	Not important	5	3
	Don't know	1	1
T2. How important is it to strengthen respect and obedience for authority?*	Very important	60	66
	Somewhat important	34	29
	Not important	6	4
	Don't know	1	1

Notes: *Cramer's V significant at $p < 0.01$.
Some questions were subject to wording variations. See Appendix 1 for details.

real movement over time. On item C2, concerning the legitimacy of a questionable drug search, there has been a small shift in opinion toward the civil libertarian position. On item C3, which asks about the administration of a breathalyzer test in the absence of legal counsel, opinion has moved in the other direction, but only slightly.

Compared with civil liberties, there is higher overall support for equality rights as well as greater change over time. Item E1 is a general query about whether we have gone too far in pushing equal rights. Most Canadians say no at both points in time. However, in 1987, only 30 percent agreed with the statement; in 1999 this climbed to 40 percent. This partial backlash against equality rights is not, however, mirrored in the responses given to a series of questions that probe respondents' feelings toward various groups that frame their claims in the language of equality rights and which have — in some cases thanks to explicit Charter guarantees — won some important court battles to secure those claims. Items E2 to E6 ask in turn about women, Canada's two official languages, ethnic and racial minorities, native peoples and homosexuals. E2 and E3 show no significant movement of opinion from 1987 to 1999. E4 and E6 reveal increasing public sympathy toward ethnic and racial minorities and homosexuals, with very substantial movement in the latter case. The only item that registers a decline in support is E5 as support for the "special rights" of native peoples has dropped eight points over the 12-year period.

Thus, there has been a shift of opinion against equal rights as a general concept, yet on balance Canadians are becoming even more favourably disposed toward the various groups that couch their claims in the language of equality rights. Significant changes are also revealed in the responses given to two questions probing attitudes toward tradition and authority (T1 and T2). The majorities in favour of both principles have grown over the period, as more respondents in 1999 are inclined to deem them very important. In the case of tradition, there is a 14 percent increase, in the case of authority, a more modest 6 percent.[14] These changes are consistent with increasing opposition to equality rights in general (E1) and with the notion that there was a shift to the right in Canadians' values over the course of the 1990s. Yet they run counter to the substantial and rising support for the various minorities and outgroups that have, for the most part, challenged tradition and authority in staking their claims.[15]

As evidenced by these diverging trends, Charter values, at least at the level of popular opinion, are not of one piece. Majorities tend to respond favourably to *both* equality and authority items, while opinion on civil liberties tends to be divided. To characterize the public as simply in favour of or opposed to Charter values would be misleading. It is more appropriate to look at each of the three value domains separately.

Table 2 uses simple additive indices to summarize the trends in each value domain.[16,17] This confirms the basic patterns: little movement in the area of

Table 2: Rights and Values, Summary Indices, 1987 and 1999

		1987 (%)	1999 (%)
Civil liberties	Low	23	22
	Medium	40	41
	High	37	37
Equality rights*	Low	36	29
	Medium	32	34
	High	32	38
Tradition and authority*	Low	26	18
	Medium	34	29
	High	40	53

Notes: *Cramer's V significant at p < 0.01.
See Appendix 2 for details of index construction.

civil liberties, a significant rise in support for the equality rights of specific groups, and a very substantial rise in support for the principles of tradition and authority. There is, then, *prima facie* evidence of some type of shift to the right over the 1987 to 1999 period, yet this does not appear to be part of a more general phenomenon entailing decreasing support for either civil liberties or the equality of particular outgroups.

COHORT ANALYSIS OF CHARTER SUPPORT AND ITS UNDERPINNINGS

From our preliminary overview, it is apparent that value change in Canada over the past dozen years cannot be readily summarized by a single theoretical account. If Canadian values have not been moving consistently in the direction predicted by postmaterialist theory or Charter-transformation accounts, neither have they been shifting uniformly to the right. In this section, we take a closer look at these divergent trends and consider their implications for different theoretical understandings of Canadian value change and the contours of Charter support.

For this purpose we turn to cohort analysis, a useful tool for unpacking aggregate social change. It is especially illuminating when it reveals cohort effects — constant levels for some variable of interest in particular birth cohorts across different points in time, which are taken to indicate stability at the individual level. When the level of the relevant variable differs across cohorts, it is plausible to expect long-term aggregate change based on population turnover. Cohort effects mean that societal attitudes will gradually change as younger cohorts replace older ones. The mechanical predictability of this process makes it a potentially powerful tool for the social scientist. It is the notion that cohort effects underlie the long-term ascendance of postmaterialist values that largely accounts for the appeal of the theory.

If cohort effects can be at once predictable and consequential, the same is not generally true of the other two phenomena sometimes detected in longitudinal analysis, age and period effects. Age effects — consistent differences between age groups (as opposed to birth cohorts) at different points in time — can be predictable, but are typically of lesser consequence. They will only produce aggregate change if the relative weight of different age groups in the population changes significantly over time. Otherwise age effects simply lead to the reproduction of abiding age divisions over time.

Period effects, on the other hand, can be consequential, but are generally less predictable. Consisting of a uniform shift in opinion across different age groups and birth cohorts over a given period, they are consequential because they necessarily produce aggregate social change. But they do not easily lend themselves to predictions about the future. Sometimes period effects are treated as *sui generis* phenomena that can only be explained by the specifics of a particular time and place. More general explanations are sometimes advanced — in the postmaterialist literature, period effects are often linked to shifting economic circumstances, for example — and this can facilitate prediction. But it does represent another step in the analysis that introduces an added degree of uncertainty to any prognostications about the future. The sort of mechanical prediction possible when cohort effects are detected is generally not possible with period effects.

Understanding how cohort, age, and period effects have conditioned Canadian opinion on the rights and values identified above may help us see where opinion is likely to move in the future. Sorting out these effects can, however, be a tricky business. The three are linked, since each can be expressed as a linear combination of the other two (e.g., knowing the year, or period, and someone's age tells you their birth year). Consequently, a particular effect can always be re-interpreted as a product of the other two effects acting in combination. Plausibility becomes an important criterion for ranking interpretations.

The basic rules of thumb are as follows. First, differences between birth cohorts help in distinguishing the three effects; otherwise interpretation can be difficult. Second, stability of attitudes within birth cohorts is taken to indicate cohort effects. Third, movement within cohorts over time — intra-cohort change — is suggestive of either an age or period effect. Sometimes the two are easily distinguished. However, as we will see below, intra-cohort change is often consistent with either an age effect, a period effect or the two in

Table 3: Rights and Values, Cohort Analysis, 1987–1999

		Total	Cohort				
			1933 and earlier	1934– 1945	1946– 1957	1958– 1969	1970– 1981
Civil liberty	1987	37	27	32	41	42	
	1999	37	23	26	33	39	50
Equality rights	1987	33	21	34	33	39	
	1999	38	27	31	37	39	47
Tradition and authority	1987	40	57	45	41	26	
	1999	53	52	65	60	51	40
	Min N, 1987	(2,018)	(467)	(341)	(629)	(581)	
	Min N, 1999	(962)	(84)	(130)	(265)	(302)	(179)

Notes: Percentages appearing in the table are as follows (see Appendix 2 for full details of index construction):
Civil rights: supportive of civil liberty on at least 2 of 3 questions;
Equality rights: supportive of minority/outgroup on at least 4 of 5 questions, or supportive on 3 of 5 and replying "don't know" on other 2;
Tradition and authority: consider both "very important."

combination. Therefore, it is sometimes sensible to separate aggregate change into two components only: (i) intra-cohort change (whether due to age or period effects); and (ii) population turnover, that is change produced by cohort effects. The first is the component of change due to changing attitudes at the individual level. The second is the component of change deriving from stable attitudes at the individual level. Formal methods are helpful in breaking aggregate change into these two components.

We apply these principles in considering the evolution of opinion within birth cohorts on the various Charter underpinnings described above. Table 3 shows a birth cohort breakdown for the three indices that aggregate responses to two or more survey items: a civil rights index, an equality rights index and a tradition-authority index (see Table 2). In each case, the figures in Table 3 represent the percentage within cohorts scoring "high" on the relevant index.

CIVIL LIBERTY

As Table 3 indicates, the absence of aggregate change in attitudes toward civil liberties does not mean that no change is taking place within sub-sections of the population. Quite the contrary: all cohorts from 1987 show significant decreases in support for civil liberties between 1987 and 1999. It is only the higher level of support in the new cohort in 1999 (those born from 1970 to 1981) that keeps the overall figure constant.

One possible explanation for this pan-cohort decrease in support is an age effect, wherein people tend to become less supportive of civil liberties as they age. Indeed, the evolution of opinion within the 1987 cohorts is very nearly what would be predicted by a pure age effect: each cohort in 1999 looks very much like those of the same age did in 1987. So, for example, the percentage of strong supporters of civil liberties drops from 41 percent to 33 percent in the 1946–57 cohort, nearly the same level as in the same age group 12 years previously (32 percent for the 1934–45 cohort). Yet the data are also more or less consistent with a period effect. The reduced support for civil liberties over the 12-year period is not identical in each of the cohorts but it is roughly comparable, ranging between 3 and 8 percent. A second plausible interpretation of the data, then, is that each cohort would have maintained its 1987 level of support for civil liberties through to 1999 but for a period effect that influenced all cohorts.

Whichever interpretation is correct, neither does a good job of explaining the level of support for civil liberties in the youngest cohort, those born between 1970 and 1981. In the absence of any evidence about formative influences on new cohorts, the simplest prediction is that they will take the same value as the cohort immediately preceding them took at the same age. If a period effect is operative, it would be anticipated that this value would shift accordingly, since there is no reason to presume that the youngest cohort — those just coming of age and perhaps *most* susceptible to shifting tides of opinion — would be immune to its influence. It follows that a comparison of the 1970–81 cohort in 1999 and the youngest cohort in 1987 (the 1958–69 cohort) should reveal either a stable level of support for civil liberties (42 percent), or a decrease in support for civil liberties comparable to that in the older cohorts (42 percent less some 3 to 8 percent). Instead, the data in Table 3 show an *increase* in support for civil liberties in this youngest group over the 12-year period (from 42 percent to 50 percent[18]).

This higher than expected level of support for civil liberties suggests there have been formative influences affecting the youngest cohort. Those born between 1970 and 1981 are the only cohort that has, in its entirety, grown up with the Charter and the civil liberty guarantees embodied therein. Their stronger sympathy for civil liberties may well derive in part from the fact that they have taken on Charter values during their formative years. Whether the high level of support within this cohort will decline as the group ages (if age effects predominate) or shift more unpredictably over different periods (if period effects predominate) is more uncertain.[19]

EQUALITY RIGHTS

Turning to equality rights, visual inspection of the data in Table 3 suggests that opinion in this area is not subject to age effects. At both points in time, older Canadians are less likely to be strong supporters of equality rights than younger Canadians. Yet only one cohort (1934–45) shows signs of decreased support for equality rights as it has aged over the 1987 to 1999 period, and this is not a statistically significant change. Support is either constant within cohorts or slightly increased.

Nor does there seem to be a strong period effect at work. There is relatively little change within cohorts, and that which has taken place is not evenly distributed across the cohorts. Moreover, the change within all cohorts lies within the margins of random sampling error. The simplest account of the data in Table 3 is that support for equality rights is a relatively stable attitude within cohorts that is immune to change from aging or period shifts.

More formal methods can be used to determine what proportion of the total change in a variable is due to population turnover — that is, driven by cohort effects — and what proportion derives from intra-cohort change (whether due to aging or period effects). For this, we use all three categories of the equality rights index, as shown in Table 1: low (assigned a value of 1), medium (2) and high (3). The mean value on the index for 1987 is 1.96; for 1999 it is 2.09. Algebraic decomposition methods indicate that approximately 70 percent of this change is attributable to population turnover and only 30 percent to intra-cohort change.[20] In the case of equality rights, cohort effects are the dominant influence on aggregate change.

These results are consistent with the postmaterialist thesis. Support for the equality rights of various groups is considerably higher among younger Canadians. This higher level of support is maintaining itself over time as those younger cohorts age, resulting in aggregate social change. The cohort differentiation evident in Table 3 is, in fact, considerably stronger than it is for the four-item postmaterialist index developed by Ronald Inglehart and applied extensively in countries around the world. When Inglehart's index has been administered in Canada, it has revealed scant differences between birth cohorts, rendering Canada (along with the United States) a somewhat anomalous case.[21] Examining some of the attitudes associated with postmaterialism, however, reveals significant age differences in the Canadian data, which longitudinal analysis suggests are stable cohort differences.

If the data suggest that support for equality rights is likely to continue to grow in the future, they also suggest that the pace of change may pick up. In the 1999 data, the gap in support for equality rights between adjacent cohorts ranges from 2 percent to 6 percent for the older cohorts, but is 8 percent between the youngest and next to youngest cohorts. The postmaterialist literature would predict otherwise: Inglehart's four-item index, when administered to populations in the established democracies, typically reveals that the level of support for postmaterialist values has continued to increase in successive cohorts but the gaps between cohorts are growing smaller.[22] That Table 8 reveals a larger jump in the youngest cohort suggests some other factor is at play in Canada over and above the forces generating increased sympathy for postmaterialist values in rising cohorts worldwide. The obvious candidate is the Charter itself. As was the case for civil rights, it appears that the Charter has had some formative impact on the 1970–81 cohort that is producing levels of support for Charter-based rights and values over and above what other sources of change would lead us to expect.

Some important qualifications are in order, however. This overall picture of cohort stability and gradually increasing sympathy for the equality rights of various groups skates over some important differences between the various items that make up our equality rights index. It will be recalled, for example, that overall support for the "special rights" of native peoples dropped eight points over the 12-year period, whereas approval of homosexuals' teaching in schools jumped by 23 percent (see Table 1). Clearly, the individual attitudes that make up the index are not all moving in lockstep.

Nor do the individual items show the same degree of cohort stability exhibited by the index as a whole. Table 4 shows a cohort breakdown of attitudes for all items in the equality rights index in 1987 and 1999. It is immediately apparent that the cohort patterns for the index as a whole are not replicated for the individual items. Consider, in particular, attitudes on the gay rights and native rights questions. In both cases, it is clear that there has been movement within all cohorts. On the gay rights item, there has been a considerable upward shift in every cohort — a period effect presumably, since the data indicate that older people are less supportive of gay rights. The movement is smaller in older cohorts, but significant nonetheless. The net result is that about three-quarters of the change on this item derives from intra-cohort change (i.e., individual change) and about one-quarter from population turnover.[23]

It is also the case that the significant cohort differentiation on the gay rights item is largely responsible for the cohort differentiation for the index as a whole. Differences across the cohorts are more modest and less consistent on the other items. The importance of this one item to the index as a whole suggests some caution is in order in generalizing our results, though clearly attitudes toward gay rights are an important indicator of changing attitudes toward equality rights.

The pattern of change on the native rights item is also noteworthy. Table 4 shows decreases in support ranging from 8 to 13 percent across the 1987 cohorts. The uniformity of the shift suggests that, as with attitudes toward gay rights, a period effect is at work. But in this case, individual change and population turnover are working in opposite directions. Individual change acting

Table 4: Equality Rights, Cohort Analysis, 1987–1999

		Total	Cohort				
			1933 and earlier	1934–1945	1946–1957	1958–1969	1970–1981
Very important to guarantee equality between men and women	1987	72	63	69	75	76	
	1999	70	51	67	69	74	74
Very important to preserve French and English as the two official languages of Canada	1987	48	48	50	45	48	
	1999	44	43	51	42	45	41
Very important to make a special effort to protect ethnic and racial minorities	1987	42	41	43	42	42	
	1999	52	54	45	47	54	58
Unique rights of natives should be preserved	1987	47	47	45	46	50	
	1999	39	34	34	38	40	44
Approve of gay teachers in schools	1987	50	31	49	56	58	
	1999	73	43	61	75	76	84
	Min N, 1987	(2,049)	(473)	(347)	(639)	(585)	
	Min N, 1999	(976)	(87)	(132)	(267)	(305)	(180)

alone would produce an overall drop in support of about ten points; population turnover — the replacement of older cohorts by younger ones slightly more supportive of Aboriginal rights — reduces this slightly to eight points.

Looking at the regional breakdown for the native rights questions (Table 5) sheds further light on the sources of change. In the Atlantic region, Ontario, and the Prairies (including Alberta), attitudes toward the special rights of native peoples did not change over the 1987 to 1999 period. Instead, the entire

Table 5: Native Rights by Region, 1987 and 1999

		Total	Region				
			Atlantic	Quebec	Ontario	Prairies	BC
Unique rights	1987	47	41	47	56	37	41
of natives should	(N)	(2,072)	(372)	(433)	(619)	(352)	(296)
be preserved							
	1999	39	43	24	54	36	29
	(N)	(994)	(82)	(245)	(372)	(170)	(125)

decrease is due to declining support for native rights in two provinces, BC (a 12-point drop) and Quebec (23 points). These are, of course, the two places where native claims proved most contentious over the course of the 1990s.[24] In Quebec, the decade began with the Oka crisis, which saw natives protesting the development of a golf course on land claimed as sacred burial ground; in BC, there have been similar standoffs. The treaty negotiation process has created controversy in BC, the most recent example being the Nisga'a treaty, while in Quebec native claims to self-determination in the event of separation have produced animosity among some sovereignist supporters. That the decreased support for native rights is concentrated in this fashion suggests that it is due to period effects rooted in political developments particular to these two provinces.[25]

Thus, opinion on native rights has evolved in a different direction from the other items in our equality rights index,[26] but the anomaly is explicable. Nor are such anomalies entirely unexpected. Our contention, consistent with the postmaterialist literature, is not that cohort effects underwrite each individual item in our equality rights index, but rather that there is a favourable disposition, more prevalent in younger cohorts, that conditions, without wholly determining, attitude toward a host of equality-related issues.[27] This is leading to greater sympathy, on average, for various groups that couch their claims in the language of equality rights. Since this process appears to be underwritten by cohort effects, it is likely to continue apace, with positive consequences for Charter support.

TRADITION AND AUTHORITY

Table 3 shows that there has been a sizable aggregate increase in support for the principles of tradition and authority (13 percent). The table also reveals that this increase has occurred within all birth cohorts except the oldest. One explanation for this pattern of change is that age effects are an important influence on the attitudes in question. The 1987 data reveal significant differences across age groups, with older Canadians showing stronger support for the principles of tradition and authority. Thus, intra-cohort change over the 12-year period could reflect a tendency for people to embrace more conservative values with age.

In all cases, however, the change over the 12-year period exceeds that which would be predicted by age effects alone, suggesting that a period effect has also been operative. Table 6 shows a simple calculation of this period effect. The predicted value for each cohort in 1999 is simply the actual value for the same age group — that is, the next-eldest birth cohort — in 1987. Comparing this to the actual value for each cohort in 1999 indicates by how much the 12-year shift exceeds the value predicted by age effects alone. This estimated period effect is positive in all cases, ranging between 8 and 15 percent.

Thus, an age and period effect in combination seems a plausible interpretation for the cohort data on tradition and authority. Looking back once more to Table 3, however, it also seems possible that the entire change over the 12-year period is due to a period effect that has differentially affected the cohorts — that is to say, no impact on the oldest cohort (those born in 1933 and earlier), a small impact on the next to oldest (1934–45) and youngest (1970–81), and a larger impact on the two intermediate ones. But whatever the combination of aging and period effects responsible for the changes witnessed over the 1987 to 1999 period, it is clear that intra-cohort change greatly outweighs the effects of population turnover in this instance. In fact, the impact of population turnover serves only to mute slightly the considerable effects of change at the individual level. More precisely, in the absence of population turnover, aggregate change on the tradition and authority index would have been 16 percent instead of 13 percent.

Table 6: Age and Period Effects for Tradition and Authority

| | Cohort | | | | |
	1933 and earlier	*1934– 1945*	*1946– 1957*	*1958– 1969*	*1970– 1981*
Predicted value, 1999, if age effect only	–	57	45	41	26
Actual value, 1999	52	65	60	51	40
Difference — estimate of period effect		8	15	10	14

These findings run counter to the postmaterialist contention that support for authority and tradition has been declining as a consequence of the gradual ascendance of postmaterialist values. While the postmaterialist literature does allow that period effects can influence value preferences, these fluctuations have generally been linked to economic conditions. Bad economic times — high rates of inflation, first and foremost, unemployment to a lesser degree — produce temporary shifts away from postmaterialist values.[28] However, our survey took place in the late 1990s, a time of relative economic prosperity in Canada. Inflation remained very low and unemployment, after remaining stubbornly high through much of the 1990s, was on the decline. It is true, too, that postmaterialist theory does not claim to predict individual attitudes with great precision; it allows for significant slippage between postmaterialism per se (as measured by Inglehart's four-item index) and the host of attitudes said to be influenced by this underlying value disposition. However, attitudes toward authority are usually treated as one of the key correlates of postmaterialism.[29] It is difficult to imagine postmaterialist theory remaining robust if this core finding starts to come into question. And finally, if there are age effects at work in the Canadian context, the reconciliation with postmaterialist theory is that much harder. The postmaterialist literature may allow for some fluctuation induced by period effects but otherwise predicts stability within cohorts. Age effects — people turning away from postmaterialist values as they age — are held to be insignificant.

In sum, the divergent trends in our data are confirmed in the cohort analysis. There has been, on the one hand, rising support for the equality rights of various outgroups and minorities, which is in keeping with the contours of postmaterialist theory. But at the same time, there has also been rising support for tradition and authority, which runs counter to postmaterialist predictions. As part of this difference, the underlying cohort patterns on the measures differ. Opinion on our equality rights index seems to show cohort effects, whereas the shift to the right apparent in evolving attitudes toward tradition and authority, appears to be driven in significant measure by period effects. An important implication is that the former trend is more likely to prove enduring than the latter.

THE UNDERPINNINGS OF CHARTER SUPPORT

In this final section, we consider how these underlying values trends have influenced overall Charter support. Table 7 shows standardized coefficients for two regression models of Charter support, one for the 1987 survey, the other for the 1999 survey. In addition to the value indexes we have also included a number of standard demographic variables including birth year, education, income, gender, and region. Although the variables examined here together explain only a modest portion of the available variance, the analysis sheds some clear light on why Charter support remains high.

Immediately apparent in comparing the results for the two years is that while a number of factors were significantly related to support for the *Charter of Rights and Freedoms* in 1987, only one remains so in 1999. The single remaining factor is support for equality rights. By 1999, evaluations of the Charter were based nearly exclusively on questions of equality.

It is also notable that while the value placed upon civil liberties once had a significant influence on Charter support, that relationship is now negligible, as indicated by the decline in the civil liberty regression coefficient from significance in 1987 to essentially zero in 1999.[30] Despite the considerable impact of the Charter on police actions and the administration of justice, civil liberty

Table 7: Charter Support in 1987 and 1999, Standardized Regression Coefficients

	1987 Beta	1999 Beta
Civil liberties index	0.08*	0.03
Equality rights index	0.22*	0.26*
Tradition and authority index	0.05	0.02
Birth year	−0.02	0.03
Education	0.10*	0.05
Income	0.04	0.04
Gender (female)	−0.09*	−0.06
Atlantic	0.00	0.05
Quebec	0.08*	0.04
Prairie	0.00	0.07
British Columbia	−0.02	−0.05
Adjusted R-square	0.09	0.08
(N)	(1,478)	(699)

Notes: *Statistically significant, p 0< .01.
The dependent variable is respondents' views on the Charter: very good thing [for Canada] (1); good thing (0.75); don't know (0.5); bad thing (0.25); or very bad thing (0). For the independent variables birth year is categorized as described in Table 3; income is scored from low to high in $10,000 increments; education is categorized as low (high school or less), medium (some postsecondary), or high (completed university); gender and region variables are dummy variables.

concerns today no longer influence Canadians' assessments of their Charter. The results for tradition and authority — the absence of any impact in either year — appear somewhat counter-intuitive too. A consistent theme in the discourse of Charter critics is that it has foisted new values and policy priorities on Canadians that run counter to tried and true conventions and do not enjoy broad popular support. It might therefore be anticipated that support for the values of tradition and authority would be associated with negative views of the Charter. Such is clearly not the case.[31]

Turning to demographics, education, gender,[32] and region, these variables show small effects in 1987, but in 1999 they are all insignificant, along with the other demographic variables.[33] Thus while education was once independently associated with greater support for the Charter, this is no longer the case.[34] Demographic effects on Charter support are clearly overshadowed by the influence of values.

These results point to an account of why support for the *Charter of Rights and Freedoms* has remained firm in the face of significant value change over the last dozen years or so. It is due to the fact that people's views of the Charter primarily depend upon the value they place on equality. This was the case in 1987 and it is even more so today. By contrast, opinions about tradition and authority have essentially no impact on evaluations of the Charter. This, in effect, largely insulates Charter support from any impact due to the higher regard Canadians are now placing on these values. The regressions also reveal that the value of civil liberties has become more or less irrelevant in Canadians' overall assessment of the Charter.

CONCLUSION

The purpose of our investigation was twofold: to examine the evolution of Canadian values over the past dozen years in order to assess the proposition that there has been a marked shift to the right; and to use this analysis to understand why support for the Charter remains as high today as it was in 1987, with an eye to assessing how that support is likely to evolve in the future.

The initial overview of value change suggested there are divergent trends at work. In particular, there has been a significant rise in the value placed upon the principles of tradition and authority and growing opposition to the general concept of equal rights. These trends have not been accompanied by any mounting hostility toward the equality rights of specific outgroups, however. In fact, these groups, on the whole, enjoy greater public support today than in 1987. Meanwhile, the support Canadians show for civil liberties has remained essentially constant.

Our analysis of birth cohorts helps identify the sources of value change across these different domains. The results indicate that the strong and growing support for equality rights, indexed by attitudes toward various outgroups, will likely persist well into the future, as it is largely driven by cohort effects. The shift to the right, evident in the growing support for tradition and authority, is in contrast, evidently not due to cohort effects. While it is difficult to distinguish between age and period effects in interpreting such change, it seems that the rightward shift is, in large part, a period effect. Its future evolution, therefore, remains uncertain.

The implications of these conclusions for the theoretical proposition about the inexorable rise of postmaterialism, and the related notion that division over the Charter's merits is generationally structured, are mixed. Higher levels of support for the equality rights of specific groups within rising cohorts and intra-cohort stability over time, are consistent with the postmaterialist thesis, but the significant shift to the right evident in other trends is not. Characterizing differing views of the Charter as a debate between young postmaterialists and older materialists contains a grain of truth but is obviously an oversimplification. So too is any suggestion that public attitudes on the whole run counter to Charter values.

Regression analysis of the value basis of Charter support sheds light on the relative importance of liberty, equality, and authority for Canadian attitudes toward the Charter. It turns out that tradition and authority have virtually no direct impact on Charter assessments. Similarly, the weak effect of civil liberties in 1987 has now largely evaporated. At this juncture, it is clearly attitudes toward equality rights that are the major influence upon assessments that Canadians make about the Charter.

Thinking through the net effect of value change on support for the Charter with the help of both cohort and regression analysis, we come in the end to a fairly clear understanding of why the Charter remains popular with Canadians. The recent rightward period effect has had little direct influence on Charter assessments. Hence, irrespective of whether it persists or not, evaluations of the Charter are unlikely to be adversely affected. Moreover, the effect of population turnover on support on equality rights has already begun to enhance public support for the Charter, and it is likely to continue to do so. As generational replacement occurs, support for the Charter will likely persist or even grow. Judging by the underlying contours of Canadian value change, widespread esteem for the Charter in future years seems assured.[35]

NOTES

1.   Joseph F. Fletcher and Paul Howe, "Canadian Attitudes toward the Charter and the Courts in Comparative Perspective," *Choices* 6, 3 (2000):4-29.

2.   Fletcher and Howe, "Canadian Attitudes toward the Charter and the Courts in Comparative Perspective"; and Joseph F. Fletcher and Paul Howe, "Supreme

Court Cases and Court Support: The State of Canadian Public Opinion," *Choices* 6, 3 (2000):30-56.

3. Caution is in order when identifying trends over time on the basis of only two observation points. However, when aggregate change is pulled apart in ways that shed light on the underlying motors of change, as in the analysis below, we can extrapolate from the observed data with greater confidence. On methods and potential pitfalls of longitudinal analysis, see Glenn Firebaugh, *Analyzing Repeated Surveys* (Thousand Oaks, CA: Sage, 1997).

4. Neil Nevitte, *Decline of Deference* (Peterborough: Broadview Press, 1996). See also Neil Nevitte, Herman Bakvis and Roger Gibbins, "Ideological Contours of 'New Politics' in Canada," *Canadian Journal of Political Science* 22, 3 (1989):473-503; and Herman Bakvis and Neil Nevitte, "In Pursuit of Postbourgeois Man: Postmaterialism and Intergenerational Change in Canada," *Comparative Political Studies* 20, 3 (1987):357-89.

5. See essays on this theme in Alan C. Cairns, edited by Douglas E. Williams, *Disruptions* (Toronto: McClelland & Stewart, 1991).

6. See the critique of Cairns' Charter-oriented account by Ian Brodie and Neil Nevitte and Cairns' response in *Canadian Journal of Political Science* 26, 2 (1993):235-72.

7. It has been suggested that the Reform Party represents a right-wing manifestation of postmaterialist values. See Richard Sigurdson, "Preston Manning and the Politics of Postmodernism in Canada," *Canadian Journal of Political Science* 27, 2 (1994):249-76; and on the broader question of the relationship between left-right and materialism-postmaterialism, Nevitte, Bakvis and Gibbins, "Ideological Contours of 'New Politics' in Canada," and James Savage, "Postmaterialism of the Left and Right," *Comparative Political Studies* 17, 4 (1985):431-51. However, presumably right-wing postmaterialism would entail particular emphasis on certain elements of the postmaterialist creed, such as individual freedom and responsibility, rather than strong sympathy toward outgroups.

8. F.L. Morton and Rainer Knopff, *The Charter Revolution and the Court Party* (Peterborough: Broadview Press, 2000).

9. This, at least, seemed to be the case for members of the Reform Party (see Peter McCormick, "New Beginning or Dead End," in *Party Politics in Canada*, 6th ed., ed. Hugh G. Thorburn (Toronto: Prentice Hall, 1991), p. 347). Matters may have changed with the recent surge in membership in response to the Alliance leadership race. It also seems to be the case that there is, at this point, no particular age skew to Reform voters. See the regression models in Neil Nevitte, André Blais, Elisabeth Gidengil and Richard Nadeau, *Unsteady State: The 1997 Canadian Federal Election* (Toronto: Oxford University Press, 2000), pp. 148-49. This does not, however, preclude the possibility that older supporters of the Alliance have largely been drawn to the party by its position on value-based issues.

10. Respondents are asked to choose one of four items as "most important in the long run." These are: (i) maintaining order in the nation, (ii) giving the people

more say in important government decisions, (iii) fighting rising prices, and (iv) protecting freedom of speech. They are then asked to pick the second most important. Respondents choosing (i) and (iii) are classified as materialists, those choosing (ii) and (iv) are classified as postmaterialists, while those who choose one of each are placed in a "mixed" grouping.

11. Paul M. Sniderman, Joseph F. Fletcher, Peter H. Russell and Philip E. Tetlock, *The Clash of Rights: Liberty, Equality and Legitimacy in Pluralist Democracy* (New Haven: Yale University Press, 1996).

12. The 1999 survey was conducted for the Montreal-based Institute for Research on Public Policy. The questionnaire was developed by Paul Howe and Joseph Fletcher. The fieldwork was carried out by Opinion Search, an Ottawa-based polling firm and took place from 1 March to 20 March 1999. Potential respondents were called up to ten times to try to secure an interview. The response rate of 30 percent, while low by the standards of an academic survey, is not uncommon for a commercial survey, as response rates have been declining in the past few years throughout the polling industry. It is, however, much lower than the 63.5 percent response rate achieved on the 1987 Charter Project.

   In an effort to ensure that the longitudinal comparisons we draw below are sound, various measures were undertaken. First, we compared respondents in the 1987 study who had been easy to reach with those more difficult to reach — and found no significant differences in their opinions. Thus, we can say with certainty that if the response rate in 1987 had been comparable to that on the current survey, there would have been no difference in the results. We can also say (albeit with less confidence) that had the response rate on the current survey been higher, the results would not have differed in any significant way.

   Second, both datasets were examined to ensure that the sample accurately reflected the Canadian population in terms of basic demographic traits, such as age, sex, province of residence, and education. One variable where the 1999 data were askew was education: the sample contained a disproportionate number of Canadians with high levels of formal education (this is commonly the case for survey samples with low response rates). To compensate, weights were applied to the data to bring the sample in line with population parameters (i.e., the highly educated sub-sample was given reduced weight, the less educated sub-sample greater weight). Weights (of lesser significance) were also applied for province of residence, sex, and household size. All data reported in the tables are weighted (all sample sizes, however, are unweighted). For further details on these weighting procedures, please contact the authors.

13. Long lists of the variables found to be significantly correlated with postmaterialism are in Ronald Inglehart, *Modernization and Postmodernization* (Princeton: Princeton University Press, 1997), Table 9.1, pp. 268-69; and Ronald Inglehart and Paul R. Abramson, "Measuring Postmaterialism," *American Political Science Review* 93, 3 (1999), 670, Table 3. Interestingly, views on legal rights and protections are not among the variables mentioned – even though "protecting freedom of speech" is one of the two standard items used to classify people as postmaterialists. Our view is that support for civil liberties clearly does fit with the other items in the postmaterialist syndrome, such as suspicion of authority and respect for individuality.

14. Are these patterns unique to Canada? The best source of comparative data is the World Values Survey. The 1981 and 1990 waves revealed decreasing levels of support for authority in most countries where the surveys were administered and provided much grist for the postmaterialist mill. Analyses of the most recent wave in 1995–97 have only just started to appear. These suggest that the changes in Canada may be more dramatic than elsewhere but are not wholly aberrant. Whereas postmaterialist theory would predict continued decline in support for authority over time, several of the established democracies saw either an increase in support (Spain) or essentially no change (Finland, Sweden, US, Norway) over the 1990 to 1996 period. Three others (the former West Germany, Switzerland, and Lithuania) did see significant decreases. See Ronald Inglehart, "Postmodernization Erodes Respect for Authority, but Increases Support for Democracy," in *Critical Citizens,* ed. Pippa Norris (Oxford: Oxford University Press, 1999), Table 12.1, p. 248.

15. We do not attempt to resolve this tension here, focusing instead on the implications of these divergent trends for Charter support. But a few words might be said on the matter. First, our data would seem to suggest that the rise in support for tradition and authority is driven by variables other than those captured in our civil rights and equality rights items. Second, the seeming contradiction on the equality rights items may be partly an artifact of question construction. If we assume that equality rights are better protected today than in 1987, then there is no necessary inconsistency between a growing sense that "we have gone too far in pushing equal rights" and constant, or even increasing, absolute levels of support for the equality rights of different outgroups.

     For a more detailed analysis of the place of equality rights in the political discourse of the 1990s, see Hamish Telford's chapter in this volume.

16. Our purpose in forming these indices is simply to obtain a general impression of the Canadian public's value preferences at two points in time using a handful of available survey items. As such, we rely here on the face validity of the questions and do not offer a rigorous assessment of their reliability and validity. Nevertheless, in work toward a subsequent paper we have fit a latent variable structural equation model incorporating these indicators, which essentially supports the appropriateness of what we do here at a more rudimentary level.

17. Excluded from the equality rights index is the item that asked whether we have "gone too far in pushing equal rights." We have seen that opinion on this item moved in a different direction over the 1987 to 1999 period than did opinion on the equality rights of specific groups, and have reason to believe this may be an artifact of the question wording (see note 15).

18. The difference between the two groups is statistically significant ($p < 0.05$). This is based on a comparison of mean values for the two groups for the full civil rights index.

19. A word of caution about our measuring instruments. The questions from our 1987 baseline survey were designed in the first instance to understand how attitudes toward rights are affected by invoking specific scenarios, on the supposition that context matters. Thus two of the items in our civil rights index ask about specific scenarios, one about "a drunk driver," the other "a young man ... walk-

ing near a house where they know drugs are being sold." The latter question shows the strongest relationship with age. Thus, it may be attitudes toward certain social practices that are partly driving our results, and further verification using different questions would be appropriate.

20. For a description of these methods, see Firebaugh, *Analyzing Repeated Surveys*, pp. 20-35.

21. See, for example, the age breakdown on postmaterialism for the 1990 World Values Survey reported in Ronald Inglehart, Miguel Basañez and Alejandro Moreno, *Human Values and Beliefs: A Cross-Cultural Sourcebook* (Ann Arbor: University of Michigan Press, 1998), p. 466.

22. See data in Inglehart, Basañez and Moreno, *Human Values and Beliefs: A Cross-Cultural Sourcebook*, p. 466. For further discussion of age differences in the Canadian case, see Inglehart and Abramson, "Measuring Postmaterialism," p. 673.

23. For further discussion, see Fletcher and Howe, "Canadian Attitudes toward the Charter and the Courts in Comparative Perspective," p. 41.

24. Our 1999 survey preceded the Supreme Court ruling in the *Marshall* Decision on native fishing rights in New Brunswick, which may have negatively affected attitudes in that region.

25. For an earlier analysis finding a positive relationship between postmaterialist values and attitudes toward native peoples, see Monika J. Wohlfeld and Neil Nevitte, "Postindustrial Value Change and Support for Native Issues," *Canadian Ethnic Studies* 22, 3 (1990):56-68.

26. For more on evolving attitudes toward Aboriginal rights in BC and Quebec, respectively, see Gordon Gibson's and Daniel Salée's chapters in this volume.

27. More specifically, the model of attitude formation we have in mind is as follows: attitudes toward each individual item are conditioned by a general disposition toward the equality rights of outgroups, but also by a host of specific factors unique to each item. General dispositions do follow the cohort pattern seen for the index as a whole: more favourable in younger than older cohorts and relatively stable over time. The other factors, on the other hand, may not. They may, for example, engender less sympathetic attitudes toward particular outgroups in younger cohorts and may be subject to fluctuation over time. For any given item, these unique factors may swamp the effect of general dispositions, negating the cohort effect associated with the latter. When, however, attitudes on a number of items are aggregated, these unique influences tend to average out and the general disposition common to the items comes to the fore.

   Factor analysis could be used to test these propositions more formally. The steps involved would be the identification of a common factor across the items, the calculation of factor scores for each respondent, and an assessment of cohort stability over time on those scores. A simple summation of the equality items is, however, a rough approximation of this method.

28. Paul R. Abramson and Ronald Inglehart, *Value Change in Global Perspective* (Ann Arbor: University of Michigan Press, 1995), pp. 25-39.

29. See Nevitte, *Decline of Deference*; Inglehart, *Modernization and Postmodernization*, pp. 293-323; and Inglehart, "Postmodernization Erodes Respect for Authority, but Increases Support for Democracy."

30. This corroborates our earlier finding that views on Supreme Court cases involving important civil liberties showed little correlation with opinions on the Supreme Court or the Charter. See Fletcher and Howe, "Supreme Court Cases and Court Support: The State of Canadian Public Opinion," pp. 48-51.

31. The absence of influence is perhaps explained by the interrelationships between the independent variables. Additional analysis, not shown here, reveals that tradition and authority had a significant negative impact upon both the equality and liberty variables in 1987 and upon the latter in 1999. Part of what is likely happening is that sympathetic views toward tradition and authority generate opposition to civil liberties and equality rights, which in turn are related to Charter assessments (equality rights especially). But when all the variables are analyzed conjointly, the influence of attitudes toward tradition and authority fails to register as it is picked up instead by the civil liberties and equality rights variables.

32. The negative coefficient for gender reflects the fact that women were more likely in 1987 to have no opinion on the Charter (coded as 0.5) rather than a negative opinion of the Charter.

33. Language cannot be successfully untangled from region in our samples. To avoid problems of collinearity, it is therefore omitted from the equations presented here. Entering language in lieu of region does not produce significantly different results. For greater detail on the regional breakdown for Charter support, and for other related variables, see Fletcher and Howe, "Canadian Attitudes toward the Charter and the Courts in Comparative Perspective" and "Supreme Court Cases and Court Support: The State of Canadian Public Opinion."

34. There remains, of course, a simple correlation between education and Charter support, but controlling for other variables, principally equality, eliminates its influence.

35. Our analysis points the way toward further research. First of all, it is clear that the values we examine here are not the whole story. The value and demographic variables in the regression equations explain only a small percentage of the variance in both survey years. This points to the need in future analyses to consider different categories of variables, such as the institutional or regime preferences of Canadians and perhaps their basic social and political loyalties. Further analysis should also probe more into the interplay among the predictors. The hints at success here with only limited effort suggest some potential for such an approach. Finally, greater attention to the measurement of variables may well strengthen the analysis. The informal measurement approach employed here serves to highlight some key relationships, but further refinement may clear up some ambiguities in the analysis.

APPENDIX 1
Wording Variations in Measurement

Some questions were subject to wording variations. In order to maintain reasonable sample sizes, all respondents are used in some parts of our analysis; in other instances, we exclude some respondents. See text for details.

The questions with wording variations are as follows:

C2. I would like you to consider now an instance where the police see a young man they do not recognize walking very near a house where they know drugs are being sold. They search him and find he is carrying drugs. Do you think this search is a reasonable search, or does it violate the young man's rights? In 1987, there were four versions of the question: one used the phrase "young West Indian" in place of "young man"; another added the phrase "Many police feel very strongly that they have to be able to search people like this, in order to prevent crime from going out of control" before the question itself ("Do you think this search..."); and another incorporated both changes. For the basic version, 57 percent said it was a reasonable search. For the other three versions, it was 58 percent, 53 percent, and 54 percent respectively; the average for these three versions was 55 percent. Given that the differences are small, we have used all versions of the 1987 question in our analysis.

C3. Consider this case: The police asked an obviously drunk driver to take a breathalyzer test without telling him that he had a right to consult a lawyer. Should a judge allow the breathalyzer evidence to be used in court or should he exclude it, even if the driver may go free as a result? In 1987, for a random half-sample the question read "...without telling him that he *might* consult a lawyer." There was no statistically significant difference between the two versions.

E5. Should native peoples be treated just like any other Canadian, with no special rights, or should the unique rights of Canada's native peoples be preserved? In both 1987 and 1999, for a random half-sample, the question was preceded by "Canada's constitution recognizes the unique rights of Canada's native peoples." There was no statistically significant difference between the two versions in either year.

APPENDIX 2
Explanation of Indices

Civil Liberties, Item Coding

C1. Free speech ought to be allowed for all political groups even if some of the things that these
groups believe in are highly insulting and threatening to society.

Basically disagree – 1
Basically agree – 3
Don't know – 2

C2. I would like you to consider now an instance
where the police see a young man they do not
recognize walking very near a house where they
know drugs are being sold. They search him and
find he is carrying drugs. Do you think this search
is a reasonable search, or does it violate the young
man's rights?

Reasonable search – 1
Violated his rights – 3
Don't know – 2

C3. Consider this case: The police asked an obviously drunk driver to take a breathalyzer test
without telling him that he had a right to consult
a lawyer. Should a judge allow the breathalyzer
evidence to be used in court or should he exclude
it, even if the driver may go free as a result?

Allow evidence – 1
Exclude evidence – 3
Don't know – 2

Civil liberties index created by summing scores for all three items, recoded as
follows:

Low: 3-4
Medium: 5-6
High: 7-9

Equality Rights, Item Coding

E2. How important is it to guarantee equality
between men and women in all aspects of life?

Not important – 1
Somewhat important – 2
Very important – 3
Don't know – 2

E3. How important is preserving French and English as the two official languages of Canada?

Not important – 1
Somewhat important – 2
Very important – 3
Don't know – 2

E4. How important is it to make a special effort to protect ethnic and racial minorities?

Not important – 1
Somewhat important – 2
Very important – 3
Don't know – 2

E5. Should native peoples be treated just like any other Canadian, with no special rights, or should the unique rights of Canada's native peoples be preserved?

Like any other Canadian – 1
Unique rights preserved – 3
Don't know – 2

E6. Do you approve or disapprove of allowing homosexuals to teach in school in (respondent's province)?

Disapprove – 1
Approve – 3
Don't know – 2

Equality rights index created by summing scores for all five items, recoded as follows:

Low: 5-10
Medium: 11-12
High: 13-15

Tradition and Authority, Item Coding

T1. How important is preserving traditional ideas of right and wrong?

Not important – 1
Somewhat important – 2
Very important – 3
Don't know – 2

T2. How important is it to strengthen respect and obedience for authority?

Not important – 1
Somewhat important – 2
Very important – 3
Don't know – 2

Tradition and authority index created by summing scores for both items, recoded as follows:

Low: 2-4
Medium: 5
High: 6

12

Mosaic and Melting-Pot: The Dialectic of Pluralism and Constitutional Faith in Canada and the United States

Samuel V. LaSelva

Parmi les différences qui marquent le Canada et les États-Unis, le contraste entre la mosaïque culturelle canadienne et le melting-pot américain est le plus saisissant, le plus familier et le plus intrigant. En 1971, le Premier ministre Trudeau soutenait que le modèle de la mosaïque faisait du Canada un endroit unique. Le Canada, expliquait-il, est une société multiculturelle; elle offre à tous les Canadiens l'opportunité de satisfaire ses propres inclinations culturelles et de partager celles des autres origines. Dans des écrits précédents, Trudeau décrivait le Canada comme «meilleur que le melting-pot américain» et appartenant «au monde de demain». Le but de cet essai est d'explorer les origines, les fonctions et l'importance des concepts de mosaïque culturelle et de melting-pot, ainsi que les principales critiques les concernant. L'auteur conclut que lorsqu'il est bien interprété, le contraste entre la mosaïque culturelle et le melting-pot en dit long à propos des politiques culturelles du Canada et des États-Unis, et éclaire leurs compréhensions divergentes du fédéralisme, du multiculturalisme et du projet constitutionnel.

Statements that contrast the political cultures of Canada and the United States are not difficult to find, and among such statements the contrast between the mosaic and the melting-pot is the most striking, the most familiar, and the most intriguing. One of the earliest dramatic portrayals of the melting-pot is Israel Zangwill's play, first performed in Washington, and lionized by President Theodore Roosevelt.[1] But the melting-pot idea is much older than Zangwill's play; it is almost as old as the Republic itself. Writing in 1782, de Crevecoeur described America as a country where immigrants leave behind their ancient prejudices and are "melted into a new race of men." "The American," he said, "is a new man, who acts upon new principles."[2] As for the mosaic, it is less ancient than the melting-pot and can be traced only to the 1920s; by 1965, however, John Porter could call it Canada's most cherished value.[3] In 1971, Prime Minister Trudeau insisted that "the mosaic pattern ... makes Canada a very special place." Canada, he explained, "is a multicultural society; it offers to every Canadian the opportunity to fulfil his own cultural instincts and to share those from other sources."[4] In earlier writings, Trudeau described Canada as "better than the American melting-pot" and as belonging to "tomorrow's world."[5]

The mosaic and melting-pot also have their critics. One of the best-known criticisms of the mosaic pattern is that, far from treating all ethnic groups as equal, some groups are denied basic opportunities and accorded second-class status.[6] Another is that the mosaic rests on a sinister moral relativism incapable of distinguishing right from wrong and productive of mosaic madness.[7] And still another, that the mosaic legitimates ethnic solitudes, diminishes human dignity, and severs the ties of brotherhood that should unite Canadians.[8] All of these criticisms accept that Canada is a mosaic, but regard the mosaic pattern as dysfunctional or even pernicious. As for the melting-pot, the core criticism is that the American people are not *one*. Rather, "they are a mosaic of peoples, of different bloods and different origins, engaged in rather different economic fields, and varied in background and outlook."[9] What adds depth to this criticism is the charge that the melting-pot idea not only lacks moral neutrality, but also privileges a particular way of life, one suited to the ruling classes and inhospitable to all the rest.[10] But *if* the United States is also a mosaic of peoples, what differentiates it from Canada? And why should it not suffer too from mosaic madness and kindred maladies?

These questions do not have simple answers. Moreover, it is possible to acknowledge that Canada and the United States are ethnically diverse, while recognizing other crucial differences between them, differences that reintroduce the very distinction between the mosaic and the melting-pot. One such difference is that Canada is both a multinational and a territorial federation, whereas the United States has never been a federation of peoples. As Carl Fredrich noted, "Canadians ... had [and continue to have] a very special problem ... which found no parallel in the American experience: that was how to arrange a federal system that would satisfy their French-speaking citizens."[11] Another difference is that American pluralism rests on a distinctive and recognizable constitutional faith, which defines what it means to be an American in normal times, and serves as a touchstone even in times of great crisis. "There is an American spirit," wrote Frederick Jackson Turner. "There are American ideals. We are members of one body, though it is a varied body."[12] If Canadian federalism differs from the American variant, and if Americans have a constitutional faith that distinguishes them from Canadians, then Canada and the United States are unlikely to be a mosaic of peoples in quite the same way. Much the same idea can be expressed by saying that Canadian pluralism differs from the American variety. For although both Canada and the United States can be described as federal and multicultural societies, they are not federal and multicultural in the same way and the differences between them define two radically different brands of pluralism. The contrast between the mosaic and the melting-pot turns out to be meaningful after all. It reveals striking dissimilarities in constitutional faith, draws attention to the distinctive challenges faced by Canadians and Americans, and highlights the need to take seriously differences in political culture.

THE DIALECTIC OF NATIONHOOD: CANADA AND THE UNITED STATES

Multiculturalism can be part of either a mosaic or of a melting-pot. To understand how this can be so, it is necessary to begin with the nation, and to distinguish the different kinds of nations. Once Canada and the United States are distinguished as nations, the differences between the mosaic and the melting-pot become clearer, as do their divergent implications for multiculturalism. The United States is the first new nation; it was born of a revolution that proclaimed allegiance to the inalienable rights of man. Canada is different, as Christopher Dunkin emphasized in the Confederation Debates. The US Constitution, Dunkin said, was adopted after a "successful war of independence," in which the men who framed it had gone "shoulder to shoulder" through a great trial, and "their communities ... had been united as one man." Moreover, Americans had tried "the system of mere confederation" and were ready "to build up a great nationality that should endure in the future." By contrast, Canadian Confederation was preceded, not by a common struggle, but by a struggle that "pitted our public men one against another, and ... even our faiths and races against each other." Dunkin believed that there was no common nationality to which Confederation could appeal, or that would serve to hold Canadians together. "Have we any class of people," he asked rhetorically, "whose feelings are going to be directed to ... Ottawa, the centre of the new nationality that is to be created?"[13] If the United States was the first new nation, Canada would have to be either a very different nation or no nation at all.

In the debates of 1865, Dunkin not only predicted that Canadian Confederation lacked a destiny, but he also insisted that those who supported it were devoid of greatness. Once again, the contrast was with the United States. "The framers of the American constitution," he said, "were great men ... [and] their work was a great work." Part of their greatness was their discovery of federalism and their creation of "a true federation." But the Fathers of Confederation, Dunkin insisted, were unable to grasp that "a Legislative union is one thing; a Federal union is another." Their creation was neither a legislative union, nor a federal union, but merely combined the disadvantages of both. American Senators were picked by their states, had real powers, and functioned as a federal check. The Canadian Upper House, Dunkin said, could perform no such function because its members were appointed by the general government, rather than the provinces. As for lieutenant-governors, Dunkin believed that their interference in local affairs would merely fuel conflicts of authority between the provinces and the central government. Confederation also allocated the largest powers to the general government; yet such a distribution of powers would revive "old jealousies and hostility," and awaken the "war of races." Confederation, Dunkin said, contained much to quarrel over; with quarrels come collisions, and soon Confederation "is at an end."[14]

Dunkin had few solutions for the difficulties that troubled him, other than his belief that "what is wanted ... is an effective federalization of the [British] Empire as a whole, not a subordinate federation here and there."[15] But even if such a solution had been available to Canadians in 1867, which it was not, there was still the question of federalism. What Dunkin failed to grasp was that federal governments are not all of a kind; they can and do differ since they respond to different kinds of societies. Moreover, Canadians did not have the same reasons for adopting federalism in 1867 as Americans had in 1787, nor did they have the same aspirations for it. Dunkin understood that Canada and the United States were different, but he did not fully grasp either the extent of the differences or their deeper significance. He chose to emphasize that Americans, having fought a war of independence, were ready to build a new nationality; whereas Canadian Confederation, coming after a war of races, "was very different indeed." The contrast contains a grain of truth; but it was a strange truth to emphasize in 1865, when the American Civil War raged. The Civil War was no less tragic than the war of races; both wars were deeply implicated in distinctive conceptions of nationhood, and, when taken together, they revealed truths about the United States and Canada that Dunkin overlooked.

Unlike Dunkin, Macdonald had far more to say about the American Civil War and its significance for Canada. In the Confederation debates, he described the US Constitution as "one of the most skilful works which human intelligence ever created"; but he instantly added that it was "not the work of Omniscience." The US Constitution "commenced ... at the wrong end" because it declared that "each state was a sovereignty in itself."[16] By contrast, the Canadian constitution, said Macdonald, would confer all the great powers of legislation, as well as the residuary power, on the central government, thereby avoiding the fatal defect in the US Constitution that had resulted in the Civil War. For Macdonald, the American Civil War demonstrated that the US Constitution was not to be emulated so much as improved upon, and the improvement consisted of an attempt to reduce the provinces to little more than administrative units of the central government. Macdonald soon realized, however, that the provinces would not accept the subordinate role that he wished to assign to them. "It is difficult to make the local Legislatures understand," he complained in the years after Confederation, "that their powers are not so great as they were before the Union."[17] Nor was Macdonald any more successful in explaining the causes of the American Civil War. The issue that most divided Americans in the years before the Civil War was not state sovereignty but the meaning of liberty.

More than anyone else, Abraham Lincoln had the deepest insights into the Civil War and its meaning for the American constitutional faith. He is known to history as the great emancipator; yet, as president, he emphasized that "if [he] could save the Union without freeing any slave [he] would do it." As long as he could remember, he regarded slavery as a horrendous moral evil; yet he was painfully aware that northerners and southerners "read the same Bible," "pray[ed] to the same God," and worshipped the same Constitution. He was no enemy of federalism or states' rights. He acknowledged that the framers had made crucial concessions to slavery, but their concessions, he insisted, did not justify the expansion of slavery into new states. At the beginning of the Civil War, he said that there was only one "substantial issue." "One section of our country believes slavery is right, and ought to be extended, while the other believes that it is wrong and ought not to be extended." But as the Civil War deepened, so did his understanding of it. Eventually, he realized that the most divisive issue was the meaning of liberty. "The American people," he said, "are much in want of ... a good definition of liberty.... All declare for liberty," but they do not "mean the same thing" by it.[18]

Liberty is the core of the American constitutional faith, yet Americans have never agreed about its meaning or about how it is best realized. In 1787, the American constitutional experiment was mired in a debate about liberty, and the attempt to create a "More Perfect Union" almost failed. The key problem for post-revolutionary America had been classically defined by Montesquieu; he believed that large countries (empires) turn into despotisms and destroy republican liberty.[19] Had Americans thrown off the tyranny of George III merely to replace it by one of their own creation? So long as this question remained unanswered, most Americans could see no alternative to the ineffectual Articles of Confederation other than Alexander Hamilton's unacceptable proposals for consolidated government. Eventually, James Madison provided a solution. Smallness, he said, was fatal to republicanism because it magnified the power of faction; but consolidated government was also unacceptable because it destroyed liberty. Small republics and great empires were both extreme cases and each was equally destructive of liberty. To secure liberty, it was necessary to create a compound republic, whose constitution was both national and (con)federal in character. By compounding the diverse economic interests of a large territory with a federal system of semi-sovereign political units, Americans could obtain, so Madison believed, the commercial and military advantages of energetic union, while guaranteeing republican liberty and the autonomy of the states.[20]

The Constitution which Madison helped to create did not solve all the problems of freedom. Not only did its framers leave Negro slavery intact, but their attempt to bury the slavery problem within the intricacies of federalism proved to be philosophically untenable. For slavery found a strong ally in classical republican theory and eventually burst the boundaries of Madisonian federalism. Classical republicanism equates freedom with independence; it regards tyranny and poverty as the great enemies of freedom; it holds that those who lack independence are unfit for freedom. In America, such ideas made it easier to justify the enslavement of Negroes; they also made it possible to equate the emancipation of the Negro with the destruction of freedom.[21] The cry of many southerners, in the years before the Civil War, was that they were the true defenders of freedom and the republican heritage. Lincoln replied that the permanent acceptance of slavery was incompatible with the ideal of human equality enshrined in the Declaration of Independence. He also insisted that the slavery argument, once admitted, could not be confined to Negroes but would engulf the American people and destroy the American experiment.[22] Lincoln's prayer was for "a new birth of freedom," so that a nation "conceived in liberty" would not perish from the earth.[23] The United States did not perish; slavery was abolished; and the faith in freedom continued to define the essence of the American constitutional faith.

In the Confederation debates, Dunkin and Macdonald demonstrated little understanding of the American constitutional faith. Nor were the lessons they drew for Canada from the American Civil War any more satisfactory. As Macdonald revealed, his preference was for a legislative union because such a union was "the best, the cheapest, the most vigorous, and the strongest system of government we could adopt."[24] This preference was bolstered by his understanding of the American Civil War and accorded with his Tory conception of the nation as an entity that transcends all lesser divisions and loyalties. Nevertheless, a legislative union, he was compelled to admit, was "impracticable," not only because Lower Canada refused to accept it, but also because the Maritimes had developed strong local identities that worked against it. Even so, Canada would still differ from the United States, he insisted, because only minimal concessions had been made to federalism. The emergence of a strong provincial rights movement after 1867, with its articulation of the compact theory of Confederation, shattered Macdonald's Tory vision of Canada; it also made federalism the defining feature of the Canadian polity. If Canada was to differ from the United States, the difference could not lie in the Macdonaldian constitution or its failed attempt to banish "states' rights" from the constitutional landscape.[25]

The failure of the Macdonaldian constitution did not, however, confirm Dunkin's darkest predictions for Canada. After 1867, conflicts of jurisdictions occurred, clashes between French and English continued, yet Confederation endured. What Dunkin had perceptively but only vaguely glimpsed was the importance of constitutional faith for nationhood. This insight led him to contrast the United States and Canada with respect to their founding moments, and to forecast that a future built on a war of independence would differ from one premised on a war of races. But Dunkin's forecast rested on half truths. In 1787, the constitutional faith of Americans did enable them to build a great nation. The United States, as Lincoln said even during the American Civil War, was a nation "conceived in liberty." Canada was different indeed. But the difference did not lie in the impossibility of a Canadian nation or in an eternally recurring war of races. As George Cartier emphasized, such views failed to grasp that Confederation envisioned a new kind of nation, one that differed from the American model and moved beyond the war of races by rejecting ethnic unification. Madison defended American federalism on the grounds that it protected republican liberty. Cartier regarded Canadian federalism as a device that enabled different races and ethnicities to live together under a common political nationality. In the debates of 1865, no one knew for certain if Canada would flourish or even survive. For it to do so, however, it would have to develop a constitutional faith unlike anything America had produced.

MULTICULTURALISM: INDIVIDUAL FREEDOM AND MUTUAL RECOGNITION

If 1787 is compared with 1867, and the Civil War with the war of races, differences between the United States and Canada become evident. But can the differences be described in terms of a mosaic and a melting-pot? And what happens if, instead of looking backward, one looks forward to the phenomenon of multiculturalism that has become a prominent feature of both Canada and the United States? One response would be to say that both Canada and the United States are now a mosaic of peoples, and the differences between the two countries are increasingly negligible. But such a response is unsatisfactory. Canada is (among other things) a multinational polity, whereas the United States is a territorial federation. This difference is foundational and affects almost every other aspect of these two countries. A multinational polity and a territorial federation are both pluralistic societies, but the character of their pluralism is different. Moreover, multiculturalism does not have the same significance in the United States as it has in Canada, nor does it create the same challenges. In the United States, the deepest questions raised by multiculturalism are questions about individual liberty. In Canada, they have to do with mutual recognition. The questions differ because Canada and the United States are different kinds of countries and rest on different constitutional faiths.

However, liberty and mutual recognition are often treated as secondary issues or even neglected altogether by critics of multiculturalism. For most critics, in both Canada and the United States, the key issue raised by multiculturalism has to do with relativism, and the negative consequences that flow from it. What the critics contend is that multiculturalism rests on a corrosive moral relativism that makes public dialogue impossible. "To the extent citizens begin to retribalize into ethnic or 'other-fixed identity groups,' " writes Jean Bethke Elshtain, "democracy falters. Any possibility for human dialogue ... vanishes as so much froth."[26] Elshtain is concerned about contemporary America. A Canadian parallel is Reginald Bibby's *Mosaic Madness*. Canada, writes Bibby, "is leading the world in pluralism and relativism ... [and] the news is not that good." Many Canadians, he suggests, have come to accept cultural relativism as a given and, for them, "truth has been replaced by personal viewpoint." Like Elshtain, Bibby's concern is that multicultural relativism "blinds [Canadians to] the merits of ideas and behaviour" and makes dialogue impossible. Moreover, Bibby acknowledges that his critique of Canadian multiculturalism owes a considerable debt to American authors, in particular to Robert Bellah's *Habits of the Heart* and Allan Bloom's *The Closing of the American Mind*. "Inadvertently, these Americans," he writes, "have provided critiques more appropriate to Canada than the United States."[27]

Two confusions plague Bibby's critique of Canadian multiculturalism: the conflation of relativism with pluralism; and the failure to distinguish adequately Canadian pluralism from the American variety. Although relativism and pluralism are frequently assimilated, the difference between them is plain enough. "'I prefer coffee, you prefer champagne. We have different tastes. There is no more to be said.' That is relativism." But, as Isaiah Berlin goes on to explain, pluralism is different; it holds that "there are many different ends that men may seek and still be fully rational, ... capable of understanding each other and sympathising and deriving light from each other." In Berlin's analysis, pluralism can apply to individuals or to societies or to civilizations; and it holds, contrary to Platonic monism, that there is no single scheme of values "true for all men, everywhere, at all times." Not only may values "clash within the breast of a single individual," and within a single society, but there is also a plurality of civilizations, each with its own pattern, and "not combinable in any final synthesis."[28] What Bibby does not take seriously enough is that there are different kinds of pluralism; that Canadian pluralism differs from American pluralism; and that the differences have significant implications for multiculturalism.

One way of clarifying those implications is by shifting the focus from relativism to fragmentation. Next to relativism, one of the deepest fears of American critics of multiculturalism is that public acceptance of it will make the United States more like Canada. In particular, their concern is that multiculturalism and other kinds of group rights will erode national unity and spawn separatist movements. In *The Disuniting of America*, Arthur Schlesinger contends that "self-styled 'multiculturalists' are very often ethnocentric separatists."[29] In *Ethnic Dilemmas*, Nathan Glazer warns of the dangers of group rights; he also contrasts Canada and the United States. Glazer acknowledges that both countries are multi-ethnic states, but that is where the similarity ends. Historically, the policy of the United States has been to regard group identities as temporary and to oppose the conferral of group rights. The American ideal, Glazer writes, has been to see these groups as "integrating into, eventually assimilating into, a common society." However, in Canada group membership is so central and permanent that it is unrealistic to envision "a common citizenship." Glazer takes a bleak view of the Canadian model; he urges Americans to shun cultural pluralism on the grounds that it would reduce their country to a confederation of unattached and antagonistic groups. If assimilation is rejected for cultural pluralism, he warns, "we have a sure recipe for conflict."[30]

Glazer equates pluralism with fragmentation. His defence of assimilation or what he calls the "American ideal" is based on the belief that "difference, alas, is always liable to become a source of conflict."[31] By eliminating difference, assimilation also eliminates conflict. But this argument becomes absurd if taken literally or judged by the standards of American constitutionalism. No one familiar with Madison's discussion of the extended republic in *Federalist* number 10 or his defence of checks and balances in number 51 can really suppose that the American system is designed to eliminate conflict. If anything, it seeks to institutionalize and structure conflict. Presumably, Glazer does not object to all conflicts and all differences. Since much of his discussion deals with ethnic differences, his warnings might be taken to apply only to them. But there are difficulties even here. Glazer lumps together the different demands made by different kinds of ethnic groups, and wrongly supposes that all of their demands lead to fragmentation. Most multicultural groups are not disguised separatists; on the contrary, they want recognition of their special characteristics so that they can participate more fully within the mainstream of society. As Will Kymlicka emphasizes, "the common rights of citizenship, originally defined by and for white, able-bodied Christian men, cannot accommodate the special needs of these groups. Instead, a fully integrative account of citizenship must take these differences into account."[32]

Not only does Glazer misunderstand multiculturalism, but his own (crude) defence of assimilation is difficult to reconcile with the American ideal. Glazer rightly emphasizes that the American model presupposes membership in a common society. What he fails to note, however, is that the ideal of liberty forms the core of American constitutional faith. If Americans value liberty, they cannot be outright or crude assimilationists, because the affirmation of liberty is not necessarily inconsistent with cultural pluralism. In *Multicultural Citizenship*, Will Kymlicka details many of the ways that cultural pluralism sustains individual liberty in a multi-ethnic state. Liberals committed to individual autonomy, he suggests, should endorse multicultural group rights for minorities, because individual choices are made within a cultural context. When immigrants are forcibly assimilated, they experience significant harms. They are denied the ability to form their own life plans or even to evaluate and revise the beliefs that make their lives meaningful. Moreover, forcible assimilation denies equality by privileging the dominant culture and by compelling members of the minority culture to adopt it.[33] Justice for minorities requires, Kymlicka contends, recognition of the cultural preconditions of freedom so that both individual autonomy and social equality can be vindicated. As a country whose constitutional faith enshrines individual freedom, the United States has little reason to glorify crude assimilationist practices or to neglect the multicultural preconditions of individual autonomy.

In Canada, a liberal theory of multiculturalism has less resonance, even though Canadian multiculturalism became law under a Liberal government and received its strongest endorsement from a prime minister imbued with liberal principles. When Pierre Trudeau introduced official multiculturalism in the House of Commons in 1971, he portrayed Canada as a country with "two official languages [and] no official culture," a country in which no ethnic group took "precedence over any other."[34] Official multiculturalism was described as "the most suitable means of assuring the cultural freedom of Canadians" on the ground that it would help to break down discriminatory attitudes and would help to guarantee fair play for all. Ethnic groups, Trudeau said, should be "encouraged to share their cultural expression and values with other Canadians and so contribute to a richer life for us all." Outside the House of Commons, Trudeau insisted that there was "no such thing as a model or ideal Canadian." For him, Canada was "a land of people with many differences ... but a single desire to live in harmony."[35] Such an image of Canada is edifying. But neither Trudeau's liberal multiculturalism, nor the larger constitutional vision that envelops it, had the results he desired. Canada has not become more harmonious, national unity is not more firmly established, and Canadian pluralism is not easily accommodated within the boundaries established by Trudeau's liberalism.

The problem with Trudeau's liberalism is not that it understands multiculturalism but misunderstands other things about Canada.[36] The problem goes deeper. If official multiculturalism is placed too firmly within a liberal framework, Canada becomes a more difficult country to understand because

certain kinds of questions are obscured or downgraded. "Multinational societies can break up, in large part because of a lack of (perceived) recognition of
one group by another." So wrote Charles Taylor after the failure of the Meech
Lake Accord. Taylor believed that such a process of breakup was occurring in
Canada; and subsequent events (the failed Charlottetown Accord, the near
successful sovereignty referendum, and the Supreme Court decision legiti-
mating secession) add weight to his prognosis. Taylor's larger objective was
to draw attention to "The Politics of Recognition" and to emphasize that "a
number of strands in contemporary politics turn on the need, sometimes the
demand, for recognition."[37] As he explained, the need for recognition is a
driving force behind nationalist movements, some forms of feminism, and the
politics of multiculturalism. Taylor's work contains the beginning of an understanding of multiculturalism that is less indebted to the liberal tradition
than Trudeau's, and takes fuller account of the distinctive features of Canadian pluralism. In Canada, a concern for individual choice helps to sustain a
commitment to multiculturalism; but a liberal theory of multiculturalism is
no substitute for a politics of mutual recognition, at least if the spectre of
breakup is to be avoided.

CONSTITUTIONAL FAITHS: MOSAIC AND MELTING-POT

Even as multicultural polities, Canada and the United States face different
destinies. The main challenge for the United States is to respond to
multiculturalism in a way that both affirms its constitutional faith in liberty
and grants appropriate recognition of cultural particularisms. This challenge
is more difficult to meet than might at first appear. Many American feminists
question the value of multiculturalism on the grounds that "most cultures have
as one of their principal aims the control of women by men."[38] For them, the
recognition of multicultural group rights is not part of the solution, since it
perpetuates patriarchy and limits the freedom of women. Canadian feminists
also raise questions about the patriarchal character of many multicultural
groups and sometimes point to the same concerns about equality and individual freedom as their American counterparts. But, in Canada, there is the
additional complicating factor of multinationality which divides women and
can also divide their country. In the United States, the questions raised by
feminists bring into play the American faith in freedom which constitutionalizes
key components of the melting-pot. In Canada, they become mired in the complexities of the mosaic and exacerbate doubts about the possibility of a
constitutional faith that can keep the mosaic from flying apart.

For Americans, the Declaration of Independence, the Constitution, and the
Gettysburg Address are landmarks of their constitutional faith. Each of these
documents celebrates human freedom, but not one of them deals specifically

with the freedom of women. That is one reason why American feminists — even liberal feminists — proceed cautiously when confronted by the rhetoric of liberty. One of their basic concerns is that the freedom of women will be sacrificed to the power of men. In *Is Multiculturalism Bad for Women?* Susan Moller Okin raises a concern of this kind. She notes that assimilation is "now often considered oppressive" and a common demand is to "devise new policies that are more responsive to persistent cultural differences." She knows also that some defenders of cultural group rights appeal to liberal principles and rest their case on liberal conceptions of autonomy. Nevertheless, she believes that "feminists ... should remain skeptical." Too often cultural minorities are treated as if they are all of a kind and just as often their biases against women are overlooked. And when attempts are made to correct these biases, "advocates of group rights pay little or no attention to the private realm," where the most subtle forms of gender exploitation occur. In such circumstances, "group rights are ... in many cases actually antifeminist. They substantially limit the capacities of women and girls of that culture to live with human dignity equal to that of men and boys, and to live as freely chosen lives as they can."[39]

But such concerns are less damaging to a liberal theory of minority rights than might at first appear. Part of Okin's essay consists of a critique of Will Kymlicka, whom she describes as the foremost contemporary defender of cultural group rights. "His arguments for multiculturalism," she complains, "fail to register what he actually acknowledges elsewhere: that the subordination of women is often informal and private, and that virtually no culture in the world today ... could pass his 'no sex discrimination' test if it were applied in the private sphere."[40] However, this criticism neglects a key part of his argument. As Kymlicka emphasizes in his reply to Okin, "liberals can accept external protections which promote justice between groups, but must reject internal restrictions which reduce freedom within groups." The existence of domestic oppression requires a constructive elaboration of the kind of internal restrictions opposed by liberal defenders of minority rights, rather than an abandonment of such rights. Moreover, multiculturalism and feminism have more in common than is often allowed. Both reject the traditional liberal conception of individual rights. Both oppose crude notions of equality as sameness. They are, Kymlicka insists, "allies engaged in related struggles for a more inclusive conception of justice."[41] Okin accepts these replies and modifies her critique accordingly. "What we need to strive for," she concludes, "is a form of multiculturalism that gives issues of gender and intragroup inequality their due ... [by treating] all persons as each other's moral equals."[42]

That a liberal feminist (Okin) and a liberal multiculturalist (Kymlicka) are able to arrive at common ground is edifying for those who endorse liberal values. But agreement among liberals will not necessarily satisfy the critics of liberalism or settle difficult questions about the American constitutional faith. Part of the critical response to Okin and Kymlicka has been that they either misunderstand the deeper meaning of cultural difference or dilute its significance by fitting it within a liberal framework. A criticism of this kind is developed, for example, by Bhirkhu Parekh in "A Varied Moral World." Parekh argues that both Kymlicka and Okin "fail to appreciate the full force of the challenge of multiculturalism." He writes: "Like Kymlicka she [Okin] takes liberalism as self-evidently true, asks how it can accommodate minority cultures, and more or less reduces multiculturalism to a discussion of group rights." When such a stance is adopted, the real challenge of multiculturalism is overlooked, namely, its rejection of liberal hegemony and self-righteousness. "From a multicultural perspective," Parekh suggests, "the liberal view of life is culturally specific and neither self-evidently true nor the only rational or true way to organize human life." What liberals too often neglect is that "no culture exhausts the full range of human possibilities." If this is so, then, according to Parekh, the way for liberals to respect the multicultural perspective is by acknowledging the "limitations of the great liberal values" and by accepting a framework in which "different cultures ... cooperatively explore their differences."[43]

As a critique of liberal feminism and liberal multiculturalism, Parekh's views have their limitations. What they do help to highlight, however, are complexities in the American constitutional faith. America is not just a melting-pot; it is a melting-pot built on a complex constitutional faith. No American has been more aware of this fact than was Justice Frankfurter. He believed that to become an American one had to shed old loyalties, take on the loyalties of an American citizen, and become attached to the principles of the Constitution.[44] Expanding on this idea, Robert Bellah describes the existence of an American civil religion that includes the Declaration of Independence and the Gettysburg Address. Of course the American civil religion, Bellah goes on to say, has also "suffered various deformations and demonic distortions."[45] Joe McCarthy's campaign against communist sympathizers is as much a part of the American civil religion as Lincoln's struggle to free the slaves. At its best, the American civil religion has exercised long-term pressure for a humane solution to the "Negro problem"; at its worst, it has demanded rigid conformity to a restrictive way of life. These complexities of the melting-pot are well understood by some American feminists. In their fight against sexist pornography, for example, they do not reject the Constitution. On the contrary, they argue for a generous interpretation of the 14th Amendment, the very provision that secured citizenship for the slaves.[46] America is a special kind of melting-pot, because American freedom can be used both to support the rights of minorities and to suppress them.

The Canadian constitutional faith is different, in part because Canadian pluralism is unlike the American variety. In fact, the dissimilarities are so great that the existence and even the possibility of a Canadian constitutional faith can be questioned. Those who put their faith in Canada's mosaic pattern must somehow respond to Gad Horowitz's sobering critique. "A functioning democracy," he suggests, "requires a well developed sense of national unity, a feeling on the part of ordinary people that they are part of that national com-munity." But in Canada, this feeling is absent because the strongest identifications are with regions and ethnic groups. What results from the mo-saic pattern, Horowitz goes on to say, is stagnation in politics and inequality of opportunity in economic and social life. Horowitz knows that some mosaic celebrators praise Canada for being a non-nationalistic nation, a nation that is not a nation, a land of many cultures. Their desire is to be left alone, and not to be pressed into any moulds. "When this way of talking is not fake," Horowitz responds, "it is literally nihilistic." The mosaic, he continues, "preserves noth-ing of value. It is literally nothing. It is the absence of a sense of identity, the absence of a sense of community."[47] For Horowitz, the mosaic pattern means only stagnation, inequality, ghettoization, Americanization, and disunity. If one of the functions of a constitutional faith is to promote national unity, then the mosaic pattern seems especially ill-suited to performing such a task.[48]

Horowitz's critique predates most of the disruptions that disfigure Cana-da's contemporary constitutional landscape. In a time of relative constitutional stability, Horowitz glimpsed the dark side of Canadian pluralism, its slide into fragmentation and its creation of antagonistic solitudes. For many Cana-dians, the dark side of pluralism is all that they have known. Moreover, the adoption of the *Charter of Rights and Freedoms* and the failure of the Meech Lake and Charlottetown Constitutional Accords have not resulted in a more harmonious Canada. If anything, Canadians are more divided than before, and constitutional reform is increasingly regarded as the god that failed. "After years of constitutional introspection," writes Alan Cairns, "Canada is on the brink of fracturing. Our search for the constitutional reforms that were to be the vehicle of our salvation has in fact driven us further apart."[49] This same process of fracturing can be detected within groups that compose Canadian society. One of the most striking features of the failed Meech Lake Constitu-tional Accord was the divisions it created within the women's movement. Among those opposed to the Accord were the voices of many English-speak-ing women, whereas the Federation of Quebec Women supported it.[50] The dark side of Canadian pluralism — glimpsed by Horowitz's critique of the mosaic and illustrated by divisions within the women's movement — brings into question the ability of Canadians to live under a common constitution. If Canadians cannot live together, they may have to live apart or even to look into the abyss.[51]

In the (Quebec) Secession Reference, the Supreme Court arrived at a simi-lar conclusion. It did so by recognizing a right to initiate constitutional change and a duty to negotiate the breakup of Canada. However, the Secession Refer-ence also has another side that looks not to the dissolution of Canada but to the special nature of the Canadian union. In its decision, the Court said that although Canada is a democracy, it is not a majoritarian democracy, because Canadian democracy is predicated on federalism, the rule of law, and respect for minority rights. This was another way of saying that Canada is a mosaic rather than a melting-pot. Such an interpretation receives considerable support from the Court's discussion of Confederation. In earlier decisions, including the Patriation Reference, the Court viewed Confederation through Macdonald's eyes and often emphasized the unitary features of the Canadian constitution. In the Secession Reference, however, the Court said that "the significance of the adoption of a federal form of government cannot be exaggerated." It emphasized that Canadian federalism "was a legal response to the underlying political and cultural realities that existed at Confederation and continue to exist today."[52] The Court also noted that the protection of minority rights was a central consideration at the time of Confederation. Confederation was no longer equated with the Macdonaldian constitution. Instead, the Court focused on Cartier and his idea of a Canadian political nationality.

By identifying Confederation with Cartier's idea of a political nationality rather than Macdonald's centralism, the Court not only jettisoned an unworkable constitutional theory but also took a step toward the discovery of a distinctively Canadian constitutional faith. In the passage quoted by the Court, Cartier is reported as saying that the idea of unity of races is a utopian impossibility. The Canadian federation would be composed of different races and ethnicities and everyone would add to the glory of the new country. "We are of different races," Cartier said, "not so that we can wage war on one another, but in order to work together for our well-being." Once united in Confederation, Canada would "form a political nationality independent of the national origin or the religion of any individual."[53] There exists no better description of Canada as a mosaic than Cartier's vision of Confederation. Moreover, Cartier did not believe that the mosaic would fly apart or lack a common patriotism, otherwise he would not have spoken of a Canadian political nationality. The American nation rests on a constitutional faith in freedom, which makes it an unusual kind of melting-pot. The Canadian mosaic also requires a constitutional faith, one that provides it with ties that bind and sustains a distinctive kind of nationhood.

CONCLUSION: PLURALISM AND THE TIES THAT BIND

Compared to the American, the Canadian constitutional faith seems both elusive and unrealized. "The Canada to which we really owe loyalty," wrote Northrop Frye, "is the Canada that we have failed to create." Frye also said that although every nation has a buried or uncreated ideal, "no nation has been more preoccupied with it than Canada."[54] But what is the buried ideal to which Canadians owe their allegiance? Frye did not answer this question. It is reasonably certain, however, that the Canadian ideal cannot be the same as the American. For although both countries celebrate pluralism, their pluralism differs, with the result that different ideals are available to them. That Canadian and American pluralism are of different kinds is the starting point of the theory of consociationalism. When Canada is described as a consociational democracy, the emphasis is on the absence of a strong national identity to hold Canadians together, with a corresponding focus on the role of political elites in brokering accommodations between the solitudes that compose it. By contrast, the United States is characterized as a country held together by a relatively homogeneous and secular political culture, in which groups with overlapping membership compete to promote their respective interests. Consociationalism is one important way of conceptualizing the differences between the Canadian mosaic and the American melting-pot.[55]

But the consociational model has its limitations. What it does not notice is that behind America's secular political culture there is a constitutional faith and a civil religion built on freedom. Faith in freedom is a key component of the strong national identity that holds Americans together. But freedom, as American history shows, is a paradoxical concept. When Americans agree about the meaning of their freedom, their society is most characterized by political stability and cultural homogenization. At such times, it becomes possible even to describe an American way of life. But Americans do not always agree about the meaning of freedom. They certainly did not agree in the three or so decades before the American Civil War, and the United States increasingly became two nations rather than one. Not only did the South equate slavery with freedom, but it constructed an elaborate nationalist ideology to justify secession from the Union. "Artificially constructed as it was," writes James McPherson, "Confederate ethnic nationalism was nevertheless powerful."[56] What some contemporary American feminists fear is that the equation of slavery (for women) with freedom (for men) is also the objective behind multicultural citizenship. In each case, the counter to that equation is the new birth of freedom that came with the Civil War and provides Americans with a national ideal. "In *giving* freedom to the *slave*," said Lincoln, "we *assure* freedom to the *free*."[57]

With respect to Canada, one of the deepest flaws of the consociational model is that it postulates solitudes and reduces Canadian nationhood to nothing more than a *modus vivendi*. Not only is the model inadequate as an explanatory device, but it also misunderstands Canadian history. If American history can be read as a story about freedom, Canadian history is no less compelling as a struggle to achieve fraternity or solidarity or mutual recognition. Reflecting on the breakup of Canada, a leading constitutional scholar asked why Canadian federalism is worth preserving. He answered: "Regardless of things that divide us, we have this recognition in Canada that we are our brothers' keepers."[58] Fraternity and mutual recognition are constant themes of Canadian history; they also recur in contemporary discussions of multiculturalism. In *Selling Illusions*, Neil Bissoondath insists that "brotherhood goes beyond the skin to essential notions of humanity." He then adds: "It is here that multiculturalism has failed us."[59] What Bissoondath fails to notice is the other side of multiculturalism, in which it becomes part of a politics of mutual recognition that affirms basic humanity without denying cultural differences. If mutual recognition based on a complex understanding of fraternity or solidarity is integral to Canada, then not only does the mosaic differ from the melting-pot, but there is much about Canada's partially buried ideal of nationhood that remains to be both discovered and achieved.

The process of discovery requires Canadians to reflect more deeply on the achievements of Confederation and the moral values that sustain it. But neither historical reflection nor moral clarity will necessarily secure Canada's continued existence as a nation. Within contemporary Canada, demands for Aboriginal self-government strain the Canadian political nationality and may even require a recasting of it so as to introduce new forms of mutual recognition and more complex understandings of solidarity.[60] There are also the long-standing aspirations of Quebec. The Fathers of Confederation accommodated Quebec, but it remains to be seen how special status for Quebec can be combined with a no less compelling claim to equality by other provinces within contemporary Canada.[61] When Americans had to reformulate their ideal of nationhood during the greatest crisis of their history, it was Abrahram Lincoln who was instrumental in accomplishing the transformation. "No man since Washington," wrote Lord Bryce, "has become to Americans so familiar and beloved a figure as Abraham Lincoln. He is to them the representative and typical American, the man who best embodies the political ideals of the nation."[62] The paradox of Lincoln is that he revered America's past as a heritage of liberty, yet envisioned a different future based on a new birth of freedom. In this way, he both returned to de Crevecoeur's idea of a melting-pot and reshaped it. The Canadian mosaic also needs to be refashioned, but it awaits its Lincoln.[63]

NOTES

1. Arthur M. Schlesinger, *The Disuniting of America* (New York: Norton, 1992), p. 32.

2. Hans Kohn and Daniel Walden, eds., *Readings in American Nationalism* (New York: Van Nostrand Reinhold, 1970), p. 87.

3. Porter's view is reported in Jean Burnet, "Multiculturalism in Canada," in *Ethnic Canadians*, ed. Leo Driedger (Toronto: Copp Clark Pitman, 1987), p. 66.

4. Pierre Elliott Trudeau, *Conversation with Canadians* (Toronto: University of Toronto Press 1972), p. 33.

5. Pierre Elliott Trudeau, *Federalism and the French Canadians* (Toronto: MacMillan, 1968), p. 179.

6. John Porter, *The Vertical Mosaic* (Toronto: University of Toronto Press, 1965), pp. 60-103.

7. Reginald W. Bibby, *Mosaic Madness* (Toronto: Stoddart, 1990), pp. 1-3.

8. Neil Bissoondath, *Selling Illusions: The Cult of Multiculturalism in Canada* (Toronto: Penguin, 1994), pp. 45-77.

9. Horace M. Kallen, *Culture and Democracy in the United States* (New York: Boni and Liveright, 1924), p. 58-59.

10. See, for example, Iris Marion Young, *Justice and the Politics of Difference* (Princeton: Princeton University Press, 1990), pp. 96-121.

11. Carl J. Fredrich, *The Impact of American Constitutionalism Abroad* (Boston: Boston University Press, 1967), p. 60.

12. Fredrick Jackson Turner, *Frontier and Section* (Englewood Cliffs, NJ: Prentice-Hall, 1961), p. 152.

13. *Parliamentary Debates on the Subject of the Confederation of the British North American Provinces* (Quebec: Hunter, Rose, 1865), pp. 514, 511 (Dunkin). Subsequently cited as *Confederation Debates*.

14. *Confederation Debates*, pp. 490, 493, 501, 494, 505, 530 (Dunkin).

15. *Confederation Debates*, p. 526 (Dunkin).

16. *Confederation Debates*, pp. 32-33 (MacDonald).

17. Quoted in Norman McL. Rogers, "The Genesis of Provincial Rights," *Canadian Historical Review* 14 (1933):17.

18. Richard N. Current, ed., *The Political Thought of Abraham Lincoln* (New York: Bobbs-Merrill, 1967), pp. 215, 315, 176, 329.

19. Montesquieu, *Selected Political Writings* (Indianapolis: Hackett, 1990), pp. 170-76. See also Martin Diamond, "The Federalist's View of Federalism," in *Essays in Federalism*, ed. George C.S. Benson (Claremont Men's College: Institute for Studies in Federalism, 1961), pp. 23-33.

20. Douglass Adair, *Fame and the Founding Fathers* (Indianapolis: Liberty Fund, 1998), pp. 132-50.

21. Edmund S. Morgan, *American Slavery — American Freedom* (New York: Norton, 1975), pp. 369-87.

22. Current, *The Political Thought of Abraham Lincoln*, p. 83.

23. Ibid., pp. 284-85.

24. *Confederation Debates*, p. 27 (Macdonald).

25. Rogers, "The Genesis of Provincial Rights," p. 18.

26. Jean Bethke Elshtain, *Democracy on Trial* (Toronto: Anansi, 1993), p. 75.

27. Bibby, *Mosaic Madness*, pp. 3, 2, vii, vi.

28. Isaiah Berlin, *The Crooked Timber of Humanity* (New York: Knopf, 1991), pp. 11, 30, 12, 9-10.

29. Schlesinger, *The Disuniting of America*, p. 123.

30. Nathan Glazer, *Ethnic Dilemmas 1964-1982* (Cambridge: Harvard University Press, 1983), pp. 268, 336.

31. Glazer, *Ethnic Dilemmas*, pp. 336.

32. Will Kymlicka, *Multicultural Citizenship* (Oxford: Clarendon Press, 1995), p. 181.

33. Ibid., pp. 32, 76.

34. Trudeau "Statement on Multiculturalism," in *Canadian Political Thought*, ed. H.D. Forbes (Toronto: Oxford University Press, 1985), p. 349.

35. Trudeau, *Conversation with Canadians*, p. 33.

36. See, for example, Kenneth McRoberts, *Misconceiving Canada* (Toronto: Oxford University Press, 1997) and Guy Laforest, *Trudeau and the End of a Canadian Dream* (Montreal: McGill-Queen's University Press, 1995).

37. Charles Taylor *et al.*, *Multiculturalism and "The Politics of Recognition"* (Princeton: Princeton University Press, 1992), pp. 25, 64.

38. Susan Moller Okin *et al.*, *Is Multiculturalism Bad for Women?* (Princeton: Princeton University Press, 1999), p. 13.

39. Ibid., pp. 9, 11, 12.

40. Ibid., p. 22.

41. Kymlicka in Okin, *Is Multiculturalism Bad for Women?*, pp. 32, 34.

42. Okin, *Is Multiculturalism Bad for Women?*, p. 131.

43. Parekh in Okin, *Is Multiculturalism Bad for Women?*, pp. 73-74.

44. Justice Frankfurter's views are discussed in Sanford Levinson, *Constitutional Faith* (Princeton: Princeton University Press, 1988), pp. 3, 101-02.

45. Robert Bellah "Civil Religion in America," in *American Civil Religion*, ed. Russell E. Richey and Donald G. Jones (New York: Harper and Row, 1974), pp. 33, 36.

46. Catharine MacKinnon, *Only Words* (Cambridge: Harvard University Press, 1993), pp. 71-110.

47. Gad Horowitz, "Mosaics and Identity," in Forbes, *Canadian Political Thought*, pp. 360, 361, 363.

48. See Robert F. Harney, "'So Great a Heritage as Ours': Immigration and the Survival of the Canadian Polity," *Daedalus* 117, 3-4 (1988):89-93; and John Harles, "Multiculturalism, National Identity, and National Integration: The Canadian Case," *International Journal of Canadian Studies*, Spring (1998):219, 236-39.

49. Alan C. Cairns, "Constitutional Reform: The God that Failed," *Transactions of the Royal Society of Canada*, series vi, vol. vii (1996):48.

50. Lynn Smith, "The Distinct Society Clause in the Meech Lake Accord: Could it Affect Equality Rights for Women?" in *Competing Constitutional Visions: The Meech Lake Accord*, ed. K.E. Swinton and C.J. Rogerson (Toronto: Carswell, 1988), pp. 45-47, 53-54.

51. Alan C. Cairns, *Looking into the Abyss: The Need for Plan C*, C.D. Howe Institute Commentary No. 96(Toronto: C.D. Howe Institute, 1997), pp. 14-15.

52. *Reference re Secession of Quebec*, [1998] 161 D.L.R. (4th) 407, 413.

53. *Reference re Secession of Quebec*, 407.

54. Northrop Frye, *The Modern Century* (Toronto: Oxford University Press, 1967), p. 123.

55. See Arend Lijphart, "Consociational Democracy," and S.J.R. Noel, "Consociational Democracy and Canadian Federalism," both in *Consociational Democracy*, ed. Kenneth McRae (Toronto: McClelland & Stewart, 1974), pp. 70-89, 262-68.

56. James M. McPherson, *Is Blood Thicker than Water?* (Toronto: Vintage Canada, 1998), p. 75. See also his *Abraham Lincoln and the Second American Revolution* (New York: Oxford University Press, 1991).

57. Current, *The Political Thought of Abraham Lincoln*, p. 234.

58. W.R. Lederman, *Continuing Canadian Constitutional Dilemmas* (Toronto: Butterworths, 1981), p. 208.

59. Bissoondath, *Selling Illusions*, p. 71.

60. Samuel V. LaSelva, "Aboriginal Self-Government and the Foundations of Canadian Nationhood," *BC Studies* 120 (1998/99):41.

61. Alan Cairns, "Constitutional Change and the Three Equalities," in his *Reconfigurations: Canadian Citizenship and Constitutional Change* (Toronto: McClelland & Stewart, 1995), pp. 216-37.

62. See Lord Bryce's introduction to Abraham Lincoln, *Speeches and Letters* (London: J.M. Dent, 1949), p. vii.

63. I am grateful to Harvey Lazar, Hamish Telford, and an anonymous reviewer for their comments on an earlier version of this paper.

13

Framing Citizenship Status in an Age of Polyethnicity: Quebec's Model of Interculturalism

Alain-G. Gagnon and Raffaele Iacovino

La notion de citoyenneté dans les États de démocratie libérale relève à la fois des aspects formels et symboliques de l'appartenance. Cet article explore les aspects symboliques de la citoyenneté — ex: comment les États structurent les contours d'une appartenance à la communauté politique — en la situant dans un contexte comparatif où sont pris en compte le multiculturalisme canadien, le modèle québécois d'interculturalisme et le projet assimilationniste américain. Quels sont les points d'ancrage symboliques qui délimitent l'appartenance dans une communauté de démocratie libérale? Comment fait-on pour évaluer la performance de ces ancrages dans un monde traversé de plus en plus par la polyethnicité propre à un nombre grandissant de communautés politiques nationales. Cet article cherche aussi à décortiquer le concept du multiculturalisme en tant que paradigme idéologique et à développer des critères normatifs permettant d'évaluer les modèles actuels de pluralisme culturel au Canada, au Québec et aux États-Unis. Nous en venons à la conclusion que, conceptuellement, c'est le modèle de l'interculturalisme qui en arrive au meilleur équilibre entre l'habilitation des identités collectives, en tant que composantes actives de la communauté politique, et la nécessité d'une base commune pour poursuivre le dialogue, en vue d'une grande cohésion sociale.

What is truly revolutionary is this attempt to devise a democratic vision by employing the policy instruments of the nation-state in the reconstruction of the symbolic order and the redistribution of social status among racial and ethnocultural groups in Canadian society.[1]

This chapter will address the impact of polyethnicity on political communities by focusing specifically on the symbolic aspect of citizenship — the markers of a country's self-identification through which citizens are said to exhibit a sense of social cohesion and allegiance for effective democratic participation in a given polity.[2] What are the symbolic "anchors" that frame and define sentiments of belonging in a democratic polity? How do we evaluate such criteria in light of the challenge of polyethnicity? Have citizens' ties to Canada been undermined by the policy of multiculturalism? Such questions will be explored through a comparative conceptual assessment of the Canadian policy of multiculturalism, the Quebec model of interculturalism, and the American assimilationist model, which will serve as somewhat of a benchmark for liberal-democratic attempts to address the impact of polyethnicity.

Multiculturalism has indeed filtered into academic and popular parlance. However, in its relevance to matters of citizenship — as a basis for democratic life — it remains an elusive concept. In looking at the concept of multiculturalism in Canada, Mazurek notes that

> as with "justice," "beauty" and "love," everyone seems to approve of multiculturalism, everyone seems to know what it is, yet everyone seems to define and practice it differently ... We have yet to settle upon agreement of what, exactly, multiculturalism is.[3]

Indeed, according to Golfman, assessments of multiculturalism have been "engendered by its arguably ontological status."[4] This ambiguity surrounding the meaning of multiculturalism is particularly striking considering that in Canada,

> an increasing number of jurisdictions have either statutory instruments or written policies on multiculturalism. Thus in a relatively short time multiculturalism acquired a high legitimacy similar to that assigned to such lofty concepts as *democracy* or *equality*. Given the short history of the concept and the manner in which it was introduced to the top of the hierarchy of legal norms, it is surprising that it lacks definition or even established usage.[5]

For the purposes of this conceptual analysis, the label "multiculturalism" will be treated both as an abstract ideological paradigm and as a tangible policy of the Canadian state with regard to the incorporation of immigrants, or ethnocultural minorities more generally. With regard to the former use of the term, multiculturalism can be delineated as a philosophical approach that seeks to address the impact of polyethnicity on prevailing uniform models of citizenship in liberal democracies, which have traditionally centred on formal legal/procedural definitions of citizenship. As such, the term does not merely serve as a descriptive tool, in a sociological sense, to depict the socio-cultural character of particular political communities. The challenge of multiculturalism lies precisely in its implicit assumption of cultural pluralism as a value concept — and thus as an aspect of citizenship that matters to policymakers in democracies. Juteau summarizes this point succinctly:

> Equality and pluralism are values that command some support in occidental liberal democracies. Beyond this point, however, appear disagreements, opposition and conflicts. Which pluralism to retain, which measures for redistribution to develop, which policies of cultural recognition to adopt? ... Almost all societies

are multicultural, the question is not whether we want a multicultural society, rather, it is to decide in which type of multicultural society we wish to live.[6]

Integrating immigrants or ethno-cultural groups into established host societies ultimately implies normative questions regarding the capacity of individuals in such groups to participate in the democratic life of the polity. Evaluating models of integration rests on the salience of cultural identity with regard to citizen dignity, understood here as "empowerment" or "the means to participate" in circumscribed political communities. Multiculturalism, as an ideological/philosophical challenge to classical liberal conceptions of citizenship, represents an appropriate field of study for political scientists precisely because attempts to foster "citizen dignity" are largely the result of state policy aimed at crafting a symbolic order for the larger society. To quote Wilson,

> Multiculturalism is constructed as a doctrine that provides a *political framework* for the official promotion of *social equality* and *cultural differences* as an integral component of the social order. It is government having the authority in the realm of the mind and an articulation that its responsibilities there are among the most important it has.[7]

Political actors can thus be conceptualized as "caretakers" of socio-political markers of allegiance, defining both the terms of formal membership and the symbolic markers for "belonging" in framing citizenship status. Of interest here is multiculturalism as the prerogative of policymakers, and its manifestation in a series of initiatives aimed toward an overall model for self-definition, for belonging, in a larger political community — and whether it can serve as a marker for identification, an equalizing device for members of minority groups.

Although multiculturalism occupies much terrain in the broad area of citizenship, it must be made clear that citizenship involves much more than its symbolic components — the idea that state actors actually debate and craft bases of belonging to a given political community. Citizenship extends further into the realms of formal representation (electoral systems, representation), and issues related to social entitlements (the relationship between the state, the market, and society). Indeed, citizenship involves multiple mechanisms, practical and symbolic, of social and political inclusion. This chapter thus does not claim to cover the issue of citizenship exhaustively. It merely attempts to address an increasingly salient aspect of citizenship that has gained prominence in political communities of liberal democratic states. This may be due in part to migration and the subsequent growth of identity politics, nation-building projects, or, in the case of small nations such as Quebec, the quest for recognition as a host society in its own right — its affirmation as a "global society." In short, the aspect of citizenship discussed here relates to sentiments of belonging and solidarity. The salience of these questions in the larger area of citizenship cannot be disregarded, as Micheline Labelle and

François Rocher make clear in response to a recent proposal[8] that the Quebec government hold a national commission on Quebec citizenship:

> The challenge is not merely legal in nature, knowing how to define the range of rights enjoyed by citizens and denouncing the obstacles for their exercise. The symbolic dimensions of citizenship are particularly important to the extent that, within every state ... citizenship and sentiments of belonging to the politico-national community are notions often used interchangeably.[9]

Multiculturalism can thus be characterized as an intellectual movement associated with the value of cultural identity as it pertains to democratic citizenship. From this premise comes the latter use of the term — multiculturalism as a policy of the Canadian state. Indeed, Canadian multiculturalism will serve as a tangible gauge for many of the normative expectations involved in the abstract ideological discourse surrounding multiculturalism as a value principle. In this chapter we will proceed to unpack the concept of multiculturalism as an ideological paradigm, and develop certain normative criteria with which to judge the current model of cultural pluralism in Canada. Regardless of strict definitions, multiculturalism, or the "politics of difference," is a response to the late twentieth-century phenomenon that has been called the "age of migration," challenging countries to redefine the rules of political life.[10]

CHALLENGING LIBERALISM: THE IMPACT OF MULTICULTURALISM

According to Christian Joppke, multiculturalism is an intellectual movement premised around the concepts of equality and emancipation. Its appeal lies in the defence of particularistic, mostly ascriptively defined group identities that reject western universalism as the basis for allegiance to a given collectivity. Western universalism in this view is seen as "falsely homogenizing and a smokescreen for power."[11] As such, multiculturalism implies the salience of multiple cultures coexisting within a limited state-bounded territory, rejecting the modern Jacobin view of the nation-state and the homogenization of identities. The key issue is that such "cultural communities" are said to regulate not only specific aspects, but the entire life conduct and sources of meaning of the individual. Joppke summarizes:

> Defenders of multiculturalism have argued that the exercise of individual rights and liberties depends on full and unimpeded membership in a respected and flourishing cultural group. But the tension between liberalism and multiculturalism is real, as the latter is based on the ontological primacy of the group over the individual and, if necessary, takes into the bargain the suppression of individual claims.[12]

In short, this approach views assimilation or acculturation as a violation of the integrity or dignity of the individual, whose cultural habits should be recognized fully as an integral element of a person's identity. Any stifling of particular cultural expressions by way of the symbolic construction of a larger socio-cultural identity limits the individual's capacity for self-realization, thus negating the liberal-democratic ideal that individuals, as members of the larger society, be given the means by which to explore their own life chances and directions. As such, ascriptive aspects of identity — particular cultural sources of meaning — are said to act as prerequisites to self-realization. Stripping such sources of meaning in the name of universal markers of identity, in the construction of a national (Jacobin) identity that is meant to provide common purpose, denies the individual the empowerment to determine the direction of his/her life through participation in the affairs of society. Iris Marion Young argues that if one conceptualizes such cultural differences as "relationally constituted structural differentiations," then the supposed link between citizenship and the common good is upheld, because:

> It becomes clear that socially situated interests, proposals, claims and expressions of experience are often an important resource for democratic discussion and decision-making. Such situated knowledges can both pluralize and relativize hegemonic discourses, and offer otherwise unspoken knowledge to contribute to wise decisions.[13]

The polemic between universal and particular bases of allegiance thus demarcates the contours of the debate. With the increasing polyethnic composition of nation-states, the debate has emerged largely as a challenge to the homogenizing tendencies of classical liberal models of citizenship. The idea of multiculturalism can be embedded in a wider area of post-national consciousness — some say postmodern, or "identity politics" — as an attack on the assimilation implied by nation-states with the aim of attaching a sense of common purpose to citizenship status.[14]

The sentiments associated with equal citizenship status have long been regarded by liberal theorists as integral to democratic political communities — for fostering the civic-spiritedness, mutual trust and allegiance required for meaningful self-government, self-realization and political stability. Kymlicka notes that the classical liberal response to polyethnicity has been to develop common (undifferentiated) bases of citizenship in a universal vein. In this view, the integrative function of citizenship requires that cultural differences be treated with "benign neglect," in order that a shared civic identity is forged regardless of collective, or group-based identity differences. Iris Marion Young notes that proponents of such arguments view any particular demands based on sociological "differences" as detrimental to the functioning of democracy due to the contention that citizens concern themselves less with the common good and more with their own group-based, or "special" interests.[15] Kymlicka summarizes this view:

> Citizenship is by definition a matter of treating people as individuals with equal rights under the law.... [If it is group differentiated], nothing will bind the various groups in society together, and prevent the spread of mutual mistrust or conflict. If citizenship is differentiated, it no longer provides a shared experience or common status. Citizenship would yet be another force for disunity, rather than a way of cultivating unity in the face of increasing social diversity. Citizenship should be a forum where people transcend their differences, and think about the common good of all citizens.[16]

In short, according to the classical liberal view, culture, like religion, should be left to the private sphere and should not concern the state. The only way for a democracy to flourish is for the political community to be predicated on universal bases of belonging which are "civic" and amenable to identification across cultures.

For defenders of multiculturalism, however, the notion of benign neglect is in itself infused with cultural meaning. It simply represents a preservation of the status quo in many previously homogeneous nation-states. State inactivity thus reflects a failure to adapt to dynamic polyethnic realities in society. Minority cultures are rendered unequal participants and second-class citizens if their sources of meaning are neglected in the public realm. As such, the ideal of equality cannot be achieved if citizens are forced to conform to a "civic" denial of identity, a renewed self-definition for individual citizens. Isajiw notes that the force of multiculturalism arises out of a particular sentiment in which citizen dignity is tied to the collective dignity of one's ethnic community. Multiculturalism represents a set of values whereby the recognition of identity needs is linked to the instrumental power of members of ethnic communities.[17] Charles Taylor explains:

> The demand for recognition in [the politics of multiculturalism] is given urgency by the supposed links between recognition and identity ... The thesis is that our identity is partly shaped by recognition or its absence, often by misrecognition of others, and so a person or group of people can suffer real damage, real distortion, if the people or society around them mirror back to them a confining or demeaning or contemptible picture of themselves. Nonrecognition or misrecognition can be a form of oppression, imprisoning someone in a false, distorted or reduced mode of being.[18]

The recognition of cultural pluralism by the state is thus a call for increased citizen empowerment. How are citizens in a polyethnic society equally empowered to share and participate in the affairs of the polity, without sacrificing self-fulfilling "modes of being"? How have states adapted to such challenges?

The theoretical contours outlined above reveal that normative evaluations of integration rest on two broad considerations. The first is that full citizenship status requires that all cultural identities be allowed to participate in democratic life equally, without the necessity to tone down conceptions of identity to the level of the individual. Empowerment implies that citizens are permitted to maintain their cultural differences when impacting the affairs of the polity through democratic participation. This implies some acceptance that policy outcomes will reflect some groups' differentiated initiatives by the central state. The second concerns the salience of unity in any society. Here the key element is a sense of common purpose in public matters in order that deliberation is not confined to pockets of self-contained, fragmented collectivities in juxtaposition. These two broad poles are at issue in any model of integration and subsequent conceptualizations of citizenship status. In short, a balance must be struck between the *equal empowerment of group identities* as active constituents of the larger political community and the need for a *common ground for dialogue*, for the purposes of unity — a *centre* that also serves as an identity marker in the larger society and denotes in itself a pole of allegiance for all citizens.

Prior to proceeding with the comparative study, however, it must be noted that such policies cannot be assessed in the absence of a clear understanding of political processes related to the strategy of nation-building. This qualification is particularly salient in the Canadian case, where the precarious nature of pan-Canadian identity has traditionally been in itself somewhat of a "national symbol" (sic) due to the persistent existential question in Quebec. Indeed, as will be demonstrated below, policymakers at the federal level charged with defining the bases of belonging to Canada have not only faced the challenges associated with the incorporation of diverse cultural identities, but have been confronted with a national minority with established political institutions within a well-circumscribed territory as well. This fact represents a qualitatively different challenge confronting Canada in comparison to the United States. As Joppke makes clear, each society's actual response to immigration and polyethnicity does not merely stem from an abstract model that is subsequently applied to the real world:

> The concrete meaning of multiculturalism and its linkage to immigration differs significantly across these societies. These differences are conditioned by distinct traditions of nationhood, the specific historical contexts in which immigration has taken place, and the existing immigration regimes.[19]

As such, the case of Quebec, although formally a province of Canada, nevertheless merits independent consideration, because the Quebec state has negotiated extensive authority over immigration. Moreover, Quebec constitutes a distinct political community with a well-defined collective cultural project that includes the integration of immigrants into that project. Other provinces, by contrast, have been content to leave this policy area in the hands of the federal government. In short, Quebec should be viewed as a host society in its own right, with its own historical and cultural development, its own sense of nationhood, and a distinct discourse with regards to the general orientations and choices of society.

There are indeed political imperatives at work in such policy outcomes. This chapter has attempted to clarify the meaning of the term "multiculturalism" — distinguishing between its use as a general label for an emerging tradition in political thought and the actual policy bearing its name in Canada — in order to alleviate the ambiguities surrounding the concept. An assessment of Canadian multiculturalism cannot forgo the fact that in the final analysis it is a policy and not an "ontological" principle devoid of contingencies. The ideal of multiculturalism must not be confused with the Canadian policy, as this is prone to stifling debate concerning the value of the policy in framing citizenship status.

CULTURAL PLURALISM IN THE US: THE "MELTING-POT" METAPHOR

The case of the United States can be deemed a benchmark in evaluating state policy with regard to polyethnicity. To a large extent, the liberal emphasis on "benign neglect" in cultural matters, as a basis for common citizenship status, has permeated American discourse and has been traditionally embraced as somewhat of a founding principle of American identity. The US response to polyethnicity has followed a doctrine of assimilation. John Miller traces this approach as a founding ideal of what it means to be American:

> [America] is a nation dedicated to the proposition that all men are created equal. This extraordinary notion animates the American people, whose very sense of peoplehood derives not from a common lineage but from their adherence to a set of core principles about equality, liberty and self-government. These ideas, recognised at the founding of the United States, are universal. They apply to all humankind. They know no racial or ethnic limits. They are not bound by time or history. And they lie at the centre of American nationhood. Because of this, these ideas uphold an identity into which immigrants from all over the world can assimilate, as long as they, too, dedicate themselves to the proposition.[20]

Minority cultures of all stripes were expected to shed their values, cultures, and languages and unconditionally adopt those of the larger society. This approach can be characterized as one in which the idea of benign neglect in the identity, or cultural sphere, ensures that all citizens may participate equally in democratic life. It is reductionist in the sense that the markers for identity are laid out in a procedural manner, a legalistic approach to citizenship which emphasizes the primacy of individual rights in the public sphere. The question of culture itself is relegated to the private sphere, culture is not considered to be a political concern. Katz explains:

our Bill of Rights, in contrast to every other modern bill of rights, is almost entirely procedural. It has virtually no substantive protections.... [it] consists almost entirely of what could be called civil and political rights ... [and] our procedural rights relate almost exclusively to individuals.[21]

Katz argues that the interpretation of equality in the United States is still very much a product of mid-nineteenth-century views as espoused in the Fourteenth and Fifteenth Amendments. The former amendment states that "all persons born or naturalized in the United States, and subject to the jurisdiction thereof, are citizens of the United States and of the States wherein they reside."[22] This provision has been interpreted by the courts in a manner that denied the amendments' possible use as a basis for addressing minority group rights. Equality demanded that individuals be protected from state intrusions but was not designed to eliminate "private" discrimination. The idea of equal citizenship before the law came to represent the "equal" protection of all citizens from discriminatory measures by *state action.* Any other form of discrimination experienced by groups was a question of *private conduct* and hence dismissed as constituting a political issue. Katz summarizes:

our tradition ... became at least partly one of constitutional discrimination against groups rather than protection of them, and it was based on the growing prescription of individual equality and equal protection of the laws.[23]

Such a tradition has been largely upheld in the United States in its formulation of citizenship status. The one significant caveat has been the rather recent attempt to address the reality of groups that have suffered discrimination, historically, through these interpretations of equality. Under the banner of "affirmative action," an attempt was made to grant minority groups special access to educational institutions, broadcasting, employment, etc., in order that such institutions may better reflect the proportion of group identification in the general population. This was deemed a necessary measure in order to compensate for "lost ground." However, such provisions were qualified to a large degree. The Courts' test of constitutionality of these measures was such that the groups that were discriminated against had to prove that the nature of the intention of particular cases of discrimination was blatant, and not a consequence of the "latent" effects of private actions. In other words, the burden of proof required in order to benefit from such group-based provisions of equal status rested on minority groups themselves, not on empirical structural inequalities.

In the final analysis, this tradition with regard to citizenship status in the United States prevails. Indeed, the question of the effects of affirmative action on the melting-pot metaphor as a symbol for national identity has resulted in virulent reaction.[24] If multiculturalism has achieved somewhat of an "ontological status" in Canada, in the United States it is deemed by many to run counter to the very defining principles of American democracy. Again, equality in this view rests on reductionist principles — a matter of non-discrimination and the equal opportunity to participate. It is in this light that American sociologist Nathan Glazer describes the role of culture as it pertains to state policy:

> [immigrants] had come to this country not to maintain a foreign language and culture but with the intention ... to become Americanized as fast as possible, and this meant English language and American culture. They sought the induction to a new language and culture that the public schools provided — as do many present-day immigrants, too — and while they often found, as time went on, that they regretted what they and their children had lost, this was their choice ... The United States, whatever the realities of discrimination and segregation, had as a national ideal a unitary and new ethnic identity, that of American.[25]

For Schlesinger, Jr. as well, the key to American stability in the face of increasing polyethnicity has and will remain embedded in the melting-pot:

> The United States had a brilliant solution for the inherent fragility, the inherent combustibility, of a multiethnic society; the creation of a brand new national identity by individuals who, in forsaking old loyalties and joining to make new lives, melted away ethnic differences — a national identity that absorbs and transcends the diverse ethnicities that come to our shore ... The point of America was not to preserve old cultures, but to produce a new American culture.[26]

The basis of such identification is a "civic culture" — the notion that individuals are bound by equal adherence to a set of principles. Jürgen Habermas has labelled this approach "constitutional patriotism." The state here is interpreted as the "domain of law," while collective identity based on national allegiance is the "affective realm." Thus citizenship implies a civic patriotism, void of national identity. Political legitimacy as such stems from the procedures of democracy itself rather than any attachment to historical or cultural attributes.[27] Schlesinger, Jr. calls this set of principles the "American Creed," which is rooted in the practical obligations of civic participation and a patriotic commitment to a "democratic faith." In this view, democracy is not the product of citizen dignity through the recognition of diverse cultural contexts, but the precursor to unity. Procedural democracy comes to be the much heralded symbol of identification which all Americans share. In sum, the American response to polyethnicity has been to deny differences altogether and focus on the symbolic virtue of a "central" American identity, based on a procedurally (legally) defined conception of equal individual rights.

THE POLITICS OF MULTICULTURALISM IN CANADA

The idea of multiculturalism in Canada came into awareness largely as a result of a negative response to the recommendations of the Royal Commission on Biculturalism and Bilingualism (B&B) in the mid-1960s by a "third force" — groups that represented immigrant ethnic communities.[28] The commission was spearheaded by Prime Minister Pearson as a response to the rise of a reinvigorated Quebec nationalism through the Quiet Revolution, and the subsequent questioning of Quebec's collective place in a federation dominated largely by Anglo-Canadians in economic, cultural, and political affairs.[29] To quote Breton:

> The immediate motive ... was the rise of the independence movement [in Quebec] and the government's initial response. The transformation of institutional identity, language and symbols to help members of the French segment of the society recognize themselves generated identification and status concerns ... among those of non-British, non-French origin.[30]

Representatives of the "third force" sought recognition of their cultural contribution to Canada, and felt that they would be relegated to second-class citizenship status if the country were to be formally recognized as bicultural and bilingual. In Harney's words:

> Since the spokesmen for the third element rejected the idea of a separate *Canadien* nation, they tended to see the argument over dualism and the Commission's bilingual and bicultural mandate as one about power, not history.... As an exasperated Ukrainian leader put it, "Is it necessary for all these people to establish their own ethno-cultural enclaves before their cultural and linguistic aspirations are truly respected and encouraged?"[31]

The result of such politicking was Book IV of the B&B Commission's recommendations, the precursor to official multiculturalism, entitled *The Contribution of the other Ethnic Groups*. The recommendations were to form the subsequent thrust of multiculturalism policy as initiated by the Trudeau government.

Prime Minister Trudeau rejected the "two-nations" conception of the country whereby French and English Canada were to be recognized equally as founding nations, with each enjoying majority status in their respective territorial and institutional domains. Trudeau opted instead to adopt a policy of official multiculturalism in a bilingual framework. As such, it was believed that language could be dissociated from culture, and individuals would be free to decide whether or not to endeavour to preserve their ethnic identities. Implicit in such an approach is the primacy of individual rights, the right of all individuals to dissociate freely themselves from their cultural communities. Also, the languages of participation in Canadian society, French and English, were left to individual choice. The notion that language use was to correspond to sociological realities, as the original mandate of the B&B Commission implied, was abandoned. The community for the integration of immigrants was to be Canada, defined as a bilingual host society. In Trudeau's view:

> We cannot have a cultural policy for Canadians of French and British origin, another for Aboriginals, and still another for all the others. Although we will

have two official languages, there will be no official culture, and no ethnic group will have priority.... All men will see their liberty hindered if they are continually enclosed in a cultural compartment determined uniquely by birth and language. It is thus essential that all Canadians, regardless of their ethnic origins, be required to learn at least one of the two languages in which the country conducts its public affairs.[32]

Indeed, as Kallen contends, the final policy outcome represented a compromise to the "multicultural and multilingual" vision espoused by the "third force" and the "two-nations" demand of Quebec nationalists.[33] By separating language and culture, Canadian identity was to be constructed on universal principles, relegating culture to the private sphere. In short, the federal government's policy objectives ran as follows:[34]

- The Government of Canada will support all of Canada's cultures and will seek to assist, resources permitting, the development of those cultural groups which have demonstrated a desire and effort to continue to develop a capacity to grow and contribute to Canada, as well as a clear need for assistance.

- The Government will assist members of all cultural groups to overcome cultural barriers to full participation in Canadian society.

- The Government will promote creative encounters and interchange among all Canadian cultural groups in the interest of national unity.

- The Government will continue to assist immigrants to acquire at least one of Canada's official languages in order to become full participants in Canadian society.

New concerns over racial and ethnic equity led to a reiteration of the policy in the 1988 *Canadian Multiculturalism Act* by the Conservative government of Brian Mulroney. As Abu-Laban notes, the Act furthered the impact of multicultural policy by focusing not only on cultural maintenance, but by emphasizing more explicitly concerns regarding discrimination. The Act now contained a provision whereby the minister of multiculturalism may "assist ethno-cultural minority communities to conduct activities with a view to overcoming any discriminatory barrier and, in particular, discrimination based on race or national or ethnic origin."[35] Such a response by the state emanated from greater concerns surrounding the changing composition of minority ethnic groups due to recent waves of immigration. The new Act, however, did little to change the general thrust of the original policy, and simply refined and strengthened the terms of recognition with respect to the contribution of cultural groups.[36]

Of more significance was the entrenchment of multiculturalism in the 1982 *Canadian Charter of Rights and Freedoms*. The existing policy of multiculturalism within a bilingual framework was reinforced. Under the interpretative clause in section 27, the policy would henceforth "be interpreted in a manner consistent with the preservation and enhancement of the multicultural heritage of Canadians." Multiculturalism thus became a "visible component of the patriated constitution," leading to the perception among ethnocultural groups that they had achieved the status of "legitimate constitutional actors."[37] In Wilson's words, "Armed with long memories and the constitutional gains of 1982, these recently enfranchised 'Charter Canadians' took our political decision-makers by surprise in serving notice that they were now serious players in the constitutional stakes."[38] In the final analysis, the Charter, as Rainer Knopff and F.L. Morton argue, can be seen as a compromise between the dualism envisioned by Trudeau and the concerns of the "third element." Dualism was now constitutionally entrenched with English and French serving as official languages across Canada, as well as in the provision of both English and French minority education, with the former targeting Quebec and the latter aimed at the rest of Canada. At the same time, section 27 added an interpretive clause that took into account the "preservation and enhancement of the multicultural heritage of all Canadians." In short, Trudeau's early vision to establish pan-Canadian identity markers devoid of any one particular linguistic or cultural attribute was now formally entrenched at the constitutional level in the Charter.[39]

"INTERCULTURALISM": QUEBEC'S MODEL OF CULTURAL PLURALISM

Quebec's persistent attempts to establish itself as a "host society" can be traced back to the Quiet Revolution, the increased activity of the state in many dimensions of the lives of Quebecers, and can be qualified as a project to gradually construct Quebec citizenship. The idea of Quebec citizenship cannot be divorced from the larger issue of Quebec's national affirmation in the face of pan-Canadian attempts at nation-building. In developing its own model for integration, Quebec has in effect developed a response to the Canadian policy of multiculturalism, a response that affirms the primacy of the Quebec state in the areas of politics and identity and challenges the reductionist notion that Quebec is a monolithic ethnic group. The treatment of diversity, when placed in a larger historical context, can be seen as but one of the many areas of contention between opposing visions regarding Canada's constituent political communities, or national groupings. Will Kymlicka highlights this progression toward a formal Quebec citizenship:

> The notion of a distinctly Québécois citizenship has seen a spectacular progression. In the space of a lifetime, the dominant identification of Quebecers has been profoundly transformed. From Canadians, they became French-Canadians, then Franco-Québécois and finally, Québécois.... These transformations cannot

be interpreted as a simple evolution of a sort of sentiment of belonging to the tribe. Rather, they represent a continuing progression of Québécois identity, in which its foundations have passed from non-citizenship to citizenship.[40]

Historically, the main impetus for the increasing salience of the discourse on Quebec citizenship has been the idea of the French language as the primary vehicle for the preservation and flourishing of Québécois identity. Language was indeed the precursor to concerns over immigration and integration. With an alarming decline in the birth rate in Quebec, state actors became concerned with the tendency of allophones to gravitate linguistically toward the anglophone community. Immigration and integration thus became inextricably tied to the fate of the Quebec nation. With a Ministry of Immigration in place since 1968, the Quebec government was very active in almost all aspects of immigration except recruitment and reception.[41] Some of its activities included an employment search service for newly arrived immigrants, support for community groups with the aim of adaptation, and the funding of cultural and linguistic heritage programs, including the translation of literature into French, in the hopes of building bridges between the allophone and francophone communities. From 1969 to 1980, the ministry's budget grew from $2.8 million to $20 million. The Quebec government took a wide range of measures in the areas of language acquisition and cultural adaptation, the initial steps toward a more fully articulated model of integration.

As Michael Behiels argues, however, many such positive measures, as perceived by allophones, were at times overshadowed by language legislation which culminated in the Charter of the French Language (Bill 101) in 1977. This was interpreted as a hardline approach, out of line with the bridge-building measures in progress, and was frequently opposed by allophones and anglophones.[42] With the adoption of the Charter, the PQ government established the vision of a linguistically unilingual and ethnically pluralistic political community in Quebec, a vision that would nourish subsequent models of integration to this day. As early as 1981, the Quebec model began taking shape, with publication of *Autant de façons d'être Québécois*.[43] The essence of the publication was that, unlike Canadian multiculturalism, Quebec integration would stress the idea of "convergence." We will return to this point below. Of significance here is the fact that the Quebec model explicitly challenged the Canadian variant as a basis for citizenship. The jurisdictional battles of the Quiet Revolution and the linguistic conflicts of the 1970s culminated in a fully articulated discourse centred on citizenship in Quebec. As such, it can no longer be disputed that Quebec constitutes a host society whose model of integration deserves serious attention.

Quebec has adopted as its official position a discourse on interculturalism to deal with its polyethnic composition. This view contends that the incorporation of immigrants or minority cultures into the larger political community is a reciprocal endeavour — a "moral contract" between the host society and the particular cultural collectivity, with the aim of establishing a forum for the empowerment of all citizens — "a common public culture."[44]

The moral contract is summed up as follows:

1. a society in which French is the common language of public life

2. a democratic society where participation and the contribution of everyone is expected and encouraged

3. a pluralist society open to multiple contributions within the limits imposed by the respect for fundamental democratic values, and the necessity of inter-community exchange.[45] (our translation)

The Government of Quebec describes the general thrust of this model as such.

The "moral contract" affirms that, in its options for society, it follows that rights and responsibilities apply as much to immigrants, on the one hand, as to the receiving society itself (including Québécois of cultural communities already integrated or on their way to being integrated) and its institutions, on the other hand. Being a Québécois means being engaged in fact in Quebec's choices for society. For the immigrant established in Quebec, adopting Quebec as an adopted land, there requires an engagement like all other citizens, and to respect these very choices of society. It is the simultaneous existence of complementary rights and obligations attributed to all parties — and to engage in solidarity in relationships of reciprocal obligation — which justifies the vocabulary of "moral contract" to designate the general environment governing such relations with the aim of fully integrating immigrants.[46] (our translation)

The common public culture in this view does not consist solely of the juridical sphere; it is not a procedural definition like the American model. Instead, the basic tenets of the moral contract are such that the established "modes of being" in economic, political, and socio-cultural realms are to be respected as markers of identification and citizenship status, with the institutions of democratic participation acting as a point of convergence for groups of specific collective identities in order that all may share equally in democratic life. Carens highlights this feature of the model:

Immigrants can be full members of Quebec's society even if they look and act differently from the substantial segment of the population whose ancestors inhabited Quebec and even if they do not in any way alter their own customs and cultural patterns with respect to work and play, diet and dress, sleep and sex, celebration and mourning, so long as they act within the confines of the law.[47]

In establishing a model based on the convergence of collective identity, the French language is to serve as the common language of public life; this is seen as an essential condition for the cohesion of Quebec society. Indeed, the French language constitutes the basis for Quebec's self-definition as a political community. In this view, language is not conceptualized as an individual right. Rocher *et al.* elaborate:

In Quebec,... the French language is presented as a "center of convergence" for diverse groups which can nevertheless maintain and let flourish their specificity. While the Canadian policy privileges an individualist approach to culture, Quebec's policy states clearly the need to recognize French as a collective good that requires protection and encouragement.[48] (our translation)

The notion of "public life" is shady and nuanced, indeed, what constitutes a "public exchange" is not often clear. As a general rule, the confines of public space are not relegated solely to the activities of the state, but encompass "the public space of social interaction" as well. For example, students may, as a matter of individual right, communicate in any language they wish on the playground of a francophone school. However, language use in the classroom is considered public space. More examples of what constitutes "private interaction" are relations with family members, friends, colleagues or anyone involved in the social circle of the individual in question in which the choice of language use is of a consensual nature. Again, in Rocher *et al.*'s words,

It must be emphasized that valuing French as the common language does not imply in itself the abandonment of a language of origin, for two reasons. The first is related to the democratic nature of society which must respect individual choices. The second is a question of utility: the development of languages of origin is considered an economic, social and cultural asset. It must be stressed that there exists a fundamental distinction between the status of French as a common language of public life and that of the other languages.[49] (our translation)

Thus an emphasis on the proficient use of the French language is taken as a minimal condition of the exercise of common citizenship — as an instrument of democracy. To quote Giroux,

it is of importance that the French language is taken first and foremost as a condition of the exercise of citizen rights; the modern nation cannot claim to be a forum for discussion and decision-making without the existence of a community of language.[50] (our translation)

Moreover, the host society expects as a matter of obligation that members of minority groups fully integrate into the larger community, with the expectation that all citizens are to contribute and participate in the social fabric of the common public culture. As a democratic community, this implies that once citizenship is attained, all members are equally encouraged to "participate in defining the general direction of our society ... at all stages and in all sectors where the judgement of citizens can be manifested and heard."[51] (our translation)

With regard to the eventuality of conflict arising between individuals or groups, the method of resolution must correspond to democratic norms. This point is important because it highlights a fundamentally different perspective than the American emphasis on procedural judicial channels. The Quebec model stresses that in the initial manifestation of conflict, deliberative measures such as mediation, compromise, and direct negotiation, are preferred, leaving as much initiative and autonomy to the parties in question. Legalistic measures and the recourse to specified rights are to be an option of last resort. In other words, this model values deliberation, mutual understanding, and generally, dialogue as fundamental characteristics of democratic life, in the realm of civil society, and aims to foster a cohesive and participatory conception of citizenship.

It is in the model's treatment of pluralism that the idea of "interculturalism" emerges — an idea whereby the notion of difference does not imply a society built on the juxtaposition of ethnic groupings, in a "mosaic," nor does it reduce citizenship status simply to procedural safeguards from state intrusion through the codification of fundamental individual rights, and the assimilation of particular identities to such universal principles.[52] The Quebec model of cultural pluralism operates fundamentally in the tradition of parliamentary democracy, with an emphasis on deliberation and representation. Pagé summarizes:

> In conceptualising a common civic space, it is common civic norms which constitute the basis for social cohesion. The norms are situated above particular ethnic cultures and have a scope general enough to govern the actions of a society consisting of individuals belonging to a plurality of ethnic groups. *These norms are established by democratic institutions, which are capable of accounting for pluralism in seeking always, through decisions arrived at by democratic voting, as large as possible a consensual base, which does not limit itself only to the majority ethnic group or an ensemble of minority groups.* [53] (our translation)

Within the framework of basic principles — a commitment to the peaceful resolution of conflict, a charter of human rights and freedoms in order to provide legal recourse to the protection of individual and group rights, equality between the sexes, a secular state, and equality and universality of citizen access to social provisions (i.e., health)[54] — interculturalism attempts to strike a balance between individual rights and cultural relativism by emphasizing a "fusion of horizons," through dialogue and consensual agreement. Through the participation and discourse of all groups in the public sphere, the goal of this approach is to achieve the largest possible consensus regarding the limits and possibilities of the expression of collective identitive differences, weighed against the requirements of social cohesion and individual rights in a common public context. The recognition of cultural differences is assumed in such a view — the sources of meaning accrued from cultural identity are acknowledged as an explicit feature of citizen empowerment — yet an obligation is placed on all parties to contribute to the basic tenets of a common public culture.

ASSESSING THE MODELS

As aforementioned, two general considerations are salient in assessing the models as they pertain to polyethnicity and democratic citizenship. First, the model must consider unity as a basis for democratic stability — which provides a shared sentiment — a common ground for dialogue. In other words, a pole of allegiance which acts as an identity centre of convergence is required for active participation in a democratic polity. Second, the recognition of difference and a respect for the sources of meaning of minority cultures are integral elements of both the equality of citizenship status — of citizen dignity or empowerment. For traditional liberal thought, such goals are incompatible. The involvement of group-differentiated recognition is said to mitigate the former ideal, in which equality emanates from shared adherence to universal principles and culture is treated with benign neglect in the public sphere. Recognizing cultural distinctions shatters such unity and renders citizens unequal.

Returning to the normative backdrop for evaluating integration as developed above, it is clear that the Canadian strategy was related to both the goal of unity and the fostering of citizen dignity through the recognition of particular cultural affiliations. First, it seeks to achieve unity through a pan-Canadian nation-building project that emphasizes the primacy of individual rights in a constitutional *Charter of Rights and Freedoms* and a choice of language use, between French or English, across the country. Superimposed on individual rights is the official recognition of all constituent cultures, equally. Such recognition, however, is largely a symbolic concession, the fabrication of an identitive marker based on the voluntary adherence to particular cultural allegiances. In Weinfeld's words:

> In the absence of any consensus on the substance of Canadian identity or culture, multiculturalism fills a void, defining Canadian culture in terms of the legitimate ancestral cultures which are the legacy of every Canadian: defining the whole through the sum of its parts.[55]

While forging a common identity throughout the country based on the "sum of its parts," it was hoped that the identity marker for unity could be universal — the equal recognition of all cultures, within a regime governed by individual rights and bilingualism. In this way, adherence to particular cultural attachments could be voluntary for all *individuals*, while at the same time claiming to "empower" citizens of minority cultures through reductionist means. Canada's symbolic order was to be based on the negation of any particular cultural definition. Bourque and Duchastel argue that the Canadian response, by conceptualizing citizenship in such terms, has in effect altered social relations to the point of damaging the exercise of democracy. The Canadian political community in this sense is predicated on the judicialization of social interactions, to the detriment of the deliberative aspects of representative democracy. The idea of public space for citizen participation, reflection and deliberation within the political community is reduced to a narrow forum of rights-bearers. Deliberative assemblies give way to the "legalization" of social relations, preventing parliaments from being responsible for organizing social life and, ultimately, preventing citizens from identifying with others in the political community.[56]

According to Kymlicka, the final outcome of multiculturalism as a symbol for identification in Canada is analogous to the United States in its failure to differentiate between national minorities and polyethnic communities. The fundamental difference between the two is that the former seek self-determination while the latter seek inclusion. Canada's policy fails to address this distinction, and multiculturalism becomes a mechanism by which to quell legitimate national aspirations. Thus it fundamentally shares with the US model a certain homogenization, or universalization of identity, albeit through cultural relativism. Kymlicka argues that the American reluctance to recognize minority nations is a direct result of its assimilationist model, a fear that such recognition will trickle down to polyethnic communities and thus undermine the bases for unity.[57] Canada's policy stems from similar fears. However, Canada's response was to elevate the status of cultural groups to the same level as that of national minorities. Both are universal, both are bound by nation-building projects that stress unity, and both fail in any significant way to recognize group-differentiated rights as a federal principle.[58]

As such, the Canadian response was not predicated on a genuine commitment to the "ideology of multiculturalism" as a pillar upon which to frame citizenship status. The goal was unity in the face of a national minority challenge. Quebec's national identity was placed, constitutionally, alongside every other minority culture as a basis for identification.[59] In Giroux's words:

> The partial recognition of ancestral rights reveals, *a contrario*, a refusal to recognize the Quebec nation.... As such, demands by national minorities, those of cultural communities, and those of the majority group are regarded, without being defined or explicitly taking into consideration the criteria of legitimacy attributed to a nation which allow for a viable and effective democratic order....
> In effect, without valid criteria for inclusion and exclusion, all demands become acceptable; thus it becomes possible to pit group demands against one another and to transform pluralism into a zero-sum game.[60]

In Taylor's terms, multiculturalism as such fails to appreciate the "deep diversity" in Canada, in which difference can be recognized on tiered levels in view of particular groupings' political aspirations and historical/territorial/linguistic realities. In adopting a strategy for unity similar to the American approach — uniformity from coast to coast based on universal principles — the Canadian policy in effect failed to recognize that national minorities, as opposed to polyethnic communities, seek to provide a "centre" for identification, their own pole of allegiance necessary for unity and common purpose. In other words, national identity in Quebec assumes a self-determining project for society. The community of reference for all citizens under the banner of multiculturalism, however, is Canada. Bourque *et al.* summarize:

> This ideology ... defines itself in relation to the territorial state: it circumscribes a community of belonging to the state within a country — Canada. It thus privileges, clearly, national dimensions of the production of the community, even though the discourse struggles to find a coherent representation of the Canadian nation. This Canadian nationalism finds its full significance in its opposition to the "counter-nationalisms" of Quebec and the Aboriginals.[61]

The arguments put forth above are predicated on the notion that Canada's similarity to the United States flows from the implicit assumption that equality stems from an emphasis on the individual, and what such individuals share with others across the country. The Canadian constitution essentially protects individuals from collective intrusions. It can be argued that the failure to achieve unity and common purpose is not inherent in the model of multiculturalism adopted. Rather, disunity is a product of federal dynamics, Canada is not a nation-state that can claim the status of a single and unified host society. As such, we can assess the policy independently of the Quebec question which, to a large extent, may explain the motivation for the policy but not its actual effects as a model for integration. If we disregard the variable of multinationality in Canada, has multiculturalism been successful in integrating immigrants and ethnic groups? Indeed, if we begin with the assumption that Canada constitutes a single political community, or host society, we can then proceed to evaluate the success of multiculturalism without considering disunity in terms of the fragmentation of "national allegiance." Unity can thus be conceptualized as the extent to which minority groups feel as though they belong to a single community called Canada and actually participate in the general affairs of the larger society.

As a response to critics who view multiculturalism as a divisive force in Canada, Kymlicka provides some empirical data which demonstrate the success of multiculturalism in terms of the integration of minority cultures.[62] Indeed, the line of criticism in this chapter does not challenge the integrative success of the policy. The claim is that due to the imperatives of nation-building, for the purposes of unity in the face of the Quebec question, Canada chose to adopt a "lowest common denominator" formula that rejected the recognition of culture as an aspect of belonging altogether. Again, Trudeau's "just society" is predicated on the notion that any emotive attachment to a polity is destructive and backward, and that progress requires an emphasis on reason, which is universal, to serve as a guiding principle in any citizenship regime. If we look closely at Kymlicka's indicators for integration, however, it may be argued that although integration has been rather successful, it came at the expense of the recognition and preservation of minority cultures, which in the final analysis is the defining feature of ideological multiculturalism. Does the Canadian model provide genuine space for ascriptively defined groups, and not merely individuals, to make their mark on the general directions and values of the larger society? Has the imperative of integration and pan-Canadian universality rendered the country "multicultural" in name only?

The Canadian model operates along the primacy of individual rights in a constitutional *Charter of Rights and Freedoms*, with an interpretive clause for the recognition of diverse cultural affiliations. The interpretive clause is the only element different from American assimilation. There is no democratic imperative for the recognition of diverse minority cultures besides a legal/ procedural provision that may be invoked if the minority group in question chooses to do so. This is a key conceptual distinction between the Canadian and Quebec models and it stems from the nature of the expectations of democracy itself. The fact that Canadian identity — the way citizens relate to each other and to the state in determining societal preferences — is predicated on such terms implies that there is no public culture on which minority cultures can make their mark. Again, multiculturalism in Canada does not reflect the recognition of diverse cultures; rather, to be blunt, it refers to the denial of culture altogether in defining the limits and confines of public space. Public space is based on individual participation via a Bill of Rights.

To return to Kymlicka's data on the success of Canadian multiculturalism in terms of integration, we note a dearth of evidence regarding the extent to which minority cultures feel as though they have been able to persist in living according to the sources of meaning garnered by their cultural affiliations. To his defence, this endeavour would require a large-scale empirical study, and the fact that he was able to successfully operationalize "integration" merits credit in its own right, as it deepens the conceptual discourse surrounding these models of integration. However, the success of minority groups within indicators such as "naturalization rates"; "political participation," including the institutional avenues of participation; "official language competence"; "intermarriage rates" and lack of territorial enclaves of cultural groups[63] are addressed to those critics who view multiculturalism as divisive to the forging of a strong Canadian identity. They do not speak to the explicit concern for the preservation and flourishing of minority cultures within the political community — the capacity of such groups to participate and affect the public affairs of the country without shedding their particular group identities. The debate itself thus takes place outside the imperatives of ideological multiculturalism. In other words, these criteria may very well be addressing a regime committed to assimilation.

The virtue of Quebec's model of interculturalism is that it strikes a balance between the requirements of unity — an identity centre — and the recognition of minority cultures. Quebec's model of integration is not assimilatory as is that of the US, nor does it conceptually fall into cultural relativism and fragmentation in its commitment to cultural pluralism. The idea of empowerment as it pertains to marginalized ethno-cultural groups is such that integration is a necessary prerequisite to participate fully in the construction of a "common public culture" as an identity centre. Identification with and participation through a variety of cultures is not ruled out as a basis for citizenship status, yet the possibility of enclosure and ghettoization is discouraged because the recognition of particular cultural identities is *de facto* the *recognition of the right and obligation to participate* in the polity, not the recognition of culture as existing in self-contained communities, in a vacuum of space and time. In other words, recognition is an *outcome* of participation; it is in contributing to the development of a common public culture, to larger consensual bases of allegiance and identification, without a rejection of the established symbolic order offered by Quebec society as it has evolved historically, that members of minority cultural groups can make a difference regarding their status as citizens.

Indeed, as a response to critics who view the legal imposition of French on individuals as an affront to liberal principles of individual rights over society, Joseph Carens turns to this participatory aspect of the model to defend the liberal-democratic merits of the Quebec model. In his words:

> The duty to learn French is intimately connected to the duty to contribute and to participate in society, which is connected, on this account, to fundamental democratic principles. Learning French is, among other things, a necessary means to participation in society so that if one can defend the duty to participate, and I think one can, one can defend the duty to learn French.[64]

In the final analysis, the recognition of minority cultures is built into the model; the "moral contract" is an integrative principle whereby ethnocultural groups are given the empowerment to contribute, in a common language, and to make their mark on the basic principles of the common public culture. Harvey summarizes the model of interculturalism as:

> the conservation of a language of origin, a history other than that of the receiving country, the preservation of distinct familial, religious and social commitments, the establishment of welcoming groups to help in the integration of those arriving from the same country, the continuity of relations with the country of origin, are all accepted, welcome, and enriching for the host society. *All of this is also in the domain of negotiation, of active reciprocal tolerance, involving an evolution with the passing of time* ... Intercultural pluralism is the domain ... in which a host country can and also must encourage originality in the ways of life of those arriving. Sensibilities, aesthetics, and models of belonging and association can remain identical to those within the cultural structures of the countries of origin. Pride in cultural origins must be permitted ... except in the case of contradiction with the common public culture.[65] (our translation)

Difference is recognized within the limits of societal cohesion and political community, not as a *fundamental starting point* for common identification and unity. In short, the Quebec model satisfies the challenge for models of cultural pluralism that Paquet highlights below:

> Citizenship has become a crucible in which a *new identity* is always in the process of being forged, when it becomes understood that any identity or citizenship is always in transition, and therefore *intégration sans assimilation* becomes a concept that is not an oxymoron.... In that sense, citizenship conditions may be negotiated in a manner that would recognize both the *diversity* of the social fabric and the need for some *unifying* concept to provide a linking force.... The notion of citizenship would recognize the patchwork quilt social fabric without losing sight of the need to channel the energy of this varied group into a well-defined direction.[66]

Interculturalism as a model for addressing polyethnicity represents a forum for citizen empowerment, not retrenchment. From the initial premise that a national culture consists of a "daily plebiscite," in Renan's conceptualization, the Quebec model rests on the idea that the common public culture be inclusive of all groups in its changing and evolutionary fabric. Jeremy Webber has located this dynamic aspect of a national identity in the idea that communities are forged through public debates in a common language through time. Shared values in themselves do not provide the sense of allegiance necessary for a national collectivity to thrive. Indeed, disagreements about the major orientations of society are perhaps emblematic of a healthy political community because they demonstrate that people are concerned with the state of the community. The democratic quality of a constantly changing political community lies precisely in the idea that citizens are able to identify with and impact on the current streams of public debate in society, and this requires that citizens interact within the framework of a common vernacular.[67] In short, Carens states it succinctly: "In integrating immigrants, Quebec is transforming not only their identity but its own as well."[68] As such, the French language is not meant to define a static culture into which immigrants and cultural minorities are expected to "melt." Rather, French is the conduit through which the disagreements, contentions, and conflicts inherent in a culturally diverse society can be aired in a situation of normal politics. In the end, participation implies some degree of political conflict. In the Quebec model this attribute of a national identity is explicitly acknowledged; everybody is given the means by which to identify with and impact on the public debates of the day. The political community is based on a shared language, and challenges to the prevailing tenets of the "national culture" are not viewed as threatening, but are encouraged as a normal and healthy effect of democratic deliberation.

This discussion is not meant as a radical argument for post-national identity politics, indeed, the normative merits of unity in any given state have been explicitly acknowledged. Nor is it meant to prescribe a formula for unity in a specifically federal context. It merely seeks to demonstrate that Canadian multiculturalism has been and continues to be a product of nation-building efforts, and not a genuine commitment to the main tenets of ideological multiculturalism. In other words, it continues to be an element of a political strategy by the central state to forge a strong commitment, by its citizens, to Canada as a single and unified political community. Canadian multiculturalism should not be viewed as an example of the emerging ideology of multiculturalism and its implications for the redefinition of the legitimacy of nation-states in the case of polyethnic societies. The main tenets of Canadian citizenship status are not that far off from those of the United States. This is reminiscent of a statement by Joppke in looking at the effects of multiculturalism in the real world:

> liberal states are reluctant to impose particular cultural forms on its [sic] members, aside from a procedural commitment to basic civic rules.... There is a widely held sense that forced assimilation or acculturation violates the integrity and dignity of the individual, whose cultural habits should be a matter of his or her choice alone. To a certain degree, liberal states today are necessarily multicultural.[69]

Indeed, the place of culture in Canadian conceptions of citizenship is liberal, it is about building a nation based on universal principles. A model of cultural pluralism along the lines of Quebec interculturalism, we argue, makes a more serious effort to balance the prerogatives of unity with the preservation and flourishing of minority cultures. The enduring problem confronting the Quebec model, one that would have to be taken into account in any future attempts at empirical verification, is the idea of competing interpretations of citizenship by those targeted for integration in the first place. As Labelle and Levy have demonstrated in interviews with leaders of ethnocultural groups, there is ongoing ambivalence with regards to the legitimacy of the Quebec model in the eyes of ethnocultural groups. Any initiative by the Quebec state is often interpreted as a secessionist ploy, or a denial of Canadian space, to which allophones largely adhere. One leader put it succinctly:

> We emigrate to Canada, Canada grants us citizenship, Canada is a land of refuge and reception, Canada is hegemonic in its immigration policies; [and] Quebecers of French-Canadian origin themselves suffer from ambivalence and share a double-reference — they define themselves ... as a national minority, as an ethnic group, or as a Québécois majority and they themselves practice identity exclusion, reserving for themselves *Quebecness*.[70]

The Quebec model is unlike the others in that it is embedded in a larger struggle for national affirmation. The fact that it can legitimately be included as a model for integration at the very least demonstrates the strides that Quebec has made in the area of citizenship, and it is hoped that such conceptual overviews can spark some interest in more empirically-based research in the future. Whether or not such research can be undertaken in a context of competing models of citizenship, within a single territory, should not undermine efforts to include conceptually the model of interculturalism in debates about recognition and integration in liberal democracies.

NOTES

We wish to thank Will Kymlicka, Harvey Lazar, Douglas Brown, and the two anonymous referees for their thoughtful comments.

1. V. Seymour Wilson, "The Tapestry Vision of Canadian Multiculturalism," *Canadian Journal of Political Science* 26,4 (1993):653.

2. Kymlicka and Norman note that citizens' perceptions about their political communities, their sense of belonging and level of commitment, have become an increasingly salient concern for contemporary political theorists, and that this is partly due to the challenge of integrating minority groups in established liberal democracies. In their words, "the health and stability of a modern democracy depends, not only on the justice of its institutions, but also on the qualities and attitudes of its citizens: e.g. their sense of identity, and how they view potentially competing forms of national, regional, ethnic or religious identities; their ability to tolerate and work together with others who are different from themselves; their desire to participate in the political process in order to promote the public good and hold political authorities accountable; ... Without citizens who possess these qualities, the ability of liberal societies to function successfully progressively diminishes." Will Kymlicka and Wayne Norman, eds., *Citizenship in Diverse Societies* (Oxford: Oxford University Press, 2000), p. 6.

3. Kas Mazurek, quoted in Vince Seymour Wilson, "Canada's Evolving Multiculturalism Policy," in *Canada's Century: Governance in a Maturing Society*, ed. C.E.S. Franks *et al.* (Montreal: McGill-Queen's University Press, 1995), p. 165.

4. Noreen Golfman, "Locating Difference: Ways of Reading Multiculturalism," *Mosaic* 29, 3 (1996):175.

5. Marek Debicki, "The Double Mythology of Multiculturalism in Canada," in *Twenty Years of Multiculturalism: Successes and Failures*, ed. Stella Hryniuk (Winnipeg: St. John's College Press, 1992), p. 29.

6. Danielle Juteau, "Citoyenneté, intégration et multiculturalisme canadien," in *Dual Images: Multiculturalism on Two Sides of the Atlantic*, The Royal Academy of Canada and the Institute for Political Science of the Hungarian Academy of Sciences (Budapest, 1996), pp. 173-74.

7. Wilson, "The Tapestry Vision of Canadian Multiculturalism," p. 654.

8. Alain-G. Gagnon, "Plaidoyer pour une commission nationale sur la citoyenneté québécoise," *Le Devoir,* 15 June 2001, p. A-7.

9. François Rocher and Micheline Labelle, "De la légitimité d'une loi fondamentale québécoise: La citoyenneté et l'unité canadienne," *Le Devoir,* 20 June 2001.

10. Will Kymlicka, *Multicultural Citizenship: A Liberal Theory of Minority Rights* (New York: Oxford University Press, 1995), p. 193.

11. Christian Joppke, "Multiculturalism and Immigration: A Comparison of the United States, Germany and Great Britain," *Theory and Society* 25(1996):449.

12. Ibid., p. 452.

13. Iris Marion Young, *Inclusion and Democracy* (Oxford: Oxford University Press, 2000), p. 7.

14. For more on multiculturalism's challenge to liberal models of citizenship, see Andrea Semprini, *Le multiculturalisme* (Paris: Presses universitaires de France, 1997).

15. Young, *Inclusion and Democracy,* See in particular ch. 3, where Young offers a review of arguments which "construct group specific justice claims as an assertion of group identity, and argue that the claims endanger democratic communication because they only divide the polity into selfish interest groups," p. 83.

16. Kymlicka, *Multicultural Citizenship*, pp. 174-75.

17. W.W. Isajiw, "Social Evolution and the Values of Multiculturalism." Paper presented at the Ninth Biennial Conference of the Canadian Ethnic Studies Association, Edmonton, Alberta, 14-17 October 1981, cited in Evelyn Kallen, "Multiculturalism: Ideology, Policy and Reality," *Journal of Canadian Studies* 17, 1 (1982):52.

18. Charles Taylor, "The Politics of Recognition," in *Multiculturalism: Examining the Politics of Recognition*, ed. Amy Gutman (Princeton, NJ: Princeton University Press, 1994), p. 25.

19. Joppke, "Multiculturalism and Immigration," p. 454. Joppke compares Germany, Great Britain and the United States.

20. John J. Miller, *The Unmaking of Americans: How Multiculturalism has Undermined the Assimilation Ethic* (New York: The Free Press, 1998), p. 24.

21. Stanley M. Katz, "The Legal Framework of American Pluralism," in *Beyond Pluralism: The Conception of Groups and Group Identities in America*, ed. Wendy F. Katkin, Ned Landsman and Andrea Tyree (Chicago: University of Illinois Press, 1998), p. 12.

22. Ibid., p. 14.

23. Ibid., p. 15.

24. See, for example, Arthur M. Schlesinger, Jr., *The Disuniting of America* (New York: W.W. Norton and Company, 1998); Dinesh D'Souza, *The End of Racism: Principles for a Multiracial Society* (New York: Free Press, 1995); Alvin J. Schmidt, *The Menace of Multiculturalism: Trojan Horse in America* (Westport, CT: Praeger Publishers, 1997); and Miller, *The Unmaking of Americans.*

25. Nathan Glazer (1983 and 1978), quoted in Will Kymlicka, "Ethnicity in the USA," in *The Ethnicity Reader: Nationalism, Multiculturalism and Migration*, ed. Montserrat Guibernau and John Rex (Cambridge: Polity Press, 1997), p. 243.

26. Schlesinger, Jr., *The Disuniting of America*, p. 17.

27. Jürgen Habermas, *Écrits politiques* (Paris: Cerf, 1990).

28. For more on the historical significance of the "third element" in the enactment of formal multiculturalism in Canada, see Robert F. Harney, "So Great a Heritage as Ours: Immigration and the Survival of the Canadian Polity," *Daedalus* 117 (1988):51-97.

29. Yasmeen Abu-Laban, "The Politics of Race, Ethnicity and Immigration: The Contested Arena of Multiculturalism into the Twenty-First Century," in *Canadian Politics*, 3d ed., ed. James P. Bickerton and Alain-G. Gagnon (Peterborough: Broadview Press, 1999), p. 465.

30. Raymond Breton, "Multiculturalism and Canadian Nation-Building," in *The Politics of Gender, Ethnicity and Language in Canada*, ed. Alan C. Cairns and Cynthia Williams (Toronto: University of Toronto Press, 1986), p. 48.

31. Harney, "So Great a Heritage as Ours," p. 69.

32. Pierre Elliott Trudeau (1971), cited in Linda Cardinal and Claude Couture, "L'immigration et le multiculturalisme au Canada: la genèse d'une problématique," in *Les politiques publiques canadiennes*, ed. Manon Tremblay (Sainte-Foy: Les Presses de l'Université Laval, 1998), pp. 249-50. According to Kas Mazurek, Trudeau's motivation for multiculturalism within a bilingual framework was not motivated by a genuine commitment to the flourishing and preservation of minority cultures. Rather, it was part of Trudeau's vision for Canada based on his conception of a "just society," in which attachment to the country for all Canadians was to be established on reason and fair socio-economic opportunity, not emotional ties to any particular ethnic group. Mazurek, "Canada's Evolving Multiculturalism Policy," p. 20. For more on Trudeau's ideological inclinations and the "just society," see Michael Behiels, *Prelude to Quebec's Quiet Revolution: Liberalism vs. Neo-Nationalism, 1945-1960* (Montreal: McGill-Queen's University Press, 1985).

33. Kallen, "Multiculturalism," p. 54.

34. *House of Commons Debates*, 8 October 1971. Statement of Prime Minister Trudeau.

35. Abu-Laban, "The Politics of Race, Ethnicity and Immigration," p. 12.

36. Cardinal and Couture, "L'immigration et le multiculturalisme au Canada," p. 251.

37. Abu-Laban, "The Politics of Race, Ethnicity and Immigration," p. 13.

38. Wilson, "The Tapestry Vision of Canadian Multiculturalism," p. 657.

39. Rainer Knopff and F.L. Morton, *Charter Politics* (Scarborough: Nelson Canada, 1991), p. 88.

40. Will Kymlicka, *Théories récentes sur la citoyenneté* (Ottawa: Multiculturalism and Citizenship Canada, 1992), p. 40, quoted in Micheline Labelle, *Immigration et diversité ethnoculturelle: Les politiques québécoises*, Cahiers du Programme d'études sur le Québec, McGill University, No. 13 (September 1998), p. 13.

41. The Couture-Cullen Agreement, signed in 1978, would grant extensive powers in recruitment and reception to the Quebec government.

42. Michael D. Behiels, *Quebec and the Question of Immigration: From Ethnocentrism to Ethnic Pluralism, 1900-1958* (Ottawa: Canadian Historical Association, 1991).

43. Marcel Gilbert, *Autant de façons d'être Québécois. Plan d'action à l'intention des communautés culturelles* (Quebec: Ministry of Communications, Direction générale des publications gouvernementales, 1981).

44. For more on the conceptualization of the principles of the "common public culture" as it is understood in Quebec, see Julien Harvey, "Culture publique, intégration et pluralisme," in *Relations* (October 1991); and Gary Caldwell, "Immigration et la nécessité d'une culture publique commune," in *L'Action Nationale* 78, 8 (1988).

45. Gouvernement du Québec, *Au Québec pour bâtir ensemble. Énoncé de politique en matière d'immigration et d'intégration* (Quebec: Ministère des Communautés culturelles et de l'Immigration du Québec, Direction des communications, 1990), p. 15.

46. Gouvernement du Québec, Conseil des relations interculturelles, "Culture publique commune et cohésion sociale: le contrat moral d'intégration des immigrants dans un Québec francophone, démocratique et pluraliste," in *Gérer la diversité dans un Québec francophone, démocratique et pluraliste: principes de fond pour guider la recherche d'accommodements raisonnables* (1994), p. 11.

47. Joseph H. Carens, *Culture, Citizenship and Community: A Contextual Exploration of Justice and Evenhandedness* (Oxford: Oxford University Press, 2000), p. 131.

48. François Rocher, Guy Rocher and Micheline Labelle, "Pluriethnicité, citoyenneté et intégration: de la souveraineté pour lever les obstacles et les ambiguïtés," *Cahiers de recherche sociologique* 25 (1995):221.

49. Ibid., p. 225.

50. France Giroux, "Le nouveau contrat national est-il possible dans une démocratie pluraliste? Examen comparatif des situations française, canadienne et québécoise," *Politique et Societés* 16, 3 (1997):137.

51. Gouvernement du Québec (1990), *Au Québec pour bâtir ensemble*, p. 13.

52. Harvey, "Culture publique, intégration et pluralisme," "Intégration dit contact culturel intermédiaire entre l'assimilation et la juxtaposition, tenant compte des deux cultures en contact et constituant une nouvelle synthèse et une nouvelle dynamique," p. 239.

53. Michel Pagé, "Intégration, identité ethnique et cohésion sociale," *Pluriethnicité et société: construire un espace commun*, ed. Ouellet and Pagé (Québec: Institut québécois de recherche sur la culture (IQRC), 1991), pp. 146-47. (Our emphasis).

54. Gouvernement du Québec, *La gestion de la diversité et l'accommodement raisonnable* (Montreal: Ministère des Communautés Culturelles et de

l'Immigration, 1993), quoted in Rocher *et al.*, "Pluriethnicité, citoyenneté et intégration," p. 225.

55.   Morton Weinfeld, "Myth and Reality in the Canadian Mosaic: 'Affective Ethnicity,' " *Canadian Ethnic Studies* 13 (1981):94.

56.   Gilles Bourque and Jules Duchastel, "Multiculturalisme, pluralisme et communauté politique: le Canada et le Québec," in *Mondialisation, Citoyenneté et Multiculturalisme*, ed. Mikhaël Elbaz and Denise Helly (Sainte-Foy : Les Presses de l'Université Laval, 2000).

57.   Kymlicka, "Ethnicity in the USA," p. 240. See also Bourque and Duchastel, "Multiculturalism," p. 159, where the authors argue that Canadian multiculturalism is in large part a product of the refusal that the country be defined in multinational terms. The Canadian political community was thus in itself founded on this negation of multinationality precisely because of the perceived imperative to negate Quebec's place as a "national minority."

58.   For more on the distinction between national minorities and polyethnic communities in the framing of citizenship status, see Gilles Paquet; "Political Philosophy of Multiculturalism," in *Ethnicity and Culture in Canada*, ed. J.W. Berry and J.A. Laponce (Toronto: University of Toronto Press, 1994), pp. 60-79.

59.   For more on the idea that official multiculturalism represents a wholesale redefinition of Canada's constitutional order in terms of collective identity references, see Fernand Dumont, "La fin d'un malentendu historique," in *Raisons Communes* (Montréal: Boréal, 1995), pp. 33-48; and Gilles Bourque and Jules Duchastel, "La représentation de la communauté," in *L'identité fragmentée* (Montréal: Éditions Fides, 1996), pp. 29-51.

60.   Giroux, "Le nouveau contrat national est-il possible dans une démocratie pluraliste?" p. 141.

61.   Gilles Bourque, Jules Duchastel and Victor Armony, "De l'universalisme au particularisme: droits et citoyenneté," in *L'Amour des Lois*, ed. Josiane Ayoub, Bjarne Melkevik and Pierre Robert (Sainte-Foy/Paris: Presses de l'Université Laval/l'Harmattan, 1996), p. 240.

62.   Kymlicka's work is mainly directed toward the contentions of Neil Bissoondath. Bissoondath argues that in the Canadian model minority cultures are recognized, *a priori*, in a vacuum of space and time, which tend towards ghettoization and fragmentation in terms of allegiance to a larger polity. Bissoondath develops this point forcefully, labelling the phenomenon "cultural apartheid." The contention here is that multiculturalism in effect defines culture provisionally — in a static sense — and prohibits full social interactivity. In other words, the dynamic nature of cultural sources of meaning are neglected, resulting in the stagnant "folklorization" or "commodification" of cultural production, reducing culture to "a thing that can be displayed, performed, admired, bought, sold or forgotten ... [it is] a devaluation of culture, its reduction to bauble and kitsch." As such, neither unity nor citizen dignity accrued from cultural recognition is achieved here. This is the result of recognizing cultures in juxtaposition without any expectation that such cultures may contribute to the overall direction of the

larger society in an evolutionary interplay of ideas. The substantive elements of minority cultures — their bases of meaning — are virtually pre-determined and unchanging, disregarding the very real effects of displacement into a new context. See Will Kymlicka, *Finding Our Way: Rethinking Ethnocultural Relations in Canada* (Toronto: Oxford University Press, 1998); and Neil Bissoondath, *Selling Illusions: The Cult of Multiculturalism in Canada* (Toronto: Penguin Books, 1994), p. 83.

63. Kymlicka, *Finding Our Way*, pp. 17-19.

64. Joseph H. Carens, *Culture, Citizenship and Community*, p. 128.

65. Harvey, "Culture publique, intégration et pluralisme," p. 241. (Our emphasis.)

66. Paquet, "Political Philosophy of Multiculturalism," p. 74.

67. Jeremy Webber, *Reimagining Canada: Language, Culture, Community and the Canadian Constitution* (Montreal: McGill-Queen's University Press, 1994). See in particular Chapter 6, "Language, Culture and Political Community," pp. 183-229.

68. Carens, *Culture, Citizenship and Community*, p. 133.

69. Joppke,"Multiculturalism and Immigration," p. 454.

70. Labelle, *Immigration et diversité ethnoculturelle*, p. 14.

14

Communities in Conflict: Nova Scotia after the *Marshall* Decision

Ian Stewart

Le 17 septembre 1999, la Cour suprême du Canada a acquitté Donald Marshall Jr. des charges de pêche et de vente d'anguilles sans permis qui pesaient sur lui. Selon la cour, Marshall était protégé par les termes du Traité de Paix et d'Amitié de 1760 passé entre la couronne britannique et les Micmacs. À court terme, la décision Marshall a provoqué de nombreuses confrontations entre les pêcheurs autochtones et non-autochtones. À long terme, on peut douter que la communauté non-autochtone réponde favorablement aux plaintes autochtones actuelles. Premièrement, il y a désaccord à propos de l'origine de ce droit autochtone de pêche et par conséquent, de sa pertinence. Deuxièmement, il y a une réticence croissante dans la communauté non-autochtone d'accepter cette sorte de droit particulier réclamé par plusieurs porte-parole micmacs. Troisièmement, il y a un même niveau d'aversion chez les non-autochtones à reconnaître des droits collectifs en opposition à des droits individuels. Finalement, la relative rareté des ressources qui peuvent être récoltées érafle le mince vernis de bonne volonté non-autochtone envers les Micmacs de la Nouvelle-Écosse.

Twice in his lifetime, Donald Marshall, Jr. has come to symbolize the contradictions which exist between Nova Scotia's Aboriginal and non-Aboriginal populations. The details of the first of these are familiar to most Canadians. In 1971, Marshall, a young Mi'kmaq from Cape Breton, was wrongfully convicted of murder and served 11 years behind bars before his innocence was established. Under some pressure, John Buchanan's Progressive Conservative government appointed a Royal Commission to account for this miscarriage of justice. The commission's report, released in January 1990, was scathing. Noting that "the criminal justice system failed Donald Marshall, Jr. at virtually every turn,"[1] that, by contrast, senior Cabinet ministers Billy Joe MacLean and Rollie Thornhill had seemingly received preferential treatment under the law, the commissioners recommended sweeping alterations to the administration of justice in Nova Scotia. To its credit, the provincial government enacted most of the changes sought by the commission; the goal, as articulated by then Attorney General Joel Matheson, was "to ensure that all Nova Scotians receive fair and equal treatment before the law."[2] Of course not all Royal Commissions are acted upon so promptly. In this instance, however, it was clear that their recommendations coincided with the dominant understanding of justice in Nova Scotia, one in which, as implied by Attorney General Matheson, "fairness" and "equality" were regarded as essentially synonymous.

Within a decade, Donald Marshall, Jr. was once again the central figure in a court case with profound implications for the Aboriginal and non-Aboriginal peoples of Nova Scotia. On this occasion, his alleged offense was less severe; Marshall had been charged (and, initially, convicted) with fishing eels out of season and selling his catch without a licence. Ultimately, Marshall's conviction was quashed by the Supreme Court of Canada who ruled, by a 5 to 2 majority, that his actions were sanctioned under eighteenth-century treaties signed between the Mi'kmaq and the British Crown. I will explore some of the implications of this decision later in the chapter. It is important to emphasize at the outset, however, that the outcome of the second Marshall case represents a more fundamental challenge to Nova Scotia's non-Aboriginals than did the first. At issue is whether the overwhelming proportion of Nova Scotians can accept a conception of justice in which fairness is best served by difference, rather than equality.[3] Ultimately, I conclude that, notwithstanding the decisions of the Supreme Court, it will be difficult for non-natives to countenance a special and collective Aboriginal right to fish.

It seems fair to say that the Mi'kmaq have struggled, almost since the first contact with Europeans, to find an appropriate niche in Nova Scotia society. Admittedly, the provincial coat of arms gives a Mi'kmaq brave equal prominence with the royal unicorn. The provincial motto of "Munit Haec et Altera Vincit," however, can be loosely translated as "One defends and the other conquers," and there can be little confusion about which is which.[4] For almost a hundred years prior to the mid-eighteenth century, the British and the French were at war more often than not. In the Nova Scotia theatre, the Mi'kmaq were typically allies of the latter, having been not only early converts to Roman Catholicism, but also the recipients of the more generous French approach to gift-giving.[5] Only with the final defeat of the French in North America were the British also able to exercise dominance over the Mi'kmaq, and a series of treaties was drawn up to formalize this arrangement. Thereafter, the decline of the Mi'kmaq was precipitous. One observer notes that by 1783, "the Indians (of Nova Scotia) were to be feared no longer, courted no more. They had been transformed from dreaded warriors into dispossessed wanderers within a single generation."[6] Although the Mi'kmaq had been pushed off their traditional hunting lands and ravaged by imported diseases, a penurious colonial administration provided only enough relief funds to avoid outright starvation, and attempts to establish Mi'kmaq farming communities invariably foundered on the insouciant defiance of European squatters.

By the mid-nineteenth century, a system of Mi'kmaq reserves had been established, and the sharp decline in population (from an estimated high of 100,000 to less than a tenth of that figure)[7] had been arrested. Since Confederation, the number of Nova Scotia Mi'kmaq has edged steadily upward; the provincial Aboriginal Affairs office reports that, as of 1998, there were 11,748 registered Mi'kmaq in Nova Scotia (of which approximately one-third lived off reserve).[8] Given that this figure constitutes just over 1 percent of the Nova Scotia population and given, as well, that the principal legislative competence over Aboriginal peoples resides in Ottawa, it is not surprising that the Mi'kmaq voice has seldom been heard in provincial politics. Admittedly, Nova Scotia enfranchised its Aboriginal voters prior to World War II (well before any other jurisdiction in the country);[9] however, the province has never had a Mi'kmaq member of the Legislative Assembly, and internecine squabbling between bands in Cape Breton and the mainland has hamstrung any attempts to institute special Aboriginal representation at Province House.

Accompanying this political marginalization has been a disquieting level of socio-economic deprivation. Most Canadians are familiar with the depressing litany of social ills that pervade many Aboriginal communities: few opportunities for economic advancement, high levels of substance abuse, and the like. Unfortunately, the Nova Scotia Mi'kmaq do not deviate markedly from this general pattern. In December 1999, for example, the Membertou band made national headlines when it was revealed that four boys between the ages of nine and thirteen had attempted a multiple suicide.[10] Accompanying such social anomie has typically been an entrenched economic malaise. One study from the late 1970s discovered that 72 out of 80 families in Nova Scotia's second largest reserve collected welfare at some point in the year;[11] a second revealed that less than one-quarter of adult Mi'kmaq enjoy regular employment,[12] and more recent studies have been scarcely more encouraging.[13] Much of the reaction to the *Marshall* Decision, from both Aboriginals and non-Aboriginals alike, must be understood in the context of this endemic socio-economic distress.

That the Supreme Court would uphold Donald Marshall, Jr.'s Aboriginal rights should not, in retrospect, have been particularly surprising. Admittedly, the decision seemed to catch the federal government offguard, despite warnings of potential trouble from both the RCMP and CSIS well in advance of the ruling. Somewhat defensively, Indian Affairs Minister Bob Nault acknowledged that it's "always possible that we could be better prepared, but how far can you go with this when in fact the courts have been unpredictable up to now."[14] To be fair, the ruling may also have surprised Nova Scotia's Mi'kmaq community. As Chief Frank Meuse, Jr. of the Bear River First Nation put it: "The DFO didn't have a contingency plan, but then again neither did we."[15]

In fact, the Supreme Court has not been especially "unpredictable" in its rulings on Aboriginal matters. On the contrary, it is possible to detect a growing judicial sympathy for Aboriginal rights. Under the principle of *stare decisis*, one might have expected the Supreme Court to adhere to the 1888 decision of the Judicial Committee of the Privy Council in the *St. Catherines Milling* case. With that ruling, the Aboriginal link to the land was adjudged to be usufructory, rather than an instance of ownership; full title, therefore, rested with the Crown. It was not until 1973 that the Supreme Court revisited and revised this understanding. In the *Calder* case, six of seven justices acknowledged that Aboriginal title to the land had, in fact, existed, although three of this group adjudged it to have been extinguished in the particular case of the Nisga'a.

Judicial enthusiasm for Aboriginal rights was almost certainly accelerated by the newly patriated constitution. Section 35(1) of the *Constitution Act, 1982* declared that the "existing aboriginal and treaty rights of the aboriginal peoples of Canada are hereby recognized and affirmed." Notwithstanding the opacity of this provision (Did its framers intend this box be empty or full, frozen or evolving?), the Supreme Court was thus provided with an opening to expand Aboriginal rights "to far beyond what courts were willing to recognize or accept only a few decades ago."[16] Although their particulars need not detain us here, some cases are especially noteworthy, including *Simon* (which deemed that Aboriginal treaty rights trumped provincial hunting regulations), *Sioui* (which widened the legal definition of treaties), *Sparrow* (which concluded that the Aboriginal right to fish for food still existed in BC and that any federal restrictions required strict justification), and *Delgamuukw* (which rejected Aboriginal sovereignty, but which first laid down a set of criteria for the establishment of Aboriginal title; second, determined that this could only be extinguished by the federal government; and third, concluded that in the particular case of the Gitksan and Wet'suwet'en peoples, this had yet to happen).[17] Small wonder, therefore, that during the constitutional discussions of the mid-1980s, provincial premiers were adamant that it would be legislatures, rather than courts, that would define the terms and conditions of Aboriginal self-government.[18] Even so, had the ill-fated Charlottetown Accord of 1992 actually been entrenched in the Canadian constitution, the court's role in affirming and interpreting Aboriginal rights would certainly have been greatly expanded. Section 35.1 (3) of that document specified that, consistent with their "inherent right of self-government," the Aboriginal peoples had the authority:

(a) to safeguard and develop their languages, cultures, economies, identities, institutions and traditions, and

(b) to develop, maintain and strengthen their relationships with their lands, waters and environment, so as to determine and control their development as peoples, according to their own values and priorities and to ensure the integrity of their societies.[19]

Needless to say, had those provisions been constitutionalized, no one would have been caught off guard by the *Marshall* Decision.

To the uninitiated, the Court's decision in the *Marshall* case may seem somewhat surprising. Certainly, the facts of the case were not in dispute. All sides agreed that, Donald Marshall, Jr. had caught and sold eels without the appropriate licences and that moreover, he had done so with a prohibited net and out of season. Marshall's lawyers contended that, notwithstanding the negative verdicts rendered at both the initial trial and at the Nova Scotia Court of Appeal, Marshall was protected by the terms of a 1760 Treaty of Peace and Friendship between Governor Charles Lawrence and Mi'kmaq Chief Paul Laurent. Under the relevant section of that document, the Mi'kmaq pledged, "that we will not traffick, barter or Exchange any Commodities in any manner but with such persons or the managers of such Truck houses as shall be appointed or Established by His Majesty's Governor at Lunenbourg or Elsewhere in Nova Scotia or Accadia."[20] On the face of it, this clause would seem to restrict, rather than enhance, the position of the Mi'kmaq vis-à-vis the British Crown, by enforcing an eighteenth-century equivalent of "the company store."

In reality, truck houses had only a brief existence in Nova Scotia. The British Crown had promised in the Treaty of 1752 to establish truck houses "wherever the Indians desired," although the Mi'kmaq were still "to have full liberty to market all supplies anywhere in the colony."[21] In fact, this pledge was basically ignored for the succeeding eight years. Only after the Treaty of 1760 did the British appoint six truck masters.[22] Unfortunately, the volume of trade was insufficient to keep their enterprises solvent, and the entire system was scrapped in 1764. For the next four years, the terms of Anglo-Mi'kmaq trade were significantly liberalized, although it was still confined to five specific locales in the province. In 1768, however, even this more modest arrangement was overturned; thereafter, matters of trade with the native people were to be left to the discretion of the colonial authorities.

Taken at face value, it may seem implausible that this brief treaty-mandated experiment with truck houses in the mid-eighteenth century could serve as the basis of a successful defence for Donald Marshall, Jr. Nevertheless, five of seven Supreme Court justices thought otherwise. First, the justices concluded that even in the absence of any textual ambiguity, extrinsic evidence about the motivations and beliefs of the treaty's signatories should be considered.[23] The justices were persuaded that the actual terms of the treaty did not come close to capturing fully the understanding of the British and Mi'kmaq negotiators. As the judgement declared:

It is the common intention of the parties in 1760 to which effect must be given. The trade clause would not have advanced British objectives (peaceful relations with a self-sufficient Mi'kmaq people) or Mi'kmaq objectives (access to the European "necessaries" on which they had come to rely) unless the Mi'kmaq were assured at the same time of continuing access, implicitly or explicitly, to a harvest of wildlife to trade.

Second, much was made of the ongoing moral obligation of the Crown to avoid profiting from "sharp practices" in its dealings with the Mi'kmaq. If British negotiators made oral promises about trading arrangements with their native counterparts, then these must be respected even in the absence of any specific textual reference to same. Justice Binnie spoke for the majority on this point when he claimed: "I do not think an interpretation of events that turns a positive Mi'kmaq trade demand into a negative Mi'kmaq covenant is consistent with the honour and integrity of the Crown."

Third, although two of their colleagues explicitly dissented on this point, a majority of the justices maintained that the Mi'kmaq right to harvest and trade wildlife did not lapse with the termination of the truck houses specified in the treaty. "The promise of access to 'necessaries' through trade in wildlife was the key point," they insisted, "and where a right has been granted, there must be more than a mere disappearance of the mechanism created to facilitate the exercise of the right to warrant the conclusion that the right itself is spent or extinguished." And in the absence of such extinguishment, section 35 (1) of the *Constitution Act, 1982* guarantees a "higher protection" for the Mi'kmaq treaty right to hunt, fish, and trade.

Finally, the Court also sketched out some limitations on the potential exercise of this treaty right. The justices were convinced that the Treaty of 1760 had been designed, in part, to assist the Mi'kmaq in securing "necessaries"; the late twentieth century analogue of this concept was deemed to be "a moderate livelihood." Therefore, the Mi'kmaq had a treaty right to hunt and fish in order to secure "food, clothing and housing supplemented by a few amenities"; this right did not, however, mandate "the open-ended accumulation of wealth," and present-day governments would be perfectly justified in setting catch limits to prevent same.

The blanket prohibitions of the *Fisheries Act*, under which Marshall had been charged, were manifestly inconsistent with the thrust of this ruling. Moreover, Marshall and his fishing companion had only received $787.10 for the 463 pounds of eels that they had caught in Pomquet Harbour; by almost any standard, this was closer to "a moderate livelihood" than to "the open-ended accumulation of wealth." Accordingly, on 17 September 1999, the Supreme Court acquitted Donald Marshall, Jr. on all charges.

The response to the ruling was immediate. Within a week, tensions between Aboriginal and non-Aboriginal fishermen had escalated dramatically. For the latter, the *Marshall* Decision signified an obvious challenge to their livelihood. If large numbers of Aboriginal fisherman were permitted to operate year-round (even if only to garner "a moderate livelihood"), would fish stocks fall precipitously? With the failure of the cod fishery serving as an ongoing reminder of "the tragedy of the commons," few non-Aboriginals seemed sanguine about the outcome. "There's a mess here. I just hope that nobody gets hurt," declared Harold Theriault, President of the Bay of Fundy Inshore Fishermen's Association. "There's fear here and anger. I was even getting threats myself."[24]

In contrast, Aboriginal spokesmen were jubilant. "The non-Indians don't want to share," claimed Chief Lawrence Paul, co-chair of the Atlantic Policy Congress of First Nations Chiefs. "But due to the Supreme Court decision, the rules of the game have changed and they'll have to share, whether they like it or not."[25] And while the *Marshall* case may have been precipitated by an unsanctioned harvest of eels, many perceived the decision to extend to other natural resources. Hence, lawyers for Joshua Bernard, a New Brunswick Mi'kmaq charged with illegally cutting timber on Crown land, were quick to claim that the Supreme Court's ruling would result in their client's acquittal. "The *Marshall* case is extremely significant," noted Bruce Wildsmith. "We're going to have to put the point to [Judge Dennis Lordin] and he is going to have to decide whether logs are in the same position as eels."[26] Others saw the Court's decision as extending well beyond traditional Mi'kmaq activities of hunting, fishing, and gathering. Rick Simon, the Atlantic regional vice-chief for the Assembly of First Nations suggested, for instance, that the Mi'kmaq were now assured access to such resources as minerals and even the natural gas fields off Sable Island. "As far as we're concerned," claimed Simon, "the principle is the same for any business" and "the right to earn a moderate living without government interference" is "not limited to hunting, fishing, and logging."[27]

Somewhere between the despair of the non-Aboriginal fishermen and the jubilation of the status Indians could be found the response of the non-status natives. Members of this group could legitimately claim some ties by blood to the Mi'kmaq elders who, over two centuries previously, had signed treaties with the British Crown. Accordingly, they insisted that, notwithstanding the lack of legal status under the *Indian Act*, they were fully entitled to all rights and benefits flowing from the *Marshall* Decision. "Because all of the people don't meet the Indian Act requirements (of) our great white brother of who is and isn't an Indian ... people are being excluded from their rights," claimed Tim Martin of the Native Council of Nova Scotia. "The [1760–61] treaties applied to everyone in the Mi'kmaq nation. The treaties don't talk about status and non-status Indians."[28] It soon became clear that no other group was prepared to support this position. Status Indians were particularly anxious that the federal government crack down on "poachers" from the non-status community. "The line in the sand right now is the Indian Act," claimed Rick

Simon of the Assembly of First Nations. "Everyone else's not supposed to be in the water."[29] Non-Aboriginal fishermen echoed this sentiment; if the *Marshall* Decision extended treaty rights to non-status fishermen with as little as 12 percent native ancestry, then the prospects of a sustainable fishery would be appreciably dimmed. Ottawa may have been unprepared for the *Marshall* Decision, but on this matter they moved with some alacrity; two weeks after the ruling, the Department of Fisheries and Oceans (DFO) announced that the *Marshall* treaty rights did not apply to non-status Indians and that even this group's right to a food fishery was being suspended.

That it was DFO who stepped forward as the mouthpiece of the federal government at this time was highly significant. The Supreme Court may have ruled that a treaty right to an Aboriginal fishery existed, but that right cut messily across two federal departments: the Department of Fisheries and Oceans and the Department of Indian Affairs and Northern Development (DIAND). Determining which of these would be the lead actor on Ottawa's behalf must have involved two considerations. First, the federal government had to determine what, in jurisprudential terms, is dubbed "the leading aspect" of the issue; simply put, was an "Aboriginal fishery" more about "Aboriginals" or more about "fish?" Since few outside the legal community are able to answer such questions with any degree of confidence, the second consideration was likely decisive. Was Ottawa intent on shrinking the import of the *Marshall* ruling? If not, a prominent role would likely have been allocated to the Department of Indian Affairs and Northern Development and its minister, Bob Nault. After all, DIAND has an organizational culture geared to advancing the interests of its principal clients: Canada's Aboriginal peoples. Indeed, over half the Aboriginals who work in the federal civil service are located within the friendly confines of DIAND.[30] On those occasions in the fall of 1999 when Bob Nault spoke publicly, it was to offer soothing reassurances of Ottawa's fealty to the spirit of the *Marshall* ruling. While DFO spokespersons were explicitly denying rights to non-status Indians, Nault was much more ambivalent on the matter. "We're not saying they're going to be excluded," he told reporters at one point. "We're basically saying we're talking about a whole series of things and that's one of them."[31] On another occasion, Nault indicated, to the consternation of both opposition parliamentarians and provincial governments, that the implications of the *Marshall* Decision would likely extend well beyond the Atlantic fishery to include other resources in other parts of the country.[32] And with many voices calling for the Supreme Court to clarify the ambiguities in its decision, Nault stressed that he was opposed to further judicial involvement. "I've made it very clear to the ministers in the Atlantic provinces that I would prefer that we not do that," Nault observed, "because it also makes the relationship even that less trustworthy when Aboriginal peoples just continue to see governments trying to limit their rights and/or somehow delay the implications of their rights being in play."[33]

It was thus left to DFO and its minister, Herb Dhaliwal, to take the harder line against the Mi'kmaq. With the established regulatory regime of the fisheries thrown into at least temporary disarray by the *Marshall* ruling, clashes between Aboriginal and non-Aboriginal fishermen inevitably ensued. Much media attention was focused on Burnt Church, New Brunswick, where melees on the water were accompanied by fist-fights and arson on land (including the torching of a sacred native religious arbour on the reserve).[34] But Burnt Church was merely the most extreme instance of a more generalized phenomenon. Convinced that native fishermen (both status and non-status) were catching too many lobsters (and reported catches of $5,000/day might have been construed as exceeding the Supreme Court's "moderate livelihood" stipulation), non-native fishermen vandalized boats and traps with equal enthusiasm.[35] In Yarmouth, an armada of non-Aboriginal boats effectively blockaded eight Aboriginal boats inside the harbour. Under pressure from Herb Dhaliwal, some, but not all, of the Mi'kmaq chiefs agreed to a 30-day fishing moratorium. In the words of Chief Laurence Paul, chairman of the Assembly of Nova Scotia Mi'kmaq:

> As far as I can tell, we don't have any choice. The minister tells me he is reluctant to set aside the *Marshall* decision, but he has the authority to do it if he feels public safety is threatened ... I think we either declare the moratorium ourselves, or the government will.[36]

It was during this partial moratorium that the West Nova Fisherman's Coalition appealed to the Supreme Court for a rehearing and possible stay of the *Marshall* judgement. Erroneously, Indian Affairs Minister Nault was dismissive of this stratagem: "The courts have never, as I understand, ever allowed that to proceed in that fashion so I'm of the view that they'll basically say: 'Well, that's our ruling and you guys get on with doing your job.'"[37] In fact, when the Supreme Court denied the appeal on 17 November, they were substantially more verbose than Nault had predicted. In a 30-page ruling, the justices made several key points. First, the *Marshall* ruling applied only to a small-scale eel fishery; the justices had not intended their ruling to have any direct applicability to other natural resources. The issue of access to timber, minerals, natural gas and the like had simply not been raised at the *Marshall* trial and had thus not been considered by the Court. Indeed, one could not even generalize from the decision to other types of fisheries. "Conservation and other issues" raised in the harvesting of eels would differ significantly from those relevant to a salmon, crab, cod or lobster fishery. "The complexities and techniques of fish and wildlife management vary from species to species and restrictions will likely have to be justified on a species-by-species basis."[38]

Second, the Court indicated that Marshall's acquittal should not be interpreted to mean that the Mi'kmaq have an unregulated treaty right to fish anything, even including eels. In the initial trial, the Crown had denied the existence of a treaty right to the eel fishery and had thus not attempted to legitimize the licensing restrictions and closed seasons they had imposed on the harvesting of eels (by Aboriginals and non-Aboriginals alike). Once the Court discovered the existence of the treaty right, the Crown's failure to justify its regulating regime demanded that Marshall be acquitted. The clear, albeit unspoken, message from the Court was that, notwithstanding the existence of the treaty right, even an Aboriginal eel fishery could be the subject of state regulation, as long as adequate justification for the infringement of the treaty right could be provided.

Finally, the Court emphasized that the Aboriginal treaty right is a "limited" right. This right does not trump the regulatory capacity of the state. With some unhappiness, the justices complained that the West Nova Fisherman's Coalition (and presumably others) had been labouring under "a misconception of what was decided on September 17, 1999." In a lengthy passage that deserves to be quoted in full, the court rammed this point home:

> The federal and provincial governments have the authority within their respective legislative fields to regulate the exercise of a treaty right where justified on conservation or other grounds. The *Marshall* judgement referred to the Court's principal pronouncements on the various grounds which the exercise of treaty right may be regulated. The paramount regulatory objective is conservation and responsibility for it is placed squarely on the Minister responsible and not on the aboriginal or non-aboriginal users of the resource. The regulatory authority extends to other compelling and substantial public objectives which may include economic and regional fairness, and recognition of the historical reliance upon and participation in, the fishery by non-aboriginal groups. Aboriginal people are entitled to be consulted about limitations on the exercise of treaty and aboriginal rights. The Minister has available for regulatory purposes the full range of resource management tools and techniques, provided their use to limit the exercise of a treaty right can be justified on conservation or other grounds.

On the face of it, the Supreme Court's 17 November ruling would seem to have been a hammer blow against Aboriginal aspirations for a self-managed, guaranteed-access fishery. Chief Lawrence Paul, co-chairman of the Atlantic Policy Congress of First Nations Chiefs, was livid upon first hearing of the ruling. "I'm flabbergasted and disappointed," he asserted. "The Supreme Court of Canada ... lost a lot of credibility with me today."[39] Nevertheless, Aboriginal spokespersons have continued to act on their (apparently mistaken) initial understanding of the *Marshall* Decision. Many Mi'kmaq bands have drafted their own conservation rules, issued their own licences, lobster tags, and the like, and fished without regard for DFO regulations. When, in February 2000, DFO seized two native crab boats for fishing in the wrong area off Nova Scotia's eastern shore, the response was immediate. One Mi'kmaq spokesperson noted that his people "believe deeply that the Supreme Court has upheld their right to hunt and fish without heavy handed federal regulation." The community feeling was: "We have the right and the minister doesn't have the authority or justification for limiting that right."[40]

In response, the federal government has had to follow two conflicting imperatives. On the one hand, they have acknowledged the existence of a Mi'kmaq treaty right to engage in fishing for a moderate livelihood. Accordingly, they allocated $160 million to integrate Aboriginals into the existing fishery, by buying back the licences, boats, and gear of non-Aboriginal fishermen. On the other hand, Ottawa has felt compelled to demonstrate that regulation of the fishery ultimately lies in their hands. Hence, DFO spent an extra $13 million in 2000 to upgrade its surveillance equipment and hire more full-time enforcement officers in the Maritime provinces. Officially, the fisheries minister denied that Ottawa's decision to beef up its regulatory presence off the east coast was linked to the *Marshall* ruling. "If there is illegal or unauthorized fishing, whether it's aboriginal or non-aboriginal, I think that all of us want to make sure that we deal with it," noted Dhaliwal.[41] Yet the timing of the announcement can hardly have been coincidental, coming a scant ten days after the Burnt Church band announced that it was setting its own fishery rules: "We're just going to fish. It's our commercial right and we're going to exercise that right."[42] Since the *Marshall* Decision, Ottawa has tried to negotiate individual fishery management schemes with each of the Mi'kmaq bands in the Maritime provinces. In 2000, most of the 35 bands in the region did, in return for financial assistance, accept a specific allocation of the resource. Yet two high-profile bands (Shubenacadie and Burnt Church) steadfastly refused to sign on, and in the autumn months, tensions between the Burnt Church natives, the non-Aboriginal fishermen, and DFO enforcement officers again reached dangerously high levels.[43]

Whatever the short-term outcome of such confrontations, it behooves us to consider the long-term prospects of accommodating Aboriginal and non-Aboriginal interests in the east coast fishery (and elsewhere, for that matter). The discourse between the two groups has increasingly been couched in the vernacular of rights (in particular, the rights of the Aboriginal people). This is, however, a relatively recent phenomenon. Alan Cairns noted that prominent native activist Harold Cardinal had not even heard of "Aboriginal rights" in the mid-1960s; by 1982, however, the term had permeated our collective consciousness to such an extent that its constitutionalization raised few eyebrows.[44] Subsequent court rulings have made unambiguous references to the existence of "Aboriginal rights," and the *Marshall* Decision, notwithstanding the hedges and qualifications contained therein, did likewise. Can such rights be accommodated to the satisfaction of all interested parties? Sadly, there seem to be legitimate grounds for pessimism.

That a rights-based discourse can inhibit compromise and consensus is well-known, and the debate associated with the *Marshall* ruling is certainly consistent with that truism. Consider, for example, the words of Phil Fontaine, then National Chief of the Assembly of First Nations, who, while calling for further negotiations between all parties, emphasized that natives must have "the only role when it comes to self-regulation of the fishing industry" and that this was "non-negotiable."[45] Or consider the words of Chief Lawrence Paul:

> Our position ... is we're going out to fish.... The non-native fisherman may complain, but we're there because we have a right. They're there because they have a privilege, granted through a license. Rights win over privileges every time.[46]

Even if such assertions are partially a function of pre-negotiation posturing, they effectively close down the prospects for interest accommodation. There is an absolutist quality to rights, which goes some way to explaining why the *Marshall* Decision (notwithstanding the lengthy attempt to clarify same) has so frequently been misconstrued. And if rights are not fully respected, the response is likely to be incendiary. Hence, Alex Denny, head of the Mi'kmaq Grand Council, warned the federal government against even attempting to negotiate catch limits with the natives. "Every solitary one of us will end up in a jail," asserted Denny, "and that will include the Grand Council because I'm going out [to fish]."[47]

It is important to emphasize that this polarizing rights rhetoric has not been exclusively the preserve of the status Mi'kmaq. Note the words of Mike Pictou, a non-status native. "I'm getting set to start another little war down here, I guess," claimed Mr. Pictou. "I know that I was born with these rights and the Supreme Court said it. So I'm going to go out and fish."[48] And while non-native fishermen have been less prone to participate in a rights discourse, their tone has been equally intransigent. Hence, Wayne Spinney, a spokesperson for the non-Aboriginal fishermen of southwestern Nova Scotia made a public call "to negotiate one-on-one" with Mi'kmaq representatives. Mr. Spinney's conception of "negotiation," however, seemed somewhat one-sided. "They are going to have to, sooner or later, consider our ultimatum," he claimed. "And that is our season, our rules, our regulations. No other way. That's it."[49]

Yet even leaving aside the typically bellicose nature of rights-based discourse, there are four reasons to doubt that Nova Scotia's non-Aboriginal community will respond favourably to current Aboriginal claims. First, there is disagreement about the wellspring of, and therefore the significance of, an Aboriginal right to fish. Second, there is a growing unwillingness in the non-Aboriginal community to countenance the sort of special, ascriptive right claimed by many Mi'kmaq spokespersons. Third, there is a similar level of non-Aboriginal reluctance to recognize collective, as opposed to individual, rights. Finally, the relative scarcity of the resource to be harvested easily punctures the thin veneer of non-Aboriginal goodwill toward Nova Scotia's Mi'kmaq peoples. We will consider each of these obstacles in turn.

To the non-Aboriginal, the *Marshall* ruling affirmed that the Mi'kmaq have a treaty right to fish, that is, a right based on a contract. There may be disagreement about the significance of the contract; one observer dismissed the Treaties of 1760–61 as nothing more than "200-year-old documents of British military convenience."[50] There may also be disagreement about the interpretation of that contract; Tom Flanagan, for one, claims that the *Marshall* ruling could only have been reached on the basis of "judicial legerdemain."[51] There may even be disagreement about whether the terms of that contract have been either fulfilled or extinguished, as was found by two of the seven Supreme Court justices. At the most, therefore, the non-Aboriginal community is prepared to acknowledge a limited Aboriginal right to fish derived exclusively from an historic contract.

To the Mi'kmaq people, however, their right to fish does not flow solely, or even principally, from the Treaties of 1760–61. Rather, they perceive those documents as merely ratifying a pre-existing right. There are generally claimed to be two sources of this right. The first of these is spiritual; as the 1980 Declaration of First Nations put it: "The rights and responsibilities given to us by the Creator cannot be altered or taken away by any other nation."[52] The second source of this right, which also preceded the Treaties of 1760–61, is derived from the principle of first occupancy. Certainly, the Royal Commission on Aboriginal Peoples found this to be axiomatic. Aboriginal rights, according to the commission, are "rights that inhere in Aboriginal nations because of time-honoured relationships with the land, which predate European contact."[53] Or, as Phil Fontaine succinctly puts it: "The fact is, we are a special people. We were here first."[54] Yet if all Canadians are either immigrants or the offspring of same and if our increasingly secular society confines spirituality to the private sphere, then non-Aboriginals will be disposed to believe that Aboriginal fishing rights start and end with the Supreme Court's interpretation of the Treaties of 1760–61. To the Mi'kmaq, by contrast, considerations of spirituality and prior occupancy provide the moral foundation upon which treaty rights rest. From their perspective, hedging the latter is an affront to the former. Such cross-community disagreements about first premises are not conducive to a successful accommodation of diverse interests.

The second obstacle to a full recognition of Aboriginal fishery rights lies in their ascriptive character. Joanne Barnaby may claim that "aboriginal rights are only fundamental *human* rights that have yet to be recognized for aboriginal peoples,"[55] but, at least in the present context, this formulation is manifestly in error. A Mi'kmaq right to fish, whatever its foundation, is clearly a special right held by a particular group of people defined by law and/or by blood. While few would go as far as Oren Lyons ("We are the aboriginal people and we have the right to look after all life on this earth"[56]), Aboriginal spokespersons assume the existence of a privileged relationship with the resource. Nor, as is often the case with affirmative action programs, would this special right lapse should the present-day economic disadvantages of the Aboriginal peoples be ameliorated.[57] On the contrary, Mi'kmaq fishery rights would stand as on-going claims against the wider community.

Such assumptions, however, are destined to make many non-Aboriginals uncomfortable. Canada may be a rights-conscious society, but rights that are universalistic, rather than particularistic, are much more likely to generate widespread enthusiasm.[58] Consider the response of non-Aboriginal political elites to the *Marshall* ruling. Initially, Nova Scotia Premier John Hamm urged the federal government to pursue a stay of the decision; notwithstanding Chief Laurence Paul's outburst that the prospect made him "want to puke," this option was apparently seriously considered by Prime Minister Chrétien.[59] Ultimately, the decision was made to pursue a regulatory regime that would accommodate the Aboriginal fishing rights identified in the *Marshall* ruling. For Nova Scotia's fisheries minister, Ernie Fage, however, this regime could make few concessions to special Aboriginal rights. "In our view, we need one fishery with one set of rules," he asserted. "That is one management plan, one conservation plan and the economic consequences of integrating [natives] into the fishery are certainly the responsibility of the federal government."[60] When federal parliamentarians addressed this question, they came to similar conclusions. An all-party Commons committee recommended an extensive buy-back of existing fishing licences and their generous distribution to east coast Mi'kmaq. Thereafter, scant recognition of Aboriginal particularism would be apparent. "We're all pretty much in agreement that there should be one fishery, one set of regulations, one season so that the same rules apply both to non-natives and natives," noted one committee member. "There can't be all these different rules dictating different things for different people. That was a very central theme to the whole thing."[61] Alan Cairns has attempted to synthesize the tension between universalism and particularism by employing the concept of "citizens plus" to characterize a possible status for Aboriginals in Canada. It is clear from the foregoing, however, that both federal and provincial elites would rather emphasize the "citizens" than the "plus" portion of this formulation. Canada's native peoples, however, are likely to resist programs that would provide short-term recognition of their special rights, only to submerge them subsequently in a homogenizing universalism. As Patricia Montoure-Angus puts it, Canada's non-Aboriginals are preoccupied with this notion that no one, including natives, "deserves special treatment and rights. This reasoning must be understood for what it is — the colonial mentality."[62] Colonial or not, this perspective represents a formidable obstacle to Aboriginal aspirations of enjoying special rights in the fishery.

The third such hurdle lies in the putatively collective nature of Aboriginal rights. Somewhat paradoxically, liberal individualism has penetrated deeply into the collective psyche of Canadians (or, at least, of English Canadians).

Protecting individual rights coheres easily with this philosophy; protecting group rights does not. Much of the unease with which English Canada regarded the ill-fated Meech Lake Accord centred around the notorious "distinct society" clause, a provision that empowered the Quebec state, in the name of preserving and promoting the distinctive attributes of the Quebec collectivity, to infringe, if necessary, upon individual rights and freedoms. Admittedly, Canada has already constitutionalized some collective rights. In the *Constitution Act, 1982*, the rights of linguistic minority groups were entrenched; as well, some provinces were given the authority to infringe on individual mobility rights, and all provinces were given the authority, not only to employ the notwithstanding clause, but also to opt out from certain constitutional amendments. It is worth noting, however, that the backlash against collective rights has grown significantly in recent times; some of these provisions from the *Constitution Act, 1982* would be much harder to entrench today than they were 20 years ago.

Will non-Aboriginals countenance a collective Aboriginal right to fish? Much depends on the likelihood of conflict between collective and individual rights in the fishery. Traditional Aboriginal government, it is often noted, was "based upon a principle of consensual agreement regarding the interests of the nation in the political sphere."[63] Can we be sure that "consensual agreement" will endure in the management of their treaty right to fish? The Royal Commission on Aboriginal Peoples is certainly confident on that score. After all, noted the commission, treaties "are made between nations, and every individual member of the allied nations assumes personal responsibility for respecting the treaty."[64] Others are less certain. Boldt and Long, for example, recognize that in traditional Indian society, "individual self-interest was viewed as inextricably intertwined with tribal survival. That is, the general good and the individual good were virtually identical."[65] They acknowledge, however, that the arrival of the *Canadian Charter of Rights and Freedoms* has created an intellectual climate that, not unlike the imposition of Christianity in earlier times, threatens to subvert the traditional Aboriginal world-view. Conflict over changing gender roles has been one obvious manifestation of this emerging tension, as native women seek to secure individual rights in the face of unsympathetic collective norms. Extrapolating from this example is a risky enterprise. Dan Russell, for one, believes that although the activities of hunting, fishing, and trapping "are surely collective community rights, they do not precipitate the kind of confrontation between rights occasioned by the issue of gender equality."[66] For purely pragmatic reasons, the federal government must be hoping that Russell is correct. After all, it was the assumption that the *Marshall* ruling had conferred a collective right for an Aboriginal fishery that permitted DFO to exclude non-status Indians from the equation on the simple expedient that they lacked a community. Moreover, while negotiating the terms of entry to the commercial fishery with 35 separate bands has been manifestly difficult for the federal government, dealing with individual Mi'kmaq would have been exponentially more burdensome.

Nevertheless, there are grounds for doubting the long-term viability of a collective Aboriginal right to fish (even assuming that non-natives can successfully repress their growing unhappiness with any and all collective rights). The original *Marshall* ruling of September 1999 and the subsequent clarification on November 1999 used strikingly different terms to characterize Aboriginal fishing rights. In the initial decision, the justices endorsed catch limits that "could reasonably be expected to produce a moderate livelihood for individual Mi'kmaq families." Another part of the ruling noted:

> The accused caught and sold the eels to support himself and his wife. His treaty right to fish and trade for sustenance was exercisable only at the absolute discretion of the Minister. Accordingly, the close season and the imposition of a discretionary licensing system would, if enforced, interfere with the accused's treaty right to fish for trading purposes, and the ban on sales would, if enforced, infringe his right to trade for sustenance.

References to "the appellant's treaty rights" pepper the judgement. Such language seems to indicate that, at least initially, the Supreme Court conceived of the right to fish in individual terms.

In the Supreme Court's November clarification, however, the language employed to characterize the treaty right was markedly divergent. Hence, the justices now emphasized that "the treaty right permits the Mi'kmaq community to work for a living through continuing access to fish and wildlife," and that "the appellant established that the collective treaty right held by his community allowed him to fish for eels." Tellingly, the term "the appellant's treaty rights" from the first judgement is generally replaced in the clarifying ruling by "the Mi'kmaq treaty right."

These semantic distinctions are not without import, and the Supreme Court may well be guiding the central players in this tableau toward a collectivist solution. Certainly, the federal government's policy of signing interim management agreements with all, or at least most, of the 35 bands on the east coast is consistent with this approach. Whether it can be sustained in the long term, however, is open to question. There is nothing sacrosanct about the existing band structure; thus, it need not be the institutional device through which Mi'kmaq collective treaty rights are expressed. The number of Nova Scotia bands has increased in this century, and that figure might change again if the sorts of mergers envisioned by the Royal Commission on Aboriginal Peoples come to pass. But if the decision to lodge communal fishing rights in existing bands can only be legitimized as an administrative convenience, the way is open for secessionist challenges by dissident groups unhappy with band fishing policy. Moreover, and notwithstanding the carefully collectivist rhetoric of the Supreme Court's 17 November decision, the door may not have been entirely closed on the individual exercise of Aboriginal treaty rights. It is not self-evident, even in the unlikely eventuality that Ottawa is able to come to an agreement with all Mi'kmaq bands for long-term management of the fishery (as opposed to the interim arrangements which lapsed in Spring 2001), that individual Mi'kmaqs could thus be denied access to the resource. After all, Donald Marshall, Jr. was acquitted in the absence of an administrative arrangement between his band and the federal government; in the presence of same, would he have been convicted on the grounds that his treaty rights had thus been fulfilled? Few court watchers would make book on such a ruling, especially (but not only) if the band's internal allocation of fishing resources could be shown to violate some canon of natural justice.

The final obstacle to the successful accommodation of Aboriginal and non-Aboriginal interests in the east coast fishery is the relative scarcity of the resource. No doubt when the Treaties of 1760–61 were signed, the oceans teemed with fish and neither party to the agreement likely imagined a future where this would not be the case. Sadly, appetite and technology have, over time, combined to put the fishery stocks under siege. Canada's Aboriginal peoples are often credited with having a particularly enlightened concern for resource conservation. Thus, Aboriginal elders

> teach a world-view based on the knowledge that all things in life are related in a sacred manner and are governed by natural or cosmic laws. Mother Earth is therefore held to be sacred, a gift from the Creator. In their relationship to the land, people should accommodate themselves to it in an attitude of respect and stewardship.[67]

It is not clear, however, that this Aboriginal attitude of "respect and stewardship" toward natural resources has remained unalloyed in modern times. Consider the defence strategy employed by a Mi'kmaq band accused of overfishing snow crab. As Sydney lawyer Tony Mozvik put it, "we're going to say if overfishing existed at all — which we deny — but if it did, we had rights under the *Marshall* decision that allowed us to do it."[68] Or take note of the increase in moose hunting by Aboriginals in the four months after the release of the *Marshall* ruling. One Mi'kmaq, in particular, had already bagged 24 moose (or 0.1 percent of the entire provincial moose population); that this hunter had decided to stop when his total reached 30 will hardly reassure conservationists.[69] This does not imply, however, that non-Aboriginals hold the moral high ground on this issue. There has been much public posturing by non-natives that stocks will not permit a full-scale entry of Aboriginals into the fishery. Chief Lawrence Paul was characteristically blunt about such pronouncements: "I think the bottom line on the whole thing is not conservation, it's not about saving fish stocks, the bottom line is greed."[70] Seen from afar, the magnitude of the proposed Aboriginal fishery does not seem to present an obvious threat to conservation. Access to the lucrative lobster industry has raised tensions between natives and non-natives this past summer; in dispute are the Mi'kmaq plans to set, according to one estimate, 5,800 lobster traps in the waters around Atlantic Canada. Given that federal fisheries officers plucked 1,700 native-owned traps from Miramichi Bay alone in a series of midnight raids this August,[71] that estimate may be too conservative. On the other hand, even if the number of 5,800 was multiplied tenfold, it would still constitute only 2 percent of the annual total of legal lobster traps set by the non-native fishermen of Atlantic Canada.[72] And that figure does not even take into account the healthy underground trade in lobsters, whereby some non-Aboriginal fishermen routinely set more traps than their legal entitlement. As Chief Frank Meuse, Jr. recounted with a chuckle, when a group of non-Aboriginal vigilantes decided to clear St. Mary's Bay of unauthorized traps on the assumption that they had been set by Mi'kmaqs, they were actually just "cutting their own traps up."[73]

Yet even if the scale of the proposed Aboriginal fishery seems relatively modest, it is worth recalling that this clash represents a pure conflict of claim, an instance of zero-sum bargaining in which any gain achieved by one side necessitates a corresponding loss by the other. Those who are advantaged by the existing fishery regime will not easily countenance even a minor reduction in their well-being, unless there is substantial and pervasive support for the aspirations of the interlopers.

Do such feelings exist among the wider populace toward Aboriginal peoples? Alan Cairns, for one, has serious doubts. He suggests that most non-Aboriginal Canadians are ill-informed about native history and regard them with what he characterizes as a "shallow goodwill." Cairns warns, however, that in cases of direct conflict (over, for example, land and resources), non-native sympathy "tends to be overpowered by self-interested fears."[74] A recent survey undertaken by Nova Scotia's Office of Aboriginal Affairs confirmed Cairns' analysis. Levels of understanding and interest in Mi'kmaq issues were generally found to be low.[75] However, amongst those surveyed who professed to be very concerned about these matters, 41 percent believed that the Mi'kmaq have more opportunities than other Nova Scotians; only 27 percent believed the reverse. Other findings of note include data showing that levels of support for Mi'kmaq aspirations declined with direct exposure to Mi'kmaq claims, that 57 percent believed the Treaties of 1760–61 were outdated, while only 30 percent maintained they should be honoured, and only 6 percent endorsed the principle that the Mi'kmaq should self-regulate their access to resources (as opposed to 60 percent who believed there should be co-regulation between the Mi'kmaq and the government, and 33 percent who felt that the government alone should determine resource access).

To recapitulate: we should not be optimistic about the ease with which an Aboriginal right to fish can be accommodated. Mi'kmaq resolve is strengthened by their belief that the Treaties of 1760–61 were merely confirmations of a pre-existing right, rather than the sole source of said right. At the same time, non-natives tend to be suspicious of rights claims that are both special and collective, even if there is some question about whether the latter attribute can be sustained in practice. Finally, conflicts over scarce commodities can be particularly intractable, especially when heightened exploitation is believed to put at risk an otherwise renewable resource. That a recent survey commissioned by the Nova Scotia government revealed significant popular doubts about Aboriginal aspirations should not, upon reflection, have been overly surprising.

The *Marshall* case may have originated in Nova Scotia, but its impact has been and will continue to be felt over a much wider area. Obviously, the neighbouring Maritime provinces, with their substantial number of Mi'kmaq bands, have also had to adapt to the altered regulatory regime engendered by the Supreme Court's decision. Yet the *Marshall* decision has even reverberated as far afield as British Columbia. Not wishing to be caught offguard a second time, DFO has recently concluded fishing agreements with 14 Vancouver Island bands whose nineteenth-century treaties had guaranteed their rights to "carry on [their] fisheries as formerly."[76] Given that this wording seems manifestly more explicit than that contained within the 1760 Treaty of Peace and Friendship, Ottawa prudently chose to pre-empt yet another court challenge.

And what of Donald Marshall, Jr., whose eel harvesting in the fall of 1993 precipitated the whirlwind that has followed? As tensions rose last fall between Aboriginal and non-Aboriginal fishermen, Marshall appealed for calm and urged all sides to pull their nets out of the water and come to a negotiated agreement. "We waited this long," noted Marshall, "I think we could wait a little longer."[77] The editorial page of Halifax's major newspaper lauded Marshall's restraint:

> If there is a Solomon in this case, it is surely Donald Marshall. Here is a truly remarkable man. He survived 11 years wrongful imprisonment for a murder he didn't commit, fought all the way to the Supreme Court once to establish his innocence and traveled the long road back there for his people's treaty rights. If he can still say at the end of all this that life is precious and patience is needed even in expressing your rights, then who are the rest of us — native or non-native — not to listen?[78]

Sadly, there is a darker side to this parable. Many rights cannot be exercised without adverse consequences for others and this appears to be yet another instance. It has been reported that "old hands in the Acadian community of Pomquet, and young hands too, say the eels have pretty much disappeared since Donald Marshall, Jr. fished the species commercially in 1993."[79] That Donald Marshall, Jr. had the right to harvest 463 pounds of eels from Pomquet harbour is no longer in dispute. What remains more problematic, however, is whether any other Mi'kmaq fishermen will again enjoy the particular exercise of this right in fact, as well as in law.

NOTES

1.   *The Chronicle-Herald*, 27 January 1990, p. A1.

2.   Government of Nova Scotia, *Marshall Update/Justice Reform Review*, 20 May 1992, p. 1.

3.   Certainly, those charged with re-drawing Nova Scotia's electoral boundaries have been sensitive to the cultural norms against advancing justice through unequal treatment. Minority groups may claim that effective representation requires that they be grouped in "protected" constituencies which are smaller than the provincial average. Yet as Smith and Landes note, in "the harsh light of the public's gaze, only convincing and compelling justifications for abridging voter equality are likely to succeed" (Jennifer Smith and Ronald G. Landes, "Entitlement Versus Variance Models in the Determination of Canadian Electoral Boundaries," *International Journal of Canadian Studies* 17(1998):30).

4.   L.F.S. Upton, "Indian Policy in Colonial Nova Scotia, 1783-1871," in *Atlantic Canada Before Confederation*, ed. P.A. Buckner and David Franks (Fredericton: Acadiensis Press, 1985), p. 89.

5.   R.O. Macfarlane, "British Indian Policy in Nova Scotia to 1760," in *The Native Peoples of Atlantic Canada*, ed. Harold Franklin McGee, Jr. (Ottawa: Carleton University Press, 1983), p. 54.

6.   Upton, "Indian Policy in Colonial Nova Scotia," p. 89.

7.   Grand Chief Donald Marshall, Sr., Grand Captain Alexander Denny, and Putus Simon Marshall, "The Mi'kmaq: The Covenant Chain," in *Drumbeat*, ed. Boyce Richardson (Toronto: Summerhill Press, 1982), p. 77.

8.   See <http://www.gov.ns.ca/abor/contrent/first.htm>.

9.   James S. Frideres, *Native Peoples in Canada: Contemporary Conflict,* 4th ed. (Toronto: Prentice-Hall, 1993), pp. 5-6.

10.   *The Chronicle-Herald*, 1 December 1999, p. A1.

11.   Tord Larsen, "Negotiating Identity: The Micmac of Nova Scotia," in *The Politics of Indianness*, ed. Adrian Tanner (St. John's: Institute of Social and Economic Research, 1983), p. 59.

12.   Fred Wien, *Socioeconomic Characteristics of the Micmac in Nova Scotia* (Halifax: Institute of Public Affairs, 1983), p. 46.

13.   *The Chronicle-Herald*, 5 January 1998, p. C2.

14.   *The Chronicle-Herald*, 18 December 1999, p. A4.

15.   Interview with the author, Bear River, 1 September 2000.

16.   C.E.S. Franks, "Rights and Self-Government for Canada's Aboriginal Peoples," in *Aboriginal Rights and Self-Government: The Canadian and Mexican*

Experience in North American Perspective, ed. Curtis Cook and Juan D. Lindau (Montreal: McGill-Queens University Press, 2000), p. 109.

17. For a fuller discussion of these and other cases, see Royal Commission on Aboriginal Peoples, *Report, Vol. 1: Looking Forward, Looking Back*, (Ottawa: Supply and Services Canada, 1996), pp. 218-26. See also Tom Flanagan, *First Nations? Second Thoughts* (Montreal: McGill-Queen's University Press, 2000), pp. 122-31; and Patrick Macklem and Roger Townshend, "Resorting to Court: Can the Judiciary Deliver Justice for First Nations?" in *Nation to Nation*, ed. Diane Engelstad and John Bird (Concord: House of Anansi Press, 1992), pp. 78-82.

18. J. Anthony Long and Memo Boldt, eds., *Governments in Conflict? Provinces and Indian Nations in Canada* (Toronto: University of Toronto Press, 1988), p. 17.

19. *Draft Legal Text of Charlottetown Accord*, 9 October 1992, pp. 37-38.

20. See <http://www.gov.ns.ca/abor/pubs/1760Treaty.PDF>.

21. MacFarlane, "British Indian Policy in Nova Scotia to 1760," p. 59.

22. Much of this historical information is derived from Elizabeth Ann Hutton, "Indian Affairs in Nova Scotia, 1760-1834," in *The Native Peoples of Atlantic Canada*, ed. McGee, Jr., pp. 63-70.

23. The full text of the *Marshall* Decision can be found at <http://www.gov.ns.ca/abor/pubs/MARSHALL.PDF>.

24. *The Chronicle-Herald*, 22 September 1999.

25. *The Chronicle-Herald*, 23 September 1999, p. A3.

26. *The Chronicle-Herald*, 21 September 1999.

27. *The Chronicle-Herald*, 23 September 1999, p. A1.

28. *The Chronicle-Herald*, 1 October 1999, p. A10.

29. *The Chronicle-Herald*, 23 September 1999, p. A3.

30. Kenneth Kernaghan and David Siegel, *Public Administration in Canada* (Toronto: Methuen, 1987), p. 487.

31. *The Chronicle-Herald*, 22 October 1999, p. A5.

32. See *The Chronicle-Herald*, 15 October 1999, p. A11 and *The Chronicle-Herald*, 18 November 1999, p. A2.

33. *The Chronicle-Herald*, 26 October 1999, p. A9.

34. *The Chronicle-Herald*, 7 October 1999, p. A4.

35. The value of commercial lobster licences varies considerably across the 21 lobster fishing districts in the waters around the Maritime provinces. In district 34 of southwest Nova Scotia, for example, the estimated landed value per lobster licence is over $150,000 per annum. The corresponding number in district 23 (which includes the waters around Burnt Church) is a much more modest $42,000 per annum. Ken S. Coates, *The Marshall Decision and Native Rights* (Montreal: McGill-Queen's University Press, 2000), p. 216.

36. *The Chronicle-Herald*, 5 October 1999.

37. *The Chronicle-Herald*, 20 October 1999, p. A2.

38. The full text can be found at <http://www.gov.ns.ca/abor/pubs/marstwo.pdf>.

39. *The Chronicle-Herald*, 18 November 1999.

40. *The Chronicle-Herald*, 16 February 2000, pp A1-A2.

41. *The Chronicle-Herald*, 25 March 2000, p. A4.

42. *The Chronicle-Herald*, 15 March 2000.

43. Negotiations between DFO and the 35 Mi'kmaq bands in the Maritimes have proceeded much more slowly in 2001. As of 1 April 2001, none of the bands had signed an interim arrangement with Ottawa. There are indications, however, that a three-year deal between DFO and the Millbrook First Nation is imminent. See <http://www.herald.ns.ca/stories/2001/05/11/f131.raw.html>.

44. Alan C. Cairns, *Citizens Plus: Aboriginal Peoples and the Canadian State* (Vancouver: UBC Press, 2000), p. 169.

45. *The Chronicle-Herald*, 19 October 1999, p. A2. The new national chief of the AFN, Matthew Coon Come, has made similar observations. In the spring of 2001, Atlantic chiefs have declined to make short-term fishing arrangements with the federal government for fear of putting at risk their long-term claims to treaty rights. "The Chiefs are united in their resistance to this immoral approach," asserted Coon Come, "and I commend them for this." At <http://www.afn.ca/ Press%20Releases%20&%20Speeches/National Chief Supports Atlantic Chiefs and Communities in Fisheries Negotiations.htm>.

46. *The Chronicle-Herald*, 8 November 1999, p. A1.

47. *The Chronicle-Herald*, 2 February 2000, p. A1.

48. *The Chronicle-Herald*, 27 January 2000, p. A4.

49. *The Chronicle-Herald*, 21 October 1999, p. A5.

50. *The Chronicle-Herald*, 29 September 1999, p. D2.

51. Flanagan, *First Nations*, p. 140.

52. Harold E.L. Prens, *The Mi'kmaq: Resistance, Accommodation and Cultural Survival* (Fort Worth: Harcourt Brace, 1996), p. 214.

53. Report of the Royal Commission on Aboriginal Peoples, *Volume 2: Restructuring the Relationship* (Ottawa: Supply and Services Canada, 1996), p. 569.

54. Flanagan, *First Nations*, p. 11.

55. Joanne Barnaby, "Culture and Sovereignty," in *Nation to Nation,* ed. Engelstad and Bird, p. 44.

56. Oren Lyons, "Traditional Native Philosophies Relating to Aboriginal Rights," in *The Quest for Justice: Aboriginal Peoples and Aboriginal Rights*, ed. Menno Boldt and J. Anthony Long (Toronto: University of Toronto Press, 1985), p. 19.

57. Michael Asch, *Home and Native Land* (Toronto: Methuen, 1984), p. 76.

58. Here, I take issue with Seymour Lipset's classic attempt to differentiate the political cultures of Canada and the United States. Lipset concluded that "Canada

is more particularistic (group-attitude conscious) than the seemingly more universalistic United States." (S. M. Lipset, "Revolution and Counterrevolution: The United States and Canada," in *The Canadian Political Process: A Reader*, 2d ed, ed. Orest M. Kruhlak, Richard Schultz and Sidney I. Pobihushchy (Toronto: Holt, Rinehart and Winston, 1973), p. 15.

59. See *The Chronicle-Herald*, 1 October 1999, p. A1 and *The Chronicle-Herald*, 5 October 1999, p. A1.

60. *The Chronicle-Herald*, 22 October 1999, p. A1.

61. *The Chronicle-Herald*, 16 December 1999, p. A16.

62. Patricia Monture-Angus, *Journeying Forward: Discovering First Nations' Independence* (Halifax: Fernwood, 1999), p. 31.

63. Gerald R. Alfred, *Heeding the Voices of Our Ancestors* (Toronto: Oxford University Press, 1995), p. 80.

64. Report of the Royal Commission on Aboriginal Peoples, *Volume 1: Looking Forward, Looking Back*, p. 128.

65. Menno Boldt and J. Anthony Long, "Tribal Philosophies and the Canadian Charter of Rights and Freedoms," in *Governments in Conflict*, ed. Boldt and Long, p. 167.

66. Dan Russell, *A People's Dream: Aboriginal Self-Government in Canada* (Vancouver: UBC Press, 2000), p. 96.

67. Peter Kulchyski, Don McCaskill and David Newhouse, *In the Words of Elders* (Toronto: University of Toronto Press, 1999), p. xvi.

68. *The Chronicle-Herald*, 7 January 2000, p. A8.

69. *The Chronicle-Herald*, 20 January 2000, p. A11.

70. *The Chronicle-Herald*, 23 September 1999, p. A3.

71. *The Globe and Mail*, 29 August 2000, p. A6.

72. *The Globe and Mail*, 22 August 2000, p. A13.

73. Chief Frank Meuse, Jr., interview with the author, Bear River, 1 September 2000.

74. Cairns, p. 89.

75. A detailed summary of both the methodology and the findings can be found at <http://www.gov.ns.ca/abor/pubs/Report_Aboriginal_Issues.PDF>.

76. Coates, *The Marshall Decision and Native Rights*, p. 159.

77. *The Chronicle-Herald*, 2 October 1999, p. C3.

78. Ibid.

79. *The Chronicle-Herald*, 22 January 1999, p. C1.

15

Where One Lives and What One Thinks: Implications of Rural-Urban Opinion Cleavages for Canadian Federalism

Fred Cutler and Richard W. Jenkins

Ce chapitre examine le mythe populaire selon lequel les habitants des régions rurales auraient des valeurs intolérantes et des attitudes qui pourraient être un obstacle à un compromis constitutionnel. Les auteurs ont ainsi développé une typologie qui classifie les lieux de résidence au Canada selon quatre types: rural, petite ville, urbain et métropolitain. À l'aide des données de Statistiques Canada, ils ont fait correspondre les répondants de l'Étude sur le référendum canadien et ceux de l'Étude sur l'élection canadienne (1992-1993) à leurs lieux de résidence respectifs et ils les ont ensuite classifiés selon la typologie élaborée. Ils ont utilisé les questions de sondage quant à leur attitude envers les féministes, les homosexuels, le Québec, les immigrants, les minorités visibles et les Autochtones, ainsi que des questions quant aux politiques envers ces groupes. Ces réponses ont ensuite été comparées selon les quatre types. Dans l'ensemble, peu de résultats pouvaient confirmer l'avis selon lequel les Canadiens habitants des zones rurales seraient significativement moins tolérants et accommodants envers les minorités. Le péquenaud intolérant serait donc un mythe. Les petites différences trouvées s'expliquent largement par un contrôle des résultats à l'aide de la variable éducation. Il est donc très improbable qu'un clivage rural-urbain en politique canadienne soit un obstacle lors d'éventuelles négociations constitutionnelles au Canada.

In a federal state it may be inevitable that regional and provincial cleavages dominate politics and the analysis of it.[1] These units are institutionalized either formally in the case of provinces or more informally in the case of regions (even here there are regional institutions); thus they have the ability to define political conflict. Yet other important fault lines can be layered beneath or cut across conflicts institutionalized by a federal system.

One such cleavage which has received a good deal of anecdotal attention in Canada, especially with the rise of the Reform/Alliance Party in the 1990s, is a reputed urban-rural divide. A crude stereotype characterizes rural English-speaking Canadians as resentful of the affluence of the big cities, feeling that their interests (especially agricultural interests) are ignored, sceptical of or hostile to Quebec's demands for greater powers, wanting a reduction in the number of immigrants accepted into Canada, less willing to accept the claims of Aboriginal people, at odds with the majority view on issues such as gun registration, and morally conservative. If this picture were even partially accurate, the urban-rural divide in Canadian public opinion would be a serious obstacle to the kind of multinational and multicultural accommodation required for progress on Canada's constitutional agenda. But increasing urbanization might eventually remove this obstacle, if, in fact, it is something about the non-urban setting that gives rise to distinct political attitudes.

Secondarily, it is easy to confuse rural-urban cleavages with regional cleavages on matters of public opinion. Much popular commentary outside western Canada portrays "the west" and "westerners" as hewers of wood and ploughers of fields and links this to political attitudes, when in fact the west is not substantially less urbanized than the rest of the country. The notion of a distinct western public opinion may therefore be inappropriately linked to notions of distinct rural opinion. Deeper investigation of the rural-urban cleavage in Canada is an important step toward clarifying regional differences of opinion that may be more directly relevant to the future of Canadian federalism.

The purpose of this chapter is to examine the political consequences of the locales in which people live. First, how viable are common understandings about the way rural-dwellers' attitudes differ from those of urbanites on questions of moral traditionalism? Though these are not directly relevant to federalism, if there are sharp cleavages based on geography there may be a strong effect on party politics, such as, which social groupings are integrated into which electoral coalitions. Moreover, questions of moral traditionalism relate directly to social identities, and these have been particularly relevant to the constitutional debate with the growth of a rights-based discourse since the constitutional negotiations of the early 1980s. Second, are cultural, ethnic, and national attitudes, in particular those relevant to accommodation of different social groups, influenced by the kinds of communities in which Canadians live?

We begin the inquiry with a brief account of the changing patterns of urban and rural living. On the basis of this discussion, a general typology of the communities people live in is developed. It is then possible, using Canadian Election Study survey data, to compare the political attitudes of people living in different types of communities. Finally, we conduct exploratory multivariate analyses that allow us to differentiate the independent influence of community context on political attitudes. This enables us to assess whether differences, if there are any, are largely a function of who lives where or are a function of social, economic, and demographic characteristics of the varied communities in which Canadians find themselves. Ultimately, we find that while an urban-rural cleavage exists on questions of moral traditionalism (as some stereotypes might have it), that cleavage narrows to near insignificance on questions directly related to accommodation of Canada's ethnic and national minorities.

THE IMPORTANCE OF PLACE IN PUBLIC OPINION RESEARCH

By their nature, public opinion surveys do not take place or community seriously. Surveys reify the individual and separate that individual from his or her local context.[2] Respondents are selected by a random process that is usually designed to generate a representative cross-section of the national electorate. Often over-sampling of particular areas takes place so that inferences can be made about particular regions or provinces (i.e., Quebec), but more local conditions and factors are ignored.

There is, however, a tradition of taking local context seriously in the study of political behaviour dating back to the early election research.[3] A number of recent studies support the view that "individuals' political views are subject to social influence."[4] How then could place matter for our understanding of public opinion in Canada?

Two possibilities suggest themselves. The first is that place could matter from a compositional perspective. Different places have different types of people reflecting differences in economic, demographic, religious, and other social characteristics. Cleavages then, could be understood to be the product of the distribution of where people with different characteristics reside or the patterns of their migration. Since people with higher levels of education are more accommodating to Quebec and tend also to reside in urban areas, we might expect a rural-urban cleavage to emerge.[5]

The second possibility is that place could matter because people who share similar places have similar interests and/or are exposed to similar experiences and social communication. Do people who live in small towns see the world through small-town glasses? Duncan and Epps suggest the existence of a rural ideology or "countrymindedness" which accounts in part for the success of the Australian National Party in rural areas of Australia.[6]

The particular importance of rural-urban context for political beliefs and voting has been the subject of a number of studies outside Canada. Charnock has found by merging census and survey data in Australia that although the vote is largely a product of national patterns, party support is conditional on the local characteristics in which the voters find themselves.[7] The local economic conditions of the district and the degree to which the district is rural (based on primary occupation) affect party support even when the respondent's occupation and income are controlled.[8]

One would certainly expect local effects to be evident in Canada given the geography of election results. Gidengil and her colleagues show variations in the determinants of voting behaviour in the different regions.[9] Cutler shows that local economic conditions and other relevant local characteristics have sensible and sometimes quite powerful influences on citizens' thinking on political issues and ultimately on their voting behaviour.[10] Other work demonstrates that a very simple localism operates in Canadian voters' response to party leaders' geographic affiliations: all else being equal, voters prefer a party whose leader is from nearby to one from far away.[11] Few would doubt that, in general, place matters for public opinion and electoral behaviour in Canada.

Residential mobility means that untangling these competing possibilities for rural and urban differences is not simple. Some of what we observe will reflect where people choose to live, which may invite us to wrongly attribute differences to the places themselves. For example, an intolerant person may simply choose to reside in a place where minorities are absent. Nevertheless, it is important that we come to terms with the implications of where people live for their political attitudes.

COMMUNITIES IN CANADA: DEVELOPING AN URBAN-RURAL TYPOLOGY

Despite the magnitude of its geography, Canada is largely an urban society. According to the 1996 census, 60 percent of Canadians live in one of the 25 census metropolitan areas (CMAs), 77.9 percent of people live in urban areas, and only 2.5 percent of the population is categorized as rural farm population.[12] The general historical trend has been one of urbanization. A number of recent reports suggest that rural areas have grown in population, but it is clear that the rural share of the population is declining.[13] More importantly, urban spillover and more general, urban-dominated growth[14] are such that rural and small-town growth is largely taking place in areas near the commuting zones of larger urban centres.[15]

Given the discussion above, if a geographic cleavage underlies political attitudes and conflict, then we must understand local contexts in more nuanced terms than a simple urban-rural dichotomy would allow. We suggest that it makes sense to speak of four types of political communities: rural, small town, urban, and metropolitan. The obvious basis for distinguishing local contexts is city size (e.g., population density) with greater density being associated with greater urbanization, as long as proximity to urban centres is also factored in.[16] After briefly identifying the basis for the community types discussed here, we provide evidence that the community types have population characteristics consistent with the classification.

Statistics Canada defines a rural area as a place where the population is less than 1,000 and population density is less than 400 per square km.[17] This definition has the advantage of being easy to impose on census data, but the disadvantage of not allowing one to take into account the broader characteristics of the community. For example, a small place on the outskirts of Toronto may be different from a small place in northern Ontario. Approximately 9 percent of those people who fall within the boundaries of a CMA or CA (census agglomeration area), live in local contexts that are rural in terms of population.[18]

Cross-cutting the urban-rural distinction are Statistics Canada's definitions of urban centres. Cities in Canada are designated as CMAs if they have a population of 100,000 or more in their urban core and CAs if they have a population of 10,000 but less than 100,000. CAs and CMAs also include surrounding urban and rural areas that "have a high degree of social and economic integration with the urban core"[19] such as Richmond Hill or Manotick, Ontario.[20] The distinction between CA or CMA places and other locales provides a good basis for distinguishing urban from rural places.[21] Certainly the CMAs, in particular those where the bulk of the CMA population resides (Montreal, Toronto, Calgary, Edmonton, Winnipeg, Ottawa, Hamilton, Quebec City, and Vancouver), fit our perception of urban locales.

The four types of community discussed here balance strict population-based criteria with a recognition that closeness to major urban centres is indicative of the urban character of a community. We therefore defined all those people who live in areas covered by a CMA or CA as urban before further distinguishing these respondents. Doing so means that some respondents are treated as urban when they actually reside in relatively small communities. What links all respondents from urban areas is the importance of the urban core. For those people who live within a CMA or CA, the urban centre will define work, leisure and shopping activities for a significant proportion of the population.

The rural/small-town category includes municipalities with large populations that fall short of being designated a CA, but nevertheless are quite large. It is possible, however, to distinguish between rural areas and small town areas within our general rural category because Statistics Canada classifies each census subdivision (CSD) as rural or urban based on the population criteria discussed above. Rural areas are those communities dominated by agriculture and other primary resource industries, but also communities with very low population densities located some distance from major urban centres.[22] Small towns are those communities that are large enough to provide many of the services required by their populations and are not located near major population centres. The towns of Amherstburg, Ontario (pop. 8,790) and Perth, Ontario (pop. 5,565) along with places like Tisdale, Saskatchewan (pop. 3,045) are considered small town in our classification. Note, however, that common parlance would call many of the places with populations over 10,000 as "small town" (e.g., Salmon Arm, BC, Collingwood, ON, or North Battleford, SK), but in our classification they are called "urban" — the line must be drawn somewhere.

There are a number of alternative ways that one could distinguish between the various types of urban communities. Within both CMAs and CAs there are downtown or core neighbourhoods, suburban neighbourhoods, and fringe communities of various sizes. While one should not foreclose the possibility of finding significant differences between core and suburban locales within large cities,[23] the conventional story about urban and rural cleavages suggests that the large cities themselves are somehow different from the rest. Based on this logic, we classify as "metropolitan" areas the 25 communities designated as CMAs by Statistics Canada.[24] Urban communities are those areas that do not fall within one of the CMAs but are located within the sphere of major cities (CAs with population over 10,000). Included in the urban category are Barrie, Ontario (pop. 62,710); Lethbridge, Alberta (pop. 60,915); and Bathurst, New Brunswick (pop. 14,405). These areas obviously vary in population size, sharing only their socio-geographical independence from one of the CMAs. Importantly, we do not want to treat small communities on the edge of major centres as equivalent to small towns elsewhere in Canada.

We thus have four types of places: rural, small town, urban, and metropolitan. About half of our respondents come from metropolitan areas, 20 percent from areas that fall within CAs, and about 30 percent from rural or small-town locales. An added feature of the classification is that it cuts across provincial and regional differences; community type is not another measure of regionalism. To assess the degree to which this classification speaks to real differences in the aggregate characteristics of these different communities, Table 1 compares the distribution of various CSD-level variables and gives a breakdown of the classification by province.[25]

As we would expect, the classification does a reasonable job of sorting individuals in terms of the size of the CSD in which they live. On average, rural areas have populations smaller by 1,800 persons than those classified as small towns. The urban areas are also significantly larger than the small-town category.[26] Table 1 also shows that there are significant differences in the composition of these different places. We would expect urban areas to be more diverse from an ethnic perspective and to contain more educated respondents, and this appears to be the case.

The number of immigrants, as a percentage of the population of the CSD, gets higher as one moves from smaller to larger places, but the most important difference, consistent with patterns of immigration, is between metropolitan and all of the rest of the places. Respondents who live in metropolitan areas encounter a significant immigrant presence. They are also more likely to come into contact with people whose mother tongue is not one of the official languages.

The percentage of people employed in farm occupations suggests that the distinction between rural and small town is a meaningful one. On average, 10 percent of people living in rural areas are employed in farming (and thus a great many

Table 1: Provincial Composition and Characteristics of Our Place Types

	Rural	Small Town	Urban	Metropolitan
Province				
Newfoundland	37%	18%	18%	26%
Prince Edward Island	43%	11%	45%	0%
Nova Scotia	31%	15%	21%	32%
New Brunswick	23%	9%	41%	25%
Ontario	8%	9%	26%	55%
Manitoba	17%	13%	9%	58%
Saskatchewan	22%	15%	18%	43%
Alberta	9%	14%	12%	62%
British Columbia	7%	13%	27%	51%
Population in CSD				
Mean	3,060	4,840	36,263	342,758
SD	4,428	3,256	30,525	291,576
Immigrants as a Percentage of Population (CSD)				
Mean	5.02	7.26	8.53	21.26
SD	5.18	4.96	5.85	11.51
Percentage Official Language Mother Tongue (CSD)				
Mean	92.56	91.22	91.9	79.83
SD	10.5	9.52	5.47	10.93
Percentage in Farm Occupations (CSD)				
Mean	10.63	3.43	2.02	0.88
SD	12.59	4.02	2	1.34
Family Low Income (Statcan) Rate (CSD)				
Mean	11.09	11.71	12.47	14.3
SD	6.63	5.12	4.22	5.57
Percentage with less than Grade 9 Education				
Mean	21	17	13	10
SD	10	8	5	5
Percentage with University Degrees				
Mean	5	6	8	15
SD	4	3	3	6

more will be in families where one earner has such an occupation), compared with only 3 percent for the respondents living in a small town.

POLITICAL VALUES AND CULTURE

Countries around the world must accommodate significant cultural and ethnic differences within their own borders. For many observers, the willingness of citizens to value diversity is an important axis of political conflict in contemporary societies.[27]

In Canada, pluralism and ethnic accommodation are institutionalized in policies of official bilingualism and multiculturalism,[28] in the rights of Aboriginal peoples delineated in the constitution, and in the *de facto* special status of Quebec in federal-provincial relations. Of course, these federal policies are not universally applauded. Their legitimacy has been questioned by successive Quebec governments who have not viewed official bilingualism as a satisfactory policy position for the realization of "national" goals and the protection of "national" culture, and by many Aboriginal people who continue to press for the entrenchment of an "inherent right" to self-government in the constitution.

After the failure of the Meech Lake Accord the public's attitudes on questions of accommodation have become more important to the achievement of progress on the constitutional agenda.[29] The failure of the elite accommodation model means that future constitutional proposals, negotiation, and ratification will be tied more closely to what citizens will ultimately accept in a referendum. Thus any divisions within Canadian society on issues related to the accommodation of diversity will likely force their way into political activity of all kinds, particularly electoral politics. If a rural-urban divide is responsible for patterns of conflict in electoral politics, the results of that politics, particularly because seat shares are amplified from vote shares, may further entrench a perception that rural and urban interests are in opposition.

For example, some observers have suggested a link between what is seen as a city versus country divide in support for the Reform/Alliance Party and that party's positions on provincial equality, minority (Charter) rights, immigration, and Aboriginal affairs. The implication would be that people who live in areas where Reform/Alliance Party candidates were elected are sympathetic to that party's platform, including strict equality of the provinces and rejection of distinct society wording, reducing the number of immigrants, revoking the *Multiculturalism Act*, and limiting the distinct treatment of Aboriginal people in Canadian law. Even before the rise of the Reform/Alliance Party, Canadians living outside large urban areas were roughly stereotyped as less keen on government policies that were put in place to better accommodate Canada's linguistic and cultural diversity.

At a higher geographic level, but still relevant here, the report on the 1997 election study shows that "westerners are not more fiscally conservative, less willing to accommodate Quebec, or more socially conservative than their Ontario counterparts."[30] Feelings about Quebec, though, were only important in the voting decisions of westerners. And "westerners were a little less sympathetic to out groups than voters in Ontario and it was only in the West that voters who were less sympathetic towards out groups were attracted to Reform."[31] This is no doubt responsible for a stereotype (and our working hypothesis) of rural Canadians as being less tolerant or accommodative. But it conflates western with rural: the association is overdrawn. Statistics Canada classifies as urban 77 percent of those living west of the Manitoba-Ontario border; Ontario's figure is a mere 6 percent higher (83 percent).

The possibility remains open, then, that a rural-urban cleavage cuts across the more prominent west-Ontario "divide": rural westerners *and* rural Ontarians may prefer the policies proposed by the Reform/Alliance Party. But there is a range of policy- and non–policy-related explanations beyond preferences on federal and cultural accommodation that could account for the geographic patterning of Reform/Alliance success. It is possible that non-urban Canadians west of the Ottawa River have provided relatively strong support to Reform/Alliance due to the perception that Reform/Alliance speaks for farm interests, has a strong element of moral traditionalism, is more overtly Christian, advocates smaller government and lower taxes, or wishes to relax party discipline in Parliament.[32] The data hint otherwise, showing that the rural base for Reform/Alliance support is not as strong as it is often portrayed. Although the Reform/Alliance nationally enjoyed an advantage in small towns, its level of support was not sharply differentiated by place type: support was 21 percent (rural), 31 percent (small town), 19 percent (urban), and 22 percent (metro) across our four place types. Moreover, half of the party's support in 1993 came from metropolitan areas.[33] These numbers undermine the notion that there is a wide urban-rural divide in Reform/Alliance support and, by association, the attitudes under investigation here.

This chapter nevertheless addresses the possibility that an urban-rural divide on constitutionally relevant attitudes presents an obstacle to the accommodation of the aspirations of Quebec, Aboriginal peoples, and racial or cultural minorities. We focus on attitudes toward Quebec, racial or ethnic minorities, and Aboriginal people. Reporting on the 1992 referendum study, Johnston and his colleagues showed a very strong association between feeling for Quebec and voting in the Charlottetown Accord referendum.[34] Attitudes toward minority rights and the degree to which the constitution ought to reflect Canada's *three* founding peoples were weaker, but still important, influences on Canadians' 1992 referendum decision. If there is an urban-rural cleavage on questions such as these, it will undoubtedly manifest itself in noticeable urban-rural patterns in voting on any future constitutional referendums.

DATA AND METHODOLOGY

The 1992 Canadian Referendum (RS) and 1993 Canadian Election Study (CES) provide measurements of Canadians' attitudes on questions of cultural accommodation. And crucially, it is possible to link respondents to units of census geography through a procedure undertaken by the authors, allowing us to accurately place people in one of our four place types.[35] Our procedure takes the respondents' report of their postal code (the first three digits) and links this to census geography with the Statistics Canada Postal Code Conversion File. This gives us access to all of the census variables for various levels of aggregation, the most important of which is the population of the respondent's census subdivision (CSD). Once respondents are classified into a community type, we can then compare attitudes in the four places.

To begin, we look for an urban-rural divide on moral traditionalism, which provides us a baseline for understanding the significance of rural-urban differences. If there is a rural-urban cleavage, we would expect to find it on these kinds of questions, so we have a good initial test of the utility of our community typology. There are a number of questions that explicitly tap these attitudes, allowing us to establish whether our classification of places captures a widely suspected urban-rural difference in cultural and political attitudes. Two feeling thermometer variables are relevant: feelings about feminists and feelings about homosexuals. Two policy questions translate general group feelings into concrete policy terms. The first concerns whether society would be better off if more women stayed home and the second asks whether homosexuals should be allowed to marry.

Next, we move on to questions more directly relevant to the federal condition in Canada. Four questions tap attitudes about Quebec. One question measures generalized feelings about Quebec, simply asking how warmly people feel on a "feeling thermometer" (0° to 100°). Johnston and his co-authors show that a 0° to 100° difference in the feeling thermometer translates into a whopping 45 percent difference in the likelihood of support for the Charlottetown Accord.[36] Two questions raise policy considerations about the privileged place of Quebec in national politics. One asks very generally "how much should the federal government do for Quebec — more, less, or the same?" The other more specific policy question solicits support or opposition to the use of "distinct society" wording in the constitution. The importance of these attitudes to rest of Canada acceptance of a constitutional deal is obvious. Finally, we simply break down respondents' reports of how they voted in the Charlottetown referendum.

Policy and feelings are at least theoretically distinct; these questions are not simply measuring the same thing. One can, for example, have positive feelings about Quebec even if those feelings do not translate into support for the policy measures because these may be guided by other fundamental ideological orientations (i.e., liberal individualism in the case of distinct society).

The referendum study of 1992 and the CES of 1993 asked a number of questions relevant to minority rights, Aboriginal peoples, and feelings about racial minorities. One set taps general attitudes about immigration and racial minorities. The first two questions explicitly raise the issue of racial minorities, one in terms of policy and the other in terms of feelings. The format is identical to the Quebec questions: one asks how much should be done for racial minorities and the other is a feeling thermometer. The third question takes a different approach to the policy question by asking whether more or fewer immigrants should be admitted to Canada.

Another question gets at the more abstract notion of majoritarianism versus minority rights. It asks: "Which is more important in a democratic society: letting the majority decide, or protecting the rights and needs of minorities?" Johnston and his colleagues show that a minority-rights view on this question increased support for the Charlottetown Accord by 7 percent. [37]

Separately, we examine three questions relating to Aboriginal peoples: whether Canada has three founding peoples, whether the constitution should recognize Aboriginal self-government, and whether Aboriginal people should be able to make their own laws. Those giving affirmative answers to the three-founding-peoples question and the self-government question were respectively 12 percent and 15 percent more supportive of Charlottetown.[38]

Taken together, attitudes on these issues constitute the popular foundation of the kind of constitutional compromise that was embodied in the Charlottetown and Meech Lake Accords. Whether or not the overall level of support for the accommodative side of these questions implies that the foundation is solid or crumbling, this inquiry will tell us if the structure leans dangerously toward the country or the city. Most commentators would assume that the house is subsiding on the side facing away from the city, but there is little evidence thus far for this view.

RESULTS

MORAL CONSERVATISM

Our expectations here are clearly validated, according to Table 2. People living in different places have different attitudes on questions associated with "morality" by the conservative right and with "progressiveness" by the liberal left. Smaller places are home to more conservative attitudes. Although Canadians from all places are not overwhelmingly liberal, here the stereotype of rural intolerance is not misplaced.

Table 2: Moral Traditionalism by Community Type

	Rural	Small Town	Urban	Metropolitan	N
Feelings					
Homosexuals	34.2°*	37.2°*	43.1°*	48.9°*	
Feminists	50.3°	52.5°	52.2°	55.5°	(2,094)
Homosexual Marriage (%)					
Strongly disagree	54.7	54.6	48.1	40.8	
Somewhat disagree	12.1	11.9	11.2	15.0	
Don't know	5.7	5.4	5.1	5.3	
Somewhat agree	20.1	22.7	25.1	24.2	
Strongly agree	7.4	5.4	10.6	14.8	(2,069)
Mean (−2 to + 2)	−0.87*	−0.88*	−0.61*	−0.43*	(2,069)
Society Better Off if More Women Stayed Home (%)					
Strongly disagree	26.2	26.2	29.9	37.9	
Somewhat disagree	19.1	20.4	20.3	18.8	
Don't know	3.0	2.3	1.3	1.3	
Somewhat agree	22.8	24.2	26.7	20.3	
Strongly agree	28.9	26.9	21.9	21.7	(2,081)
Mean (−2 to + 2)	0.09*	0.05*	−0.09*	−0.31*	(2,081)

Note: *significantly different from at least one other column at $p < 0.05$.

Feelings about homosexuals clearly define the rural-urban cleavage. There is an almost linear relationship between people's feelings about homosexuals and the nature of the community in which people find themselves. Feelings about feminists exhibit much smaller differences, but the same pattern is evident. The policy issues reveal that these differences in feelings are accompanied by significant differences in attitudes about marriage for homosexuals and women's participation in the workforce. On each issue there is a ten percentage point gap between the rural and metropolitan communities. In fact, most of the difference is between rural and small-town communities on the one hand, and urban categories on the other.

The rural-urban cleavage holds up when we control for other potential sociodemographic influences on these attitudes, including age, education, religion, gender, marital status, and region. For feelings about homosexuals, the regression coefficients (available from authors) corresponding to the differ-ences in Table 2 indicate that people in smaller areas are on average less positive than in metropolitan areas: 15° (rural), 12° (small town), and 6° (urban) less positive. Introducing the controls reduces the differences to 9°, 8°, and 3°. The gap remains, but is reduced in half on the question of homosexual mar-riage.[39] On the other issue, whether women should work outside the home, the difference across community types goes away with the controls. Educa-tion, religious identification, and gender are the most important variables for accounting for political attitudes related to moral traditionalism.

These results reveal three things. First, there is evidence of a cleavage on social conservative attitudes consistent with expectations about the cultural differences between rural and urban life. Second, the results show that the classification of respondents into four different types of community environ-ments is able to identify cleavages based on community size. And third, that the socio-demographic composition of the place types (e.g., education levels) are likely suspects in the search for an explanation for any cleavages we ob-serve. Establishing the utility of this classification for understanding rural-urban differences in public opinion permits us to be more confident of any conclusions we derive on the issues more directly relevant to Canadian federalism, to which we now turn.

NATIONAL UNITY AND QUEBEC

The conventional view is that there is a sizable urban-rural cleavage on issues related to national unity, with rural Canada sharing a particularly negative view of Quebec. Table 3 suggests that rural and small-town Canada is not a significant barrier to an accommodation with Quebec.

One can detect a statistically significant difference in group feelings by community size, but the differences are relatively small.[40] People living in rural and small-town Canada on average have less positive attitudes toward Quebec, either measured simply as feelings toward Quebec or in relation to their more general feelings about Canada. The relationship between feelings and community size is not, however, linear. Here, living in a small town com-pared with a rural area makes no difference; both are equally negative to Quebec. People living in a metropolitan area are most positive toward Que-bec. Those living in urban non-metropolitan areas have more intermediate feelings. Although significant, the largest difference is only a matter of six or seven points on the 100 point scale, which is half the size of the difference on feelings about homosexuals. Given Johnston *et al.*'s results on the relation-ship between feelings and Charlottetown vote, the seven-point feeling difference found here would suggest only a 3 percent difference in support for the Accord.[41]

Table 3: Quebec Attitudes by Community Type

	Rural	Small Town	Urban	Metropolitan	N
Rating of Quebec	53°*	52°*	56°*	59°*	(2,094)
Canada rating minus					
Quebec rating	37°*	36°*	33°*	30°*	(2,094)
Do for Quebec (%)					
Much less	15	14	18	17	
Somewhat less	20	27	19	22	
About the same	54	49	52	50	
Somewhat more	5	6	8	8	
Much more	6	4	3	4	(2,094)
Mean (−2 to +2)	−0.32*	−0.42	−0.40	−0.40	(2,094)
Charlottetown YES (%)	44	31*	44	44	(1,386)
Distinct society					
Agree	38*	34*	46*	49*	(693)

Note: *significantly different from at least one other column at p < 0.05.

When it comes to policy, the "do for Quebec" question indicates that rural communities tend to differ from the other places, but the difference is small and it is in the wrong direction. Consider that 35 percent of rural Canadians want to do less for Quebec compared with 39 percent of those living in metropolitan areas.[42] On support for the Charlottetown Accord, which clearly goes to the question of the political impact of the cleavage, the evidence is again mixed. Rural Canada was no more opposed to the Accord than urban and metropolitan Canada. Small-town Canada stands out as 13 percent more likely to oppose the Accord, but this raises more questions since rural Canada did not share this tendency. The only question that generates a clear urban-rural divide (over 10 percent) is on agreement with distinct society status for Quebec, asked after the referendum campaign of 1992. Here the key difference is between rural and small town on the one hand, and the two urban categories on the other. In fact, almost a majority of urban dwellers of the two types agree that "we should recognize Quebec as a distinct society."

The cleavage width is generally small, but it could be objected that failing to control for regional variations might have the effect of suppressing the rural-urban cleavage. Common parlance suggests wide regional differences in attitudes toward Quebec, with the west being particularly francophobic, even if more rigorous analyses have not found large regional differences in these attitudes.[43] Controlling for region has no effect on the relationship between feelings or voting on Charlottetown and community size. Regional controls, though, erase the seemingly perverse positive impact of being rural on the "do for Quebec" question.

The variable that on an individual level most clearly accounts for attitudes about Quebec is education. Educational achievement is associated with where one lives, and as Johnston *et al.* argue, having a postsecondary education is associated with increased feeling toward French Canada and a greater willingness to accommodate Quebec demands. Controlling for education reduces the impact of community size on feeling considerably: differences of −6°, −7°, and −3° for rural, small town, and urban respectively are halved with the inclusion of education.[44] Education has no effect on reducing the influence of being from a small town on voting for the Accord.

Although our sample is restricted to those people living outside Quebec, we should not forget the potential impact of interprovincial migration, in particular, migration of people who lived in Quebec for some period of their life. Francophones who have migrated are especially more likely to have a much stronger attachment to the province than other Canadians outside Quebec. Controlling for whether a person's mother tongue is French does help account for the Quebec attitudes. In particular, in a multivariate model controlling for other demographics as well, the effect of being from a small town on voting "yes" to Charlottetown is reduced almost by half. In part this reflects the fact that people who learned French at an early age and can still speak it are unlikely to live in small-town areas in English Canada as compared with our other community types.

The results, then, are mixed. Small-town and rural Canada may be less sympathetic to distinct society and may harbor more negative attitudes about Quebec, but more positive feelings in urban and metropolitan areas do not translate into wanting to do more for Quebec. Even these modest feeling differences should not be overstated. We find two differences worth noting. There is a clear rural-urban divide on the question of distinct society even if this is not reflected in the other questions. Secondly, small-town Canada was particularly unlikely to support Charlottetown compared with the other places. Nevertheless, in comparison with the previously observed cleavage on questions of moral traditionalism, these differences do not suggest that the rural-urban cleavage is as significant as conventional wisdom suggests. The distinctiveness of rural and small-town Canada on these questions appears to be mainly due to lower levels of educational attainment and a smaller number of mother-tongue francophones in these less urbanized places.

MINORITIES, IMMIGRATION AND ABORIGINAL PEOPLES

Table 4 indicates that there is a slight gradient in opinion on how much to "do for racial minorities" and feeling about racial minorities: attitudes are more positive as community size increases. For the former question, the mean opinion among rural Canadians is to do slightly less for racial minorities (–0.07) while among metropolitan Canadians it is to do slightly more (+0.07). The feeling thermometer replicates this gradient: from 63° (rural) to 70° (metropolitan). On the immigration level question the urban-rural cleavage looks wider: 15 percent more rural residents want fewer immigrants admitted than metropolitan dwellers. However, in both kinds of place, majorities want to reduce the number of immigrants admitted to Canada. All told, attitudes facilitating accommodation of racial minorities and immigrants in Canadian society are more prevalent in urban and metropolitan settings, but the cleavage is not as overwhelming as stereotypes would suggest.

But might this simply reflect the fact that nearly all racial minorities and immigrants live in urban Canada?[45] In short, no. Estimating a multivariate regression model of these attitudes with variables indicating whether respondents are non-white or immigrated from Europe does nothing to diminish the differences we observe on the feeling and immigration level questions. It reduces the "do for racial minorities" difference by less than one-third. Even among Canadians who are not immigrants or visible minorities, there is a small rural-urban cleavage on these issues.

The more abstract questions of minority-majority relations and Canada's founding peoples show absolutely no variation across our four place types. The fact that no differences are found on these relatively abstract theoretical and historical attitudes suggests that any differences are related to either raw feelings about other groups or different interests, not differences in basic values or political principles.

Turning to the questions directly concerning the status of Aboriginal peoples, Table 4 shows that on the question of recognizing Aboriginal self-government and Aboriginal people making their own laws, metropolitan Canadians are about 10 percent more supportive than other Canadians.[46] On both questions though, urban and rural residents are on the same side of the issue: *for* recognizing Aboriginal peoples' right to self-government, but *against* them making their own laws (or, rather, in favour of them abiding by the same laws as other Canadians). Here again, we find a cleavage, but one that is likely not strong enough to be terribly influential for the broad patterns of electoral politics or support for constitutional amendments.

These findings show that there is some truth to common understandings about urban-rural differences in political attitudes that might generally be labelled "tolerance of diversity." The question becomes: Why do these opinions vary according to where citizens live? Is it something about the people who

Table 4: Racial Minorities, Immigration and Aboriginal Peoples: Attitudes by Community Type

	Rural	Small Town	Urban	Metropolitan	N
Do for Racial Minorities (%)					
Much less	8	7	7	9	
Somewhat less	18	20	18	15	
About the same	53	52	49	46	
Somewhat more	14	13	20	19	
Much more	7	8	7	10	(2,094)
Mean (–2 to +2)	–0.07*	–0.05*	0.02*	0.07*	(2,094)
Immigration Level					
Fewer	74	68	66	61	
Same	15	16	19	20	
More	11	16	15	19	(2,094)
Mean (–1 to 1)	–0.63*	–0.53*	–0.51*	–0.42*	(2,094)
Feeling about racial minorities	63°*	64°*	67°*	70°*	(2,094)
Minority rights more important	28	28	28	27	(720)
Three founding peoples	73	73	73	72	(720)
Recognize Aboriginal self-government	59	59	59	71*	(720)
Aboriginal people make own law	15*	14*	19*	25*	(2,095)

Note: *significantly different from at least one other column at $p < 0.05$.

live there (a compositional explanation), or their interaction (a social interaction explanation), or something intrinsic to the places themselves (a contextual/environmental explanation)?

Again, education is much of the story. Outside of cities educational attainment is distinctly lower. In the analysis of voting on the Charlottetown Accord, Johnston and his colleagues conclude that university-educated voters were the only subgroup in favour of the Accord because they "were just relatively minority-oriented."[47] Here, simply controlling for the individual's level of education cuts the urban-rural differences on the "do for racial minorities" and feeling about racial minorities in half, as it did for Quebec feelings. On the immigration level question education reduces the difference relative to the metropolitan category from –0.2 (rural), –0.1 (small town), and –0.08 (small urban) to –0.05, –0.08, and 0.

Education's effect does not, however, extend to Aboriginal affairs. While better educated respondents are indeed more positive about self-government, education is not responsible for the urban-rural differences on either self-government question at the bottom of Table 4. Nor do the differences go away when a host of other controls are introduced, most notably the person's feeling about racial minorities. Although feelings about racial minorities are more positive in metropolitan areas, the advantage in support in metropolitan areas is only reduced from 12 percent to 10 percent for the recognition of self-government and from 9 percent to 7 percent on the "own laws" question when we control for these feelings. Non-Aboriginal attitudes on questions of self-government appear surprisingly distinct from other political attitudes and general feelings toward other minorities in Canadian society. There are two potential explanations for the urban-rural differences on these questions. One is that they are driven by raw feelings toward Aboriginal Canadians: urban Canadians are probably slightly less likely to rely on negative stereotypes of Aboriginal Canadians and more likely to use general feelings of tolerance to inform their judgement. Or, urban Canadians will simply not have to deal with the implications of self-government, whereas some non-urban Canadians will. Unfortunately, we cannot adjudicate between these two possibilities.

None of the remaining variation on any of these questions can be attributed to something about the communities in which citizens live, even using the very detailed descriptors of characteristics of communities available from the census. That is, we have very accurate, exhaustive measurements of the kinds of places respondents live: including immigrant origins, religion, education, occupational composition, and so on. We wondered whether the prevalence of immigrants or visible minorities would affect opinion on racial minorities or immigration, and whether the prevalence of Aboriginal people would affect Aboriginal affairs opinions. Other compositional factors might influence these attitudes — education, income, occupation, religion — but we found no evidence of contextual/environmental influences. This is not simply due to the weakness of the measures or of contextual influences in general; Cutler shows that characteristics of locales can be powerful influences on opinion *if there is an obvious local interest*.[48] On these questions there is no clear local interest that might influence opinion, and so we find no contextual effects.[49]

For adherents of a provincial political culture view of Canadian politics, we found no evidence that the differences in Table 4 were simply a proxy for provincial effects. In fact, most of the differences increased when we included province in a model of the opinions.

DISCUSSION

We began with common wisdom of a wide gulf between rural and urban Canada, but our results suggest that this expectation is rooted in an unfair stereotype. The intolerant rural hick is a straw man. A cleavage does exist but it is neither as wide nor as deep as is often suggested. On questions of moral traditionalism we find the largest differences, even after controlling for individual-level factors, but the differences are not as apparent when we move to ethnic and linguistic tolerance. The cleavage is most obvious when we tap group feelings and smaller or non-existent when we move to questions of policy. On the whole, the differences are unlikely to be an obstacle to future constitutional and social accommodation.

The bottom line is that some of the urban-rural cleavage on these questions can be put down to education, while the remainder appears to be something about a non-urban political culture. These two components of an explanation fit together if education is considered as a mechanism of socialization to the dominant, mainstream values of a society. In contemporary times, those values are determined and promulgated in urban settings. Rural residents are described as "behind-the-times" in many aspects of culture, in part because novelty or progressiveness begins in the metropolis and "catches on" there through social contagion. Tied to this is undoubtedly a self-selection mechanism when it comes to leaving the country and moving to the city. Whether this occurs because the rural economy has been in decline or because in smaller communities social pressures are stronger and thus conservative, more conservative individuals, in the deep and technical sense of the psychology of personality, tend to stay put. These phenomena combine to impart to rural areas their traditional, conservative character, which has some, perhaps weak, implications for national political affairs.

When public opinion has obvious geographic patterns, even if the clarity of these patterns is greatly exaggerated, there is the potential for political parties to align themselves according to these cleavages. The spatial distribution of seats for the Saskatchewan Party and the NDP in Saskatchewan after the 1999 election seems to be a prototypical example. There are clearly few incentives for federal parties to adopt such a strategy, partly because they will risk losing urban support[50] and partly because rural interests are nowhere near as homogeneous at the national level as they are within each province. On national unity issues the potential audience for an anti-Quebec appeal is not spatially defined. There is more scope for such appeals on minority, immigration, and Aboriginal issues, but it is only on questions of moral traditionalism that there is a clear opportunity for a geographically based appeal. Of course, the relative size of the community types means that an appeal aimed at small-town and rural Canada must be fashioned in such a way as not to alienate urban Canadians since urban support is essential for political success. This is all the more difficult since the electorally influential mass media originates from the large urban centres — so parties must make even regionally specific appeals to an audience the majority of which is urban. Of course, this partially explains the fact that the Reform/Alliance Party support is not particularly rural. Yet it also leaves open the possibility that a party advocating intolerance could have national success under the right conditions.

None of this is meant to diminish the reputed importance of rural and small-town grievances, essentially independent of issues, or what Charnock terms "countrymindedness."[51] In fact, our results offer some insight into the issue. First, the lack of a large attitude cleavage means there is a reduced likelihood that parties will emerge to capitalize on the sense of grievance. Second, the importance of education for explaining the existing differences suggests that the cleavage may be a legacy of previous political conflict and socialization. When one considers that Canada is likely to become progressively more urban and educated, we might expect a further reduction of the cleavage and a political system less responsive to rural Canada in the future.

NOTES

Financial support in the form of postdoctoral fellowships from the Social Science and Humanities Research Council of Canada is gratefully acknowledged. Richard Jenkins would also like to acknowledge the financial assistance of Queen's University. The authors would like to thank Elisabeth Gidengil, the editors, and the anonymous reviewers for their helpful comments on an earlier version of this paper.

1.   Charnock suggests that the federal nature of Australia has led researchers interested in accounting for voting patterns to devote attention to federal rather than other types of regional effects. David Charnock, "Spatial Variations, Contextual and Social Structural Influences on Voting for the ALP at the 1996 Federal Election: Conclusions From Multilevel Analyses," *Australian Journal of Political Science* 32, 2(1996):237-54.

2.   This process also has the effect of suggesting that individuals have opinions in a vacuum such that a number of people have argued that the survey is a blunt instrument for understanding attitudes and their role in politics. Susan Herbst, *Numbered Voices: How Opinion Polling has Shaped American Politics* (Chicago: University of Chicago Press, 1993); see also the literature on deliberative polls, for example, James Fishkin, *The Voice of the People: Public Opinion and Democracy* (New Haven: Yale University Press, 1995).

3.   Bernard Berelson, Paul Lazersfeld and William McPhee, *Voting: A Study of Opinion Formation in a Presidential Campaign* (Chicago: University of Chicago

Press, 1954). For a review see John W. Books and Charles L. Prysby, *Political Behavior and the Local Context* (New York: Praeger, 1991).

4. Michael MacKuen and Courtney Brown, "Political Context and Attitude Change," *American Political Science Review* 81, 2(1987):471-90; Robert Huckfeldt and John Sprague, "Networks in Context: The Social Flow of Political Information," *American Political Science Review* 81, 4(1987):1197-216; and K. Jones, R.J. Johnston and C.J. Pattie, "People, Places and Regions: Exploring the Use of Multi-level Modelling in the Analysis of Electoral Data," *British Journal of Political Science* 22(1992):343-80.

5. Richard Johnston, André Blais, Elisabeth Gidengil and Neil Nevitte, *The Challenge of Direct Democracy: The 1992 Canadian Referendum* (Montreal and Kingston: McGill-Queen's University Press, 1996).

6. C.J. Duncan and W.R. Epps, "The Decline of "Countrymindedness": New Players or Changing Values in Australian Rural Politics." *Political Geography* 11, 5(1992):430-48.

7. David Charnock, "National Uniformity, and State and Local Effects on Australian Voting: A Multilevel Approach," *Australian Journal of Political Science* 31, 1(1996):51-66; Charnock, "Spatial Variations, Contextual and Social Structural Influences on Voting for the ALP at the 1996 Federal Election."

8. Charnock uses a multi-level modelling strategy in which the respondent's socio-demographic characteristics are entered along with characteristics of the division in which the respondent resides (there are no attitudinal variables).

9. Elisabeth Gidengil, André Blais, Richard Nadeau and Neil Nevitte, "Making Sense of Regional Voting in the 1997 Canadian Federal Election: Liberal and Reform/Alliance Support Outside Quebec," *Canadian Journal of Political Science* 32, 2(1999):247-72.

10. Fred Cutler, "Local Economies, Local Policy Impacts, and Government Support in Canada," *Canadian Journal of Political Science* (forthcoming, 2002).

11. Fred Cutler, "The Simplest Shortcut of All: Socio-Demographic Similarity, Information, and Voting," *Journal of Politics* (forthcoming, 2002).

12. Larry S. Bourne, "Urban Canada in Transition to the Twenty-First Century: Trends, Issues, and Visions" in *Canadian Cities in Transition*, 2d ed., ed. Trudi Bunting and Pierre Filion (Oxford: Toronto, 2000).

13. Richard Dupuy, Francine Mayer and René Morissette, *Rural Youth: Stayers, Leavers and Return Migrants,* Cat. No. 11F0019MPE. (Ottawa: Statistics Canada, 2000); Robert Mendelsohn and Ray D. Bollman, "Rural and Small Town Population is Growing in the 1990s," Working Paper No. 36. Cat. No. 21-601-MIE98036. (Ottawa: Statistics Canada, 1998).

14. Philip D. Keddie and Alun E. Joseph, "Reclassification and Rural-versus-Urban Population Change in Canada, 1976-1981: A Tale of Two Definitions," *Canadian Geographer* 35, 4(1991): 412-20.

15. Mendelsohn and Bollman, "Rural and Small Town Population is Growing."

16. Distance to the nearest urban centre is used by Keddie and Joseph to distinguish between urban core, rural hinterland, and remote hinterland areas in their analysis

of population growth rates. For a discussion of how to define rural areas see Ken Deavers, "What is Rural?" *Policy Studies Journal* 20, 2(1992):184-89.

17. Statistics Canada. Postal Code Conversion File.

18. Larry S. Bourne, "Urban Canada in Transition to the Twenty-First Century: Trends, Issues, and Visions" in *Canadian Cities in Transition*, 2d ed., ed. Trudi Bunting and Pierre Filion (Oxford: Toronto, 2000).

19. Ibid.

20. A census subdivision (CSD) is included in a CMA or CA if some part of it lies within the urban core of the CMA or, if 50 percent of the employed workforce work in the urbanized core or, if 25 percent of the workforce of the CSD lives in the urban core (Mendelsohn and Bollman "Rural and Small Town Population").

21. Dupuy *et al.*, *Rural Youth* and Mendelsohn and Bollman, "Rural and Small Town Population," use this criteria for distinguishing between rural and small town on the one hand and urban on the other.

22. Researchers at Statistics Canada have experimented with other ways of differentiating the non-CMA/CA population. Howatson-Leo and Earl suggest a method based on metropolitan influence (commuting flows out of a CSD to a CMA/CA. Further work has led to the development of a census metropolitan area and census agglomeration influenced zones (MIZ) for this area to complement the breakdown of the urban areas into urban core, urban fringe and rural fringe. Linda Howatson-Leo and Louise Earl, "A New Approach to NON-CMA/CA Areas," Working Paper No. 31. Cat. No. 21-601-M1E96031. (Ottawa: Statistics Canada, 1996). Sheila Rambeau and Kathleen Todd, "Census Metropolitan Area and Census Agglomeration Influenced Zones (MIZ) With Census Data," Geography Working Paper Series. Cat. No. 92F0138MIE, 2000-1. (Ottawa: Statistics Canada, 2000); Chuck McNiven, Henry Puderer and Darryl Janes, "Census Metropolitan Area and Census Agglomeration Influenced Zones (MIZ): A Description of the Methodology," Geography Working Paper Series. Cat. No. 92F0138MIE, 2000-2. (Ottawa: Statistics Canada, 2000).

23. The possibility of these types of differences was considered, but settling on an appropriate basis for breaking up areas is not intuitively obvious. Are Mississauga or Brampton suburbs of Toronto? They are both part of the Toronto CMA, but calling them suburbs of Toronto seems to overstate the distinction. A suburban designation may be more appropriately applied to geographical areas within municipalities (CSD). Our own analysis using the 1996 census data and the 1997 CES data indicates that the rural fringe, urban fringe, and urban core classification of CSDs within CMA/CAs is not superior to the one used here.

24. These include St. John's, Halifax, Saint John, Chicoutimi-Jonquiere, Quebec, Sherbrooke, Trois-Rivières, Montreal, Ottawa-Hull, Oshawa, Toronto, Hamilton, St. Catharines-Niagara, Kitchener, London, Windsor, Sudbury, Thunder Bay, Winnipeg, Regina, Saskatoon, Calgary, Edmonton, Vancouver, and Victoria.

25. We also compared the distribution of census tract (CT) characteristics but found no significant differences.

26. There are, of course, a number of anomalies that result from the strict application of the rules identified above. Caledonia (Ontario), Lunenburg (Nova Scotia) and Aylesford (Nova Scotia) all have CSD populations above 20,000 but are assigned a rural designation (this affects five respondents). Highly populated rural areas are the exception; half of the respondents classified as rural live in rural communities with fewer that 1,200 people.

27. Herbert Kitschelt, *The Radical Right in Western Europe: A Comparative Analysis* (Ann Arbor, MI: University of Michigan Press, 1995); Hans-Georg Betz, *Radical Right-Wing Populism in Western Europe* (New York: St. Martin's Press, 1994); and Richard W. Jenkins, "How Campaigns Matter: Priming and Learning as Explanations for Reform's 1993 Campaign Success," *Canadian Journal of Political Science* (forthcoming, 2002).

28. Leslie A. Pal, *Interests of State: The Politics of Language, Multiculturalism, and Feminism in Canada* (Montreal: McGill-Queen's University Press, 1993).

29. Ronald Watts, "Canada: Three Decades of Periodic Federal Crises," *International Political Science Review* 17(1996):360, 365-66; Matthew Mendelsohn, "Public Brokerage: Constitutional Reform/Alliance and the Accommodation of Mass Publics," *Canadian Journal of Political Science* 33, 2(2000):245-72.

30. Neil Nevitte, André Blais, Elisabeth Gidengil and Richard Nadeau, *Unsteady State: The 1997 Canadian Federal Election* (Toronto: Oxford University Press, 2000), p. 95.

31. Ibid.

32. There may be a rural interest in relaxed party discipline because it would allow for rural MPs to vote together on matters where a rural interest cuts across party lines.

33. It is possible that this breakdown may differ regionally. In the west the numbers are: 37 percent (rural), 42 percent (small town), 30 percent (urban), and 26 percent (metro). While in Ontario they are: 18 percent (rural), 23 percent (small town), 18 percent (urban), and 18 percent (metro). Thus the urban-rural divide pales in comparison with the west-Ontario one: even small-town Ontarians do not support the party as strongly as urban westerners, two-thirds of whom are from outside Alberta. The Reform/Alliance Party looks more like a western party and less like a rural party. In that sense, regional and provincial alienation look to be more important attitudinal factors for federalism in Canada.

34. Richard Johnston, André Blais, Elisabeth Gidengil and Neil Nevitte, *The Challenge of Direct Democracy: The 1992 Canadian Referendum* (Montreal: McGill-Queen's University Press, 1996), p. 170.

35. It probably would have been just as efficient to ask people whether they live in a rural area, small town, small city, suburb, or urban core. But this would not have enabled the addition of many measurements of the characteristics of the places people live in, as the current method allows.

36. Johnston *et al., The Challenge of Direct Democracy,* p. 170.

37. Ibid.

38. Ibid.

39. Of course, we are unable to control for the sexual orientation of respondents and, given the likely preference of homosexual persons for urban centres, this may explain some of the remaining difference.

40. This is simply to say that the difference we observe would be generated by chance in less than one case of 20 random trials.

41. We simply multiply the seven point difference by the coefficient 0.45 listed in Table 7-6 of Johnston *et al.*, *The Challenge of Direct Democracy*, p. 170.

42. This is not just an artifact of the distribution of "don't knows" across the four community types.

43. Elisabeth Gidengil, André Blais, Richard Nadeau, and Neil Nevitte, "Making Sense of Regional Voting in the 1997 Canadian Federal Election: Liberal and Reform/Alliance Support Outside Quebec," *Canadian Journal of Political Science* 32, 2(1999):247-72.

44. The only exception is that the urban coefficient gets modestly stronger with this control.

45. For our four place types, the percentage visible minorities is 0.2 percent, 0.5 percent, 1 percent, and 5.2 percent; the percentage immigrant is 5.6 percent, 8 percent, 10 percent, and 22 percent.

46. For further results and discussion of public opinion on Aboriginal self-government, see Paul Howe and Joseph Fletcher, this volume.

47. Johnston *et al.*, *The Challenge of Direct Democracy*, p. 281.

48. Fred Cutler, "Explaining Geographic Variation in Electoral Behaviour: Local Environments and Canadian Voting." PhD Dissertation, University of Michigan, 2000.

49. There could be a local interest for a very tiny portion of the non-Aboriginal Canadian population who live on or very close to reserves. This group is likely to be so small as to be missing entirely from the CES sample.

50. Richard Johnston and Janet Ballantyne, "Geography and the Electoral System," *Canadian Journal of Political Science*. 10, 4(1977):857-66.

51. Charnock, "National Uniformity, and State and Local Effects on Australian Voting."

V

Chronology

16

Chronology of Events
January 2000 – December 2000

Victoria Crites

An index of these events begins on page 435

4 January 2000 *Environment*	Documents reveal that the federal government has long been considering legislation to ban bulk fresh-water exports. However, only five provinces have thus far signed on to an accord with Ottawa that would create a national ban on bulk fresh-water exports, since the accord was introduced nearly a decade ago. Currently, Canada only sells its water in bottles and approximately 80 percent is shipped from Quebec to the United States. Quebec, Alberta, Saskatchewan, and Manitoba refused as recently as two months ago to sign on.
6 January 2000 *New Brunswick*	New Brunswick Premier Bernard Lord's "200 days of change" come to an end and Premier Lord seems to have accomplished 19 of his 20 promises. He is still working on one of the most controversial promises — that of eliminating tolls from all roadways in New Brunswick.
7 January 2000 *Political Parties*	Reform Party leader Preston Manning sends a letter to all 65,000 party members, in which he promises to quit as leader if the delegates to an upcoming national convention reject his initiative for a new United Alternative party. Manning's announcement comes as a surprise to

Reformers and prompts BC MP Jay Hill, who has been against the United Alternative proposal, to say now that he will stand behind Manning and his plan.

8 January 2000
British Columbia/
Political Parties

Former BC Finance Minister Joy MacPhail withdraws from the provincial New Democratic Party (NDP) leadership race and puts her support behind front runner Ujjal Dosanjh. Now only three candidates remain: Dosanjh, Gordon Wilson, and Agriculture Minister Corky Evans. NDP party members will elect a new leader and premier at a convention in Vancouver 18–20 February. The new leader will replace the interim premier, Dan Miller, who has held the office since Glen Clark resigned amidst scandal last August.

12 January 2000
Supreme Court

Chief Justice Beverley McLachlin is officially sworn in as head of Canada's Supreme Court at a Rideau Hall ceremony. Prime Minister Jean Chrétien, several federal ministers and Supreme Court judges were in attendance. McLachlin replaces the retiring Antonio Lamer.

12 January 2000
Supreme Court

Ontario's Attorney General Jim Flaherty says it is his duty as government protector of the vulnerable to defend Ontario's right to prosecute child pornographers. Therefore, he intends to appear before the Supreme Court of Canada next week when they hear arguments about the controversial child pornography possession legislation.

13 January 2000
Budget

Ottawa's Finance Department reports a budget surplus of $7.8 billion in the first eight months of the 1999–2000 fiscal year. The surplus is expected to provoke further demands for tax cuts in the upcoming budget, to be announced in late February.

13 January 2000
Newfoundland

Newfoundland's Premier Brian Tobin shuffles his Cabinet, which causes speculation regarding the future of the Voisey's Bay mining project and the Churchill River hydro-electric proposal as Tobin replaces Roger Grimes, his energy and mines minister, who has been the chief negotiator on the projects. Opposition House Leader Loyola Sullivan suggests that Grimes and Tobin could not agree on how best to proceed with the proposals. The major Cabinet shuffle also results in new postings in health, finance, justice, and municipal affairs.

13 January 2000
Agriculture

Federal Agriculture Minister Lyle Vanclief announces an aid program designed to give struggling farmers access to $1 billion over the next two years. The program will be cost-shared, with Ottawa picking up 60 percent of the tab and the provinces, the remainder.

14 January 2000
Premiers' Meeting

Quebec Premier Lucien Bouchard announces the date for the next Premiers' Meeting. It is set to take place in Quebec City on 3 February. The premiers and territorial leaders will gather to discuss a strategy to pressure the federal government into sharing some of the budget surplus, which is estimated to reach $95 billion over the next five years. The highest priority for all the premiers is the allocation of more money for health and education. All premiers are expected to attend.

15 January 2000
Quebec

Quebec Premier Lucien Bouchard declares that his government's first priority is health care. Next on the list of priorities are: youth and education, tax cuts, and then, sovereignty. When asked about the possibility of a sovereignty referendum this year, Bouchard responds by saying that "winning conditions" must be met before Quebecers wade into another referendum, and stabilizing the health-care system is an important aspect of stability — one of the necessary "winning conditions." Bouchard's declaration comes on the heels of the flu crisis, which exacerbated the health-care situation in Quebec over the New Year's holiday. Emergency rooms across the province are still overcrowded.

17 January 2000
Aboriginal Peoples

The Snuneymuxw (Nanaimo) First Nation rejects a joint federal-British Columbia government offer which included $40.3 million and 2,128 hectares of land. The 1,500 member band, which is currently living on 263 hectares south of Nanaimo, wants 4,300 hectares of Crown land plus 14,450 hectares of private land (potentially to be purchased from those willing to sell). The Snuneymuxw stated that they plan to take the land claim to court if the government docs not substantially improve its offer. Peter Smith, of BC's Ministry of Aboriginal Affairs, says the package offer was the beginning of the process, not the end.

17 January 2000   Phil Fontaine, the Chief of the Assembly of First Nations,
Aboriginal Peoples   says that the federal government's Clarity Bill is a "major
                         cause of concern," for the 43 First Nations living in Que-
                         bec. Fontaine explains that although he partially supports
                         the goal of the proposed legislation, he is concerned that
                         the legislation does not take into account the viewpoint of
                         First Nations people residing in Quebec with respect to
                         any possible future secession negotiations between Que-
                         bec and the federal government.

18 January 2000   Ontario Premier Mike Harris calls on the federal govern-
Ontario   ment to give Canadians a 20 percent cut in income tax.
                         The request was forwarded in writing to federal Finance
                         Minister Paul Martin by Ontario's Finance Minister Ernie
                         Eves. Harris's provincial government has cut personal in-
                         come taxes by 30 percent since it was elected in 1995.

18 January 2000   Ontario Premier Mike Harris says that he will not be per-
Ontario   suaded by pressure from Ottawa to provide funding for
                         all private religious schools. A recent United Nations rul-
                         ing found that Canada is violating international law
                         because Ontario does not fund non-Catholic religious
                         schools. Ontario remains the only province that does not,
                         in some way, fund religious schools.

19 January 2000   The Supreme Court of Canada's hearings on the con-
Supreme Court   troversial child-porn possession law wrap up today after
                         the nine judges hear two days of arguments. At dispute
                         is the question: Is the infringement upon Charter rights
                         justifiable (under section 1 of the Charter) in the pur-
                         suit of child protection? Vancouverite Robin Sharpe,
                         who was charged under the law nearly five years ago in
                         BC, successfully challenged it; both a BC trial court
                         and the BC Court of Appeal have struck down the law
                         as a breach of the constitutional protection provided
                         by the Charter. Lawyers for the federal and BC govern-
                         ments say they are using the court to put children's
                         rights ahead of those who would create or possess child
                         pornography, while civil liberties groups argue that the
                         law is too broad and should be redefined to criminalize
                         only those who abuse children in the production of child
                         pornography.

19 January 2000
HRDC

An internal audit by Human Resources Development Canada (HRDC) reveals that as much as $1 billion in annual federal grants has been spent with few checks into how that money was being used. The audit discovered that at least 80 percent of the projects funded show no evidence of any financial monitoring by the federal government. Also, 87 percent of the projects received no supervision by officials, and 25 percent of the files did not even show what kind of activity Ottawa was funding. Opposition Reform Party's human resources critic Diane Ablonczy says this discovery will diminish Canadians' confidence in the government's ability to handle their money. Human Resources Minister Jane Stewart admitted to "sloppy administration," but said they were working to correct the problem. The audit examined programs funded by HRDC from April 1997 to June 1999.

25 January 2000
Quebec

The Quebec government refuses to renew a ten-year-old federal-provincial agreement that provides funds to ensure access to English-language health services in Quebec. The agreement was a 50–50 deal where the federal government contributed $359,000 per year as did Quebec. The program funds a group of coordinators who act as liaisons between Quebec's English community and the provincial health-care network. The deal was originally penned in 1989 when Lucien Bouchard was then a senior Cabinet minister in the federal Conservative government. At that time, Bouchard wrote, "It seems eminently possible to follow in Quebec, without contradiction, the objectives of the promotion of the French language and the respect of the minority English population." The deal was renewed in 1994 by Jacques Parizeau's PQ government. Bouchard's current PQ government justifies its denial of the renewal by accusing Ottawa of intruding into a provincial jurisdiction.

29 January 2000
Political Parties

After much debate, at the Reform Party's annual three-day meeting, the new name is official: the Canadian Conservative Reform Alliance or the Canadian Alliance for short. Reform delegates worked on the new policy platform for the new party, which is similar to the Reform Party platform, but now supports official bilingualism and a specific flat tax rate of 17 percent. Reform Party members will vote on joining the Canadian Alliance through February and March. A two-thirds majority is required for the Canadian Alliance to become a registered party.

31 January 2000
Political Leaders

Saskatchewan Premier Roy Romanow declares that Ottawa must give struggling farmers more support than the recently announced $1 billion over the next two years. Romanow explained that farmers are facing the worst crisis since the Depression due to low commodity prices and he intends to lobby his fellow premiers at the upcoming Premiers' Meeting in Quebec City on 3 February.

1 February 2000
Aboriginal Peoples

At a native conference, Alex Denny, the leader of the Mi'kmaq Grand Council warns that more violent clashes between native and non-native fishers are likely to occur again in the spring. Federal negotiators have been working out deals with individual bands in New Brunswick since the Supreme Court rendered the *Marshall* Decision last September. The decision upheld an Aboriginal treaty signed in 1760 that allows Aboriginal people in Atlantic Canada to fish year-round in order to maintain a "reasonable livelihood." Disputes over whether or not this means *any* restrictions apply to Aboriginal fishing led to rising tensions and some violent incidents between the native and non-native communities in New Brunswick last fall.

3 February 2000
Premiers' Meeting

As expected, the health-care issue dominated the Premiers' Meeting that was held in Quebec City. The premiers emerged at the end of the day united in support of their letter to Prime Minister Chrétien asking for an immediate rescue of Canada's failing health-care system. This should include both a cash infusion and a possible future restructuring of the system itself. The premiers also repeated their call for transfer payments to the provinces to be restored to the levels that existed prior to the extensive cuts, which the Liberals began implementing in 1994. Also mentioned was support by the provinces for the tax cuts that have already been promised by Chrétien for the upcoming federal budget.

21 February 2000
HRDC

At a news briefing today, David Good, an assistant deputy minister at HRDC explains that it is difficult for businesses to make a go of it in the depressed regions of the country that the Canada Jobs Fund targets. His comments were an attempt to reply to the recently released audit that found that the Canada Jobs Fund gave more than $12 million to 51 companies between 1997 and 1999 that went bankrupt or simply closed down before any projects were completed or any jobs created.

21 February 2000
Supreme Court

The Supreme Court of Canada begins hearing arguments made on behalf of eight provinces and territories that are challenging the federal government's power to realize a national system of gun control. The challengers include Alberta, Ontario, New Brunswick, Saskatchewan, Manitoba, Nova Scotia, Northwest Territories, and the Yukon. With Alberta leading the way, the provinces claim that since guns are private property, their regulation falls under provincial rather than federal jurisdiction. Justice Frank Iacobucci pointed out that the *Firearms Act* is about not only the registration of guns, but about the registration of gun users, and moreover that Parliament has said that the issue is rooted in concern for public safety and criminal law.

The *Firearms Act*, which was passed by Parliament in 1995, compels all gun owners to be licensed by the end of this year and every gun to be registered by the end of 2002. Over the next two days, the Court will also hear from the Coalition for Gun Control and several victims' organizations.

21 February 2000
Atlantic Canada

Provincial spokespersons in Newfoundland, Nova Scotia, and Prince Edward Island state that the provinces will not be seeking taxes from those cash settlements the federal government recently awarded to merchant marine veterans. The four provinces had previously threatened to seize the cheques issued by Veterans Affairs Canada in order to garner a portion in taxes. The federal Cabinet allocated $50 million for the program, which will include lump-sum payments of up to $24,000; the payments have been declared non-taxable by Revenue Canada.

22 February 2000 *Atlantic Canada*	The two-day truckers' blockade at the Nova Scotia-New Brunswick border of the Trans-Canada highway ends. The blockade had been organized to protest the steep rise in diesel fuel prices. A trucker's protest on Parliament Hill prompts Prime Minister Jean Chrétien to remark, "these prices have increased around the globe. The level of taxation by the federal government on these products is the lowest of probably any other country in the world." Similar trucking industry protests are also happening in the United States.
23 February 2000 *Aboriginal Peoples/* *Clarity Bill*	Chief Ted Moses of the Grand Council of the Crees tells the parliamentary committee on Bill C-20 that his nation supports the goal of clear rules for a sovereignty referendum, but he also believes that the bill ignores the constitutional rights of Aboriginals. Moses emphasized the need for Aboriginal participation in any secession negotiations with Quebec.
23 February 2000 *Clarity Bill*	Joe Clark tells the parliamentary committee studying the Clarity Bill (Bill C-20) that the bill would tie the hands of future politicians with respect to preventing Quebec's possible separation. Clark says that the bill would make it impossible for politicians to employ "ambiguity … and find ways in which we might save Canada."
23 February 2000 *Justice*	The Federation of Saskatchewan Indian Nations demands that the province hold a public inquiry into the allegations surrounding the Saskatoon police force. More than 100 complaints of police threats and abuse have been called into the federation since two police officers were suspended in connection with a complaint from Darrell Night who alleges that the officers took his coat, dropped him outside town and told him to walk home. The RCMP is currently investigating the incident and the freezing deaths of four other Aboriginal men.
25 February 2000 *New Brunswick*	The federal Fisheries Department plans to buy back more than 1,000 commercial fishing licences, as well as boats and equipment from fishermen who are ready to either retire or change careers. The move is aimed at easing the pressure on fish stocks in Miramichi Bay, New Brunswick and will allow more expansion within the native

fishery. However, Robert Levi, the chief of Big Cove reserve in New Brunswick says that Aboriginal fishermen do *not* require licences under the *Marshall* Decision, rather they only need to proceed in an "orderly and regulated fashion."

28 February 2000
Budget

Federal Finance Minister Paul Martin delivers the annual federal budget. The message of the budget is a focus on the future and the underlying theme is, as Martin puts it, "the days of deficit are gone and they are not coming back." Accordingly, Martin's budget framework is based generally on the following principles: sound fiscal management, lower taxes to promote economic growth, investment in providing Canadians with skills and knowledge for jobs, and to build an economy based on innovation. Tax relief is the cornerstone of the budget. The personal income tax system is to be fully indexed and applied retroactively to 1 January 2000, actual tax rates are to be lowered over the next five years, and the Canada Child Tax Benefit (CCTB) will increase from $1,975 to $2,265 by July 2001 and up to $2,400 over the next five years. Higher taxed industries (like high technology services) will see their tax rates lowered from 28 percent to 21 percent over the next five years and investors will now be allowed a $500,000 tax-free rollover when investing in new ventures.

Other highlights of the budget include: increased funding of $2.5 billion to the provinces for postsecondary education and health care (CHST) over the next four years (Ottawa expects the provinces to spend $1 billion next year and $500 million in each of the following three years), $900 million in funding over five years for 2,000 new research chairs at universities, $900 million in funding to Canada Foundation for Innovation (CFI: a foundation that helps postsecondary institutions, research hospitals to modernize their equipment, labs, etc.), $700 million toward environmental technologies and research, an additional $240 million in relief for prairie farms, and as promised in the Speech from the Throne — an increase in maternity and parental benefits under the employment insurance program.

29 February 2000
Budget

An angry Premier Mike Harris demands that Ottawa give an explanation of the meager health-care funding announced in yesterday's budget. The additional $2.5 billion over four years to provinces for health care, social programs and postsecondary education is not enough for even health care alone, according to Harris. He further suggests that the federal government has a top-down overhaul of the health-care system in mind and is deliberately underfunding the provinces in order to force them on board with the plan.

1 March 2000
Justice

Saskatchewan Justice Minister Chris Axworthy calls on his federal counterpart, Anne McLellan, to help formulate a plan that will restore the Aboriginal peoples' faith in the justice system. Axworthy's request comes in the wake of the unresolved freezing deaths of two Aboriginal men outside Saskatoon. Two Saskatoon police officers have been suspended with pay in connection with the incident, while an RCMP task force investigates.

1 March 2000
Health

Federal Health Minister Allan Rock offers to meet with his provincial counterparts as early as next week to discuss the problems of the health-care system. The offer comes in response to the provinces' laments about the budget's shortfall on health-care funding.

1 March 2000
Aboriginal Peoples

The new grand chief of the Council of Yukon First Nations Ed Schultz accuses the federal government of deliberately stalling on First Nations land claims agreements, while at the same time expediting the devolution of natural resources from Ottawa to the Yukon government. Schultz and other chiefs representing 11 First Nations communities warn that they may not support devolution if the federal and provincial governments do not move negotiations forward much more quickly.

2 March 2000
Ontario

Ontario Corrections Minister Rob Sampson asserts that Parliament's proposed changes to the young offender laws are insufficient. The new *Youth Criminal Justice Act* proposes lowering the age at which young people can face adult sentences from 16 years to 14 years, also the names of youth who face adult sentences would become public. Currently, the publication of the names of young offenders is banned.

3 March 2000 *Environment*	An environmental agreement is signed between Diavik Diamond Mines, the Northwest Territories (NWT) and the federal government which will potentially allow Diavik to start work on its $1.3 billion mine. Aboriginal and environmental groups have expressed concerns regarding the effects of Diavik's construction plans in the northern area. Diavik still requires a building permit from Indian Affairs Minister Robert Nault and a licence from the NWT water board. Diavik has already awarded $90 million in construction contracts.
3 March 2000 *Quebec*	Quebec Premier Lucien Bouchard states that on an upcoming trip to Paris he plans to denounce Ottawa's Clarity Bill as being undemocratic. In early April, Bouchard plans to meet with France's Prime Minister Lionel Jospin to discuss political, economic, and cultural issues. Federal Intergovernmental Affairs Minister Stéphane Dion sees this appeal to the international community as a sign of desperation within the separatist cause.
8 March 2000 *Newfoundland/ Aboriginal Peoples*	Amid continuing stories of sky-high suicide rates and substance abuse in native communities, the Newfoundland government announces plans to form a committee to study the problems of Aboriginal communities in Labrador. Provincial Justice Minister Kelvin Parsons pointed to factors such as isolation, insufficient housing, high unemployment, substance abuse and unresolved land claims as the largest burdens on Aboriginals in Newfoundland and Labrador. Premier Brian Tobin is slated to lead the committee.
9 March 2000 *Political Leaders*	Alberta Treasurer Stockwell Day announces his bid for the leadership of the nascent Canadian Alliance Party. In turn, Reform Party leader Preston Manning, in an effort to focus on his own political future, says he will hand over his duties as opposition leader in the House of Commons to deputy leader Deborah Grey if Reformers vote for the new Canadian Alliance Party. The referendum results on the new party will be released 25 March and the subsequent leadership vote is set for 24 June.
9 March 2000 *Health*	Alberta Premier Ralph Klein announces that the provincial health ministers will meet the week of 21 March to discuss the problems plaguing Canada's health-care

system. Klein also expressed the hope that a follow-up premiers' meeting on health care will happen in April.

9 March 2000
Aboriginal Peoples

The Supreme Court of Canada is scheduled to hear the Benoit case which will examine the question of whether or not Ottawa granted tax-free status to Aboriginals under Treaty 8 when it was signed in 1899. The Benoit family of Ft. McMurray, Alberta argues that the federal government violates the treaty by compelling Aboriginals who earn off-reserve income to pay income tax and to pay GST on goods and services purchased off-reserve. Bonnie Moon, of the federal Justice Department, says that if the Benoits win, she expects that other treaty natives would file similar lawsuits.

13 March 2000
Aboriginal Peoples

A two-year pilot project aimed at providing culturally-sensitive justice programs in Northern Manitoba will cost $703, 088 and is set to be cost-shared by the federal and Manitoba governments. Six First Nations of Manitoba will participate in the community-based project.

13 March 2000
Political Leaders

In an interview with *le Journal de Montreal,* Prime Minister Jean Chrétien states that he intends to stay on the job. While acknowledging that some Liberals would like to see Finance Minister Paul Martin replace him, Chrétien emphasized that he is in charge of the party and is preparing for the next election. He also pointed out that 60 percent of Canadians are satisfied with his government according to recent polls and this suggests that winning conditions exist for a Liberal government at the election. "What more could you ask for?" Chrétien mused.

14 March 2000
Aboriginal Peoples

Aboriginal fishermen walk away from the federal negotiating table in Fredericton. A councillor at the Burnt Church First Nation, Kathy Lambert says the reserve has given up hope of an agreement with Ottawa and instead they intend to come up with their own plan for managing the fisheries. Federal Fisheries Minister Herb Dhaliwal recently stated that he hopes to have agreements in place prior to the opening of fishing season on Miramichi Bay on 1 May.

15 March 2000 *Clarity Bill*	The House of Commons overwhelmingly passes Bill C-20, the Clarity Bill, by a vote of 208 to 55; this was accomplished after 36 hours of recorded votes on nearly 400 Bloc Québécois amendments, which were all defeated. Two NDP amendments that proposed changing the bill to include Aboriginal peoples as political actors in the referendum review process passed. Bill C-20 is based on the 1998 Supreme Court of Canada decision which outlined broadly the required criteria for a province to secede. The bill states that the federal government will only negotiate secession with a province if there has been a clear question and a clear expression of the will of the citizens of that province. The Bloc Québécois has vigorously opposed the bill, calling it undemocratic. Stéphane Dion claims that the bill protects the interests of all Canadians in that it helps to protect federalism. It remains for the Senate to approve it before it becomes legislation.
21 March 2000 *Reform Party/* *Quebec*	At a hearing on Quebec's Bill 99, Reform MP Grant Hill says that the Reform Party would propose changes to the federation that would accommodate Quebec's long sought-after demands, thereby resolving the national unity problem. Hill stated that the Reform Party would propose a legislated "withdrawal of the federal government from health, education, language and culture, family policy, natural resources, manpower training, municipal affairs, sports and recreation, and housing and tourism." Joseph Facal, Quebec's intergovernmental affairs minister said he was appreciative of Hill's remarks. The Bloc Québécois created Bill 99 in response to the Liberals' Clarity Bill.
22–23 March 2000 *Agriculture*	In what is said to be an excellent example of cooperation among federal, provincial, and territorial governments, agriculture ministers from these governments, in a meeting in Ottawa, agree on a tentative plan that includes basic safety-net programming and an income disaster component. After ratification, the plan is later signed at the annual meeting of agriculture ministers and deputy ministers in Fredericton on 5 July. At the latter meeting, there is also agreement on the general principles of a proposed Canadian Farm Income Program — an initiative for disaster assistance programming. CFIP will contribute $2.2 billion of the $5.5 billion, three-year agreement by ministers.

23 March 2000
Aboriginal Peoples

Chief Ted Moses of the Grand Council of the Crees declares that the Cree are not a part of the Quebec people and they will not be assimilated. Moses's comments are in response to the Quebec government's Bill 99, which refers to "the Quebec people." The Cree have denounced the proposed legislation as "colonial and anti-democratic." The bill is currently before a legislature committee.

23 March 2000
Political Parties

After a Liberal caucus meeting, MPs emerge united behind Prime Minister Jean Chrétien as their leader. In recent weeks, squabbling between Liberal supporters of Paul Martin and Chrétien loyalists had intensified over Martin's prospects for leadership. At the caucus meeting, Chrétien discussed plans for a possible fall election and reminded his caucus that there will be no leadership race until he retires.

24 March 2000
Quebec

Ottawa pledges $700,000 in funding in order to ensure that Quebec anglophones will have access to health and social services. The money will pay for English health-access coordinators whose continued employment in the province was in question earlier this year when the Quebec government refused to renew a long-standing intergovernmental agreement that had obligated the Quebec government and Ottawa to share the cost of the coordinators.

30 March 2000
Aboriginal Peoples

Some Aboriginal fisheries start opening for the season in Atlantic Canada while federal Director General of Resource Management David Bevan declares, "fishing will be orderly and regulated." The Fisheries Department is currently negotiating agreements with several First Nations bands in the area in an attempt to ease tensions between the native and non-native fishing communities. Tensions remained and have often erupted into violence, since the Supreme Court's *Marshall* Decision last September upheld the 1760 Aboriginal treaty right to "hunt, fish and gather" in order to maintain a moderate living. Subsequently, the Supreme Court also released a statement clarifying that the federal government still had the right to regulate Aboriginal access to resources like lobsters, trees or minerals. Bevan said that three of 34 bands have signed agreements and negotiations continue on a band-by-band basis.

4 April 2000
Political Parties

Stockwell Day, candidate for the leadership of the Canadian Alliance Party, drops in on Tory leader Joe Clark's fundraiser in Regina in order to let Clark know that the "door is open" to the federal Tories. Day emphasized that many Tory members are coming over to the Canadian Alliance. Clark, in turn, suggested that Day's momentum would not hold, especially given his tough opponent in the leadership race, Preston Manning.

4 April 2000
Aboriginal Peoples

The First Nations National Accountability Coalition releases a report condemning the spending practices of several bands. The report is the result of the hearings that were held across the country to gather information on band management and spending. Leona Freed, president of the coalition says that unless changes occur, many band members are ready to engage in uprisings. Among the coalition's recommendations are: direct delivery of federal funds to band members rather than through chiefs and councils; a native ombudsman for dispute resolution; and an overhaul of the election method for chiefs and council that would eliminate the "family connection advantage" and promote competitive appointments. The Canadian Alliance Party helped to finance the hearings.

7 April 2000
Senate

The Prime Minister's Office announces the appointments of entertainer Tommy Banks and former lieutenant-governor/farmer Jack Wiebe to the Senate. Liberals in the Senate now number 55, Progressive Conservatives total 40 and there are five independents and five vacancies. Recently, Prime Minister Chrétien expressed confidence that the Senate will likely ratify Bill C-20 and these appointments should further support his conviction.

7 April 2000
Clarity Bill

Intergovernmental Affairs Minister Stéphane Dion states that Ottawa will not define specifically what percentage of the vote in a Quebec referendum would constitute a clear majority. Many circumstances would need to be considered, says Dion, including the views of all political parties in Quebec and those of Aboriginal peoples. Bill C-20, which was passed by the House of Commons on 15 March, outlines the rules for any province's future secession. The bill stipulates that a clear question in a referendum and a clear expression of the will of the people must occur if secession negotiations with the federal government are to begin.

9 April 2000
Quebec

Quebec's Intergovernmental Affairs Minister Joseph Facal says that public hearings on Bill 99 have made it clear that the bill requires revisions. More than 60 submissions were made over the course of the hearings. Yet, despite the many requests for changes to the bill, many feel that the bill has failed to stir nationalist emotions among Quebecers.

20 April 2000
Supreme Court

The Supreme Court agrees to hear the precedent-setting case in which the Osoyoos First Nation is appealing the decision made by the BC Court of Appeal that denied the band the right to tax the nearby town of Oliver for an irrigation canal that runs through reserve land. The case will not be heard for at least several months.

27 April 2000
Atlantic Canada/
Fisheries

Ministers responsible for fisheries in Quebec, Nunavut, the Atlantic provinces and federal government meet in St. John's to discuss the implementation of the *Marshall* Decision in the Maritimes, with universal support for access to the commercial fishery for affected First Nations groups, based on the Supreme Court of Canada ruling. The Nova Scotia minister emphasizes the importance of keeping the commercial sector informed of the details on the interim agreements.

4 May 2000
Environment

Prime Minister Jean Chrétien and BC Premier Ujjal Dosanjh visit Clayoquot Sound to mark the region's designation as a UN biosphere reserve. The beautiful, densely-forested area was the focus of international scrutiny when protestors took on the logging companies there in the early 1990s. A huge road blockade in 1993 led to over 800 protestor arrests. International pressure combined with a near riotous demonstration at the BC legislature led then-premier Mike Harcourt and his NDP government to change its logging industry policy. Prime Minister Chrétien is set to formally hand over $12 million in federal funds for the reserve to begin an endowment fund dedicated to research and training.

7 May 2000 *Aboriginal Peoples*	On a visit to Yellowknife, Minister of Indian Affairs Robert Nault announces the creation of an intergovernmental forum between Aboriginal leaders, the territories, and Ottawa. The aim of the forum is to organize agreements that will transfer more money and control over northern resources (such as diamonds and natural gas) to the territories from Ottawa. NWT Premier Stephen Kakfwi stated that this move toward local control could result in the Northwest Territories becoming Canada's first "have" territory.
8 May 2000 *National Unity*	Premier Lucien Bouchard rallied 1,800 delegates at a Parti Québécois convention on the weekend by affirming the party's objective of independence and promising that the next vote on sovereignty will be held "as soon as possible." The stance earned Bouchard a 91 percent confidence vote despite the fact that he failed to offer any firm sovereignty deadlines to party hardliners.
8 May 2000 *Aboriginal Peoples*	Settlement of a land claims agreement creates a new First Nation in Northern Alberta. The Alberta government will transfer 7,689 hectares of unoccupied Crown land and $3.2 million to the federal government. The federal government agrees to transfer a one-time payment of $28 million and 1,000 hectares of land within Wood Buffalo National Park to the Smith's Landing First Nation. Chief Jerry Paulette says the historic agreement fulfils the obligations the government made to his people under Treaty 8, signed in 1899. Smith's Landing First Nation has 272 band members.
8 May 2000 *Political Leaders*	Progressive Conservative leader Joe Clark challenges the Canadian Alliance leader, who is yet to be decided, to run against him in a by-election in the Calgary centre riding. Clark issued the challenge at a Tory fundraising banquet, where he also called the Alliance Party's policies "racist, homophobic and anti-French." Clark has yet to hold a seat in the House of Commons since he took over the leadership of the Tory Party nearly two years ago.
9 May 2000 *Health/ Ontario*	The Ontario government pledges $25,000 in compensation for each person who contracted hepatitis C from infected blood, but was excluded from last year's federal-provincial compensation deal. That $1.2 billion national

agreement only applied to victims who contracted the disease between 1986 and 1990, whereas the Ontario deal will extend compensation outside that window. $25,000 is the same compensation amount given to victims under the federal-provincial plan of last year.

10 May 2000
National Unity/
New Brunswick

New Brunswick creates a team of lawyers to work on constitutional matters such as Quebec sovereignty questions, native treaty rights, and French-language education. The province intends to budget $800,000 for the current seven-member team.

12 May 2000
Aboriginal Peoples

Federal Indian Affairs Minister Robert Nault and BC Premier Ujjal Dosanjh attend festivities in the Nass Valley of British Columbia as hundreds of Nisga'a members celebrate the formal enactment of the historic Nisga'a Treaty. The treaty gives self-governing powers, approximately 2,000 square kilometres of land and cash to the 5,000-member band. The deal, which has been approved by the Nisga'a people, the federal government, and the BC government, is being challenged on a constitutional basis by the BC Liberal Party.

15 May 2000
Atlantic Canada

Canada's four Atlantic premiers sign an agreement that creates the Council of Atlantic Premiers. The premiers believe that the Council will give the Atlantic provinces more clout in Ottawa and strengthen regional unity. One of the first items on the Council's agenda is to pressure Ottawa to remove the ceiling on equalization payments to provinces.

17 May 2000
Aboriginal Peoples

Federal Indian Affairs Minister Robert Nault announces a new $75 million fund created to stimulate Aboriginal economic development. Nault explains that the money will not be used on a per capita basis, but rather on strategic investments in the hope of reducing long-standing, high unemployment in Aboriginal communities.

19 May 2000
National Unity

Quebec Intergovernmental Affairs Minister Joseph Facal and federal Intergovernmental Affairs Minister Stéphane Dion mark the twentieth anniversary of the first sovereignty referendum (20 May 1980) by discussing sovereignty at an academic conference. Facal declared that he is confident that Quebecers will "choose the path of a modern sovereignty," while Dion told attendees that most Quebecers are very attached to Canada and would prefer to see improvements in Canada and Quebec's place in the federation since "Canada belongs to Quebecers just as much as it does to other Canadians."

22 May 2000
Clarity Bill

Ontario Liberal Senator Anne Cools claims that the Prime Minister's Office has deliberately excluded senators who might be critical of Bill C-20 from studying it. She argues that the PMO set up a special Senate committee to study the bill that does not include members of the Standing Senate Committee on Legal and Constitutional Affairs — of which Senator Cools is a member. Senate Leader Bernie Boudreau replied to Senator Cools and other Liberal senators who are critical of the bill by saying that the Senate's role in constitutional affairs is a limited one.

23 May 2000
Premiers' Meeting

The Western Premiers' Conference gets underway today in Brandon, Manitoba. The two-day meeting will focus largely on health-care issues but is set to include discussions on the environment and the deterioration of services in the airline industry since the Air Canada /Canadian Airlines merger.

24 May 2000
Premiers' Meeting

Alberta Premier Ralph Klein spends much of the Western Premiers' Conference defending his controversial Bill-ll legislation. The bill, which allows for overnight stays in private clinics for medicare-covered procedures, has been widely criticized both inside and outside Alberta as a step toward a two-tier health-care system. Saskatchewan Premier Roy Romanow, although critical of the bill, suggests that the premiers should focus on the bigger picture — the ailing health-care system, which simply provokes provincial responses like Bill-11. Premier Gary Doer of Manitoba agreed and remarked that in the past five years the four western provinces have had to come up with an additional $7.5 billion in health-care funding while Ottawa has withdrawn $2.4 billion. The premiers are united in calling on the federal government to restore health and social transfer payments to pre-1995 levels.

25 May 2000 *Agriculture*	A meeting between the four western premiers and two US governors (North Dakota and Idaho) concludes at the International Peace Garden on the Canada-US border. A number of issues were discussed, including the role of the Canadian Wheat Board in grain marketing, but nothing was resolved. The one conclusion of the short afternoon meeting was an agreement among all the attendees that agriculture subsidies to both Canadian and US farmers require study.
27 May 2000 *Aboriginal Peoples*	An agreement to begin negotiations on Aboriginal self-government is signed by the federal government, the Saskatchewan government, and the Federation of Saskatchewan Indian Nations. Saskatchewan has 74 First Nations groups which are collectively represented by the federation. The agreement outlines guiding principles for developing new relationships between the three governing bodies, which is intended to facilitate extensive future negotiations in specific areas such as justice, lands and resources, health, housing, and taxation.
30 May 2000 *Health*	Provincial and territorial health ministers meet in Quebec City, unanimously agreeing on the following requests and initiatives: immediate unconditional reinstatement of the Canadian Health and Social Transfer to 1994–95 levels of funding; an appropriate CHST escalator; to continue to explore innovation and adaptation deemed necessary to ensure the sustainability of a quality publicly-funded health-care system.
31 May 2000 *Atlantic Canada*	Federal Natural Resources Minister Ralph Goodale announces the creation of a binding arbitration panel to end the 14-year-old dispute between Newfoundland and Nova Scotia over the boundary line in the North Atlantic. The dispute can be traced back to the 1986 Canada-Nova Scotia Offshore Petroleum Accord, which drew a boundary that gave a larger share of a potentially oil-rich 60,000 kilometres to Nova Scotia. Retired Supreme Court Justice Gerard LaForest will head the panel.
13 June 2000 *Clarity Bill*	Federal Intergovernmental Affairs Minister Stéphane Dion tells the Quebec Cree that if they challenge Bill C-20, they would likely fail because of the bill's constitutional

strength. Grand Chief of the Cree Ted Moses has said that his people may challenge the bill unless the Aboriginal right to be included in any secession negotiations is explicitly recognized in the bill. Dion says it is unnecessary to include Aboriginal participation in the bill since the constitution already guarantees Aboriginal people the right to participate in any negotiations that would affect their interests.

15 June 2000
Supreme Court

In a unanimous judgement, the Supreme Court upholds Parliament's 1995 gun control legislation. The nine justices clearly reject the provinces' arguments that guns do not fall under federal jurisdictional powers. The decision stated that, "Gun control has traditionally been considered valid criminal law because guns are dangerous and pose a risk to public safety."

Justice Minister Anne McLellan took the opportunity to announce changes to the gun control system that are geared to simplify and reduce the costs of the registration process, in an effort to encourage more gun owners to comply with the *Firearms Act*.

19 June 2000
Political Parties

Membership in the Canadian Alliance jumps significantly — from approximately 78,000 members in March to over 200,000 this month. Ken Kalopsis, the party's co-president also adds "the memberships reflect interest in every part of the country."

19 June 2000
Finance

Ottawa outlines a new $90 million fund designed to create awareness of the federal government's activities across the country. The fund, which is to be spent over the next three years, will largely be used directly for advertising purposes ($57 million). The remainder will support projects at the Canada Information Office to ensure federal presence in the provinces. This new fund is in addition to the $45 million that is already earmarked in the annual budget for federal government advertising.

20 June 2000
Political Parties

Current and former Tory Party members in Quebec and Ontario receive free and unsolicited Canadian Alliance membership cards in the mail. The cards bore their addresses but other people's names. The incident adds to the Alliance's growing credibility problem, since a recent check into the approximately 2,800 new members in the Gaspé revealed that at least 600 of the new memberships are spurious.

21 June 2000
Aboriginal Peoples

The government of Nunavut decides to back a major Aboriginal group in its court challenge of the federal government's gun control legislation. Nunavut Tunngavik Incorporated, the firm that administers the Nunavut Land Claims Agreement, argues that the *Firearms Act* contradicts the land claim agreement which extends to the Inuit the right to hunt without fees or licences.

23 June 2000
Aboriginal Peoples

One day after the BC Treaty Commission releases its annual report, in which it states that the treaty process is at a stand-still, Grand Chief Ed John of the First Nations Summit calls on Premier Ujjal Dosanjh to become involved in the treaty negotiations before the process dies entirely. John claims that both the federal and provincial governments are not living up to the agreement made in a 1991 Claims Task Force Report where all parties promised that no pre-conditions would apply to the negotiations. John states that both the federal and provincial governments are maintaining positions that preclude discussions on shared resources and jurisdictional powers.

24 June 2000
Political Parties

The two-day Canadian Alliance Leadership Convention ends today without a definitive leader being chosen. Candidate Stockwell Day received 44 percent of party member support, while Preston Manning garnered 36 percent and Tom Long 18 percent. Of the 205,000 Alliance members, only about 120,000 voted in the leadership contest. Both the Manning and Day camps are expected to campaign aggressively until the run-off ballot, which is to be held 8 July.

6 July 2000
Aboriginal Peoples

The BC Court of Appeal decides that Canada's fisheries minister does have the right to set up a separate commercial fishery for natives. The BC Fisheries Survival Coalition has been struggling for seven years to put a stop to the Aboriginal fishery in BC claiming that a "race-based fishery" is unfair to all Canadians. The coalition is considering taking its case to the Supreme Court of Canada.

7 July 2000 *Aboriginal Peoples*	Federal officials and representatives of the Westbank First Nation of BC sign an Aboriginal self-government agreement, which dispenses with much of the *Indian Act*. The signing marks the end of nearly ten years of negotiations.

8 July 2000
Political Leaders

In a much-anticipated run-off vote, Stockwell Day claims victory as the leader of the newly named Canadian Alliance Party with 64 percent of the vote. Day is formerly the Treasurer of Alberta.

12 July 2000
Aboriginal Peoples

Matthew Coon Come, a Cree leader from northern Quebec, receives 58 percent of the vote at the Assembly of First Nations to become its new national chief. Of the 494 votes cast by eligible chiefs, Coon Come garnered 287 supporters, while current chief Phil Fontaine conceded defeat with 207 votes. Coon Come gained national prominence when, as the Cree Grand Chief he fought the Hydro-Quebec project planned on Cree land. As the new AFN national chief, Coon Come says he plans to use international organizations like the United Nations to shame Canada into recognizing Aboriginal rights and sharing natural resources.

Coon Come's campaign emphasized that the AFN under Fontaine's leadership had become too much of a service provider for Ottawa rather than an organization aggressively fighting for native concerns, whereas the Fontaine camp focused on the accomplishments of the AFN in recent years because of Fontaine's "bridge-building" approach. Marilyn Buffalo, former president of the Native Women's association won only 13 votes and Lawrence Martin, Grand Chief of the Mushkegowuk First Nation (near Timmins, Ontario) received 26 votes.

16–18 July 2000
Atlantic Canada

The 25th Annual Conference of the New England Governors and Eastern Canadian Premiers takes place in Halifax. A number of resolutions are made, such as each member government of the conference will make efforts to identify and, if possible, remove unnecessary impediments restricting the further development of the knowledge economy, and to work collaboratively in its further development; a call to respective university-level organizations to explore significant expansion of university-level exchange programs; the establishment of the Standing

Committee on Trade and Globalization; a call to the United States Environmental Protection Agency and Environment Canada to intensify efforts for the implementation of effective emission reduction strategies.

18 July 2000
Environment

Pollution Probe, a Toronto-based environmental group, presents an environmental report card to the Atlantic premiers at the conclusion of the two-day conference of Atlantic Canadian premiers and New England governors held in Halifax. Prince Edward Island received an "F," Nova Scotia a "B-," and New Brunswick and Newfoundland both received "Ds." The aim of the conference was to promote business relations between New England and Atlantic Canada. However, several Canadian and US environmental groups were also given some time at the meetings during which they emphasized the goals of reducing acid rain and mercury emissions.

25 July 2000
Local Government

Walkerton, Ontario receives $3.5 billion in an interest-free loan from the provincial government to replace pipes that cannot be cleared of the E. coli virus. In May of this year, Walkerton's water supply was contaminated with the E. coli virus causing the deaths of seven residents and illness for over 2,000 residents. A public inquiry into the cause(s) of the tragedy is currently underway.

25 July 2000
Political Leaders

Joe Clark announces his intention to run in the Kings-Hants Nova Scotia riding. Current MP Scott Bryson will step aside to allow the federal Progressive Conservative leader to run in the traditional Tory stronghold riding. The by-election now remains to be called by Prime Minister Chrétien, and although he has six months to do so, Clark has made it known that he would like to be in the House of Commons by September.

25 July 2000
Aboriginal Peoples

The BC Supreme Court rejects the BC Opposition Liberal Party's challenge of the Nisga'a Treaty. Justice Paul Williamson said in his 76-page ruling that "[a]lthough the right of Aboriginal people to govern themselves was diminished [by Canada's Confederation] it was not extinguished." The BC Liberal Party plans to appeal the ruling.

4 August 2000
British Columbia/
Aboriginal Peoples

Justice Douglas Halyard of the BC Supreme Court reserves his decision in the Haida court challenge to Weyerhauser's licence to log in the Queen Charlotte Islands. The BC Forest Ministry first issued the licence in 1961 to MacMillan Bloedel and it was transferred to US-based Weyerhauser after the company took over MacMillan Bloedel. The Haida Nation argues that the licence (which covers one-quarter of the Queen Charlotte Islands) should not have been transferred without settling the outstanding Haida land claim first.

5 August 2000
Health

Ontario Intergovernmental Affairs Minister Norm Sterling says the federal government is stalling on paying its share of health-care costs and furthermore, it is trying to break up the unity among provincial governments on the health-care issue. Sterling's comments were a reaction to a letter sent this week to premiers from Prime Minister Jean Chrétien. The letter outlined Ottawa's position on health care.

9–11 August 2000
Annual Premiers'
Conference

The forty-first Annual Premiers' Conference takes place in Winnipeg, with a strong focus on the future of federal transfers in Canada. The premiers release a final report on the sustainability of the health-care system called "Understanding Canada's Health Care Costs," which includes a number of facts and reasons that support a call by the provinces and territories for the federal government to restore cash funding to 1994–95 levels, or before the CHST was implemented. Fiscal imbalance is also a hot topic, with discussion once again returning to a call for a restoration of federal transfers — the premiers support their argument with "A Federation Out of Balance," a paper commissioned by the western finance ministers. Overall, the major agreement among premiers is a call to the prime minister to restore the $4.2-billion to the CHST along with some guarantee of annual funding increases. Jean Chrétien has stated that he wants an agreement on health-care reform before any increased funding takes place.

Early childhood development is also discussed, with the premiers agreeing on the importance of family and community support for the well-being and proper physical, emotional and social development of children. The premiers list a number of priorities, principles and recommendations to enhance progress on this issue, particularly on cooperation and assistance from the federal government.

The premiers release the *Fifth Annual Status Report on Social Policy Renewal*, which provides updates on the status of the Social Union Framework Agreement and the National Children's Agenda, as well as a number of other social programs.

15 August 2000
Environment

Federal Environment Minister David Anderson promises that Aboriginal people will have input into upcoming legislation regarding the protection of endangered species. National Chief of the AFN Matthew Coon Come applauded the announcement and added that guaranteed harvest levels would be a part of the establishment of a list of endangered species. Environmental groups such as the World Wildlife Fund and the Sierra Club acknowledged the importance of recognizing Aboriginal traditional knowledge where endangered species are concerned.

17 August 2000
Supreme Court

The Supreme Court of Canada agrees to hear arguments and decide whether sections of BC's *Heritage Conservation Act* surpass provincial jurisdiction when it comes to the protection of Aboriginal artifacts and historical sites. The Kitkatla First Nation located near Prince Rupert is appealing a January 1999 ruling by the BC Court of Appeal that said that BC did have the power to make decisions regarding native sites. Lawyers for the Kitkatla band argue that the Kitkatla people specifically have the Aboriginal right to a coastal tract of land that has been logged by Interfor Ltd. since 1982, and the area contains marked trees of significant cultural and spiritual value to the band. The case will not be heard for several months.

23 August 2000
Aboriginal Peoples

Lasting tensions in Miramichi Bay, New Brunswick boil over as several Aboriginal fishermen throw rocks at Department of Fisheries and Oceans officers who were seizing native lobster traps. One officer is in hospital awaiting reconstructive surgery to his face. Two native boats sank during the violent clash, while the RCMP helped fisheries officers seize 553 native lobster traps and one native boat and arrest two native fishermen. Indian Affairs

Minister Robert Nault plans to be in Burnt Church in a few days for more discussions on the issue. The RCMP are expected to maintain a strong presence in the Burnt Church area while the tensions continue.

25 August 2000 *Quebec*	Premier Lucien Bouchard tells a news conference in Granby, Quebec that Quebecers will not support Canadian Alliance leader Stockwell Day because Day's values are too different from those of Quebecers. Particularly, Bouchard pointed to Day's support of the death penalty and his opposition to abortion and gun control as fundamentally irreconcilable with Quebec voters. Bouchard also took the opportunity to tell the press that he is frustrated because Prime Minister Chrétien never calls him.
31 August 2000 *Aboriginal Peoples*	Approximately 30 Tyendinaga Mohawks block off a major commuter bridge east of Belleville, Ontario in support of the Mi'kmaq natives of New Brunswick. The blockade was in place from early morning to early evening, but protestors were allowing motorists to pass after handing them information on the Mi'kmaq cause.
5 September 2000 *Alberta*	Alberta Premier Ralph Klein announces more than $200 million in spending initiatives which include funds for postsecondary institutions and energy-rebate cheques for taxpayers and businesses. Alberta's budget is currently in a $5 billion surplus position thanks to even higher than expected oil and natural gas revenues. Klein also hinted at the possibility of a spring election.
5 September 2000 *Ontario*	Thousands of Ontario students return to school today amidst the fight between Ontario teachers and the provincial government over class size and extracurricular activities. Students will also be getting used to a new "code of conduct" which includes mandatory singing of the national anthem every morning.
5 September 2000 *British Columbia*	An all-day kindergarten class funded by user fees gets underway at West Bay elementary school in Vancouver. User-pay public education is a first in BC where 12 families are each paying $350 per month to allow their children to stay in school until 3:00 pm, rather than 11:30 am when other public-financed classes end. BC Education Minister

Penny Priddy says she has "huge difficulties" with the program and wonders whether it will lead to a trend toward privatization within the province's public school system.

7 September 2000
Justice

Manitoba's Justice Minister Gord Mackenzie plans to bring the issue of establishing a national child-support collection system to the annual meeting of Canada's ministers of justice set to take place next week in Iqualuit. Mackintosh hopes to streamline the jurisdictional process for enforcing support orders when they apply to parents who are delinquent in paying support and have moved to other provinces.

8 September 2000
Justice

The Ontario government calls on the federal government to make DNA testing mandatory upon arrest. Blaine Harvey, a spokesman in the federal solicitor general's office, responds by stating that Ottawa has already considered the idea but ruled it out because it "posed too great a Charter risk." Ontario's Attorney General Jim Flaherty acknowledged the challenge that exists under the *Charter of Rights and Freedoms*. However, he suggested that the law could be "designed in such a way to withstand constitutional challenge." The issue is expected to be discussed at the justice ministers' meeting in Iqualuit next week.

8 September 2000
Health

Ontario Premier Mike Harris announces that if Quebec does not sign off on a potential new health-care deal with the federal government, then he will not sign either. The surprise announcement was made at a joint press conference with Quebec Premier Lucien Bouchard.

10 September 2000
First Ministers' Meeting

The First Ministers' Meeting is launched over dinner at 24 Sussex Drive. The meeting, which is expected to centre on health-care reform and funding, will take place tomorrow.

11 September 2000
First Ministers' Meeting

The First Ministers' Meeting concludes with Prime Minister Chrétien announcing a health-care deal that gives the provinces an additional $23.4 billion in transfers over the next five years for health and social programs (of that, $2.2 billion is earmarked for early childhood education), plus an extra one-time payment of $2.3 billion specifically for diagnostic equipment. The prime minister and the premiers appeared to be uniformly satisfied with the agreement, which appears to many to be a signal that a federal election is on the horizon.

Also briefly discussed at the meeting was the $2.65 billion infrastructure program, which was part of last February's budget. The plan is geared to repairing Canada's aging roads and water and sewage systems. However, no details of the plan were worked out. Ontario and Quebec both have concerns (Ontario about its share of the money and Quebec about how the federal-provincial jurisdictions will be worked out).

11 September 2000 *Elections*	Two new MPs will be joining the House of Commons. Joe Clark surprises nobody by winning the Kings-Hants riding of Wolfville, Nova Scotia in a by-election. Likewise, Stockwell Day wins his seat easily in his chosen riding of Okanagan-Coquihalla, BC.
11 September 2000 *Political Leaders*	Former Ontario Premier Bob Rae is appointed as mediator in the Mi'kmaq fishing dispute in Burnt Church, New Brunswick.
12 September 2000 *Political Parties*	Quebec Progressive Conservative MPs Diane St-Jacques and David Price defect to the federal Liberal Party. Pundits see this as another sign of an upcoming federal election as Prime Minister Chrétien holds a news conference introducing the two new Liberal MPs as being part of a strong team.
18 September 2000 *Local Government/ Environment*	The city of Hamilton, Ontario is fined $300,000 under the federal *Fisheries Act* and an additional fine of $150,000 levied by the provincial Ministry of the Environment for allowing toxic waste to seep into Red Hill Creek and then Hamilton Harbour from a nearby landfill. The city pleaded guilty to the charges after a study was completed by the Environmental Bureau of Investigation. The investigation had been prompted by water samples that were collected and brought forward by environmentalist Lynda Lukasik and other Hamilton residents.
21 September 2000 *Environment*	A House of Commons Environment Committee unanimously recommends a federal environmental assessment

of the already Ontario government-approved plan for Toronto to dump its garbage into an abandoned mine near Kirkland Lake, Ontario. The committee also plans to hold a public hearing on the issue. Liberal MP Benoit Serre of Temiskaming-Cochrane riding in Northern Ontario declared that the Adams Mine project must be stopped, while the Chief of the AFN, Matthew Coon Come said the project could be a disaster for Aboriginal peoples in the northern regions of Canada. Federal Environment Minister David Anderson has asked the arm's-length organization — the Canadian Environmental Assessment Agency — to advise on the matter.

25 September 2000
Political Leaders

Saskatchewan NDP Premier Roy Romanow resigns after nine years as premier and 35 years of political service. Romanow was first elected to the Saskatchewan legislature in 1967 and between 1971 and 1982 and he served as both deputy premier and Saskatchewan's attorney general. In 1979, after being appointed Saskatchewan's first minister of intergovernmental affairs, Romanow became an integral part of the federal-provincial negotiations, which led to the deal to "bring home" the constitution in 1982.

26 September 2000
Aboriginal Peoples

Federal Fisheries Department boats launch another raid on Aboriginal lobster traps in Miramichi Bay, New Brunswick. Although there were no direct confrontations between the fisheries' boats and native boats, the RCMP and Coastguard helicopters maintained a presence in the area. More than 1,300 native lobster traps have already been seized, but native fishermen have been trying to replace them on an ongoing basis. The Mi'kmaq band council has declared that the lobster fishery will close down 17 October.

28 September 2000
Political Leaders

Former Prime Minister Pierre Elliott Trudeau dies in his home in Montreal. Born in 1919, Trudeau graduated from the University of Montreal's law faculty in 1944. He also went on to study at Harvard, the London School of Economics, and in Paris. In the 1950s, Trudeau co-founded the small but influential magazine *Cité Libre*. Entering politics in 1965, Trudeau remained an advocate of a "just society" and an opponent of Quebec nationalism throughout his career. As justice minister in 1967, Trudeau gained public attention when he spearheaded the amendments to the criminal code that liberalized the laws pertaining to homosexuality and abortion.

In 1968, he was elected leader of the Liberal Party and in short order became prime minister when the Liberals won the June election. The *Official Languages Act* was introduced under his guidance in 1969. Trudeau remained prime minister until the Liberals lost to Joe Clark's Tories in 1979. After the Tory government failed in 1980, Trudeau returned to his posting as prime minister, which gave him the opportunity to patriate the constitution and introduce the *Charter of Rights and Freedoms* in 1982. Trudeau retired from politics in 1984, returning to a career in law in Montreal.

28 September 2000
Aboriginal Peoples

National Chief of the AFN Matthew Coon Come delivers an intense speech to a group of 300 at the University of Alberta. He declares that Ottawa is proceeding illegally in the Burnt Church fishing dispute and he accuses Canadian Alliance leader Stockwell Day of having a dangerous lack of understanding with respect to Aboriginal issues. Coon Come also accused Fisheries Minister Herb Dhaliwal of endangering lives by "playing cowboys and Indians." Coon Come warned that more disputes and road blocks were on the way if political leaders did not begin to take Aboriginal negotiations seriously.

30 September 2000
Political Leaders

Prime Minister Jean Chrétien receives Pierre Trudeau's coffin in Ottawa. Trudeau will lie in state in Parliament's Hall of Honour today and tomorrow, then in Montreal on Monday. A state funeral will be held Tuesday at Notre Dame Basilica in Montreal.

4 October 2000
Environment

The Pembina Institute, an environmental think-tank, delivers a report stating that Canada's five largest provinces (BC, Alberta, Ontario, Quebec, and Saskatchewan) have failed to take any real action to reduce greenhouse gas emissions. Since the provinces have jurisdiction over areas like fossil fuel production, their action is fundamental to Canada's international environmental commitments. The United Nation's Kyoto Protocol was signed by Canada in 1997 and is due to be ratified by all the signatories by 2005. Under the agreement, Canada promises to reduce

its gas emissions to 6 percent below 1990 levels some-
time between 2008 and 2012.

5 October 2000
Political Parties

A new poll by Leger Marketing show the Liberals have
risen in popular support to 48 percent, while the Canadian Alliance has slipped to 19 percent. The poll also shows
that support for the Tories is at 10 percent, the Bloc
Québécois at 9 percent and the NDP at 10 percent. Ru-
mours about a fall election persist and Prime Minister
Chrétien has stated that he intends to invoke Trudeau's
legacy on the campaign trail as he considers himself a key
defender of Trudeau values. Chrétien explained that these
values include tolerance, compassion, and social justice.

10 October 2000
Finance

Thirteen private sector economists meet today with Finance Minister Paul Martin to complete economic
projections for the next five years. The group projects that
the federal government will have approximately $121.5
billion to use toward a combination of new spending, tax
cuts, and debt repayment between now and 2006. The
panel also pointed out that the Canadian Alliance Party's
tax reduction plan would cost Ottawa between $22 and
$25 billion per year, which would use up all of $121.5
billion, leaving nothing for spending or debt reduction.
Martin is expected to base his upcoming mini-budget on
the forecasts offered by the group of economists.

11 October 2000
Local Government

Toronto City Council approves the controversial 20-year
contract to send Toronto's garbage north to an abandoned
mine near Kirkland Lake, Ontario. Hundreds of anti-dump
protestors have gathered at City Hall over the past four
days and many of the protestors vow that they will not
allow Toronto to go forward with the plan. Both the Ontario and Quebec environment ministers have now signed
off on the project, but City Council gave the federal government the option to decide whether or not they would
carry out any environmental assessment on the project.
The deadline for the federal government's decision on the
assessment is 15 February 2001.

13 October 2000
Political Parties

Prime Minister Jean Chrétien appears to have successfully
persuaded Royal Bank economist John McCallum and
Newfoundland premier Brian Tobin to run for the Liberal
Party in the still-to-be-announced federal election.

14 October 2000 *Environment*	Canada and the US reach a draft agreement to cut smog-causing emissions on both sides of the border. The pact calls for Ontario to reduce by 50 percent emissions from power plants that burn coal, oil, and natural gas by 2007. In return, the US would reduce their emissions of nitrogen oxide by 35 percent. Ontario Environment Minister Don Newman criticized the federal government for not demanding more of the US. Newman lamented that the 35 percent reduction in US emissions is the standard that the US Environmental Protection Agency has already set for the US. Federal Environment Minister David Anderson, on the other hand, stated that he was pleased with the deal and that, in fact, Ontario presented the biggest obstacle in obtaining tighter restrictions in the pact.
15 October 2000 *Political Parties*	Brian Tobin prepares to step down as premier of Newfoundland, so that he can enter federal politics. The move fuels further speculation that the federal Liberals are about to make an election announcement.
17 October 2000 *Environment*	Ontario rejects a national program to cut greenhouse gas emissions. Instead, the province insists that its own air-quality plans should set national standards. At a meeting of environment ministers, Ontario's Environment Minister Don Newman expressed disappointment with Ottawa's plan, while federal Natural Resources Minister Ralph Goodale said that it was regrettable that Ontario did not endorse the plan "but the door is still open." Environmentalists at the meeting criticized Newman, charging that Ontario's plan was too weak. Since Mike Harris's Conservative team formed the government, severe cuts have been made to the Environment Ministry and the province has been criticized for its use of coal-fired power plants.
17 October 2000 *Political Leaders*	Lloyd Axworthy officially steps down as minister of foreign affairs and confirms that he is moving to a position at the University of British Columbia. John Manley is appointed the new minister of foreign affairs and Brian Tobin replaces Manley as the minister of industry.
18 October 2000 *Budget*	Finance Minister Paul Martin unveils his mini-budget in the House of Commons. The key component of the mini-budget is the largest tax cut in Canadian history. The

five-year, $100 billion tax plan is aimed at largely reducing the tax burden for Canadians at all income levels, but will especially benefit the middle-class (or upper-middle-class, depending on your definition) with the creation of a fourth income tax bracket for those earning between $60,000 and $100,000. Most of the tax changes are slated to come into effect on 1 January 2001 after the new legislation is passed. Also included in Martin's plan was a pledge to pay down the public debt by another $10 billion in the 2000–2001 fiscal year. The debt currently sits at $564.5 billion.

20 October 2000
Political Leaders

New federal Industry Minister Brian Tobin meets with shipyard owners and union leaders who are jointly demanding a national shipbuilding policy that they say would put thousands back to work. Les Hollaway, the director of the Marine Workers Federation expects cooperation, given that the minister had expressed support for the plan in his previous capacity as the Newfoundland premier.

22 October 2000
Elections

After a visit to Governor-General Adrienne Clarkson, Prime Minister Chrétien officially calls the much-anticipated early federal election for 27 November. The last federal election was held on 2 June 1997, just a little over three years ago.

24 October 2000
Political Parties

Former Prime Minister Brian Mulroney introduces Joe Clark at the Progressive Conservatives' first major campaign event. Tory organizers are hopeful that Mulroney's presence will help revive support for the party.

25 October 2000
Political Leaders

Canadian Alliance leader Stockwell Day promises to give Newfoundland a break on resource development. Day pledged that, if elected, he would suspend Ottawa's clawback of equalization payments.

1 November 2000
Elections

Prime Minister Jean Chrétien releases the Liberals' election platform in the form of the *Red Book III*. Since most of the plans have already been detailed over the past few months, the Liberals emphasize their focus on new technologies, the Internet, and education.

| 6 November 2000
Elections | A new poll by Léger Marketing shows that the Liberals and the Bloc Québécois are tied in popularity with Quebec voters. Although the Bloc has the majority of francophone support, once all voters are considered each party has exactly 43 percent of popular support in the province. |

| 6 November 2000
Elections | Alliance leader Stockwell Day spends the day campaigning with Peter Stock, the Alliance candidate in the Ontario riding of Simcoe-North. The move triggers renewed criticism of the Alliance Party as "anti-gay." Peter Stock is the director of the Canadian Family Coalition, which promotes the strict definition of family — as two married people of the opposite sex and their children — as the only definition that should be recognized by law. Alliance spokesperson Phil von Finckenstein says that the Alliance Party welcomes people of all backgrounds and viewpoints and although Peter Stock is a party member, he does not speak for the party as a whole. |

| 9 November 2000
*Newfoundland/
Quebec* | Newfoundland Energy Minister Paul Dicks releases the province's new plan to dramatically cut back on the $12 billion hydro-electric joint project with Quebec, originally proposed by former Premier Brian Tobin. Dicks said the project is now cut down in size to a $3.7 billion project and there is no longer any intention to include Quebec. "It's a lot cleaner for [Quebec] to buy power than to get into a construction project with another province," Dicks explained. Quebec Premier Lucien Bouchard seems to agree. Bouchard responded to Newfoundland's plan by saying that Hydro-Québec will buy the electricity and that prices are under discussion. Dicks also added that the province will not move forward with the plan unless a potential US buyer of electricity is also secured in advance. |

| 16 November 2000
*Newfoundland/
Aboriginal Peoples* | After an emergency meeting is held to discuss the intensifying crisis of gas-sniffing and suicidal children in Sheshatshiu, the largest Innu community in Labrador, the Innu leaders call on the Newfoundland government to remove the high-risk children from the community for their own safety. Newfoundland Health Minister Roger Grimes says that the province has no intention of forcibly removing |

children from their parents' homes without permission from the parents. Rather, he plans to first send additional social workers to the overwhelmed community to talk with and assess the 30–40 children considered to be at risk. Innu Nation president Peter Penashue says the unprecedented move is necessary because of the rapidly increasing rate of addiction for youth in the communities and that the removal of children would allow the parents to get counselling and treatment for their own addictions. Penashue added that the Innu call on the Newfoundland government because they do not have the authority to remove children from unsafe environments, but the province does have that authority.

20 November 2000
Political Leaders

Prime Minister Jean Chrétien rejects calls by Alliance leader Stockwell Day, Tory leader Joe Clark and NDP leader Alexa McDonough to hold an inquiry into his actions with respect to his involvement in securing a $615,000 loan for the owner of the Auberge Grand-Mère, which is located in his riding. Chrétien insists that he acted appropriately, that all details are already public information and therefore an inquiry is unnecessary.

21 November 2000
Nova Scotia

A child poverty report released in Nova Scotia shows that 19.1 percent of the province's children live in poverty, which is an increase of 18.6 percent over the 1989 level. Annual child poverty reports continue to compare their figures with the 1989 numbers since that was the year in which the House of Commons unanimously passed a resolution to end child poverty by 2000. Poverty groups report that child poverty is on the rise in nearly every province, and nationally approximately 1.3 million children are poor, which is a 43 percent increase since 1989.

22 November 2000
Political Leaders

Ethics Counsellor Howard Wilson rules that Prime Minister Jean Chrétien did nothing inapproprate by calling a bank president on behalf of a constituent — the owner of the Auberge Grand-Mère. Wilson concludes that the prime minister had no personal financial interest in the arrangement and his communication with the then-president of the Business Development Bank of Canada, François Beaudoin, "did not violate any government rule."

The Auberge Grand-Mère is owned by Yvon Duhaime, who purchased the hotel from a company partly owned by Chrétien in 1993, before Chrétien became prime minister. However, the deal to also sell the shares Chrétien held in the golf course adjoining the hotel fell through in 1993, and he did not receive payment for them until 1999. Ethics Counsellor Wilson pointed out that Chrétien's business dealings have been held in a blind trust since 1993 and thus Wilson again ruled that the prime minister had no conflict of interest. Critical of the fact that Wilson was appointed by the prime minister and that Wilson reports to him directly, Stockwell Day, Alexa McDonough and Joe Clark all pledged to continue to press the issue. Interestingly, many of the provinces (including Ontario and BC) have their ethics counsellors report directly to the legislature instead of the premier so as to keep them separate and independent.

26 November 2000
Political Leaders/
Aboriginal Peoples

Prime Minister Jean Chrétien meets with Innu leaders in his home riding of Shawinigan on the day before the federal election. The Innu leaders travel from Labrador to discuss the much-publicized crisis of youth addicted to gas-sniffing in the communities of Davis Inlet and Sheshatshiu. Also, Industry Minister Brian Tobin makes the twin announcement that "millions" will be spent to build a detox centre to help addicts and their families in both communities; and the Innu people will now be included under the *Indian Act*, which will qualify the Innu for tax exemptions and food subsidies not previously available to them.

26 November 2000
Elections

The 36-day election campaign draws to a close today and the party leaders make their last-minute efforts to sway undecided voters. Speaking in his Shawinigan riding, Prime Minister Jean Chrétien tells Canadians that they should elect a majority Liberal government as a strong bulwark against the Quebec separatist movement. Alliance leader Stockwell Day recorded a 15-minute "infomercial" in which he urged Canadians not to vote Liberal because their leader "cannot be trusted to spend Canadians' money wisely."

27 November 2000   As many pundits had predicted, the Liberals garnered their
Elections   third majority under the leadership of Jean Chrétien in
                   today's federal election. Additionally, the Liberal Party
                   made significant headway in Quebec, winning 36 seats to
                   the 38 seats won by the Bloc Québécois (the BQ lost six
                   seats). The Canadian Alliance, while increasing its over-
                   all number of seats, failed to make its critical breakthrough
                   in Ontario, winning only two seats in the province. The
                   lowest voter turnout since Confederation (62.8 percent)
                   gave the Liberal Party 40.8 percent of the popular vote,
                   which translated to 172 seats; the Canadian Alliance
                   formed the Official Opposition with 25.5 percent of the
                   vote and 66 seats; the Bloc Québécois won 38 seats; the
                   NDP 13 seats; and the Progressive Conservatives 12 seats.
                   Of the 301 elected MPs, 62 are women.

30 November 2000   The entries for the leadership of Saskatchewan's New
Saskatchewan   Democratic Party are known and the seven candidates that
                   party members will choose from are: Environment Min-
                   ister Buckley Belanger, farm activist Nettie Wiebe, former
                   Social Services Minister Lorne Calvert, former Justice
                   Minister Chris Axworthy, lawyer Scott Banda, Labour
                   Minister Joanne Crofford and Highways Minister Maynard
                   Sonntag. Members will vote for the new leader at a con-
                   vention on 27 January in Saskatoon, or by mail. The new
                   leader will become premier, since Roy Romanow an-
                   nounced his retirement in September. Lorne Calvert is
                   considered by some to be the front-runner.

30 November 2000   Canadian Alliance aide Bob Runciman, who acted as co-
Political Parties chairman of the Alliance's Ontario election campaign
                   suggests that a "new party on the right," is the only way to
                   challenge the federal Liberals. Runciman also claims that
                   there is not a lot of difference between the platforms of
                   the Canadian Alliance and the Progressive Conservatives,
                   and therefore a merger between the two parties should be
                   possible. Runciman further suggested that PC Leader Joe
                   Clark was an obstacle to such a plan and that possibly
                   even Stockwell Day may have to step down as a new party
                   would need a new leader.

1 December 2000   Health Canada cuts funding to a native treatment centre
Finance   on the Sagkeeng reserve 145 kms northeast of Winnipeg.

The funding is cut as a result of centre staff refusing to cooperate with a forensic audit that was ordered by Health Canada in October after the controversial story about 70 treatment centre employees taking a Caribbean cruise funded by the centre. Health Canada has been providing more than $7 million annually to help the centre treat those suffering from drug, alcohol, and solvent abuse.

1 December 2000
Ontario

The Ontario government introduces legislation that will separate Ontario income tax rates from federal tax rates starting in January 2001. Ontario Finance Minister Ernie Eves emphasized that tax forms will still be processed the same way; Ontario will simply now be levying tax on an individual's income rather than collecting a percentage of federal income tax. The freedom to levy their own rates allows Ontario to give tax cuts beyond those offered by the federal government, Eves explained.

1 December 2000
Quebec

Quebec Premier Lucien Bouchard cancels his trip to Mexico City to attend President-Elect Vicente Fox's inauguration ceremony after he receives a downgraded invitation from the Mexican government. Bouchard angrily accused Ottawa of sabotaging his visit to Mexico as a national leader, claiming that Ottawa must have contacted Mexico after Bouchard received an invitation that was meant for heads of state. However, the Mexican government was quick to point out their error and send out the correct invitation as soon as the error was caught.

4 December 2000
Atlantic Canada

The Council of Atlantic Premiers calls on the prime minister to hold a First Ministers' Conference in January to discuss increasing equalization payments to poorer provinces. The Council explained that even with current equalization payments, the ability of their provinces to generate funds is far below the national average. Equalization payments to Quebec, Manitoba, Saskatchewan, and the Atlantic provinces totalled $9.8 billion this year. Premier Bernard Lord of New Brunswick stressed the importance of resolving the issue quickly since most provincial budgets are due in March of next year.

4 December 2000
Quebec

Quebec Premier Lucien Bouchard defeats a motion to use public funds to re-establish the Council for Sovereignty.

He argues that this is not the right time to push for sovereignty with public money when health-care services in the province already exceed the budget by \$430 million. However, the separatist hardliners see the Council for Sovereignty as an important step in showing that the PQ is serious about working toward sovereignty, and that commitment, they argue, requires public funding.

9 December 2000
Aboriginal Peoples

Speaking in Port Alberni, BC, Deputy Minister of Indian Affairs Shelley Serafini apologizes on behalf of the federal government to the Nuu-chah-nulth people who were the victims of abuse at residential schools. The lawyer for seven former residents of the Alberni Indian Residential School on Vancouver Island questioned the timing of the apology since a prolonged civil trial in which his clients are seeking damages for alleged physical and sexual abuse is due to close in two days. The result of the civil suit is expected to be precedent-setting with approximately 5,000 outstanding claims of former students of residential schools throughout Canada.

10 December 2000
Local Government

Tens of thousands of peaceful protestors gather in downtown Montreal to show their anger over Bill 170, which mandates municipal mergers in Quebec. The PQ government plans to amalgamate the 28 municipalities that surround Montreal, creating a megacity. Protestors from all 28 communities took turns voicing their concerns over the potential loss of services and community spirit that could result from the merger. Bill 170 is expected to pass in the Quebec National Assembly on 18 December. Further plans to merge the Quebec City and Hull regions are in the planning stages by the provincial government.

11–12 December 2000
Finance

Provincial and territorial finance ministers meet in Winnipeg to follow up on issues raised at the Annual Premiers' Conference, and state that a number of these have remained unresolved, resulting in a call to their federal counterpart for an immediate meeting to address the following issues: expenditure and tax pressures; strengthening equalization and the Canadian Health and Social Transfer, which includes the removal of the equalization ceiling; transfers outside CHST and equalization; taxation issues, such as tax collection agreements.

13 December 2000 *Budget*	Finance Minister Paul Martin announces that there will be no traditional February budget next year since the Liberals are not planning any new spending initiatives. Martin further explained that the mini-budget that was announced in October goes into effect on 1 January 2001 and is expected to guide the government's spending for the next year provided that there are no drastic changes in the economy.
15 December 2000 *Supreme Court*	One of the Supreme Court's most anticipated decisions this year blames Canada Customs for 15 years of harassing a Vancouver gay and lesbian bookstore, but only strikes down one provision under section 152(3) of the *Customs Act* that supported the actions of Customs agents. Reaction to the 6–3 majority decision are mixed. The president of the Civil Liberties Association John Dixon called the decision a "landslide victory," but many other civil libertarians expressed disappointment that the court did not clarify or alter the existing "community tolerance" standard for obscenity (under section 163(8) of the Criminal Code) which allows the seizure of materials if the "community believes it could potentially cause harm." The striking down of the *Customs Act* provision reverses the onus of proof from the importers to Canada Customs agents; agents will now have to prove within 30 days that any seized materials are obscene. Previously, importers had to prove that a seized item was not obscene.
18 December 2000 *Ontario/Local Government*	Stan Koebel, former manager of the Walkerton, Ontario public utilities admits, at a public inquiry into the E coli water contamination crisis, that he had neither the skills nor the education to perform the job he held for the past 12 years. Koebel corroborated the evidence given earlier this week by his brother (who also worked at the utilities commission) that they had mislabelled bottles and falsified reports in an attempt to keep up with their jobs. Koebel also said that since the Ontario Progressive Conservatives amalgamated local municipalities and deregulated public utilities, he held managerial responsibility for both the electrical and water utilities and was spending only 5 percent of his time managing the town's water supply.

21 December 2000
Aboriginal Peoples

The Ontario Court of Appeal rules that the social costs of returning more than 1,000 hectares of land in Sarnia, Ontario outweigh the necessity of returning the land to the Chippewa band over a bureaucratic error made back in 1853. The land in question was originally protected by a 1827 treaty which stipulated that the Chippewa band members must collectively consent to any sale of their land. However, three Chippewa chiefs did sell the land and surrendered it improperly to a land speculator. And no record of the band's collective consent has ever been found. Earl Cherniak, the lawyer for the Chippewa band says that the court's decision will affect all land claims cases since the idea of applying discretion to the sanctity of Aboriginal title is new.

22 December 2000
Aboriginal Peoples/
Health

A Health Canada report prepared in light of last May's water crisis in Walkerton, Ontario, states that at least 10 percent of native reserves' water supplies are at risk. Several reserves' water-treatment plants show higher than acceptable limits for contaminants, while many of the reserve water managers have insufficient training for their position. Seventy-nine treatment plants were highlighted as potential problems and of those, 30 are in Saskatchewan, 27 in BC, and 14 in Ontario. One of the Saskatchewan reserves — the Yellowquill First Nation — has been under a boil-water order for four years because of farm run-off in their reservoir. Gilles Rochon, the director general for community development for Indian Affairs, says that his department is reviewing existing regulations and water funding for reserves.

Chronology: Index

Aboriginal Peoples 17 January, 1 February, 23 February, 1 March, 8 March, 9 March, 13 March, 14 March, 23 March, 30 March, 4 April, 7 May, 8 May, 12 May, 17 May, 27 May, 21 June, 23 June, 6 July, 7 July, 12 July, 25 July, 4 August, 23 August, 31 August, 26 September, 28 September, 16 November, 26 November, 9 December, 21 December, 22 December

Agriculture 13 January, 22–23 March, 25 May

Alberta 5 September

Annual Premiers' Conference 9–11 August

Atlantic Canada 21 February, 22 February, 27 April, 15 May, 31 May, 16–18 July, 4 December

British Columbia 8 January, 4 August, 5 September

Budget 13 January, 28 February, 29 February, 18 October, 13 December

Clarity Bill 23 February, 15 March, 7 April, 22 May, 13 June

Elections 11 September, 22 October, 1 November, 6 November, 26 November, 27 November

Environment 4 January, 3 March, 4 May, 18 July, 15 August, 18 September, 21 September, 4 October, 14 October, 17 October

Finance 19 June, 10 October, 1 December, 11–12 December

First Ministers' Meeting 10 September, 11 September

Fisheries 27 April

Health 1 March, 9 March, 9 May, 30 May, 5 August, 8 September, 22 December

HRDC 19 January, 21 February

Justice 23 February, 1 March, 7 September, 8 September

Local Government 25 July, 18 September, 11 October, 10 December, 18 December

National Unity 8 May, 10 May, 19 May

New Brunswick 6 January, 25 February, 10 May

Newfoundland 13 January, 8 March, 9 November, 16 November

Nova Scotia 21 November

Ontario 18 January, 2 March, 9 May, 5 September, 1 December, 18 December

Political Leaders 31 January, 9 March, 13 March, 8 May, 8 July, 25 July, 11 September, 25 September, 28 September, 30 September, 17 October, 20 October, 25 October, 20 November, 22 November, 26 November

Political Parties 7 January, 8 January, 29 January, 23 March, 4 April, 19 June, 20 June, 24 June, 12 September, 5 October, 13 October, 15 October, 24 October, 30 November

Premiers' Meeting 14 January, 3 February, 23 May, 24 May

Quebec 15 January, 25 January, 3 March, 21 March, 24 March, 9 April, 25 August, 9 November, 1 December, 4 December

Reform Party 21 March

Saskatchewan 30 November

Senate 7 April

Supreme Court 12 January, 19 January, 21 February, 20 April, 15 June, 17 August, 15 December

Queen's Policy Studies
Recent Publications

The Queen's Policy Studies Series is dedicated to the exploration of major policy issues that confront governments in Canada and other western nations. McGill-Queen's University Press is the exclusive world representative and distributor of books in the series.

School of Policy Studies

Knowledge, Clusters and Regional Innovation: Economic Development in Canada, J. Adam Holbrook and David A. Wolfe (eds.), 2002
Paper ISBN 0-88911-919-8 Cloth ISBN 0-88911-917-1

Lessons of Everyday Law/Le droit du quotidien, Roderick Alexander Macdonald, 2002
Paper ISBN 0-88911-915-5 Cloth ISBN 0-88911-913-9

Improving Connections Between Governments and Nonprofit and Voluntary Organizations: Public Policy and the Third Sector, Kathy L. Brock (ed.), 2002
Paper ISBN 0-88911-899-X Cloth ISBN 0-88911-907-4

Governing Food: Science, Safety and Trade, Peter W.B. Phillips and Robert Wolfe (eds.), 2001 Paper ISBN 0-88911-897-3 Cloth ISBN 0-88911-903-1

The Nonprofit Sector and Government in a New Century, Kathy L. Brock and Keith G. Banting (eds.), 2001 Paper ISBN 0-88911-901-5 Cloth ISBN 0-88911-905-8

The Dynamics of Decentralization: Canadian Federalism and British Devolution, Trevor C. Salmon and Michael Keating (eds.), 2001 ISBN 0-88911-895-7

Innovation, Institutions and Territory: Regional Innovation Systems in Canada, J. Adam Holbrook and David A. Wolfe (eds.), 2000
Paper ISBN 0-88911-891-4 Cloth ISBN 0-88911-893-0

Backbone of the Army: Non-Commissioned Officers in the Future Army, Douglas L. Bland (ed.), 2000 ISBN 0-88911-889-2

Precarious Values: Organizations, Politics and Labour Market Policy in Ontario, Thomas R. Klassen, 2000 Paper ISBN 0-88911-883-3 Cloth ISBN 0-88911-885-X

The Nonprofit Sector in Canada: Roles and Relationships, Keith G. Banting (ed.), 2000
Paper ISBN 0-88911-813-2 Cloth ISBN 0-88911-815-9

Institute of Intergovernmental Relations

Federalism, Democracy and Disability Policy in Canada, Alan Puttee (ed.), 2002
Paper ISBN 0-88911-855-8 Cloth ISBN 1-55339-001-6, ISBN 0-88911-845-0 (set)

Comparaison des régimes fédéraux, 2ᵉ éd., Ronald L. Watts, 2002
ISBN 1-55339-005-9

Health Policy and Federalism: A Comparative Perspective on Multi-Level Governance, Keith G. Banting and Stan Corbett (eds.), 2001
Paper ISBN 0-88911-859-0 Cloth ISBN 1-55339-000-8, ISBN 0-88911-845-0 (set)

Disability and Federalism: Comparing Different Approaches to Full Participation, David Cameron and Fraser Valentine (eds.), 2001
Paper ISBN 0-88911-857-4 Cloth ISBN 0-88911-867-1, ISBN 0-88911-845-0 (set)

Federalism, Democracy and Health Policy in Canada, Duane Adams (ed.), 2001
Paper ISBN 0-88911-853-1 Cloth ISBN 0-88911-865-5, ISBN 0-88911-845-0 (set)

Federalism, Democracy and Labour Market Policy in Canada, Tom McIntosh (ed.),
2000   ISBN 0-88911-849-3, ISBN 0-88911-845-0 (set)

*Managing the Environmental Union: Intergovernmental Relations and Environmental Policy
in Canada,* Patrick C. Fafard and Kathryn Harrison (eds.), 2000   ISBN 0-88911-837-X

Canada: The State of the Federation 1999/2000, vol. 14, *Toward a New Mission Statement
for Canadian Fiscal Federalism,* Harvey Lazar (ed.), 2000
Paper ISBN 0-88911-843-4 Cloth ISBN 0-88911-839-6

Canada: The State of the Federation 1998/99, vol. 13, *How Canadians Connect,*
Harvey Lazar and Tom McIntosh (eds.), 1999
Paper ISBN 0-88911-781-0 Cloth ISBN 0-88911-779-9

Stretching the Federation: The Art of the State in Canada, Robert Young (ed.), 1999
ISBN 0-88911-777-2

Comparing Federal Systems, 2d ed., Ronald L. Watts, 1999   ISBN 0-88911-835-3

John Deutsch Institute for the Study of Economic Policy

*Towards Evidence-Based Policy for Canadian Education/Vers des politiques canadiennes
d'éducation fondées sur la recherche,* Patrice de Broucker and/et Arthur Sweetman (eds./dirs.),
2002   Paper ISBN 0-88911-946-5 Cloth ISBN 0-88911-944-9

*Money, Markets and Mobility: Celebrating the Ideas of Robert A. Mundell, Nobel Laureate
in Economic Sciences,* Thomas J. Courchene (ed.), 2002
Paper ISBN 0-88911-820-5 Cloth ISBN 0-88911-818-3

The State of Economics in Canada: Festschrift in Honour of David Slater,
Patrick Grady and Andrew Sharpe (eds.), 2001
Paper ISBN 0-88911-942-2 Cloth ISBN 0-88911-940-6

The 2000 Federal Budget, Paul A.R. Hobson (ed.), Policy Forum Series no. 37, 2001
Paper ISBN 0-88911-816-7 Cloth ISBN 0-88911-814-0

Room to Manoeuvre? Globalization and Policy Convergence, Thomas J. Courchene (ed.),
Bell Canada Papers no. 6, 1999   Paper ISBN 0-88911-812-4 Cloth ISBN 0-88911-812-4

Women and Work, Richard P. Chaykowski and Lisa M. Powell (eds.), 1999
Paper ISBN 0-88911-808-6 Cloth ISBN 0-88911-806-X

Available from: McGill-Queen's University Press
c/o Georgetown Terminal Warehouses
34 Armstrong Avenue
Georgetown, Ontario L7G 4R9
Tel: (877) 864-8477
Fax: (877) 864-4272
E-mail: orders@gtwcanada.com

Institute of Intergovernmental Relations
Recent Publications

Political Science and Federalism: Seven Decades of Scholarly Engagement, Richard Simeon, 2000 Kenneth R. MacGregor Lecturer, 2002
ISBN 1-55339-004-0

The Spending Power in Federal Systems: A Comparative Study, Ronald L. Watts, 1999
ISBN 0-88911-829-9

Étude comparative du pouvoir de dépenser dans d'autres régimes fédéraux, Ronald L. Watts, 1999   ISBN 0-88911-831-0

Constitutional Patriation: The Lougheed-Lévesque Correspondence/Le rapatriement de la Constitution: La correspondance de Lougheed et Lévesque, with an Introduction by J. Peter Meekison/avec une introduction de J. Peter Meekison, 1999   ISBN 0-88911-833-7

Securing the Social Union: A Commentary on the Decentralized Approach, Steven A. Kennett, 1998   ISBN 0-88911-767-5

Working Paper Series

2002

1. *Redistribution, Risk, and Incentives in Equalization: A Comparison of RTS and Macro Approaches* by Michael Smart, Department of Economics, University of Toronto

2. *Revisiting Equalization Again: RTS vs Macro Approaches* by Robin Boadway, Department of Economics, Queen's University

3. *The Stablization Properties of Equalization: Evidence from Saskatchewan* by Paul Boothe, University of Alberta and C.D. Howe Institute

4. *The Case for Switching to a Macro Formula* by Dan Usher, Department of Economics, Queen's University

5. *Using GDP in Equalization Calculations: Are There Meaningful Measurement Issues?* by Julie Aubut, C.RD.E. and François Vaillancourt, Département de sciences économiques and Fellow, C.R.D.E., Université de Montréal

6. *What Do We Already Know about the Appropriate Design for a Fiscal Equalization Program in Canada and How Well Are We Doing?* by Paul Hobson, Department of Economics, Acadia University

7. *Macroeconomic Versus RTS Measures of Fiscal Capacity: Theoretical Foundations and Implications for Canada* by Stephen Barro

8. *Quiet Cooperation: Relations Among Labour Ministries in Canada* by Ronald Saunders

2001

1. *Tax Competition and the Fiscal Union: Balancing Competition and Harmonization in Canada.* Proceedings of a Symposium held 9-10 June 2000, edited by Douglas Brown, Queen's University

2. *Federal Occupational Training Policy: A Neo-Institutionalist Analysis* by Gordon DiGiacomo, Consultant in Workplace Relations, Greely, Ontario

3. *Federalism and Labour Market Policy in Germany and Canada: Exploring the Path Dependency of Reforms in the 1990s* by Thomas R. Klassen, Trent University and Steffen Schneider, University of Augsburg, Germany

4. *Bifurcated and Integrated Parties in Parliamentary Federations: The Canadian and German Cases* by Wolfgang Renzsch, Otto-von-Guericke Universität Magdeburg, Germany

5. *The Two British Columbias* by Phillip Resnick, University of British Columbia and *The West Wants In! (But What is the West? and What is "In?")* by Peter McCormick, University of Lethbridge

6. *Federalism and Labour Policy in Canada* by Gordon DiGiacomo

7. *Quebec's Place in the Canada of the Future* by Benoît Pelletier

8. *The Evolution of Support for Sovereignty – Myths and Realities* by Claire Durand, Université de Montréal

2000

1. *The Agreement on Internal Trade: An Institutional Response to Changing Conceptions, Roles and Functions in Canadian Federalism* by Howard Leeson, University of Regina

1999

1. *Processes of Constitutional Restructuring: The Canadian Experience in Comparative Context* by Ronald L. Watts, Queen's University

2. *Parliament, Intergovernmental Relations and National Unity* by C.E.S. Franks, Queen's University

3. *The United Kingdom as a Quasi-Federal State* by Gerard Hogan, Queen's University

4. *The Federal Spending Power in Canada: Nation-Building or Nation-Destroying?* by Hamish Telford, Queen's University

For a complete list of working papers see: www.iigr.ca

These publications are available from:
Institute of Intergovernmental Relations, Queen's University, Kingston, Ontario K7L 3N6
Tel: (613) 533-2080 / Fax: (613) 533-6868; E-mail: iigr@qsilver.queensu.ca